AFRICA AT A
TURNING POINT?

AFRICA AT A TURNING POINT?

Growth, Aid, and External Shocks

Edited by

Delfin S. Go
John Page

THE WORLD BANK
Washington, D.C.

© 2008 The International Bank for Reconstruction and Development / The World Bank
1818 H Street NW
Washington DC 20433
Telephone: 202-473-1000
Internet: www.worldbank.org
E-mail: feedback@worldbank.org

1 2 3 4 11 10 09 08

This volume is a product of the staff of the International Bank for Reconstruction and Development / The World Bank. The findings, interpretations, and conclusions expressed in this volume do not necessarily reflect the views of the Executive Directors of The World Bank or the governments they represent.

The World Bank does not guarantee the accuracy of the data included in this work. The boundaries, colors, denominations, and other information shown on any map in this work do not imply any judgement on the part of The World Bank concerning the legal status of any territory or the endorsement or acceptance of such boundaries.

Rights and Permissions
The material in this publication is copyrighted. Copying and/or transmitting portions or all of this work without permission may be a violation of applicable law. The International Bank for Reconstruction and Development / The World Bank encourages dissemination of its work and will normally grant permission to reproduce portions of the work promptly.

For permission to photocopy or reprint any part of this work, please send a request with complete information to the Copyright Clearance Center Inc., 222 Rosewood Drive, Danvers, MA 01923, USA; telephone: 978-750-8400; fax: 978-750-4470; Internet: www.copyright.com.

All other queries on rights and licenses, including subsidiary rights, should be addressed to the Office of the Publisher, The World Bank, 1818 H Street NW, Washington, DC 20433, USA; fax: 202-522-2422; e-mail: pubrights@worldbank.org.

ISBN: 978-0-8213-7277-7
eISBN: 978-0-8213-7278-4
DOI: 10.1596/978-0-8213-7277-7

Cover design: Naylor Design.

Library of Congress Cataloging-in-Publication Data has been requested.

Contents

Boxes

Figures

Tables

Foreword

Much of sub-Saharan Africa missed two decades of economic progress between 1975 and 1995. As a result, the average income per person remained virtually unchanged between independence and the turn of the 21st century. Since the mid-1990s, an acceleration of economic growth in much of Africa has produced rising incomes and faster human development, but sustained poverty reduction will depend on lasting and shared growth. Africa's frequent growth accelerations and collapses in the past provide a cautionary note for those who would like to interpret the progress of the past decade as a "turning point" in the continent's economic performance.

How durable is Africa's recent growth acceleration? Answering that question requires answers to several other questions concerning the causes of Africa's recent economic growth and the external environment within which its economies operate. How much of current performance is due to favorable commodity prices or the recovery of external assistance, and how much is due to hard-won economic policy reforms? How much has aid been scaled up, and what are the issues surrounding the management and delivery of greater aid? Relative to factors such as policy failures, conflicts, and natural disasters, how important are commodity price shocks in explaining output variability in Africa?

To address these and related questions, the Office of the Chief Economist of the Africa Region at the World Bank has sponsored several regional and country studies addressing the topics of growth, aid, and external shocks in Africa. This volume—the first in a new series of Africa Development Essays—pulls together 12 of these papers. The essays share recent empirical and policy findings of particular interest and will, I hope, contribute to the debate about Africa's growth prospects.

The essays in this volume show the vitality of research on Africa conducted by colleagues in and outside the World Bank. We look forward to further volumes of essays that will present research by World Bank staff members and other scholars directed at key policy issues in Africa's development.

John Page
Chief Economist
Africa Region, World Bank
Washington, DC

Abbreviations

Afreximbank	African Export–Import Bank
AGOA	African Growth and Opportunity Act
AMC	Advanced Market Commitment
ATI	African Trade Insurance Agency
bbl	barrel
CEM	Country Economic Memorandum
CEMAC	Economic and Monetary Community of Central Africa
CES	constant elasticity of substitution
CET	constant elasticity of transformation
CFAA	Country Financial Accountability Assessment
CGE	computable general equilibrium
CPAR	Country Procurement Assessment Report
CPI	consumer price index
CPIA	Country Policy and Institutional Assessment
CRED	Centre for Research on the Epidemiology of Disasters
CV	coefficient of variation
DAC	Development Assistance Committee
DM index	Deaton-Miller index
DNOC	domestic national oil company
DSA	debt sustainability analysis
DWE	direct welfare effect
EAC	East Africa Community

EBID	ECOWAS Bank for Investment and Development
EC	European Commission
ECCAS	Economic Community of Central African States
ECOWAS	Economic Community of West African States
EITI	Extractive Industries Transparency Initiative
EM-DAT	Emergency Disasters Database
EPM	*Enquête Auprès des Ménages*
ESMAP	Energy Sector Management Assistance Program
ESWs	Economic and Sector Works
FDI	foreign direct investment
FFG	Fund for Future Generations
FMIS	financial management information system
FRA	Fiscal Responsibility Act
FSA	fiscal sustainability analysis
GAVI	Global Alliance for Vaccines and Immunization
GDP	gross domestic product
Gemloc	Global Emerging Markets Local Currency (Bond Fund)
GNI	gross national income
GPG	global public good
HIPCs	heavily indebted poor countries
ICOR	incremental capital-output ratio
ICRG	International Country Risk Guide
IDA	International Development Association
IDS	Institute of Development Studies
IES	Income and Expenditure Survey
IFFIm	International Financing Facility for Immunization
IFS	International Financial Statistics
IMF	International Monetary Fund
INTOSAI	International Organization of Supreme Audit Institutions
IO	input-output
IWE	indirect welfare effect
LFS	Labor Force Survey
LIBOR	London interbank offered rate
MAMS	Maquette for MDG Simulations
MCA	Millennium Challenge Account
MDGs	Millennium Development Goals
MDRI	Multilateral Debt Relief Initiative

MGA	Malagasy ariary
MIGA	Multilateral Investment Guarantee Agency
MLD	mean log deviation
MOF	ministry of finance
MTEF	medium-term expenditure framework
NGO	nongovernmental organization
NPISH	nonprofit institution serving households
NPV	net present value
NSWG	National Stakeholders Working Group
ODA	official development assistance
OECD	Organisation for Economic Co-operation and Development
OLS	ordinary least squares
OPFR	oil price fiscal rule
ORC	oil-rich country
PEFA	public expenditure and financial accountability
PER	Public Expenditure Review
PFM	public financial management
PIU	project implementation unit
PPP	purchasing power parity
PRS	poverty reduction strategy
PRSP	Poverty Reduction Strategy Paper
PSC	production-sharing contract
PV	present value
ROSC	Reports on the Observance of Standards and Codes
SADC	Southern African Development Community
SAI	Supreme Audit Institution
SAM	social accounting matrix
SD	standard deviation
SIGFE	Sistema Integrado de Gestão Financeira de Angola
SimSIP	Simulations for Social Indicators and Poverty
SMH	Société Mauirtanienne des Hydrocarbures
SPA	Strategic Partnership with Africa
StAR	Stolen Assets Recovery
TFP	total factor productivity

TIP	Three 'I's of Poverty
TPP	*Taxes sur les Produits Pétroliers*
TWE	total welfare effect
VAR	vector autoregression
WAEMU	West African Economic and Monetary Union
WDI	*World Development Indicators*
WEO	World Economic Outlook
WTI	West Texas Intermediate

All amounts are presented in U.S. dollars unless otherwise indicated.

Introduction

Delfin S. Go and John Page

Sub-Saharan Africa (hereafter Africa) is the world's biggest development challenge. Much of Africa missed two decades of economic progress between 1975 and 1995, with the result that the average income per person was virtually unchanged between independence and the turn of the 21st century. Lagging the rest of the developing world in nearly every indicator of human well-being, Africa is also the region where, according to current projections, most of the Millennium Development Goals are unlikely to be met.

Yet there is renewed hope in recent years. Since the mid-1990s, an acceleration of economic growth in much of Africa has produced rising incomes and faster human development. This growth acceleration has raised questions and expectations about Africa's development. Is there a turnaround in Africa's economy? What will determine whether growth persists?

This book is a collection of essays that seeks to answer three interrelated sets of questions about Africa's recent growth recovery. The first set of essays addresses questions about the drivers and durability of Africa's growth. How different is current economic performance compared to Africa's long history of boom-bust cycles? Have African countries learned to avoid past mistakes and pursued the right policies? How much of the current performance depends on good luck—such as favorable commodity

1

prices or the recovery of external assistance—and how much depends on hard-won economic policy reforms.

A second set of essays looks at the role of donor flows. External assistance plays a larger role in Africa's growth story than in any other part of the developing world. As a result, the economic management of external assistance is a major public policy challenge, and donor behavior is a significant source of external risk. How much has aid been scaled up, and what are the issues of managing and delivering greater aid? Are there worrisome historical patterns and volatility to donor flows for Africa? What are the recent findings and lessons regarding the macroeconomic absorption and the fiscal spending of aid? How good is our understanding of the microdrivers of success in reaching the MDGs, and how are they related to expenditure efficiency? Under what circumstances is real exchange rate appreciation or "Dutch disease" an issue with regard to greater aid flows? How should the sequencing of public expenditures toward the attainment of MDGs in low-income countries be analyzed?

External shocks are often blamed for the unstable economic performance of African countries. The third set of essays looks at questions arising from commodity price shocks—especially from changes in the price of oil. Relative to factors such as policy failures, conflicts, and natural disasters, how important are commodity price shocks in explaining output variability in African countries? Compared to the oil price shocks in the 1970s, why have recent higher oil prices apparently had less impact on Africa's growth? Oil is also now an important source of revenue for several oil-exporting countries in Africa; what are the economic challenges faced by those countries? How should one analyze the macroeconomic and distributional impact of external and oil price shocks?

Part I: Patterns of Long-Term Growth in Sub-Saharan Africa

The first chapter, "Africa's Economy at a Turning Point?," by Arbache, Go, and Page, examines the recent acceleration of growth in Africa. Unlike the past, the performance is now registered broadly across several types of countries—particularly the oil-exporting and resource-intensive countries and, in more recent years, the large- and middle-income economies, as well as coastal and low-income countries. The analysis confirms a trend break in the mid-1990s, identifying a growth acceleration that is due not only to favorable terms of trade and greater aid, but also to better policy. Indeed, the growth diagnostics show that more and more African countries have been able to avoid mistakes with better macropolicy, better governance, and fewer conflicts; as a result, the likelihood of growth decelerations has declined significantly. Nonetheless, the sustainability of that growth is fragile, because economic fundamentals, such as savings, investment, productivity, and export diversification, remain stagnant. The good news in the story is that African economies appear to have learned how to avoid the mistakes that led to the frequent growth collapses between 1975 and 1995. The bad news is that much less is known about the recipes for long-term success in development, such as developing the right institutions and the policies to raise savings and diversify exports, than about how to avoid economic bad times.

Chapter 2, by Arbache and Page, is titled "The Long-Term Pattern of Growth in sub-Saharan Africa." Using the most recent purchasing power parity data for 44 sub-Saharan African countries, Arbache and Page examine the characteristics of long-run growth in Africa between 1975 and 2005. They find that low and volatile growth is the outstanding defining characteristic of Africa's growth experience since 1975, but they find no evidence that growth volatility is associated with economic performance over the long run. The analysis confirms that the 1990s mark a turning point in Africa's growth. It also finds that income distribution is becoming more unequal across countries, "clubs" are beginning to emerge, initial conditions matter a great deal for income distribution but not for growth, and geography and natural resources do not seem to matter for growth.

Part II: Aid—Volume, Volatility, and Macroeconomic Management

In chapter 3, "Assessing the Macroeconomic Framework for Scaling Up Aid," the authors, Go, Korman, Page, and Ye, survey the issues and challenges regarding the macroeconomic management of scaled-up foreign aid. The chapter summarizes recent country case studies undertaken at the International Monetary Fund and the World Bank regarding the absorption and spending of aid, as well as "fiscal space" studies of the feasibility of raising Millennium Development Goals (MDGs)–related expenditures. The chapter also describes how the analytical framework for aid management has expanded at the World Bank to address the challenges brought about by the advent of the country-based poverty reduction strategies, the MDGs, debt relief from the Heavily Indebted Poor Countries and Multilateral Debt Relief initiatives, and aid volatility and unpredictability. The last part of the essay summarizes selected country cases with respect to fiscal space issues and scenarios for accelerating progress toward the MDGs in Ethiopia, Ghana, Kenya, Madagascar, Rwanda, Tanzania, and Uganda.

Chuhan-Pole and Fitzpatrick investigate the evolution of foreign aid, particularly in sub-Saharan Africa, in chapter 4, "Providing More and Better Aid." The authors document notable changes in several dimensions of aid—its size, composition, sources, destinations, volatility, and predictability. For example, they find that development assistance is still the main source of external finance for sub-Saharan Africa. But although bilateral donors are allocating a larger share of their aid to the region, much of the increase reflects debt relief. Moreover, there is only limited evidence of a scaling up of development assistance to strong policy performers. The authors also argue that the reliability and predictability of aid remain important issues, although there are some signs of improvement. For example, better performers experience less year-to-year variation in aid flows, and there is some evidence that aid is becoming more predictable. The growing importance of global programs and nontraditional donors and the challenge they present to aid coherence are also discussed. The chapter concludes by looking at progress in the alignment of aid to national programs and the harmonization of donor practices and suggests reforms for delivering aid more effectively.

In chapter 5, Devarajan, Go, Page, Robinson, and Thierfelder argue that aid is about the future, and if recipients can plan consumption and investment decisions optimally over time, an aid-induced appreciation of the real exchange rate (Dutch disease) does not occur. In their essay, "The Macroeconomic Dynamics of Scaling Up Foreign Aid," this key result is derived without requiring extreme assumptions. The economic framework is a standard neoclassical growth model, based on the familiar Salter-Swan characterization of an open economy, with full dynamic savings and investment decisions. It requires the model to be fully dynamic in both savings and investment decisions. An important assumption is that aid must be predictable for intertemporal smoothing to take place. If aid volatility forces recipients to be constrained and myopic, Dutch disease problems become an issue.

How does one analyze MDG scenarios for a low-income country in Africa? In chapter 6, "Foreign Aid, Taxes, and Government Productivity: Alternative Scenarios for Ethiopia's MDG Strategy," Lofgren and Diaz-Bonilla present simulations based on MAMS (Maquette for MDG Simulations), an analytical framework pioneered and developed at the World Bank for this purpose. The authors find that, for Ethiopia and other countries in sub-Saharan Africa, very rapid growth in government service provision and spending would be needed to reach the MDG targets by 2015. Even if the necessary financing could be mobilized, strong efforts would be required to maintain an acceptable level of government productivity. Unless foreign aid is expanded more rapidly than seems plausible at this point, governments would face difficult trade-offs under which some MDGs might be achieved, but only at the expense of reduced progress on others. In such settings, it seems preferable to direct policy analysis toward the design of alternative strategies for different levels of foreign aid, thereby aiming at achieving feasible targets emanating from the specific country context. Finally, this chapter strongly suggests that an economy-wide perspective, like the one taken here, is needed to explore how such strategies influence key aspects of economic performance, including economic growth, the structure of production and incomes, and labor market conditions.

With prospects of scaling up aid not entirely certain, Ratha, Mohapatra, and Plaza look at the prospects of other resource flows to Africa. In chapter 7, "Beyond Aid: New Sources and Innovative Mechanisms for Financing Development in Sub-Saharan Africa," they describe the pattern and composition of resource flows to Africa and propose some creative ways to raise additional external financing. Some of the existing mechanisms—including multilateral guarantees to mobilize private capital for infrastructure projects, innovative structuring of future aid commitments, an international fund to encourage foreign investment in local currency bond markets, and the World Bank–United Nations Office of Drugs and Crime Stolen Asset Recovery initiative to repatriate Africa's illicit flight capital—can be used more intensively. African countries are now acquiring sovereign ratings and floating debt instruments in international capital markets. New players, such as China and India, have emerged on the African scene but are raising concerns. The authors argue that given the shortage and short-term nature of private capital flows and the concentration of foreign direct investment in enclave investments, Africa needs innovative financing mechanisms to raise additional external financing. The authors estimate that sub-Saharan African countries can potentially raise $1 billion to $3 billion by reducing the cost of international migrant remittances, $5 billion to $10 billion by issuing diaspora bonds, and $17 billion by securitizing future remittances and other future receivables. Because more than half of sub-Saharan African countries are not rated by the three major rating agencies, the authors make a case for establishing sovereign ratings, because such ratings can improve the market access not only for sovereigns but also for private sector entities. Model-based shadow ratings show that several unrated African countries may be more creditworthy than currently believed.

Part III: Managing External Shocks

The last part of the volume addresses another source of growth uncertainty in Africa: external shocks. Complementing the growth diagnostics of the first two chapters, chapter 8, by Raddatz, "Have External Shocks Become More Important for Output Fluctuations in African Countries?," uses a panel vector autoregression model to perform a series of variance decompositions and quantifies the relative importance of external and internal shocks as sources of macroeconomic fluctuations in African economies in 1963–89 and 1990–2003. Raddatz finds an increase in the relative importance of external shocks—including the international business cycle, commodity prices, interest rates, aid flows, and natural disasters—as sources of output instability in Africa in the past 15 years. He argues that this growing importance is due to two factors: (1) a decline in the variance of internal shocks and (2) an increase in the response of output to most external shocks. Raddatz also documents a decline in the variance of most external shocks (except aid flows) from 1990 to 2003. This favorable change in the external environment partly mitigates the effect of the two internal factors, but it is insufficient to compensate for their full impact. The chapter also shows that in oil-exporting African countries oil price shocks have had different output effects than changes in other commodity prices. In the oil exporters, changes in oil-driven external shocks account for much of the decline in output volatility during the period 1990–2003—a decline also supported by a reduction in the variance of internal shocks in oil exporters.

The next two chapters look at the rising importance of oil revenue for oil-exporting countries. The recent boom in oil prices poses significant opportunities for accelerating growth and poverty reduction in Africa. In chapter 9, titled "Harnessing Oil Windfalls," Devlin, Lewin, and Ranaweera describe fiscal approaches to managing oil windfalls. The chapter first outlines factors influencing the size and variability of current oil windfalls and the size of the government "take" from oil. Africa's oil windfall is large, but exhaustible and volatile. The authors argue that the windfall in and of itself does not translate into a permanent increase in wealth. A medium-term fiscal policy framework in which policy makers can make decisions about savings and investment is needed to avoid some of the real appreciation of the exchange rate and its detrimental impact on the economy and non-oil exports and to shift some of the benefits of current oil windfalls to future generations. Implementing such fiscal policies, however, requires a well-functioning system of fiscal controls—processes and institutions—as well as political incentives conducive to balancing the welfare of current and future generations. Thus, the chapter concludes by identifying fiscal mechanisms needed to enhance transparency and accountability in the use of oil windfalls and to mitigate rent-seeking behavior.

In chapter 10, Budina and van Wijnbergen focus on the role of fiscal and debt management policies in managing oil-driven volatility by making an in-depth analysis of the country case of Nigeria. Nigeria is one of the world's top oil exporters. However, its macroeconomic management of its oil windfall has been extraordinarily poor. The authors show that fiscal policy has increased rather than smoothed out oil price volatility and emphasize the challenge of managing volatility in a poor institutional environment. Budina and van Wijnbergen assess the sustainability of recently adopted fiscal policy rules and their robustness under alternative scenarios. In those scenarios, they focus mostly on downside risk factors, given Nigeria's history of debt overhang problems. The authors emphasize the insurance role of foreign exchange reserves and develop a framework to analyze the consequences of oil revenue spending rules for fiscal sustainability. Although relevant to contemporary Nigeria, the analytical framework is also of wider interest to other oil-rich countries.

As crude oil prices reach new highs, there is renewed concern about how external shocks will affect growth and poverty in Africa's oil-importing countries. The last two chapters present two country cases and two contrasting methods of addressing this question adapted to the availability of resources and data. In chapter 11, Andriamihaja and Vecchi estimate the effect of a rise in petroleum prices on living standards in Madagascar, combining information on expenditure patterns from the *Enquete Aupres des Menages* 2005 with an input-output model describing how petroleum price increases propagate across economic sectors. The attractiveness of the approach—besides its relative ease of implementation—derives from efficiently combining micro- and macrodata that are commonly available for most countries in a rigorous welfare analysis. Decomposing the total welfare effect, the authors identify both a *direct* welfare effect (heating and lighting one's house become more expensive) and an *indirect* effect (the price of food and anything else that has to be transported from factory to shop rises). Andriamihaja and Vecchi find that a 17 percent rise in oil prices, as observed in 2005, produces, on average, a 1.75 percent increase in household expenditures (1.5 percent for high-income households; 2.1 percent for households in the bottom expenditure quintile). About 60 percent of the increase in expenditures is due to the indirect effect, mostly through higher food prices. Although energy price increases hurt the poor more in percentage terms, subsidizing would involve a substantial leakage in favor of higher-income households. This paradox raises the issue of identifying more cost-effective policies to protect poor households against energy price increases.

Essama-Nssah, Go, Kearney, Korman, Robinson, and Thierfelder describe in chapter 12 an elaborate macro-micro framework for examining the structural and distributional consequences of a significant external shock—an increase in the world price of oil—on the South African economy. The authors merge results from a highly disaggregated computable general equilibrium model and a microsimulation analysis of earnings and occupational choice based on sociodemographic characteristics of the household. The model provides changes in employment, wages, and prices that are used in the microsimulation. Looking at the marginal effect, the authors find that a 125 percent increase in the price of crude oil and refined petroleum (which was the observed cumulative increase from 2003 to 2006) reduces employment and gross domestic product by approximately 2 percent and reduces household consumption by approximately 7 percent. The oil price shock tends to increase the disparity between rich and poor. The adverse impact of the oil price shock is felt by the poorer segment of the formal labor market in the form of declining wages and increased unemployment. Unemployment hits mostly low- and medium-skilled workers in the services sector. High-skilled households, on average, gain from the oil price shock. Their income rises, and their spending basket is less skewed toward food and other goods that are most affected by changes in oil prices. The actual impact may vary and be ameliorated by compensating factors, as appears to be the case to this point in South Africa.

The essays in this volume offer a range of analytical and policy perspectives on Africa's current growth. Taken together, they suggest that the 21st century may mark a turning point in Africa's postindependence economic performance. Today, Africa's macroeconomies are better managed than at any time in the past three decades. Countries have learned how to avoid the debilitating economic collapses that characterized the 20 years from 1975 to 1995 and are now poised to move to a second decade of growth. But, the achievements of the past decade provide no basis for complacency. As the essays in this volume show, laying the policy and institutional basis for longer-term growth, managing volatile commodity prices and aid flows, and turning growth in *average* incomes into growth in *all* incomes remain formidable—but manageable—challenges if Africa is to reach its turning point.

PART I

Patterns of Long-Term Growth in Sub-Saharan Africa

CHAPTER 1

Is Africa's Economy at a Turning Point?

Jorge Arbache, Delfin S. Go, and John Page

There is something decidedly different and new about the economic land-scape of sub-Saharan Africa (Africa or the region hereafter). After stagnat-ing for much of 45 years, economic performance in Africa is markedly improving. In recent years, for example, growth in gross domestic product (GDP) in Africa is accelerating to its strongest point at about 6 percent a year, while inflation registered below the two-digit level, its lowest point. This much-improved economic performance is confirmed by several recent assessments.[1]

Although the current economic growth is still short-lived relative to Africa's long history of growth crisis and is certainly nowhere close to the standard of East Asia, it is nonetheless noteworthy and a cause for guarded optimism. The performance at least calls for a closer examination. Several interesting questions can immediately be raised: Is Africa finally overcom-ing the challenges of growth and poverty to claim the 21st century, as posed, for example, by Gelb et al. (2000), Collier (2007), and Ndulu et al. (2007)? In particular, is there indeed a turning point? How widespread are the recent gains among the 47 countries in the region? What are the key factors underlying the recent improvements in Africa's economic perform-ance? Why have the recent oil price increases not dampened its growth performance? Is the growth robust and supported by improvements in the economic fundamentals? What major risks and challenges remain? Will Africa attain the Millennium Development Goals by 2015?

The rest of the chapter looks at these questions and is organized as follows. The recent acceleration of growth in Africa is discussed in the next section. Then, the growth diagnostics in the following section carefully examine the differences since 1995, the likely causes of the recent growth, and its robustness. The chapter then looks at the key actions that are necessary to promote and sustain growth and discusses why growth should be shared. The chapter concludes by summarizing sub-Saharan Africa's economic prospects.

The Recent Acceleration of Growth in Africa

Is the growth failure in sub-Saharan Africa finally reversing? An upward shift in the recent growth rates suggests that a trend break may have taken place around the mid-1990s.[2] Annual GDP growth was a sluggish 2.9 percent in the 1980s and 1.7 percent during 1990–94. Since 1994, however, the pace of economic expansion has approached the threshold of moderate growth of 5 percent a year. Even if the record is measured more conservatively with regard to per capita income, the shift is perceptible: relative to its prolonged stagnation or contraction, per capita income grew by 1.6 percent a year in the late 1990s and by 2.1 percent to 3.0 percent a year since 2000. Despite the recent oil price shock, growth has remained good. From 2004 to 2006, the annual growth in GDP and per capita income, when weighted by each country's GDP, approaches 6 and 4 percent, respectively. Although improvement in aggregate output does not necessarily indicate broad economic development of the region, the current growth episode has nonetheless lasted 12 years altogether, a period that is neither trivial nor brief.

In fact, average incomes in Africa have been rising in tandem with those in other regions (figure 1.1). The top performers in Africa are doing very well compared with fast-growing countries in other regions (figure 1.2).

How Widespread Is the Current Growth Acceleration?

The recent economic expansion seems to be registering across an increasing number of countries (figure 1.3). The number of countries with economic declines dropped from 15 to 18 in the early 1990s to about 2 to 5 countries in recent years. Only one country has significant economic

FIGURE 1.1

African Per Capita Income Relative to Other Developing Countries

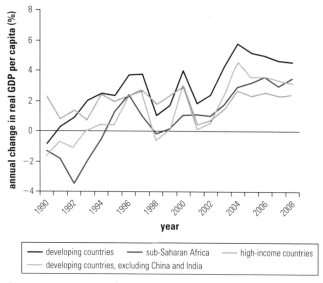

Source: World Bank various years g.

FIGURE 1.2

Africa's Five Fastest-Growing Economies Relative to Asia

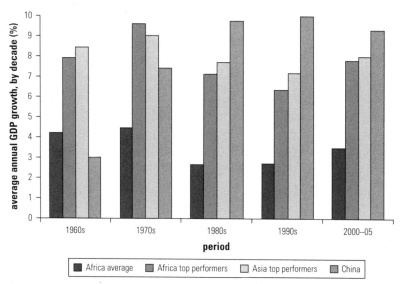

Source: World Bank various years g.

FIGURE 1.3

Growth Pattern of African Countries: Number of Countries by Different GDP Growth Range

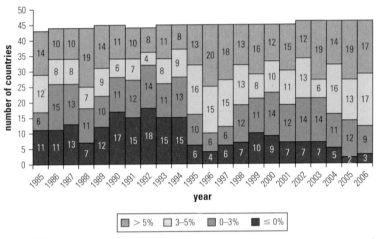

Sources: AFRCE various years; World Bank various years g.

contraction—Zimbabwe.[3] In contrast, about 40–45 countries have positive growth, and 14–19 countries are growing by more than 5 percent a year.

During 2000–06, about 26 countries had GDP growth exceeding 4 percent a year, while as many as 14 countries exceeded 5.5 percent. Countries with at least 4 percent GDP growth now constitute a sizable portion of sub-Saharan Africa—about 70 percent of the region's total population and 80 percent of the region's GDP. As a group, these countries have been growing consistently at nearly 7 percent a year, whether considered in the more recent period or a longer period since the mid-1990s. The classification of countries in table 1.1 is fairly stable in the two time periods. There are some exceptions near the cut-off point: the performance of São Tomé and Principe, Sierra Leone, South Africa, and Zambia has improved in performance during the more recent period (2004–06), whereas that of Malawi and, to a smaller extent, Cameroon and Mauritius has deteriorated.

Performance by Different Types of Countries

Nonetheless, the range of growth among individual countries can vary widely, anywhere from −5.5 percent to a high of 23.1 percent. Alternative

TABLE 1.1
GDP Growth Rates for Individual Countries in Sub-Saharan Africa

GDP growth > 4% in 2000–06[a]			GDP growth < 4% in 2000–06[b]		
Country	2000–06 (%)	1995–2006 (%)	Country	2000–06 (%)	1995–2006 (%)
Equatorial Guinea	23.1	36.2	Mauritius	3.9	4.4
Sierra Leone	11.6	1.7	Cameroon	3.7	4.1
Chad	10.9	7.4	Kenya	3.6	3.3
Angola	10.6	9.8	Niger	3.5	3.6
Liberia	8.9	12.1[c]	Lesotho	3.4	3.2
Mozambique	7.6	7.9	Madagascar	3.2	3.2
Sudan	7.3	5.8	Guinea Congo, Dem	2.8	3.6
Tanzania	6.3	5.2	Rep. of	2.6	0.6
Ethiopia	6.2	5.7	Malawi	2.6	4.4
Burkina Faso	6.1	6.6	Comoros	2.4	2.2
Cape Verde	5.7	6.9	Swaziland	2.4	2.8
Nigeria	5.6	4.4	Burundi	2.2	0.3
Uganda	5.6	6.4	Togo	1.7	2.3
Rwanda	5.5	9.7	Eritrea	1.3	2.6
Botswana	5.3	6.3	Guinea-Bissau	1.2	0.3
Ghana	5.0	4.8	Gabon	1.1	1.4
São Tomé and Principe	5.0	3.7	Central African Rep.	0.2	1.1
Mauritania	4.9	4.6	Seychelles	0.1	2.3
Gambia, The	4.9	4.6	Côte d'Ivoire	−0.3	2.0
Congo, Rep. of	4.9	3.6	Zimbabwe	−5.5	−2.6
Mali	4.9	5.1			
Zambia	4.8	3.4			
Namibia	4.5	4.1			
Benin	4.2	4.6			
South Africa	4.1	3.5			
Senegal	4.1	4.3			
Average	6.8	6.9	Average	1.8	2.3

Source: World Bank various years g.

Note: The cut-off point of 4 percent is based primarily on performance during 2000–06. Somalia is not included for lack of data. At the World Bank, Djibouti is classified as part of the Middle East and not as part of sub-Saharan Africa.

a. These countries represent 70 percent of the population of sub-Saharan Africa and 78 percent of GDP.

b. These countries represent 30 percent of the population of sub-Saharan Africa and 22 percent of GDP.

c. Data for Liberia were available only for 1999–2006.

taxonomies of countries are often necessary to characterize the growth story better. Table 1.2 presents the growth performance for frequently used country groups for the 1980s, the 1990s, and the more recent periods. The numbers show that, unlike the past, the recent acceleration of growth is broadly registered across different types of countries.

TABLE 1.2
Real GDP Growth in Sub-Saharan Africa

Categories of countries	1980–2006 (%)			Recent periods (%)			Since mid-1990s (%)
	1980–89	1990–99	2000–06	2000–03	2004–06	2007[a]	1995–2006
Sub-Saharan Africa							
Simple average:							
Region	2.9	3.3	4.6	4.3	5.1	5.3	4.9
Region, excluding Zimbabwe	2.9	3.3	4.9	4.5	5.3	5.6	5.0
Weighted average:							
Region	2.3	2.1	4.6	3.9	5.9	6.1	4.1
Nigeria	1.7	2.8	5.6	5.2	6.2	7.3	4.4
South Africa	2.2	1.4	4.1	3.4	5.0	5.0	3.5
Rest of sub-Saharan Africa	2.7	2.5	4.9	4.0	6.5	6.1	5.1
Oil exporting countries	3.5	5.9	8.4	8.4	8.4	8.2	9.1
Oil importing countries	2.8	2.7	4.1	3.7	4.7	5.0	4.1
By endowment and location:							
Resource-intensive countries	3.2	1.3	5.7	6.1	5.1	4.9	3.8
Coastal countries	2.9	3.4	3.8	3.4	4.4	5.0	4.3
Landlocked countries	2.9	2.5	3.0	2.1	4.2	4.3	3.6
By income level and fragile states:							
Middle-income countries	5.6	4.5	3.7	3.5	4.0	4.7	4.2
Low-income countries	2.1	3.5	4.9	4.3	5.6	6.1	5.2
Fragile countries	2.2	0.5	2.8	2.4	3.2	3.6	2.5
Regional groups							
EAC	3.4	3.9	5.1	4.5	6.0	6.4	5.0
SADC	3.6	2.6	4.0	3.1	5.2	5.7	4.0
CFA franc zone	2.8	4.9	4.9	5.1	4.7	4.3	5.9
WAEMU	2.1	3.5	3.2	2.9	3.5	4.0	3.6
CEMAC	3.8	6.8	7.3	8.0	6.4	4.7	9.0
ECOWAS	2.4	2.8	4.7	4.8	4.5	5.2	4.4
ECCAS	2.8	3.6	6.3	6.0	6.9	6.6	7.1
COMESA	3.0	2.3	3.5	2.4	5.0	5.8	3.8
IOC	2.9	3.5	2.4	2.1	2.9	5.1	3.0
Other categories							
Flexible exchange rate regime	2.3	2.4	5.1	4.3	6.1	7.1	5.1
Fixed exchange rate regime	3.5	3.9	4.3	4.3	4.4	4.1	5.1
MDRI	2.1	2.7	5.3	5.1	5.6	6.0	5.0

Sources: IMF various years; World Bank various years a.

Note: CEMAC = Economic and Monetary Community of Central Africa; COMESA = Common Market for Eastern and Southern Africa; EAC = East African Community; ECCAS = Economic Community of Central African States; ECOWAS = Economic Community of West African States; IOC = Indian Ocean Commission; MDRI = Multilateral Debt Relief Initiative; SADC = Southern African Development Community; WAEMU = West Africa Economic and Monetary Union. All statistics are annual percentage rates and simple averages unless otherwise mentioned.

a. Estimates based on AFRCE various years, World Bank 2007a, and IMF 2007a.

An immediate issue in characterizing group performances is the choice of central tendencies. Population weights are best if the desired reference is the typical African in the group. If the typical country and its representative economic experience and policies are the targets as in this analysis, simple averages are more appropriate to give equal weights to individual countries.[4] This method is used to characterize growth in table 1.2. The overall regional growth is, however, also presented by weighted average by GDP.

Large Countries

Nigeria and South Africa are the two largest economies in sub-Saharan Africa, accounting for almost half the regional GDP and one-fourth the population. Their slow growths in the past have tended to pull down any regional growth averages, especially if GDP weights were used. However, as may be seen in table 1.2, the growth performance of Nigeria and South Africa has improved significantly since 2000. During 2004–06 in particular, their GDP growth reached about 6.2 and 5.0 percent a year, respectively. The rest of sub-Saharan Africa continued to do better at 6.5 percent a year during 2004–06. The weighted average (about 6 percent) for the whole region is better than its simple average (about 5 percent) for the same period, which suggests that large countries in general are doing well.

Oil-Exporting Countries

Higher oil prices since 2000 now directly benefit eight countries where net oil exports make up 30 percent or more of total exports: Angola, Cameroon, Chad, Republic of Congo, Equatorial Guinea, Gabon, Nigeria, and Sudan. Côte d'Ivoire is also producing oil, but its net exports of oil are still low. Angola and Nigeria are the largest oil exporters, accounting for about 20 percent and 53 percent, respectively, of Africa's total oil exports. As a group, the oil exporters represent about 25 and 29 percent of Africa's GDP and population, respectively. Moreover, fuel now makes up about 40 percent of Africa's total merchandise exports.

Partly as a result of the recent higher oil prices, real GDP growth in oil-exporting countries accelerated to about 8.4 percent a year during 2000–06. This growth represents the strongest economic expansion among the possible country groupings shown in table 1.2. Growth during the 1990s was also significant at 5.9 percent a year.

Oil-Importing Countries by Endowment and Location

Although growth in oil-importing countries lagged behind the regional average, it has also been improving, reaching 4.7 percent during 2004–06. This group is large and diverse, encompassing the majority of African countries and a wide range of characteristics. For digging deeper, the classification of countries by endowment and location, as suggested by Collier and O'Connell (2006), is useful. Countries are grouped in a nonoverlapping way as non-oil resource-intensive countries, coastal, and landlocked countries.[5]

The six *non-oil resource-intensive countries* represent roughly 4.9 percent of Africa's GDP and 4.2 percent of its population.[6] Like the oil exporters, the group also did very well relative to its own past performance: 5.1 percent during 2000–06 or 5.7 percent since 2000.

The 19 *coastal countries* account for about 53 percent of the regional GDP and 32 percent of the total population.[7] This group has been growing by 3.4 percent a year since 2000—a rate that has further improved to 4.4 percent a year during 2004–06.

The 13 *landlocked countries* were traditionally the laggards in growth.[8] Although they represent as much as 32 percent of the total population in the region, they take up only 17 percent of the regional income. Annual growth in GDP since 2000 has averaged only 3 percent but has improved to 4.2 percent recently. The individual records are mixed. Although the group includes noted growth failures such as the Central African Republic and Zimbabwe, it nonetheless has several bright spots, as reported in table 1.1: Burkina Faso, Ethiopia, Mali, Rwanda, and Uganda.

Oil-Importing Countries by Income and Fragile States

An alternative classification of the oil-importing countries is by income level and fragile states—that is, low- and middle-income countries plus fragile states. The International Monetary Fund, (IMF) for example, has used this classification (see IMF 2007a).[9]

The eight *middle-income countries* correspond to less than 8 percent of the region's total population but to 40 percent of regional income.[10] South Africa alone represents 6.3 percent of the population and 35 percent of Africa's GDP. The individual performances in this group have been mixed: whereas South Africa's performance has been improving in recent periods, the performance of others (such as the Seychelles, Swaziland, and to some extent Mauritius) has slowed down. Zimbabwe, which used to be in this group, is now a fragile low-income country. As a result of the mixed performance of several countries, average growth for the group has fallen slightly from the 1980s and 1990s. However, growth during 2004–06 has again rebounded to about 4 percent a year.

Fifteen countries may be classified as *low income* and non–oil exporting.[11] They are home to 45 percent of the total population but only 25 percent of the total income in the region. However, the recent performance of the group is heartening: growth has been steadily improving, from 2.1 percent a year in the 1980s to 3.5 percent in the 1990s and 4.9 percent since 2000. In recent years, growth has been approaching 5.6 percent annually. The top performers in this group include Ghana, Mozambique, Senegal, and Tanzania plus the bright spots mentioned for landlocked countries: Burkina Faso, Ethiopia, Mali, Rwanda, and Uganda.

Fragile states without significant oil resources—14 countries—still account for 18 percent of the total population and 10 percent of total income in the region.[12] For the most part, GDP growth in this group is stuck at less than 2.5 percent, but it improved to 3.2 percent during 2004–06. The challenges faced by this group are many and daunting, as has been portrayed persuasively by sources such as Collier (2007) and the World Bank (2007b, 2007c). Even so, there are hopeful signs; a few countries have managed to turn around at least their output growth (as reported in table 1.1): The Gambia, Liberia, São Tomé and Principe, and Sierra Leone.

Regional Groupings

There are several overlapping regional groupings in sub-Saharan Africa. Among those presented in table 1.2, the East Africa Community (EAC),[13] the Economic and Monetary Community of Central Africa (CEMAC),[14] and the Economic Community of Central African States (ECCAS)[15] did the best, at 6.0, 6.4, and 6.9 percent, respectively, during 2004–06. The Southern African Development Community (SADC)[16] and the Economic Community of West African States (ECOWAS)[17] did as well as the regional average in recent years. Regional groups below the African average include the western part of the franc zone—the West African Economic and Monetary Union (WAEMU)—and the island economies in the Indian Ocean Commission.[18] WAEMU has the fixed exchange rate but not the oil resources of the eastern part.[19]

In sum, there is therefore evidence that economic growth is accelerating and registering across several types of countries, not just oil-exporting and resource-rich countries, but also oil-importing, landlocked, and—to some extent—fragile countries. Are country patterns with respect to growth becoming less defined? In chapter 2, Arbache and Page found no obvious pattern when classifying countries according to long-term growth, geography, and geology, thus suggesting that initial conditions and other factors may play an important role in explaining performance. They found, however, that income typology—classification of countries above and below the median GDP per capita—to be suitable to predict human development indicators and economic performance when tested against others. In any case, the next section analyzes the recent growth record more rigorously over a longer period of time.

Growth Diagnostics: What Is Different since 1995?

How different is the recent experience in the context of Africa's history of frequent growth accelerations and collapses? This section examines the issue on the basis of findings from a series of growth diagnostics and statistical tests conducted by Arbache and Page using long time-series and most recent purchasing power parity data for 45 African countries. In the next chapter, one of those studies is used to examine the characteristics and patterns of long-term growth in sub-Saharan Africa for cross-country income structure, convergence, country level, growth persistence, and evidence for the formation of country groups or clubs. The growth diagnostics of this section are derived from the two other studies on growth cycles and their robustness (Arbache and Page 2007a, 2007b), as well as various briefs by the Office of the Chief Economist of the World Bank's Africa region (AFRCE various years).

Africa's Growth: 1975–2005

The analysis uses GDP per capita (or per capita income hereafter) with regard to purchasing power parity (PPP) at 2000 international prices and its growth rate. Data on per capita income (PPP at 2000 international prices) and its growth rate are taken from the World Bank's (various years g) *World Development Indicators* (*WDI*), unless otherwise specified. The sample includes all sub-Saharan countries except Liberia and Somalia, for which there are no data. Because the emphasis is on the representative country, unweighted country data in the aggregate analysis are used unless otherwise stated. The time-series spans 1975–2005.[20] Thus, there is an unbalanced panel of data with $T = 31$ and $N = 45$. This period follows the

FIGURE 1.4
Per Capita Income

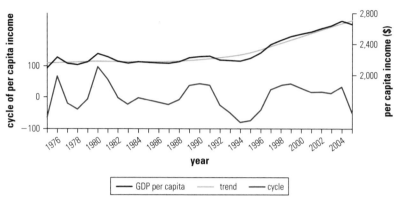

Source: Arbache and Page 2007a.

first oil shock and includes the commodity prices plunge, when many African economies collapsed and several conflicts erupted; the introduction of structural reforms, which brought significant changes in many economies; and the recently observed growth recovery.

Figure 1.4 shows that mean per capita income in Africa had a slow, positive long-term trend, consisting of about 20 years of virtual stagnation with a point of inflexion upward in the mid-1990s. Since then, actual income has remained above the trend most of the time and the variance appears to have declined.[21] The same is true if growth rates of per capita income are used. Figure 1.5 shows Africa's growth path over the same

FIGURE 1.5
Growth Rate of Per Capita Income

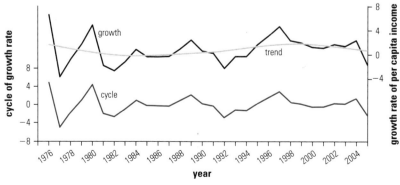

Source: Arbache and Page 2007a.

TABLE 1.3

Per Capita Income, Mean Growth, and Variation for Different Periods in Africa

Period	Growth rate			GDP per capita ($)
	Mean (%)	Standard deviation	Coefficient of variation	
1975–2005	0.70	6.27	8.96	2,299
1975–84	0.13	6.92	53.23	2,180
1985–94	−0.23	5.87	−25.52	2,183
1995–2005	1.88	5.99	3.19	2,486
1975–94	−0.07	6.33	−90.43	2,182
(1995–2005) − (1985–94)	2.11	0.12	28.71	303
(1995–2005) − (1975–94)	1.95	−0.34	93.61	304

Source: Arbache and Page 2007a.

period. Trend growth declined until the late 1980s and increased thereafter, although there is evidence of a slowdown in recent years. Variance has declined since the mid-1990s, and actual growth has tended to be above and closer to the trend (table 1.3).

A Trend Break in 1995

At the regional level, growth in per capita income increased substantially during 1995–2005 and was accompanied by a sharp reduction in the coefficient of variation. This story is consistent with that about aggregate GDP growth discussed earlier. The per capita growth rate rose from −0.23 percent of the previous decade to 1.88 percent during 1995–2005, and the absolute value of the coefficient of variation fell from (−25.5) percent to 3.2 percent (table 1.3). This shift implies an increase of 2 percent in growth, which is about three times the long-term growth rate of 0.7 percent. Income per capita went up to $2,486 in 1995–2005, which represents an increase of about $300, or 11 percent, compared with previous periods. Recursive residual estimations, Chow breakpoint tests, and Chow forecast tests do not reject the hypothesis that a structural break in the growth series occurred between 1995 and 1997 (Arbache and Page 2007b).

Hence, statistical evidence suggests that structural breaks occurred in the mid-1990s for per capita income or its growth, thereby making it legitimate to break up the series before and after this period. To put the recent growth experience in better perspective, however, one must look at Africa's long history of economic boom-bust cycles.

History of Growths and Collapses

Although there has been a recent trend break, Africa's growth over the past three decades has been both low and highly variable (Ndulu et al. 2007). Between 1975 and 2005, per capita income PPP grew by 0.7 percent per year, by far the lowest figure among developing regions. At the same time, country growth rates were highly volatile. Interestingly, however, there is no evidence that growth volatility was associated with Africa's poor long-term economic performance (see chapter 2, by Arbache and Page). This result is unexpected (Ramey and Ramey 1995; Hnatkovska and Loayza 2004) and may be misleading. Perhaps because no statistical association exists between Africa's long-term growth rate and its volatility, most attempts to explain Africa's growth performance have focused on investigating the determinants of growth over time and across countries using standard models and techniques (Collier and Gunning 1999; O'Connell and Ndulu 2000; Ndulu et al. 2007). Instead, given Africa's high growth volatility, it may be more relevant and rewarding to examine the causes and consequences of medium-term deviations from the long-run trend: growth accelerations and decelerations.

Identification of Good Times and Bad

As a means of investigating this phenomenon, the economic performance of African countries is classified into growth acceleration and deceleration on the basis of a variation of the methodology in Hausmann, Pritchett, and Rodrik (2005). What constitutes good times for a given country? There are four conditions: First, the four-year forward-moving average of GDP per capita growth minus the country's four-year backward-moving average is greater than zero for a given year. Second, the four-year forward-moving average of growth is above the country's long-run trend. Third, the four-year forward-moving average of GDP per capita exceeds the four-year backward-moving average. Fourth, the first three conditions are satisfied for at least three years in a row, followed by the three subsequent years after the last year that satisfies the first three conditions. And what constitutes bad times?—the opposites of the first three conditions for good times.

In contrast to Hausmann, Pritchett, and Rodrik (2005), this methodology does not impose common parameters for identifying growth acceleration in a cross-section of countries. Instead, it identifies growth acceleration *and* deceleration by *endogenizing* each country's economic conditions into the method, thus allowing for a much wider and more informative investigation of growth volatility. For example, a period with a modest average per capita growth rate of, say, 3 percent may not be substantial for many countries, but it may well be a genuine growth boom for a country enduring very low growth rates. This method takes care of this kind of issue, avoids unsupported generalizations, and provides more sensible results.

Using this methodology, one finds that African countries have experienced numerous episodes of growth acceleration in the past 30 years, but also a comparable number of growth collapses. In short, Africa's long-run record of slow and volatile growth reflects a pattern of alternating, identifiable accelerations and declines, rather than random variations of growth rates around the long-run trend. In addition, growth volatility—when viewed as the product of accelerations and declines—is not neutral and indeed matters for economic and social outcomes. To begin to address the public policy questions posed by these results, one must look for correlates associated with acceleration and deceleration episodes and examine the probability that an economy will undergo a growth acceleration or deceleration.

Growth Acceleration and Deceleration over Time

Table 1.4 shows the unconditional probability of accelerations and decelerations and their respective growth rates for different periods. For the entire period from 1975 to 2005, there is a slightly higher probability of growth acceleration than deceleration: 25 percent of the 1,243 country-year observations (total of valid observations per country per year) refer to countries experiencing growth acceleration, while 22 percent refer to countries experiencing growth decelerations.[22]

Between 1975 and 2005, countries in Africa that experienced growth accelerations managed to grow on average by 3.6 percent during those episodes, compared with the regionwide average of 0.7 percent. During decelerations, countries contracted on average by −2.7 percent. Given the almost equal probabilities of growth accelerations and decelerations, most of the benefits of growth accelerations on Africa were offset by growth collapses, leading to an overall tepid rate of growth. Had Africa avoided its growth collapses, it would have grown at 1.7 percent a year in per capita terms instead of 0.7 percent. Figure 1.6 shows the actual and simulated GDP per capita at these growth rates. Income per capita would have been at least 30 percent higher in 2005 had bad times been avoided.[23] This finding

TABLE 1.4

Likelihood and Growth Rates of Economic Acceleration and Deceleration in Africa, 1975–2005

Period	All country-years in the period		Country-years with growth acceleration		Country-years with growth deceleration		Country-years with trend growth
	Observations (country-years)	Growth (%)	Frequency of country-years	Growth (%)	Frequency of country-years	Growth (%)	Frequency of country-years
1995–2005 (after trend break)	494	1.88	0.42	3.76	0.12	−1.29	0.46
1975–94 (before trend break)	749	−0.07	0.14	3.39	0.29	−3.14	0.57
1985–94	433	−0.23	0.21	3.21	0.36	−3.18	0.43
1975–84	316	0.13	0.04	4.61	0.18	−3.06	0.78
1975–2005 (all years)	1,243	0.7	0.25	3.64	0.22	−2.74	0.53

Source: Arbache and Page 2007a.

FIGURE 1.6
Actual and Simulated GDP Per Capita

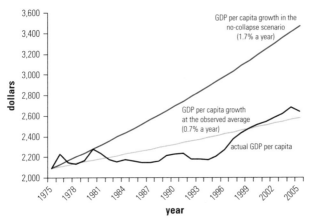

Source: Arbache and Page 2007b.

is consistent with Easterly (1998), who argued that the incremental capital-output ratio, ICOR (or its inverse, the marginal returns of investment) of African countries such as Zambia fluctuated too much, so that growth opportunities were missed. Growth decelerations matter a great deal in the fight against poverty in Africa.

The relative frequency of good and bad times over the past three decades follows Africa's long-run pattern of growth. Accelerations were more frequent in 1995–2005; decelerations were more common in the two preceding decades. Forty-two percent of the 494 country-year observations for 1995–2005 occurred in countries experiencing growth accelerations, and only 12 percent in countries undergoing growth decelerations. The remaining 46 percent of observations belong to years in which countries were experiencing neither growth acceleration nor deceleration. In 1975–1984, growth decelerations were 350 percent more frequent than accelerations.[24] In 1985–1994, this ratio had dropped to 71 percent, mainly because of a sharp rise in accelerations to 21 percent from 4 percent.

In 1995–2005, the average growth rate for countries during acceleration episodes was 3.8 percent, the second-highest average among the three 10-year periods. Interestingly, it was in 1975–1984, a period of very modest regional economic growth, that average growth during accelerations reached its highest rate. This finding reflects a compositional effect at work. In the past decade, even long-stagnant economies, such as the Central

African Republic, Ethiopia, Mali, Mozambique, Sierra Leone, and Tanzania, experienced some sustained growth, pushing down the averages during acceleration episodes, whereas in 1975–1984, the high average growth rate was mainly due to a few growth accelerations overall and very rapid growth in the Republic of Congo.

The average (negative) growth rate for countries experiencing growth decelerations in 1995–2005 was less than half that in previous decades, contributing to the more positive overall economic performance of the period. Economic declines had both the highest frequency—double that of the next highest decade—and the greatest impact on countries during the 1985–1995 period.

Nonetheless, some caution arises from the fact that a significant amount of time—53 percent—pertains to country-years with neither growth acceleration nor growth deceleration for the entire period from 1975 to 2005. These are supposed to be "normal times," when countries were growing at the trend line. For much of the time before 1995, however (as shown in figure 1.4), that trend is very flat, the growth stagnant. From a very high 78 percent during 1975–84, that likelihood also fell to about 43 percent during 1975–94. Since 1995, the probability of growing at the trend is still high at 46 percent, but the trend has shifted up to 1.9 percent a year.

Country Pattern of Growth Cycles

Over the entire 30-year period, richer countries have had more growth accelerations, and poorer countries have experienced more growth collapses. This result is, of course, to some extent endogenous; average income per capita will tend to rise in countries with more frequent growth accelerations and fall in countries with more frequent collapses. But this result also holds in each 10-year period, where the compounding effects may be assumed to be less important. It may indicate that richer countries can better take advantage of propitious circumstances and that poorer countries are less able to avoid bad times. There is one interesting exception. Income per capita for countries experiencing growth accelerations in 1995–2005 is slightly below the average for the region overall, thus indicating that growth successes have been spreading to poorer countries in the past decade.

Table 1.5 shows the frequency of growth acceleration and deceleration episodes by country category and compares them with the mean. In general, there is no substantial difference in the probabilities of growth

TABLE 1.5

Frequency of Growth Acceleration and Deceleration by Country Category

Country category	Growth acceleration		Growth deceleration	
	Frequency of country-years	Above or below all countries' mean	Frequency of country-years	Above or below all countries' mean
All countries' mean	0.25	n.a.	0.22	n.a.
Coastal countries	0.26	Above	0.22	Equal
Landlocked countries	0.23	Below	0.22	Equal
Coastal countries without resources	0.24	Below	0.23	Above
Landlocked countries without resources	0.22	Below	0.22	Equal
Oil exporters	0.29	Above	0.23	Above
Non-oil exporters	0.24	Below	0.22	Equal
Resource-rich countries	0.30	Above	0.21	Below
Non-resource-rich countries	0.23	Below	0.23	Above
Major conflict countries	0.16	Below	0.17	Below
Minor conflict countries	0.19	Below	0.32	Above

Source: Arbache and Page 2007b.

Note: n.a. = not applicable.

acceleration and deceleration episodes for a given country category. Although geography does not appear to matter, geology and conflict do.[25] As might be expected, oil exporters and resource-rich countries have more frequent growth accelerations but, somewhat unexpectedly, the same frequency of growth decelerations as the regional average. Conflict is also important in determining good times and bad. Major conflict countries had fewer growth accelerations than the regional average but also fewer decelerations. They also had significantly lower average growth than the regional average. Taken together, these results suggest that major conflict countries were trapped in a low-level equilibrium. Minor conflict countries have a substantially higher probability of a growth deceleration than the average and are much more likely to experience bad times than good times.

Table 1.6 shows the unconditional probabilities of growth acceleration and deceleration at the country level and the growth rates during these episodes. The gaps between growth rates during accelerations and decelerations at the country level tend to be high, generating the high growth volatility observed in Africa. The high average growth rates observed in many economies during acceleration episodes also show the resilience and capacity of the region's economies to grow when economic and political

TABLE 1.6
Frequency of Growth Acceleration and Deceleration and Growth Rate at the Country Level

Country	Frequency of growth acceleration	Frequency of growth deceleration	Growth rate, 1976–2005 (%)	Growth rate during growth acceleration years (%)	Growth rate during growth deceleration years (%)
Angola	0.48	0.28	0.70	3.93	−5.48
Benin	0.27	0.23	0.59	1.60	−0.99
Botswana	0.43	0.00	6.24	6.87	
Burkina Faso	0.43	0.00	1.21	1.39	
Burundi	0.20	0.23	−0.47	1.48	−4.45
Cameroon	0.23	0.23	0.81	2.21	−5.34
Cape Verde	0.42	0.00	3.26	3.57	
Central African Rep.	0.23	0.53	−1.27	0.89	−1.95
Chad	0.20	0.20	1.34	7.66	−1.66
Comoros	0.24	0.28	−0.14	0.11	−1.89
Congo, Dem. Rep. of	0.00	0.30	−3.94		−7.60
Congo, Rep. of	0.20	0.43	0.61	10.05	−2.25
Côte d'Ivoire	0.20	0.63	−1.57	1.82	−3.81
Equatorial Guinea	0.42	0.00	10.55	20.88	
Eritrea	0.00	0.00	1.96		
Ethiopia	0.25	0.25	0.42	3.71	−3.05
Gabon	0.00	0.40	−0.91		−1.52
Gambia, The	0.00	0.23	0.29		−0.99
Ghana	0.43	0.20	0.60	2.15	−4.33
Guinea	0.37	0.00	0.98	1.78	
Guinea-Bissau	0.23	0.20	−0.70	0.76	−1.87
Kenya	0.20	0.40	0.48	1.76	−0.75
Lesotho	0.23	0.00	3.27	3.83	
Madagascar	0.00	0.43	−1.38		−2.12
Malawi	0.23	0.37	0.22	1.68	−2.12
Mali	0.33	0.23	0.86	2.75	−3.09
Mauritania	0.00	0.00	0.10		
Mauritius	0.28	0.00	4.22	5.65	
Mozambique	0.32	0.00	2.08	5.08	
Namibia	0.32	0.00	0.15	2.14	
Niger	0.00	0.43	−1.01		−3.55
Nigeria	0.53	0.20	0.27	1.99	−4.79
Rwanda	0.20	0.20	1.68	2.27	2.12
São Tomé and Principe	0.47	0.00	0.31	0.99	
Senegal	0.27	0.23	0.36	1.75	−1.38
Seychelles	0.53	0.00	2.46	4.01	
Sierra Leone	0.20	0.47	−0.57	7.95	−2.92
South Africa	0.23	0.40	0.12	1.96	−1.72
Sudan	0.30	0.00	1.72	3.90	
Swaziland	0.27	0.00	1.15	4.63	
Tanzania	0.47	0.00	1.69	3.69	
Togo	0.20	0.60	−0.60	4.27	−2.61
Uganda	0.30	0.00	1.92	3.69	
Zambia	0.23	0.50	−1.23	2.35	−2.38
Zimbabwe	0.20	0.27	−1.26	2.61	−5.34

Source: Arbache and Page 2007b.

Note: An empty cell means that the country experienced neither growth acceleration nor deceleration.

conditions favor growth. The magnitude of economic contractions during deceleration episodes similarly indicates the severity of the consequences when economic and political conditions are unfavorable.

Sixteen countries in our sample have avoided growth decelerations altogether. Many—Botswana, Cape Verde, Equatorial Guinea, Lesotho, Mauritius, Mozambique, and Uganda—are among the region's top performers in per capita income growth over the three decades, but not all. Burkina Faso, Guinea, Namibia, São Tomé and Principe, and Swaziland are not among the region's growth leaders. Avoiding growth collapses is important for long-run success at the country level, but it is not the only factor contributing to robust long-term growth.

Seven countries—the Democratic Republic of Congo, Eritrea, Gabon, The Gambia, Madagascar, Mauritania, and Niger—have never had a growth acceleration. Of those seven, only Eritrea shows good long-term per capita income growth. Four of the seven had long-run declines in per capita income.

Do Growth Accelerations and Decelerations Matter?

Although growth accelerations and decelerations are important features of Africa's low and volatile long-run growth, do they matter for economic and social outcomes beyond their direct consequences on the rate of growth? If growth accelerations and decelerations have effects that are not neutral, one would expect economic, social, and governance indicators during such episodes to be different than such indicators during normal times. We investigate the non-neutrality of growth volatility by examining differences in mean values in countries experiencing growth acceleration and deceleration episodes and simple correlations between changes in key economic and social variables and the presence or absence of growth accelerations and decelerations. Table 1.7 shows simple sample averages during growth accelerations, decelerations, and "normal" times (defined as the absence of either). It also gives the correlation coefficients between a number of economic, social governance, and institutional characteristics and the frequency of acceleration and deceleration episodes.

What appears to increase the odds for good times?—in general, higher savings and investment, more foreign direct investment (FDI), and a more competitive exchange rate. What appears to increase the odds for bad times?—bad macroeconomic policy (high inflation), political instability,

TABLE 1.7

Means of Economic, Social Governance, and Institutional Characteristics during Growth Accelerations and Decelerations and Their Correlations with the Frequency of Acceleration or Deceleration Episodes

Characteristic	Mean during normal times or trend growth	Growth acceleration		Growth deceleration	
		Mean	Correlation coefficient	Mean	Correlation coefficient
Savings, investment, and consumption					
Savings (% GDP)	11.4	15.3*	0.180*	7.1*	−0.177*
Investments (% GDP)	20.0	23.1*	0.176*	15.5*	−0.236*
Private sector investment (% GDP)	12.2	13.8*	0.125*	9.2*	−0.166*
Foreign direct investments net flow (% GDP)	2.51	4.20*	0.130*	0.72*	−0.135*
Consumption (% GDP)	93.4	88.8*	−0.091*	89.7*	−0.058*
Macroeconomic management					
Consumer price index (%)	27.2	15.2	−0.034	184.7*	0.084*
GDP deflator (%)	26.9	16.7	−0.028	175.0*	0.078*
Public debt (% GNI)	87.3	112.3*	0.077*	115.7*	0.089*
Government consumption (% GDP)	17.2	16.0	−0.038	15.2*	−0.084*
Real effective exchange rate (2000 = 100)	130.2	115.1*	−0.107*	186.4*	0.168*
Current account (% GDP)	−5.96	−5.83	0.056	−6.03	0.011
Structure of the economy					
Agriculture value added (% GDP)	29.8	28.6	−0.050	31.9*	0.069*
Industry value added (% GDP)	25.3	26.9	0.061*	24.6	−0.042
Service value added (% GDP)	44.9	44.3	−0.044	43.5	−0.040
Trade					
Trade (% GDP)	74.7	76.2	0.065*	58.7*	−0.176*
Exports (% GDP)	30.1	31.6	0.056*	26.5*	−0.083*
Imports (% GDP)	44.6	44.4	0.054	32.5*	−0.217*
Terms of trade (2000 = 100)	109.5	102.2*	−0.102*	114.5	0.082*
Aid					
ODA (% GDP)	14.2	13.8	0.001	12.1	−0.059*
ODA per capita (US$)	57.3	69.5*	0.100*	41.8*	−0.122*
Policies, institutions, and governance					
CPIA (scale 1 = low, 6 = high)	3.17	3.19	0.065	2.75*	−0.206*
Voice and accountability (−2.5 = low, +2.5 = high)	−0.65	−0.45*	0.168*	−1.08*	−0.209*

(Continues on the following page)

TABLE 1.7
(continued)

Characteristic	Mean during normal times or trend growth	Growth acceleration		Growth deceleration	
		Mean	Correlation coefficient	Mean	Correlation coefficient
Political stability (−2.5 = low, +2.5 = high)	−0.47	−0.45	0.051	−1.07*	−0.200*
Government effectiveness (−2.5 = low, +2.5 = high)	−0.65	−0.58	0.100	−1.03*	−0.203*
Regulatory quality (−2.5 = low, +2.5 = high)	−0.61	−0.49	0.129*	−0.97*	−0.176*
Rule of law (−2.5 = low, +2.5 = high)	−0.62	−0.65	0.037	−1.14*	−0.227*
Control of corruption (−2.5 = low, +2.5 = high)	−0.55	−0.57	0.025	−0.92*	−0.182*
Minor conflict (frequency)	0.09	0.08	−0.046	0.16*	0.082*
Major conflict (frequency)	0.12	0.05*	−0.070*	0.07*	−0.044
Human development outcomes					
Life expectancy (years)	50.8	51.3	0.062	48.2*	−0.136*
Dependency ratio	0.93	0.91	−0.067*	0.93	0.053
Under-5 mortality (per 1,000)	150.4	145.8	−0.108	188.7*	0.237*
Infant mortality (per 1,000 live births)	86.2	84.2	−0.108	114.1*	0.277*
Primary completion rate (% of relevant age group)	53.2	52.7	0.049	40.9*	−0.178*

Source: Arbache and Page 2007b.

Note: * = *t*-test significant at the 5 percent level. The means of variables are tested against the means of normal times corresponding to the respective periods of growth acceleration or deceleration. However, the subsample means of normal times are generally similar to those of the entire period in the second column. See Arbache and Page (2007b) for the details, including the corresponding standard errors.

and bad governance. The specific results in table 1.7 also reveal an asymmetric relationship between growth accelerations and decelerations and some economic indicators.

Savings, Investment, and Consumption
The major changes in national accounts during growth episodes take place in investments and savings rather than in consumption. Savings and investments are higher during accelerations, compared with normal times, and substantially lower during deceleration episodes. FDI during accelerations is six times the figure for deceleration episodes.

Correlations show that countries that have high savings and investment have a higher probability of growth acceleration and less probability of deceleration. Consumption is relatively lower during growth accelerations, which is consistent with the higher allocation of resources for investment. But consumption is also lower during decelerations, which is probably due to the fall in the purchasing power of households.

Structure of the Economy

The share of the agriculture sector is slightly higher in countries experiencing decelerations, whereas industry's share is slightly larger in countries going through accelerations. Correlations suggest that countries that rely more on agriculture have more spells of growth deceleration, possibly because of a higher exposure to insects, droughts, and other natural disasters, but also because of swings in agriculture commodity prices.

Trade is substantially lower during decelerations. Exports and especially imports drop sharply. Correlations indicate that countries that trade less are more exposed to growth decelerations. Somewhat surprisingly, the terms of trade are lower during growth accelerations. This result may indicate that although high commodity prices trigger growth, they may not be the main factor behind medium-term growth spells in Africa.

Economic Management

Macroeconomic management appears to be an important factor in both good times and bad times. Decelerations are accompanied by high inflation; one recent example is Zimbabwe. There is a positive correlation between inflation and the frequency of growth decelerations. Public debt is higher during both acceleration and deceleration episodes than it is during normal times, and government consumption falls during both accelerations and decelerations. Correlations suggest that countries that increased their debt also experienced more growth accelerations and decelerations, which may support the view that prudent debt management is important for reducing growth volatility.

The real effective exchange rate is more competitive during growth accelerations and highly appreciated during decelerations. Correlations suggest that exchange rate appreciation is associated with growth deceleration, whereas depreciation is associated with acceleration. There is no evidence that current accounts change during growth acceleration and deceleration.

Aid

Official development assistance (ODA) as a percentage of GDP is similar in both good and normal times but falls during growth decelerations. Per capita ODA, however, is higher during growth accelerations and lower during decelerations. The correlation analysis suggests that a higher share of ODA in GDP is associated with fewer growth collapses and that countries with higher ODA per capita experience more growth accelerations and have fewer collapses. These results indicate that ODA has been procyclical, reinforcing arguments for greater predictability of ODA to underpin sustained growth.

Policies, Institutions, and Governance

Policies and institutions are also closely associated with both good and—especially—bad times. The World Bank's Country Policy and Institutional Assessment (CPIA) score, a broad measure of policy and institutional performance, is lower during decelerations, but not significantly different between accelerations and normal times. The correlation coefficients suggest that countries with lower CPIA scores tend to experience more economic collapses.

All the governance indicators—political stability, government effectiveness, rule of law, and control of corruption—are lower for growth decelerations than for the region as a whole.[26] Correlation coefficients are negative, suggesting that a deterioration of governance is accompanied by more frequent growth decelerations. Voice and accountability scores are higher during growth accelerations. The correlations also suggest that countries that experience more growth accelerations have more voice and accountability and better regulatory quality.

Minor conflicts are more frequent during growth deceleration episodes than during normal times. Major conflicts are less frequent during acceleration and deceleration episodes than for the region as a whole. The correlation coefficients suggest that minor conflicts are associated with collapses and that major conflicts hamper the chances of a growth acceleration.

These results reinforce the findings of other empirical studies (Dufrénot, Sanon, and Diop 2006; Ndulu et al. 2007) of the close relationship between institutions and governance and economic performance in Africa. However, they also reveal that governance appears to be more relevant to understanding how to avoid a growth deceleration than how to promote an acceleration.

Human Development Outcomes

Growth variability also affects a number of important human development indicators. Life expectancy is substantially lower in countries experiencing growth decelerations than in countries experiencing normal times. The correlation coefficient is negative, suggesting that more collapses are associated with lower life expectancy. The dependency ratio is slightly lower during growth accelerations, and the correlation coefficient is negative, as expected. Mortality for children under age 5 and infant mortality are substantially higher during growth decelerations than in normal times, but these indicators do not improve during growth accelerations (see box 1.1). Correlation coefficients suggest that growth collapses are associated with

---

BOX 1.1

Asymmetric Effects of Good and Bad Times on the Poor: The Case of Infant Mortality

During normal times, the average infant mortality rate across sub-Saharan Africa is 86.2 per 1,000. During good times, the ratio falls slightly to 84.2, which is not statistically different. But there is a major increase in infant mortality to 114.1 during bad times. This evidence is illustrated by the kernel density distribution. During normal or accelerating times, the kernel is skewed to the right (see panels a and b in the figure below). But during decelerating times, the kernel curve is clearly skewed to the left, and a second peak emerges, representing the countries experiencing much worse infant mortality levels (panel c).

Among the countries in the second peak are Malawi and Mali in 1980, both of whose infant mortality rate was 176. Remarkably, as growth accelerated, these countries experienced substantially lower figures: 115 in 1995 for Malawi and 124 in 2000 for Mali. Other countries in the second peak include Angola in 1990 and 1995; Niger in 1985 and 1990; and Sierra Leone in 1985, 1990, and 1995. These examples highlight the asymmetric relationship between (1) growth acceleration and deceleration and (2) social indicators, suggesting that growth volatility matters and is marginally more important for the poor than growth acceleration.

BOX 1.1 (continued)

Infant Mortality: Kernel Density Estimation

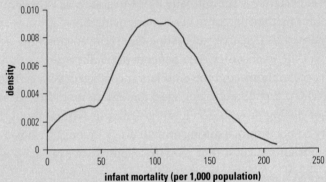

a. During normal times

density / infant mortality (per 1,000 population)

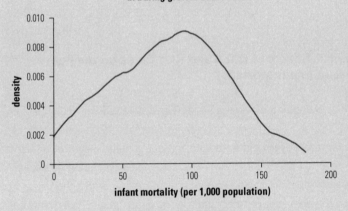

b. During growth acceleration

density / infant mortality (per 1,000 population)

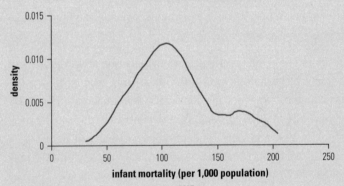

c. During growth deceleration

density / infant mortality (per 1,000 population)

Source: World Bank, *Africa Development Indicators,* 2007.

increases in mortality. The primary completion rate is substantially lower in countries experiencing growth decelerations and is negatively correlated with growth collapses.

Explaining the Probability of Growth Accelerations and Decelerations

Table 1.8 shows the conditional probabilities of a country experiencing a growth acceleration and deceleration at the aggregate level. Models 1–4 refer to growth accelerations and models 5–12 to growth decelerations. These regressions represent a further search for stylized facts about acceleration and deceleration episodes. No causality is inferred from the relationships, and no attempt has been made to control for endogeneity of some of the right-hand-side variables.

Model 1 shows that a 1 percent change in investment is on average associated with a higher probability of a growth acceleration of about 0.1 percent. So, an increase of, say, 10 percent in investment is associated with an increase of 1 percent in the probability of a growth acceleration. Voice and resource endowment (models 2 and 3) are also positively associated with a growth acceleration. However, all coefficients are significant at only the 10 percent level, and the R^2 are low. Model 4 shows a regression with all these correlates together. Only voice and resource endowment remain significant at the 10 percent level.

All estimated coefficients of models 5–11 have the expected sign and are significant at the 5 percent level. They show that more investment, higher ODA per capita, increased imports, and better governance indicators are associated with fewer growth decelerations. Model 12 shows the coefficients for all the nongovernance indicators together. In this case, only investment remains significant. The governance indicators were not regressed together because of their very high collinearity.

Only investment is significantly associated with the conditional probability of both acceleration and deceleration episodes. This finding suggests that investment is likely to be an important factor for predicting spells of growth and collapse at the aggregate level, but one cannot assert with confidence that it is a leading indicator, because of its probable endogeneity. Better governance indicators reduce the likelihood of growth decelerations, but they are not closely associated with more frequent accelerations.

TABLE 1.8
Conditional Probability of Growth Acceleration and Deceleration at the Aggregate Level

Variable	Dependent variable: frequency of growth acceleration per country				Dependent variable: frequency of growth deceleration per country							
	Model 1	Model 2	Model 3	Model 4	Model 5	Model 6	Model 7	Model 8	Model 9	Model 10	Model 11	Model 12
Ln investment	0.110 (1.70)			0.047 (0.72)		−0.253 (−3.23)						−0.233 (−1.97)
Voice (governance indicator)		0.056 (1.187)		0.061 (1.98)								
Resource-rich country			0.082 (1.77)	0.082 (1.73)								
Ln ODA per capita					−0.078 (−2.17)							−0.036 (−0.84)
Ln imports							−0.145 (−2.40)					0.020 (0.21)
Political stability (governance indicator)								−0.068 (−2.08)				
Government effectiveness (governance indicator)									−0.127 (−2.63)			
Rule of law (governance indicator)										−0.115 (−2.60)		
Control of corruption (governance indicator)											−0.132 (−2.68)	
R^2	0.06	0.08	0.06	0.16	0.10	0.19	0.12	0.09	0.14	0.14	0.15	0.21
N	45	44	45	44	45	45	45	44	44	44	44	44

Source: Arbache and Page 2007b.

Note: t-test in parentheses.

TABLE 1.9

Predicting Growth Acceleration and Deceleration: Panel Data

Variable	Dependent variable: dummy of growth acceleration		Dependent variable: dummy of growth deceleration	
	Odds ratio	p-value	Odds ratio	p-value
Savings	1.152	0.000	0.929	0.000
Investment in fixed capital			0.956	0.062
Foreign direct investments net flow	1.146	0.000	0.811	0.000
GDP deflator			1.010	0.016
Consumption	1.051	0.004		
Government consumption	0.904	0.000		
Trade			0.980	0.008
Minor conflict			1.744	0.045
Major conflict	0.435	0.064		
LR (χ^2)	127.6	0.000	97.4	0.000
N	825		647	

Source: Arbache and Page 2000b.

Note: Fixed-effect logit regression.

Table 1.9 shows fixed-effect logistical models that predict the presence of a growth acceleration or deceleration at the country level. Increases in savings, foreign direct investment, and consumption increase the odds of a growth acceleration, whereas government consumption and major conflicts reduce the odds. In the deceleration regression, increases in savings, investment, FDI, and trade reduce the odds of a growth deceleration, whereas inflation and minor conflicts increase the odds of collapse.[27] Only savings, FDI, and conflict appear in both regressions. These results suggest that policies aimed at attaining sustained growth and preventing growth collapses need to focus on ways to increase savings, attract foreign investments, and reduce conflicts.

Good Luck or Good Policy: How Robust Is the Recent Growth?

Today's Africa is clearly different from the Africa of the early 1990s, when it was coming out of the declines after the first two oil price shocks, the debt problems, and stagnation of the adjustment years. Thanks to the recent acceleration of growth, there is definitely a higher economic base to work with. But how sustainable is that growth? Are the main contributing factors good luck or good policy? As the growth diagnostics so far indicate, the answer hinges not only on policy and governance but also on economic fundamentals, such as factor accumulation and productivity as well as trade and export diversification—and the significance of the changes in these fundamentals. This section evaluates Africa's recent growth against the lessons learned in the previous sections.

Commodity Prices and Terms of Trade

External circumstances have certainly been favorable since the mid-1990s: the global economy has been expanding at 3.2 percent a year, global trade expanded by 40 percent a year, and the share of FDI in the world GDP nearly doubled from 1.15 percent in 1995 to more than 2.23 percent in 2005. As a result of greater demand, commodity prices, including oil prices, heave been pushed to new high levels. Hence, the better economic performance in the recent period is certainly partly due to the higher export prices of many African countries (figure 1.7). Higher oil prices now benefit about 8–10 oil-exporting countries in sub-Saharan Africa, as discussed in the previous section. Non-oil commodity prices have also risen significantly. Of the 40 commodity prices monitored regularly, only cotton prices declined from

FIGURE 1.7
Commodity and Oil Prices

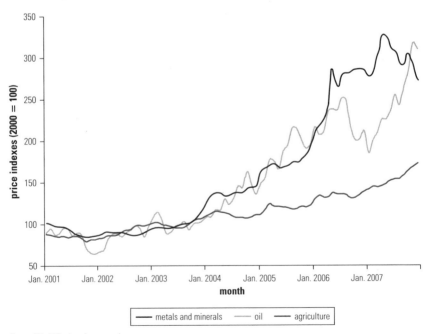

Source: World Bank various years b.

FIGURE 1.8

Terms-of-Trade Index in Sub-Saharan Africa, 1973–80 and 1999–2006

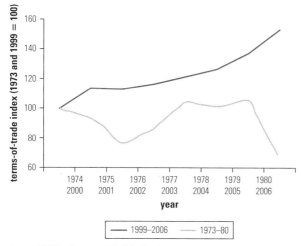

Sources: AFRCE various years; World Bank various years g.

the high prices of the 2003 drought year. Hence, gains from higher export prices for commodities such as gold, aluminum, copper, and nickel more than offset the losses from higher oil import bills in several oil-importing countries, such as Burundi, Ghana, Guinea, Mali, Mozambique, Rwanda, Uganda, Zambia, and Zimbabwe. Overall, compared with the previous major oil price cycle during 1973–1980, the aggregate terms of trade for sub-Saharan African countries have fared much more favorably in the current oil price cycle, relative to their respective starting points (figure 1.8).[28]

For oil-importing countries, the weakening of the U.S. dollar has also meant that the oil price in euros or local currency has not risen as much. For sub-Saharan Africa in particular, the real price increases of oil were in fact significantly lower than the recent nominal price increases quoted in dollars, after adjusting for exchange rate movements and domestic inflation. Since 2000, the nominal price of oil has tripled, whereas the real price has doubled (see figure 1.9). Although the nominal price was approaching $100 a barrel toward the end of 2007, the real oil price for oil importers in Africa was only 2.6 percent higher than in 2006.

Nonetheless, although economic performance remains strong in many African countries (as seen in table 1.1), several non-resource-rich countries will have to be monitored because their terms-of-trade losses were exacerbated by unfavorable changes in both oil and import prices. These

FIGURE 1.9
Nominal and Real Price of Oil in Sub-Saharan Africa

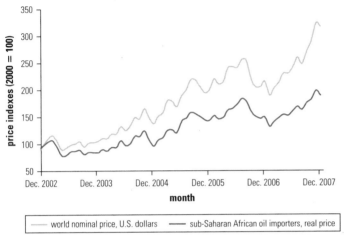

Source: World Bank various years b.

countries include Benin, Burkina Faso, Cape Verde, Comoros, Eritrea, Ethiopia, The Gambia, Kenya, Lesotho, Madagascar, Mauritius, Niger, Senegal, the Seychelles, and Togo. In most cases, the additional negative shock came from prices of staple imports, such as wheat, rice, and vegetable oils. Eritrea, for example, had an estimated negative terms-of-trade impact of greater than 5 percent of GDP from higher food prices, while Lesotho, Mauritania, Senegal, and Togo had an estimated negative terms-of-trade impact in excess of 2 percent of GDP because of changes in food prices.

Effect of External Shocks on Growth

The importance of terms-of-trade shocks in sub-Saharan Africa has been evolving. Historical data suggest that external shocks are important determinants of growth in Africa (see, for example, Deaton and Miller 1995; Collier and Dehn 2001). Collier (2007) finds this is especially true in resource-rich countries. Moreover, Collier and Dehn (2001) observe that aid may mitigate the negative consequences of external shocks. However, Hausmann, Pritchett, and Rodrik (2005) argue that positive external shocks are strongly correlated only with short-term economic expansions, not with sustained growth episodes. Collier and Goderis (2007) confirmed that positive shocks have short-term effects on outputs, but negative shocks have lasting damaging effects. IMF (2007a) finds that most ongoing growth spells in Africa are taking place amid negative terms-of-trade shocks since the current growth began, suggesting that other factors have been more important in recent years. Looking at these issues carefully, Raddatz, in chapter 8, finds that the relative importance of external shocks as sources of output instability in African countries has actually increased in the past 15 years and that this increase is the result of two reinforcing factors: (1) a decline in the variance of internal shocks, including policy failures or conflicts, and (2) a relative increase in the vulnerability of output to external shocks, while output variability in general is declining among African countries. Contrary to the importance attributed to oil prices in policy circles, Raddatz also finds that they are not particularly important for output volatility in the typical African country, but only among those countries that are net oil exporters. Without compensating developments, such as higher export prices, exogenous flows, or adjustment policies, however, the marginal impact of an oil price shock can be quite significant, as shown in chapter 11 by Andriamihaja and Vecchi on Madagascar and chapter 12 by Essama-Nssah, Go, Kearney, Korman, Robinson, and Thierfelder on South Africa.

Aid Flows and Debt Relief

Moreover, new commitments to scale up foreign aid from industrial countries have already led to greater external resources and debt relief for poor countries. Recent aid commitments and actual disbursements (inclusive of debt relief) have already recovered to the high points of the early 1990s (see figure 1.10). Moreover, additional and significant debt relief became a reality when the World Bank and IMF approved the financing and implementation of the Multilateral Debt Relief Initiative (MDRI) starting on July 1, 2006. Sixteen countries in sub-Saharan Africa, together accounting for 23 percent of the regional income but 43 percent of the total population, have now reached the completion point for significant debt relief under the enhanced Heavily Indebted Poor Country Initiative and have qualified for further assistance from the MDRI. Benefiting from debt relief, MDRI countries did very well recently and grew by over 5.3 percent during 2000–06 (table 1.2).[29]

Nonetheless, the promises made at the Gleneagles summit to scale up aid have yet to materialize. In particular, aid still has to go much beyond the high points of the 1990s to double by 2010, as pledged by donors. Chapter 4, by Chuhan-Pole and Fitzpatrick, reviews several issues relating to aid: its trends, its distribution with regard to debt relief and new flows, its reliability with regard to volatility and predictability, and its progress

FIGURE 1.10

Official Development Assistance to Sub-Saharan Africa

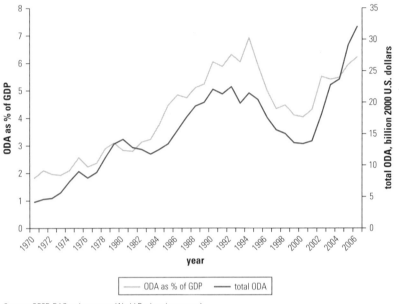

Sources: OECD-DAC various years; World Bank various years h.

toward donor alignment and harmonization. The scaling up of aid also presents several challenges in the macroeconomic management of aid, and
chapter 3, by Go, Korman, Page, and Ye, reviews the issues regarding the
absorption and spending of aid, the efficiency and composition of additional
public expenditure, and the evolution of the macroeconomic framework to
integrate microeconomic aspects at the World Bank, as well as several case
studies on fiscal space issues. Moreover, chapter 5, by Devarajan, Go, Page,
Robinson, and Thierfelder, argues that the specter of Dutch disease from
additional aid is intrinsically related to the predictability of aid: if aid is certain and sufficient to allow intertemporal substitution to take place in consumption and supply, the issue of real exchange appreciation ceases to be
an issue. Moreover, the scaling-up debate is taking place amid rapid globalization and development of capacity, which changes results.

Better Leadership

However, the current acceleration of growth is not all due to luck; better
policy seems to be taking place in sub-Saharan Africa. Africa today enjoys
better economic prospects because its leaders have undertaken major

reforms during the past 10 years and are taking increasing control of their economic destiny. African governments are making regional initiatives in conflict resolution and are taking action to improve governance under the African Union and the New Partnership for Africa's Development initiatives. These initiatives are designed to

- Push African countries to be assertive about ownership and to assume leadership and accountability for their development programs.

- Improve the reputation of the region through certification of good practices in governance for a critical mass of African countries under the African Peer Review mechanism.

- Increase regional connectivity to improve capacity to trade within the region and with the outside world.

- Enhance the capacity of a rationalized system of regional bodies to provide regional public goods, such as cross-country transportation and power sharing, coordination in managing pandemics, and protection of regional commons such as the Nile and the Great Lakes.

Overall Policy and Institutional Environment

Although there is no perfect or leading indicator of the overall quality of policy and institutional environment, the World Bank's CPIA provides a consistent framework for assessing country performance on 16 items, which are grouped into four wide-ranging clusters: economic management, structural policies, policies for social inclusion and equity, and public sector management and institutions.

The average CPIA scores for African countries have been rising. The average CPIA score in 1995 was 2.8. By 2006, it had risen to 3.2. The number of African countries with scores equal to or greater than the threshold of 3.5 for international good performance had also risen, from 5 countries in 1997 to 17 in 2006.

Economic performance among African countries is highly correlated with the quality of policy (see figure 1.11). Countries with CPIA scores of greater than or equal to 3.5 by 2006 tend to have higher growth and lower inflation than those with scores lower than 3.5 (excluding Zimbabwe). The low-income countries (excluding oil-exporting countries) with good policy and institutional environment are in fact doing very well: growth averaged 5.1 percent and inflation was 6.9 percent.

FIGURE 1.11

Economic Performance of African Countries by Quality of Policy, 2000–06

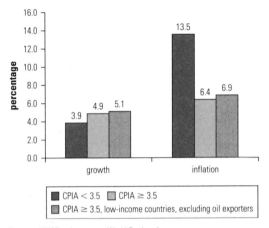

Sources: AFRCE various years; World Bank various years g.

Macroeconomic Management

The most striking improvement in policy is observed for macroeconomic stabilization. Inflation among African countries has come down dramatically since 1995 (figure 1.12). The number of countries able to keep inflation below 10 percent a year increased from 11–26 in the early 1990s to about 31–35 since 2000. From the 1980s to the present, there were as many as 10 different African countries with hyperinflation (greater than 50 percent) at one point or another. The extreme values can run over thousands of percentage points. The countries with hyperinflation have included Angola, the Democratic Republic of Congo, Guinea, Guinea-Bissau, Mozambique, São Tomé and Principe, Sierra Leone, Sudan, Uganda, Zambia, and Zimbabwe.

In recent years, all these countries except Zimbabwe have been able to contain inflation drastically. The regional average has fallen below 10 percent since 2002.[30] This performance is all the more remarkable in view of the significant increase in oil prices that started in 1999.

Another indicator of macroeconomic stabilization, the overall fiscal balance, also improved.[31] The average fiscal deficit as a percentage of GDP in African countries declined from 5.7 percent during the 1980s and 1990s to 2.9 percent during 2000–06. Fiscal policy in oil-exporting countries has also improved. Unlike the unchecked wasteful spending in the past, windfalls from oil revenue are increasingly being saved. At the start of the

FIGURE 1.12

Inflation Pattern of African Countries: Number of Countries by Inflation Range

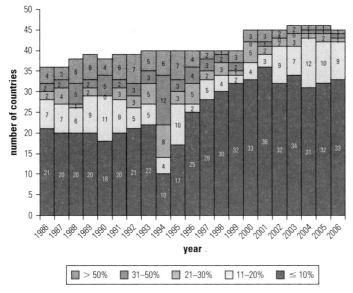

Sources: AFRCE various years; World Bank various years g.

current oil price shock, fiscal deficits were increasingly reduced, and by 2004–06, the overall fiscal surplus averaged about 8 percent for the group. More needs to be done, and two chapters in this volume examine the issues relating to fiscal policy and rules: in chapter 9, Devlin and Lewin examine the fiscal management of oil revenue to improve its effect on growth, while in chapter 10, Budina and van Wijnbergen look at the role of fiscal policy in managing oil revenue volatility in the case of Nigeria.

Adjustment to Higher Oil Prices

For the past seven to eight years, most oil-importing countries in Africa have already been slowly adjusting to the new and higher trend of oil prices, and their ability to continue the adjustment will be the key to future growth, especially if higher oil prices persist. Since 2003, the majority of African countries have allowed frequent and full pass-through of higher oil prices to domestic prices. The pass-through is less pronounced in oil-exporting countries. A few countries, such as Côte d'Ivoire and Ethiopia, have at one point or another suspended the use of formulas in favor of less frequent and ad hoc adjustments. Many countries have also tried to protect the poor by limiting price increases and taxation of kerosene. For

14 African countries for which data are available, petroleum subsidies increased from 0.75 percent of GDP in 2003 to 1 percent in 2005. On average, petroleum taxes are important sources of revenue and constitute close to 2 percent of GDP in indirect taxes.

In a recent Energy Sector Management Assistance Program (ESMAP)[32] study of 31 developing countries, the amount of pass-through in gasoline and diesel was found to be positively correlated with a country's terms of trade and inflation (GDP deflator) and negatively correlated with a country's oil vulnerability, overall fiscal position, and per capita income or growth; interestingly, it is also negatively correlated with whether a country is an oil producer or exporter. The debt-to-GDP ratio affects gasoline pricing negatively but not diesel pricing. The 31 developing countries in the sample showed less pass-through of oil cost when compared with industrial countries, particularly with respect to diesel (table 1.10). However, the results for 11 African countries confirmed that African countries have not been delaying adjustment to their fuel prices, even when compared with developed countries; hence, the risks of an unsustained fiscal position appear to be less than in past episodes of oil price shocks. Overall, diesel prices tended to be protected from increases to protect the poor—although such increases are implemented relatively less often in African

TABLE 1.10
Pass-Through Coefficients for Gasoline and Diesel in Local Currency

Country	Gasoline	Diesel
Reference industrial countries (6 countries)	1.13	0.96
Developing countries (31 countries)	1.03	0.88
Non-sub-Saharan African countries (20 countries)	0.92	0.73
sub-Saharan African countries (11 countries)	1.22	1.16
Cameroon	0.91	0.98
Ethiopia	0.48	0.64
Ghana	1.33	1.21
Kenya	0.97	0.79
Madagascar	1.46	1.55
Malawi	1.14	1.22
Mozambique	1.10	1.01
Rwanda	0.98	0.76
Tanzania	1.57	1.52
Uganda	1.23	1.14
Zambia	2.20	1.93

Source: Bacon and Kojima 2006.

countries. Outside of a few instances in which market mechanisms were directly suspended, African governments have been actively intervening in the fuel markets in other ways to help the poor or consumers: by adjusting taxes and subsidies, regulating margins, mandating conservation measures and cash transfers, and so forth.[33]

Exchange Rate Regimes

Unlike the past, countries with flexible exchange regimes now account for about 76 percent of Africa's GDP and 68 percent of the region's population. In recent years, and during the current oil price shock, these countries have also tended to grow better than the regional average and better than countries with fixed exchange rates (table 1.2). In franc zone countries, a strong currency tied to the euro is bringing about concerns regarding real exchange rate appreciation and its impact on export competitiveness (box 1.2).

BOX 1.2

Real Exchange Rate in Franc Zone

Countries with fixed exchange rate regimes are mostly in the franc zone, where the CFA franc is tied to the euro. There is, however, an increasing divergence between the eastern and western part of the zone. The CEMAC countries benefit from large oil inflows, and their growth performance was better in the 1990s and has been better since 2000. The WAEMU countries did not adjust as well to higher oil prices, partly because their exports were hurt by an exchange rate tied to a strong euro. The growth of these countries decelerated to 2.7 percent since 2000, with some improvement during 2004–06 at 3.5 percent a year. Real exchange rate changes for selected countries indicate appreciations during 2000–06: 17 percent in Benin, 9 percent in Burkina Faso, 18 percent in Chad, 13 percent in Côte d'Ivoire, 1 percent in Mali, and 8 percent in Togo (see the figure showing real effective exchange rates). The country-level appreciations (with the exception of Mali) are sufficiently large to be worrisome from the viewpoint of export competitiveness, although whether an adjustment of the CFA franc is necessary depends (among other things) on whether the strength of the euro relative to the U.S. dollar will persist.

BOX 1.2 **(continued)**

Real Effective Exchange Rates in Franc Zone Countries

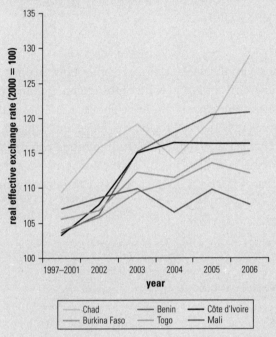

Source: AFRCE various years.

The structure of CFA zone economies is such that an appreciation of the exchange rate will reduce the real price of exports much more rapidly than the unit cost of labor, with negative consequences for export competitiveness. But the impact will vary considerably at the sector level in each country. The case in point is the cotton sector. Because cotton prices are quoted in U.S. dollars, cotton producers in the CFA franc zone are increasingly confronted with export prices that are significantly lower in euros or CFA francs than in dollars (see the figure showing the price of cotton). This disparity puts downward pressure on farm-gate prices and will add to the potential fiscal cost of any scheme to stabilize farm prices or provide financial assistance to poor farmers. In the case of the cotton sector, the issue goes beyond the exchange rate, however, and reflects declining relative cotton prices driven by new technologies used by new competitors, such as Brazil, China, and India.

BOX 1.2 (continued)

Monthly Price of Cotton in U.S. Dollars and Euros

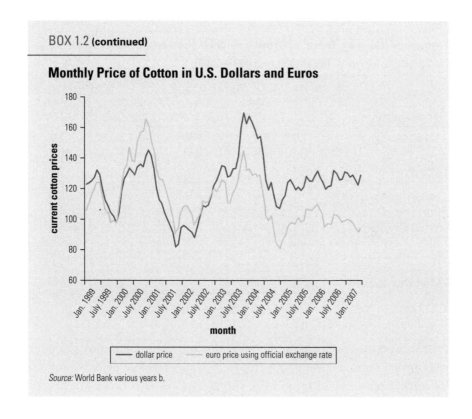

Source: World Bank various years b.

Reduction of Policy Mistakes across Countries

Hence, though external circumstances have been favorable, there is also strong evidence that African countries have increasingly learned to avert economic mistakes and have avoided bad leadership, conflict, corruption, and macroeconomic instability. Such reduction of policy mistakes is central to preventing growth collapses—a key point from the growth analysis described earlier.

To look at how widespread the phenomenon is, table 1.11 compares the unconditional probabilities of growth acceleration and deceleration by country groups during 1995–2005 against the averages for the entire sample, 1975–2005. The likelihood of growth decelerations has clearly declined by half across the board for different types of countries to about 12–14 percent, which is the average for Africa during 1995–2005. In addition, the probability of major conflict has declined the most: from 17 to 6 percent. Likewise, the likelihood of growth acceleration has improved for different types of countries. That said, oil exporters and resource-rich countries have experienced more growth accelerations than all other

TABLE 1.11

Frequency (Country-Years) of Growth Acceleration and Deceleration, by Country Category, 1995–2005 and 1975–2005

Country category	Growth acceleration		Growth deceleration	
	Likelihood (1975–2005)	Likelihood (1995–2005)	Likelihood (1975–2005)	Likelihood (1995–2005)
All countries' mean	0.25	0.42	0.22	0.12
Coastal countries	0.26	0.44	0.22	0.12
Landlocked countries	0.23	0.34	0.22	0.14
Coastal countries without resources	0.24	0.38	0.23	0.14
Landlocked countries without resources	0.22	0.34	0.22	0.14
Oil exporters	0.29	0.49	0.23	0.12
Non-oil exporters	0.24	0.40	0.22	0.12
Resource countries	0.30	0.55	0.21	0.08
Non-resource countries	0.23	0.36	0.23	0.14
Major conflict countries	0.16	0.35	0.17	0.06
Minor conflict countries	0.19	0.32	0.32	0.13

Source: Arbache and Page 2007a.

country subsets—well above the mean for the entire period or all countries during same recent period. This finding suggests that better commodity prices and terms of trade were still significant factors; for the recent period at least, possessing mineral resources has not been a curse to growth.

Economic Fundamentals before and after 1995

If growth is robust, economic fundamentals should have become stronger in the past decade. Table 1.12 compares sample means of economic fundamentals during 1995–2005 for all countries and all episodes (growth acceleration, growth collapses, and normal times), as well as for the subset of countries undergoing growth accelerations with sample means of the same variables in 1985–94. The table examines all countries and then compares resource-rich and non-resource-rich economies.[34]

Progress among all African countries was observed in the means of several economic fundamentals for all economic episodes, but the record was not uniform. Savings were higher than in the previous decade, as indicated by the *t*-test. Although aggregate investments did not change significantly, private investment and FDI went up. In particular, FDI increased by threefold in the period 1995–2005, to 5 percent from 1.5 percent in the previous decade. Nonetheless, neither the magnitudes of savings and

TABLE 1.12

Differences of Means of Key Economic Variables before and after 1995

Variable	All countries			Non-resource-rich countries			Resource-rich countries		
	1995–2005	1985–1994	t-test	1995–2005	1985–1994	t-test	1995–2005	1985–1994	t-test
During all episodes									
Savings (% of GDP)	12.05	10.47	*	10.88	10.8		14.85	9.68	*
Investments (% of GDP)	20.26	19.4		18.93	18.78		23.4	20.92	**
Private sector investment (% of GDP)	12.51	11.46	**	11.23	10.6		15.43	13.47	
FDI net flow (% of GDP)	4.95	1.50	*	3.63	1.41	*	8.23	1.75	*
Consumption (% of GDP)	91.12	92.09		95.85	95.24		79.9	84.15	*
Trade (% of GDP)	76.58	68.43	*	72.73	66.11	*	85.77	74.1	*
Exports (% of GDP)	32.27	28.06	*	28.86	25.67	*	40.32	33.92	*
Imports (% of GDP)	44.27	40.36	*	43.86	40.44	*	45.25	40.18	*
Real effective exchange rate (2000 = 100)	103.52	182.78	*	100.06	186.64	*	109.18	174.71	*
Terms of trade (2000 = 100)	102.4	113.7	*	101.63	110.01	*	104.53	123.17	*
Current account (% of GDP)	−5.58	−6.17		−6.43	−6.5		−3.71	−5.53	
Consumer price index (%)	33.98	71.8		16.98	81.52		77.81	41.91	
GDP deflator (%)	45.85	65.48		30.46	76.85		71.77	37.28	
Public debt (present value, % of gross national income)	128.41	85	*	114.53	77.38	*	163.61	104.23	*
Government consumption (% of GDP)	15.48	17.24	*	15.12	16.55	*	16.44	18.91	*
During growth acceleration									
Savings (% of GDP)	12.9	20.94	*	12.13	20.27	*	14.1	22.83	*
Investments (% of GDP)	21.55	25.47	*	19.39	25.12	*	24.9	26.39	
Private sector investment (% of GDP)	13.51	14.15		11.6	13.46	*	16.45	16.23	
Foreign direct investments net flow (% of GDP)	5.02	2.4	*	2.35	2.08		9.44	3.24	
Consumption (% of GDP)	88.78	88.23		91.89	94.93		83.97	70.92	*
Trade (% of GDP)	70.27	86.1	*	60.76	86.21	*	85.22	85.81	
Exports (% of GDP)	29.47	35.8	*	24.48	32.49	*	37.21	44.36	
Imports (% of GDP)	40.71	50.3	*	36.27	53.71	*	47.69	41.58	
Real effective exchange rate (2000 = 100)	108.96	128.77	*	109.54	125.87	*	108.35	136.18	**
Terms of trade (2000 = 100)	104.38	99.06	**	105.51	100.72		102.08	94.14	
Current account (% of GDP)	−6.5	−4.46		−6.61	−6.7		−6.33	1.16	**
Consumer price index (%)	14.16	17.06		9.14	16.76	*	23.28	18.45	
GDP deflator (%)	15.54	18.73		9.21	19.12	*	25.1	17.71	
Public debt (present value, % of GNI)	120.91	94.52	**	89.75	94.98		172.42	93.14	*
Government consumption (% of GDP)	15	17.7	*	13.3	16.74	*	17.85	20.16	

Source: Arbache and Page 2007a.

Note: * = t-test that means are not equal was significant at the 5 percent level; ** = t-test that means are not equal was significant at the 10 percent level.

investments as a percentage of GDP nor their changes were large, relative to levels in other successful sustained-growth economies (such as those in South and East Asia).

Trade as a share of GDP increased significantly (by about 8 percent) with exports and imports increasing by 4 percent each. The small change in the current account balance was not statistically significant, remaining close to about 6 percent. The real exchange rate appreciated substantially to an index of 103.5 from 138.0 in 1985–94, most likely as a result of favorable commodity prices since 2000. This trend raises concerns that the export competitiveness of nonprimary exports will continue to be an issue. On average, the terms of trade became slightly less favorable in the more recent decade, also reflecting the offsetting patterns before and after 2000. Average inflation was cut by half, but the change was not statistically significant because of large variations in the consumer price indexes of individual countries. The present value of public debt increased significantly, but it is likely that these data do not reflect fully the debt relief in more recent years. Government consumption decreased by about 2 percent of GDP to 15.5 percent from 17.2 percent, while no significant difference was observed for private consumption.

Table 1.12 also presents the results for non-resource-rich and resource-rich countries. For non-resource-rich countries, improvements were also observed for FDI, trade, exports, and imports in the full sample, but they were slightly more muted when compared with the results for all countries. The means for the real exchange rate, terms of trade, public debt, and government were significantly different in the two decades and more or less followed the same pattern as for all countries. In contrast, the means for savings and private investments in non-resource-rich countries were not significantly different in the two periods. The reduction in inflation remains insignificant because of great variation.

The results are somewhat more favorable for the resource-rich countries. Savings and aggregate investments in resource-rich countries experienced substantial increases (by about 5 percent of GDP) in 1995–2005. FDI showed an impressive jump to 8.2 percent of GDP from 1.8 percent, confirming that most FDI flows to Africa are concentrated in the mineral sectors. No significant change was observed for private investment. Mineral wealth did not lead to a higher level of private and public consumption, suggesting that windfall revenue was increasingly saved. However, public debt still increased. Trade, particularly exports, increased more than imports, but not enough to turn the current accounts into surplus. The real exchange rate appreciated, as expected, but as for other countries, the terms of trade became less favorable. Inflation did not improve, and the level was high on average for 1995–2005.

Important compositional effects were at work, affecting the differences of means for the subset of countries experiencing growth accelerations. Savings for all African countries undergoing growth accelerations, for instance, fell significantly, from 21 percent in 1985–94 to 13 percent in 1995–2005. Two factors were at work. Because the probability of a growth acceleration was higher during 1995–2005, the number of observations was larger (for example, 201 country-years for savings), pulling in a wider variety of country circumstances, including economies with low savings rates. In contrast, the probability of a growth acceleration was much lower for 1985–94, and the number of observations was therefore few (for example, 84 country-years for savings). However, the countries that did grow during this more difficult period had substantially better economic indicators than those experiencing normal or bad times. In addition to savings, compositional effects for all countries were also observed in aggregate investment, trade, exports, imports, and terms of trade. This factor was less important for FDI, the real exchange rate, public consumption, and public debt.

In general, there were more significant compositional effects for non-resource-rich countries than for resource-rich countries during growth accelerations. The effect was common only for savings. In non-resource-rich countries, these compositional effects were also observed for aggregate investment, private sector investment, trade, exports, and imports. One area in which the non-resource-rich countries did much better during growth accelerations was inflation: not only was the level much lower in the second period, but also the means in the two periods were significantly different.

Overall, there is therefore modest evidence of improvements in economic fundamentals, in particular for resource-rich countries. The data are, however, somewhat mixed, and the robustness of Africa's growth remains fragile.

Africa Relative to Other Regions

Table 1.13 puts sub-Saharan Africa in perspective and compares key economic indicators with those of other developing regions in 1995–2005.

TABLE 1.13
Differences between Simple Sample Average by Regions, Weighted Data, 1995–2005

Variable	Sub-Saharan Africa	East Asia and the Pacific	Latin America and the Caribbean	Middle East and North Africa	South Asia	All low- and middle-income countries
Per capita GDP growth (%)	1.34	6.75	1.13	2.23	4.27	3.89
Savings (% of GDP)	17.47	38.45	21.04	23.85	22.39	26.01
Investments (% of GDP)	17.69	32.77	19.17	22.49	22.88	23.65
Private sector investment (% of GDP)	13.11	19.27	16.39	13.92	16.36	16.83
FDI net flow (% of GDP)	2.60	3.22	3.24	1.16	0.79	2.73
Consumption (% of GDP)	84.10	68.03	80.85	75.64	80.54	76.23
Trade (% of GDP)	62.31	66.85	42.72	57.38	31.90	55.43
Exports (% of GDP)	30.62	35.04	21.47	28.15	14.81	27.95
Imports (% of GDP)	31.68	31.78	21.25	29.22	17.09	27.47
Terms of trade (2000 = 100)	101.89	90.89	101.50	n.a.	104.10	96.28
GDP deflator (%)	7.16	4.91	6.17	5.20	5.67	6.48
Government consumption (% of GDP)	16.00	13.47	14.52	15.04	10.83	14.34

Source: Arbache and Page 2007a.

Note: The simple sample means refer to all years between 1995 and 2005.

Inflation was single digit and only slightly below that of other regions. On aggregate, FDI and trade compare well with such indicators in other regions (there are issues, however, as discussed next). The growth rate was still behind that of the low- and middle-income countries but comparable to that of Latin America and the Caribbean. Savings and investments were still well below those of other regions. Both private consumption and government consumption were higher than those of other regions, reflecting the low income of African countries.

Trade and FDI

Trade reforms have brought down tariffs in Africa, and the trade regimes do not discriminate against exports relative to other regions worldwide. However, African exports, particularly non-oil exports, are growing slowly (figure 1.13). In fact, in sharp contrast to the case for China and for Asia's top performing countries, exports are not growing in importance in the region's output and are declining in importance for Africa's top performers. As a result, Africa's share of world trade is falling (figure 1.14). And

FIGURE 1.13

Non-Oil Exports as a Percentage of GDP, by Region

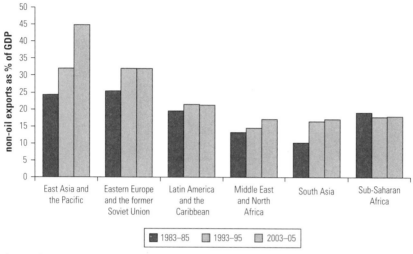

Source: IMF various years.

Note: Export shares are unweighted averages.

FIGURE 1.14

Africa's Share of World Trade

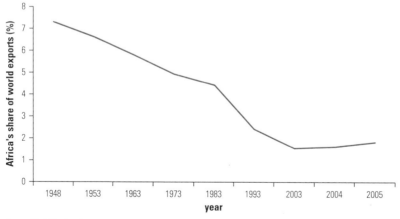

Source: World Bank various years g.

Africa's exports remain heavily concentrated compared with those of other regions (figure 1.15).

Although FDI as a share of GDP has grown since 1990 (see figure 1.16), the absolute amount is still modest at $13.3 billion in 2006 and is concentrated primarily in one country, South Africa, and in one line of business,

FIGURE 1.15

Concentration and Diversification of Exports, by Region: 2000–04 Average

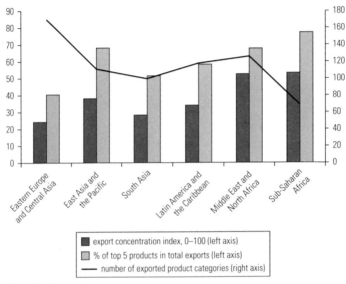

Source: World Bank various years h.

FIGURE 1.16

Net FDI as a Percentage of GDP, by Region

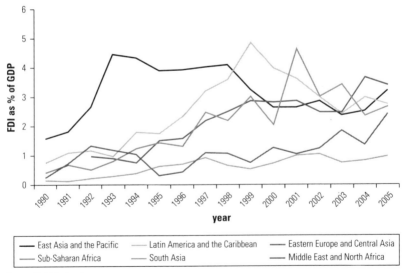

Source: World Bank various years g.

extractive industries. Outside of FDI, migrant remittances appear to be increasing, but a large portion of the flows bypass formal financial channels and these remittances are difficult to account for. Exogenous private flows such as these could certainly become important sources of balance of payment finance to supplement and counter the fluctuations of foreign aid. In chapter 7, Ratha, Mohapatra, and Plaza examine the issues and estimate their potentials.

Accumulation and Productivity of Capital

Africa's growth deficit in the past is also the product of low productivity, not just low savings and investment. Growth accounting shows that physical capital per worker has grown less than 0.5 percent a year, half the world average. In addition, a main culprit in Africa's disappointing growth is total factor productivity, which has been negative since the 1960s and −0.4 percent between 1990 and 2003 (Bosworth and Collins 2003). With Africa's low productivity, it can be argued that low investment in Africa is not a constraint to its development (Devarajan, Easterly, and Pack 2003). Given the importance of capital accumulation, more recent evidence about the quality and quantity of investment among some individual countries should be examined.

For top performers in Africa, the investment rates are becoming comparable to the high-performing Asian countries (table 1.14). Ghana and Mozambique, for example, are on par with India and the Lao People's Democratic Republic, although their investment rates are still below China's and Vietnam's. Moreover, the aggregate efficiency of investment among top performers in Africa, as reflected by incremental capital-output ratios, is not behind that found in many Asian countries. That said, the ICORs in Africa are less stable and are easily affected by output variation caused by drought (Rwanda in 2003), flood (Mozambique in 2000), or other factors. Also, the improvement of the productivity of investment noted among top performers needs to spread across Africa, where the overall ICOR is still high at 5.5.

Human Capital

Although there is evidence that the contribution of human capital has increased (Berthélemy and Söderling 2001), the overall record is still mixed. The contribution of human capital in Africa has kept pace with that

TABLE 1.14

GDP Growth, Investment Rates, and ICOR for Selected Countries in Asia and Africa, 2000–06

Country	GDP growth (%)	I/Y (%)	ICOR (%)
Top Asian performers			
China	9.5	39.7	4.2
Cambodia	9.2	19.0	2.2
Vietnam	7.5	33.4	4.5
India	6.9	27.8	4.7
Lao PDR	6.4	25.1	4.0
Top African performers[a]			
Mozambique	7.6	26.4	3.1 (5.1)[b]
Tanzania	6.3	20.2	3.3
Ethiopia	6.2	18.4	3.0
Burkina Faso	6.1	18.5	3.3
Uganda	5.6	20.7	3.8
Rwanda	5.5	19.4	3.7 (5.8)[c]
Ghana	5.0	25.7	5.2
Average of all sub-Saharan Africa	4.9	20.5	5.5

Sources: World Bank various years g; authors' calculations.

Note: I/Y = investment as percentage of GDP; ICOR = incremental capital-output ratio.

a. Middle-income countries, oil exporters, and resource-intensive countries are excluded.

b. Figure in parentheses represents the flood year in Mozambique (2000).

c. Figure in parentheses represents the drought year in Rwanda (2003).

in the rest of the world, mainly a result of rising average years of schooling, but health indicators need to be improved.

In particular, gross primary-school enrollment rates rose from 79 percent in 1999 to 92 percent in 2004. Health outcomes are more varied but are also improving in many countries. Between 1990 and 2004, the average literacy rate (in the 29 countries for which data exist) rose from 54 percent to 62 percent, while the range improved from 11–81 percent to 26–87 percent. This convergence is the result of rising primary-school enrollments. Regionwide gross enrollment rose from 79 percent in 1999 to 92 percent in 2004. Some 87 percent of Africans live in countries where the average enrollment rate is over 75 percent, and fewer than 2 percent live in countries where the rate is under 50 percent. Six of the seven top countries worldwide with expanding primary completion rates (by more than 10 percent a year between 2000 and 2005) are in Africa (Benin, Guinea, Madagascar, Mozambique, Niger, and Rwanda). There have been no comparable improvements in secondary and tertiary education. Although East Asian countries increased secondary enrollment rates by 21 percentage points and tertiary enrollment rates by 12 percentage points over 12 years, Africa raised its secondary rates by only 7 percentage points and its tertiary rates by just 1 percentage point.

Africa is the only region in the world where life expectancy has declined. Life expectancy in the region in 1960 was 15 years below that for non-African developing countries. By the 1990s, it had fallen below the non-African developing-country average by nearly 20 years. Between 1990 and 2005, life expectancy at birth in sub-Saharan Africa declined from 49.2 years to 47.1. Although life expectancy increased in 25 countries by an average of eight years, it declined in 21 more populous countries by an average of four years. HIV/AIDS, malaria, and armed conflict have contributed to the falling life expectancy. Progress against malaria, tuberculosis, and HIV/AIDS is mixed but showing some positive signs. The spread of AIDS has slowed in Africa, but the continent still bears the brunt of the epidemic. Rapid increases in tuberculosis infections in Africa are linked to the greater likelihood of tuberculosis appearing from latent infections among HIV carriers. Malaria remains Africa's leading killer of children under age five, but a strong new global partnership has formed to address the disease.

HIV/AIDS threatens further progress. Africa is the only region that has experienced a reversal of trend in life expectancy, mostly attributable to the HIV/AIDS epidemic. Africans account for 60 percent of the world's people living with HIV/AIDS. This fact has a profound social and economic impact, which can be seen in the large numbers of premature deaths of people in their prime employment, reproduction, and parenting years and in the large numbers of orphans that burden Africa's families and economies.

The Blueprint for Success Is Still Not Secured

All in all, these results indicate a mixed picture with regard to the robustness of growth in Africa. Growth was certainly higher, more likely, and more widespread, and it was favored by better commodity prices, aid inflows, and policy, as well as by higher productivity in top performers. But there is no strong evidence that it was unambiguously fueled or accompanied by accumulation of capital, that higher productivity is spreading across all countries, or that export diversification has been attained. Although a group of diversified, sustained growers is emerging, economic performance varied substantially. Certainly, the story on policy reforms and institutional changes is unfinished (as will be discussed further). Therefore, there are questions about whether the region was experiencing a robust growth period, despite the high growth rates. Without greater productivity and factor accumulation, changes in global demand for oil and metals or other external adverse shocks, including aid flows, could jeopardize the current growth boom.

Relative to the lessons learned about avoiding mistakes, the results also indicate that much less is generally known about the factors and institutions for bringing about success in development (Dixit 2007) or policies to create greater savings rates, productivity, and export diversification. Institutional context, for example, can change incentives and reduce policy results drastically, as Easterly (2001) has argued. Although they are difficult to measure and quantify, there are certainly some outward signs of recent improvement.

For example, figure 1.11 suggests a correlation between (1) better policy and institutions and (2) economic performance since 2000 for all African countries, as well as low-income countries, excluding oil exporters. The high growth rates in oil- and resource-rich countries also confirm that the management of mineral resources has improved and windfalls are not wasted to the same extent as in the past. Moreover, there are now 19 African countries adopting the Extractive Industries Transparency Initiative (EITI), which has the goal of verification and full publication of company and government revenues from oil, gas, and mining, and 6 countries have issued one or more EITI reports.

Nonetheless, these improvements have not yet been reflected consistently in many governance indicators since data started becoming available. Figure 1.17 compares the governance indicators of 1996—the first year of the series—and 2006. Actually, all indicators worsened. But a closer look shows that resource-rich countries—oil-rich countries in particular—were among the main causes of the worsening in governance and also that these indicators were particularly low there during growth acceleration. These results highlight the importance of the political economy issues associated with mineral- and oil-rich countries in Africa as found in the recent empirical literature (see, for example, Kaufmann, Kraay, and Zoido 1999; Dufrénot, Sanon, and Diop 2006; Ndulu et al. 2007; Seldadyo, Nugroho, and de Haan 2007).

FIGURE 1.17
Governance Indicators Scores, 1996 and 2006

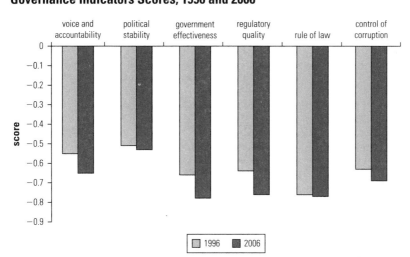

Source: Arbache and Page 2007a, based on data from World Bank various years i.

Note: Scores can range from −2.5 to +2.5.

Key Areas of Actions to Sustain Growth

The avoidance of economic collapses will continue to depend on good policy, leadership, and aid. To sustain an accelerating growth, however, the region will have to tackle several barriers and constraints to greater productivity and investment. Addressing these barriers will require both continuing reforms and greater external assistance.

Lowering the Cost of Doing Business and Building an African Private Sector

Firm studies such as Eifert, Gelb, and Ramachandran (2005) highlight one of the barriers to greater productivity. Research shows that efficient African enterprises can compete with Chinese and Indian firms in factory floor costs (figure 1.18). They become less competitive, though, because of higher indirect business costs, including infrastructure (figure 1.19). In China, indirect costs are about 8 percent of total costs, but in African countries they are 18–35 percent.

Building the African private sector will be crucial both for growth and for fostering a national consensus for growth-oriented policies. Improving

FIGURE 1.18

Factory Floor Costs in Selected Sub-Saharan African Countries, China, and India

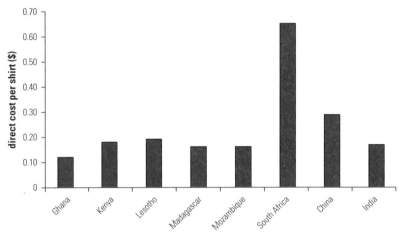

Source: Cadot and Nasir 2001.

FIGURE 1.19

Net Productivity versus Factory Floor (Gross) Productivity in Selected Sub-Saharan African Countries, India, and China

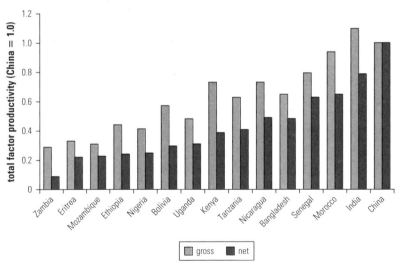

Source: Eifert, Gelb, and Ramachandran 2005.

FIGURE 1.20
Manufacturing Costs for Selected Countries

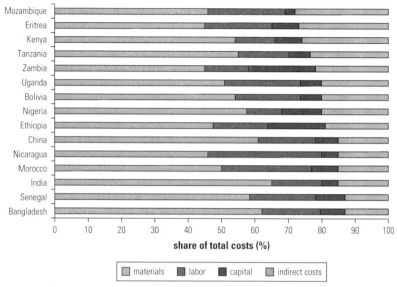

Source: Eifert, Gelb, and Ramachandran 2005.

the investment climate and enhancing the capacity of African entrepreneurs to invest and engage in business are central to this effort.

Africa remains a high-cost, high-risk place to do business. Overall, the cost of doing business in Africa is 20–40 percent above that for other developing regions, including the costs associated with bureaucracy, corruption, risk, and essential business services (figure 1.20). During 2006/07, the average rank of African countries was 136 in the Doing Business indicators (figure 1.21), but four middle-income countries rank in the top third: Mauritius, 32; South Africa, 35; Namibia 43; and Botswana, 51. Value-chain analysis by Subramanian and Matthijs (2007) also indicated several choke points in the supply chain for African firms: high cost of import logistics and time, low speed to market delivery, high cost of export logistics, and high incidence of rejects.

The picture is somewhat brighter for additional reforms, albeit still uneven. Forty-six sub-Saharan countries introduced at least one business environment reform in 2006/07, and Ghana and Kenya were among the top 10 reformers (Tanzania was also on the list in 2005/06). Kenya rose from 82 to 72, and Ghana from 109 to 87. But all others had ranks of 90 or higher. Nonetheless, several countries saw improvements: Mozambique

FIGURE 1.21

Ease of Doing Business, by Region, 2007

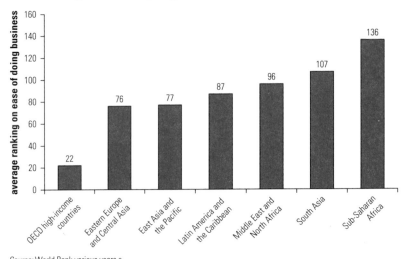

Source: World Bank various years c.

Note: OECD = Organisation for Economic Co-operation and Development.

went from 140 to 134, Madagascar from 160 to 149, and Burkina Faso from 161 to 165. In 2005/06, the region came in third behind Eastern Europe and Central Asia and Organisation for Economic Co-operation and Development countries with regard to countries that made at least one positive reform.

Improving the performance of Africa's financial systems is also high on the agenda for enterprise development. Firms in Africa identify financing constraints as even more severe than lack of infrastructure in limiting their business development.

Closing the Infrastructure Gap

An export push requires an infrastructure push in Africa, because many of the bottlenecks pertain to lack of infrastructure (figures 1.22 and 1.23). Sub-Saharan Africa lags at least 20 percentage points behind the average for International Development Association countries on almost all major infrastructure measures.[35] In addition, quality of service is low, supplies are unreliable, and disruptions are frequent and unpredictable (figure 1.24)— all pushing up production costs, a critical impediment for investors (table 1.15). There are also large inequities in access to household infrastructure services, with coverage rates in rural areas lagging those in urban

FIGURE 1.22

Reform Measures Needed to Achieve 10 Percent Increase in Africa's Exports

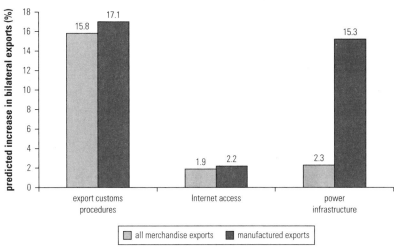

Source: Broadman et al. 2007.

FIGURE 1.23

Road Density, by Region

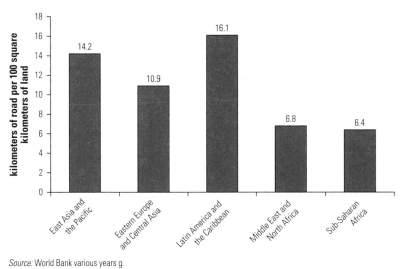

Source: World Bank various years g.

FIGURE 1.24
Time to Clear Goods at Ports in Selected Sub-Saharan African Countries and China and India

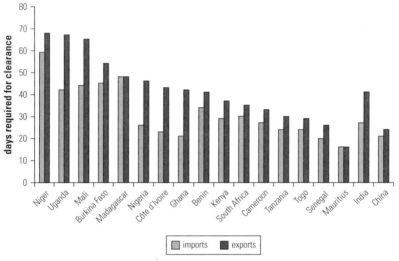

Source: World Bank various years c.

TABLE 1.15
Effect of Unreliable Infrastructure Services on the Productive Sector

Service problem	Sub-Saharan Africa	Developing countries
Electricity		
Delay in obtaining electricity connection (days)	79.9	27.5
Electrical outages (days per year)	90.9	28.7
Value of lost output attributable to electrical outages		
(% of turnover)	6.1	4.4
Firms maintaining own generation equipment (% of total)	47.5	31.8
Telecommunications		
Delay in obtaining telephone line (days)	96.6	43.0
Telephone outages (days per year)	28.1	9.1

Source: World Bank various years e.

Note: Data for sub-Saharan Africa are for 6 countries; data for developing countries are for 55 countries.

areas. The region's unmet infrastructure needs are estimated at $22 billion a year (5 percent of GDP), plus another $17 billion for operations and maintenance.

Recent progress is encouraging. Except roads, indicators of infrastructure access rose between the 1990s and 2000s (table 1.16). The Africa

TABLE 1.16
Improvements in African Infrastructure Access

Service	1990s	2000s	Percentage of change
Telephones (per 1,000 people)	21	90	328.6
Improved water (% of households)	55	65	18.1
Improved sanitation (% of households)	31	37	19.3
Grid electricity (% of households)	16	23	43.8

Source: World Bank various years a.

Partnership Forum reported steady improvements in effectively using existing infrastructure and in increasing public investments. Countries are also undertaking regulatory and policy reforms, especially for water, telecommunications, and transport (Africa Partnership Forum 2006b). Twenty of the largest African countries have or are formulating reform agendas for water and sanitation.

Compared with other regions, Africa has been slow to mobilize the private sector for the provision and financing of infrastructure. The Infrastructure Consortium reports that private sector interest has gradually spread. There is an upward trend in private sector provision and management of infrastructure, which stood at $6 billion in 2006, up from $4 billion in 2004. Most private flows (84 percent) go to telecommunications and energy. Concessions have now been awarded to operate and rehabilitate many African ports and railways and some power distribution enterprises, but financial commitments by the concessionaire companies are often small. The small commitments reflect both the value of the management improvements that the concessionaire is expected to bring and the limited scale and profitability of the enterprises taken over. An important facilitator in some cases has been the insurance instruments developed over the past 15 years by such bodies as the U.S. Overseas Private Investment Corporation and the Multilateral Investment Guarantee Agency and by the World Bank's Partial Risk Guarantee offerings.

There has been significant progress in information and communication technology. Access to communications services has increased dramatically over the past three years, with the proportion of the population (excluding South Africa) living under the mobile telephone footprint rising from 3 percent in 1999 to 50 percent in 2006. This increase has been matched by an equally rapid increase in the use of communications services. By the end of 2006, there were 123 million mobile subscribers. Average penetration rates in the region doubled between 2004 and 2006 to reach 16 percent.

Integrating the Region's Economies

The small size of African economies and the fact that many countries are landlocked call for regional approaches to common problems: infrastructure in trade corridors; common institutional and legal frameworks (customs administration, competition policy, regulation of common property resources, such as fisheries); and transborder solutions to regional health issues.

African leaders have become more aware of the benefits of regional approaches, especially in matters related to trade and infrastructure. The New Partnership for Africa's Development has adopted regional integration as one of its core objectives, and the African Union is leading efforts to rationalize regional economic communities. Most countries in Africa are party to multiple treaties or conventions addressing joint development and management of shared water resources (including navigation and fisheries), hydropower, trade corridors, irrigation, and flood control. Progress has been most notable in regional infrastructure, particularly regional power pools (in West Africa and southern Africa) and in launching customs unions (in West Africa, East Africa, and southern Africa). Progress on regional infrastructure is slowed by the technical complexity of multicountry projects and the time required for decisions by multiple governments. There is less progress in creating regional approaches to education and in systematically addressing regional health issues.

Making Agriculture More Productive

Sustained growth that reduces rural poverty will require that more countries achieve 5 percent annual growth in agricultural value added. Although growth in agricultural value added has been strong since 2000, averaging 4.6 percent in 2004, too little of it has come from higher productivity or yields.[36] Although land productivity is increasing in 38 of 46 countries, only 6 have a rate of increase of 5 percent or more.[37] Labor productivity is increasing in 29 countries, with 10 achieving increases of 3 percent a year or higher.[38]

Productivity growth will require an expansion of irrigated areas, as well as better performance of rain-fed agriculture. But less than 4 percent of cultivated land is irrigated. Because of the long lead time before investments are completed and operational, this proportion changed little in recent years. Improvements in management of soil fertility have been slow, as has been the adoption of better seeds. Spending for agricultural research and technology remains low, although it is starting to increase along with overall spending on agricultural programs in the region (Africa Partnership Forum 2006a). On a positive note, there has been an increase in the use of water management techniques (water harvesting, reduced tillage).

Using Natural Resource Rents Well

Resource-based rents are widespread and growing because of new discoveries and favorable prices. During the 1990s, 65 percent of all FDI was concentrated in oil, gas, and mining. Between 2000 and 2010, $200 billion in oil revenue will accrue to African governments. The 2004 oil windfall alone, on average, resulted in a 26 percent increase in government revenue in oil-exporting countries.

However, in Africa, mineral-dependent countries tend to do worse in social indicators than non-mineral countries at the same income level, including having higher poverty rates, greater income inequality, less spending on health care, higher prevalence of child malnutrition, and lower literacy and school enrollments. But mineral-exporting economies can achieve shared growth. Indonesia and Malaysia have all used natural resource wealth to provide a basis for a more diversified economy in which the poor have been able to participate and contribute to the process of growth (figure 1.25).

Elements of a strategy for mineral revenue management include the following:

- Promote transparency in accounting for revenues by adopting the EITI.

- Establish fiscal rules, including setting savings rules and maintaining fiscal discipline in decentralized fiscal systems.

- Strengthen public financial management and the Medium Term Expenditure Framework.

- Monitor and evaluate outcomes.

See also chapter 9, by Devlin and Lewin, and chapter 10, by Budina and van Wijnbergen, for further discussion on fiscal management of oil revenue and the case of Nigeria.

FIGURE 1.25

Income Growth by Population of Different Income Levels in Three Countries

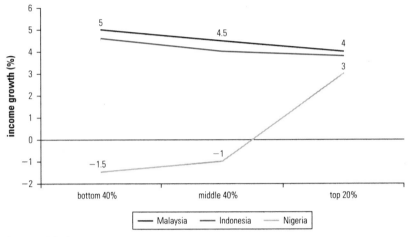

Source: World Bank.

Increasing Regional and Global Support

Developing and implementing regional strategies for increasing connectivity to the world and within Africa are crucial. Cross-country infrastructure projects are particularly important, but so too are institutional reforms, such as common customs procedures, that lower transactions costs. Complementary action by the global development community to reduce barriers to trade and to scale up aid to enhance the region's capacity to trade is also required.

Sharing the Benefits of Growth

Growth alone will not be enough to reach the Millennium Development Goals (MDGs) for Africa. At the same time that Africa's governments are pursuing a new growth strategy—and with the same vigor—they will also need to focus on delivering more and better services for human development.

Many MDGs Will Not Be Met

Despite the recent good performance, Africa's GDP per capita is still 50 percent of the level of East Asia (figure 1.26), and the growth rate is far short of the 7 percent needed if poverty is to be halved by 2015. The mean income/expenditure of the poor—those earning less than one PPP dollar a

FIGURE 1.26

Per Capita GDP of Sub-Saharan Africa, East Asia, and Low-Income Countries

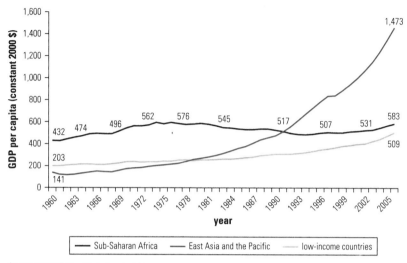

Sources: World Bank various years d, various years g.

day—is much lower in Africa than in East Asia or South Asia (figure 1.27). Africa is far behind all other regions in terms of the United Nations human development index (figure 1.28). It will also remain behind on most MDGs (figure 1.29); if current trends continue, it will not meet the 2015 targets. In 1990, 47 percent of Africans lived in poverty. In 2004, 41 percent did, and with present trends, 37 percent will in 2015.

FIGURE 1.27

Average Expenditure of the Poor, by Region

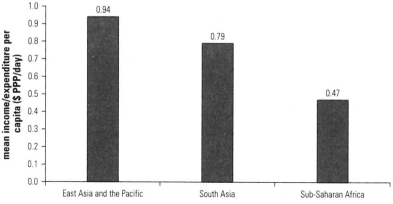

Source: World Bank various years f.

FIGURE 1.28

The Human Development Index

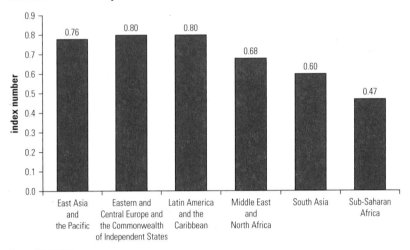

Source: UNDP 2006.

FIGURE 1.29

Gap between the MDGs and Projected Levels, Given Current Trends

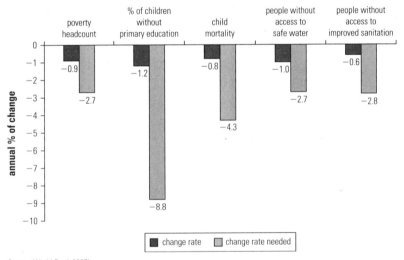

Source: World Bank 2007b.

Although sub-Saharan Africa is one of two regions not expected to reach most of the MDGs by 2015 (the other is South Asia), there is substantial variation among countries in both the level of attainment of the goals and the pace of progress. Mauritius has met four goals. Botswana has met three and will likely meet one more. And South Africa has met three. Among other countries, 9 will meet two goals, and 13 will meet at least one. But despite better progress—especially in education, malaria, and HIV/AIDS—23 African countries are unlikely to meet any of the MDGs. Scaling up the efforts on MDGs presents several challenges in low-income countries, and chapter 6 by Lofgren and Diaz-Bonilla examines the trade-offs and scenarios in the case of Ethiopia.

Sharing the Benefits of Public Services Will Be Key

Africa has the lowest and most unequal access to essential services. In the 1960s and into the 1970s, many African countries widened access to essential social services and saw significant improvements in many social indicators. However, this progress did not prove sustainable. Africa has the lowest access to all essential services. Service delivery is costly for African governments because of long distances and sparsely populated areas.

The rural populations have extremely limited access to services of decent quality, including education, health care, safe drinking water, paved roads, and telecommunications. They also lack access to factors of production, such as means of transportation, fertilizer, and improved seeds.

Women in Africa provide more than half the region's labor but lack equal access to education and factors of production. Gender differentials in the areas of labor force participation and labor productivity are constraints to economic growth. A study in Kenya, for example, concluded that giving women farmers the same level of agricultural inputs and education as men could increase their yields by more than 20 percent.

Service Delivery Must Reach the Poor, Rural Populations, and Women

African rural populations and the poor have a distinct disadvantage in their access to services (figure 1.30). To build and sustain service delivery, African countries will need to do the following:

- Improve social sector policies.

- Strengthen financial management and costing.

- Decentralize service delivery, capacity building, and training.

FIGURE 1.30

Rural-Urban Gaps in Access to Services, Selected Countries

a. Access to health center within 5 kilometers or 1 hour

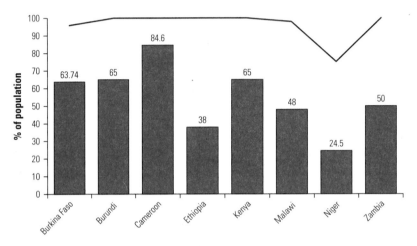

b. Access to market within 5 kilometers or 1 hour

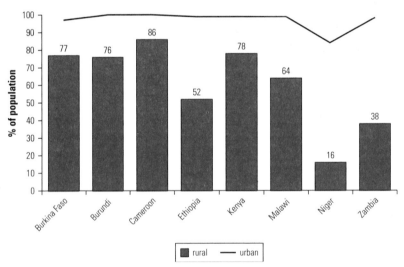

Source: World Bank Africa Region.

- Integrate sectors into multisectoral budgetary programming to underpin the implementation of the national poverty reduction strategy.

Since 1999, when the Poverty Reduction Strategy Paper (PRSP) became the key policy framework for development partners, many African governments have consciously started to invest more in pro-poor service

FIGURE 1.31

**Pro-poor Spending as Percentage of Total Government Spending,
1999 and 2004**

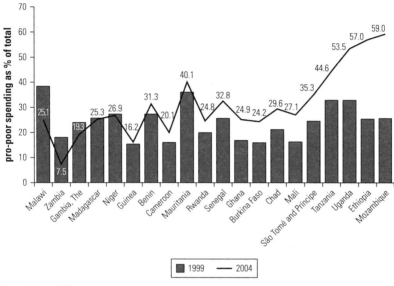

Source: Country PRSPs.

delivery, especially in the areas of health, education, HIV/AIDS, rural
development (roads), agriculture, and water (figure 1.31).

So, Is Africa at a Turning Point?

Based on the records, the verdict is guarded. There is indeed an acceleration of growth in sub-Saharan Africa, but its sustainability is fragile.
African countries in general are increasingly able to avoid mistakes and
economic collapses, but increasing and sustaining growth are a difficult
challenge. In the short to medium term, much depends on the continuation of favorable terms of trade, aid, and debt relief, as well as good policy.
In the medium to long term, it is essential to raise the economic fundamentals, which are still lagging. Particularly needed are higher exports,
more private sector growth, greater productivity of investment, higher foreign investment and remittances from migrant workers, greater regional
efforts at tackling the infrastructure gaps, and improved agriculture. These
economic fundamentals can be raised through continuing reforms and

improved governance. In the long term, there is no substitute for improving human development and sharing the benefits of growth.

Predictions of Africa's imminent recovery or demise have proved wrong on numerous occasions in the past 40 years. Some of its economies have been badly managed and have declined, whereas others have prospered. But the energy, imagination, and entrepreneurship of its people have overcome both limited opportunities and bad policies to place the region at a position in this new century where better governments and better policies can make a difference. Shared growth can become a reality in Africa.

Notes

We thank Betty P. Dow, Cristina Savescu, and Xiao Ye for excellent research assistance.

1. These assessments include AfDB and OECD (2007); AFRCE (various years); EIU (2007); IMF (2007a, 2007b); and World Bank (2007a, 2007b, 2007d). AFRCE briefs, from which much of this chapter is derived, are biannual economic briefs prepared by the Chief Economist Office of the Africa Region at the World Bank. The briefs cover recent economic growth in sub-Saharan Africa, issues about the scaling up of foreign aid, and the effect of external shocks. In addition, papers by Arbache and Page (2007a, 2007b) are key sources of the growth analysis.
2. The statistical significance of this hypothesis is tested in the growth analysis in the next section.
3. This assessment does not include Somalia, where no good data are available, and the numbers for Sudan may not fully cover its southern regions. Both current and past data face the same limitations.
4. If there is any pattern growth, small countries in the resource-rich groups (oil and non-oil) tend to benefit more from higher commodity prices and additional revenue than larger countries in the groups. As a result, simple averages will tend to be higher than weighted averages. The reverse pattern between simple and weighted averages seems to be the case in countries that are not rich in resources.
5. Strictly speaking, oil-exporting and oil-importing countries may belong to two or more subgroups simultaneously. For purposes of describing the performance, however, the classification is not overlapping, so that the subgroups add up to 100 percent. Collier (2007) and Collier and O'Connell (2006) also argue that oil and non-oil resource endowments are dominant characteristics relative to the others.
6. These countries are Botswana, Guinea, Namibia, São Tomé and Principe, Sierra Leone, and Zambia.
7. These countries are Benin, Cape Verde, Comoros, Côte d'Ivoire, Eritrea, The Gambia, Ghana, Guinea-Bissau, Kenya, Liberia, Madagascar, Mauritania,

Mauritius, Mozambique, Senegal, the Seychelles, South Africa, Tanzania, and Togo.

8. These countries are Burkina Faso, Burundi, the Central African Republic, the Democratic Republic of Congo, Ethiopia, Lesotho, Malawi, Mali, Niger, Rwanda, Swaziland, Uganda, and Zimbabwe.

9. The classification, like that of oil-importing countries by endowment and location, is not overlapping (see note 5).

10. These countries are Botswana, Cape Verde, Lesotho, Mauritius, Namibia, the Seychelles, South Africa, and Swaziland.

11. These countries are Benin, Burkina Faso, Ethiopia, Ghana, Kenya, Madagascar, Malawi, Mali, Mozambique, Niger, Rwanda, Senegal, Tanzania, Uganda, and Zambia.

12. These countries are Burundi, the Central African Republic, Comoros, the Democratic Republic of Congo, Côte d'Ivoire, Eritrea, The Gambia, Guinea, Guinea-Bissau, Liberia, São Tomé and Principe, Sierra Leone, Togo, and Zimbabwe.

13. Kenya, Tanzania, and Uganda.

14. Cameroon, the Central African Republic, Chad, Equatorial Guinea, Gabon, and the Republic of Congo.

15. Angola, Burundi, Cameroon, the Central African Republic, Chad, the Democratic Republic of Congo, the Republic of Congo, Equatorial Guinea, Gabon, Rwanda, and São Tomé and Principe.

16. SADC comprises Angola, Botswana, the Democratic Republic of Congo, Lesotho, Madagascar, Malawi, Mauritius, Mozambique, Namibia, South Africa, Swaziland, Tanzania, Zambia, and Zimbabwe. SADC is the largest regional group in table 1.2 (about 52 percent of Africa's GDP).

17. ECOWAS comprises Benin, Burkina Faso, Cape Verde, Côte d'Ivoire, The Gambia, Ghana, Guinea, Guinea-Bissau, Liberia, Mali, Niger, Nigeria, Senegal, Sierra Leone, and Togo.

18. WAEMU comprises Benin, Burkina Faso, Côte d'Ivoire, Guinea-Bissau, Liberia, Mali, Niger, Senegal, and Togo.

19. The Indian Ocean Commission comprises Comoros, Mauritius, Madagascar, and the Seychelles.

20. The *WDI's* GDP per capita PPP series starts in 1975.

21. The Hodrick-Prescott filter is used in figures 1.4 and 1.5 to smooth the estimate of the long-term trend component of the GDP series.

22. As a means of checking the robustness of the results, growth accelerations and decelerations were also identified by replacing 0 with $+1$ percent and -1 percent for acceleration and deceleration, respectively, in condition 1, but the results did not change substantially. Therefore, only the base-case results are reported, because they are less restrictive.

23. The simulated growth rate without collapses takes into account the growth rate during all country-years but growth deceleration years. The additional GDP per capita results from the difference in compound growth at 1.7 percent and 0.7 percent in 1975–2005.

24. Calculated as $((0.18/0.04) - 1)*100$.
25. See country assignment in table A.2 in Arbache and Page (2007b).
26. Governance indicators are available for the following years: 1996, 1998, 2000, 2003, 2004, and 2005.
27. Random-effect models, including dummies for oil-producing countries, and landlocked and resource-rich countries returned statistically insignificant results. Hausmann tests suggest that fixed-effect estimates are preferable to random effect.
28. The recovery of terms of trade in non-oil-exporting developing countries since the late 1990s is, however, still below the peaks of the early 1980s. Data are from the World Bank's *World Economic Indicators.*
29. So far, MDRI countries include Benin, Burkina Faso, Cameroon, Ethiopia, Ghana, Madagascar, Malawi, Mali, Mozambique, Niger, Rwanda, Senegal, Sierra Leone, Tanzania, Uganda, and Zambia.
30. Excluding the hyperinflation in Angola and Zimbabwe. In Angola's case, inflation fell over 300 percent in 2000 to about 13 percent in 2006.
31. Low-income countries in Africa are generally constrained from borrowing in international capital markets. As a result, the current account balance, the other significant macrobalance, is not a policy-dependent variable or a good indicator of macroeconomic management. Imports in these countries tend to adjust to export revenues and aid inflows.
32. See Bacon and Kojima (2006). ESMAP is a global technical assistance partnership that has been administered by the World Bank and sponsored by bilateral official donors since 1983.
33. See Bacon and Kojima (2006) for various case studies of African countries.
34. So that the subsets' sample sizes are consistent, oil-exporting countries are not accessed separately.
35. An important exception is the penetration of fixed-line and mobile telephones, where sub-Saharan Africa leads low-income countries by as much as 13 percent. The largest gaps are for rural roads (29 percentage points) and electricity (21 percentage points).
36. Growth in Angola, Burkina Faso, Cape Verde, the Republic of Congo, Eritrea, Ethiopia, Ghana, Mauritius, Mozambique, Nigeria, and Tanzania has been through an expansion of cropped area.
37. This rate is the five-year moving average based on 2001–05.
38. This rate is the five-year moving average based on 2000–04.

References

AfDB and OECD (African Development Bank and Organisation for Economic Co-operation and Development). 2007. *African Economic Outlook.* Paris: OECD.

AFRCE (Office of the Chief Economist, Africa Region). Various years. "Biannual Economic Briefs." World Bank, Washington, DC.

Africa Partnership Forum. 2006a. "Progress Report: Agriculture." Africa Partnership Forum, Moscow.

———. 2006b. "Progress Report: Infrastructure." Africa Partnership Forum, Moscow.

Arbache, Jorge Saba, and John Page. 2007a. "Is Africa's Recent Growth Robust?" World Bank, Washington, DC. [forthcoming as an Africa Region Working Paper No. 111].

———. 2007b. "More Growth or Fewer Collapses? A New Look at Long Run Growth in Sub-Saharan Africa." Policy Research Working Paper 4384, World Bank, Washington, DC.

Bacon, Robert, and Masami Kojima. 2006. "Coping with Higher Oil Prices." Report of the Energy Sector Management Assistance Programme, World Bank, Washington, DC.

Berthélemy, Jean-Claude, and Ludvig Söderling. 2001. "The Role of Capital Accumulation, Adjustment, and Structural Change for Economic Take-off: Evidence from African Growth Episodes." *World Development* 29 (2): 332–43.

Bosworth, Barry, and Susan M. Collins. 2003. "The Empirics of Growth: An Update." *Brookings Papers on Economic Activity* 2: 113–206.

Broadman, Harry G., with Gozde Isik, Sonia Plaza, Xiao Ye, and Yutaka Yoshino. 2007. *Africa's Silk Road: China and India's New Economic Frontier.* Washington, DC: World Bank.

Cadot, Olivier, and John Nasir. 2001. "Incentives and Obstacles to Growth: Lessons from Manufacturing Case Studies in Madagascar." Regional Program on Enterprise Development, Discussion Paper 117. World Bank, Washington, DC.

Collier, Paul. 2007. *The Bottom Billion.* Oxford, U.K.: Oxford University Press.

Collier, Paul, and Jan Dehn. 2001. "Aid, Shocks, and Growth." Policy Research Working Paper 2688, World Bank, Washington, DC.

Collier, Paul, and Benedikt Goderis. 2007. "Commodity Prices, Growth, and the Natural Resource Curse: Reconciling a Conundrum." Department of Economics, University of Oxford.

Collier, Paul, and Jan Willem Gunning. 1999. "Explaining African Economic Performance." *Journal of Economic Literature* 37 (1): 64–111.

Collier, Paul, and Stephen A. O'Connell. 2006. "Opportunities and Choices." Draft chapter 2 of the synthesis volume of the African Economic Research Consortium's Explaining African Economic Growth project. Nairobi, African Economic Research Consortium.

Deaton, Angus, and Ronald I. Miller. 1995. "International Commodity Prices, Macroeconomic Performance, and Politics in Sub-Saharan Africa." Princeton Studies in International Finance 79, Princeton University, Princeton, NJ.

Devarajan, Shantayanan, William Easterly, and Howard Pack. 2003. "Low Investment Is Not the Constraint on African Development." *Economic Development and Cultural Change* 51 (3): 547–71.

Dixit, Avinash. 2007. "Recipes for Development Success." *World Bank Research Observer* 22 (2): 131–57.

Dufrénot, Gilles, Gilles Sanon, and Abdoulaye Diop. 2006. "Is Per-Capita Growth in Africa Hampered by Poor Governance and Weak Institutions? Examining the Case of the ECOWAS Countries." West Africa Economic and Monetary Union, Ouagadougou.

Easterly, William. 1998. "The Ghost of Financing Gap: Testing the Growth Model in the International Financing Institutions." IMF Seminar Series 1998-2, International Monetary Fund, Washington, DC.

———. 2001. *The Elusive Quest for Growth*. Cambridge, MA: MIT Press.

EIU (Economist Intelligence Unit). 2007. *Sub-Saharan Africa: Regional Overview*. London: EIU.

Eifert, Benn, Alan H. Gelb, and Vijaya Ramachandran. 2005. "Business Environment and Comparative Advantage in Africa: Evidence from the Investment Climate Data." Working Paper 56, Center for Global Development, Washington, DC.

Gelb, Alan, Ali A.G. Ali, Tesfaye Dinka, Ibrahim Elbadwi, Charles Saludo, and Gene Tidrick. 2000. *Can Africa Claim the 21st Century?* Washington, DC: World Bank.

Hausmann, Ricardo, Lant Pritchett, and Dani Rodrik. 2005. "Growth Accelerations." *Journal of Economic Growth* 10 (4): 303–29.

Hnatkovska, Viktoria, and Norman Loayza. 2004. "Volatility and Growth." Policy Research Working Paper 3184, World Bank, Washington, DC.

IMF (International Monetary Fund). 2007a. "Sub-Saharan Africa Regional Economic Outlook: Fall 2007." SM/07/319, IMF, Washington, DC.

———. 2007b. *World Economic Outlook: Spillovers and Cycles in the Global Economy*. Washington, DC: IMF.

———. Various years. *World Economic Outlook*. Washington, DC: IMF.

Kaufmann, Daniel, Aart Kraay, and Pablo Zoido. 1999. "Governance Matters." Policy Research Working Paper 2196, World Bank, Washington, DC.

Ndulu, Benno J., Lopamudra Chakroborti, Lebohang Lijane, Vijaya Ramachandran, and Jerome Wolgin. 2007. *Challenges of Africa Growth: Opportunities, Constraints, and Strategic Directions*. Washington, DC: World Bank.

O'Connell, Stephen A., and Benno J. Ndulu. 2000. "Africa's Growth Experience: A Focus on Sources of Growth." Growth Working Paper 10, African Economic Research Consortium, Nairobi.

OECD-DAC (Organisation for Economic Co-operation and Development–Development Assistance Committee). Various years. Database on official development assistance. OECD, Paris.

Ramey, Garey, and Valerie A. Ramey. 1995. "Cross-Country Evidence on the Link between Volatility and Growth." *American Economic Review* 85 (5): 1138–51.

Seldadyo, Harry, Emmanuel Pandu Nugroho, and Jokob de Haan. 2007. "Governance and Growth Revisited." *Kyklos* 60 (2): 279–90.

Subramanian, Uma, and Matthias Matthijs. 2007. "Can Sub-Saharan Africa Leap into Global Network Trade?" Policy Research Working Paper 4112, World Bank, Washington, DC.

UNDP (United Nations Development Programme). 2006. *Human Development Report 2006—Beyond Scarcity: Power, Poverty, and the Global Water Crisis.* New York: UNDP.

World Bank. 2007a. *Global Economic Prospects 2007: Managing the Next Wave of Globalization.* Washington, DC: World Bank.

———. 2007b. *Global Monitoring Report 2007: Millennium Development Goals and Confronting the Challenges of Gender Equality and Fragile States.* Washington, DC: World Bank.

———. 2007c. "Operational Approaches and Financing in Fragile States." IDA 15, International Development Agency, World Bank, Washington, DC.

———. 2007d. "The World Bank Group's Africa Action Plan: Progress in Implementation." Report M2007-0112, World Bank, Washington, DC.

———. Various years a. *Africa Development Indicators.* Washington, DC: World Bank.

———. Various years b. Commodity Price database. Development Economics Prospect Group (DECPG), World Bank, Washington, DC.

———. Various years c. Doing Business database. World Bank, Washington, DC. http://www.doingbusiness.org/.

———. Various years d. Global Development Finance database. World Bank, Washington, DC. http://publications.worldbank.org/GDF/.

———. Various years e. Investment Climate Assessments. World Bank, Washington, DC. http://www.worldbank.org/privatesector/ic/ic_ica.htm and http://www.worldbank.org/rped.

———. Various years f. PovcalNet database. World Bank, Washington, DC.

———. Various years g. *World Development Indicators.* Washington, DC: World Bank.

———. Various years h. *World Trade Indicators.* Washington, DC: World Bank.

———. Various years i. World-Wide Governance Indicators Project database. Washington, DC: World Bank. http://info.worldbank.org/governance/wgi2007/home.htm.

CHAPTER 2

Patterns of Long-Term Growth
in Sub-Saharan Africa

Jorge Saba Arbache and John Page

Recent popular and academic writing has suggested that Africa may be at a turning point in its long economic decline (CFA 2005; Ndulu 2007). Beginning about the middle of the 1990s, growth accelerated in a number of countries, and the region's average growth rate began to approach that of other developing countries for the first time since the mid-1970s. To understand whether Africa is at a turning point, however, it is useful to examine the stylized facts of the region's post-independence long-run growth performance.

Using the most recent purchasing power parity (PPP) data for 44 sub-Saharan African countries, this chapter investigates the characteristics of long-run growth in Africa between 1975 and 2005. We were interested in examining the following issues: cross-country income structure, convergence, the country-level distribution of income, and growth persistence. Also, we examined the data for evidence of the formation of country groups or "clubs."

The time period includes the first oil shock and commodities prices plunge, when many African economies collapsed and several conflicts erupted; the introduction of structural reforms, which brought significant changes in many economies; and the growth recovery observed more recently. Given the rich and varied economic changes experienced by African countries, our time-series may well capture long-term economic trends.

The next section describes our data and methods and is followed by a section examining the characteristics of Africa's long-run growth experience. The fourth section of the chapter looks at the structure of gross domestic product (GDP) per capita across Africa. We then identify four groups of countries according to their income levels and growth experiences, and we look for some common characteristics that are associated with the groups. Next, we probe more deeply into the consequences of growth volatility for economic performance and test for some correlates of volatility.

Data and Methods

We analyzed patterns of GDP per capita growth at 2000 international PPP prices and their respective standard deviations (SDs) and coefficients of variation (CVs), which are our measures of volatility. Although there are differences between GDP per capita at PPP and non-PPP, those differences mainly are confined to levels and do not affect growth trajectories.[1]

All data are from *World Development Indicators*, unless otherwise specified. The time-series spans the years 1975 to 2005. Our sample contains all sub-Saharan African countries for which PPP GDP data exist. For Liberia, São Tomé and Principe, and Somalia, there are no GDP per capita PPP data.[2] We have an unbalanced panel of data with 44 countries and 31 periods. The mean GDP per capita between 1975 and 2005, using unweighted data, was $2,306 for the 44 countries in our sample. The mean GDP using weighted data was $1,702. Unless stated otherwise, we used unweighted country data because we are interested in examining the representative country.[3]

Along with descriptive statistics and kernel distributions, we analyzed the GDP data using bivariate and multivariate cross-country and pooled ordinary least squares (OLS) regression models and multivariate logit models. Because we are interested in identifying the long-run association between growth and other variables, rather than in modeling the determinants of growth, we are not concerned about omitted variables and problems associated with direction of causality, reverse causality, endogeneities, nonlinearities, and other potential econometric issues that usually plague growth regressions. We interpret our econometric results descriptively only.

Characteristics of Africa's Long-Run Growth

Figure 2.1a shows that mean GDP per capita had a slow, positive long-term trend, consisting of about 20 years of virtual stagnation with a point of inflexion in the early 1990s.[4] Since the mid-1990s, the variance of mean income per capita also appears to have declined. Weighting by GDP (figure 2.1b) gives a U-shaped pattern of GDP per capita, reaching a minimum in the mid-1990s. By 2005, GDP per capita had not yet recovered to the levels observed in mid-1970s.

The trajectories of the unweighted and weighted series show significant differences. Africa's larger economies stagnated or declined in the 1970s

FIGURE 2.1
GDP Per Capita

a. Unweighted data

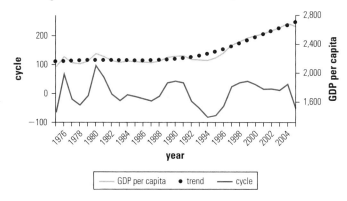

b. Weighted data

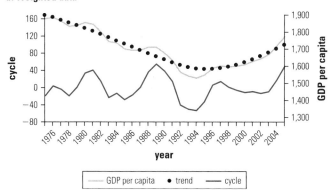

Source: Authors' calculations.

and 1980s, causing the U shape. South Africa, which represents, on average, 42 percent of the regions' GDP, grew by an average of only 0.12 percent
a year; and Nigeria, the second-largest economy, representing 12.50 percent of the region's GDP, grew by 0.28 percent, while the regional
unweighted average growth was 0.71 percent. Both the unweighted and
weighted series show a strong positive trend from the mid-1990s on. In the
period 1995–2005, the unweighted average GDP per capita growth was
1.81 percent, more than twice the long-term average.

Turning to growth rates, figure 2.2 presents the paths of unweighted
and weighted data. The mean and SD of unweighted GDP per capita
growth are 0.71 percent and 6.32 percent, respectively. Figure 2.2a

FIGURE 2.2
GDP Per Capita Growth

a. Unweighted data

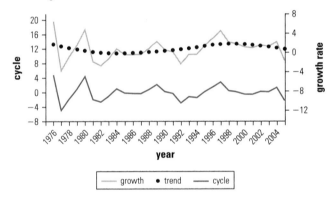

b. Weighted data

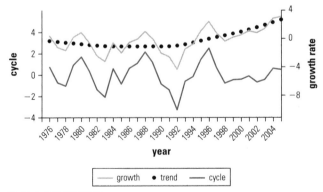

Source: Authors' calculations.

shows that growth declined until the mid-1980s, but it has had a positive trend since then. The mean and SD of weighted data are −0.17 percent and 1.7 percent, respectively. Although the trend line shapes appear similar, their means and variances are significantly different. The mean calculated from unweighted data is larger, suggesting that big economies grew less than small ones, as indicated above. Both small and large economies experienced high growth variation, however. The average SD of South Africa's growth is 2.41 percent; Nigeria's average is 5.15 percent; and the simple average of African countries is 2.26 percent.

Comparing Sub-Saharan Africa with Other Developing Regions

The African growth story looks bleak when compared with the growth performances of other developing countries. Whereas all other regions experienced significant income improvements, Africa's income shrank between the 1970s and the 2000s (see table 2.1). Africa is always among the weakest growth performers, although there has been some catching up recently.

Figure 2.3 shows that Africa has the lowest CV of GDP per capita, which is due to its long economic stagnation. Figure 2.4 shows that African

TABLE 2.1

GDP Per Capita and Growth, by Region, Weighted Data, 1975–2005

Region	1975–80	1981–85	1986–90	1991–95	1996–2000	2001–05
GDP per capita						
Sub-Saharan Africa	1,928	1,844	1,782	1,648	1,668	1,768
East Asia and Pacific	905	1,227	1,686	2,407	3,399	4,595
Latin America and Caribbean	6,020	6,295	6,315	6,450	6,978	7,205
Middle East and North Africa	4,179	4,180	4,055	4,326	4,651	5,197
South Asia	1,132	1,268	1,505	1,745	2,110	2,530
Low and middle income	2,278	2,560	2,881	3,045	3,513	4,219
Growth						
Sub-Saharan Africa	−0.06	−1.60	−0.21	−1.64	0.79	1.79
East Asia and Pacific	5.26	6.12	5.76	9.10	5.63	7.06
Latin America and Caribbean	3.31	−0.95	−0.43	1.61	1.53	1.21
Middle East and North Africa	−0.20	2.41	−1.20	1.18	1.91	2.78
South Asia	1.03	3.14	3.89	3.01	3.59	4.65
Low and middle income	2.79	1.99	1.93	1.56	3.23	4.58

Source: Authors' calculations.

Note: All sub-Saharan African countries are included in calculations.

FIGURE 2.3

Mean, Standard Deviation, and Coefficient of Variation of GDP Per Capita (weighted data), by Region and Income Level

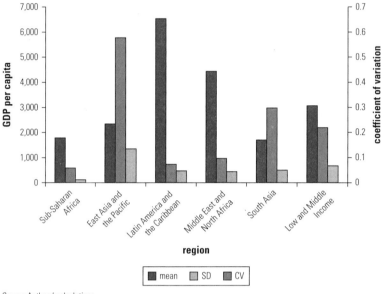

Source: Authors' calculations.

Note: CV = coefficient of variation; SD = standard deviation

FIGURE 2.4

Mean, Standard Deviation, and Coefficient of Variation of GDP Per Capita Growth (weighted data), by Region

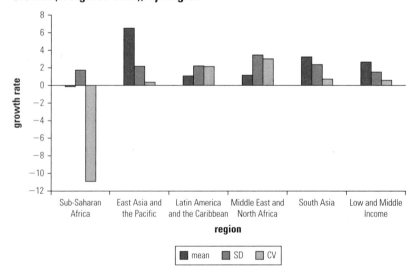

Source: Authors' calculations.

countries have the least predictable growth, as suggested by the largest CV. Numerous factors can explain this outcome, such as higher exposure to climatic shocks, changes in the international economic environment, political economy issues, and high incidence of conflicts. Guillaumont, Guillaumont-Jeanneney, and Brun (1999) found that, for Africa, these sources of instability contribute to the induction of bad policies that result in instabilities of the rate of investment and the real exchange rate and in lower total factor productivity.

Country-Level Growth Patterns

Table 2.2 presents descriptive statistics at the country level. In general, African countries' GDP per capita registered only modest increases between 1975 and 2005, and many countries—such as the Democratic Republic of Congo, Côte D'Ivoire, and Zimbabwe—showed declining per capita incomes over the period. The SD of income per capita is generally low, and the CV of many countries is close to zero. Thus, the overall pattern of income in the region was both stagnant and stable.

Consistent with the relative stability of income, growth rates for most countries were low. Despite some statistical commonalities, however, there were highly diverse growth experiences in Africa, and they can be described by the metaphor suggested by Pritchett (2000): hills, plateaus, mountains, and plains (see the illustrative examples in figure 2A.2 in the annex to this chapter). The CV of growth in many countries is very high, suggesting that growth is highly erratic. Some noteworthy cases are the Comoros (−22.6), Ethiopia (18.4), Guinea-Bissau (−11.9), and South Africa (20.6), all of which are associated, at least in part, with some kind of internal or external conflict. More remarkable is that countries at different levels of income (like Botswana and Malawi) or following diverse long-term GDP per capita patterns (like Cape Verde, the Comoros, and South Africa) also share the attribute of high growth volatility.

Table 2.3 shows the decomposition of the SD of GDP per capita and its growth within and between countries. Variation of GDP per capita is mostly due to between-country variations, whereas the variation in growth is basically due to within-country variation. In short, the GDP per capita of individual countries is relatively stable, and the bulk of the variation in Africa's average income per person occurs between countries.

TABLE 2.2
Countries' Descriptive Statistics, 1975–2005

Country	1975 (US$)	2005 (US$)	GDP per capita Average annual (US$)	Standard deviation	Coefficient of variation
Angola		2,077	1,608	242.5	0.151
Benin	860	1,015	914	56.3	0.062
Botswana	1,820	11,021	5,474	2,637.0	0.482
Burkina Faso	763	1,079	918	81.5	0.089
Burundi	738	622	785	104.1	0.133
Cameroon	1,702	2,045	2,054	345.6	0.168
Cape Verde	..	5,162	3,686	799.0	0.217
Central African Republic	1,646	1,089	1,330	201.6	0.152
Chad	972	1,270	879	133.9	0.152
Comoros	..	1,773	1,845	107.1	0.058
Congo, Dem. Rep.	2,214	635	1,271	539.4	0.425
Congo, Rep.	998	1,123	1,163	181.6	0.156
Côte d'Ivoire	2,433	1,466	1,881	429.3	0.228
Equatorial Guinea	..	..	2,859	2,110.0	0.738
Eritrea	..	986	1,078	134.5	0.125
Ethiopia	..	938	817	76.7	0.094
Gabon	9,323	6,187	7,041	1,389.3	0.197
Gambia, The	1,584	1,709	1,633	50.9	0.031
Ghana	1,885	2,206	1,756	201.1	0.115
Guinea	..	2,060	1,873	122.0	0.065
Guinea-Bissau	1,019	736	921	104.3	0.113
Kenya	963	1,103	1,051	39.7	0.038
Lesotho	1,176	2,967	2,102	517.8	0.246
Madagascar	1,290	821	947	154.6	0.163
Malawi	579	593	565	40.1	0.071
Mali	742	919	764	80.0	0.105
Mauritania	1,963	1,988	1,915	63.1	0.033
Mauritius	..	11,312	7,318	2,327.4	0.318
Mozambique	..	1,105	704	168.7	0.240
Namibia	..	6,749	5,875	415.9	0.071
Niger	985	695	829	150.5	0.181
Nigeria	961	1,003	865	90.6	0.105
Rwanda	840	1,073	1,031	123.9	0.120
Senegal	1,468	1,594	1,408	80.3	0.057
Seychelles	7,363	14,329	12,113	2,954.6	0.244
Sierra Leone	935	717	770	166.8	0.217
South Africa	9,625	9,884	9,242	517.5	0.056
Sudan	1,161	1,853	1,287	220.6	0.171
Swaziland	3,103	4,292	3,664	578.0	0.158
Tanzania	..	662	529	53.3	0.101
Togo	1,708	1,340	1,490	182.5	0.123
Uganda	..	1,293	976	181.3	0.186
Zambia	1,351	910	981	182.3	0.186
Zimbabwe	2,784	1,813	2,526	253.2	0.100

Source: Authors' calculations.

Note: .. = negligible; max = maximum; min = minimum.

GDP per capita growth				
Average annual (%)	Standard deviation	Min	Max	Coefficient of variation
0.70	8.31	−27.13	17.21	11.92
0.60	2.96	−7.64	6.38	4.95
6.24	3.36	−0.58	16.07	0.54
1.21	3.30	−4.36	7.16	2.72
−0.46	4.65	−8.92	9.18	−10.02
0.81	6.51	−10.51	18.42	8.00
3.26	2.52	−1.56	8.51	0.77
−1.27	4.42	−10.70	6.47	−3.48
1.34	9.57	−23.04	25.23	7.13
−0.14	3.23	−7.85	6.24	−22.65
−3.95	5.07	−16.59	3.54	−1.28
0.61	6.77	−11.77	19.76	11.14
−1.57	4.51	−15.14	7.81	−2.87
10.55	17.62	−6.16	67.09	1.67
1.96	9.11	−16.30	20.92	4.66
0.42	7.78	−13.87	16.43	18.41
−0.91	9.60	−26.25	31.80	−10.60
0.29	2.92	−6.09	7.24	9.90
0.60	3.78	−10.08	6.70	6.33
0.97	1.55	−2.64	3.41	1.59
−0.70	8.36	−29.98	14.81	−11.95
0.48	2.29	−3.89	5.49	4.78
3.27	5.47	−5.77	19.04	1.67
−1.38	4.68	−15.19	6.92	−3.39
0.22	5.41	−11.03	15.13	24.57
0.86	5.49	−13.45	10.92	6.36
0.10	3.40	−6.62	6.96	34.58
4.22	1.66	1.69	8.46	0.39
2.07	7.34	−17.45	14.75	3.54
0.15	2.89	−5.11	5.03	19.82
−1.00	5.45	−19.42	10.04	−5.43
0.28	5.15	−15.54	8.20	18.67
1.68	12.25	−47.00	37.48	7.28
0.36	4.12	−6.77	12.19	11.57
2.47	6.91	−9.23	19.28	2.80
−0.57	7.97	−19.26	21.82	−14.04
0.12	2.41	−4.33	4.17	20.64
1.72	5.52	−8.80	13.09	3.21
1.15	3.64	−5.19	11.13	3.17
1.69	2.65	−2.73	5.06	1.57
−0.60	6.44	−17.14	12.05	−10.68
1.92	3.15	−6.59	8.09	1.64
−1.23	4.01	−10.92	4.31	−3.26
−1.26	5.71	−11.25	10.46	−4.53

TABLE 2.3
Decomposition of the SD of GDP Per Capita and Growth, 1975–2005

Variable	Mean	SD overall	SD between countries	SD within countries
GDP per capita	2,306	2,633	2,490	809
GDP per capita growth	0.71	6.32	2.26	5.95

Source: Authors' calculations from panel data.

Growth in contrast is highly unstable in individual countries. The bottom line is a high growth variation around a stable GDP per capita mean; the ratio of within-country SD to total SD of growth is 94 percent, although it is only 31 percent for GDP per capita.

Figure 2.5 shows the comparative kernel density plot of GDP per capita. There has been slow economic growth as evidenced by the slight movement toward the right of the GDP per capita of 2005 compared with that of 1975 (figure 2.5a). The kernel plot identifies persistence and stratification, formation of convergence clubs, and the polarization of the distribution over time into twin peaks (Quah 1993a, 1993b) of relatively rich and poor African countries.

The most significant shift toward polarization occurred between 1985 and 1995 (figure 2.5c), a period when many countries were devastated by conflicts. Between 1995 and 2005 (figure 2.5d), we observe a substantial slide to the right, meaning increasing income throughout Africa. The second peak virtually disappears when we remove Botswana, Cape Verde, Gabon, Mauritius, Namibia, the Seychelles, and South Africa from the data. For that reason, they could be considered regional champions.[5]

The comparative kernel density of GDP per capita growth is depicted in figure 2.6. It reveals that growth is becoming a more accurate predictor of economic performance and that growth is converging over time (see figure 2.6a). The SD dropped from 8.2 percent in 1976 to 3.6 percent in 2005. The decade 1976–85 marked the most significant change in growth distribution toward convergence (figure 2.6b). Since then, there has been an increasingly more acute peak around the mean (figures 2.6c and 2.6d).

To examine further how the income distribution evolved over time, figure 2.7 shows the CV of GDP per capita and the SD of growth.[6] From 1986 until 2002, the distribution of GDP per capita became increasingly

FIGURE 2.5

Density of GDP Per Capita across Countries, 1975–2005

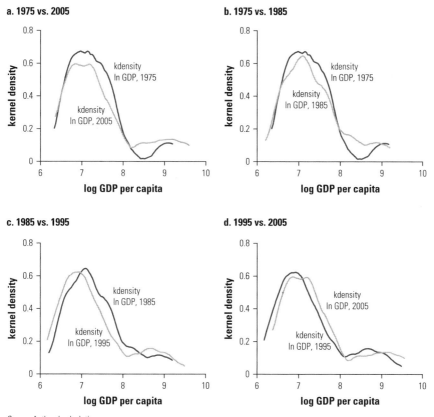

Source: Authors' calculations.

more dispersed, but, since then, there has been some convergence. The distribution of growth, however, shows a negative long-term trend toward convergence.

The reduction of growth dispersion did not lead to overall convergence of income, however. The opposite slopes of curves in figure 2.7 indicate that the poorest countries were growing less, allowing the richest countries to maintain or even increase the income gap. Accordingly, the ratio of income of the richest 10 percent of countries to the poorest 10 percent of countries was 10.5 in 1975, but it increased to 18.5 in 2005. In 1975–80, South Africa's GDP per capita was 17 times higher

FIGURE 2.6

Density of GDP Per Capita Growth across Countries, 1976–2005

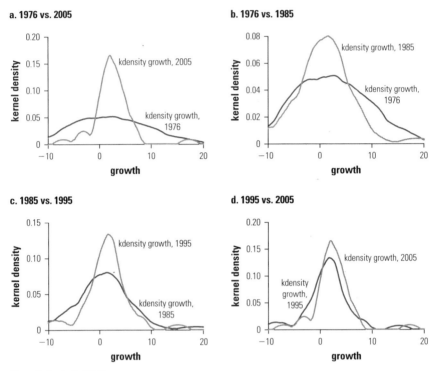

Source: Authors' calculations.

than that of Malawi. In 2000–05, the gap between the then-highest GDP per capita—the Seychelles—and Malawi had grown to 24 times. Africa is becoming an increasingly more unequal region in terms of its distribution of income among countries, despite the convergence of growth rates.[7]

Growth Persistence

Another important aspect of long-term growth is whether it is persistent. Figure 2.8 shows the regression of average GDP per capita growth as a function of growth in 1976. We ran the following cross-country model:

$$\Delta \overline{Y}_i = \alpha + \beta(\Delta Y_i^{76}) + \varepsilon \tag{2.1}$$

FIGURE 2.7

GDP Per Capita Coefficient of Variation and Growth Standard Deviation, 1975–2005

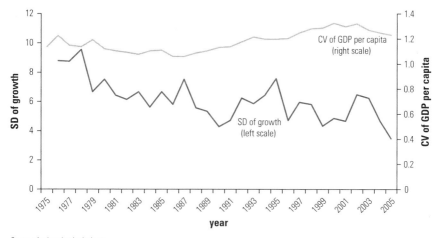

Source: Authors' calculations.

FIGURE 2.8

Average Growth as a Function of Initial Conditions

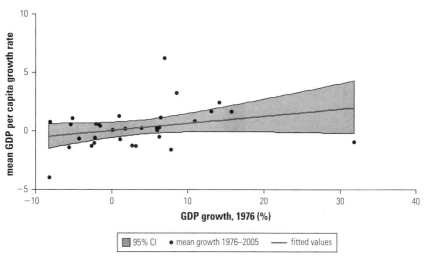

Source: Authors' calculations.

Note: CI = confidence interval.

where $\Delta \overline{Y}_i$ is the average growth of country i, and ΔY_i^{76} is the growth rate of country i in 1976, the first year in our series. The coefficient is positive and insignificant ($\beta = 0.061, t = 1.65$).[8] So, there is no evidence of growth persistence.

We stratified the data before and after 1990 to assess whether there is persistence during the period when many economies experienced growth accelerations. We ran the following models:

$$\Delta \overline{Y}_i^{76-90} = \alpha + \beta(\Delta Y_i^{76}) + \varepsilon \qquad (2.2)$$

$$\Delta \overline{Y}_i^{91-05} = \alpha + \beta(\Delta Y_i^{91}) + \varepsilon \qquad (2.3)$$

where $\Delta \overline{Y}_i^{76-90}$ is the average GDP per capita growth between 1976 and 1990, $\Delta \overline{Y}_i^{91-05}$ is the average GDP per capita growth between 1991 and 2005, and ΔY_i^{91} is the growth rate of country i in 1991.

The results are shown in figures 2.9a and 2.9b. Although the coefficient is statistically significant at the 7 percent level only in the first period ($\beta_{1976-90} = 0.110, t = 1.89$), it is significant in the second period ($\beta_{1991-05} = 0.218, t = 3.64$), thus suggesting that growth becomes somehow more

FIGURE 2.9

Average Growth as a Function of Initial Conditions, by Time Range

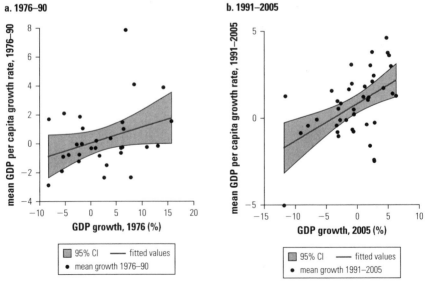

Source: Authors' calculations.

predictable from the 1990s on—a finding that is in line with the kernel density exercises. The weak persistence is thus a phenomenon of the 1970s and 1980s.

We also calculated the correlation coefficients of growth over time. Statistically significant (nonsignificant) coefficients suggest that country growth rates follow predictable (unpredictable) patterns. The results, presented in table 2.4, indicate that the large majority of coefficients is not statistically significant, including the vectors of 1991 and 2005. This suggests that growth is erratic, even when, on average, it shows some persistence, as seems to be the case in the second period under analysis. Also, it confirms the finding in table 2.3 that most growth variation comes from within individual countries rather than across countries, as suggested in the decomposition of SD in table 2.3.[9] Even though there is some persistence in more recent years, the results imply that past growth does not help predict future growth and that the growth process in Africa may be erratic.

GDP Per Capita Convergence

We examined further whether the income per capita of the poorest African countries tends to converge toward the regions' richest ones. For convergence to occur, poor countries have to grow faster (Barro 1991; Barro and Sala-i-Martin 1991). We ran the following unconditional regression:

$$\Delta \overline{Y}_i = \alpha + \beta Y_i^{75} + \varepsilon \tag{2.4}$$

where $\Delta \overline{Y}_i$ is the average growth rate of country i, and Y_i^{75} is the GDP per capita of country i in 1975.

The regression in figure 2.10 shows no support for the overall convergence hypothesis, which may result from the high income heterogeneity between African countries and from stratification of data in clubs, as suggested by figure 2.5. Although the estimated coefficient is negative as expected, it is not significant ($\beta = -0.122$, $t = -0.29$).[10] McCoskey (2002) examined whether there is income convergence in Africa using long panel data, and likewise found no evidence of convergence.

We also split the sample into before 1990 and after 1990 to assess convergence in the second period when growth accelerated. We ran the following models:

$$\Delta \overline{Y}_i^{76-90} = \alpha + \beta(Y_i^{75}) + \varepsilon \tag{2.5}$$

$$\Delta \overline{Y}_i^{91-05} = \alpha + \beta(Y_i^{75}) + \varepsilon \tag{2.6}$$

TABLE 2.4

Correlation Coefficients of GDP Per Capita Growth, 1976–2005

Year	1976	1977	1978	1979	1980	1981	1982	1983	1984	1985	1986	1987	1988	1989
1976	1.00													
1977	−0.19	1.00												
1978	−0.32	*0.44*	1.00											
1979	0.12	−0.01	0.27	1.00										
1980	−0.18	−0.10	−0.13	0.18	1.00									
1981	−0.07	−0.16	0.10	−0.07	0.10	1.00								
1982	−0.07	−0.11	0.15	0.16	0.13	*0.43*	1.00							
1983	0.20	−0.05	−0.08	−0.08	0.16	0.26	0.29	1.00						
1984	−0.08	0.00	0.17	−0.02	0.02	0.15	0.07	0.09	1.00					
1985	−0.14	0.18	0.34	−0.22	−0.16	−0.03	0.09	0.10	−0.07	1.00				
1986	−0.05	*0.36*	0.08	0.27	−0.01	−0.15	−0.19	−0.03	−0.18	−0.12	1.00			
1987	−0.30	0.28	0.31	0.12	0.15	0.02	0.10	0.01	−0.02	−0.05	*0.43*	1.00		
1988	0.34	0.02	−0.09	−0.15	0.09	−0.17	−0.03	0.22	0.04	*0.45*	−0.04	−0.01	1.00	
1989	0.43	0.05	0.05	0.14	−0.01	−0.23	−0.15	0.19	0.23	−0.07	0.22	0.33	*0.52*	1.00
1990	0.19	−0.09	0.08	*0.40*	0.18	−0.20	−0.06	−0.12	0.22	0.12	−0.07	0.20	*0.41*	*0.43*
1991	*0.44*	0.01	0.04	−0.13	0.02	0.10	0.14	0.22	−0.03	0.25	−0.12	0.08	*0.42*	*0.35*
1992	*0.43*	0.14	0.16	0.12	−0.09	−0.08	0.00	0.32	−0.02	0.19	0.09	0.13	0.36	0.41
1993	0.28	−0.12	0.12	0.46	−0.02	−0.08	−0.03	−0.19	−0.03	−0.24	0.12	0.17	−0.08	0.17
1994	−0.25	0.10	−0.06	−0.34	−0.09	−0.10	−0.04	−0.20	0.20	0.15	0.00	0.09	0.27	0.27
1995	0.33	0.01	0.11	0.19	0.08	−0.06	0.02	0.11	−0.11	−0.09	0.03	−0.23	−0.04	−0.08
1996	0.15	−0.14	0.30	0.15	0.04	0.13	0.04	−0.11	−0.01	−0.07	−0.13	0.04	0.06	0.13
1997	0.32	0.19	0.33	0.01	−0.12	−0.13	−0.10	0.00	0.16	0.29	0.06	−0.07	0.50	*0.42*
1998	0.10	0.28	−0.04	0.16	0.28	−0.28	0.05	0.26	−0.29	0.11	0.25	0.06	0.09	0.08
1999	−0.01	0.27	0.29	0.12	−0.26	−0.04	0.02	0.03	0.07	0.03	*0.49*	*0.35*	0.09	0.23
2000	0.20	0.00	0.20	0.32	0.03	0.11	0.33	0.13	*0.39*	−0.15	−0.02	0.27	0.09	*0.36*
2001	0.08	0.21	−0.06	0.00	−0.01	0.01	0.15	0.25	−0.07	−0.21	0.19	0.16	−0.04	0.13
2002	0.04	0.22	0.10	−0.06	0.27	0.12	0.19	0.11	0.05	−0.09	0.03	0.22	−0.16	−0.09
2003	−0.04	0.26	−0.12	−0.18	−0.04	−0.33	−0.02	0.38	−0.07	−0.01	0.08	0.10	0.19	0.05
2004	−0.07	0.17	−0.09	*−0.61*	−0.11	−0.10	0.14	*0.54*	0.08	*0.41*	−0.26	0.02	0.32	−0.03
2005	0.03	0.11	−0.10	0.00	0.15	−0.05	0.27	0.19	0.00	*−0.36*	0.07	0.22	0.02	0.04

Source: Authors' calculations.

Note: Coefficients in italic type are statistically significant at the 5 percent level. N = 44.

The estimated coefficients of both periods are not significant, thus suggesting no convergence at all.

Cross-Country Structure of GDP Per Capita

We now assess in more detail the structure of income per capita. A stable structure implies little income mobility, which, in turn, suggests that policies, external shocks, conflicts, and other factors may not substantially change the distribution of GDP per capita across countries in the long run.

1990	1991	1992	1993	1994	1995	1996	1997	1998	1999	2000	2001	2002	2003	2004	2005
1.00															
0.39	1.00														
0.09	0.30	1.00													
0.48	0.38	0.09	1.00												
0.10	0.03	−0.36	−0.25	1.00											
−0.07	0.14	0.44	0.17	−0.71	1.00										
0.28	0.31	0.13	0.37	−0.14	0.40	1.00									
0.15	0.21	0.57	0.00	0.10	0.29	0.25	1.00								
−0.13	0.06	0.10	0.03	0.02	−0.05	−0.40	0.04	1.00							
−0.01	0.07	0.47	0.26	0.06	0.14	0.08	0.50	−0.06	1.00						
0.32	0.25	0.40	0.46	−0.07	−0.02	0.08	0.21	−0.07	0.45	1.00					
−0.12	0.13	0.10	0.00	0.02	−0.20	−0.07	−0.31	0.22	−0.06	0.30	1.00				
−0.10	0.30	−0.13	−0.02	−0.16	0.04	0.09	−0.37	0.21	−0.38	0.05	0.54	1.00			
−0.15	0.04	0.18	−0.09	0.01	−0.05	−0.02	−0.13	0.09	0.13	0.24	0.49	0.21	1.00		
−0.24	0.20	0.22	−0.39	0.05	−0.01	−0.15	−0.06	0.12	−0.04	0.00	0.30	0.27	0.64	1.00	
−0.26	−0.05	0.22	0.01	−0.26	0.18	−0.05	−0.21	0.03	0.14	0.47	0.46	0.35	0.64	0.37	1.00

We ran the following regression:

$$\overline{Y}_i = \alpha + \beta Y_i^{75} + \varepsilon \tag{2.7}$$

where $\overline{Y}_i$ is the mean GDP per capita of country i, and Y_i^{75} is the GDP per capita of country i in 1975. The result described in figure 2.11 shows a line near 45 degrees ($\beta = 0.901$, $t = 7.41$) and suggests that, apart from a few cases, the average GDP per capita closely mirrors that of 1975, thus reflecting inertia, stratification, and the importance of initial conditions in economic output. Nevertheless, there are some outliers, such as Botswana and Namibia, whose average GDPs per capita are well above the 1975

FIGURE 2.10

Average Growth as a Function of Initial Conditions, 1975

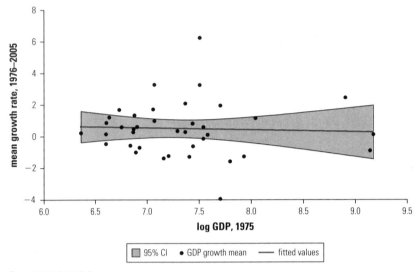

Source: Authors' calculations.

FIGURE 2.11

Mean GDP Per Capita, 1975–2005, as a Function of 1975 GDP Per Capita

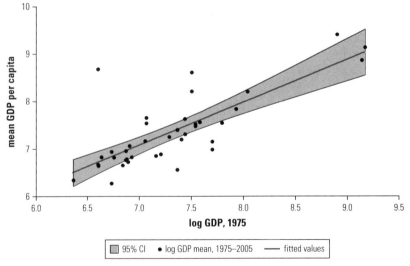

Source: Authors' calculations.

levels, and Eritrea and Mozambique, whose average GDPs per capita were well below those levels.[11]

We calculated the correlation coefficients of GDP per capita over time. Statistically significant coefficients suggest that the GDP per capita hardly changed and its structure remained relatively stable. Table 2.5 shows that most coefficients are large, thus supporting the evidence of inertia and stable structure.

To assess further the GDP per capita structure, we calculated the ratio of 43 countries' GDP per capita to that of South Africa, the largest African economy, for 1975 and 2005. Table 2.6 shows that 19 countries experienced a relative improvement in their GDP per capita of 2 percent or more in relation to South Africa; 13 experienced slight or no change at all; and 11 experienced steep deterioration. These figures suggest little income mobility among African countries. The modest changes observed in relation to South Africa may be surprising in view of the long period of stagnation it endured until the late 1990s. Notable exceptions are Botswana, Cape Verde, and Equatorial Guinea—all mineral exporters that strongly improved GDP per capita. It is interesting to note that resource-rich oil exporters do not always improve their relative positions (Angola, Chad, and Nigeria). This finding suggests that mineral resources may help but do not determine successful development stories.

The limited income mobility over time suggests that African countries experience similar economic cycles, despite conflicts and other factors observed on the continent that could have affected productivity and changed the positions in the GDP per capita ranking league table. This empirical evidence suggests contagion, interdependence, regional spillovers, and externalities among African countries.[12] Recorded and unrecorded trade, regional migration, remittances, and regional conflicts are among the potential channels through which countries affect others, eventually keeping productivity and GDP per capita relatively unchanged over time.

Checking for Common Country Features

The previous sections have identified some stylized facts about the long-term GDP per capita growth that cut across African countries. Despite sharing common attributes, however, African economies are quite diverse and their diversity is increasing. In this section, we examine if countries indeed follow common GDP per capita patterns and if there is a country typology based on economic outcomes.

TABLE 2.5

Correlation Coefficient of GDP Per Capita, 1975–2005

Year	1975	1976	1977	1978	1979	1980	1981	1982	1983	1984	1985	1986	1987	1988	1989
1975	1.00														
1976	0.99	1.00													
1977	1.00	1.00	1.00												
1978	0.97	0.96	0.98	1.00											
1979	0.96	0.95	0.97	1.00	1.00										
1980	0.97	0.95	0.97	1.00	1.00	1.00									
1981	0.98	0.96	0.98	0.99	0.99	1.00	1.00								
1982	0.97	0.95	0.97	0.99	0.99	1.00	1.00	1.00							
1983	0.97	0.96	0.97	0.99	0.99	0.99	1.00	1.00	1.00						
1984	0.97	0.95	0.97	0.99	0.98	0.99	0.99	1.00	1.00	1.00					
1985	0.94	0.93	0.94	0.98	0.98	0.98	0.98	0.98	0.99	0.99	1.00				
1986	0.93	0.92	0.94	0.97	0.98	0.98	0.98	0.98	0.98	0.99	1.00	1.00			
1987	0.89	0.87	0.90	0.95	0.96	0.97	0.95	0.96	0.96	0.97	0.99	0.99	1.00		
1988	0.88	0.87	0.89	0.94	0.95	0.96	0.95	0.95	0.96	0.96	0.99	0.99	1.00	1.00	
1989	0.87	0.86	0.88	0.94	0.95	0.95	0.94	0.94	0.95	0.96	0.98	0.99	1.00	1.00	1.00
1990	0.87	0.86	0.88	0.94	0.95	0.95	0.93	0.94	0.95	0.95	0.98	0.99	0.99	1.00	1.00
1991	0.86	0.86	0.88	0.94	0.95	0.95	0.93	0.94	0.94	0.95	0.98	0.98	0.99	0.99	1.00
1992	0.84	0.84	0.86	0.92	0.94	0.93	0.91	0.92	0.92	0.93	0.96	0.97	0.98	0.99	0.99
1993	0.83	0.83	0.85	0.92	0.94	0.93	0.90	0.91	0.92	0.93	0.96	0.96	0.98	0.98	0.99
1994	0.83	0.83	0.85	0.91	0.93	0.92	0.90	0.91	0.92	0.92	0.96	0.96	0.98	0.98	0.99
1995	0.84	0.85	0.86	0.92	0.94	0.93	0.91	0.92	0.93	0.94	0.96	0.97	0.98	0.98	0.99
1996	0.84	0.84	0.86	0.92	0.94	0.93	0.91	0.92	0.93	0.93	0.96	0.96	0.98	0.98	0.99
1997	0.82	0.82	0.84	0.91	0.93	0.92	0.89	0.90	0.91	0.92	0.95	0.95	0.97	0.97	0.98
1998	0.80	0.81	0.82	0.90	0.92	0.91	0.88	0.89	0.90	0.90	0.94	0.94	0.96	0.97	0.98
1999	0.78	0.78	0.80	0.88	0.91	0.90	0.86	0.88	0.88	0.89	0.93	0.94	0.96	0.96	0.97
2000	0.76	0.77	0.79	0.87	0.90	0.88	0.85	0.86	0.87	0.88	0.92	0.93	0.95	0.96	0.97
2001	0.77	0.78	0.80	0.88	0.90	0.89	0.86	0.87	0.88	0.89	0.93	0.93	0.95	0.96	0.97
2002	0.75	0.76	0.78	0.86	0.88	0.87	0.84	0.85	0.87	0.88	0.92	0.92	0.95	0.96	0.97
2003	0.77	0.77	0.80	0.87	0.89	0.89	0.86	0.87	0.88	0.89	0.93	0.93	0.96	0.96	0.97
2004	0.77	0.78	0.80	0.87	0.89	0.89	0.86	0.87	0.89	0.90	0.93	0.94	0.96	0.97	0.97
2005	0.77	0.77	0.79	0.86	0.88	0.88	0.86	0.87	0.89	0.90	0.93	0.93	0.96	0.97	0.97

Source: Authors' calculations.

Note: All coefficients are statistically significant at the 5 percent level. N = 44.

Country Groups

We split the time-series into two subperiods, 1975–90 and 1991–2005. Such periods are long enough to allow for the data to capture macroeconomic cycles and to get rid of short-run noises. For each year, we calculated the median of sub-Saharan Africa's GDP per capita, which served as a benchmark, and then checked for every year if each country's GDP per capita is above or below the benchmark. A country whose GDP per capita remained above the median for most years of 1975–90 was assigned category "A,"

1990	1991	1992	1993	1994	1995	1996	1997	1998	1999	2000	2001	2002	2003	2004	2005
1.00															
1.00	1.00														
1.00	1.00	1.00													
0.99	1.00	1.00	1.00												
0.99	1.00	1.00	1.00	1.00											
0.99	1.00	1.00	1.00	1.00	1.00										
0.99	1.00	1.00	1.00	1.00	1.00	1.00									
0.99	0.99	1.00	1.00	1.00	1.00	1.00	1.00								
0.98	0.99	0.99	1.00	0.99	1.00	1.00	1.00	1.00							
0.98	0.98	0.99	0.99	0.99	0.99	0.99	1.00	1.00	1.00						
0.97	0.98	0.99	0.99	0.99	0.99	0.99	0.99	1.00	1.00	1.00					
0.98	0.98	0.99	0.99	0.99	0.99	0.99	1.00	1.00	1.00	1.00	1.00				
0.97	0.98	0.98	0.98	0.99	0.99	0.99	0.99	0.99	1.00	1.00	1.00	1.00			
0.98	0.98	0.98	0.98	0.99	0.99	0.99	0.99	0.99	0.99	0.99	1.00	1.00	1.00		
0.98	0.98	0.98	0.98	0.99	0.98	0.99	0.99	0.98	0.99	0.99	0.99	0.99	1.00	1.00	
0.97	0.97	0.97	0.97	0.98	0.98	0.98	0.98	0.97	0.98	0.98	0.98	0.99	0.99	1.00	1.00

meaning that its GDP per capita was generally "above" Africa's benchmark. A country whose GDP per capita remained below the median for most years was assigned category "B," meaning "below" Africa's benchmark.[13] The same exercise is applied for the second period, 1991–2005. It is also possible that a country switches categories, and we account for that by having four possible combinations.[14] In short, the combinations are

- **AA**—Countries whose GDP per capita is above Africa's median GDP per capita for most years of the first and second periods

TABLE 2.6
GDP Per Capita Disparities
Ratio of GDP per capita, by country, in relation to South Africa

Country	1975 or earliest year	2005 or most recent year	Country	1975 or earliest year	2005 or most recent year
Angola	0.19	0.21	Lesotho	0.12	0.30
Benin	0.09	0.10	Madagascar	0.13	0.08
Botswana	0.19	1.12	Malawi	0.06	0.06
Burkina Faso	0.08	0.11	Mali	0.08	0.09
Burundi	0.08	0.06	Mauritania	0.20	0.20
Cameroon	0.18	0.21	Mauritius	0.40	1.14
Cape Verde	0.23	0.52	Mozambique	0.07	0.11
Central African Republic	0.17	0.11	Namibia	0.65	0.68
Chad	0.10	0.13	Niger	0.10	0.07
Comoros	0.19	0.18	Nigeria	0.10	0.10
Congo, Dem. Rep. of	0.23	0.06	Rwanda	0.09	0.11
Congo, Rep. of	0.10	0.11	Senegal	0.15	0.16
Côte d'Ivoire	0.25	0.15	Seychelles	0.76	1.45
Equatorial Guinea	0.13	0.73	Sierra Leone	0.10	0.07
Eritrea	0.09	0.10	Sudan	0.12	0.19
Ethiopia	0.09	0.09	Swaziland	0.32	0.43
Gabon	0.97	0.63	Tanzania	0.05	0.07
Gambia, The	0.16	0.17	Togo	0.18	0.14
Ghana	0.20	0.22	Uganda	0.08	0.13
Guinea	0.19	0.21	Zambia	0.14	0.09
Guinea-Bissau	0.11	0.07	Zimbabwe	0.29	0.18
Kenya	0.10	0.11			

Source: Authors' calculations.

- **BB**—Countries whose GDP per capita is below Africa's median GDP per capita for most years of the first and second periods

- **BA**—Countries whose GDP per capita switches from below to above Africa's median GDP per capita from the first to the second period

- **AB**—Countries whose GDP per capita switches from above to below Africa's median GDP per capita from the first to the second period.

The results of this exercise are presented in table 2.7. AA countries have a substantially larger average GDP per capita, $3,424, which is about four times higher than that of BB countries; and AAs have higher mean growth, 1.05 percent, than do BBs, 0.37 percent. *T*-statistics do not reject the hypothesis of equality of growth means of AA and BB, but they do reject

TABLE 2.7
Country Groups' Basic Statistics

Country group	Countries	Countries (n)	Average GDP per capita (US$)			Average growth (%)			SD of growth 1976–2005	CV of growth 1976–2005	Share of Africa's GDP (%)		Share of Africa's population (%)	
			1975	2005	1975–2005	1976–90	1991–2005	1976–2005	1976–2005	1976–2005	1975–80	2000–05	1975	2005
AA	Angola, Botswana, Cameroon, Cape Verde, Comoros, Côte d'Ivoire, Gabon, The Gambia, Ghana, Guinea, Lesotho, Mauritania, Mauritius, Namibia, Senegal, Seychelles, South Africa, Swaziland, Togo, and Zimbabwe	20	3,424	4,241	3,648	1.07	1.02	1.05	1.44	1.37	64.3	62.6	31.7	31.1
BB	Benin, Burkina Faso, Burundi, Chad, Rep. of Congo, Eritrea, Ethiopia, Guinea-Bissau, Kenya, Madagascar, Malawi, Mali, Mozambique, Niger, Nigeria, Rwanda, Sierra Leone, Tanzania, Uganda, and Zambia	20	931	933	880	−0.07	0.81	0.37	1.73	4.67	28.3	32.1	56.2	56.7
BA	Equatorial Guinea and Sudan	2	1,161	1,853	1,787	−0.71	8.84	4.06	9.16	2.25	3.1	4.0	4.8	4.5
AB	Central African Republic and Dem. Rep. of Congo	2	1,930	862	1,301	−2.18	−3.04	−2.61	3.46	−1.32	4.3	1.4	7.3	7.6

Source: Authors' calculations.

Note: T-test does not reject the hypothesis of equality of means of growth rates (1976–2005) between AA and BB, but does reject the equality of means of GDP per capita.

the equality of means of GDP per capita. When we split the series by period, we observe that AA countries grew substantially more than BBs in the first period, but BB countries undertook an impressive growth acceleration in the second period (from −0.07 percent to 0.81 percent), closing the gap with AAs. Table 2.7 also shows that countries at different levels of income experience high growth volatility, which confirms that volatility is a distinctive phenomenon of African economies.

In the first period, AA countries had a 64 percent share of regional GDP. That share fell slightly to 63 percent in the second period. BBs increased from 28 percent to 32 percent. This relative stability may be surprising in view of the economic and political ups and downs experienced by these countries over time. The AAs' share of the African continent's population was only about 31 percent, whereas BB countries hosted about 56 percent of the population.

BA countries comprise Equatorial Guinea and Sudan, both oil exporters. These economies grew by 4 percent a year, but the expansion was confined to the second period when the annual growth was 9 percent (from −0.7 percent in the first period). That enabled their GDP per capita to increase by 60 percent between 1975 and 2005.

The AB economies collapsed mainly as a result of conflicts, but the economic disintegration intensified in the second period when the annual growth rate was −3 percent. That disintegration led the average GDP per capita to shrink from $1,930 in 1975 to only $862 in 2005. It is more striking that in 1975 these economies were responsible for 4.3 percent of the region's GDP, but in 2005 their share had fallen to a mere 1.4 percent. The BAs' income rise, along with the plunge of the ABs', helps explain the increasing dispersion of income per capita as identified in figure 2.5.

Figure 2.12 shows the GDP per capita by country group over time. AA countries have the highest GDP per capita, as expected, and the gap separating them from other countries has increased more recently. BAs' GDP per capita increased in the second period; the ABs' collapsed; and the BBs' remained flat all the way, only showing some modest improvement in the more recent past. Because AB and BA groups accounted for less than 6 percent of the region's GDP in the 2000s, and for about 12 percent of the population, it is reasonable to think that AA and BB countries alone guide the regional economy.

The CV of GDP per capita of AA countries increased from 0.027 in 1975–90 to 0.073 in 1991–2005; the BBs remained almost unchanged,

FIGURE 2.12
GDP Per Capita, by Country Group, 1975–2005

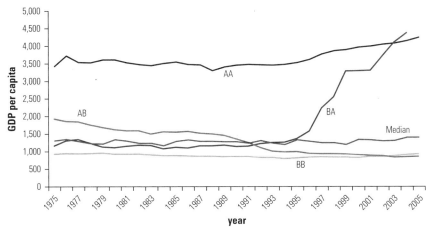

Source: Authors' calculations.

Note: See table 2.7 for a list of countries in groups AA, AB, BA, and BB.

increasing only from 0.038 to 0.041. Thus, the increasing income inequality identified in figure 2.7 is mainly driven by the large and rising income dispersion among AA countries.

We examined whether there is income convergence within country groups. For each group we ran unconditional growth regressions against GDP per capita in 1975. The results showed no convergence between AA countries or between the more homogeneous BB countries.

Figure 2.13 shows a more detailed examination of the share of country groups in the regional GDP. Apart from some swap in ranking between AB and BA groups, there is no significant change over time. This accords with the previous finding that initial conditions matter.

Table 2.8 sorts countries by country groups, long-term growth performance, mineral resources, and geography—the last two variables increasingly being identified in the literature as predictors of economic performance in Africa (Collier and O'Connell 2004). No pattern emerges, however. Within AA and BB country groups, there are oil-rich and non-mineral-intensive countries, landlocked and coastal countries, and both growing and shrinking economies. Table 2.8 also shows landlocked, non-resource-intensive countries growing at high rates (such as Burkina Faso, Rwanda, and Uganda) and shrinking oil exporters (such as Côte d'Ivoire

FIGURE 2.13

Share of Country Groups in Total GDP, 1975–2005

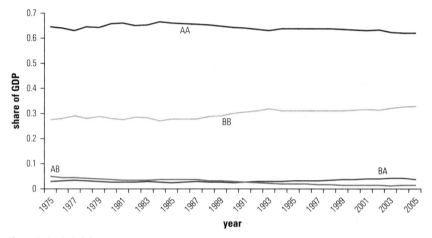

Source: Authors' calculations.

Note: See table 2.7 for a list of countries in groups AA, AB, BA, and BB.

and Gabon). These highly diverse experiences suggest that initial conditions and institutions may be more important than geographic attributes in explaining Africa's long-term GDP per capita.[15]

The feature that most distinguishes AA from BB countries is certainly not growth rates; rather, it is the AAs' much larger capability to create income and wealth. Shrinking AA economies, such as Côte d'Ivoire, Gabon, and Zimbabwe, have GDP per capita far above such BB growers as Mozambique, Tanzania, and Uganda (the GDPs per capita of the first three countries are $1,811, $7,041, and $2,526, respectively; those of the latter three countries are $704, $529, and $976, respectively). As a consequence, the AAs have more means to fight poverty and foster development if the right policies are in place. One cannot sort countries into a distinct pattern of winners and losers, however, based only on country groups. Actually, growing countries, whatever their groups, are those that are more likely to reshape the continent's economy in the long run.

The Role of Initial Conditions at the Country-Group Level

To assess whether initial conditions play a role at the country-group level as well, we ran regressions of average GDP per capita on initial conditions

TABLE 2.8
Countries Sorted by Group and Classified by Growth and Other Characteristics

Country group	Shrinking economies (average growth below 0)	Stagnant economies (average growth between 0 and 0.71%)	Growers (average growth above 0.71%)
AA	Comoros (−0.14)[a] Côte d'Ivoire (−1.57)[c] Gabon (−0.91)[c] Togo (−0.60)[a] Zimbabwe (−1.26)[d]	Angola (0.70)[c] Gambia, The (0.29)[a] Ghana (0.60)[a] Guinea (0.62)[b] Mauritania (0.10)[a] Senegal (0.36)[a] South Africa (0.12)[a]	Botswana (6.24)[b] Cape Verde (3.26)[a] Cameroon (0.81)[c] Lesotho (3.27)[d] Mauritius (4.22)[a] Namibia (1.15)[b] Seychelles (2.47)[a] Swaziland (1.15)[d]
BB	Burundi (−0.46)[d] Guinea-Bissau (−0.70)[a] Madagascar (−1.38)[a] Niger (−1.00)[d] Sierra Leone (−0.57)[b] Zambia (−1.16)[b]	Benin (0.60)[a] Congo, Rep. of (0.61)[c] Ethiopia (0.42)[d] Kenya (0.48)[a] Malawi (0.22)[d] Nigeria (0.28)[c]	Burkina Faso (1.21)[d] Chad (1.34)[c] Eritrea (1.96)[a] Mali (0.86)[d] Mozambique (2.07)[a] Rwanda (1.68)[d] Tanzania (1.69)[a] Uganda (1.92)[d]
BA	n.a.	n.a.	Equatorial Guinea (10.55)[c] Sudan (1.72)[c]
AB	Central African Republic (−1.27)[d] Congo, Dem. Rep. of (−3.95)[d]	n.a.	n.a.

Source: Authors' calculations.

Note: n.a. = not applicable. The average growth rate for the period 1976–2005 was 0.71 percent. The average growth rates for individual countries appear in parentheses.

a. Oil exporter.

b. Non-oil-resource-intensive country.

c. Non-resource-intensive, coastal country.

d. Non-resource-intensive, landlocked country.

and SD of growth, and the same model with average growth as the dependent variable. We estimated coefficients for AA and BB countries separately. The models are the following:

$$\overline{Y}_i = \alpha + \beta Y_i^{75} + \lambda SD(\Delta Y_i) + \varepsilon \tag{2.8}$$

$$\Delta \overline{Y}_i = \alpha + \beta Y_i^{75} + \lambda SD(\Delta Y_i) + \varepsilon \tag{2.9}$$

The results for GDP per capita suggest an almost perfect inertia for AA countries, as the estimated and statistically significant coefficient is 0.93. A hypothetical increase of $1 in the 1975 GDP per capita therefore would

TABLE 2.9

Impact of Initial Conditions on GDP Per Capita

Data	GDP per capita in 1975	SD of growth	R^2	N
Dependent variable: GDP per capita				
AA and BB countries	1.00 (9.24)	−144.8 (−1.52)	0.70	39
AA countries	.923 (4.83)	−181.7 (−0.69)	0.63	18
BB countries	0.147 (1.35)	9.32 (0.61)	0.16	18
Dependent variable: growth				
AA and BB countries	−0.000 (−0.27)	−0.012 (−0.10)	0.00	39
AA countries	−0.000 (−0.28)	−0.165 (−0.63)	0.04	18
BB countries	0.000 (0.47)	0.100 (0.96)	0.09	18

Source: Authors' calculations.

Note: See table 2.7 for a list of countries in groups AA, AB, BA, and BB. *T*-statistics appear in parentheses.

be almost entirely transmitted to the mean GDP per capita (see table 2.9). The estimated coefficient for BB economies is 0.15, but it is not statistically significant. These results suggest that initial conditions seem to play a larger role in explaining the economic performance of the better-off countries.

In the growth models, initial conditions are not statistically significant for both groups. This finding suggests no income convergence within and between groups, as already pointed out.

Robustness of Country Groups

This section examines the robustness of country groups by testing their statistical significance. We estimated coefficients of country groups in GDP per capita pooled and fixed-effect regression models, as follows:

$$Y_{it} = \alpha_i + \beta G_g + \phi C_{it} + \lambda t_t + \eta t_t^2 + \varepsilon_{it} \qquad (2.10)$$

$$\Delta Y_{it} = \alpha_i + \beta G_g + \phi C_{it} + \lambda t_t + \eta t_t^2 + \varepsilon_{it} \qquad (2.11)$$

where Y_{it} is the GDP per capita of country i in year t, α_i is the country fixed-effect, ΔY_{it} is the growth rate of country i in year t, G_g is the dummy of country-group g, C_i is the dummy of country i, t_t is time, t_t^2 is time squared, and ε is the error term.

Table 2.10 shows the results. Country groups' coefficients are statistically significant at the 5 percent level; they are sizable and have the expected signs. After controlling for country fixed-effects, country groups, and time and its quadratic term, model 2 of table 2.10 explains 94 percent

TABLE 2.10

Impact of Country Groups on GDP Per Capita Level and Growth, Pooled OLS Regressions

Explanatory variables	Dependent variable: GDP per capita		Dependent variable: GDP per capita growth	
	Model 1	Model 2	Model 3	Model 4
AA	1.237 (41.1)	1.929 (31.12)	0.603 (1.63)	−0.612 (−0.30)
BA	0.619 (8.29)	0.879 (14.76)	4.761 (5.17)	9.107 (4.53)
AB	0.362 (5.31)	0.914 (15.35)	−2.979 (−3.55)	−5.49 (−2.98)
R^2	0.57	0.94	0.05	0.13
F-test	342 (0.00)	402 (0.00)	13.09 (0.00)	3.81 (0.00)
N	1,268	1,268	1,224	1,224
Country dummies included	No	Yes	No	Yes
Wald test that groups' coefficients are equal	108.01 [0.00]	253.9 [0.00]	21.21 [0.00]	34.06 [0.00]
Wald test that groups' coefficients are zero	569.7 [0.00]	333.8 [0.00]	15.05 [0.00]	22.71 [0.00]

Source: Authors' calculations.

Note: OLS = ordinary least squares. See table 2.7 for a list of countries in groups AA, AB, BA, and BB. *T*-statistics appear in parentheses; *p*-values appear in brackets. Time and time squared are included in all models.

of the GDP per capita dispersion. If one moves residence from a BB country, the base group, to an AA country, she or he would enjoy a 193 percent income rise, on average. A person moving to a BA country could expect income improvement of 88 percent, and someone moving to an AB economy could expect 91 percent improvement. Wald tests strongly reject the notion that country groups' coefficients are zero or equal.

Model 4 in the table presents the impacts of country groups on growth, after controlling for country fixed-effects. Only the coefficient of AAs is not significant, suggesting that they tend to grow at the same pace as BBs. As expected, BAs' coefficient is high, whereas ABs' coefficient is very low. Wald test rejects the hypothesis that groups' coefficients are all zero or equal. These results suggest that country groups are relevant in predicting income and growth.

If country groups indeed capture common country features, they need to fit not only income and growth data, but also other relevant economic and social variables. To assess this hypothesis, we ran models similar to the ones above, but with other dependent variables. Table 2.11 shows that most country-group dummy coefficients are statistically significant at the 5 percent level and have the expected signs. Model 1 in table 2.11, for

TABLE 2.11
Selected Economic and Human Development Variables as a Function of Country Group, Pooled OLS Regression

Variable	Agriculture value added Model 1	Industry value added Model 2	Service value added Model 3	Trade Model 4	Fixed capital formation Model 5	Savings Model 6	Current account Model 7	Debt Model 8	Dependency ratio Model 9	Life expectancy Model 10	Aid per capita ($) Model 11
AA	−16.80	8.17	8.60	39.73	4.94	6.17	2.71	−27.36	−.07	7.92	34.88
BA	2.06	6.17	−8.23	18.50	9.15	3.28	−4.28	22.47	−.10	2.58	11.53
AB	5.11	.94	−6.05	−6.63	−7.06	−.45	3.30	−3.45	−.03	−1.29	−7.63
R^2	.33	.09	.18	.26	.11	.03	.03	.20	.19	.26	.14
F-test	122.06	27.3	56.16	89.66	30.86	8.70	7.51	60.80	64.97	40.51	42.54
N	1,252	1,252	1,252	1,239	1,227	1,227	1,025	1,167	1,328	567	1,270
Wald test that groups' coefficients are equal	116.4	9.10	89.57	54.90	46.04	4.37	8.52	15.16	9.61	26.18	22.21
Wald test that groups' coefficients are zero	195.8	40.48	93.24	142.60	48.86	13.33	9.87	19.80	79.80	61.72	48.25

Source: Authors' calculations.

Note: See table 2.7 for a list of countries in groups AA, AB, BA, and BB. BB is the base country group. The dependent variable is presented above each model number. Dependent variables of models 1 through 8 are measured as percentage of GDP. Time and time squared are included in all models. Coefficients in italics are significant at the 5 percent level.

example, shows that agriculture value added as a share of GDP in AA countries is, on average, about 17 percent below that of BB countries, the base group, and that in AB countries, it is 5 percent higher. Accordingly, BB countries are more heavily dependent on agriculture. Country groups plus time and time squared can explain about 33 percent of the variance of agriculture value added.

Model 2 shows that AA and BA countries have a greater share of industry in GDP than do BB countries. Model 3 shows that AA countries have a larger service sector. Model 4 shows that AA and BA economies are substantially more open than are BB economies. Considering the dynamic and static benefits of openness to growth, as suggested by the new growth literature (Grossman and Helpman 1991a, 1991b), it may help explain the poorer economic performance of BB economies.

Models 5 and 6 indicate that AA countries invest and save more than BBs do. Although the AAs' coefficient of fixed capital is perhaps modest, the productivity of investment, as suggested by Devarajan, Easterly, and Pack (2003), also may be important to explain the better economic outcomes of these countries. Models (7) to (10) show that AA countries have a better external balance, lower debt ratios, lower dependency ratio, and a significantly longer life expectancy. Perhaps it is surprising that model (11) shows that AA countries enjoy more aid per capita than do BBs.

These results are in harmony with the better economic and human development indicators of AA countries, as compared with BBs. They also suggest that there seem to be "two Africas," roughly represented by AA and BB country groups.

Figure 2.14 illustrates the previous econometric results. Dependency ratios of AA and BB countries were somewhat comparable until the early 1980s, but then the ratio started to fall sharply in AA countries and continued to climb in BB countries, thus enlarging the gap between the two groups. The gaps are also big for life expectancy and under-5 mortality. In the 1960s, aid per capita was comparable for various groups, but the gap started to widen toward the end of the decade. In 1990, AA countries received, on average, almost three times more aid than did BB countries ($112 and $41, respectively). The gap has since narrowed, mainly as a result of a reduction in the aid received by AA countries.

Finally, we estimated multinomial logit regressions of country clubs against each of these variables at a time: GDP per capita, growth, savings,

FIGURE 2.14
Selected Variables, by Country Group, 1960–2005

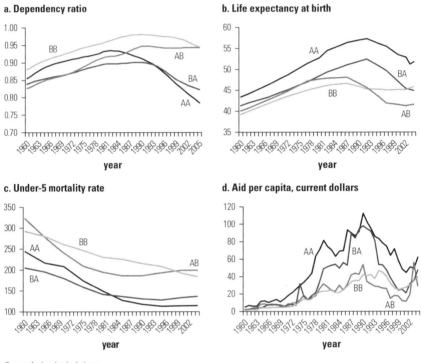

a. Dependency ratio

b. Life expectancy at birth

c. Under-5 mortality rate

d. Aid per capita, current dollars

Source: Authors' calculations.

Note: See table 2.7 for a list of countries in groups AA, AB, BA, and BB.

capital, trade, agriculture value added, life expectancy, and other independent variables. The estimated model is as follows:

$$\text{Prob}(G_i = j|X) = \alpha + \beta X_i^t + \varepsilon \tag{2.12}$$

where $\text{Prob}(G_i = j|X)$ is the probability of country-group dummy G_i taking value j given X_i^t; the independent variables for country-group i and time tj are country-groups AA, BB, BA, and AB.[16]

The model with GDP per capita as an independent variable returns the following coefficients: AA = 13.67 (z = 15.78), BA = 10.89 (z = 11.95), and AB = 6.81 (z = 9.20). The model for growth as an explanatory variable provides these coefficients: AA = 0.02 (z = 1.69), BA = 0.09 (z = 4.48), and AB = −0.07 (z = −3.58). In regard to life expectancy, for example, the coefficients are AA = 7.99 (z = 9.99), BA = 3.14 (z = 2.06), and

AB = -1.34 ($z = -0.88$). These and the nonreported results have the expected signs and hierarchy, and they confirm the robustness of country groups to predict income and human development outcomes.

Growth Volatility

High growth volatility is one of the most distinctive features of African economies. In this section, we examine its relationship to economic performance and a number of factors that are correlated with it.

Growth Volatility and Economic Performance

The defining characteristics of the long-run pattern of growth described above are low output growth and high volatility. The literature long has attempted to explain the poor economic performance in Africa in the postwar period. Barro (1991), Levine and Renelt (1992), and Sala-i-Martin, Doppelhofer, and Miller (2004), among others, found a structural low-growth effect in Africa that remained even after controlling for investment, fertility, education, macroeconomic policies, and other conventional variables. Growth accounting exercises show that growth in physical capital per worker in Africa has been less than 0.5 percent a year since 1960, far slower than the world average of 1 percent. Capital deepening was negative between 1990 and 2003, suggesting low capital investment in the region (Bosworth and Collins 2003). The contribution of human capital to growth kept pace with the rest of the world and has increased lately, mainly as a result of rising average years of schooling. But the main contributor to Africa's disappointing growth is total factor productivity change, negative since the 1960s and -0.4 percent between 1990 and 2003.

History and initial conditions are also found to play an important role in Africa's fate. According to Acemoglu, Johnson, and Robinson (2003), for example, countries that inherited institutions that supported rent-extracting activities from their colonial past were most likely to experience high volatility and economic crisis. Once they control for these institutions, the "Africa-dummy" tends to lose significance in cross-country growth models. Those authors concluded that poor economic policies are a result—not the cause—of poor economic outcomes. O'Connell (2004) suggested that political polarization at the time of independence is strongly associated with conflicts.

The literature on economic volatility in developing countries is large and focuses mainly on macroeconomic and financial sector issues. The standard macroeconomic view links volatility to bad macroeconomic policies. Accordingly, high inflation, misaligned exchange rates, large government sectors, and budget deficits will result in economic crisis. More recently, there has been increased focus on institutions (Acemoglu, Johnson, and Robinson 2003).

Given the magnitude of growth volatility in Africa, we examined whether it is associated with poor economic performance. Theoretically, this relationship can be positive or negative, depending on the mechanisms driving the relationship (Imbs 2002). But Ramey and Ramey (1995) and Hnatkovska and Loayza (2004) found empirical evidence of a negative relationship between the SD of growth and macroeconomic volatility for large cross-country data sets. Hnatkovska and Loayza also showed that this effect is particularly evident for institutionally underdeveloped countries undergoing intermediate stages of financial development or unable to conduct countercyclical fiscal policies. Thus, we also expected to find a negative and statistically significant relationship.

We estimated the following bivariate, unconditional regressions:

$$\Delta \overline{Y}_i = \alpha + \beta SD(\Delta Y_i) + \varepsilon \tag{2.13}$$

$$\overline{Y}_i = \alpha + \beta SD(\Delta Y_i) + \varepsilon \tag{2.14}$$

where $\Delta \overline{Y}_i$ is the average growth rate of country i, $\overline{Y}_i$ is the average GDP per capita of country i, $SD(\Delta Y_i)$ is the SD of growth of country i, and ε is the error term.

The results in figure 2.15 suggest a negative but statistically insignificant association between volatility and growth ($\beta = -0.075$, $t = -0.68$, figure 2.15a) and between volatility and GDP per capita ($\beta = -0.023$, $t = -0.61$, figure 2.15b).[17]

One explanation for the lack of relationship is that it may require a conditional model using policy and structural country characteristics as controls. An alternative explanation for the lack of a direct, long-run relationship is that African economies are already in their steady-state equilibrium pattern and short-term volatility is not able to divert them significantly from their long-term track. This hypothesis is consistent with the poverty trap argument. Another potential explanation is the inherent endogeneity of these variables (Easterly and Levine 2003;

FIGURE 2.15

GDP Per Capita Growth and Level as a Function of Growth Volatility, 1975–2005

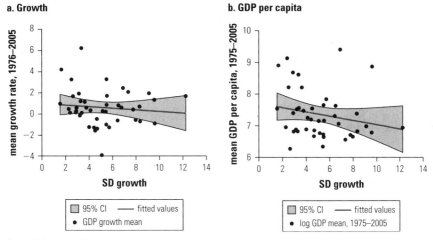

a. Growth

b. GDP per capita

Source: Authors' calculations.

Rodrik, Subramanian, and Trebbi 2004; and others). Acemoglu, Johnson, and Robinson (2003), for example, argued that high growth volatility and poor macroeconomic performance are both symptoms—and therefore not independent—of institutionally weak societies, in which distortionary macroeconomic policies are tools that groups in power deploy to reap rents and remain in power. This, in turn, leads the economies to further difficulties in dealing with political and economic shocks (Acemoglu and Robinson 2001) and makes economic adjustments in face of external shocks more difficult (Rodrik 1999), all leading to more political and economic instability.

Growth Volatility and Its Correlates

Although it does not seem to affect long-term economic performance significantly, volatility certainly must have short-term welfare effects via uncertainty, risks, and other channels on investments, savings, and credit, for example. In this section, we are interested in identifying variables other than institutions most likely to be associated with long-term growth variance in Africa.[18] We ran cross-country bivariate and multivariate models of the SD of GDP per capita growth as a function of selected economic variables as follows:

$$SD(\Delta \overline{Y}_i) = \alpha + \beta \overline{X}_i + \varepsilon \qquad (2.15)$$

where $SD(\Delta \overline{Y}_i)$ is the average SD of growth of country i, and $\overline{X}_i$ is a vector of variables of country i. For brevity, only statistically significant variables at 5 percent and 10 percent are reported and discussed here. The results are presented in table 2.12.[19]

Models 1 and 2 of table 2.12 show that a 1 percent change in the SD of savings and capital formation is associated with a 0.4 percent change in growth volatility. These results are expected for poor countries where investments are highly volatile because they rely on residents and nonresidents who usually bring in capital during an export bonanza but pull out as soon as crises appear or terms of trade change. Public investments are usually sensitive to foreign aid flow and political cycles, which are volatile variables, too.

Model 3 shows that the rise of one point in the diversification of exports index is associated with a reduction of 0.3 percent in growth volatility. This result is in line with the stylized fact that less-diversified economies are poorly protected from fluctuations in market conditions. Economies highly dependent on few products or a single product are vulnerable to external shocks and may suffer from the Dutch disease, which discourages domestic industry via an overvalued exchange rate. Table 2A.2 in the annex shows that export diversification in Africa is generally low, especially in oil-rich countries such as Angola, the Democratic Republic of Congo, Equatorial Guinea, Gabon, Nigeria, and Sudan. The average diversification index in the region is 4.8 (the index goes from 0 to 100), which suggests that export revenues strongly rely on few tradable items.

Model 4 shows that a 1 percent change in the SD of openness is associated with a 0.2 percent change in growth volatility. Where foreign trade exerts an important influence in aggregate demand, volatility of openness may play a role in growth volatility. Because export revenues in poor countries usually are crucial to pay for imports of capital goods and raw material, to service foreign debt, and to use as collateral in foreign financial markets, adverse changes in trade may have significant implications for growth. Volatility of openness may result from internal factors, such as regulatory and trade policies; from external factors that also affect the exchange rate, terms of trade, and foreign demand; and from conflicts and natural disasters, like draughts and insect attacks in agriculture-intensive countries.

TABLE 2.12

Variables Associated with GDP Per Capita Growth Volatility, Cross-Country OLS Regression

Variable	Model 1	Model 2	Model 3	Model 4	Model 5	Model 6	Model 7
SD of savings	0.418 (4.53)						0.371 (2.91)
SD of capital formation		0.405 (6.00)					0.162 (1.42)
Diversification of exports index			−0.300 (−2.76)				−0.074 (−.99)
SD of openness				0.210 (5.40)			0.030 (.53)
SD of aid per capita					0.262 (3.17)		0.020 (.31)
Life expectancy at birth						−0.170 (−2.81)	−0.099 (−2.91)
R^2	0.33	0.46	0.17	0.41	0.20	0.16	0.72
F-test	20.55	36.06	7.63	29.13	10.06	7.91	13.66
N	44	44	38	44	43	44	38

Source: Authors' calculations.

Note: T-statistics appear in parentheses. Savings and capital formation refer to percentage of GDP. Diversification index refers to mean of diversification of exports (the higher, the better). Openness refers to exports + imports divided by GDP. The dependent variable is the SD of GDP per capita growth.

The weighted average openness ratio in Africa is 46 percent, whereas it is 37 percent and 35 percent, respectively, in low- and middle-income countries and in the world. (Table 2A.3 in the annex shows a proxy of openness—the merchandise trade as a share of GDP and its SD). Africa is more open but also more exposed to adverse trade shocks via a high SD of openness and low diversification of exports. In Ghana, for example, the SD of openness is 17 percent. Given that the average openness is 55 percent, it has varied in the range of 38 percent to 72 percent of GDP over time, which should have non-negligible effects on the Ghanaian growth volatility.[20]

Model 5 suggests that a 1 percent rise in volatility of aid per capita is associated with an increase of 0.2 percent in growth volatility. This result stresses the importance and impact that aid has on the economy. Among the main channels through which aid has such an effect are certainly the government budget—which has increased over time—and investments in areas such as utilities and infrastructure.

Model 6 suggests that an additional year in life expectancy is associated with a reduction of 0.17 percent in growth volatility. Low probability of survival affects consumption and savings decisions. The lower the probability of survival, the lower will be the benefits of long-term investment, including formal education, because the returns to human capital accrue mainly over adult life. A shortened expected life span reduces incentives for capital accumulation and affects growth via lower levels of human and physical capital investments. Ndulu (2007) found that life expectancy is among the most influential variables associated with growth in Africa, and that it helps explain the growth gap between Africa and other developing regions. Lorentzen, McMillan, and Wacziarg (2005) found that a high adult mortality rate explains almost all of Africa's slow growth.

Model 7 presents a model with all the previous variables. The SDs of savings and life expectancy remained statistically significant, thus suggesting they are among the most influential variables associated with growth volatility.

Summary and Conclusions

This chapter has described the long-term features of GDP per capita growth in sub-Saharan African countries. Our main goal was to identify the relevant cross-section and long-term patterns and regularities. The main findings are the following:

- *Growth has been low and volatile.* Africa has grown little over the last three decades, and this low growth has helped widen the income gap with other regions. Africa has the lowest CV of income per capita, but the highest CV of growth. African countries have erratic growth around a low mean. Growth is extremely volatile across Africa, and this phenomenon is not restricted to economies with any specific economic or geographic attributes. The pervasiveness of growth volatility in the region suggests significant spillover and contagion effects between countries. Volatility in savings, investments, and openness and low life expectancy are among the factors associated with long-run growth volatility in Africa.

- *The 1990s may mark a turning point.* It seems that the 1990s marked a shift in African economy when the growth rate improved significantly across the continent. It is necessary, however, to disentangle the main contributing factors—whether external factors, productivity growth, investments, better institutions, less conflict, or terms of trade, among others—or whether the shift reflects a structural break toward a more sustainable and inclusive growth pattern.

- *The cross-country income distribution is becoming less equal.* The growth rate is converging in Africa and is becoming a more accurate predictor of economic performance. This fact is explained mainly by growth convergence between the poorest countries. Despite recent improvements in growth performance in many poor countries, the richest countries have grown more in the long run, and that has increased the income gap. We identified an increasingly stratified distribution of income and the formation of clubs, which prevents overall income convergence. As a consequence, some growth champions are emerging in Africa, but laggards also are becoming more significant. We proposed a typology for grouping countries based on relative economic performance that looks useful to describe the long-term economic potential of countries and to predict economic and human development outcomes.

- *Geography and natural resources do not seem to matter for growth.* We found high and increasing economic diversity in Africa, and no identifiable pattern emerged from classifying countries by geography or mineral resources. These facts suggest that institutions may play an important role through policies and other channels in explaining long-term economic performance.

- *Initial conditions matter a great deal for income distribution but not for growth.* Initial conditions seem to be the single-most important factor explaining income levels, and this is especially relevant for richer countries. Whatever the channels and the mechanics behind this phenomenon, it exerts a strong and persistent influence on income determination and on the structure of income between countries. We did not find evidence that initial conditions are associated with long-run growth.

Taken together, our results leave us with a puzzle. Low and volatile growth is the outstanding defining characteristic of Africa's growth experience since 1975. But, over the long run, we find no evidence that growth volatility is associated with economic performance. Considering that volatility is not neutral, this result is unexpected. One explanation may be that African countries are in their steady state and that growth volatility and economic performance are both symptoms of deeper characteristics, such as institutions and initial conditions. A second explanation is that long-term analysis can mask important medium-term patterns in a country's growth. If there are such patterns, it may be more relevant and rewarding to look for the causes of growth accelerations and decelerations—and what sustains growth—(as proposed by Hausmann, Pritchett, and Rodrik [2005] and Arbache and Page [2007]), rather than to investigate the determinants of growth over time and across countries.

Annex

TABLE 2A.1

Basic Statistics of GDP Per Capita PPP and Non-PPP Data, Weighted, Sub-Saharan Africa

Statistic	Mean (1975–2005)	SD (1975–2005)	CV (1960–2005)	CV (1975–2005)
GDP per capita	533.6	32.8	0.08	0.06
GDP per capita PPP	1,702	108.3	—	0.06
GDP per capita growth	−0.16	1.74	3.44	−11.12
GDP per capita PPP growth	−0.17	1.70	—	−10.01

Source: Authors' calculations.

Note: — = not available.

TABLE 2A.2
Export Diversification Index, 2003

Country	Index	Country	Index
Angola	1.1	Kenya	16.0
Benin	2.1	Madagascar	8.1
Burkina Faso	2.2	Malawi	3.0
Burundi	1.6	Mali	1.3
Cameroon	4.4	Mauritania	3.8
Cape Verde	9.2	Mauritius	11.7
Central African Republic	3.4	Mozambique	2.0
Chad	2.6	Niger	1.9
Comoros	1.3	Nigeria	1.3
Congo, Dem. Rep. of	3.0	Rwanda	2.4
Congo, Rep. of	1.6	Senegal	12.2
Equatorial Guinea	1.2	Seychelles	2.7
Eritrea	5.2	Sierra Leone	3.8
Ethiopia	4.0	Sudan	1.6
Gabon	1.6	Tanzania	21.7
Gambia, The	5.2	Togo	5.3
Ghana	4.0	Uganda	7.3
Guinea	4.2	Zambia	5.0
Guinea-Bissau	4.8	Zimbabwe	8.1

Source: Data from the Organisation for Economic Co-operation and Development.

Note: The index goes from 0 to 100—the higher, the better.

TABLE 2A.3
Merchandise Trade as a Share of GDP, Means, 1975–2005

Country	Mean	SD	Country	Mean	SD
Angola	86.2	30.4	Lesotho	130.6	12.9
Benin	41.9	8.3	Madagascar	30.4	8.3
Botswana	98.6	14.1	Malawi	55.6	9.1
Burkina Faso	25.7	5.1	Mali	41.4	10.2
Burundi	28.5	6.0	Mauritania	69.9	10.2
Cameroon	31.7	6.7	Mauritius	90.9	12.1
Cape Verde	45.4	4.1	Mozambique	38.4	14.4
Central African Republic	24.8	4.5	Namibia	94.0	14.7
Chad	34.1	17.5	Niger	35.0	6.3
Comoros	33.4	6.9	Nigeria	62.5	9.0
Congo, Dem. Rep. of	33.8	14.7	Rwanda	23.1	5.1
Congo, Rep. of	82.6	24.1	Senegal	51.6	11.1
Côte d'Ivoire	58.8	7.6	Seychelles	80.0	19.5
Equatorial Guinea	117.1	61.2	Sierra Leone	35.1	11.5
Eritrea	77.9	16.5	South Africa	42.2	6.1
Ethiopia	20.0	9.5	Sudan	21.0	8.3
Gabon	68.9	9.5	Swaziland	148.7	13.7
Gambia, The	69.4	16.2	Tanzania	32.5	7.8
Ghana	55.3	16.9	Togo	62.2	13.8
Guinea	42.7	7.7	Uganda	26.6	9.0
Guinea-Bissau	50.2	11.0	Zambia	59.1	8.3
Kenya	42.6	6.2	Zimbabwe	47.3	19.4

Source: Authors' calculations.

Note: Merchandise trade as a share of GDP is the sum of merchandise exports and imports divided by the value of GDP, all in current U.S. dollars.

TABLE 2A.4
Country GDP Per Capita and Median, 1975–2005

Country	1975	1976	1977	1978	1979	1980	1981	1982	1983	1984	1985	1986	1987	1988	1989
Angola	n.a.	n.a.	n.a.	n.a.	n.a.	1,909	1,728	1,667	1,677	1,719	1,725	1,726	1,817	1,874	1,836
Benin	860	845	863	849	878	909	967	956	883	921	958	947	903	905	850
Botswana	1,820	1,946	2,107	2,328	2,523	2,731	2,880	3,123	3,419	3,593	3,730	3,913	4,250	4,933	5,423
Burkina Faso	763	812	798	818	831	821	838	898	881	845	894	944	905	937	918
Burundi	738	784	856	829	820	805	875	837	839	812	877	876	894	911	898
Cameroon	1,702	1,563	1,726	2,044	2,105	2,005	2,282	2,386	2,481	2,593	2,724	2,824	2,683	2,401	2,290
Cape Verde	..	..	..	..	..	..	2,409	2,492	2,704	2,922	3,086	3,097	3,112	3,230	3,341
Central African Republic	1,646	1,698	1,722	1,700	1,616	1,503	1,439	1,505	1,344	1,431	1,449	1,465	1,362	1,356	1,353
Chad	972	981	983	959	738	679	672	692	782	778	923	861	816	914	930
Comoros	..	..	..	..	..	1,861	1,883	1,951	1,993	2,021	2,014	1,999	1,979	1,980	1,867
Congo, Dem. Rep. of	2,214	2,031	1,982	1,817	1,768	1,753	1,742	1,684	1,660	1,703	1,662	1,690	1,685	1,642	1,571
Congo, Rep. of	998	977	862	889	947	1,079	1,230	1,473	1,510	1,564	1,497	1,350	1,310	1,290	1,282
Côte d'Ivoire	2,433	2,623	2,687	2,842	2,775	2,355	2,324	2,220	2,036	1,894	1,896	1,880	1,802	1,756	1,745
Equatorial Guinea	..	..	..	..	..	..	..	..	..	..	1,266	1,188	1,209	1,219	1,185
Eritrea	..	..	..	..	..	..	..	..	..	..	..	..	..	..	..
Ethiopia	..	..	..	..	..	..	909	891	935	886	764	807	897	868	827
Gabon	9,323	12,288	10,435	7,696	7,506	7,469	7,614	7,155	7,326	7,632	7,220	6,934	5,561	6,073	6,380
Gambia, The	1,584	1,646	1,648	1,697	1,622	1,668	1,668	1,602	1,718	1,719	1,644	1,648	1,625	1,633	1,664
Ghana	1,885	1,783	1,792	1,912	1,827	1,790	1,676	1,507	1,387	1,454	1,478	1,507	1,534	1,575	1,610
Guinea	..	..	..	..	..	..	..	..	..	..	..	1,717	1,728	1,787	1,802
Guinea-Bissau	1,019	1,030	916	993	973	790	907	923	873	933	950	921	924	942	973
Kenya	963	948	1,000	1,030	1,068	1,086	1,084	1,059	1,033	1,012	1,018	1,051	1,075	1,102	1,115
Lesotho	1,176	1,276	1,519	1,755	1,761	1,669	1,637	1,633	1,539	1,657	1,701	1,677	1,708	1,859	1,982
Madagascar	1,290	1,217	1,213	1,149	1,228	1,204	1,057	1,009	989	978	961	953	937	942	953
Malawi	579	589	597	633	640	623	574	573	578	589	589	557	532	517	497
Mali	742	823	855	823	889	831	775	722	738	751	650	688	668	662	722
Mauritania	1,963	2,080	1,991	1,933	1,977	1,994	2,013	1,919	1,944	1,837	1,849	1,910	1,904	1,893	1,939
Mauritius	..	..	..	..	..	4,038	4,170	4,355	4,438	4,513	4,744	5,097	5,528	5,915	6,200
Mozambique	..	..	..	..	..	706	724	659	544	501	501	488	560	608	645
Namibia	..	..	..	..	..	6,573	6,502	6,347	6,094	5,911	5,743	5,772	5,707	5,489	5,338
Niger	985	962	1,006	1,107	1,150	1,090	1,064	1,048	968	780	815	840	815	844	826
Nigeria	961	1,018	1,047	957	992	1,004	848	823	759	703	751	748	722	770	802
Rwanda	840	972	959	1,013	1,096	1,156	1,183	1,172	1,208	1,121	1,128	1,138	1,082	1,083	1,058
Senegal	1,468	1,559	1,480	1,388	1,449	1,365	1,313	1,473	1,463	1,364	1,374	1,394	1,406	1,433	1,372
Seychelles	7,363	8,406	7,753	9,248	10,560	9,984	9,062	8,872	8,643	8,961	9,884	9,797	10,158	10,629	11,727
Sierra Leone	935	914	898	902	925	951	961	989	950	968	894	880	915	826	811
South Africa	9,625	9,631	9,422	9,503	9,649	10,051	10,335	10,041	9,606	9,837	9,469	9,231	9,193	9,353	9,365
Sudan	1,161	1,313	1,352	1,233	1,134	1,115	1,159	1,187	1,173	1,080	985	1,013	1,132	1,106	1,180
Swaziland	3,103	2,942	2,879	2,825	2,822	3,075	2,994	2,917	2,888	2,976	2,994	3,260	3,623	3,746	3,962
Tanzania	..	..	..	..	..	..	..	..	..	..	..	..	..	501	503
Togo	1,708	1,634	1,708	1,850	1,708	1,897	1,772	1,646	1,498	1,521	1,547	1,516	1,471	1,516	1,529
Uganda	..	..	..	..	..	..	844	865	834	779	754	755	787	807
Zambia	1,351	1,387	1,282	1,248	1,172	1,170	1,201	1,130	1,071	1,033	1,015	990	983	1,012	971
Zimbabwe	2,784	2,708	2,445	2,306	2,305	2,546	2,759	2,723	2,658	2,505	2,577	2,533	2,470	2,564	2,611
Median	1,290	1,313	1,480	1,388	1,449	1,586	1,538	1,505	1,463	1,454	1,464	1,465	1,406	1,395	1,363

Source: Authors' calculations.

Note: .. = negligible; n.a. = not applicable.

1990	1991	1992	1993	1994	1995	1996	1997	1998	1999	2000	2001	2002	2003	2004	2005
1,782	1,709	1,541	1,123	1,127	1,209	1,311	1,382	1,443	1,455	1,462	1,469	1,635	1,641	1,772	2,077
848	856	858	856	862	872	892	919	933	949	974	991	1,003	1,009	1,008	1,015
5,633	5,894	5,911	5,877	5,949	6,074	6,279	6,784	7,374	7,795	8,349	8,724	9,184	9,761	10,354	11,021
878	927	904	919	902	918	957	980	963	1,000	986	1,013	1,024	1,056	1,063	1,079
907	931	923	851	807	735	670	655	681	666	650	648	659	630	639	622
2,089	1,954	1,842	1,737	1,650	1,663	1,705	1,751	1,800	1,839	1,877	1,923	1,962	2,003	2,039	2,045
3,289	3,257	3,283	3,429	3,578	3,754	3,813	3,927	4,121	4,373	4,555	4,618	4,717	4,893	4,994	5,162
1,292	1,253	1,142	1,115	1,140	1,192	1,118	1,152	1,182	1,202	1,209	1,208	1,183	1,079	1,080	1,089
864	910	954	780	834	819	813	833	864	832	801	855	894	991	1,241	1,270
1,912	1,762	1,872	1,888	1,751	1,776	1,717	1,749	1,727	1,740	1,718	1,739	1,773	1,779	1,737	1,773
1,418	1,253	1,079	900	836	817	789	729	704	660	601	574	578	594	615	635
1,254	1,244	1,236	1,185	1,085	1,102	1,112	1,069	1,073	1,007	1,055	1,061	1,077	1,053	1,059	1,123
1,667	1,614	1,560	1,510	1,478	1,538	1,612	1,658	1,693	1,679	1,582	1,553	1,505	1,459	1,462	1,466
1,201	1,161	1,255	1,301	1,334	1,487	1,875	3,133	3,729	5,149	5,103	5,058	5,813	6,516	7,005	..
..	..	804	913	1,104	1,126	1,210	1,277	1,263	1,221	1,022	1,071	1,031	1,046	1,021	986
814	721	621	723	722	739	806	815	761	791	814	859	841	798	879	938
6,496	6,674	6,254	6,205	6,225	6,465	6,606	6,796	6,758	6,188	6,175	6,208	6,100	6,159	6,149	6,187
1,659	1,650	1,646	1,638	1,585	1,545	1,526	1,547	1,549	1,595	1,631	1,674	1,572	1,634	1,671	1,709
1,618	1,656	1,673	1,706	1,716	1,742	1,779	1,811	1,854	1,893	1,920	1,954	1,997	2,056	2,126	2,206
1,818	1,770	1,748	1,744	1,758	1,803	1,834	1,880	1,929	1,978	1,974	2,009	2,048	2,028	2,037	2,060
1,002	1,022	1,000	988	988	1,000	1,085	1,124	787	826	863	840	757	739	732	736
1,124	1,104	1,061	1,033	1,030	1,046	1,062	1,041	1,050	1,050	1,033	1,049	1,032	1,041	1,067	1,103
2,080	2,134	2,205	2,255	2,305	2,377	2,581	2,756	2,597	2,577	2,592	2,662	2,750	2,834	2,927	2,967
955	869	854	847	822	811	804	809	816	829	843	869	737	788	807	821
506	537	491	535	476	548	576	583	589	589	583	541	544	564	591	593
691	685	723	689	677	700	703	730	754	782	785	854	863	900	892	919
1,861	1,850	1,839	1,900	1,795	1,920	1,978	1,847	1,846	1,914	1,894	1,891	1,856	1,901	1,941	1,988
6,511	6,825	7,096	7,406	7,629	7,872	8,196	8,568	8,987	9,391	9,673	10,100	10,286	10,504	10,904	11,312
643	658	582	599	617	616	640	692	762	801	799	885	938	992	1,046	1,105
5,245	5,462	5,655	5,366	5,582	5,635	5,638	5,702	5,724	5,767	5,838	5,868	6,163	6,295	6,592	6,749
790	785	711	699	704	699	699	694	741	712	678	701	698	711	687	695
844	859	860	855	833	831	845	846	841	830	854	860	854	924	959	1,003
1,036	1,048	1,187	1,183	627	862	932	974	957	940	931	951	1,012	1,005	1,030	1,073
1,385	1,341	1,334	1,270	1,273	1,304	1,337	1,347	1,372	1,420	1,427	1,458	1,440	1,498	1,553	1,594
12,438	12,645	13,379	14,003	13,663	13,302	13,753	15,218	16,177	16,160	16,790	16,404	16,121	15,270	14,815	14,329
824	836	675	685	672	616	642	524	511	459	463	527	642	670	691	717
9,147	8,869	8,501	8,426	8,514	8,592	8,765	8,793	8,633	8,626	8,764	8,841	9,064	9,229	9,533	9,884
1,092	1,147	1,194	1,219	1,202	1,244	1,286	1,336	1,389	1,445	1,506	1,567	1,636	1,695	1,750	1,853
4,169	4,146	4,066	4,080	4,087	4,111	4,139	4,160	4,162	4,185	4,167	4,150	4,191	4,224	4,258	4,292
520	513	499	488	480	482	491	496	503	509	524	546	573	602	631	662
1,481	1,432	1,342	1,112	1,246	1,305	1,374	1,517	1,429	1,414	1,358	1,315	1,332	1,332	1,337	1,340
829	846	846	887	915	989	1,047	1,068	1,087	1,140	1,167	1,185	1,219	1,234	1,257	1,293
938	912	872	907	808	766	799	806	774	774	785	808	820	848	879	910
2,710	2,783	2,470	2,442	2,614	2,572	2,793	2,827	2,872	2,738	2,498	2,411	2,289	2,039	1,950	1,813
1,339	1,253	1,236	1,183	1,140	1,209	1,286	1,336	1,372	1,414	1,358	1,315	1,332	1,332	1,337	1,317

TABLE 2A.5
Country-Group Assignment, 1975–2005

Country	1975	1976	1977	1978	1979	1980	1981	1982	1983	1984	1985	1986	1987	1988	1989	1990
							Period 1 — 1975–1990									
Angola	n.a.	n.a.	n.a.	n.a.	n.a.	n.a.	n.a.	n.a.	n.a.	n.a.	0	0	0	0	0	0
Benin	1	1	1	1	1	1	1	1	1	1	1	1	1	1	1	1
Botswana	0	0	0	0	0	0	0	0	0	0	0	0	0	0	0	0
Burkina Faso	1	1	1	1	1	1	1	1	1	1	1	1	1	1	1	1
Burundi	1	1	1	1	1	1	1	1	1	1	1	1	1	1	1	1
Cameroon	0	0	0	0	0	0	0	0	0	0	0	0	0	0	0	0
Cape Verde											0	0	0	0	0	0
Central African Republic	0	0	0	0	0	0	0	0	1		0	0	1	0	0	0
Chad	1	1	1	1	1	1	1	1	1	1	1	1	1	1	1	1
Comoros	0	0	0	0	0	0	0	0	0	1	0	0	1	0	0	0
Congo, Dem. Rep. of	0	0	0	0	0	0	0	0	0	0	0	0	0	0	0	0
Congo, Rep. of	1	1	1	1	1	1	1	1	0	0	0	1	1	1	1	1
Côte d'Ivoire	0	0	0	0	0	0	0	0	0	0	0	0	0	0	0	0
Equatorial Guinea											1	1	1	1	1	1
Eritrea																
Ethiopia	0	0	0	0	0	0	1	1	1	1	1	1	1	1	1	1
Gabon	0	0	0	0	0	0	0	0	0	0	0	0	0	0	0	0
Gambia, The	0	0	0	0	0	0	0	0	0	0	0	0	0	0	0	0
Ghana	0	0	0	0	0	0	0	0	1	0	0	0	0	0	0	0
Guinea											0	0	0	0	0	0
Guinea-Bissau	1	1	1	1	1	1	1	1	1	1	1	1	1	1	1	1
Kenya	1	1	1	1	1	1	1	1	1	1	1	1	1	1	1	1
Lesotho	1	1	0	0	0	0	0	0	0	0	0	0	0	0	0	0
Madagascar	1	1	1	1	1	1	1	1	1	1	1	1	1	1	1	1
Malawi	1	1	1	1	1	1	1	1	1	1	1	1	1	1	1	1
Mali	1	1	1	1	1	1	1	1	1	1	1	1	1	1	1	1
Mauritania	0	0	0	0	0	0	0	0	0	0	0	0	0	0	0	0
Mauritius											0	0	0	0	0	0
Mozambique							1	1	1	1	1	1	1	1	1	1
Namibia							0	0	0	0	0	0	0	0	0	0
Niger	1	1	1	1	1	1	1	1	1	1	1	1	1	1	1	1
Nigeria	1	1	1	1	1	1	1	1	1	1	1	1	1	1	1	1
Rwanda	1	1	1	1	1	1	1	1	1	1	1	1	1	1	1	1
Senegal	0	0	0	0	0	1	1	1	0	1	1	1	1	1	1	0
Seychelles	0	0	0	0	0	0	0	0	0	0	0	0	0	0	0	0
Sierra Leone	1	1	1	1	1	1	1	1	1	1	1	1	1	1	1	1
South Africa	0	0	0	0	0	0	0	0	0	0	0	0	0	0	0	0
Sudan	1	1	1	1	1	1	1	1	1	1	1	1	1	1	1	1
Swaziland	0	0	0	0	0	0	0	0	0	0	0	0	0	0	0	0
Tanzania														1	1	1
Togo	0	0	0	0	0	0	0	0	0	0	0	0	0	0	0	0
Uganda							1	1	1	1	1	1	1	1	1	1
Zambia	0	0	1	1	1	1	1	1	1	1	1	1	1	1	1	1
Zimbabwe	0	0	0	0	0	0	0	0	0	0	0	0	0	0	0	0

Source: Authors' calculations.

Note: 1 = GDP is greater than median; 0 = GDP is not greater than median; GDP = gross domestic product; n.a. = not applicable.

						Period 2 — 1991–2005									
1991	1992	1993	1994	1995	1996	1997	1998	1999	2000	2001	2002	2003	2004	2005	Country-group
0	0	1	1	0	0	0	0	0	0	0	0	0	0	0	AA
1	1	1	1	1	1	1	1	1	1	1	1	1	1	1	BB
0	0	0	0	0	0	0	0	0	0	0	0	0	0	0	AA
1	1	1	1	1	1	1	1	1	1	1	1	1	1	1	BB
1	1	1	1	1	1	1	1	1	1	1	1	1	1	1	BB
0	0	0	0	0	0	0	0	0	0	0	0	0	0	0	AA
0	0	0	0	0	0	0	0	0	0	0	0	0	0	0	AA
0	1	1	0	1	1	1	1	1	1	1	1	1	1	1	AB
1	1	1	1	1	1	1	1	1	1	1	1	1	1	1	BB
0	0	0	0	0	0	0	0	0	0	0	0	0	0	0	AA
0	1	1	1	1	1	1	1	1	1	1	1	1	1	1	AB
1	0	0	1	1	1	1	1	1	1	1	1	1	1	1	BB
0	0	0	0	0	0	0	0	0	0	0	0	0	0	0	AA
1	0	0	0	0	0	0	0	0	0	0					BA
	1	1	1	1	1	1	1	1	1	1	1	1	1	1	BB
1	1	1	1	1	1	1	1	1	1	1	1	1	1	1	BB
0	0	0	0	0	0	0	0	0	0	0	0	0	0	0	AA
0	0	0	0	0	0	0	0	0	0	0	0	0	0	0	AA
0	0	0	0	0	0	0	0	0	0	0	0	0	0	0	AA
0	0	0	0	0	0	0	0	0	0	0	0	0	0	0	AA
1	1	1	1	1	1	1	1	1	1	1	1	1	1	1	BB
1	1	1	1	1	1	1	1	1	1	1	1	1	1	1	BB
0	0	0	0	0	0	0	0	0	0	0	0	0	0	0	AA
1	1	1	1	1	1	1	1	1	1	1	1	1	1	1	BB
1	1	1	1	1	1	1	1	1	1	1	1	1	1	1	BB
1	1	1	1	1	1	1	1	1	1	1	1	1	1	1	BB
0	0	0	0	0	0	0	0	0	0	0	0	0	0	0	AA
0	0	0	0	0	0	0	0	0	0	0	0	0	0	0	AA
1	1	1	1	1	1	1	1	1	1	1	1	1	1	1	BB
0	0	0	0	0	0	0	0	0	0	0	0	0	0	0	AA
1	1	1	1	1	1	1	1	1	1	1	1	1	1	1	BB
1	1	1	1	1	1	1	1	1	1	1	1	1	1	1	BB
1	1	0	1	1	1	1	1	1	1	1	1	1	1	1	BB
0	0	0	0	0	0	0	0	0	0	0	0	0	0	0	AA
0	0	0	0	0	0	0	0	0	0	0	0	0	0	0	AA
1	1	1	1	1	1	1	1	1	1	1	1	1	1	1	BB
0	0	0	0	0	0	0	0	0	0	0	0	0	0	0	AA
1	1	0	0	0	0	0	0	0	0	0	0	0	0	0	BA
0	0	0	0	0	0	0	0	0	0	0	0	0	0	0	AA
1	1	1	1	1	1	1	1	1	1	1	1	1	1	1	BB
0	0	1	0	0	0	0	0	0	0	0	0	0	0	0	AA
1	1	1	1	1	1	1	1	1	1	1	1	1	1	0	BB
1	1	1	1	1	1	1	1	1	1	1	1	1	1	1	BB
0	0	0	0	0	0	0	0	0	0	0	0	0	0	0	AA

FIGURE 2A.1

GDP Per Capita and Growth Rate

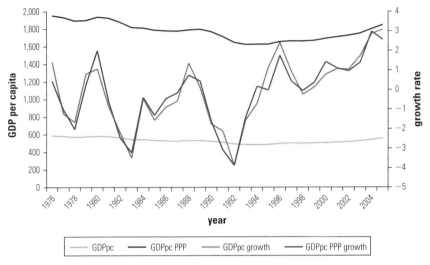

Source: Authors' calculations.

GDP Per Capita and Growth, Selected Countries

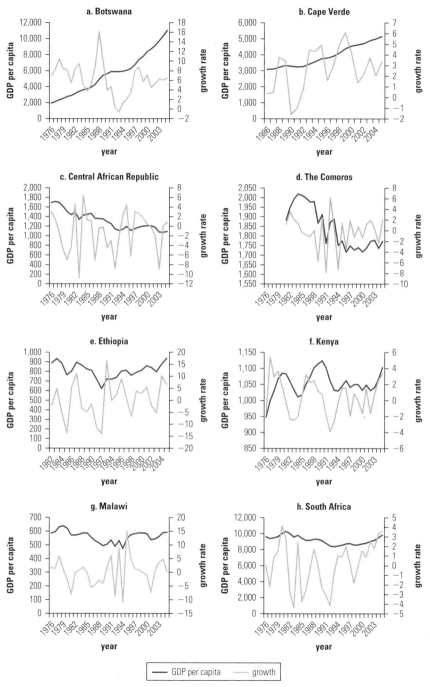

Source: Authors' calculations.

Notes

For comments and suggestions on an early version of this chapter, we would like to thank participants at the World Institute for Development Economics Research "Southern Engines of Global Growth: China, India, Brazil, and South Africa" conference, held in Helsinki, Finland, September 7–8, 2007.

1. Figure 2A.1 and table 2A.1 in the annex show that PPP and non-PPP growth data share similar statistical properties.
2. Our sample accounted for 98.4 percent of population and 99 percent of regional GDP as of 2005.
3. Although Equatorial Guinea is in our sample, we removed the country from all charts, tables, econometrics, and aggregate descriptive statistics because its extremely high growth rates in recent years distort the results.
4. We used the Hodrick-Prescott filter in figures 2.1 and 2.2 to smooth the estimate of the long-term trend component of the GDP series.
5. In 2005, those countries hosted about 8.5 percent of the regional population, but produced 45 percent of the regional GDP.
6. We present the SD of growth without extreme outliers. Among the observations removed from data are Angola (1992 and 1993), Chad (1993), and Rwanda (1992 and 1994). For example, Rwanda's growth in 1994 was −47 percent, and Angola's growth was 27 percent in 1993.
7. We show below more evidence against the neoclassical hypothesis of income convergence.
8. Gabon grew 31 percent in 1976, biasing the results. So, we removed it from the regression.
9. Easterly et al. (1993) found for a worldwide sample that correlation of growth across decades is also very low, averaging 0.3.
10. The statistical and qualitative results remain the same when we remove outliers such as Botswana and the Democratic Republic of Congo from the regression.
11. We also ran the same model (equation [2.7]) while controlling for growth SD, and the results were virtually the same.
12. Internal conflicts in Africa often spill out into wider regions—for example, Sudan–Chad, Liberia–Sierra Leone, and the Democratic Republic of Congo and several neighbors.
13. Bosworth and Collins (2003) had a similar method for grouping countries. They grouped 84 countries from all regions as higher income and lower income, according to the per capita income above or below the median. However, they took the income per capita in 1960, their first year, as reference for grouping. Garner (2006) used average long-term growth rates to classify African countries. We also tested other criteria for grouping countries, using

means instead of medians, growth instead of GDP per capita level, and clustering analysis, among others; but the present exercise provided the most robust results. We ran the median exercise removing South Africa, but the classification of countries remained basically the same.

14. Tables 2A.4 and 2A.5 in the annex show the countries' GDP per capita and median by year and respective assignments to country groups.

15. The literature has suggested that mineral-dependent countries grow more slowly not only as a result of Dutch disease, but also because of civil strife and corruption associated with the rents engendered from those resources (Collier 2007; Sachs and Warner 1995). The diverse picture presented here opposes that view. Easterly and Levine (2003) and Rodrik, Subramanian, and Trebbi (2004) suggested that geography affects income only indirectly through institutions.

16. BB is the base category. For the sake of space, we report only a few results. The complete set of results is available from the authors upon request.

17. We ran regressions removing the middle-income countries from the data (Mauritius, the Seychelles, and South Africa), but the results were virtually unchanged.

18. As reviewed above, institutions are found to be a primary source of growth volatility in developing countries (Acemoglu, Johnson, and Robinson 2003; Rodrik, Subramanian, and Trebbi 2004; and others). As discussed in the methodology section, there is certainly enormous potential for endogeneity between growth volatility and the correlates under examination. But our primary interest is in identifying long-term associations, not in explaining growth volatility.

19. We also tested other variables, including aid as a percentage of gross national income, terms of trade, exchange rate, inflation, initial conditions (GDP per capita in 1975), agriculture value added as a percentage of GDP (a variable that seeks to capture the impact of climate shocks on agriculture), population, and dependency ratio. All were nonsignificant at the 5 percent and 10 percent levels. Credit to the private sector as a percentage of GDP was statistically significant at the 10 percent level. Acemoglu and Zilibotti (1997) showed a strong relationship between initial income and volatility. They interpreted that as resulting from the fact that richer countries are able to achieve a more balanced sectoral distribution of output.

20. Berg, Ostry, and Zettelmeyer (2006) found evidence in a large set of countries that more liberal trade regimes and competitive exchange rates are associated with longer spells of growth and less growth volatility. Johnson, Ostry, and Subramanian (2007) found that a strong exporting sector, especially in manufacturing, is strongly associated with longer growth spells. They argued that manufacturing exports help change the distribution of power and help create a middle class that favors the strengthening of institutions.

References

Acemoglu, D., S. Johnson, and J. Robinson. 2003. "Institutional Causes, Macro-economic Symptoms: Volatility, Crises and Growth." *Journal of Monetary Economics* 50: 49–123.

Acemoglu, D., and J. Robinson. 2001. "A Theory of Political Transitions." *American Economic Review* 91: 938–63.

Acemoglu, D., and F. Zilibotti. 1997. "Was Prometheus Unbound by Chance? Risk, Diversification and Growth." *Journal of Political Economy* 105: 1167–200.

Arbache, J. S., and J. Page. 2007. "More Growth of Fewer Collapses? A New Look at the Long Run Growth in Sub-Saharan Africa." Policy Research Working Paper 4384. World Bank, Washington, DC.

Barro, R. 1991. "Economic Growth in a Cross Section of Countries." *Quarterly Journal of Economics* 106 (2): 407–43.

Barro, R. J., and X. Sala-i-Martin. 1991. "Convergence Across States and Regions." *Brooking Papers on Economic Activity* 1: 107–82.

Berg, A., J. D. Ostry, and J. Zettelmeyer. 2006. "What Makes Growth Sustained?" Photocopy. International Monetary Fund, Washington, DC.

Bosworth, B. P., and S. M. Collins. 2003. "The Empirics of Growth: An Update." *Brookings Papers on Economic Activity* 2: 113–206.

Collier, P. 2007. *The Bottom Billion—Why the Poorest Countries Are Failing and What Can Be Done about It.* New York: Oxford University Press.

Collier, P., and S. O'Connell. 2004. "Growth in Africa: Opportunities, Syndromes, and Episodes." Paper presented at the African Policy Institute Forum, Harare, Zimbabwe, November 15–16.

CFA (Commission for Africa). 2005. *Our Common Interest: Report of the Commission for Africa.* Available at http://www.commissionforafrica.org/english/report/introduction.html

Devarajan, S., W. Easterly, and H. Pack. 2003. "Low Investment Is Not the Constraint on African Development." *Economic Development and Cultural Change* 51: 547–71.

Easterly, W., M. Kremer, L. Pritchett, and L. H. Summers. 1993. "Good Policy or Good Luck? Country Growth Performance and Temporary Shocks." *Journal of Monetary Economics* 32: 459–83.

Easterly, W., and R. Levine. 2003. "Tropics, Germs, and Crops: How Endowments Influence Economic Development." *Journal of Monetary Economics* 50: 3–39.

Garner, P. 2006. "Economic Growth in Sub-Saharan Africa." Photocopy. Brigham Young University, Salt Lake City, UT.

Grossman, G., and E. Helpman. 1991a. *Innovation and Growth in the Global Economy.* Cambridge, MA: MIT Press.

———. 1991b. "Trade, Knowledge Spillovers, and Growth." *European Economic Review* 35: 517–26.

Guillaumont, P., S. Guillaumont-Jeanneney, and J. F. Brun. 1999. "How Instability Lowers African Growth." *Journal of African Economies* 8: 87–107.

Hausmann, R., L. Pritchett, and D. Rodrik. 2005. "Growth Accelerations." *Journal of Economic Growth* 10: 303–29.

Hnatkovska, V., and N. Loayza. 2004. "Volatility and Growth." Policy Research Working Paper 3184, World Bank, Washington, DC.

Imbs, J. 2002. "Why the Link between Volatility and Growth Is Both Positive and Negative." Discussion Paper 3561, Centre for Economic Policy Research, London.

Johnson, S., J. D. Ostry, and A. Subramanian. 2007. "The Prospects for Sustained Growth in Africa: Benchmarking the Constraints." Working Paper WP/07/52, International Monetary Fund, Washington, DC.

Levine, R., and D. Renelt. 1992. "A Sensitivity Analysis of Cross-Country Growth Regressions." *American Economic Review* 82: 942–63.

Lorentzen, P., J. McMillan, and R. Wacziarg. 2005. "Death and Development." Working Paper 11620, National Bureau of Economic Research, Cambridge, MA.

McCoskey, S. K. 2002. "Convergence in Sub-Saharan Africa: A Nonstationary Panel Data Approach." *Applied Economics* 34: 819–29.

Ndulu, B. 2007. *Challenges of African Growth—Opportunities, Constraints, and Strategic Directions.* Washington, DC: World Bank.

O'Connell, S. 2004. "Explaining African Economic Growth: Emerging Lessons from the Growth Project." Paper presented at the African Economic Research Consortium Conference, Nairobi, May 29.

Pritchett, L. 2000. "Understanding Patterns of Economic Growth: Searching for Hills among Plateaus, Mountains, and Plains." *World Bank Economic Review* 14: 221–50.

Quah, D. 1993a. "Empirical Cross-Section Dynamics in Economic Growth." *European Economic Review* 37: 426–34.

———. 1993b. "Galton's Fallacy and Tests of the Convergence Hypothesis." *Scandinavian Journal of Economics* 95: 427–43.

Ramey, G., and V. A. Ramey. 1995. "Cross-Country Evidence on the Link Between Volatility and Growth." *American Economic Review* 85: 1138–151.

Rodrik, D. 1999. "Where Did All the Growth Go? External Shocks, Social Conflicts, and Growth Collapses." *Journal of Economic Growth* 4: 385–412.

Rodrik, D., A. Subramanian, and F. Trebbi. 2004. "Institutions Rule: The Primacy of Institutions over Geography and Integration in Economic Development." *Journal of Economic Growth* 9: 131–65.

Sachs, J., and A. Warner. 1995. "Natural Resource Abundance and Economic Growth." Working Paper 5398, National Bureau of Economic Research, Cambridge, MA.

Sala-i-Martin, X., G. Doppelhofer, and R. Miller. 2004. "Determinants of Long-Run Growth: A Bayesian Averaging of Classical Estimates Approach." *American Economic Review* 94: 813–35.

PART II

Aid—Volume, Volatility, and Macroeconomic Management

CHAPTER 3

Assessing the Macroeconomic Framework for Scaling Up Foreign Aid

Delfin S. Go, Vijdan Korman, John Page, and Xiao Ye

The macroeconomic framework has evolved considerably in the past 10 years in response to policy challenges of a new country development model and the emphasis on poverty reduction and other social or human development outcomes. Among the significant developments were (1) the shift toward country-owned poverty reduction strategies (PRSs); (2) the worldwide and United Nations' undertakings to reach the 2015 Millennium Development Goals (MDGs) of reducing extreme poverty and infant mortality and improving education, health, and other human development outcomes; (3) the introduction of significant debt relief, first by the Heavily Indebted Poor Countries (HIPC) Initiative and then by the Multilateral Debt Relief Initiative (MDRI); and, no less important, (4) the promises made by industrial countries to scale up aid to poor countries. The 2002 Monterrey Consensus called for donors and international financial institutions to increase financing, improve aid predictability, and ensure that aid is aligned with national priorities. Recipient countries, in turn, are committed to improving policies and to enhancing institutions and governance so that aid is used effectively. At the 2005 Gleneagles Summit, the Group of Eight countries pledged to scale up aid significantly to the low-income countries and, in particular, to double aid to sub-Saharan Africa by 2010.

This chapter briefly surveys and assesses how these various recent developments have affected the macroeconomic framework—in terms of the policy challenges of scaling up foreign aid and the evolution and expanded scope of the analytical framework. The next section's discussion of the policy challenges of scaling up foreign aid focuses on the latest thinking and key findings at the World Bank and the International Monetary Fund, and it is not meant to be exhaustive or complete. That discussion is followed by a presentation of how the analytical framework for macroeconomic analysis also has evolved to meet the challenges of Poverty Reduction Strategy Papers (PRSPs), the MDGs, debt relief, and aid volatility. It provides a useful historical perspective. The fourth section offers some country cases dealing with scaled-up aid and MDG scenarios, including Ethiopia, Ghana, Kenya, Madagascar, Rwanda, Tanzania, and Uganda. The final section addresses remaining issues and challenges. An annex provides summary tables of recent and ongoing analytical work related to the scaling up of aid in selected countries.

Policy Challenges of Scaling Up Foreign Aid

Three basic questions describe the policy challenges of scaling up foreign aid: (1) How to spend more? (2) How to spend better? and (3) How to manage the risks of aid fluctuations? The first question deals with the macroeconomic management of scaling up aid so that the transfer of additional real resources from donors will help bring about growth and poverty reduction without incurring the harm of inflation, Dutch disease, and other issues of macroeconomic stability. The second challenge is the design of fiscal policy for growth and it deals with fiscal space issues, such as the efficiency, composition, and service delivery issues of public expenditure as well as the building of fiscal policy framework and institutions for long-term growth and poverty reduction. The last question deals with the increasing problem of unpredictability and volatility of aid. All three challenges are different slices of the basic issue, and the division is primarily for the convenience of discussion.

Macroeconomic Management of Scaling Up Aid

A sound macroeconomic framework to anchor a stable and increased expenditure path arising from greater foreign aid form an essential foundation to achieve greater development results. Issues concerning how to absorb and spend the incremental aid and the specter of real exchange rate appreciation (that is, Dutch disease) are central to the macroeconomics and management of significant aid inflows. There are now a number of studies regarding the macroeconomic management of aid, including the compilation in Isard et al. (2006) as well as Gupta, Powell, and Yang (2006). There is also an extensive body of literature on aid effectiveness, which will not be covered here.[1] In the text below, we will concentrate on new works, particularly case studies that have emerged recently at the International Monetary Fund (IMF).

Absorption and Spending of Aid

The basic purpose of aid is to allow recipient countries to raise their consumption and investment (that is, to *spend* the aid), using the transfer of external resources from donors (that is, *absorb* the aid). A macroeconomic strategy that specifically allows aid to be absorbed and spent so that it finances new public investment and social spending is instrumental in helping raise growth and reduce poverty. To account for that in the macroeconomic framework, recent formulations at the IMF look at the macroeconomic balances as *net of aid flows* and distinguish different combination of aid spending and absorption in managing the increased aid inflows (see IMF 2005, 2007a). Incremental aid is *absorbed* if it is accompanied by a widening of the current account deficit (excluding aid) by engendering resource transfers through higher imports or through a reduction in domestic resources for producing exports. That additional aid is *spent* in the budget if it leads to a widening of the fiscal deficit (excluding aid). In addressing the expenditure needs for long-term development and poverty reduction, a central concern, however, would still be about the sustainability of those external current account or fiscal programs, particularly if large deficits are involved. Hence, debt issues and sustainability are very much integral parts of the analysis.

Table 3.1 summarizes the basic short-run policy combinations available to a recipient of increased aid and their likely effects. Case 1 (*spend and absorb*) and Case 2 (*not spend but absorb*), or some combination thereof, are the desirable outcomes—with spending done by the public sector in the first case and by the private sector in the second. The risk of Dutch disease in Case 1 is very much related to the composition and productivity of public expenditure (which is discussed in the subsection regarding fiscal policy for growth). Case 2 is not devoid of Dutch disease risk if the spending of

TABLE 3.1

Absorption and Spending of Aid

Aid	Absorbed	Not absorbed
Spent	**Case 1.** Central bank sells aid dollars. Current account (net of aid) widens to allow real transfer of resources through higher imports. Aid is used for public investment and consumption. Fiscal deficit (net of aid) rises as aid is spent. No change in money supply. Risk: Dutch disease.	**Case 3.** Central bank accumulates aid dollars as foreign exchange reserves. There is no real resource transfer, and there is no effect on the current account deficit Fiscal deficit rises as aid is spent. If unsterilized: money supply rises. Risk: inflation. If sterilized: domestic public debt accumulates. Risks: higher interest rate and crowding out of private sector.
Not spent	**Case 2.** Central bank sells foreign exchange, but fiscal deficit remains unchanged. Helps achieve stabilization and provides resources for private investment. Risk: possible Dutch disease if supply response from private sector is mainly in the nontraded goods.	**Case 4.** Central bank accumulates foreign exchange as reserves; fiscal deficit net of aid is unchanged. No real transfer and no Dutch disease. Equivalent to rejection of aid (in the long run).

Sources: IMF 2005, 2007a.

the private sector leads to a supply response mainly in nontraded goods, such as in a real estate boom.[2] Case 3 (*spend but not absorb*) is a problematic response brought about by an uncoordinated monetary and fiscal policy in a strategy similar to a fiscal stimulus without aid. It will raise domestic liquidity if the additional public expenditure is not sterilized, leading to inflationary pressures and possible appreciation of the real exchange rate not due to the absorption of aid. If the fiscal expansion is sterilized by accumulating domestic public debt, it risks higher interest rate and the crowding out of the private sector. Finally, Case 4 (*neither spend nor absorb*) may build up reserves but, in the long run, is equivalent to forgoing aid altogether. As the country cases below and the subsequent discussion of fiscal policy seem to indicate, however, Case 4 (as a temporary or occasional measure within a more general strategy defined by Case 1 or 2) may be an entirely appropriate policy to follow to smooth volatile aid flows so that the expenditure path is stable and rising over time.

Country Experiences

In an IMF report, Berg et al. (2007) applied the methodology in table 3.1 in several African countries that received significant increases in aid during the period 1999–2005—namely, Ethiopia, Ghana, Mozambique, Tanzania, and Uganda. The number of cases was further expanded to 10 countries in a subsequent IMF paper (2007a). Whereas aid inflows averaged 15 percent of gross domestic product (GDP), the case studies surprisingly revealed no significant real appreciation accompanying the surge in aid in any of the sample countries. There were several factors that might have affected absorption and spending. First, there were simultaneous external or terms-of-trade shocks (for example, oil and other commodity price changes) that might have offset the effects on the real exchange rate. However, the assessment showed that the increase in aid tended to dominate the terms-of-trade movements. Further analysis revealed other explanations why countries were initially reluctant to fully absorb the incremental aid through a corresponding increase in net imports: absorption ranged from two-thirds for Mozambique to zero for Ghana and Tanzania. These factors included the need to (1) establish macroeconomic stability by reversing low levels of international reserves (for example, in Ethiopia and Ghana), (2) hedge against aid volatility and future reduction of aid inflows, and (3) avoid appreciation to maintain export competitiveness. In Mozambique, Tanzania, and Uganda, where spending (fiscal) of aid exceeded its absorption in the current account, there were inflationary pressures from the injection of domestic liquidity. In Ethiopia and Ghana, the don't-absorb-don't spend stance over the aid surge did not add to inflationary pressures. In 2001, when aid was absorbed but not spent in Ethiopia and Ghana, that approach helped reduce inflation. Nonetheless, in later years, as countries' macroeconomic positions strengthened and as the aid increases and debt relief were more established, the countries generally tended to opt for fuller spending and absorption of aid. Table 3.2 summarizes an expanded list of country experiences with regard to the absorption and spending of additional aid, outcomes in the real exchange rate, and any concerns about debt distress.

Fiscal Policy for Growth

Easing the resource constraints and making effective use (that is, spending better) of the scaled-up aid requires a sound fiscal policy as part of the

TABLE 3.2

Macroeconomic Management of Aid, Country Experiences, 1999–2004

Country	Summary
Burundi	Macroeconomic framework during 1999–2004 allowed for full spending of aid and accommodated aid volatility by adjusting net domestic asset, central bank credit to government, the floor on net foreign assets, and so forth. The IMF program during 2004–07 envisaged foreign exchange sales to control liquidity in light of sizable aid inflows, and thus allowed for a widening current account deficit. Competitiveness concerns did not materialize and the real exchange rate remained below its 2000 level. The divergence between programmed and actual aid disbursement was an issue. Debt sustainability was a concern, but debt relief was granted through the enhanced HIPC Initiative and the completion point is expected at end-2007.
Ethiopia	External assistance initially was not spent but was used to reduce fiscal deficit and stabilize the economy. Authorities chose to replenish reserves initially, which contributed to a slight deprecia-tion. Later, spending generally followed the availability of aid. However, Ethiopia did not make full use of the flexibility in the IMF program and consistently "overperformed" on fiscal and foreign reserve targets. Competitiveness was not an issue, and the birr depreciated slightly in nominal and real terms over the period. Inflation was not a key concern and was generally ameliorated by favorable food prices, except for the drought in FY 2002/03. Debt sustainability was a concern throughout and contributed to a shift toward grants and a lowering in IDA lending in FY 2002/03. Accurate aid projection remained difficult.
Ghana	Cautious approach limited aid absorption and spending because of the need to stabilize the econo-my and reduce the fiscal deficit. Aid was used to replace domestic financing and to build interna-tional reserves. Another factor was aid volatility, and the average swing in fiscal aid inflows during 1999–2005 was more than 5 percent of GDP. Following substantial depreciation in 2000, the real exchange rate was relatively stable, despite higher inflation versus trading partners. The 2006 PRGF-supported program was the first to encourage a spend-and-absorb approach. Concerns about the external debt burden led to zero ceilings on medium- and long-term nonconcessional borrowing in the IMF program (except the 35 percent grant element).
Madagascar	The IMF's initial macroeconomic program in 1999 emphasized lowering high debt and restraining borrowing following debt relief. After 2002, fiscal and current account developments largely tracked external assistance, with aid spending exceeding absorption. Aid forecast tended to be optimistic. CPI-based real exchange rate showed appreciation between 2002 and 2003, but unit labor cost-based real exchange rate did not appreciate and export growth remained healthy. HIPC and MDRI debt relief has reduced Madagascar's very high debt level, but concerns about future sustainability continue to emphasize the importance of grants and concessional financing.
Mozambique	Mozambique's IMF-supported program has had three distinct phases since 1999. Initially, the policy design was to spend and absorb an expected surge in aid. The program, starting in 2004, targeted fiscal consolidation in the face of a programmed decline in aid. More recently, the program is back to a more explicit spend-and-absorb strategy anticipating a scaling up of aid. In general, aid inflows were quite volatile and unpredictable during 2000–05. Aid peaked in 2001 due to flood-related as-sistance. The real exchange rate depreciated during 2000–03 as international reserves were accu-mulated. A real appreciation was registered in 2004 but was corrected in 2005. Since then, the real exchange rate has remained relatively stable.

Source: IMF 2007a, annex 4.

Note: CPI = consumer price index; GDP = gross domestic product; HIPC = heavily indebted poor countries; IDA = International Development Association; MDRI = Multilateral Debt Relief Initiative; PRGF = Poverty Reduction and Growth Facility.

Country	Summary
Nicaragua	Since 1999, IMF programs have focused on fiscal sustainability and external viability, resulting in partial absorption and little spending of aid inflows. Aid was used to substitute for domestic financing, leaving room to crowd in private sector. A shift to a spend-and-absorb strategy started in 2004. Nicaragua has had a crawling peg regime since 1996, which offered little flexibility in exchange rate movement. As a result, monetary management of aid inflows has become challenging and inflation targets are often missed. Concerns about the external debt burden led to zero ceilings on medium- and long-term nonconcessionary borrowing in the IMF program (except the 35 percent grant element).
Rwanda	Until the attainment of the HIPC completion point in 2005, the emphasis in the IMF-supported program was on debt sustainability, with stringent limits on external borrowing and efforts to reduce domestic debt. Aid-based fiscal spending was initially limited. A shift to a spend-and-absorb approach started in 2004. Since 2004, aid has increased rapidly, making coordination of monetary and fiscal policies a challenge. Aid absorption has increased, but was still constrained by authorities' concern about real exchange rate appreciation and export growth, resulting in higher-than-programmed reserve accumulation. The grant element in concessional lending was recently raised to at least 50 percent to avoid debt distress in the future.
Tanzania	Aid generally was fully spent, but absorption initially lagged behind because authorities were concerned about exchange rate appreciation and reluctant to use foreign exchange resources to sterilize increased capital inflows. This reluctance resulted in higher-than-programmed reserve accumulation. During 2003–05, both programmed and actual aid absorption has increased. The Dutch disease effect was deemed small, considering the cumulative 40 percent real devaluation during 2001–04. Debt sustainability is not an issue because extensive debt relief was received through the HIPC Initiative (completion in 2001) and MDRI (2006).
Uganda	The surge in aid during the period (from about 8 percent of GDP in FY 1997/98 to a peak of 12 percent in FY 2003/04) was largely spent, which was reflected in a rise in the fiscal deficit (excluding grants) from 6.5 percent to 10 percent of GDP. Emphasis was on poverty-related spending as supported by the HIPC Initiative. Aid absorption lagged, however, given that the monetary authorities sterilized the liquidity impact to control inflation and to accumulate reserves. Program design was switched later to allow larger sales of foreign exchange and greater absorption. Debt sustainability is not an issue because Uganda has reached the completion point in the Enhanced HIPC Initiative and is eligible for future MDRI debt relief.
Zambia	Aid to Zambia was generally absorbed, but repeated shortfalls in external budget support contributed to higher domestic financing. Partly as a result of policy slippages and variation in fiscal discipline (for example, large wage increases), aid as a percent of GDP during 2000–06 fell from a high of 12.3 percent to less than 6.0 percent in 2006. Double-digit inflation was problematic in the past but has been brought under control since 2004. International reserve was generally weak. The mining-based economy, however, has been growing after prolonged decline. The real exchange rate has been appreciating strongly from the combined effects of higher copper prices and private inflows—more than from changes in aid. Zambia attained HIPC completion in 2005 and received further debt relief from MDRI in 2006.

central challenges in macroeconomic management and development. The issues surrounding the determination of an increased spending path and the efficiency and composition of public expenditure in response to the additional aid have been broadly categorized recently as fiscal space issues. This is a rapidly evolving area, and our understanding of the relationship between fiscal policy and growth is still very incomplete, in terms of both an encompassing conceptual framework and data and experiences at the country and sector levels to inform policy. Several new works have emerged recently, however, including Bevan (2007), Heller (2005), Heller et al. (2006), IMF (2007b), Krumm (2007), Ter-Minassian (2007), and World Bank (2007d), In addition to issues of absorption and spending described above, the following issues are deemed important:

- *Development of an appropriate longer-term fiscal policy and expenditure framework to anchor a stable and increased spending path.* Short-term fiscal policy decisions should be anchored in a medium- and longer-term fiscal policy and expenditure framework. The usual elements in determining a medium-term expenditure framework also will apply, such as determining a realistic resource envelope, choosing an expenditure path and fiscal targets, and performing debt and fiscal sustainability analysis. However, the scaling up of aid adds several new challenges:

  a. While there should be at least a medium-term fiscal and expenditure framework based on the scaled-up aid scenario, the MDG targets and scenarios also require a longer-term perspective and some notions regarding what is feasible over the long run, however uncertain. Ideally, the medium-term expenditure framework should be anchored in the prioritization of a country's PRS. In addition, a new generation of PRS should incorporate the longer view and plans toward attaining human development outcomes, such as the MDGs. Enormous challenges remain in the sense that existing macrofiscal frameworks often are rudimentary or nonexistent. Out of 31 low-income countries examined by the Fiscal Affairs Department of the IMF, only 3 countries had a full macrofiscal framework; 5 had a comprehensive framework; 13 had only a basic framework; and 10 had no framework (see Ter-Minassian 2007).

  b. Accounting for all aid flows and their time profile so that a greater but reasonable resource envelope over the medium and longer terms can be established is increasingly complicated by the proliferation of aid channels from official and private sources. The average number of donors per country has increased from approximately 12 in the 1960s to about 30 in recent years (World Bank 2007a). Some aid also might be delivered in a regional context or to regional institutions, such as the Economic and Monetary Community of Central Africa, the Common Market for Eastern and Southern Africa, the West African Economic and Monetary Union, and so forth. In addition, earmarking and off-budget spending by donors in special or vertical funds diminish flexibility in the use of budgetary resources and hamper the formulation and implementation of expenditure plans (see World Bank 2007a, 2007j). In this regard, the development of domestic revenue effort is also important in improving both the resource picture and the capacity to finance future recurrent spending brought about by the scaled-up aid flows.

c. The fiscal policy framework should ensure a stable expenditure path and avoid disruptive cutbacks in nonwage spending in sectors, operations and maintenance, and stalling of projects. There is considerable difficulty, however, in how to smooth expenditure prudently in response to shocks. Permanent shocks may require permanent adjustment to the spending path, but short-term shocks and aid volatility could be met by adjusting domestic financing requirements or government reserves to smooth expenditure. The choice of appropriate fiscal balance or targets (domestic balance, overall balance including or excluding grants, and so forth) also may depend on circumstances, including the capacity to design and administer spending programs at the center and sector levels. To allow for various spending possibilities, the baseline scenario should be accompanied by alternative scenarios, stress tests, and measures of fiscal and debt sustainability.

d. No less important, implementing a serious reform program and a prudent macrofiscal policy obviously will help draw donor commitments for the increased aid flows needed for a higher expenditure path and toward scaled-up development results.

- *Efficiency and composition of public spending* are central to the question of how to spend better within a sound fiscal policy for growth. The attainment of growth and the MDG targets, and the risk of Dutch disease, depend very much on how aid is used among competing spending needs in the budget, the productivity of those public expenditures, and possible complementarities among public services and between private and public capital. For examples, infrastructure spending may have a more direct and short-term supply effect and higher import contents to assist aid absorption. However, social spending may improve access to clean water, health, and human development, which, in turn, will likely raise labor productivity and economic growth in the longer run.

At the World Bank, issues regarding the efficiency and composition of public spending traditionally have been handled in Public Expenditure Reviews (PERs), which continue to play an important role in strengthening countries' ability to implement sound expenditure programs across sectors. These general PERs are increasingly complemented by sector-specific PERs that examine expenditure issues within sectors. PERs are part of the standard or core diagnostic and analytical works provided by the World Bank (called Economic and Sector Works [ESWs]), which provide the underlying basis of the policy dialogue and operational works in support of the country-based model. Both types of PER tend to address the multidimensional nature of the development process. Even the sector-specific studies, such as water resource management, infrastructure, or energy sector studies, now employ a cross-sectoral approach to demonstrate the links to all types of economic activities and business climates. In addition to PERs and sector studies, Country Economic Memoranda (CEMs) and Development Policy Reviews also have adopted a multisectoral approach to growth, incorporating the links, issues, and recommendations from a variety of sectors, such as infrastructure (including transport, power, water, and telecommunications) and human development (including health and education). Table 3.3 summarizes the total and types of core ESWs delivered to low-income countries classified as receiving concessionary financing or grants under the International Development Association (IDA) for the period fiscal years 2000–07. Of the total 326 reports, PERs constituted the highest share at 27 percent, and CEMs came in second at 19 percent.

However, the distinctive feature and the challenge in the fiscal space issues brought about by scaled-up aid are the more explicit links of public service delivery to poverty reduction and human development outcomes (that is, the MDG targets), as well as the connection between MDGs and growth. Hence, studies dealing with MDGs or fiscal space issues are necessarily more long-term than are traditional PERs, and

TABLE 3.3

IDA Core Economic and Sector Work, by Type, FY2000–07

Report type	Total number	% distribution
Public Expenditure Review	88	27.0
Country Economic Memorandum/Development Policy Review	62	19.0
Country Financial Accountability Assessment	53	16.2
Country Procurement Assessment Report	52	16.0
Integrative Fiduciary Assessment	16	4.9
Poverty Assessment	55	16.9
Total	326	100.0

Source: Operations Policy and Country Services, World Bank.

they cut across several other ESW types—CEMs, poverty assessments, sector studies, and the institutional aspects of public expenditure management. In addition to the macroeconomic aspects of managing the absorption of aid and ensuring a sound fiscal framework to increase the expenditure path, the fiscal space analysis provides the necessary microeconomic and institutional underpinnings for increasing public spending effectively. Several fiscal spaces studies already have begun and were summarized in a recent policy paper at the World Bank (2007d)—(see also the selected country cases presented later in this chapter). These new studies tend to use an analytical framework called the Maquette for MDG Simulations (MAMS) at the World Bank (see the section on the analytic framework below), which was designed specifically to assess the alternative scaling up of public expenditures in terms of sector or spending composition, sequencing, and macroeconomic implications (like Dutch disease issues). Much depends, however, on the availability of detailed sector studies to inform and provide the estimates of efficiency parameters of government services. Moreover, there is still considerable uncertainty about the productivity of public expenditure (see World Bank [2007d], table A2, for a summary of recent results for developing countries).

- *Strengthening of budgetary institutions and public expenditure management* is vital to manage and implement expanded service delivery and capital expenditure programs. The importance of strengthened budget systems, fiscal management, and a medium-term expenditure framework linked to the PRS is underscored by several ESWs devoted to improving financial fiduciary systems and fiscal institutions. For IDA countries during fiscal 2000/07, there were 53 ESWs (16.2 percent of the total) classified as Country Financial Accountability Assessments (CFAAs), and another 52 (16.0 percent) were Country Procurement Assessment Reports (CPARs). In addition, a growing number of integrative reports combined PERs, CFAAs, and CPARs in various amalgamations. Not counting the large amount of technical assistance in this area from the World Bank, IMF, and other donors, there were also some 16 reports (approximately 5 percent) registered as Integrative Fiduciary Assessments.

In addition, assessments of public expenditure and financial accountability (PEFA) are now scheduled regularly for many countries (table 3.4). Started in 2001, PEFA is a joint endeavor among the World Bank, the IMF, the European Commission, the United Kingdom's Department for International Development, the Swiss State Secretariat for Economic Affairs, the French Ministry of Foreign Affairs, the Royal Norwegian Ministry of Foreign Affairs, and the Strategic Partnership with Africa. It aims to support integrated and harmonized approaches to assessment and reform in the fields of public expenditure, procurement, and financial accountability. The PEFA Public Financial Management (PFM) Performance Measurement Framework provides 28 indicators covering the entire PFM cycle and is linked to six objectives—(1) policy-based budgeting; (2) predictability and control in budget execution;

TABLE 3.4
PEFA Status of Assessments, July 2007

Assessments	Completed	Substantially completed	Commenced	Planned	Total assessments
Total number of assessments	37	21	23	29	110
First-generation PRS and IPRS (23 countries)	6	7	3	5	21 of 23 countries
Second-generation PRS (18 countries)	7	4	4	1	16 of 18 countries
Fragile states (21 countries)	2	5	2	4	13 of 21 countries

Sources: PEFA Secretariat; World Bank 2007b.

Note: IPRS = interim PRS; PEFA = public expenditure and financial accountability; PRS = poverty reduction strategy. First-generation PRS/IPRS: *Albania, Armenia, Azerbaijan,* Bhutan, *Cameroon, Cape Verde, Dominica, Georgia, Grenada (IPRS), Guyana, Honduras, Kenya, the Kyrgyz Republic, Lesotho, Mali, Moldova, Mongolia, Nepal, Niger, Pakistan, Serbia and Montenegro,* Sri Lanka. Second-generation PRS: *Benin,* Bolivia, Bosnia and Herzegovina, *Burkina Faso, Ethiopia, Ghana, Madagascar, Malawi,* Mauritania, *Mozambique, Nicaragua, Rwanda, Senegal, Tanzania, Uganda, Vietnam, the Republic of Yemen, and Zambia.* Fragile states: (PRS-I): Burundi, *Central African Republic,* Chad, Democratic Republic of Congo, Djibouti, Guinea, Guinea-Bissau, Nigeria, São Tomé and Principe, Sierra Leone, Timor-Leste; (PRS-II): Cambodia, The Gambia, *Lao People's Democratic Republic, Tajikistan;* (IPRS): *Afghanistan, Republic of Congo,* Côte d'Ivoire, *Haiti,* Liberia; (Transitional Results Matrix): Sudan. *Italics* = completed, substantially completed, commenced, or planned.

(3) accounting, recording, and reporting expenditure; (4) external scrutiny and audit; (5) comprehensiveness and transparency; and (6) budget credibility. The assessment has been implemented in 68 countries and is planned for use in 18 more countries. Repeat assessments using this tool will gradually allow tracking of PFM performance over time; and they have been completed or substantially completed in 4 countries, commenced in 2 countries, and planned in 10 countries.

Managing Aid Volatility and Risks

The uncertainties in terms of aid volatility, the long-run provision of aid (predictability), and the risk of debt distress argue for risk management to be an essential part of the macrofiscal framework to ensure a stable expenditure path. Country experiences listed in table 3.2 where aid is not fully absorbed to build up foreign reserves could be explained by the need to smooth aid levels. Low-income countries in sub-Saharan Africa generally experience the highest level of unpredictability. Whereas better-performing countries may receive higher levels of aid and greater predictability, the pattern is uneven. In a sample of 13 countries with relatively large aid inflows, the mean absolute deviation in budget aid receipts from expected levels declined between 1993–99 and 2000–05, but was still almost one-third of the expected levels in the latter period (World Bank 2007b). Figure 3.1 shows that official development assistance particularly as a percent of gross national income can vary widely, even for well-performing countries in the Africa region.

To manage the risk of aid fluctuations, Heller et al. (2006) argued for three elements to augment the medium-term macroeconomic framework: The first element is debt sustainability assessments supplemented by medium-term vulnerability analyses of alternative scenarios. The second element encompasses policies of self-protection, such as prudent fiscal policies; enhanced domestic revenue; shared strategy with donors; flexibility in aid-financed expenditure initiatives in terms of their contractual and employment commitments; and "ring-fencing" uncertain aid spending, such as the practices in Uganda and the separation of the external budget in Zambia (which, however, may fragment the budget). The third element is policies of self-insurance centered on an explicit policy of higher reserve accumulation based on the degree of vulnerability of the budget, given its composition and sources of financing. In mineral resource–rich countries, the role of fiscal policy and management has been applied to

FIGURE 3.1

ODA Trends in Some Better-Performing African Countries, 1981–2005

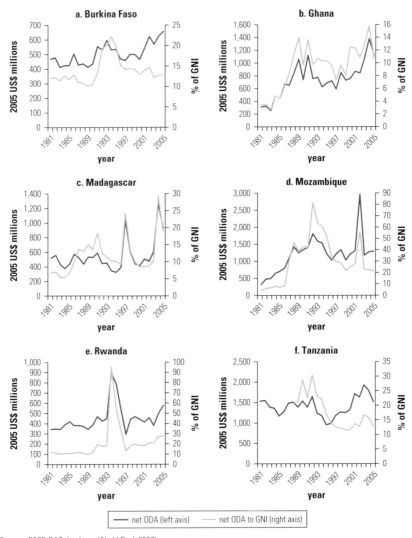

Sources: OECD-DAC database; World Bank 2007b.

Note: GNI = gross national income; ODA = official development assistance.

address revenue volatility from commodity price fluctuations in reports by Budina and Wijnbergen (chapter 10 of this volume) and Devlin and Lewin (chapter 9). In addition to debt sustainability, the same kind of analysis regarding fiscal sustainability and management will need to be extended for aid-dependent countries.

Evolution and Expanded Scope of the Analytical Framework

The scope of the macroeconomic framework, particularly in terms of formal analytical modeling, has expanded tremendously as a result of the challenges wrought by the advent of PRSPs, the MDGs, debt relief from the HIPC Initiative and the MDRI, as well as issues related to aid volatility and unpredictability. The tendency, particularly at the World Bank, is increasingly to link microeconomic aspects to the macroeconomic framework. This evolution is summarized below.

PRSPs and Poverty Reduction

Poverty reduction always has been a primary goal of development. However, the advent of the country-owned PRSPs in the late 1990s placed the issues of poverty reduction and the distribution of household incomes squarely at the center of policy discussions and argued for their urgent incorporation into the macroeconomic framework. The PRSPs also were closely associated with the introduction of significant debt relief from the HIPC Initiative, which put great importance on the allocation of the budgetary headroom created by debt relief to poverty-related public expenditures and the need for a medium-term expenditure framework anchored in the PRS. Parallel with the evolving and growing literature regarding effectiveness of aid, growth, and poverty, the shift in development approach spurred the advance in the World Bank of various techniques and tools for evaluating the impact of economic policies on poverty and income distribution. For examples, see the compilation in Bourguignon and Pereira da Silva (2003) and the sourcebook edited by Klugman (2002). A point emphasized in these references is the importance of microeconomic tools—such as benefit incidence analysis and survey tools for tracking service delivery—to augment traditional macroeconomic analysis of growth and to enhance its links to issues of poverty reduction, household welfare, and income distribution. In addition, the HIPC debt relief was seen as akin to the provision of budgetary support, and great emphasis was given to improving public expenditure management and budgetary institutions to improve the links between the prioritization in the PRS and the resource allocation in the budgetary framework. The end result has been the development and proliferation of rich approaches designed to improve the microeconomic and institutional underpinnings of the PRS and the concomitant macroeconomic framework. Hence, the evolution of the analytical framework starting in the late 1990s should be understood in the light of the policy challenges first posed by the PRS approach and HIPC debt relief.

The emphasis on country-owned PRSs also put a great deal of emphasis on country participation, including the development of the macroeconomic framework. Some of the initial efforts at the World Bank explicitly recognized the data constraint and technical capacity of policy makers in many low-income countries that were the focus of the PRSP approach and the HIPC debt relief. An early macro-microeconomic framework for that purpose, dubbed the "123PRSP Model" in Devarajan and Go (2003), took a rigorous but simplified approach to explicitly link public expenditure and debt relief to growth and poverty reduction, and it was employed in the Zambia Public Expenditure Review (see World Bank 2001). The 123PRSP Model simplified the macro framework into aggregative distinction of tradable and nontradable goods in a computable general equilibrium (CGE) framework. Effects of policy and external shocks are first derived as a change in the real exchange rate between tradable and nontradable goods, which are then mapped to the expenditure and income sources of various household groups (for example, in income deciles). Growth impact is derived from either short-term vector autoregressive analysis or long-term growth regression. Another type of simplification is found in Pereira da Silva, Essama-Nssah, and Samaké (2003); it distills the income distribution from household surveys into a parameterized Lorenz curve or equation, which then easily can be linked to macroeconomic models to examine policy and external shocks. It provides the flexibility of choosing the macroeconomic framework from simple macroconsistency models like the Revised Minimum Standard Model Extended or the IMF financial programming to more complex econometric or CGE models. Wodon, Ramadas, and Mensbrugghe (2003) also developed the SimSIP (Simulations for Social Indicators and Poverty), which can be used to assess targets related to poverty and is applicable to the MDGs (discussed further below).

The simplicity and minimal data needed from the simpler frameworks are, of course, achieved at the cost of fuller information and complexity at either the macro or the poverty module, thereby reducing the depth of analysis that is feasible. Hence, more sophisticated macro-micro frameworks also were deployed for developing countries with more data and capacity. These frameworks typically have a richer structure of the economy and make full use of household information. As an example, Bourguignon, Robilliard, and Robinson (2002) merged a disaggregative macroeconomic framework in a CGE model of Indonesia with a microsimulation model that made full use of the complete household data, with explicit treatment and full individual heterogeneity of labor skills, preferences, and characteristics at the individual and household levels. Several macro-micro frameworks have now been developed and compiled in Bourguignon, Pereira da Silva, and Bussolo (forthcoming). The microeconomics of income distribution dynamics in East Asia and Latin America are also discussed in Bourguignon, Ferreira, and Lustig (2005). In the Africa Region, a joint effort between the World Bank and the South Africa National Treasury also has implemented an elaborate framework for examining the macro-micro impact of external shocks and policy issues relating to the labor market as well as the combined incidence of taxation and public expenditures in South Africa (Essama-Nssah et al. [2007]), which is being planned as a possible template in neighboring African countries.

MDGs and Service Delivery

Following the introduction of the PRS approach and the HIPC debt relief, the recent efforts to achieve the MDGs by 2015 shifted the scope of the analytical framework considerably outward to represent an expanded vision of development that encompasses not only growth and poverty reduction but also broader human development goals related to education, health, gender, and access to water and sanitation. To help countries monitor and assess alternative plans toward the MDGs, the World Bank has developed a new analytical tool, called the Maquette for MDG Simulations (see, for example, Bourguignon, Diaz-Bonilla, and Lofgren forthcoming). MAMS' main contribution is a methodical integration of government services and their impact on the economy within a standard economywide or CGE framework. To assess alternative scaling up of public expenditures in terms of sector or spending composition, sequencing, and macroeconomic implications (like Dutch disease issues), it incorporates several key features: (1) a formal representation of the production of government services, such as education, health, and infrastructure, that also takes into account demand and supply factors as well as the efficiency of those services; (2) the interactions across the MDGs, allowing for possible complementarity or synergy—for example, improved access to clean water likely will improve health, which, in turn may increase education attendance and raise labor productivity and economic growth; (3) the economywide impact of the scaling up of services, such as the impact on relative prices and resource allocation of government and nongovernment sectors; and (4) the recursive dynamics that allow for trade-offs over time in a practical way, including relative cost and benefit of the timing of various sector spending.

To be sure, there are also simpler approaches. The SimSIP is also applicable to MDG strategy analysis, including estimation of fiscal costs (for example, see Datt et al. 2003). It is also available in a user-friendly Microsoft Excel-based format. Alternative projections of poverty, health, education, and access to water-sanitation are derived from reduced-form regressions against determinants such as GDP, urbanization, and time. Another approach to MDG analysis was applied to Niger by Agénor et al. (2005). The advantage of this approach is that much less data are needed and an MDG module performs the post-calculations of MDGs and other social indicators based on cross-country estimations of parameters. Simplification in both cases was accomplished by aggregating the macro/labor module and by limiting the feedback/interaction mechanism between the MDGs and the economy as well as among MDGs.

As a practical tool to explore key processes that generate MDG outcomes as well as the fiscal sustainability and trade-offs over time and across sectors, the MAMS framework is now being applied to 6 countries in Africa and 18 countries in Latin America (the latter group in a project managed by the United Nations Development Programme). Table 3.5 summarizes completed or ongoing applications of the MAMS in several countries. The MDG scenarios for select African countries are discussed in the country cases presented in the next section.

Debt Relief and Sustainability Analysis

A significant part of the scaling up of aid has come in the form of debt relief. As a consequence of the debt relief effort of the HIPC Initiative and, more recently, the MDRI, systematic debt sustainability analysis (DSA) is now conducted jointly by the World Bank and the IMF in developing countries, particularly low-income countries receiving multilateral aid from the IDA.[3] Using realistic macroeconomic projections for the medium and long term and under standardized stress tests or shocks, the framework assesses whether a country's current borrowing strategy may lead to future difficulties in servicing its debt. The debt sustainability framework is, therefore, a forward-looking approach that aims to guide borrowing

TABLE 3.5

MAMS Applications in Country Work

Country	Year	Issues Addressed	Product/context
Congo, Dem. Rep. of	2007	Fiscal space and debt sustainability	Public Expenditure Review
Ethiopia	2005	MDG strategy	Government MDG Needs Assessment
	2005	Poverty reduction strategy	Input to and review of poverty reduction strategy
	2006	Fiscal space, aid, trade-offs	Report: Review of Public Finance
	2007	Labor market, migration	Report on Urban Labor Markets
Ghana	2007	MDG strategy	Country Economic Memorandum
Honduras	2007	MDG strategy	Public Expenditure Review
Kenya	2007	Long-run growth, policy trade-offs	Country Economic Memorandum
Madagascar	2007	MDG strategy	Not yet determined
Malawi	2007	Government spending composition and trade-offs	Public Expenditure Review
Tanzania	2007	Government spending composition and trade-offs	Country Economic Memorandum
Uganda	2006	Growth	Country Economic Memorandum
	2007	Growth, alternative financing strategies, trade-offs	Public Expenditure Review
Venezuela, R. B. de	2007	Sustainable poverty reduction strategies	Poverty Assessment

Source: Development Economics Vice Presidency Program on MAMS, World Bank.

Note: MAMS = Maquette for MDG Simulations; MDG = Millennium Development Goal. This table does not cover MAMS applications in some Latin American countries under "Assessing Development Strategies to Achieve the MDGs in Latin America," the joint project of the World Bank, the United Nations Development Programme, and the United Nations Department of Economic and Social Affairs.

and lending decisions for low-income countries on terms that enable borrowing countries to devote resources toward achieving the MDGs, while also staying within their means to repay loans. By accounting each country's specific circumstances, the framework tries to help borrowing countries balance their need for funds with their current and prospective ability to repay their debts. Linking a country's borrowing potential to its current and prospective ability to service debt should help countries avoid accumulating excessive debts. The approach considers vulnerabilities in both external debt and public sector debt. The external debt burden indicators are distinguished in terms of policy-dependent thresholds (strong, medium, and poor policy performers), and the risk of possible debt distress is classified into low risks, moderate risks, high risks, and in debt distress.

As a standard practice, all World Bank country teams for all IDA-only countries are now required to prepare DSAs jointly with the IMF. In the last three years, approximately 50 DSAs were completed—25 of which were done in fiscal 2007 and 13 in fiscal 2006. Among the IDA countries in the Africa Region, DSAs were recently carried out for Benin, Burkina Faso, Burundi, Cameroon, Cape Verde, Chad, the Republic of Congo, Ethiopia, The Gambia, Guinea, Guinea-Bissau, Lesotho, Madagascar, Malawi, Mauritania, Mozambique, Niger, Rwanda, São Tomé and Principe, Sierra Leone, and Uganda.

Dynamics of Aid

One issue recently receiving attention is the dynamics of aid, particularly its volatility. The findings of Berg et al. (2007) emphasized the importance of intertemporal smoothing and hedging against aid volatility (see also table 3.2)—that is, the dynamics of adjustment to aid inflows. For this reason, in the last chapter of Mirzoev (2007), a stochastic general equilibrium model of a small and open economy was developed to look at the impact of various options of absorption and spending on inflation and the real exchange rate. The key features of the model include intertemporal substitution in consumption, inclusion of monetary and fiscal policy, and the uncertainty that comes from aid inflows as defined by an autoregressive AR(1) process. Capital stock is fixed, however, so that the framework is short-term.

The importance of supply response in ameliorating the problem of Dutch disease from aid inflows has been emphasized in the MAMS simulations as well as by the findings of recent studies, such as Adam (2006) and Adam and Bevan (2004). However, these studies all use recursive dynamics and do not allow for intertemporal smoothing decisions in consumption or supply. If aid is about the future, then a report by Devarajan et al. (chapter 5 of this volume) shows that intertemporal choices in consumption and supply will matter in determining impact on the real exchange rate. The study uses a very standard neoclassical growth model without additional assumptions about the productivity of public expenditures or the complementarity between public and private capital. The findings showed that, if intertemporal smoothing is allowed so that the timing and decisions regarding savings and investment are planned optimally over time, then Dutch disease ceases to be a significant issue. However, if investment and consumption are done on a yearly basis (recursive but myopic) because aid is unpredictable and uncertain, then Dutch disease is likely to be an issue even if the aid level at each point in time turns out to be the same as the dynamic case. The integration of dynamic adjustment and choices, uncertainty, and the MAMS' more micro-links to service delivery remains a daunting challenge in the formulation of the macroeconomic framework.

Selected Country Cases

In this section we describe a few African country cases focusing on the macroeconomic management of scaled-up aid and, where available, fiscal space issues, MDG scenarios, and DSA. The MDG scenarios were derived mainly from the MAMS framework. Many of the findings are preliminary and derived from ongoing or completed ESWs and fiscal space studies at the Africa Region of the World Bank. They serve as background information for policy dialogue with governments and donors. They also are intended to provide input to the country's PRS, like the Ethiopia case, and eventually to identify areas for coordinated assistance from donors toward the medium-term budgetary framework and work program. Hence, case studies are only part of a wider analytical program for the PRS and MDGs.

Ethiopia

Ethiopia is one of the poorest countries in sub-Saharan Africa and faces big challenges to achieve its MDG targets. Significant scaling up of aid to Ethiopia has already happened, but a further significant increase is needed to finance both physical and human capital investment needs. The year 2001 marked the beginning of the turning point for aid to Ethiopia; net aid flows increased to 8.6 percent of GDP, up from 5.0 percent in 2000. In subsequent years, net aid inflows increased to over 15.0 percent of GDP (Berg et al. 2007). According to a recent estimate, the foreign resources requirement for achieving the MDGs is about $19–24 billion[4] in net present value (NPV) terms over the next decade, which would require a further sharp increase in foreign aid (see World Bank 2007i).

What are the implications for such a sharp scaling up of aid for the macroeconomic framework? Various challenges of scaling up aid to Ethiopia have been analyzed in recent research reports (Berg et al. 2007; Mattina 2006). For example, a 2003 report by the Development Committee (the Joint Ministerial Committee of the Board of Governors of the World Bank and the International Monetary Fund on the Transfer of Real

Resources to Developing Countries) stated that a 60–100 percent increase
in aid could be absorbed effectively by Ethiopia if capacity-building efforts
and accelerated structural reforms were put in place.

Macroeconomic Management

Despite a surge in net foreign aid inflows by an average 8 percent of GDP
for the 2001–03 period, the country experienced a small real depreciation.[5]
Over this aid surge, the nominal exchange rate also did not appreciate as
the government maintained a close, crawling peg to the U.S. dollar. Why
did a large and steady surge in aid not result in real appreciation and,
hence, no Dutch disease? In our view, the lack of Dutch disease in Ethiopia
was due to a combination of factors, including low inflation resulting from
food surplus; a terms-of-trade shock; and, most important, the fact that
very little of the increased aid actually was absorbed into the economy.

Absorption and Spending of Aid

Increased aid was largely *not used* either for increased net imports or for net
fiscal spending. Only about 20 percent of the additional aid was absorbed,
and spending of additional fiscal aid was almost zero—as fiscal deficit net
of aid actually shrank at the time of aid surge. Instead, aid was used to
rebuild reserves and to reduce reliance on domestic deficit financing. A
number of factors led to lack of aid absorption and spending. Following the
war, reserves were at low levels and the government's stabilization program focused on reducing excessive domestic financing of the fiscal deficit.
Moreover, the government was concerned about the lack of predictability
and durability of the aid inflows. Full and quick absorption of increased aid
could lead to higher government spending and an appreciated real
exchange rate, both of which create serious adjustment costs if the aid
flows recede after a few years. Usually, donor estimates were overly optimistic, whereas the government preferred to base spending on only firmly
committed amounts, which often tended to underestimate likely aid flows.
To address this issue, both the government and donors formed the Joint
Budget and Aid Review mechanism to improve the predictability of aid.

Scaling Up and MDG Scenarios

An application of the MAMS model shows that achieving MDG-related
services will require a sharp acceleration of long-term growth from an historical average of 4 percent to at least 7 percent annually and a sharp rise

in investment from 20 percent to 38 percent of GDP—particularly, a massive increase in public investment from less than 7 percent to 21 percent of GDP (World Bank 2007i). These targets cannot be achieved without substantial scaling up of aid. What follows are the main results and recommendations of the analysis[6]:

- *Proposing growth-enhancing strategies:* To maximize productivity growth, balancing and sequencing of public investment are very crucial. For example, a disproportionate investment in social services at the expense of investment in infrastructure at early stages of scaling up of aid runs the risk of creating an unsustainable situation of a relatively small economy unable to maintain increased access to education and health.

- *Limiting Dutch disease:* To address the real exchange rate issue, the proposal is sequencing and frontloading of the aid necessary to fulfill the MDGs. The analysis envisaged directing aid at an early stage at investments in basic infrastructure (roads, energy, and irrigation) to help generate rapid growth and thereby reduce the headcount poverty rate, instead of putting excessive focus on social sectors to achieve the "social MDGs." It also projected a high import elasticity of demand that would ease pressure on domestic prices and the exchange rate from higher aid, and provided a clear picture of import effects of the scaled-up public spending.

- *Sequencing of public investment:* To minimize the total cost of reaching the MDGs, priority criteria for pubic investment are necessary. The focus of attention was basic infrastructure to enhance productivity, to improve network effects by strengthening links across and within regions and sectors, and to limit the impact on the real exchange rate because such investments have generally higher import contents.

Debt Sustainability Analysis

Based on a joint IMF–World Bank (2006c) DSA of Ethiopia, the country's risk of debt distress is moderate with its NPV of debt-to-exports ratio at 108 percent, which remained below the threshold as of end-2005. Implementation of the MDRI debt relief from IDA and the African Development Bank would improve Ethiopia's debt sustainability outlook even further by reducing its debt burden indicators. Stress test results also show that the country's external debt indicators are very sensitive to exports shocks and terms of new external borrowing. To keep the risk of debt stress at a minimum, external financing should be sought on highly concessional terms and, if possible, as outright grants. Also, it is important to prioritize public investment to foster growth and diversify exports.

Ghana

Ghana has emerged as one of the best-performing African economies, with growth consistently surpassing 5 percent since 2001 and rising to above 6 percent in 2006. Improved macroeconomic management and significant and ongoing progress on structural and institutional reforms present a real opportunity to accelerate growth and progress toward the MDGs. The 2007 Ghana CEM (World bank 2007f) simulates three growth scenarios to 2015, using the MAMS model, including a baseline scenario with annual growth at 6.9 percent, an accelerated growth with closing of infrastructure gaps scenario yielding growth at 7.4 percent, and a full MDG achievement scenario with growth rising to 7.9 percent (table 3.6).

Macroeconomic Management
Two independent empirical simulations, the Ghana MAMS and the time-series analysis in Elbadwi and Kaltani (2007), indicate that, from the macroeconomic perspective, Ghana can take on additional resources and spend them productively without suffering from Dutch disease. Ghana's

TABLE 3.6
Ghana: MDG Scenarios

MDG Indicator	Baseline growth scenario: GDP growth = 6.9%	Accelerated growth scenario with removal of infrastructural bottlenecks: GDP growth = 7.4%	Target/MDG attainment scenario: GDP growth = 7.9%
National poverty headcount ratio (%)	12	10	26
Primary completion rate (%)	89	94	100
Under-5 mortality rate (per 1,000 live births)	97	95	40
Maternal mortality ratio (per 100,000 births)	440	428	185
Access to safe water (%)	62	75	85
Access to sanitation (%)	47	70	85

Source: World Bank 2007f.

overall institutional and financial management capacity and the overall legal and regulatory setup for procurement have been improving, which suggests that the overall absorption constraint is not binding. Furthermore, based on the World Bank's Country Policy and Institutional Assessment (CPIA), Ghana has the same level of capacity as Mozambique and Uganda.

These estimates of the resource requirements to achieve the MDGs are based on the current public spending efficiency. If foreign grants are available, for example, at only 40 percent of the estimated cost, a MAMS "high-efficiency scenario" indicates that public spending efficiency will have to improve by 60 percent for Ghana to achieve all key MDGs.

The real danger lies in a sudden cessation of aid flows, which could lead to large adjustment costs. In such a scenario, to maintain growth and MDG paths, the investment-to-GDP ratio would need to reach the level of 41 percent GDP—a goal that is hardly feasible. The CEM concludes that stable and rising amounts of aid over the medium term can help the government of Ghana reach sustained and shared growth and achieve the MDGs. Such a large requirement for scaled-up resources may not be realized, however. In such a scenario, the government, the development partners, the private sector, and other stakeholders will have to decide on a feasible mix of financing options for Ghana's shared growth agenda.

Scaling Up and MDG Scenarios

The baseline growth, if realized, puts Ghana in a good position to achieve the key poverty MDG ahead of schedule. However, Ghana will not achieve many other key MDGs, including primary completion rate, under-5 and maternal mortality, and access to safe water and sanitation. In the accelerated growth scenario, the access to safe water and sanitation will be improved significantly because of additional investment in these sectors. However, other MDGs will still remain elusive.

Attaining all key MDGs will require a large amount of additional resources at an annual average of $750 million between 2007 and 2011, equivalent to 5–6 percent of GDP, and an additional $1.7 billion per year during 2012–15, equivalent to approximately 8–9 percent of GDP (see figure 3.2). This means that the aid will reach approximately 15 percent of GDP in the first period and 20 percent in the second period. Some African countries, such as Mozambique and Uganda, have demonstrated capacity to use so large a proportion of aid effectively.

FIGURE 3.2

Ghana: Scaling Up and Additional Financing Scenarios, 2004–15

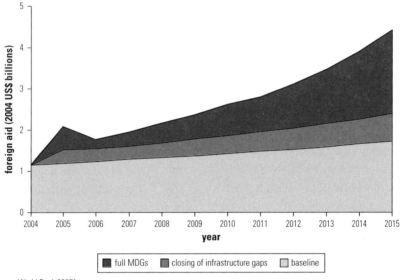

Source: World Bank 2007f.

Debt Sustainability Analysis

The IMF and the World Bank prepared a joint DSA for Ghana in 2006. One baseline scenario and three alternative scenarios were simulated, including (1) a case with the same borrowing path as in the baseline but a lower growth in exports and GDP, evaluating the risk if higher GDP and export growth should fail to materialize; (2) a case with a higher nonconcessional borrowing than the baseline, evaluating the risk of higher borrowing; and (3) a case with a higher borrowing but lower GDP and export growth path, evaluating the risks of high borrowing in the event of failed GDP and export growth acceleration. The DSA concluded that Ghana's risk of external debt distress is moderate, albeit close to the low risk category. The risks to total public debt are also moderate. However, the debt sustainability could deteriorate in the case of slower-than-forecast growth and/or substantial increases in borrowing on nonconcessional terms.

Kenya

Kenya's development policy is to reverse the effects of many years of economic decline.[7] Its development goal in the Vision 2030 is to accelerate

GDP growth to an annual rate of 10 percent. This goal is ambitious, considering that GDP growth for the last 25 years was averaging only 3.1 percent a year. However, starting in 2003/04, there has been a perceptible change for the better in Kenya's macroeconomic outcomes, suggesting a "break point" manifested in a large decline in domestic interest rates, a marked improvement in government debt dynamics, and a rise in GDP growth. In particular, GDP growth during 2005 and 2006 reached close to 6 percent a year. The better macroeconomic outcomes in recent years are being driven by several factors: (1) the lagged effects of the liberalizations of prices, trade, exchange rates, and interest rates as the results of the reforms undertaken in the late 1980s and the 1990s; (2) a solvency based on efficient own-revenue mobilization as the results of tax policy reforms and improvements made in tax administrations; and (3) a rising political stability after the successful 2002 elections.

Fiscal Policy for Growth and MDG Scenarios

Kenya is a unique case among the fiscal space studies in the sense that access to aid has often been limited, partly because of concerns regarding governance. Donors have provided relatively low and volatile aid flows or have channeled aid outside the budget because of problems of public expenditure management. To finance its expenditure path, fiscal space has been created by a strong revenue effort as well as declining domestic and external indebtedness (figure 3.3).

The level of aid in Kenya is very low relative to that of other comparable countries, such as Ghana and Uganda. During 2000–05, aid to GDP rose marginally from less than 2.0 percent in 2000 to 2.8 percent in 2005. This rise indicates potential for scaling up donor assistance. A MAMS model for Kenya was applied to explore what may be required for Kenya to achieve its growth objective. Three scenarios indicate that 6–7 percent growth is a reasonably achievable good performance, but it is still below the 10 percent growth target. For Kenya to reach its higher growth target, what is needed is a combination that brings increased aid, private savings, and foreign direct investment plus total factor productivity growth of 2.5 percent a year.

More important, however, the Kenyan government also needs to improve the efficiency and composition of its public spending, particularly in infrastructure and social services. The budget for infrastructure is about

FIGURE 3.3
Kenya: Decline in Public Debt, 1995/96–2005/06

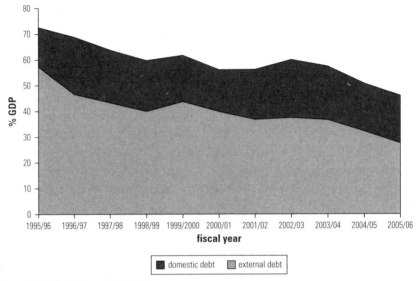

Sources: Central Bank of Kenya; Krumm 2007.

5 percent of GDP—a moderate level—but its efficiency is low. Fiscal adjustment and the decline of external budget support generally prevented any substantial spending. Moreover, low efficiency—as reflected, for example, by significant losses in transmission, distribution, and collection and by high administrative expense in the state electricity enterprise—drained resources that could be available for reinvestment. At present, the private sector provides only 1.4 percent of GDP in infrastructure spending. A recent successful sale of shares in a power generation investment (KenGen) indicates the potential in key subsectors. The 2006 joint concession for the Kenya-Uganda railway is likely to improve options for transport between Mombasa and Kampala. In prospect also are public-private partnerships for a number of energy projects, the Nairobi Urban Toll Road, and Mombasa Port.

Public spending for education and health combined for more than 10 percent of GDP, but large financial gaps have been identified in education and health sectors. For example, the shortfalls in primary and secondary education sectors for teachers' remuneration, with a full reform to gain efficiency, are estimated to be as high as $200 million. The current public spending on health is $9.47 per capita, less than half the level of the international commitment agreed as part of the Abuja Declaration.

Expenditure composition is also less than optimal, especially within social sectors. For example, in the education sector, spending is high but composition is tilted in favor of university education, which gets the highest level of government subsidy (92 percent of the unit cost is subsidized). Reducing this subsidy for higher education and shifting resources to technical education, where 75 percent of the cost is borne by participants, would improve the overall education budget. Similarly, in the health sector, resources are poorly allocated with a huge portion of the health budget being spent on wages and salaries while spending on the medicines, drugs and equipments is inadequate. This situation is a serious concern (World Bank 2007c, 2007d).

Although donors can do more to increase aid and improve aid quality, Kenya's government can also influence aid flows by improving governance and the investment climate. The initial sign of success in recent years already signals that additional aid likely will enhance growth acceleration by providing needed resources for infrastructure, education, and health sectors where public investment is required. However, the overall quality of budget execution and project management also should be improved to ensure that investment spending is efficiently translated into productive infrastructure assets.

Madagascar

Madagascar is a good example of how rapidly the right policies can propel a previously lagging country. Although most MDGs for Madagascar are far from being achieved, the path endorsed by the new government since 2002 has provided more and much needed financing to education, health, and infrastructure. Growth prospects have improved recently, with annual growth of 6 percent likely over the medium term. Although Madagascar lags behind many African countries in education, it is superior on some other MDGs, such as health. Most distressing is the poverty rate (over 70 percent), which is well above the African average. Madagascar received, on average, more than 8.0 percent of GDP a year in external aid over the period 2000–05, with a peak of 14.6 percent of GDP in 2004. Beside aid, preferential trade initiatives (such as the African Growth and Opportunity Act [AGOA]) led to a sharp takeoff in exports.

Macroeconomic Management

In recent years, fiscal spending and current account developments largely tracked external assistance. Madagascar appears to have both spent and absorbed aid.

- *Spending of aid:* Early increases in aid between 1999 and 2000 did not lead to a wider fiscal deficit because aid was used also to reduce the high debt levels. More recent increments in external assistance are generally reflected in Madagascar's overall fiscal deficit. The country is seeking to use external assistance to accelerate public investment and spending for growth and to attain the MDGs, while maintaining macro-economic stability. The current Madagascar Action Plan (its PRSP) includes two scenarios for growth and investment: a realistic aid scenario in which the 2006 IMF-supported program is based, and a more ambitious scaling-up scenario for which resources have not yet been identified.

- *Absorption of aid:* With reserves amounting to less than two and a half months of import cover in 1999, the early increases in aid were used also to increase reserve cover to three months of imports and to offset the adverse impact of cyclones on the balance of payments. In 2001, very strong export growth, partly because of the AGOA initiative, led to a substantial improvement in the current account position, despite no change in external assistance and a sharp increase in international reserves. In 2002, the current account deficit worsened sharply, without any significant change in foreign aid, reflecting the impact of political crisis. Since 2002, the current account deficit generally has widened when aid increased and has narrowed when aid fell, suggesting that aid was largely absorbed.

Fiscal Policy for Growth

There is scope for raising part of the required additional financing from domestic revenue mobilization as well as for improving the efficiency of public spending. At 10 percent of GDP, tax revenue generation in Madagascar is low. A recent fiscal space study assessed tax revenue to be below its potential by at least 3 percent of GDP (World Bank 2007d). As part of the latest PRS, the government plans to undertake a major tax reform.

The composition of the budget is generally aligned to the priorities of the government, with roads and primary education receiving 34 percent of the noninterest budget. Health and education sectors also focused on providing primary-level services. In addition, the share of administration in overall expenditures has continued to decline. However, there is still potential for improving the composition and efficiency of expenditure. For example, the relative balance between investment and recurrent spending could be further improved to enhance operations and maintenance spending. Communes control only 3–4 percent of resources, and more could be provided. Allocation to poorer districts also could be improved because they receive fewer resources and have fewer qualified personnel than would be justified by their poverty rates.

Scaling Up and MDG Scenarios

A recent application of the MAMS model analyzed two scenarios (Mensbrugghe and Tan 2006). A baseline scenario, based on current improved trends, achieved moderate progress toward the MDGs. A more ambitious scenario achieved the health and water-sanitation MDGs, almost achieved the primary completion MDG, and made significant progress toward the poverty MDG (see table 3.7). The financing requirements of this scenario are double those of the baseline scenario (aid recently has averaged about 8 percent of GDP). Despite the relatively better initial health indicators, the additional financing requirement is largest for achieving the health MDGs. If all of the large additional financing is provided by foreign aid, the real exchange rate undergoes a sizable appreciation (more than 20 percent), risking competitiveness and growth unless productivity gains are enhanced. Meeting part of the additional financing with increased domestic resource mobilization alleviates the pressure on the exchange rate.

TABLE 3.7
Madagascar: MDG Achievement Scenario

MDG indicator	1990 (actual)	2004 (actual)	2010 (projected)	2015 (projected)	2015 (target)
National poverty headcount ratio (%)	68.0	74.0	54.8	47.3	34.0
Primary completion rate (%)	35.0	45.0	84.4	97.0	100.0
Under-5 mortality rate (per 1,000 live births)	168	123	62	56	56
Maternal mortality ratio (per 100,000 births)	550	550	164	137	138
Access to improved water source (%)	40.0	46.0	66.7	77.8	70.0
Access to improved sanitation facilities (%)	14.0	32.0	44.8	57.0	57.0

Source: Mensbrugghe and Tan 2006.

Another implication of the scaled-up scenario is the need for stepped-up efforts to strengthen institutional capacities.

Debt Sustainability Analysis

Debt relief under both the HIPC Initiative and the MDRI has reduced Madagascar's previously high debt burden to a sustainable level.[8] Although Madagascar's debt indicators are now below the thresholds in the baseline scenario, the 2006 DSA assessed debt sustainability to be vulnerable to shocks (IMF and World Bank 2006d). High vulnerability to shocks puts Madagascar's risk of debt distress at the moderate level. For example, debt sustainability appears vulnerable if large export shocks materialize, because of either the expected termination of AGOA or a large natural disaster. Maintenance of debt sustainability will depend on successful promotion of growth and exports, and careful management of external borrowing, with maximum reliance on grants and highly concessional loans.

Rwanda

Rwanda has achieved an impressive recovery since the end of conflict in 1994. With strong donor support, Rwanda has progressed to its second PRS, implementing a wide-ranging policy reform agenda to secure a broad-based economic recovery. GDP growth reached over 15.0 percent a year during 1995–99, the immediate postconflict reconstruction phase, and has registered 5.3 percent a year during 2000–06. Inflation fell from over 15 percent a year from 1995 to 1999 to slightly over 6 percent during 2000–06. A number of economic and structure reforms were undertaken to strengthen the market orientation of the economy, including a flexible exchange rate, a reduction of tariff from 35 percent to 18 percent, liberalization of the monetary and financial sectors, and trade liberalization.

In particular, outcomes have been most remarkable in the area of service delivery, particularly for human development services in education, health, and water. In education, net primary school enrollment reached 92 percent in 2004 and 2005 (exceeding the PRSP target for 2008); the primary completion rate increased from 51 percent in 2004 to 55 percent in 2005 (but fell short of the target). In health, the contractual approach for community health centers, piloted in Cyangugu and Butare in 2004 and expanded to all health centers in the country, transferred about $0.50 per capita in 2006 (to be increased to $1 per capita in 2007). Various health services were increased: use of insecticide-treated nets increased from 4 percent in 2005 to 30 percent in 2006; use of assisted deliveries increased to 39 percent of the population, from 29 percent in 2000; coverage by *mutuelles* (community insurance schemes) increased from 27 percent in 2004 to 41 percent in 2005. In addition, access to potable water increased between 2001 and 2005 from 41 percent to 55 percent in rural areas and from 66 percent to 69 percent in urban areas, respectively. In 2005, an additional 598,000 people living in rural areas gained access to potable water, compared with only 167,000 in 2004. Functionality of the rural water systems increased to 75 percent, with 8 percent of the 830 piped water systems being privately managed.

Macroeconomic Management

The achievements in macroeconomic progress and service delivery have been supported by sizable aid inflows, which increased from about 11.0 percent of GDP in 2000 to about 16.5 percent of GDP in 2006. Actual donor aid was often significantly stronger than originally anticipated (by about 50 percent), except in 2003. Until 2004, the macroeconomic framework was geared to partial spending of aid for three reasons: (1) there was a desire to repay and secure a gradual reduction of domestic debt, (2) aid projection was cautious because of uncertainty, and (3) fiscal policy generally supported partial spending of aid. In 2003, however, the IMF program experienced slippages and aid plummeted for one year, leading to spending being higher than program projections and being financed by domestic borrowing. Aid has recovered since 2004 and, with foreign reserves reaching a more comfortable five months of imports, the approach supposedly switched to spending and absorbing the projected aid.

Dutch disease symptoms did not materialize as feared even after 2004. This was partly because monetary authorities were still reluctant to boost foreign exchange sales for fear of real exchange rate appreciation and its impact on export competitiveness. The more recent spending program is contingent on the monetary program as defined by the IMF and includes a contingent spending equal to 2 percent of GDP.

Fiscal Policy for Growth and Scaled-Up Aid Scenarios

For Rwanda to raise its per capita income growth three times to 6–7 percent a year, as called for in its development plan Vision 2020, several issues and constraints need to be addressed.[9] First, as a landlocked country, Rwanda has to invest to ease the infrastructure constraints to growth and export diversification. It has a dense but poorly maintained road network. Maintenance costs are twice as high as in other countries because of the terrain and climatic conditions. Energy supply and costs are also problematic because the national coverage for electricity is only 6 percent, and power outages are common. In addition, it has to transform the agricultural sector to be more market oriented and provide support and incentives for private sector development to diversify its economy with manufacturing and services. Lack of skilled labor and low productivity are also constraints.

To improve growth and the MDG outcomes, the recent fiscal space case study examined improving efficiency and prioritization in public spending as well as revenue mobilization and the scaling up of external aid. The analysis pointed out that the allocation of public spending on infrastructure and economic services is very low, which likely constrained growth from going higher. There also exist inefficiencies in resource allocation within sectors, such as education. Expenditure on education receives the largest share of the budget, but nearly a third of the recurrent budget is spent on higher education.

A significant part of the fiscal space challenge is brought about by the proliferation of aid channels, which makes it difficult to align and integrate vertical and earmarked funds with Rwanda's development strategy. Although vertical funds bring much-needed attention and financing to their focus areas, they also can undermine development effectiveness by creating potential distortion of resource allocation because of their financing size or dominance. In the case of Rwanda, for example, spending on HIV/AIDS is 22 times the amount spent on maternal and child health (Republic of Rwanda 2006). Even though malaria is the leading cause of morbidity and mortality in the country, it receives only about a third of the donor funding allocated to HIV/AIDS (figure 3.4). Moreover, only a small fraction of donor aid in the health sector enters the government budget; the rest is managed directly by donors and channeled through nongovernmental organizations, mainly to single-issue vertical programs. The fragmentation of the budget is part of the reason why key government-run health programs, such as malaria control, maternal mortality, and management of childhood diseases, are badly underfunded. Several initiatives have been started to strengthen public resource management and to

FIGURE 3.4

Rwanda: Distribution of Donor Health Sector Funding, 2005

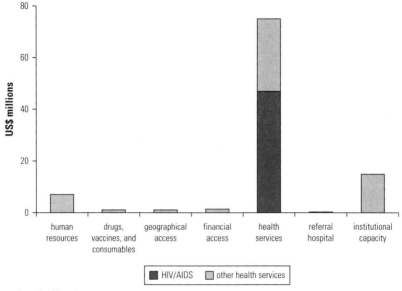

Source: Republic of Rwanda 2006.

improve expenditure programming, budgeting, procurement, and expenditure management and monitoring processes as well as tracking surveys and community-based interventions.

The fiscal framework will require significant scaling up of aid. Investment needs to be accelerated, and the financial gap to achieve the MDGs is estimated to be an additional $79 million a year over the current aid level (already near $500 million). There are limitations to domestic revenue enhancements because of the poor tax base, and a balance needs to be maintained between improved tax collection efficiency and overburdening enterprises with high tax rates, especially for small and medium enterprises. Non-aid deficit will need to be limited to levels that will not pose a risk of creating shocks to government programs as a result of aid volatility.

Debt Sustainability Analysis

Risks of debt distress were overriding concerns before the attainment of the HIPC Initiative completion point in April 2005. Rwanda is also one of the MDRI countries because of its continued satisfactory macroeconomic performance, progress in poverty reduction, and improvements in public expenditure management. The joint DSA (IMF and World Bank 2006a) has concluded that, although the MDRI lowers Rwanda's immediate risk of debt distress, its debt situation quickly could become unsustainable without a high and sustained level of grant financing and strong export growth. The DSA recommends that further structural reforms should focus on better protecting Rwanda against shocks by taking steps to diversify its exports and to accelerate its growth.

Tanzania

Tanzania has experienced a notable increase in aid since 2000, but substantial further scaling up of aid will be needed to support strong growth and accelerate progress toward the MDGs. The government has been hard at work, with support from donors, to address both micro and macro absorptive capacity constraints. The macro framework underlying the growth and poverty reduction strategy has improved significantly (IDA and IMF 2006). Public financial management has been strengthened, including improvement of the medium-term budget framework (World Bank 2006b). The mechanisms for aid coordination have improved, including the preparation of a Joint Assistance Strategy.

Macroeconomic Management
Between 2000 and 2004, net aid inflows to Tanzania have increased substantially, reflecting partly declining debt service payments following the debt relief. Moreover, as the government started to improve public financial management systems, donors started increasingly to channel their assistance through the government budget. Consequently, the net aid to the budget had quadrupled by 2004.

- *Spending of aid:* Over this aid-surge period, the increased aid to the government budget was spent mostly on priority and development programs. The aid surge led to a wider fiscal deficit net of aid—mainly because of an increase in public expenditures by about the same magnitude as the aid surge. In recent years, additional aid has been targeted to public investment to accelerate economic growth.

- *Absorption of aid:* For most of the aid-surge period, the incremental aid was not absorbed, partly because of the fear of currency appreciation and the uncertainty about donor flows. A large portion of additional aid was used to build up reserves (Berg et al. 2007). The current account narrowed for the period 2000–04, despite increased financing through higher aid inflows. This policy response succeeded in avoiding any real appreciation of the currency, but its success came at the cost of no absorption of aid—which is generally not the most desired outcome for a scaling up of aid. In recent years, however, with an improved macroeconomic framework and large reserves, absorption of aid has been improving. For example, the current account deficit before aid widened by 3.7 percent of GDP in 2004, which is well above the aid increment. Although some real appreciation of the currency occurred, the Dutch disease effect was negligible because of the cumulative 40 percent real depreciation of the currency over the 2001–03 period.

Scaling Up and MDG Scenarios

The MAMS simulations for Tanzania are preliminary, but early results show that the poverty reduction MDG is almost achievable with continuation of the recent years' higher average growth—about 5.5 percent annually (table 3.8) (World Bank 2007g). But an acceleration of growth to the 6–7 percent range, quite feasible if Tanzania's reform momentum is sustained and adequately supported by partners, would achieve the target well ahead of schedule. However, achievement of most other MDGs will require substantial further increases in aid, beyond the baseline scenario that assumes about the same level of aid relative to GDP as at present—about 10 percent. The simulations underscore the need for the additional financing to be raised on concessional terms for continued debt sustainability. They also point to the need for stronger domestic resource mobilization through higher revenues (more from expanding the revenue base

TABLE 3.8
Tanzania: Baseline Scenario of Key MDG Results

MDG indicator	2005	2010	2015	Target
National poverty headcount ratio (%)[a]	34.4	29.5	20.1	19.3
Primary completion rate (%)	54.2	62.8	71.0	100
Under-5 mortality rate (per 1,000 live births)	83.2	75.7	66.5	48.0
Maternal mortality ratio (per 100,000 births)	578	460	325	133
Access to safe water (%)	57.0	57.6	59.6	70.9
Access to sanitation (%)	91.0	91.0	91.2	92.0

Sources: World Bank 2007b, 2007g.

a. The poverty headcount is based on the national poverty line, set at per capita purchasing power parity of $0.79 a day (2000 prices).

and improving tax administration than from raising taxes) and for improvements in expenditure efficiency. The appreciation of the real exchange rate from the scaled-up aid inflows is estimated to be moderate, but the results reinforce the importance of a continued policy focus on improving Tanzania's competitiveness.

Debt Sustainability Analysis

Tanzania received substantial debt relief in 2006 under the MDRI, which was about 60 percent of Tanzania's total external debt stock at the end of 2005. As a result of debt relief, all external debt indicators were significantly below the debt threshold (IMF 2007d, appendix V). The NPV of external debt declined to 15 percent of GDP and 60 percent of exports, and debt service payments fell to 5 percent of exports.[10] This decline puts Tanzania at a low risk of debt stress, given prudent macroeconomic and debt management. Stress test analysis confirms this assessment.

Uganda

Uganda achieved one of the highest growth rates in Africa in the 1990s, with growth averaging 6.9 percent. This performance was supported by improved macroeconomic management and a range of structural reforms. Foreign aid over the past decade has averaged 10 percent of GDP. Poverty reduction activities strengthened and social services, including health and education, improved significantly. The better social services and sustained high growth have benefited poor people of Uganda, and poverty rates have fallen from 58 percent in 1992 to 38 percent in 2004 (World Bank 2006c).

During 2000–06, growth slowed to 5.1 percent a year, partly because of a sharp decline in world coffee prices—the country's major export. Uganda needs to reinvigorate efforts to achieve stronger and sustained growth and to accelerate progress toward the MDGs.

Macroeconomic Management

Uganda experienced a substantial increase in aid inflows in the early 2000s. The country followed a spend-but-don't-absorb strategy (IMF 2007a, annexes).

- *Spending of aid:* On average, over the aid-surge period, government spent incremental aid resources by increasing its spending. The fiscal deficit before aid was worsened (from 6.5 to 10.0 percent of GDP) in response to additional aid inflows.

- *Absorption of aid:* However, Uganda was not very successful in absorbing the additional aid. Most of the aid dollars were saved as international reserves instead of leading to a higher current account deficit and a real resource transfer. On the contrary, the current account balance improved during most of the years of the aid surge. One possible reason for such a policy response could be the authorities' desire to preserve the economy's competitiveness by not allowing appreciation of its currency. In fact, sale of aid-related foreign exchange by the central bank was limited to a level consistent with a depreciating nominal exchange rate. This response may also be a result of the desire to minimize the adverse impact of sharp terms-of-trade deterioration on the coffee sector.

The policy of spending but not absorbing aid entailed a rapid increase in domestic liquidity. To revamp excess liquidity and keep inflation in check, the central bank undertook heavy sterilization operations through treasury bill sales. That action had at least two negative consequences. First, interest rates that rose significantly potentially crowded out private sector investment. Second, this sterilization led to a rapid accumulation of domestic debt.

Fiscal Space and MDG Scenarios

A recent fiscal space study and the MAMS application examine alternative financing strategies for achieving higher growth and increasing investment in MDG-related services (Lofgren and Diaz-Bonilla 2006; World Bank 2007k). A particularly high priority is strengthening infrastructure because problems such as poor transport, power shortages, high transport costs, and high energy costs act as severe constraints to growth. There is significant scope for mobilizing more resources for infrastructure and other priorities through improvement of government expenditure composition and efficiency. Administration expenses and defense consume 48 percent of the budget. Insufficient maintenance expenditures result in poor maintenance of the trunk and urban roads, and losses in electricity and unaccounted water are in the range of 35–45 percent. In education, a survey of costs and outputs and an analysis of the value for money indicate that there are substantial leaks in government recurrent expenditure on primary education, including "ghost workers," excessive administrative overhead, teacher absenteeism. and other waste. Roughly one-fifth of the recurrent budget may be wasted. Data on pupil-to-teacher ratios in different grades suggest inefficiencies in teacher deployment (see figure 3.5).

FIGURE 3.5

Uganda: Waste in Primary Education, Recurrent Expenditure Only, FY 2005/06

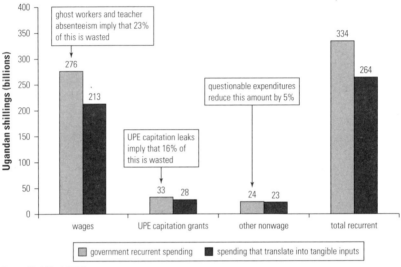

Source: World Bank 2007k.

Note: UPE = universal primary education.

The results of a MAMS simulation show that cutting unproductive expenditure and reallocating savings to sound programs in higher-priority areas, such as infrastructure, education, and health, can boost growth by 0.4–0.5 percent a year and improve a broad range of MDG indicators. Similar gains are observed if aid is scaled up and allocated to growth and MDG-oriented functions. Increasing expenditure by raising taxes, however, results in a decline of private investment growth (see table 3.9).

TABLE 3.9

Uganda: Baseline and Policy Simulations, 2020

MDG indicator	Base	Sim1	Sim2	Sim3	Sim4
National poverty headcount ratio (%)	21.0	22.8	18.7	17.0	23.0
Primary completion rate (%)	75.7	78.8	91.0	92.4	78.2
Under-5 mortality rate (%)	9.2	9.1	7.8	8.0	8.2
Improved access to safe water (%)	64.0	66.3	75.2	72.7	72.4

Source: Lofgren and Diaz-Bonilla 2006.

Note: Sim1 = 90 percent growth cut for infrastructure (roads and agriculture) and expansion of MDG-related human development; Sim2 = 50 percent growth cut for other (unproductive) government and expansion of infrastructure and MDG-related human development; Sim3 = doubled foreign aid increase and expansion of infrastructure and MDG-related human development within fiscal space limits; Sim4 = same government expansion as Sim3 and same foreign aid as Base, but financed by extra direct taxes.

The analysis points to a financing strategy that employs a mix of improved expenditure efficiency, higher aid, and domestic revenue mobilization that emphasizes improved collection and broadening of the tax base rather than higher tax rates. Over the longer term, the government aims to reduce reliance on foreign aid, an effort that will need careful design and phasing.

Debt Sustainability Analysis

According to the 2006 joint DSA, the risk of debt distress in Uganda is at the moderate level (IMF and World Bank 2006b). This primarily reflects substantial debt relief that Uganda received under the HIPC Initiative. The NPV of the debt-to-exports ratio was estimated at 179 percent in 2005, which is below its policy-dependent threshold of 200 percent.[11] Whereas these results are based on debt data before relief under the MDRI, the additional debt relief under the MDRI would reduce Uganda's NPV of debt-to-exports ratio to below 50 percent in 2007 and would decrease the debt service-to-exports ratio to 4 percent in 2007 from 16 percent in 2005. This will put Uganda at a low risk of debt stress. Looking ahead, prudent debt management policies and efficient use of new external resources will be needed to ensure that the debt burden remains low over the long term.

Summary and Challenges

The macroeconomic framework has advanced in several ways to respond to the policy challenges of scaling up foreign aid. New works regarding the macroeconomic management of aid distinguish between various degrees of absorption of aid in the current account and spending of aid in the budget, and their possible impact on the real exchange rate. The fiscal policy for growth emphasizes the development of an appropriate medium-term fiscal framework to achieve a stable expenditure path; an assessment of the efficiency and composition of public expenditures; and the building of budgetary, expenditure management, and monitoring systems. Managing the risk of aid volatility underscores risk management, which may include vulnerability assessments, polices for self-protection, and polices for self-insurance. The scope of the analytical framework also has expanded tremendously to meet the challenges of PRSPs, the MDGs, debt relief, and aid volatility. No doubt, the framework will continue to evolve in response to new issues. Some of the key remaining challenges are discussed below.

Sector Studies

The efficiency parameters of government services in bringing about the outcomes related to the MDGs need to be identified and evaluated in detailed sector studies underpinned by econometric analysis. The degrees of complementarity between government services and between MDG results are also areas for estimation in a multisector approach, such as the PER. So far, there is a lack of empirical data in many countries to estimate the relationship between expenditures on health, education, or related outcomes, or the relationship between investment and growth. What constitutes an appropriate overall approach and methodology is still quite open, but progress and estimations need to be made.

Policy and Institutional Environment

Sector studies, PERs, and MAMS scenarios are all within-country analyses. Any estimates of the productivity and complementarities of public expenditures, therefore, are conditioned by the policy and institutional environment prevailing in that country. Yet, the purpose of reforms is to improve the policy and institutional environment to improve the outcomes of public spending. To carefully incorporate the impact of changes in policy and institutional environment, sector studies have to be conducted in several countries, using a consistent methodology so that estimates can be compared across countries and against policy environments of different quality. The improved measurement of changes in policy and institutions, such as with the CPIA, also has long been an area of emphasis at the World Bank.

Scope of Public Sector and Public Expenditure

The proliferation of vertical funds in infrastructure, HIV/AIDS, and other areas makes aid accounting and projection more difficult in the management of aid absorption and spending. Faced with weak budgetary institutions and processes in recipient countries, the tendency of donors is to go outside the budget system with special donor funds to derive immediate results. However, this process fragments the budget and weakens budget institutions. Furthermore, to take into account more explicitly the complementarity or interplay between vertical funds and the government budgets, and to assess the efficiency and composition of various forms of public spending, the definition of the "public sector" will need to go beyond the budget of the central government to encompass the nongovernmental organizations and independent agencies that benefit directly from the vertical funds.

Risk Management of Aid Fluctuations

What are the optimal or practical decision rules for smoothing aid fluctuations and the resulting expenditure path? How should they be incorporated and accounted for in the macroeconomic framework. Many questions and much work remain.

Donor Coordination

Most of the observations thus far on the macroeconomic framework are made from the viewpoint of the countries receiving aid. Donors, however, also will play a critical role in determining whether their additional financing of public spending will bring about greater results. Several areas are important: (1) enhanced donor coordination to maximize interplay and interactions of projects and to avoid duplication, (2) a greater commitment to long-term and predictable levels of aid, (3) support to initiatives for a well-designed PRS and medium-term expenditure programs in support of the MDGs, and (4) support for well-defined reserve accumulation efforts for smoothing expenditure or donor pooling of some reserves. Much like the debt sustainability analysis, the integration of macro and micro aspects to the economic framework for scaling up aid and the attainment of the MDGs will require greater collaboration between the two Bretton Woods institutions.

Annex: Selected Economic Indicators

TABLE 3A.1
Overall Fiscal Balance, Including Grants, 1997–2007

Country	1997–2001	2002	2003	2004	2005	2006	2007
Ethiopia	−5.6	−7.6	−7.0	−3.2	−4.7	−4.4	−5.4
Ghana	−8.4	−5.0	−3.3	−3.1	−1.7	−6.2	−5.6
Kenya	−0.9	−3.2	−1.7	−0.1	−1.8	−3.2	−3.3
Madagascar	−3.8	−6.2	−4.8	−5.7	−4.3	36.2	−4.4
Mozambique	−3.6	−7.2	−4.1	−4.3	−2.1	−2.0	−4.6
Rwanda	−2.0	−1.9	−2.5	−0.2	0.7	−0.2	−2.1
Tanzania	−1.0	−1.0	−1.4	−3.0	−3.2	−5.2	−5.0
Uganda	−3.0	−5.3	−4.3	−1.7	−0.6	−0.9	−1.8
Non-oil countries	−1.8	−4.4	−4.4	−2.3	1.4	8.1	1.3

Source: IMF 2007c.

Note: Shading indicates projections.

TABLE 3A.2
Overall Fiscal Balance, Excluding Grants, 1997–2007

Country	1997–2001	2002	2003	2004	2005	2006	2007
Ethiopia	−8.5	−11.4	−13.6	−8.1	−9.4	−8.5	−10.7
Ghana	−11.2	−8.1	−8.0	−9.5	−6.9	−11.3	−10.2
Kenya	−1.8	−3.9	−3.6	−1.3	−3.0	−4.4	−4.5
Madagascar	−7.8	−8.4	−9.9	−13.9	−10.1	−10.9	−9.5
Mozambique	−13.8	−17.5	−13.6	−11.8	−8.6	−12.7	−16.5
Rwanda	−9.1	−9.1	−10.5	−12.3	−13.4	−13.2	−14.7
Tanzania	−4.5	−5.1	−7.2	−8.6	−10.4	−10.9	−12.7
Uganda	−8.7	−12.3	−10.9	−10.7	−8.5	−7.5	−8.2
Non-oil countries	−4.0	−7.2	−6.7	−4.3	−0.8	−1.8	−2.7

Source: IMF 2007c.

Note: Shading indicates projections.

TABLE 3A.3
Overall Fiscal Balance, Including Grants, Less ODA, 1997–2007

Country	1997–2001	2002	2003	2004	2005	2006	2007
Ethiopia	−14.9	−25.3	−27.1	−21.9	−22.0	—	—
Ghana	−18.1	−15.5	−15.9	−18.5	−12.1	—	—
Kenya	−4.2	−6.2	−5.3	−4.2	−5.9	—	—
Madagascar	−16.3	−14.6	−14.6	−34.3	−22.7	—	—
Mozambique	−28.3	−61.0	−25.7	−25.4	−21.5	—	—
Rwanda	−18.9	−22.3	−22.4	−26.8	−26.0	—	—
Tanzania	−13.1	−13.6	−18.0	−18.6	−15.6	—	—
Uganda	−15.1	−17.5	−19.9	−19.3	−14.3	—	—
Non-oil countries	—	—	—	—	—	—	—

Sources: IMF 2007c; World Bank World Development Indicators for official development assistance data.

Note: — = not available.

TABLE 3A.4
Overall External Account Balance, Including Grants, 1997–2007

Country	1997–2001	2002	2003	2004	2005	2006	2007
Ethiopia	−3.5	−4.7	−2.2	−5.3	−8.6	−11.6	−10.0
Ghana	−8.9	0.5	1.7	−2.7	−7.0	−8.2	−8.4
Kenya	−2.9	2.2	−0.2	−1.3	−3.0	−3.3	−4.1
Madagascar	−5.1	−6.0	−4.9	−9.1	−10.4	−8.9	−8.6
Mozambique	−17.3	−19.3	−15.1	−8.6	−11.0	−10.4	−11.8
Rwanda	−7.6	−6.7	−7.8	−0.3	−3.2	−8.1	−9.4
Tanzania	−7.3	−6.8	−4.7	−3.9	−5.2	−9.3	−11.0
Uganda	−6.4	−4.9	−5.8	−1.2	−2.1	−4.1	−4.4
Non-oil countries	−0.7	−2.6	−0.7	−0.4	3.6	7.2	7.2

Source: IMF 2007c.

Note: Shading indicates projections.

TABLE 3A.5
Overall External Account Balance, Excluding Grants, 1997–2007

Country	1997–2001	2002	2003	2004	2005	2006	2007
Ethiopia	−7.0	−10.5	−9.7	−11.2	−15.2	−18.1	−16.8
Ghana	−12.2	−3.1	−3.5	−8.8	−12.3	−11.2	−11.7
Kenya	−3.2	2.2	−0.6	−1.4	−3.0	−3.6	−4.1
Madagascar	−6.2	−6.1	−7.5	−12.9	−11.7	−10.1	−9.4
Mozambique	−23.8	−23.0	−19.9	−14.1	−16.3	−16.3	−20.9
Rwanda	−16.8	−16.6	−19.2	−18.2	−19.4	−18.8	−20.7
Tanzania	−12.3	−9.4	−8.2	−7.5	−5.8	−13.2	−15.0
Uganda	−12.8	−13.2	−13.5	−11.0	−10.6	−9.9	−11.3
Non-oil countries	−5.2	−6.7	−4.9	−5.4	−1.5	−1.6	−1.3

Source: IMF 2007c.

Note: Shading indicates projections.

TABLE 3A.6
Overall External Account Balance, Including Grants, Less ODA, 1997–2007

Country	1997–2001	2002	2003	2004	2005	2006	2007
Ethiopia	−12.8	−22.4	−22.3	−24.0	−25.9	—	—
Ghana	−18.6	−10.0	−10.9	−18.1	−17.4	—	—
Kenya	−6.2	−0.8	−3.8	−5.4	−7.1	—	—
Madagascar	−17.6	−14.4	−14.7	−37.7	−28.8	—	—
Mozambique	−42.0	−73.1	−36.7	−29.7	−30.4	—	—
Rwanda	−24.5	−27.1	−27.7	−26.9	−29.9	—	—
Tanzania	−19.4	−19.4	−21.3	−19.5	−17.6	—	—
Uganda	−18.5	−17.1	−21.4	−18.8	−15.8	—	—
Non-oil countries	—	—	—	—	—	—	—

Sources: IMF 2007c; World Bank *World Development Indicators* for official development assistance data.

Note: — = not available.

TABLE 3A.7
Real Effective Exchange Rates, 1997–2007

Country	1997–2001	2002	2003	2004	2005	2006	2007
Ethiopia	99.0	87.1	90.1	85.0	91.3	99.9	—
Ghana	130.5	99.8	100.5	99.4	109.5	115.9	—
Kenya	100.2	105.1	106.6	104.1	116.2	135.3	—
Madagascar	98.3	119.9	106.0	80.4	85.0	85.7	—
Mozambique	97.2	90.5	79.7	83.5	85.3	85.6	—
Rwanda	105.3	86.5	72.6	69.6	75.4	79.6	—
Tanzania	98.8	90.8	75.0	67.7	65.7	62.6	—
Uganda	109.9	93.5	81.8	84.6	88.8	87.9	—
Non-oil countries	102.1	98.7	101.1	99.8	96.7	97.5	—

Source: IMF 2007c.

Note: — = not available. Annual average for 2000 = 100.

TABLE 3A.8
Real GDP Annual Growth, 1997–2007
Percent

Country	1997–2001	2002	2003	2004	2005	2006	2007
Ethiopia	3.8	1.2	−3.5	13.1	10.3	10.6	6.5
Ghana	4.2	4.5	5.2	5.6	5.9	6.2	6.3
Kenya	2.3	0.3	2.8	4.5	5.8	6.0	6.2
Madagascar	4.6	−12.7	9.8	5.3	4.6	4.7	5.6
Mozambique	9.2	8.2	7.9	7.5	7.8	8.5	6.8
Rwanda	8.6	9.4	0.9	4.0	6.0	4.2	4.7
Tanzania	4.4	7.2	5.7	6.7	6.8	5.9	7.3
Uganda	5.5	6.9	4.4	5.7	6.7	5.4	6.2
Non-oil countries	5.1	7.0	4.8	5.9	5.6	5.1	5.0

Source: IMF 2007c.

Note: Shading indicates projections.

TABLE 3A.9
Annual Changes in Consumer Price Index, 1997–2007
Percent

Country	1997–2001	2002	2003	2004	2005	2006	2007
Ethiopia	0.6	−7.2	15.1	8.6	6.8	12.3	17.0
Ghana	22.9	14.8	26.7	12.6	15.1	10.9	9.4
Kenya	8.0	2.0	9.8	11.6	10.3	14.1	4.1
Madagascar	7.3	16.2	−1.1	14.0	18.4	10.8	9.6
Mozambique	6.7	16.8	13.5	12.6	6.4	13.2	5.9
Rwanda	4.7	2.0	7.4	12.0	9.2	5.5	5.0
Tanzania	9.8	4.6	4.4	4.1	4.4	5.8	5.5
Uganda	4.8	−2.0	5.7	5.0	8.0	6.6	5.8
Non-oil countries	9.8	8.5	11.5	11.3	14.8	15.4	13.7

Source: IMF 2007c.

Note: Shading indicates projections.

Notes

This chapter was written as a background note for a World Bank paper (2007b). Comments were received from Louise Cord and Mohammad Zia M. Qureshi. Input and information about country cases, an update of the analytical work program concerning scaled-up aid and MDG scenarios, and the macroeconomic framework also were provided by several economists at the World Bank. In particular, we would like to thank Gilles Alfandari, Gregor Binkert, Zeljko Bogetic, Maurizio Bussolo, Carlos B. Cavalcanti, Siaka Coulibaly, Kene Ezemenari, Kathie Krumm, Praveen Kumar, Hans Lofgren, Antonio Nucifora, Sudhir Shetty, Mark Thomas, Robert Utz, and Paolo B. Zacchia.

1. See, for example, a recent survey in Roodman (2007).
2. This would be more evident if the real exchange rate were defined in terms of the relative price of tradable and nontradable goods, based on the familiar Salter-Swan "dependent economy." For example, see Hinkle and Montiel (1999).
3. In April 2005, the Bank and IMF boards endorsed an operational framework for debt sustainability (see, for example, World Bank 2006a).
4. A billion is 1,000 millions.
5. This subsection draws on Berg et al. (2007).
6. This subsection draws on Lofgren and Diaz-Bonilla (2005) and Sundberg and Lofgren (2006).
7. This section is derived from various sources: Bandiera, Kumar, and Pinto (2007), Lofgren and Kumar (2007), and World Bank (2007d, 2007e).
8. The World Bank CPIA index classifies Madagascar as a medium performer. Accordingly, the thresholds applicable for Madagascar are (1) NPV of debt-to-exports ratio of 150, (2) NPV of debt-to-GDP ratio of 40, (3) NPV of debt-to-fiscal revenues ratio of 250, and (4) debt service-to-exports ratio of 20.
9. One of the central themes in Rwanda's 2007 CEM was the management and effective use of public resources, with a chapter on "Managing Aid Flows for Growth and Poverty Reduction," accompanied by a report on creating fiscal space (World Bank 2007h). The IMF also prepared a DSA in 2007 to evaluate the potential impact of scaled-up aid on Rwanda's debt sustainability.
10. The World Bank's CPIA index classifies Tanzania as a stronger performer. Accordingly, debt thresholds are NPV of debt-to-GDP ratio of 50, NPV of debt-to-export ratio of 200, and debt service-to-exports ratio of 25.
11. According to the World Bank CPIA Index, Uganda is rated as a high performer; accordingly, the indicative threshold applicable for Uganda is 200 percent for the NPV of debt-to-exports ratio.

References

Adam, C. 2006. "Dutch Disease—Where Do We Stand?" In *The Macroeconomic Management of Foreign Aid—Opportunities and Pitfalls,* ed. P. Isard, L. Lipschitz, A. Mourmouras, and B. Yontcheva, 171–96. Washington, DC: International Monetary Fund.

Adam, C., and D. Bevan. 2004. "Aid and the Supply Side: Public Investment, Export Performance, and Dutch Disease in Low-Income Countries." Discussion Paper 201, Department of Economics, University of Oxford, Oxford, UK.

Agénor, P.-R., N. Bayraktar, E. P. Moreira, and K. El Aynaoui. 2005. "Achieving the Millennium Development Goals in Sub-Saharan Africa: A Macroeconomic Monitoring Framework." Policy Research Working Paper 3750, World Bank, Washington, DC.

Bandiera, L., P. Kumar, and B. Pinto. 2007. "Kenya: Reforms, Stabilization—and Growth at Last?" Background paper for the Kenya Country Economic Memorandum, World Bank, Washington, DC.

Berg, A., S. Aiyar, M. Hussain, S. Roache, T. Mirzoev, and A. Mahone. 2007. *The Macroeconomics of Scaling Up Aid—Lessons from Recent Experience.* Occasional Paper 253. Washington, DC: International Monetary Fund.

Bevan, D. 2007. "Fiscal Policy for Growth with Stability." Background paper, World Bank, Washington, DC.

Bourguignon, F., C. Diaz-Bonilla, and H. Lofgren. Forthcoming. "Aid, Service Delivery and the MDGs in an Economy-Wide Framework." In *The Impact of Economic Policies on Poverty and Income Distribution—Macro-Micro Evaluation Techniques and Tools,* ed. F. Bourguignon, L. Pereira da Silva, and M. Bussolo. New York: Palgrave.

Bourguignon, F., F. H.G. Ferreira, and N. Lustig, eds. 2005. *The Microeconomics of Income Distribution Dynamics in East Asia and Latin America.* New York: Oxford University Press.

Bourguignon, F., and L. A. Pereira da Silva, eds. 2003. *The Impact of Economic Policies on Poverty and Income Distribution.* New York: Oxford University Press.

Bourguignon, F., L. Pereira da Silva, and M. Bussolo, eds. Forthcoming. *The Impact of Economic Policies on Poverty and Income Distribution—Macro-Micro Evaluation Techniques and Tools.* New York: Palgrave.

Bourguignon, F., A.-S. Robilliard, and S. Robinson. 2002. "Representative vs. Real Households in the Macroeconomic Modeling of Inequality." Photocopy. International Food Policy Research Institute, Washington, DC.

Datt, G., K. Ramadas, D. van der Mensbrugghe, T. Walker, and Q. Wodon. 2003. "Predicting the Effect of Aggregate Growth on Poverty." In *The Impact of Economic Policies on Poverty and Income Distribution,* ed. F. Bourguignon and L. A. Pereira da Silva, 215–34. New York: Oxford University Press.

Devarajan, S., and D. S. Go. 2003. "The 123PRSP Model." In *The Impact of Economic Policies on Poverty and Income Distribution,* ed. F. Bourguignon and L. A. Pereirra da Silva, 277–300. New York: Oxford University Press.

Elbadawi, I., and L. Kaltani. 2007. "Scaling-Up Aid for Ghana: Maintaining Competitiveness, Avoiding the Dutch Disease, and Accelerating Growth." Background paper for the Ghana Country Economic Memorandum, World Bank, Washington, DC.

Essama-Nssah, B., D. S. Go, M. Kearney, V. Korman, S. Robinson, and K. Thierfelder. 2007. "Economy-wide and Distributional Impact of an Oil Price Shock on the South African Economy." Policy Research Working Paper 4354, World Bank, Washington, DC.

Gupta, S., R. Powell, and Y. Yang. 2006. "Macroeconomic Challenges of Scaling Up Aid to Africa—A Checklist for Practitioners." Photocopy. International Monetary Fund, Washington, DC.

Heller, P. S. 2005. "Understanding Fiscal Space." Policy Discussion Paper PDP/05/4, International Monetary Fund, Washington, DC.

Heller, P. S., M. Katz, X. Debrum, T. Thomas, T. Koreanchelian, and I. Adenauer. 2006. "Making Fiscal Space Happen: Managing Fiscal Policy in a World of Scaled-Up Aid." Policy Discussion Paper PDP/06/270, International Monetary Fund, Washington, DC.

Hinkle, L. E., and P. J. Montiel, eds. 1999. *Exchange Rate Misalignment—Concepts and Measurement for Developing Countries.* Washington, DC: World Bank.

IDA and IMF (International Development Association and International Monetary Fund). 2006. "Tanzania: Poverty Reduction Strategy Paper-Joint Staff Advisory Note." Washington, DC.

IMF (International Monetary Fund). 2005. "The Macroeconomics of Managing Increased Aid Inflows: Experiences of Low-Income Countries and Policy Implications." Washington, DC.

———. 2007a. "Aid Inflows—The Role of the Fund and Operational Issues for Program Design." Photocopy. Washington, DC.

———. 2007b. "Fiscal Policy Response to Scaled-Up Aid." Photocopy. Fiscal Affairs Department, Washington, DC.

———. 2007c. *Regional Economic Outlook: Sub-Saharan Africa.* Washington, DC.

———. 2007d. "United Republic of Tanzania: Sixth Review Under the Three-Year Arrangement Under the Poverty Reduction and Growth Facility and Request for a Three-Year Policy Support Instrument." Country Report 07/138, Washington, DC.

IMF and World Bank. 2006a. "Rwanda: Joint Debt Sustainability Analysis." Washington, DC.

———. 2006b. "Uganda: Joint Debt Sustainability Analysis." Washington, DC.

———. 2006c. "The Federal Democratic Republic of Ethiopia: Joint Debt Sustainability Analysis." Washington, DC.

———. 2006d. "The Republic of Madagascar: Joint Debt Sustainability Analysis." Washington, DC.

Isard, P., L. Lipschitz, A. Mourmouras, and B. Yontcheva, eds. 2006. *The Macroeconomic Management of Foreign Aid—Opportunities and Pitfalls.* Washington, DC: International Monetary Fund.

Klugman, J., ed. 2002. *A Sourcebook for Poverty Reduction Strategies.* Washington, DC: World Bank.

Krumm, K. 2007. "AFR Fiscal Policy for Growth (aka Fiscal Space)." Africa Region, World Bank, PowerPoint presentation to the Regional Leadership Team, Washington, DC, July 18.

Lofgren, H., and C. Diaz-Bonilla. 2005. "Economywide Simulations of Ethiopian MDG Strategies." Photocopy. World Bank, Washington, DC.

———. 2006. "Patterns of Growth and Public Spending in Uganda: Alternative Scenarios for 2003–2020." Background paper for the Uganda Country Economic Memorandum, World Bank, Washington, DC.

Lofgren, H., and P. Kumar. 2007. "The Challenges of Achieving Kenya's Vision 2030: A Macro Perspective." Background paper for the Kenya Country Economic Memorandum, World Bank, Washington, DC.

Mattina, T. 2006. "Money Isn't Everything: The Challenge of Scaling Up Aid to Achieve the Millennium Development Goals in Ethiopia." Working Paper WP/06/192, International Monetary Fund, Washington, DC.

Mensbrugghe, D. van der, and S. Tan. 2006. "A MAMS Approach to Analyzing the Millennium Development Goals in Madagascar." Photocopy. World Bank, Washington, DC.

Mirzoev, T. 2007. "Modelling Aid Inflows in a Small and Open Economy." In *The Macroeconomics of Scaling Up Aid—Lessons from Recent Experience,* ed. A. Berg, S. Aiyar, M. Hussain, S. Roache, T. Mirzoev, and A. Mahone, 87–100. Occasional Paper 253. Washington, DC: International Monetary Fund.

Pereira da Silva, L. A., B. Essama-Nssah, and I. Samaké. 2003. "Linking Aggregate Macroconsistency Models to Household Surveys: A Poverty Analysis Macroeconomic Simulator, or PAMS." In *The Impact of Economic Policies on Poverty and Income Distribution,* ed. F. Bourguignon and L. A. Pereirra da Silva, 235–60. New York: Oxford University Press.

Republic of Rwanda. 2006. "Scaling Up to Achieve the Health MDGs in Rwanda." A Background Study for the High-Level Forum, Tunis, June 12–13.

Roodman, D. 2007. "The Anarchy of Numbers: Aid, Development, and Cross-Country Empirics." *World Bank Economic Review* 21(2): 255–77.

Sundberg, M., and H. Lofgren. 2006. "Absorptive Capacity and Achieving MDGs: The Case of Ethiopia." In *The Macroeconomic Management of Foreign Aid—Opportunities and Pitfalls,* ed. P. Isard, L. Lipschitz, A. Mourmouras, and B. Yontcheva, 141–67. Washington, DC: International Monetary Fund.

Ter-Minassian, T. 2007. "Making Fiscal Space Happen: Managing Fiscal Policy in a World of Scaled-Up Aid." Fiscal Affairs Department, International Monetary Fund, PowerPoint presentation to the European Commission, Brussels, March 21.

Wodon, Q., K. Ramadas, and D. van der Mensbrugghe. 2003. "SimSIP Poverty Module." Available at http://www.worldbank.org/simsip.

World Bank. 2001. "Zambia Public Expenditure Review—Public Expenditure, Growth and Poverty: A Synthesis." Report 22543-ZA, Washington, DC.

———. 2003. "Supporting Sound Policies with Adequate and Appropriate Financing." Paper prepared for the Development Committee Meeting, Dubai, September 22.

———. 2006a. "Review of Low-Income Country Debt Sustainability Framework and Implications of the Multilateral Debt Relief Initiative (MDRI)." Report IDA/R2006-0046, Washington, DC.

———. 2006b. "Tanzania—Public Expenditure and Financial Accountability Review: FY05." Background paper, Washington, DC.

———. 2006c. "Uganda: Beyond Recovery: Investment and Behavior Change for Growth." Country Economic Memorandum, vol. 1, Washington, DC.

———. 2007a. "Aid Architecture: An Overview of the Main Trends in Official Development Assistance Flows." IDA 15 background paper, Washington, DC.

———. 2007b, "Country-Based Scaling Up: Assessment of Progress and Agenda for Action." Background paper, Washington, DC.

———. 2007c. "Efficiency of Government Education Expenditures in Kenya." Background paper, Washington, DC.

———. 2007d. "Fiscal Policy for Growth and Development—Further Analysis and Lessons from Country Case Studies." Background paper, Washington, DC.

———. 2007e. "Fiscal Space for Kenya—Health Sector." Background paper for the Kenya Country Economic Memorandum, Washington, DC.

———. 2007f. "Ghana CEM: Meeting the Challenge of Accelerated and Shared Growth.: Ghana's Growth and Poverty Reduction Story." Washington, DC.

———. 2007g. "MAMS for Tanzania: Data Sources, Assumptions, and Preliminary Results." Photocopy. Washington, DC.

———. 2007h. "Rwanda: Toward Sustained Growth and Competitiveness." Country Economic Memorandum, Report 36860-RW, Washington, DC.

———. 2007i. "The Ethiopia Accelerating Equitable Growth Country Economic Memorandum." Washington, DC.

———. 2007j. "The Role of IDA in the Global Aid Architecture: Supporting the Country-Based Development Model." IDA 15 background paper, Washington, DC.

———. 2007k. "Uganda: Fiscal Policy for Growth." Public Expenditure Review, Report 40161-UG, Washington, DC.

CHAPTER 4

More and Better Aid: How Are Donors Doing?

Punam Chuhan-Pole and Brendan Fitzpatrick

In recent years, donors have committed to providing more and better aid in a number of international forums. At the 2002 International Conference on Financing for Development, held in Monterrey, Mexico, donors agreed to scale up aid resources to developing countries. Building on these commitments at their 2005 summit in Gleneagles, Scotland, the leaders of the Group of Eight major industrial countries pledged to increase aid to sub-Saharan Africa by $25 billion[1] a year by 2010, and donors agreed to increase aid by another $25 billion elsewhere. Along with pledges of higher aid volumes, donors and partner countries alike are focused on improving the effectiveness of aid through better alignment, harmonization, and coordination. This commitment to enhance the quality of aid is embodied in the 2005 Paris Declaration on Aid Effectiveness, which builds on the 2003 High-Level Forum on Harmonization in Rome.

This chapter assesses the recent progress on scaling up the quantity and quality of aid in developing countries, especially sub-Saharan Africa. It reviews whether donors are providing more aid, especially to countries with demonstrated potential to use increased resources effectively; and whether aid is becoming more predictable and long term. It also presents progress on the harmonization and alignment agenda, and addresses the special challenge presented by a changing aid landscape—proliferation of aid channels, substantial degree of earmarking, and fragmentation—to donors and partner countries.

Progress on Scaling Up Aid Volumes Is Mixed

The international community has committed itself to a global partnership to promote development and reduce poverty. In 2000 the United Nations adopted the Millennium Development Goals (MDGs)—eight goals and 18 targets to be achieved by 2015—against which the global community can measure progress toward reducing poverty. At the 2002 United Nations Conference on Financing for Development, the international community adopted the Monterrey Consensus, which created a new framework of mutual accountability for meeting these goals between developed and developing countries. That consensus recognizes the need to harness global forces to tackle poverty through

- better access by developing-country producers to industrial country markets;

- better access by poor countries to international financial resources to boost investment in health, education, and infrastructure and to reduce vulnerability to external shocks and natural disasters;

- debt relief for heavily indebted poor countries (HIPCs) to free up resources for investing in health, education, and water and sanitation and to reduce debt overhang; and

- adaptation of technological and scientific advances and medical research to benefit the poor directly.

For their part, developing countries need to pursue sound policies and make a commitment to good governance, which is central to development. Governments in developing countries need to be accountable to their citizens for the delivery of services such as health, education, and infrastructure and for their use of resources. Strengthening the quality of developing countries' public financial management is central to this framework. Building on the Monterrey Consensus, there is an urgent need for all parties—developed and developing countries alike—to scale up their actions.

During 2005 the international community sharpened its focus on aid. At their summit in Gleneagles, the leaders of the Group of Eight countries pledged to double their aid to Africa—an annual increase of $25 billion (in real terms)—by 2010, and donors worldwide agreed to expand their overall aid to all developing countries by about $50 billion. Major progress also was made in 2005 in extending and deepening debt relief to the poorest countries through the Multilateral Debt Relief Initiative (MDRI). That initiative cancels 100 percent of the debt that HIPCs owe to the African Development Fund, the International Development Association (IDA), the International Monetary Fund (IMF), and the Inter-American Development Bank (which joined the initiative in March 2007). To date, 22 post-completion point HIPCs have benefited from debt relief amounting to about $38 billion in nominal terms under the MDRI.[2] The remaining HIPCs will qualify automatically for the MDRI when they reach the completion point.

Recent Trends in Global Official Development Assistance

Have donors delivered on their pledges of higher aid? After declining sharply in the mid-1990s, official development assistance (ODA) has rebounded. Aid (measured in real terms) from members of the Development Assistance Committee (DAC) of the Organisation for Economic Co-operation and Development (OECD) climbed to a record $107 billion in 2005, up from $69 billion in 2001 and $59 billion in 1997. Although aid edged lower in 2006, the expansion in real terms in 2001–06 was about 45 percent, representing an average annual increase of 7.7 percent.[3] Over this same period, the share of ODA in donors' combined gross national income (GNI) climbed from 0.22 percent to 0.30 percent, but remained below the level of the early 1990s (figure 4.1).

Although a stepped-up focus on aid post-Monterrey has boosted aggregate aid levels since 2001, a substantial amount of the expansion in ODA is the result of higher amounts of debt relief. For example, the 2005 jump in ODA ($27.3 billion) and the subsequent pullback were driven by debt relief operations (figure 4.2). Exceptional debt relief to Iraq and to Nigeria boosted net debt relief grants to $22.7 billion in 2005, an increase of $18 billion over 2004 levels. These grants fell off in 2006 to $19.2 billion, but still represented a substantial share (nearly a fifth) of ODA; by contrast, net debt relief grants made up less than 5 percent of ODA in 2000–01.

Debt relief from the donors' perspective (budget effort) can be quite different from that of the recipients' perspective (availability of resources). Debt relief represents additional financial resources for recipients if debt is

FIGURE 4.1
Trends in DAC Members' Real ODA (Net), 1990–2006

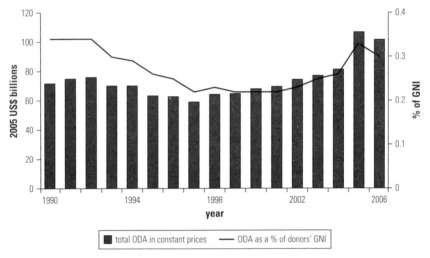

Source: OECD-DAC database.

Note: DAC = Development Assistance Committee; GNI = gross national income; ODA = official development assistance; OECD = Organisation for Economic Co-operation and Development.

FIGURE 4.2
Increase in ODA for Debt Relief, 2000–06

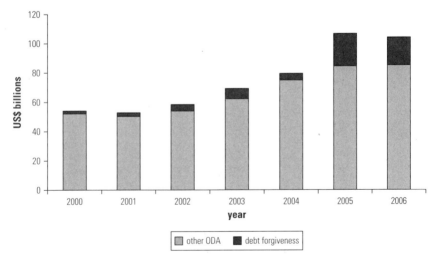

Source: OECD-DAC database.

being serviced. But if a country is not servicing its debt because of an unbearable debt burden and under reasonable conditions is clearly unable to meet its obligations to external creditors, then debt relief amounts to an accounting exercise for the recipient. Hence, one important question that arises is whether ODA debt forgiveness grants represent additional flows (cross-border flows) to recipients. At Monterrey, donors pledged that debt relief would not displace other components of ODA.

Other components of aid have grown at a much slower pace than has debt relief. ODA for core development programs—that is, ODA excluding debt relief, humanitarian aid, and administrative costs—expanded by 19 percent in 2001–06. A winding down of debt relief operations in the near term will affect ODA flows, including those in 2007. Other categories of net ODA will have to expand very rapidly in the near term if donor promises of an additional $50 billion in annual aid (over 2004 levels) are to be met by 2010. This need for expansion is prompting concern that donors may fail to deliver on their aid promises.

In recent years, a wide range of other donors—official and private—have expanded their assistance to developing countries. ODA from non-DAC reporters (that is, non-DAC countries that report aid flows to the DAC) grew threefold during 2001–05, and is set to rise further: Saudi Arabia and other Middle East countries provided about $2 billion in assistance in 2005 and the Republic of Korea and Turkey provided $750 million and $600 million, respectively. And emerging-market donors such as Brazil, China, India, the Russian Federation, and South Africa are becoming more important providers of official support to poor countries. Private giving through foundations, charities, and other nongovernmental organizations (NGOs) has grown briskly: for example, DAC statistics show that own funds raised by NGOs have more than doubled over 2001–05, reaching $14.7 billion in 2005. Data n private assistance (NGOs, private voluntary organizations, foundations, corporations, educational scholarships, and religious organizations) are quite incomplete. Indeed, a recent report (Kharas 2007) puts U.S. private international giving at $33.5 billion in 2005.

Aid to Sub-Saharan Africa: Actions Lag Promises

Aid to sub-Saharan Africa has risen in real terms from its substantial slide in the second half of the 1990s. After climbing to more than $23 billion in

FIGURE 4.3
Net ODA to Sub-Saharan Africa, 1990–2006

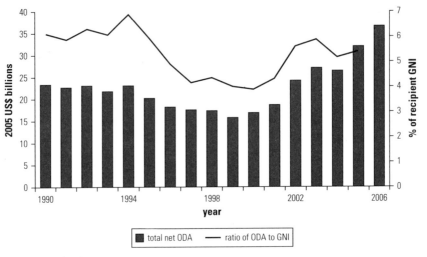

Source: OECD-DAC database.

1990, real ODA (in 2005 U.S. dollars) contracted by almost one-third during 1990–99. This pattern reversed beginning in 2000 and ODA volumes
have more than doubled since then (figure 4.3). The improving trend in
overall ODA is reflected also in a larger share of assistance going to the
region. A third of bilateral DAC flows was allocated to African countries
in 2004–05, compared with about a quarter in 1999–2000 and 29 percent
in 1994–95; the share of flows to the region is higher when ODA from
multilateral agencies is included in the totals—36 percent in 2004–05,
30 percent in 1999–2000, and 34 percent in 1994–95. Most aid to the
region is in the form of grants: bilateral donors provide practically all their
assistance as grants (95 percent of gross bilateral aid); and multilateral
ODA consists of highly concessional loans and grants, with the share of
grants rising from 41 percent in 2000 to 56 percent in 2005.

Although the positive trend in development assistance to sub-Saharan
Africa is encouraging, these flows have yet to translate into substantial
additional resources for the region. Although bilateral donors are providing larger amounts of aid to the region and are allocating a larger share of
ODA to sub-Saharan Africa, much of the increase represents debt relief
grants. For example, bilateral net ODA from DAC members rose by 23 percent to $28 billion (preliminary) in 2006, with debt relief grants accounting

FIGURE 4.4

Rising Share of Debt Relief in Aid Flows to Sub-Saharan Africa, 2000–06

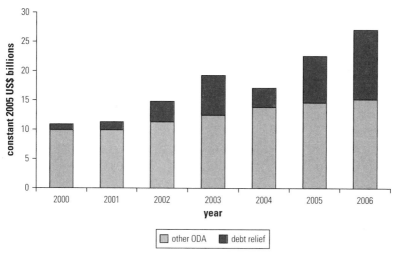

Sources: OECD-DAC database; authors' estimates.

for more than three-quarters of that increase (figure 4.4). The increase in ODA excluding these grants was about 5 percent. During 2005–06, debt relief grants averaged about 40 percent of bilateral aid. These grants also helped boost overall aid flows to the region to an estimated $37 billion in 2006, from $32 billion in 2005. The prominence of debt relief in aid flows is evident since 2001: net ODA in real terms (2005 U.S. dollars) to the region more than doubled over 2001–06, but close to 70 percent of the expansion represented debt relief.

Donor focus on sub-Saharan Africa has been prompted primarily by the region's growth performance, which has lagged that of other regions, and an increasing concentration of poverty in Africa.[4] In the 1990s, growth averaged 2.3 percent a year in the region and per capita incomes stagnated; growth has picked up more recently, however. By contrast, developing countries as a whole grew at an average annual rate of 3.8 percent and per capita income growth averaged 2.1 percent a year. The region's poverty rate—the percent of people living in extreme poverty (under $1 a day)—remained stubbornly high at approximately 47 percent in the 1990s, and only recently has begun to show a sustained decline. As donor allocations have become more selective in terms of need and as donors are directing a larger share of aid to sub-Saharan

FIGURE 4.5
Trends in Size of Aid Relative to GNI and Per Capita Aid, by Region, 1990–2006

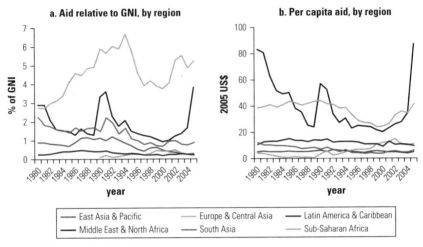

Sources: OECD-DAC database; authors' estimates.

Africa, the size of ODA relative to recipients' GNI and aid per capita levels
have risen (figure 4.5). At more than 5 percent in 2001–05, the average
size of aid relative to recipients' GNI was nearly threefold larger than
that for the Middle East and more than fivefold larger than that for
South Asia.

The share of bilateral donors in total aid to Africa grew in 1991–2005.
Bilateral donors now account for more than two-thirds of the aid to the
region, compared with approximately 60 percent in 1991–2000. The
United States is now the largest country donor to sub-Saharan Africa, followed by France, the United Kingdom, and Germany (figure 4.6). Several
bilateral donors, such as Belgium, Denmark, France, Ireland, Luxembourg,
the Netherlands, Portugal, Sweden, and the United Kingdom, allocated
over half or more of their bilateral net ODA to the region in 2004–05.
Among multilateral donors, the IDA and the European Commission continue to be the largest donors to the region.

Newer donors are gaining importance in Africa. The growing global
prominence of emerging economies means that these countries also are
becoming more significant in terms of trade, investment, and financial
flows to poor countries. For example, both China and India doubled their

FIGURE 4.6
Sub-Saharan Africa's Largest Donors, 1991–2005

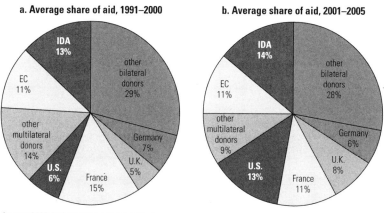

a. Average share of aid, 1991–2000   b. Average share of aid, 2001–2005

Sources: OECD-DAC database; authors' estimates.

annual growth rates of imports from Africa between 1990–94 and 1999–04, and those two countries also account for 50 percent of Asia's exports to Africa.[5] Foreign direct investment (FDI) in Africa from emerging economies, particularly Brazil, China, India, Malaysia, and South Africa, is also substantially higher. Newly emerging donors are increasing their assistance to other developing countries. For example, one study estimated that China's annual aid to Africa was about $1.0–$1.5 billion in 2004–05, up from about $310 million a year for 1989–92.[6] China also has provided debt relief to African countries (an estimated $1.5 billion) and has pledged to double its assistance to Africa by 2009 (that is, over three years).[7]

Despite an expansion in private resource flows to sub-Saharan Africa, official aid continues to be the largest source of external financing for the region. At approximately $37 billion in 2006, development assistance to the region outpaced nondebt private financial flows, such as FDI and portfolio equity inflows ($28.6 billion) and inward remittances ($9 billion). Although the share of aid in foreign financial flows has declined sharply from the highs of the early 1990s, it remains substantial at close to 50 percent (figure 4.7).[8] Recorded worker remittances to sub-Saharan Africa have been small but remarkably stable and growing in importance over time, equivalent to 23 percent to 37 percent of ODA flows since 1997.

FIGURE 4.7
Sources of External Finance for Sub-Saharan Africa, 1980–2006

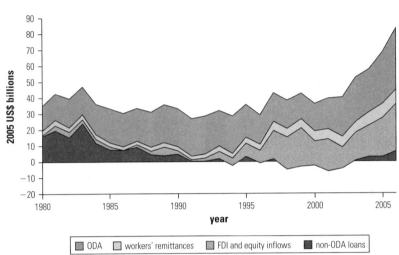

Sources: OECD-DAC database; World Bank Global Development Finance Database; authors' estimates.

Note: FDI = foreign direct investment. All categories of flows are positive, except for non-ODA loans in 1994, 1996, and 1998–2002. Non-ODA loans are nonconcessional official loans and private-source loans.

FDI and equity inflows have assumed much greater importance since the mid-1990s, exceeding the value of total aid in some years (for example, in 2001).

These figures mask sharp variations across countries. Both portfolio equity investment and FDI are highly concentrated in just a few countries, with more than 99 percent of equity inflows going to South Africa and almost 60 percent of FDI going to South Africa and the oil-rich economies of Angola, Equatorial Guinea, and Nigeria. For the lower-income countries, which have had less access to commercial loans (official or private) and have received less FDI, aid has assumed a much larger share of capital inflows; for fragile states that aren't oil exporters, aid and remittances essentially have been the only sources of capital flows. More than half of sub-Saharan African countries have relied on ODA for more than 70 percent of total capital inflows since 1995, despite the large increase in FDI and equity inflows to the region. The prospects for attracting more direct investment to the region are improving, however, as several African countries undertake tough reforms to liberalize their economies and promote macroeconomic stability. Nevertheless, much work remains to be done to enhance their investment climates. Thus, in the near to medium term, increases in ODA will remain critically important for countries in the region.

Aid to Strong Performers: Is There Evidence of a Scale-Up?

Although a range of reforming countries is well positioned to absorb more aid, the scaling up of support from development partners to these countries has been limited. Several country groups are identified. One group comprises the second-generation poverty reduction strategy (PRS-II) countries—those economies where the strengthening of the strategic and institutional framework for scaling up development results is adequately advanced to merit an early delivery on donor commitments to double aid.[9] Among the PRS-II countries, six African countries (Burkina Faso, Ghana, Madagascar, Mozambique, Rwanda, and Tanzania) were singled out initially for scaling-up efforts by the OECD-DAC and the World Bank. These countries are referred to as the "group of six strong performers." Another group comprises 22 first-generation poverty reduction strategy (PRS-I) countries.[10] For these countries, performance on country ownership, prioritization and sequencing, PRS-budget links, and monitoring and evaluation typically lags that of the PRS-II group.[11] The fragile-state group consists of 21 countries classified as fragile on the basis of their Country Policy and Institutional Assessment (CPIA) ratings.[12] The extent of scaling up of aid in these groups is measured in terms of ODA volumes, size of aid relative to gross domestic product (GDP), and per capita aid levels. All measures yield similar results.

The increase in ODA in 2001–05 varies widely across the country groups (table 4.1). The fragile-states group experienced the largest increase as their real ODA volumes rose by nearly 300 percent; many fragile states are in sub-Saharan Africa, and aid to this region expand by more than three-quarters. By contrast, the expansion of aid in strong-performing economies was mixed, with the six strong performers receiving a modest increase of 14 percent and other PRS-II and the PRS-I countries actually experiencing a decline. The expansion in real ODA, likewise, was largely concentrated in fragile states. The six strong performers in Africa also experienced a larger expansion in ODA for core development programs than did other groups. Evidence of the scaling up of aid is even less widespread when measured in terms of the ratio of ODA to GDP and aid per capita.

TABLE 4.1
Where Aid Flows Went, Selected Years, 2001–05

Aid recipients	Real net ODA by recipient (constant 2005 US$ millions)			Change 2001–05	Net ODA-to-GDP ratio (%)		
	2001	2004	2005	(%)	2001	2004	2005
All IDA/blend	38,052	40,818	50,747	33	11	13	12
PRS-I	11,546	10,141	10,592	−8	8	7	6
PRS-II[a]	10,607	11,268	9,994	−6	13	14	11
6 strong performers	5,348	6,867	6,076	14	15	20	17
Fragile states	4,686	9,115	17,766	279	12	17	18
Other countries	5,865	3,427	6,319	8	7	8	8
Memorandum items							
6 strong performers							
Burkina Faso	544	627	660	21	14	13	13
Ghana	873	1,387	1,120	28	12	15	10
Madagascar	504	1,274	929	85	8	29	18
Mozambique	1,308	1,279	1,286	−2	25	21	19
Rwanda	412	499	576	40	18	27	27
Tanzania	1,707	1,801	1,505	−12	13	16	12
Sub-Saharan Africa	16,573	23,491	29,306	77	13	16	15

Source: OECD-DAC database.

Note: GDP = gross domestic product; PRS = poverty reduction strategy. The table excludes countries with populations under 1 million.

a. Excluding six strong-performing economies.

The only country group to show any appreciable increase in those two indicators is the fragile states. For this group, the aid-to-GDP ratio rose by 5 percentage points. Fragile states' aid per capita figures also had a strong increase.

Although the data suggest that the development community's focus on fragile states is beginning to translate into increased assistance, these results have to be interpreted cautiously. For one thing, debt relief and humanitarian relief account for a substantial amount of this increase. For another, these aggregate trends mask the wide variation across different groups—aid "darlings" and aid "orphans." Large increases in aid have been concentrated in Afghanistan, the Democratic Republic of Congo, Nigeria, and Sudan, whereas some other fragile states have experienced modest changes or even declines in aid volumes.

Although recent trends point to a somewhat positive picture regarding the increase in aid to the six strong performers, there is substantial variation across these countries. Within this group, Madagascar and Rwanda have had a substantial scaling up of aid: in Madagascar, aid rose by 85 percent in real terms and ODA relative to GDP increased from 8 percent to 19 percent; Rwanda enjoyed a similar increase in its ODA-to-GDP ratio, as aid flows grew by 40 percent in real terms. Burkina Faso and Ghana also received more aid, but ODA relative to GDP was practically unchanged in both economies. By contrast, Mozambique and Tanzania actually experienced declines in real ODA.

The trend in the composition of aid to the six strong performers is favorable. The share of flexible ODA (that is, ODA minus humanitarian relief, debt relief, and technical cooperation) is rising in there. These countries also are receiving larger amounts of budget support—15 percent of aid compared with 4 percent in other sub-Saharan African countries.

Looking ahead, what are the prospects of scaling up aid to these six strong performers? Many of these countries have adopted ambitious growth-oriented development strategies that are receiving support from donors. Ghana is a promising example of where development partners are responding positively to the country's program for accelerating growth. There is a strong likelihood that ODA to Ghana will expand from an estimated $1.4 billion in 2006 to about $2 billion a year over 2007–09 (including debt relief) (World Bank 2007b). Tanzania also could experience a scaling up of resources in the context of the country's joint assistance strategy.

Empirical studies also find evidence of greater donor focus on policy performance (Amprou, Guillaumont, and Guillaumont-Jeanneney 2005; Dollar and Levin 2006).[13] The policy selectivity index that measures the elasticity of aid to the quality of recipients' policies and institutions (the World Bank's CPIA index) exhibits an improving trend for overall bilateral aid and for various types of aid (World Bank-IMF 2007).[14] Donors' aid allocations also point to a stronger focus on policy performance within sub-Saharan Africa (figure 4.8). For example, the elasticity of aid with respect to CPIA in 2001–05 was virtually double that of 1991–95. There is considerable variation among the larger donors, however, and some of these donors continue not to be very selective. A stronger focus on policy selectivity also is evident in multilateral donors' aid allocations (not shown in figure 4.8). The relationship between aid and policy is much stronger for multilateral than for bilateral aid. Using alternative measures of institutions, such as Freedom House's civil liberties and political rights

FIGURE 4.8
Donor Aid Allocations Focused on Policy, 1991–2005

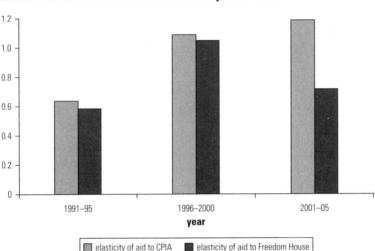

Source: Authors' calculations, based on Dollar and Levin (2006).

Note: The Freedom House indicator is the average of Freedom House's civil liberties and political rights indexes. Positive elasticities denote that countries that better protect personal freedoms or that have policies and institutions of better quality (CPIA) receive more aid. Elasticities to Freedom House were multiplied by −1 to make interpretation easier.

indexes, also shows that bilateral aid flows are responsive to the quality of institutions. But evidence regarding an increasing focus on these criteria is less clear.

Reliability of Aid Resources Remains Problematic

Aid flows tend to be variable and are characterized by a large gap between donor promises and actions. The uncertainty of aid resources has emerged as a crucial issue because these flows are particularly important in financing the MDGs in low-income countries and because they make up a sizable share of these countries' government expenditure, especially in social sectors such as health and education. In aid-dependent countries, the variability and unpredictability of donor funding undermines aid effectiveness by affecting short- and medium-term budget planning and programming, disrupting implementation of expenditure allocations, complicating macroeconomic management, and deepening the challenge of building absorptive capacity. Furthermore, scaling up aid and development effectiveness also requires more reliable information on resource availability. All of this suggests that donors need to improve aid delivery practices to ensure greater predictability of near- and longer-term aid flows and less volatility of funding.

Evidence from recent studies has indicated that both volatility and predictability of aid remain problematic, although welcome signs of change are appearing. For example, the March 2005 Paris Declaration, which was signed by more than 100 recipient countries and donors, emphasized that aid predictability is a key dimension of improving the effectiveness of aid, and the declaration included an indicator for measuring progress in that area. A few donors have moved to providing both greater transparency in aid allocations and forward commitments in multiyear frameworks. Donors also have asked the DAC to undertake monitoring surveys to collect three-year forward projections on aid at the country level. Despite the international community's recognition of the need for more stable and reliable flows, donor progress in implementing practices aimed at improving aid predictability is slow.

Aid Volatility

Several recent studies have analyzed issues related to aid volatility (Bulir and Hamann 2006; Celasun and Walliser 2007; DFID 2006; and Fielding and Mavrotas 2005). Despite using different methodologies, measures, and data sets to capture the variability of aid, the studies concluded that

1. aid flows typically exhibit large volatility,

2. aid is more volatile than government revenue,[15]

3. some forms of aid are more variable than others, and

4. volatility of aid varies by recipients.

A few studies also found evidence of increasing aid volatility in recent periods and of procyclicality of aid resources. This section of the chapter examines some of these stylized facts, with particular attention to sub-Saharan Africa.

Donor-reported data have shown substantial annual fluctuations in ODA disbursements. The variability of aid is measured by comparing the absolute values of percentage changes in annual disbursements of real gross ODA. Because some types of aid are expected to be more uncertain

TABLE 4.2
Aid Volatility in Low-Income Countries, 1980–2005
Percent

Aid recipients	1980s	1990s	2000–05
Sub-Saharan Africa	19.7	22.3	21.2
6 strong performers	15.3	19.4	15.1
Other top African performers	18.8	12.3	11.3
Other African low-income countries	21.4	25.6	25.6
All other regions	22.8	46.4	17.5

Sources: OECD-DAC database; authors' estimates.

Note: CPIA = Country Policy and Institutional Assessment. Table presents the average year-to-year percentage of absolute change in real ODA (gross disbursements less debt relief, emergency aid, and food aid); data are for low-income countries where the ratio of ODA to GDP is 5 percent or more. Top performers are countries in the top tercile of the overall CPIA score within the group of African low-income countries.

because they are in response to natural disasters or economic and social crises, these are excluded from the analysis. Thus, the focus here is on gross ODA disbursements less emergency and food aid and debt relief. The average annual absolute change in this measure of aid in 2000–05 was less than 20 percent for all low-income countries (table 4.2).[16] Low-income countries in sub-Saharan Africa have experienced the highest yearly change in aid (21.2 percent). There is wide variation across African countries, however. Top performers (as measured by the CPIA) experience uncertainty in aid receipts, but do so to a lesser degree than other countries. For example, the average annual absolute change in ODA is 15.1 percent for the six strong performers and 11.3 percent for other top African performers.

Real gross ODA was within ±10 percent of the previous year's level in approximately 37 percent of cases (figure 4.9). That is, in just over a third of cases this indicator was within 90 percent to 110 percent of the previous year's level. But the variation in ODA was outside of this range nearly two-thirds of the time, indicating a low level of aid certainty from one year to the next. Moreover, the number of cases in which countries experienced a decline in ODA from the previous year exceeded the number of cases in which aid rose. This pattern was relatively unchanged over the period 1991–2005. By contrast, other low-income countries experienced lesser year-to-year variations and an improving trend in recent years: in 2001–05, gross ODA was within ±10 percent of the previous year's level in nearly 45 percent of cases, compared with just over a quarter of cases for 1991–2000.

FIGURE 4.9

Frequency Distribution of the Year-to-Year Variation in ODA

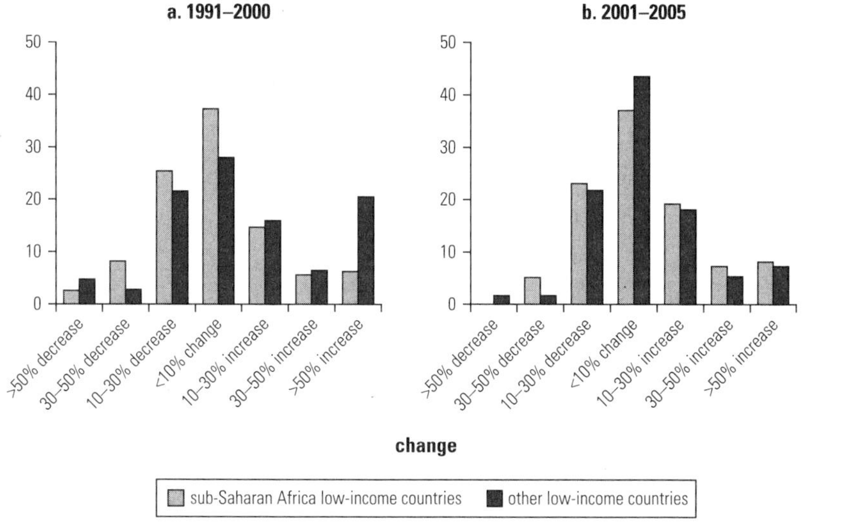

a. 1991–2000

b. 2001–2005

change

☐ sub-Saharan Africa low-income countries ■ other low-income countries

Sources: OECD-DAC database; authors' estimates.

Note: Real ODA (gross disbursements less debt relief, emergency aid, and food aid); data are for low-income countries where ODA/GDP is 5 percent or more.

Aid Predictability

The predictability of aid is the gap between expected and realized amounts of aid, where expected amounts could be announced commitments or projections based on the best information about donor intentions. Recent additions to the literature have measured predictability in two ways: (1) the degree to which donors deliver on their own aid promises, as measured by the deviation between donors' reported commitments and disbursements; and (2) the forecasting error of budget aid disbursements, based on aid projections and outruns from IMF programs or government Poverty Reductions Strategy Papers. Empirical findings based on donor-reported data, recipient information from IMF staff reports, and surveys (Strategic Partnership with Africa [SPA] and the Paris Declaration) suggest that aid predictability is low (OECD 2007; SPA 2006). However, there also is evidence that aid predictability is improving. This improvement is confined to aid in the near term, and medium-term aid resources remain unpredictable.

Donor-reported data indicate that the absolute deviation of aid commitments from disbursements is substantial, but that the size of deviations has
declined in recent periods.[17] There is considerable country-level variation
in aid predictability. In sub-Saharan Africa, annual aid disbursements devi-
ated from commitments by an average of 2.2 percent of GNI in 1991–2000
and by 0.9 percent in 2001–05 (table 4.3).[18] Several factors could explain
the lack of predictability—both aid shortfalls and excesses of commitments
over disbursements. The contributing factors on the donor side include
administrative delays, revisions of aid allocation, and political considerations. The way in which donor budgets are approved and administered
also contributes to the unpredictability of aid. The donor agencies that
make commitments are different from the institutions that make funding
decisions (parliaments) and those that disburse (ministries of finance).
This disconnection is widespread, although there is country variation. On
the recipient side, failure to meet conditions attached to disbursements or
slippage on project implementation can affect predictability.[19]

Recipient-side data are needed to assess the gap between aid projections
and disbursements. Drawing on data for 13 countries from IMF staff
reports for 1992–07, Celasun and Walliser (2007) estimated the forecasting error of budget aid disbursements—the gap between projected aid
flows based on reliable information available at the time of budget preparation and actual disbursements. Aid projections and outturns from IMF
program data point to large unpredictability of aid flows; both over- and
underprojection errors are large. The study estimated the average mean
absolute error in projecting budget aid at greater than 1.0 percent of GDP
during 1993–2005. This figure is high because budget aid averages 3.0 percent of GDP; thus, one-third of budget aid is unpredictable. However,
excess aid shortfalls almost even out over time so that disbursed aid, on
average, differs from projected aid by 0.2 percent of GDP. The study found
that predictability has improved in recent years. Improvements are particularly evident in some countries (Burkina Faso and Madagascar) but other
countries have seen little change (Tanzania) or even a worsening trend.

Evidence that aid has become more predictable in recent years is found
in other studies as well. An IMF report (2007a) found that projections of
next-year aid inflows have become more accurate. Although earlier
IMF-supported programs tended to underestimate aid because of overly
cautious aid projections, recent programs carry more accurate forecasts
and lower projection errors. The 2006 SPA survey of budget support by

TABLE 4.3

Trends in Aid Predictability, Bilateral Gross ODA, 1991–2005

Percent

Aid recipients	1991–2000			2001–05		
	Gross disbursements/ GNI	Commitments minus disbursements to GNI	Absolute value of commitments minus disbursements to GNI	Gross disbursements/ GNI	Commitments minus disbursements to GNI	Absolute value of commitments minus disbursements to GNI
Sub-Saharan Africa	10.4	–1.2	2.2	8.9	0.0	0.9
Low-income countries	12.3	–1.3	2.4	11.2	0.0	1.1
6 strong performers	15.0	–1.2	2.0	11.6	0.2	1.0
Burkina Faso	10.4	–0.8	1.4	7.3	0.4	0.9
Ghana	6.3	0.1	0.6	10.4	0.0	0.6
Madagascar	9.2	–1.6	1.8	8.8	0.5	0.9
Mozambique	32.9	–4.0	4.7	21.6	–0.4	1.9
Rwanda	18.5	–0.6	2.4	12.2	0.3	0.9
Tanzania	12.8	0.0	1.2	9.4	0.4	0.6
Other IDA countries	7.7	0.3	2.1	7.3	0.6	1.9

Sources: OECD-DAC database; authors' estimates.

Note: Data are for IDA-eligible countries. Commitments are new resources available for disbursements. Because some commitments are associated with multiyear disbursements, commitment data should be viewed as merely indicative of likely disbursements during a period.

20 donors in 15 African countries found evidence of substantial aid unpredictability. The survey also found, however, that, in recent years, donors are disbursing more of their general budget support commitments in-year, although there was some slippage in fiscal 2005/06, with in-year disbursements falling from 87.1 percent of commitments in fiscal 2004/05 to 82.8 percent. As with general budget support, sector budget support also has shown a gap between commitments and disbursements. The proportion of funds disbursed in the following year or undisbursed varies widely by country. The reasons for disbursement difficulties include political governance concerns (Ethiopia, Uganda), economic governance concerns (Uganda), and other conditions not being met. Administrative holdups, such as a delay in signing an agreement or nonreceipt of a request for payment, also were behind the gap between commitments and disbursements.

The 2006 baseline survey on monitoring the Paris Declaration (OECD 2007) spotlighted the state of play regarding aid predictability: the percent of donor aid disbursements released according to agreed schedules in annual or multiyear frameworks and the accurate recording by partners of donor aid disbursements to the government sector. The survey found that $19.9 billion of the $21.1 billion that donors scheduled for disbursement in 2005 actually was disbursed in 2005. However, the amount recorded by partners was only $14.8 billion—that is, 70 percent of scheduled disbursements (a 30 percent gap) and 75 percent of actual disbursements. Underrecording is commonly observed in almost all countries; in 8 of the 34 countries, the gap in recording was more than 50 percent. This pattern of underrecording could result from the inability of government systems to capture and process this information because of inappropriate notification processes on the part of donors or because projects may not be included in the budget.

To facilitate the process of scaling up, donors agreed in 2005 that the DAC would undertake an effort to collect information on three-year forward projections of aid at the country level. By providing information on resource availability at the country level over the next few years, donors would improve transparency in aid allocations, better coordinate aid, and enhance the predictability of resource flows. The first such monitoring exercise took place in 2006. The results were weak (that is, coverage was only 27 percent of aid flows), reflecting the challenge donors face in providing three-year forward projections at the country level.

The 2006 SPA survey results also pointed to the limited availability of donors' forward commitments of budget support. Although recipient governments place a high priority on multiyear commitments, both SPA general budget support and SPA sector support surveys suggested that medium-term commitments and programs by donors decline in outer years. Donor commitments in signed formal agreements or in announced agreements for 2006–08 are lower by 40 percent in value and by more than half in terms of the number of programs. Ninety percent of donors who had committed general budget support in 2005 made a firm commitment for 2006, but this proportion dropped off to 67 percent for 2007. The pattern of medium-term commitments is similar for sector budget support. Given the incompleteness and uncertainty of donors' forward commitments, it is not surprising that an IMF Independent Evaluation Office report (IMF 2007b) concluded that projections of medium-term aid underestimated aid flows.

Improving the Predictability of Aid

The recognition that "business as usual" will not work and that newer mechanisms are needed to ensure predictable and stable flows aligned as much as possible to a country's long-term development strategy is prompting change. For example, the DAC is following up its 2006 exercise on future aid allocations with a more focused monitoring effort. This year's aid allocation work attempts to address some of the constraints to donor predictability. A key constraint is that, although donors are increasingly discussing three-to-four-year forward-spending plans with partners, the reality of budget mechanisms poses a challenge—aid budgets have an annual cycle and are subject to parliamentary approval, which can lead to adjustments in planned spending (OECD-DAC 2007a, 2007b). Another fact that has a bearing on predictability is that multiyear programming may not cover all components of ODA or all partners. Given the reality of donor budget processes, the DAC's approach to collecting indicative spending plans is focused on collecting information on future flows of programmable aid only (as opposed to all aid) at the country level. The approach also focuses on estimating a range of possible financing paths for each recipient country, based on a wide range of future aid scenarios. The idea is for donors to use these scenarios to inform their aid allocations. Preliminary information on this year's donor survey of forward-spending plans shows a higher response rate than the 2006 donor survey showed.

The European Commission (EC) has adopted mechanisms to make aid more predictable. One of these is the graduated response to aid delivery. Within the framework of the PRS, the EC's general budget support provides fixed and variable tranche disbursements. Whereas the fixed tranche component is a traditional aid modality linked to conditionality, the variable tranche provides resources in a graduated form dependent on the achievement of agreed targets and indicators. The variable tranche usually has two subtranches: one is linked to satisfactory management of public finances and the other is linked to a set of agreed poverty reduction indicators.

Several donors, including the Netherlands, Sweden, and the United Kingdom, are showing interest in the EC's graduated response approach. A recent study by Gelb and Eifert (2005) suggested a practical way of addressing the issue of budget aid predictability. It recommended applying performance-based allocation rules with a flexible precommitment rule, such that aid levels adjust sharply only in response to major performance changes. This mechanism would allow for precommitment of aid in a multiyear framework while avoiding drawn-out periods of misallocation. In addition, donors could fund a country's reserve holdings—that is, a buffer reserve fund of two to four months of imports—so that the reserves could cushion a shortfall in disbursements arising from exogenous factors unrelated to country performance.

The EC has also launched a proposal—the MDG Contract—to make its general budget support more long term and predictable (EC 2007). It is not a new EC financial mechanism, but rather an enhanced form of general budget support for implementation under the 10th European Development Fund, which will provide €22,682 million over the period 2008–13. The proposed features of the MDG Contract include a six-year time horizon, a virtually guaranteed minimum level of support, annual monitoring with a focus on results, and a performance assessment in a multiannual framework that takes into account previous performance and future prospects. The MDG Contract will be targeted at countries with a strong track record of implementing general budget support, a medium-term framework for assessing performance, and substantive public financial management (PFM) reforms.

Consultative Group and Roundtable meetings and formal mutual accountability reviews of progress are important mechanisms for promoting more predictable and long-term financing from donors. Ghana is using a revamped Consultative Group process ("Results, Resources, and Partnership") built on the aid effectiveness principles of the Paris Declaration to link funds to ambitious country-owned strategies and development results. The June 2007 Ghana Consultative Group Annual Partnership meeting drew strong donor support for the country's development strategy. In Tanzania, a similar process emerged from the merging of the consultative Group meetings, the Annual Public Expenditure Review Consultative meeting, and the Poverty Reduction Strategy Paper Annual Review meeting.

The United States' Millennium Challenge Account (MCA) is designed to provide larger, more predictable, and longer-term commitments to countries that qualify for its funding. Countries are eligible for MCA funding on the basis of their demonstrated commitment to sound policies and good governance. The MCA selects recipients on the basis of policy and institutional changes that have already been implemented. Funding tranches are linked to specified results and not future policy changes. Each recipient government works with the Millennium Challenge Corporation, which administers the MCA, to plan and negotiate a four- to five-year agreement (compact) on how to use a specified amount of money. Each agreement includes a disbursement schedule for the entire time span of the agreement. Disbursement is not subject to the U.S. Congressional appropriations process because compacts are signed only after enough money is appropriated to the Millennium Challenge Corporation to cover the cost for all years of the compact. Disbursements also are not conditional on implementing future reforms, but are subject to the recipient's compliance with specific procurement policies or mutually agreed conditions, including maintenance of good governance. These aspects of the MCA are designed in part to increase the predictability of aid.

Accelerating Progress on Alignment and Harmonization

Improving aid delivery is central to scaling up development results. The 2005 Paris Declaration, which built on the Rome Meeting of 2003, embodies the international community's commitment to increasing the effectiveness of aid. Partner countries, donors, and the international financial institutions are taking substantial actions toward meeting the Paris commitments. Much has been achieved in implementing this agenda at the international level, within donor institutions and, most important, at the country level where harmonization and alignment activities have engaged all development partners. But the breadth and depth of actions are varied among countries. It is clear that development partners and donors will need to continue focusing on this agenda and make appropriate changes in practices, processes, and procedures to achieve the intended development impact.

Actions at the Donor and Developing-Country Levels

Following the adoption of the Paris framework in 2005, donors have taken a broad range of actions to disseminate the agreed commitments. Two-thirds of DAC donors have included the Paris Declaration as a strategic priority in official statements, indicating political ownership (OECD-DAC 2006a). Many donors also have developed action plans for implementing the Paris framework.[20] But implementing the declaration involves a broad and complex process of change. Donor agencies are organizing to strengthen internal processes. They also are making some progress on improving internal incentive systems—at both the institution and individual levels—to make these systems more compatible with a sharpened focus on harmonization, alignment, and results (also see ODI 2004). The Paris Declaration set out the principle that implementation should take place at the country level, but less than a third of donors report progress on decentralization.

The World Bank and other multilateral development banks are reflecting their commitment to the Paris Declaration by improving the effectiveness of their own programs and by pushing for greater collective implementation of the Paris principles throughout the donor community. In a number of areas, substantial actions are being taken. The multilateral donor banks have undertaken efforts to harmonize their procedures, strengthen country systems where necessary, and align with those systems where possible. Also, there is an increasing use of joint or collaborative country assistance strategies to harmonize country diagnostics, align with country priorities, and prepare a coordinated portfolio of activities. In further implementing the Paris Declaration, multilateral donor banks face a number of additional common challenges, including addressing incentive issues as a key means of promoting further progress on aid effectiveness.

Continued attention by all levels of management and evolution of internal processes where needed will be required to provide staff with an environment more conducive to harmonization and alignment.

Donor coordination also is being strengthened through the World Bank's Africa Action Plan and partnerships such as the Limelette Process. The Africa Action Plan provides an outcome-oriented framework of partnership between the World Bank and other development actors to help every African country achieve the MDGs (World Bank 2007a). The Limelette Process is a partnership between the World Bank's Africa Region and the EC.[21] Limelette IV, held in September 2007, focused on four themes: (1) greater use of budget support, (2) monitoring for results, (3) infrastructure, and (4) climate change. It emphasized deeper collaboration between the World Bank and the EC in scaling up, with particular attention to division of labor, coordination of program aid, predictability of aid, and harmonization (EC-World Bank 2007).

In 2007 the European Union adopted a voluntary Code of Conduct on Complementarity and Division of Labor in Development Policy to facilitate division of labor as a way to improve aid effectiveness. The code of conduct, which is aimed at strengthening partner-country ownership and capacity and donor coordination, exploits in-country and cross-country complementarities to reduce transactions costs through a division of labor and to address the issue of "darling" and "orphan" sectors. Among the 10 operational principles of the code of conduct for donors' actions are

- concentration in a limited number of in-country sectors (three), chosen on the basis of a donor's comparative advantage;

- in areas outside of the concentration sectors, donor redeployment of resources to budget-support or concentration sectors, or use of delegated cooperation/partnership arrangements to stay financially engaged in the sector;

- enhanced donor coordination through the support of a lead donor arrangement in each priority sector;

- adequate donor support in sectors that are relevant for poverty reduction; and

- establishment of priority countries for European Union donor engagement.

In moving forward, two issues that donors will need to address are (1) what mechanisms will be used for allocating responsibilities across sectors and countries, and (2) what indicators will be used for measuring the various principles of the division of labor. The likely obstacles in donor agencies and in recipient countries will need to be recognized and addressed as well.[22] The EC plans to report on progress in the implementation of the code of conduct by the time of the Accra High-Level Forum on Aid Effectiveness (September 2008).

A review of country-level harmonization and alignment actions and activities suggests a broad and growing attention to these issues. At least 60 countries around the world are collaborating with their development partners on country-level harmonization and alignment actions. Of course, the breadth and depth of actions differ among countries, thus reflecting the adaptation of the Paris Declaration elements to country-specific contexts and circumstances. The evidence suggests that substantial implementation of the harmonization and alignment agenda is taking place in five to eight countries; and that good but less extensive implementation is occurring in 10–15 other countries. Many of these countries are preparing or implementing harmonization road maps or action plans articulating the aid relationship with donors—that is, the shared agenda between the government and donors to make progress toward localized Paris indicators and targets, to establish mutual accountability, and to facilitate managing for results. In these countries, donors are implementing a range of mechanisms and processes to improve the alignment and harmonization of aid, including joint assistance strategies (collaborative country assistance strategies), division of labor, and revamped Consultative Group processes.

Results of the 2006 Baseline Monitoring Survey

A 2006 baseline survey covering 34 countries and 37 percent of total donor assistance provided comprehensive data for assessing where development partners and recipient countries stand with respect to the Paris agenda. The results of the survey spotlight a number of challenges that need to be addressed if the targets of the Paris Declaration are to be met. Past experience suggests that many of the targets are attainable if partner countries and donors build on the momentum fostered by the Paris Declaration.

Results for indicators pertaining to donors' implementation of the Paris agenda present a mixed picture. The survey showed that 40 percent of donors' disbursements use the partner country's PFM system and an almost equal percentage of disbursements use the partner country's procurement system. Better-quality PFM systems (as measured by the CPIA) do tend to be associated with a higher use of these systems for aid provided to the public sector. Nevertheless, there is wide variation among bilateral donors (DAC members) in the use of PFM systems for delivering aid to government sectors—from a low of 10 percent to a high of 90 percent. The survey results showed that greater attention is needed with respect to project implementation units (PIUs). In the 34 countries surveyed, 1,832 parallel PIUs are relied on to implement projects; the Paris target is to reduce that number by two-thirds (to 611) by 2010. Although a number of agencies, including the World Bank and the EC, are looking to merge existing PIUs into the structures of ministries or agencies, substantial effort will be required to achieve that goal.

The baseline survey gathered information on two dimensions of harmonization: (1) the use of common arrangements within program-based approaches, and (2) the conduct of joint missions and analysis sharing. The survey found that the donors provided 43 percent of their aid through program-based efforts, such as budget support and sectorwide approaches, relative to the Paris target of 66 percent.[23] In addition, the extent to which donors conduct joint missions is very low: the survey found that 18 percent of missions were undertaken jointly, whereas 42 percent of country analytic work was prepared jointly with another donor (relative to the 2010 Paris targets of 40 percent joint missions and of 66 percent joint analytic work). Greater donor efforts are going to be needed if the 2010 targets are to be met.

Among the better performers, the six strong performers in Africa boasted a relatively robust performance on a wide range of indicators. Many of these countries have undertaken substantial implementation of the harmonization and alignment agenda. Several of them share common factors, such as strong government leadership in setting out priorities in development assistance, an effective implementation process for the poverty reduction strategy, a mature government—donor aid relationship, and a well-functioning aid coordination mechanism. Consequently, these countries are often in the top tercile in the indicators that underpin the Paris Declaration. Other PRS-II countries show considerable variation in harmonization and alignment actions (table 4.4).

TABLE 4.4
Country-Level Progress on Harmonization and Alignment Actions and Selected Indicators of Aid Effectiveness: Six Strong Performers and Other PRS-II Countries

Actions and indicators	Strong performers				
	Burkina Faso	Ghana	Mozambique	Rwanda	Tanzania
Harmonization action plan					
Collaborative CAS					
Quality of development strategy					
Quality of financial management					
Aid on budget					
Coordinated technical assistance					
Use of country financial management systems					
Use of country procurement systems					
Parallel PIUs					
Predictability					
Program base					
Coordinated missions					
Joint analysis					
Results framework					
Mutual accountability					

Source: Adapted from IDA 2007a.

Note: CAS = country assistance strategy; PIU = project implementation unit. The group of strong performers presented in this table excludes Madagascar. Shading and patterns denote the position of the country relative to other countries (in the survey) with respect to the indicator being measured: light gray = top tercile, lines = middle tercile, and dark gray = bottom tercile. For the first two and the last indicators, light gray denotes "yes," lines denote "some progress," and dark gray denotes "no."

	Other PRS-II countries								
	Benin	Bolivia	Ethiopia	Malawi	Mauritania	Nicaragua	Senegal	Uganda	Vietnam

Challenges Moving Forward

The Paris framework has generated a momentum for change in aid delivery practices. The survey pointed to the progress that has been made and the areas that need attention. Moving forward, donor efforts to scale up harmonization and alignment increasingly will need to focus on division of labor processes, expanded use of delegated cooperation, greater use of country harmonization and alignment action plans, and improvement of incentives within agencies.

Even as important gains are being made at both the donor and country levels in improving the way aid is delivered, a changing aid environment calls for a number of remaining challenges to be addressed. Notable among these challenges are the trend toward greater use of global funds/vertical funds or earmarking and the increasing importance of emerging-market donors. The challenge for the donor community and recipients is how to better align and integrate vertical and earmarked funds in country strategies and how to strengthen the complementarities between these funds and traditional aid.[24]

The growing importance of newer donors is adding to the complexity of the aid architecture. Not much is known about the size and composition of flows from emerging donors, and better information is needed to facilitate monitoring and donor coordination. Although several emerging-market donors have signed the Paris Declaration, the extent to which they are formulating and implementing Paris Declaration action plans is not known. The May 2007 memorandum of understanding between the World Bank and the Export-Import Bank of China[25] is a welcome move to build collaboration on development, with a particular focus on Africa.

Effectively and quickly addressing the challenges described above is central to enhancing the effectiveness of aid. Donors and partners will need to pay attention to these issues in formulating and implementing their "second-generation" Paris frameworks.

Delivering Global Program Aid More Effectively

Global programs are issue-based aid vehicles that are a response of the donor community to a special challenge or problem. In recent years there has been a sharp rise in the number and size of global programs. Contributions have risen from approximately $1 billion in the 1990s to $3 billion in 2005. A few large programs, however, account for 95 percent of the contributions of global programs. For example, three programs (the Global Fund to Fight AIDS, Tuberculosis, and Malaria; the Global Environment Facility; and the Joint United Nations Programme on HIV/AIDS) received nearly 90 percent of donor contributions in 2006, and 14 of the programs that were included in the 20 major programs in 2006 were established after 1994. The biggest increase in size and concentration of funds has been in the area of health because donors have responded to the potential for "emerging" diseases, such as avian flu and severe acute respiratory syndrome (SARS), to lead to pandemics and to the high toll in lives and development associated with such diseases as HIV/AIDS.

The rapid growth in size and prominence of global programs is spurring concern over the effectiveness of these aid modalities and the sustainability of their goals. One key concern is that increasing numbers of single-issue programs, often with overlapping objectives, contribute to the challenge of better aid coordination, harmonization, and alignment. Another concern is that the size of some funds' activities can overwhelm the local capacity in low-income countries and may even create critical imbalances and development gaps. Also important is the need to undertake complementary actions and policies to improve the future sustainability of global programs' goals.

The Aid Effectiveness Challenge of Global Programs

Global programs are favored by donors because the programs are flexible. These programs enable donors to respond quickly to pressing global issues, and they provide innovative ways of doing things, and their narrow focus enables them to generate economies of scale through specialization. Moreover, the progress and results of these programs can be evaluated quickly. Furthermore, such programs can draw much-needed political attention to pressing issues. Global programs, however, also pose some challenges—namely, in their aid effectiveness and in the sustainability of their development impact and goals.

The growing prominence of global programs reflects a number of advantages to vertical approaches. These aid vehicles allow donors rapidly to mobilize and channel resources, while they provide scope for economies of scale through specialization. They also enable relatively rapid monitoring of impact on the ground.

Although vertical funds bring much-needed attention and financing to their focus areas and are increasingly important as sources of funding, they can have unintended effects. Problems can occur (especially in the short run) where these funds are narrowly targeted to a sector or subsector, are large, and scale up quickly. The challenges posed by vertical approaches to aid delivery are most evident in the health sector. One study (Lewis 2005) showed that seven African countries received HIV/AIDS funding that exceeded 30 percent of their total public health budgets; in some countries, this funding exceeds public sector health spending. Such single-issue funding can lessen attention on other health priorities. In Ghana, for example, malaria is the main cause of sickness and mortality, but donor funding to fight malaria is only 60 percent of the amount allocated for fighting HIV/AIDS. In Rwanda, donor funding in health is unevenly distributed: $47 million is directed toward HIV/AIDS; $18 million is earmarked for malaria, which is the leading cause of morbidity and mortality; and only $1 million is allocated for the management of childhood diseases (Republic of Rwanda 2006).

Verticalization also can pose obstacles for sustainability and absorption at the local/sector level. For example, 55 percent of foreign-financed projects are negotiated on an annual basis in Ethiopia and Rwanda. This short-term pattern of financing introduces uncertainty in aid amounts. Large year-to-year variations in aid levels constrain long-term plans for building capacity in the health sector—that is, hiring nurses and doctors and scaling up health services. Absorptive capacity problems at the sector level in Ethiopia are evident from the capital budget execution rate for external assistance, which is exceptionally low (15–20 percent, compared with 80 percent for domestic resources). Strengthening the absorptive capacity of the health systems, however, usually receives less attention than does HIV in donor pledges (see figure 4.10 for a depiction of aid allocations to health care in Ethiopia). With 90 global health funds (not counting other funds) and an average of 200 donor missions a year, it is important to enhance country capacity to enable a more effective aid relationship.

Policies and Actions to Deliver More Effective Global Program Aid

The trend toward more global programs is likely to continue, making the issue of aid effectiveness particularly relevant moving forward. Some of

FIGURE 4.10
Allocation of Donor Pledges, Ethiopia

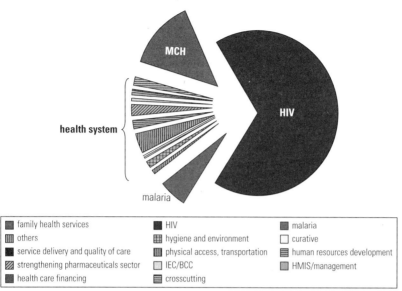

■ family health services	■ HIV	■ malaria
▥ others	▦ hygiene and environment	□ curative
■ service delivery and quality of care	▥ physical access, transportation	▤ human resources development
▨ strengthening pharmaceuticals sector	□ IEC/BCC	■ HMIS/management
■ health care financing	▤ crosscutting	

Source: Government of Ethiopia, Irish Aid, UNICEF, and World Bank. 2007.

Note: IEC/BCC = information, education, and communication/behavioral change communication; HMIS = health management information systems.

the consequences discussed above, however, are not inevitable. Countries and donors must work together to minimize these potential challenges and maximize the contribution of global funds to country-based development. The Paris Declaration goes some way to address these issues: it recognizes the need to better integrate global programs and horizontal aid in recipient countries' broader development agendas; and it reinforces the centrality of the country-based approach to development aid—the need for strong national development strategies, such as PRSs, so that aid can be aligned with country priorities and country systems. A range of complementary actions and policies is essential for realizing the rewards of vertical approaches, including country-owned development strategies, complementary investments, fiscal sustainability, and favorable investment climates conducive to growth and private sector development.

A study by the World Bank (2006) found that the ability to align with country-led strategies also depends on the characteristics of global programs. Vertical programs should be integrated with the national budget and should use national systems as much as possible. The issues concerning strategic coherence and harmonization are the most serious in the health sector. Those issues also arise in other sectors that are the focus of global programs—namely, education and environment—but are less pronounced because the approaches followed by the major programs in those sectors (the Education for All—Fast Track Initiative and the Global Environment Facility) put more emphasis on harmonization and alignment. The Fast Track Initiative, for example, uses a country-based approach to the education sector involving the local donor group, which jointly endorses the government's education sector strategy and then coordinates the scaling up of donor funding to support it.

The World Bank's strong support of the country-based development model heightens the institution's role in addressing the challenges of integrating global programs and country programs with national priorities. In addition, the Bank plays a platform or "glue" role in providing strategic coherence to other forms of aid. This glue role derives from the institution's multisector perspective, its convening power, and its global reach combined with local presence. These dimensions enable the Bank to adapt to country situations, to act as a first mover when appropriate, and to leverage other funding to scale up poverty reduction interventions (IDA 2007b). Thus, the Bank can bring greater coherence in development assistance at the macroeconomic and intrasectoral levels. It also can play a central role in enhancing harmonization and coordination among donors. Moving forward, the Bank can take a critical role in helping raise the effectiveness of aid in a changing and complex aid environment, if appropriate financing is available for the IDA.

Work on aid effectiveness and health has yielded a substantial body of evidence and a number of important streams of work have been started or are ongoing. In 2004–05, a High-Level Forum on the Health MDGs assessed aid effectiveness issues in health and proposed a set of Best Practice Principles for Engagement of Global Health Partnerships at the Country Level. These principles for improving the delivery of health aid are based on the Paris Declaration, but also include a few best-practice principles for governance of global health programs—namely, to provide clarity and transparency to decision-making roles, objectives, and procedures; to have a strong commitment to minimizing overhead costs; and to be subject to regular external audits (Working Group on Global Health Partnerships 2005).

In 2006 the World Bank and the OECD-DAC cosponsored a policy workshop to focus attention on improving country-level alignment of global programs. The Bank proposed good-practice guidance for integrating global programs (*all* global programs, not only those involving health) at the country level. The good practices are anchored in the Paris Declaration and draw on the best practices for global health partnerships cited above (OECD-DAC 2006b). This workshop was followed by a June 2007 workshop in Mauritius focused on how to enhance the links between global programs and country strategies to achieve development results. In preparation for the Ghana High-Level Meeting, the OECD-DAC organized a meeting in May 2007 to propose areas of aid effectiveness in health that could be taken forward by the World Health Organization and the World Bank. One area of interest that has been identified is support of health systems.

Most recently, donors have launched a new health program—the International Health Partnership—to address some of the donor coordination problems in health funding.[26] The new partnership emphasizes the need for better spending of resources to meet the health MDGs of reducing child and maternal mortality and tackling HIV/AIDS, malaria, and other diseases. It focuses on strengthening health systems and health infrastructure in poor countries—targeting aid to priority health needs—and on providing more long-term and predictable funding to support these countries' health plans. Burundi, Ethiopia, Kenya, Mozambique, and Zambia will be among the first seven developing countries to benefit from this new partnership.

Conclusion

At the halfway mark in the MDGs' term (2000–15), progress on scaling up the quantity and quality of aid is mixed. A proliferation of aid sources is expanding the global resources available for development, even as aid from traditional donors (DAC countries) has stalled. These newer resources often target productive sectors and physical infrastructure. Along with presenting opportunities, however, these new sources of development assistance present the international community with a big challenge—that of making aid more effective. Now, more than ever before, there is a need for closer coordination of aid activities and for greater harmonization and less fragmentation and earmarking of aid for specific applications. Such coherence is critical to successful scaling up of aid to meet the MDGs. The principles of the Paris framework address some of these challenges, but more needs to be done. Clearly, "business as usual" will not work.

Notes

This chapter draws on background notes prepared by the authors for the 2007 Development Committee, "Country-Based Scaling Up: Assessment of Progress and Agenda for Action" (World Bank 2007b).

1. In this context, a billion is 1,000 millions.
2. Cambodia and Tajikistan—two non-HIPCs—have also received MDRI debt relief from the IMF (see IDA-IMF 2007).
3. The increase in nominal terms is much larger, at nearly 100 percent.
4. The importance of policy performance in donors' aid allocations is addressed in the next section of this chapter.
5. For an analysis of the evolution in the size and pattern of Africa–Asia trade, see Broadman (2006).
6. From 1956 to May 2006, China provided an estimated $5.7 billion in aid to Africa (Wang 2007).
7. This assistance includes setting up a $5 billion China–Africa development fund to promote investment by Chinese companies in Africa, and providing $5 billion in loans and credits to the region. China also has pledged to cancel large amounts of debt that are owed to it by the poorest African countries (Taylor, 2007; Wang 2007).
8. Financial flows include workers' remittances, which are classified as current transfers in the balance of payments.
9. PRS-II countries are Benin, Bolivia, Bosnia and Herzegovina, Burkina Faso, Ethiopia, Ghana, Madagascar, Malawi, Mauritania, Mozambique, Nicaragua, Rwanda, Senegal, Tanzania, Uganda, Vietnam, the Republic of Yemen, and Zambia.
10. PRS-I countries are Albania, Armenia, Azerbaijan, Bangladesh, Bhutan, Cameroon, Cape Verde, Dominica, Georgia , Guyana, Honduras, Kenya, the Kyrgyz Republic, Lesotho, Mali, Moldova, Mongolia, Nepal, Niger, Pakistan, Serbia and Montenegro, and Sri Lanka.
11. For the performance of these groups across various measures of PRS quality and governance, see World Bank (2007b).
12. This group comprises Afghanistan, Burundi, Cambodia, the Central African Republic, Chad, the Democratic Republic of Congo, the Republic of Congo,

Côte d'Ivoire, Djibouti, The Gambia, Guinea, Guinea-Bissau, Haiti, the Lao People's Democratic Republic, Liberia, Nigeria, São Tomé and Principe, Sierra Leone, Sudan, Tajikistan, and Timor-Leste.

13. Of course, as Amprou, Guillaumont, and Guillaumont-Jeanneney (2005) pointed out, aid is allocated on the basis of several criteria, including geostrategic considerations, vulnerability to shocks, and former colonial ties.

14. The report finds that flexible ODA is the most selective with respect to policy performance (CPIA) and technical cooperation is the least selective. No significant relationship is found between the CPIA and debt relief.

15. The DFID (2006) study argued that Bulir and Hamann's (2006) results were affected by exchange rate volatility because they used the variances of aid/GDP and government revenue/GDP instead of normalizing aid and revenue by their respective averages. Nevertheless, the DFID study did find evidence that aid is relatively more volatile than revenue.

16. Using the Hodrick-Prescott filter to smooth the time-series lowers the volatility of aid but does not affect the conclusion that aid is uncertain. The filter pays more attention to long-run fluctuations and is less sensitive to short-term fluctuations. Bulir and Hamann (2006) used this technique to smooth the time-series for both aid and government revenues.

17. Commitments in the OECD-DAC database are new resources available for disbursements. Because some commitments are associated with multiyear disbursements, commitment data should be viewed as merely indicative of likely disbursements during a period.

18. Celasun and Walliser (2007) found that commitments are good at predicting disbursements, but the coefficient is not equal to 1. Some countries report disbursements as commitments, and that practice could affect this result.

19. Celasun and Walliser (2007) found that predictability increases with the number of years a country has implemented an IMF program (or successive IMF programs). The result suggests that sustained implementation of IMF programs signals a country's commitment to stable macroeconomic management, and donors respond by providing more predictable aid.

20. As of November 2006, 16 DAC members had adopted action plans on implementing the Paris Declaration. An additional three members have adopted the principles of harmonization, alignment, and results in their aid strategies and policies; and four others intend to have action plans.

21. The Limelette Process was launched in April 2003 as an annual meeting between the World Bank's Africa Region and the EC's Directorate-General for Development. It aims to exchange views on practices and to improve mutual coordination on the ground. The topic changes annually: Poverty Reduction Strategy Papers in 2003; budget support and public finance management in 2004; and infrastructure, public finance management, and trade and regional integration in 2005.

22. The World Bank and the EC are in discussions to see how the two institutions can cooperate in implementing the code of conduct in a few pilot countries.

23. The results need to be interpreted carefully because some donors' definitions of program-based approaches may not represent the use of common procedures with other donors.
24. A detailed discussion of the challenges inherent in integrating global/vertical funds with country programs is presented in the next section of this chapter.
25. The Export-Import Bank of China is China's state policy bank for international economic development and cooperation.
26. The program was announced initially by U.K. Prime Minister Gordon Brown and German Chancellor Angela Merkel in August 2007 and was unveiled formally on September 5, 2007.

References

Amprou, J., P. Guillaumont, and S. Guillaumont-Jeanneney. 2005. "Aid Selectivity According to Augmented Criteria." Agence Française de Développement, Paris.

Broadman, Harry G. 2006. *Africa's Silk Road: China and India's New Economic Frontier.* Washington, DC: World Bank.

Bulir, A., and A. J. Hamann. 2006. "Volatility of Development Aid: From the Frying Pan into the Fire?" Working Paper 06/65, International Monetary Fund, Washington, DC.

Celasun, O., and J. Walliser. 2007. "Predictability and Procylicality of Aid: Do Fickle Donors Undermine Economic Development?" Preliminary version of a paper prepared for the 46th Economic Policy Panel Meeting, Lisbon, Portugal, June 1.

DFID (U.K. Department for International Development). 2006. "Assessing the Volatility of International Aid Flows." London.

Dollar, D., and V. Levin. 2006. "The Increasing Selectivity of Foreign Aid, 1984–2003." *World Development* 34 (12): 2034–46.

EC (European Commission). 2007. "Technical Discussion Paper on a 'MDG Contract'—A Proposal for Longer Term and More Predictable General Budget Support." June 19.

EC (European Commission)-World Bank. 2007. Report on the Meeting with Civil Society on EC-World Bank Collaboration on Africa, Brussels, September 17–18. http://siteresources.worldbank.org/WBEU/Resources/17SeptemberECWBcollaborationinAfrica.pdf.

Fielding, D., and G. Mavrotas. 2005. "The Volatility of Aid." Discussion paper 2005/06, World Institute for Development Economics Research, United Nations University, Helsinki, Finland.

Gelb, A., and B. Eifert. 2005. "Improving the Dynamics of Aid: Towards More Predictable Budget Support." Policy Research Working Paper 3732, World Bank, Washington, DC.

Government of Ethiopia, Irish Aid, UNICEF, and World Bank. 2007. "Reaching the Health MDGS in Ethiopia: Facing or Escaping the Scaling Up Challenge." World Bank, Washington, DC.

IDA (International Development Association). 2007a. "IDA's Role in Enhancing Aid Effectiveness through Strengthened Alignment and Harmonization." Draft report. Washington, DC.

———. 2007b. "The Role of IDA in the Global Aid Architecture: Supporting the Country-Based Development Model." IDA/SecM2007-0450, Washington, DC.

IDA-IMF (International Development Association-International Monetary Fund). 2007. "Heavily Indebted Poor Countries (HPIC) Initiative and the Multilateral Debt Relief Initiative (MDRI)—Status of Implementation." Washington, DC.

IMF (International Monetary Fund). 2007a. "Aid Inflows—The Role of the Fund and Operational Issues for Program Design." Paper prepared by the Policy Development Review Department, Washington, DC.

———. 2007b. "The IMF and Aid to Sub-Saharan Africa." Evaluation Report, Independent Evaluation Office, Washington, DC.

Kharas, H. 2007. "The New Reality of Aid." Wolfensohn Center for Development, Brookings Institution, Washington, DC.

Lewis, M. 2005. "Addressing the Challenge of HIV/AIDS: Macroeconomic, Fiscal and Institutional Issues," Working Paper 58, Center for Global Development, Washington, DC.

ODI (Overseas Development Institute). 2004. "Incentives for Harmonisation in Aid Agencies." Study prepared for the Development Assistance Committee Working Party on Aid Effectiveness, Organisation for Economic Co-operation and Development, Paris.

OECD (Organisation for Economic Co-operation and Development). 2007. "2006 Survey on Monitoring the Paris Declaration: Aid Effectiveness Review." Paris.

OECD-DAC (Organisation for Economic Co-operation and Development-Development Assistance Committee). 2006a. "Donor Reporting on Dissemination of the Paris Declaration." Paper presented at the DAC Meeting, November 15, Paris.

———. 2006b. "Draft Good Practice Guidance for Integration and Effectiveness of Global Programs at the Country Level." COM/DCD/DEV(2006)9, Paris.

———. 2007a. "Methodology for the DAC 2007 Survey of Aid Allocation Policies and Indicative Spending Plans." Paris.

———. 2007b. "Scenarios of Future Aid Flows: DAC Technical Meeting on Aid Allocations and Scaling Up for Results." Paris.

Republic of Rwanda. 2006. "Scaling Up to Achieve the Health MDGs in Rwanda." Background study for the Organisation for Economic Co-operation and Development-Development Assistance Committee's High-Level Forum Meeting. Tunis, June 12–13.

SPA (Strategic Partnership with Africa). 2006. "Joint Evaluation of General Budget Support 1994–2004." Report developed under the auspices of the Development Assistance Committee Network on Development Evaluation, Paris.

Taylor, D. 2007. "Chinese Aid Flows into Africa" Voice of America broadcast, May 8. Available at http://www.voanews.com/english/archive/2007–05/Chinese-Aid-Flows-into-Africa.cfm?CFID=239302083&CFTOKEN=93429454.

Wang, J.-Y. 2007. "What Drives China's Growing Role in Africa?" Working Paper WP/07/211, International Monetary Fund, Washington, DC.

Working Group on Global Health Partnerships. 2005. "Best Practice Principles for Global Health Partnership Activities at Country Level." Report prepared for the High-Level Forum on the Health MDGs, Paris, November 14–15.

World Bank. 2006. "Integrating Global Partnership Programs with Country-Led National Programs: Synthesis of Findings and Recommendations." Contribution to the Organisation for Economic Co-operation and Development's Policy Workshop on Global Programmes and the Paris Agenda. COM/DCD/DEV (2006)7, December 5, Paris.

———. 2007a. "Accelerating Development Outcomes in Africa: Progress and Change in the Africa Action Plan." Paper prepared for the Development Committee Meeting, April 6, Washington, DC.

———. 2007b. "Country-Based Scaling Up: Assessment of Progress and Agenda for Action." Background report prepared for the Development Committee, Washington, DC.

World Bank-IMF (International Monetary Fund). 2007. *Global Monitoring Report 2007: Confronting the Challenges of Gender Equity and Fragile States.* Washington, DC.

CHAPTER 5

The Macroeconomic Dynamics
of Scaling Up Foreign Aid

Shantayanan Devarajan, Delfin S. Go, John Page,
Sherman Robinson, and Karen Thierfelder

Under our proposal the developed world would make a commitment to pro-
viding long-term, predictable, untied and effective aid as investment to the
countries that need it most.

—Gordon Brown, on proposing a new International Finance
Facility at the Chatham House Conference, January 22, 2003

Aid is about the future. Donors give aid so recipients will invest the money
and grow faster, reducing poverty in the future. Aid can also be about the
present, as in quick humanitarian relief for famine and other unforeseen
disasters caused by nature or human conflict. But the debate about the
scaling up of aid and debt relief to poor countries is fundamentally about
the future, linked closely to the attainment of the 2015 Millennium Development Goals (MDGs) of reducing extreme poverty and child mortality
and of improving literacy and health (United Nations Millennium Development Project 2005). Coming on the heels of recent strong commodity
prices for developing countries, particularly in sub-Saharan Africa, these
global initiatives have raised concerns about the effectiveness of aid in
general and the macroeconomic consequences of large aid flows in particular. In addition, the scaling-up debate is taking place during a period of
rapid globalization, which may mean that the effects of aid may differ from
what they were during earlier periods.

On one side of the policy debate, those people who argue for substantial aid and debt relief are passionate about how aid on the scale of a Marshall Plan will bring about a significant supply side response and reduce poverty. They are generally optimistic about possible increases in productivity from aid-assisted public expenditures such as infrastructure and social spending and about possible complementarities between public and private capital (see, for example, the epigraph by Gordon Brown at the beginning of the chapter, as well as Sachs 2005; Tyrangiel 2005; World Bank 2007). The other side is a set of cautionary tales about the absorptive capacity for extensive aid in developing countries, its incentive effects, possible Dutch disease, and macroeconomic instability, as well as serious questions about the effectiveness of aid and the marginal productivity of public investment, especially public expenditures, in education, health, and infrastructure (see, for example, Devarajan, Swaroop, and Zou 1996; Filmer, Hammer, and Pritchett 2000; Easterly 2001, 2003; Pritchett 2001).[1] Both sides of the debate are making statements about the future with scaled-up aid. It would seem that one way to resolve the narrow issue of Dutch disease or real exchange rate appreciation would be to estimate the relevant parameters empirically. Unfortunately, data problems are severe, and there has been a general lack of reliable empirical estimates of crucial relationships and parameters. Recent surveys by Adam (2006) and Radelet, Clemens, and Bhavnani (2006) conclude that the consequences of aid on Dutch disease can vary widely using available econometric estimates. Results generally depend on assumptions about the marginal productivity of additional aid and public expenditures or about the complementarities between public and private capital. Like the criticisms of growth regressions, the empirical bases of those assumptions are subject to further debate and statistical testing.

Partly because of the lack of solid empirical evidence, there is a parallel tradition of employing analytical and simulation models to assess the marginal effect of exogenous flows and shocks on the real exchange rate. The classic work on Dutch disease by Corden and Neary (1982) was quickly followed by several analyses using primarily a computable general equilibrium (CGE) framework, such as van Wijnbergen (1984), Gelb and associates (1988), and Benjamin, Devarajan, and Weiner (1989). But the analytical debate about aid from this literature is also almost always cast in a static framework, and the time dimension is at best derived from recursive dynamics. Recent work is no exception. Adam and Bevan (2004) and

Adam (2006) examine the supply side effects of aid flows in a traditional CGE framework. Even the recent absorptive capacity literature that investigates explicitly the links between public service delivery and MDGs and the allocation effects of public expenditures on social and infrastructure sectors over time—the maquette for MDG simulations in Bourguignon, Diaz-Bonilla, and Lofgren (forthcoming)—assumes that agents are myopic about intertemporal choices.

How important are these intertemporal choices with respect to the scaling up of aid and its effect on consumption, investment, and growth? In a recent International Monetary Fund paper, Berg et al. (2007) examine, for several country cases in Africa, whether recipient countries can use the transfer of external resources from donors (that is, absorb the aid) so that consumption and investment are increased (that is, spend the aid). The case studies, which covered Ethiopia, Ghana, Mozambique, Tanzania, and Uganda, surprisingly reveal no significant real exchange rate appreciation accompanying the surge in aid in any of the sample countries. The amount of absorption increase, for example, ranged from two-third of the aid flow for Mozambique to none for Ghana and Tanzania. Several factors might have affected absorption and spending, including the need (1) to establish macroeconomic stability by reversing low levels of international reserves (Ethiopia and Ghana), (2) to hedge against aid volatility and future reduction of aid inflows, and (3) to avoid real exchange rate appreciation to maintain export competitiveness. Although it is difficult to generalize findings from case studies given each country's circumstances, institutions, and policies, they nonetheless point to the importance of attempts to smooth aid flows. These aspects of aid flows are of growing concern in the continuing assessment of the macroeconomic framework at the Bretton Woods Institutions for the purpose of scaling up aid (see also, for example, chapter 3, as well as Gupta, Powell, and Yang 2006; Heller et al. 2006; IMF 2007a, 2007b; World Bank 2007). The main contribution of this chapter is to introduce choice and forward-looking behavior in a dynamic optimizing framework and to show how that may alter results, particularly about the Dutch disease issue. This chapter takes seriously the notion that aid is about the future and asks, if agents respond to aid in the same way they make intertemporal choices, how will the economy respond? Will the results differ critically from what a static model would predict? If aid is about the future, the appropriate framework should be an intertemporally dynamic model to capture important aspects of the scaling up of aid not possible with static models. In a dynamic framework of an open economy, the real exchange rate—or the relative price of tradable and nontradable goods—not only is at the receiving end of the effect of aid and shocks, but is a vital price signal for the evolution of investment and consumption. Not only will investment and consumption behavior respond to immediate changes in the exchange rate and to the expectation of how those changes will evolve in the future, but the dynamics of the real exchange rate will, in turn, be affected by the supply-and-demand responses over time. Furthermore, exogenous flows and shocks will also likely not last forever, and the anticipation of a finite duration will have a very different dynamic effect than a permanent change.

Assume that investment is "productive" in the sense that it adds to the capital stock rather than being stolen or wasted[2] and that the economy is free to allocate the investment optimally over time, including investing abroad or paying off existing foreign debt. However, additional productivity, such as the idea that expanded exports and imports might be linked to increased total factor productivity (TFP) growth, either in export sectors or more broadly, are not introduced. Adding choice and intertemporal optimality eliminates the Dutch disease problem, even without introducing links between trade and TFP or additional complementarity between public and private capital.

To be sure, there are dynamic analyses such as Devarajan and Go (1998), which examine an export price hike in a fully intertemporal and simple framework but do not explore the effect of aid or the Dutch disease as a particular subject. Turnovsky and Chatterjee (2004) examine the effect of aid and the complementarity between public and private capital in a dynamic context, but they do not distinguish between tradable and nontradable goods. Hence, they do not examine the effect on their relative price or the real exchange rate. Mirzoev (2007) is noteworthy in employing a stochastic general equilibrium model of a small and open economy that allows for intertemporal substitution in consumption and the inclusion of uncertainty in aid inflows, which is defined by an autoregressive AR(1) process. However, capital stock is fixed so that the framework is short term.[3]

A static and dynamic version of a very standard neoclassical growth model found in Devarajan, Lewis, and Robinson (1990, 1993) and Devarajan, Go, Lewis, et al. 1997), which has been called the 1-2-3 model, was used to account explicitly for how choice of model and its assumptions may change results. The simplicity of the 1-2-3 model allows us to derive the macroeconomic implications of exogenous flows and shocks in a transparent manner. Although simple, it captures, in a stylized manner, features characteristic of developing countries and anticipates policy implications obtained in more complex multisectoral CGE models. For example, the model has been applied to a variety of policy issues, such as the pre-1994 overvaluation of the CFA franc[4] in Devarajan (1997, 1999), regional integration in Devarajan, Go, Suthiwart-Narueput, and Voss (1997), and export externalities in de Melo and Robinson (1992). Devarajan, Go, and Li (1999) also provided empirical estimates of the two critical elasticities for about 60 countries. The forward-looking version of the 1-2-3 model found in Devarajan and Go (1998) provides the intertemporal dynamics for direct comparison.

In addition, this chapter examines important aspects of modern economic development, such as globalization and changing capacity, and examines how they may affect scaling up of foreign aid and real exchange rate dynamics. More specifically, the second contribution of this chapter is the introduction of "trends" in trade shares and elasticities to capture important observed historical trends or settings wherein the scaling up of aid takes place. Empirical findings about trade shares emerged long before the more recent talks about globalization and its effect on trade and growth. The importance of the long-term rise in trade proportions and how that might be affected by country size and export concentration is alluded to in the early works of Kuznets (1959, 1966). His data for the more modern period are, however, constrained by the trade contraction during the two world wars and the Great Depression. The pattern is more clearly established by the subsequent cross-country works of Chenery and Syrquin (1975, 1989). Although the direction of causality between trade and growth and the methodologies of many recent studies are still being debated, Winters, McCulloch, and McKay (2004) review the literature and conclude that the weight of evidence points strongly in the direction of trade openness (for example, higher trade shares) enhancing income levels. Similarly, trends in trade elasticities may also be important empirically against the natural tendency of Dutch disease to shrink the traded sector. Empirical estimates in Devarajan, Go, and Li (1999), for example, show that although low-income countries generally have trade substitution elasticities that are lower than one, higher-income countries with greater capability to reallocate and substitute resources tend to have significantly higher elasticities that are greater than one. That pattern points to the potential importance of an initially low-income country that is, however, slowly gaining capacity and flexibility to compete with foreign goods and to integrate itself increasingly into the world economy. The interesting finding of this chapter is that these trends will enhance the main results of the dynamic framework.

The incorporation of "trends" in trade shares is essentially an ad hoc way to capture the fact that actual import demand and export supply do not appear to have an "expenditure" elasticity of one (that is, homothetic), which is assumed in most trade functions in CGE modeling, such as the constant elasticity of substitution (CES) and constant elasticity of transformation (CET) functions described in this chapter. Historically, the expansion of trade shares is much faster than can be explained by changes in relative prices alone. Similarly, although it is feasible to include trends in trade shares and elasticities in a recursive dynamic way as in the early work by Chenery et al. (1986), it has so far not been easy to allow for both at the same time in fully dynamic CGE modeling. Because dynamic simulations are often cast over an infinite horizon and the steady state is reached only over the long term, fixing trade shares and elasticities for low-income countries at their initial lower levels in the base year is a serious shortcoming that has long required attention. One early notable exception is the dynamic CGE model of Jorgenson and Ho (1994), which incorporates a logistic curve for export shares. The econometrically estimated translog equation in their work would, however, allow for only small changes in the neighborhood of the implied average trade elasticities and in an economy that is already developed and stable—the United States. Although ad hoc, our approach in this chapter is simple and transparent; it keeps the model close to the "standard" 1-2-3 Salter-Swan model while capturing the important historical trends. Nonetheless, the new features introduced in this chapter also extend dynamic modeling for more systematic and significant shifts in trade shares and elasticities in trade-focused CGE models, therefore more apposite for developing countries still undergoing significant economic transformation.

To summarize, by comparing static and dynamic effects of exogenous flows, this chapter contributes to the aid debate by isolating the implications of intertemporal choices. By incorporating the evolution of trade shares and elasticities explicitly into the framework, this chapter extends the macroeconomic dynamics of scaled-up aid to include the effect of trade liberalization and globalization. By so doing, it also generalizes previous results of the 1-2-3 model on the real exchange rate. Following the debt literature, the dynamic model described in this chapter includes an upward-sloping supply curve of external debt to mimic borrowing constraints in developing countries. This chapter refrains, however, from any extraneous assumptions about productivity growth, whether exogenous or endogenous, including those that use production function links between public expenditures and various social and development outcomes, because they largely predetermine outcomes.

The Extended Dynamic 1-2-3 Model

The dynamic simulation framework is an expanded version of the 1-2-3t model developed in Devarajan and Go (1998), where producer and consumer decisions are both intra- and intertemporally consistent. The representative consumer maximizes the present value of the utility of consumption; producers maximize the present value of profits. The resulting forward-looking investment, together with its adjustment cost function, is similar to Abel (1980), Summers (1981), and Hayashi (1982). The parsimonious structure of the model is achieved with the basic 1-2-3 model at its core—a Salter-Swan characterization of an open economy that is well documented (see Abel 1980; Summers 1981; Hayashi 1982). With export and import prices exogenous, there is only one endogenous price per period to be solved (the price of the domestic or nontradable good), and the simplified structure is ideal for isolating the evolution of the real exchange rate expressed as the relative price of foreign and domestic goods. The implementation allows for three types of import goods, each assessed with its own import duty. Final imports compete with the domestic good. Output is a fixed coefficient combination of intermediate imports and value added, while capital imports are fixed coefficients of investment. Value added is a CES composite of labor and installed capital. A government sector is present. Government revenue comes from import tariffs, domestic indirect tax, income tax, and foreign official grants, while public expenditures include public consumption, transfers, and subsidies, all of which are normally assumed to be exogenous. Given its structural breakdown, the model can be calibrated with national and fiscal accounts data only; it can also be used to look at trade liberalization and macroeconomic and fiscal adjustments to exogenous shocks. The framework was implemented using data from Madagascar, Mozambique, and the Philippines, which was the original country case in the 1-2-3t model.

New features of the economic framework relate to the introduction of changing or exogenous trends in the trade shares and trade substitution elasticities within the same dynamic run. Increasing the share of exports in aggregate output is akin to a change in technology, which may be brought about by greater integration and by access to the world markets. Likewise, increasing the share of imports in aggregate demand is like a change in consumer preferences that may be brought about by the availability of more types of imports through greater trade. In both cases, rising trade shares are likely to be consistent with greater capacity and flexibility in the economy, which are also linked to greater substitution elasticities between foreign and domestic goods. The algebraic implications of changing elasticities and trade shares on the previous results of the 1-2-3 model on the real exchange rate are derived and discussed in Devarajan et al. (2008).

Modeling implementation of such flexible trade shares and elasticities is greatly simplified with the use of the share and index form of the CET and Armington functions (see equations [5.27] and [5.32] in the annex). The calibration of the model is straightforward. One thing to note is that the reference values of the components for the index form of the CET or CES functions will change every time as the shares of the components are adjusted to satisfy the base-year budget constraint at base-year prices.[5] That recalibration can easily be included in the system of equations of the model (see equations [5.29], [5.30], [5.34], and [5.35] in the annex). Several sensitivity tests were run, and the results are consistent with the conceptual conclusions of the preceding sections.

In addition, the external debt accumulation is carefully specified in order to examine issues of foreign aid and borrowing in developing countries. Foreign aid can come in the form of concessional loans (subsidized interest rate) or outright foreign official grants (no interest charges or repayment required). Following the literature regarding borrowing constraints or imperfect debt market for developing countries (see, for example, Bardhan 1967; Eaton and Gersovitz 1981; Obsfeld 1982; Sachs and Cohen 1982; Bhandari, Haque, and Turnovsky 1990; Kletzer 1994; van der Ploeg 1996), an upward-sloping supply curve of external debt is used, and there is a risk premium that rises with external debt. More specifically,

$$i(Debt) = i^* + \omega(Debt/GDP); \quad \omega > 0 \qquad (5.1)$$

where the world interest rate i^* is a weighted average of the interest for concessional and commercial loan—equation (5.15) in the annex. The risk premium ω rises with foreign debt as a ratio to the capacity to pay as indicated by gross domestic product (GDP) (equation [5.14] in the annex).[6]

Like the 1-2-3t model, the domestic interest rate affecting consumption and investment is a form of risk-adjusted interest parity reflecting the cost of foreign borrowing. Hence, the domestic discount rate will depend on both i and the forward evolution of the real exchange rate. For the consumer, the appropriate real exchange rate is the relative price of imports and domestic goods; for the producer, it is the relative price of exports and domestic goods. In the steady state, the economy reaches a balanced-growth path, the change in the real exchange rate ceases, and the domestic discount rate settles back to i. In a forward-looking framework and for dynamic consistency, the consumer correctly anticipates this and its single rate of time preference adjusts immediately in the first period and is used throughout the time horizon. The difference between this expanded framework and the previous 1-2-3t model is that $i(Debt)$ could change at the steady state or terminal period and will not necessarily be the risk-free i^*. Hence, the rate of time preference may also change with each simulation.

The simulations distinguish between two types of countries.[7] The first type refers to an economy with a growing and functioning private sector, and the full-scale model with endogenous and forward-looking investment and consumption is deployed. Subject to an upward-sloping supply of debt, the current account, or more precisely external borrowing, is an integral part of the optimal decisions of the consumer and producer and adjusts dynamically to bridge the gap between investment and savings. This country is referred to as the flexible dynamic country (simulations 1 and 2).

There are many reasons to believe that some agents, even those in developed countries, are credit constrained. This chapter takes this case to mean a country facing severe constraints in savings and external borrowings. A significant source of savings is derived from external financing and comes in the form of foreign aid to finance much-needed public capital. Without public expenditures and investments financed by aid, many of these countries are likely stuck at a low-level equilibrium. This second case uses a modified version where the forward-looking behavior of investment is rendered inoperative and investment in each period adjusts to available savings. External financing is exogenous and two options are considered for consumption: (1) consumption is forward-looking and dynamic because foreign aid is available and stable (simulation 3), and (2) no forward planning is feasible in consumption (consumers are myopic and optimize in each time period; there are recursive dynamics but no intertemporal decisions about consumption) because foreign aid is unpredictable and volatile (simulation 4).

The chapter annex lists the equations of the full dynamic framework, dubbed the 1-2-3Aid model. Except for the new features, calibration and implementation follow Devarajan and Go (1998).

Simulations[8]

Economy with Forward-Looking Investment and Consumption

Simulation 1: Foreign Official Grants Increase by 2 Percent of Output Permanently

A significant increase in foreign grants will not necessarily lead to a real exchange rate appreciation or a Dutch disease problem. In any economy with an active private sector undertaking significant investment but facing an existing debt stock and an upward-sloping supply of debt, the effect is to increase investment, consumption, and output over time as expected (see figures 5.1 and 5.2). However, the dynamically optimal decisions in investment and consumption will result in the real exchange

FIGURE 5.1
Investment Ratio to Base: Permanent versus Temporary Increase in Foreign Aid

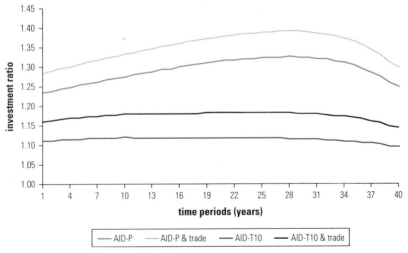

Source: Authors' calculations.

Note: AID-P = permanent increase in aid; AID-T10 = temporary increase in aid for 10 periods; trade = trend increase in trade shares and elasticities.

FIGURE 5.2

Consumption Ratio to Base: Permanent versus Temporary Increase in Foreign Aid

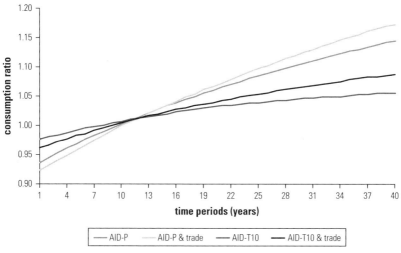

Source: Authors' calculations.

rate depreciating immediately (rather than appreciating), as well as the external debt stock declining over time (see figures 5.3 and 5.4). The effects are interrelated.

With a permanent increase in aid, domestic agents will consume and invest it optimally. To the extent that some of it is invested, the domestic price has to increase in the future to make the investment profitable (recall that the world price is exogenous). For the domestic price to rise in the future, it has to fall in the present, so that the trajectory is upward sloping, to justify the investment. For investment to jump and increase, the returns to the firm must also improve to reach a new asset market equilibrium; hence, the market discount rate affecting supply behavior will have to increase immediately (equations [5.16] and [5.17] in the annex). The firm's real exchange rate in the 1-2-3t model is Pe/Pd, and the relative price of domestic goods (relative to exports) must fall to cause the forward depreciation of the real exchange rate required to change the firm's discount rate. In the absence of an external shock, the fall in the relative price of domestic goods is brought about by an immediate contraction of consumption. As a result, the real exchange rate affecting consumption, Pm/Pd, also rises, which increases the demand-side discount rate, postponing consumption immediately but causing an increasing growth rate

FIGURE 5.3
Real Exchange Rate: Permanent versus Temporary Increase in Foreign Aid

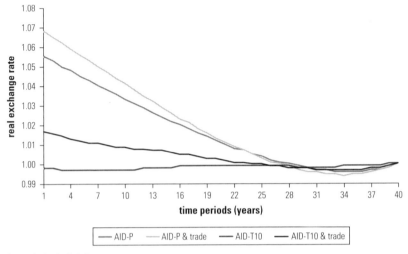

Source: Authors' calculations.

FIGURE 5.4
Debt Ratio to Base: Permanent versus Temporary Increase in Foreign Aid

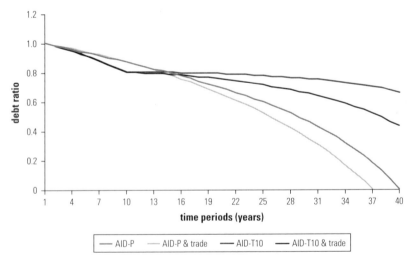

Source: Authors' calculations.

in consumption over time. The rise in consumption and investment will eventually lead to a gradual amelioration of the initial depreciation, ultimately restoring the real exchange rates to the same preshock level at the steady-state terminal period.

In the face of an upward-sloping supply curve of external debt, another optimal outcome is to substitute and pay back in effect the preexisting external debt with the interest-free foreign grants. Agents want to invest, and the highest return in the early period is to retire existing debt (effectively getting a return equal to the interest rate on foreign debt). The trade balance improves, and the real exchange rate depreciates. Investment is allocated between debt reduction and capital formation, with the depreciation increasing the return to investment in exportables. As growth occurs, debt retirement ceases, domestic investment increases, and the exchange rate appreciates, returning finally to its initial level. External debt gradually declines to almost zero over 40 years, supporting the notion that foreign grants and debt relief are essentially equivalent. Over time, the decline in debt also reduces the premium paid for borrowing, hence the discount rate directly, as well as shifts down the rate of time preference for the consumer, spurring consumption and slowing the growth of further investment slightly.

Sensitivity tests were completed by imposing different rising trends in trade shares and trade substitution elasticities to signify greater openness and integration into the world economy and greater economic capacity and flexibility over time. The effects of globalization as defined are to improve the outcomes—growth of exports, investment, consumption, and output are all increased much more rapidly (see figures 5.1 and 5.2). In the long run (that is, the steady state), the level of exports is about 21 percent higher; likewise, investment, consumption, and output are 2.5 to 4 percent higher. The initial decline of consumption and the initial depreciation (see figure 5.3) are higher, and the external debt is also reduced much more quickly.

With respect to the real exchange rate, the contrast to the static case is worth emphasizing. In the basic 1-2-3 model where aggregate output or supply is essentially fixed, the effect of an exogenous inflow is always an appreciation of the real exchange rate; the appreciation becomes less as trade shares and elasticities increase. Here, the intertemporal behavior in consumption and investment, how they are affected by the real exchange rate, and an upward-sloping credit supply function alter the outcome altogether. Increasing both trade shares and elasticities make the dynamic model more sensitive.

The absorption of scaled-up aid and its effect on the real exchange rate are uniquely products of the intertemporal decisions of investment and consumption. Consumption smoothing is the usual outcome of a Ramsey intertemporal savings function, and the rate of exchange governing present and future consumption determines household demand for goods and services over time (equation [5.2] in the annex). However, the intertemporal supply response also adds another dimension. Investment is endogenous and inherently productive, but it is dependent on present and future relative prices and how they affect the stream of profits over time and the adjustment cost to additional capital (see, for example, Abel 1980; Summers 1981; Hayashi 1982). More precisely, at each point in time, as long as the present value of the marginal returns to investment is greater than the replacement cost of capital in a Tobin's q-type formulation, investment will rise (equations [5.3]–[5.9] in the annex). However, investment expenditure automatically ceases whenever the marginal cost–benefit ratio becomes unfavorable. Likewise, the supply response is not an instantaneous jump due to adjustment costs, and no additional productivity gains are assumed or needed to the story about the real exchange rate, growth, and debt.

Any doubts from the aid literature about the effect of incremental aid with respect to the supply response, absorption, and the real exchange rate are likely because of additional assumptions regarding the lack of productivity of investment, as well as the lack of dynamic behavior, particularly about investment. Additional savings are poured altogether toward capital accumulation despite decreasing marginal returns. In this case, there is no intertemporal path in consumption and investment to suggest that a debt reduction combined with an initial depreciation may be optimal.

These results tend to support recent historical policy responses to the external debt problems in developing countries. During the debt crisis of developing countries in the 1980s, many countries first availed themselves of long-term concessionary loans to effectively replace the more short-term and costly commercial debt. Policy conditions partly required the undertaking of much-needed policy reforms as well as economic and trade liberalization. However, growth and debt sustainability remained fragile in the 1990s so that significant debt relief came from the Heavily Indebted Poor Countries Initiative, the Multilateral Debt Relief Initiative (MDRI), and the recent trend toward pure grants. As long as there is a risk associated with increased foreign borrowing as well as continuing signs of possible debt distress, the results confirm that it is optimal to draw down the external debt with outright debt relief or foreign grants. Conversely, it also suggests that aid and debt relief will not lead to a renewed and unwanted external debt accumulation, because doing so may be far from optimal and sustainable.

Simulation 2: Foreign Official Grants Increase by 2 Percent of Output Temporarily—for 10 Years

What if foreign grants are temporary, lasting for only 10 years, and are expected to be so? Here, there is a uniform upward shift to investment; that is, it increases immediately and stays at more or less the same level over the simulation period. Over time, the additional investment raises output. However, investment and output levels are all below simulation 1 throughout (see figure 5.1). Consumption declines initially and increases over time; the initial decline and subsequent increases are also less than simulation 1 (see figure 5.2).

In addition, it is still optimal to pay back debt significantly while the interest-free foreign grants last, amounting to more than half the grants each year. As a result, debt stock is reduced by about 20 percent by the 10th year. After the 10th year, the trajectory of consumption, investment, and output, as well the preshock levels of exogenous flows from other sources, will allow the continuation of debt repayments. Debt at the steady-state terminal period is reduced by a third of the original level.

Relative to a permanent increase in foreign aid (simulation 1), the real exchange rate response for a temporary aid shock depends much more on the magnitude and length of the shock. Keeping the magnitude of the shock similar to simulation 1 and the length of the aid shock at 10 years, the real exchange rate remains practically constant throughout. If anything, there is a slight appreciation that is hardly perceptible. However, if the aid shock lasts longer, 15 or more years (instead of 10), the real exchange rate will depreciate immediately, albeit much less than in simulation 1 (see figure 5.3).

Sensitivity tests were also completed by imposing different rising trends in trade shares and trade substitution elasticities. Like simulation 1, the effect is to intensify the changes in consumption, investment, output, and debt. There is also now a slight and immediate depreciation, which is ameliorated over time (similar to the case of a permanent increase in foreign aid, simulation 1).

Economy with Severe Borrowing Constraint and Dearth of Public Capital

Simulation 3: Foreign Official Grants Increase by 2 Percent of Output

In an economy with a severe borrowing constraint, the current account balance is rigid or exogenous. Because aid is permanent, consumers still make optimal intertemporal consumption choices (equation [5.2] in the annex). Investment decisions, however, are not based on a comparison of the marginal returns to additional capital relative to its replacement cost. Instead, investment is completely driven by the intertemporal decision to consume or save (hence, equations [5.3]–[5.8] are rendered inoperative). Additional resources from the exogenous inflows will bid up prices of domestic goods so that the real exchange rate appreciates immediately (see figure 5.5). The higher prices and the forward exchange rate favor postponing consumption, and, hence, consumption falls in the initial years (see figure 5.6). Investment rises throughout from additional savings, and over time, income and consumption also rise as a result of the increased supply (see figure 5.7). The increased supply will slowly reduce the initial

FIGURE 5.5
Real Exchange Rate: Permanent Increase in Foreign Aid, with Borrowing Constraints

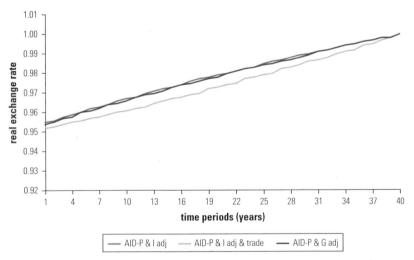

Source: Authors' calculations.

Note: I adj = investment adjusts; G adj = government consumption adjusts.

FIGURE 5.6
Consumption Ratio to Base: Permanent Increase in Foreign Aid, with Borrowing Constraints

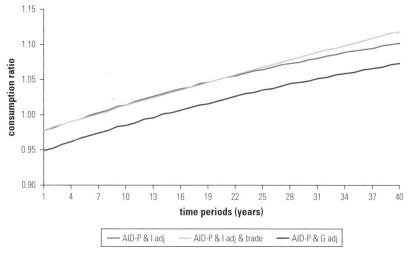

Source: Authors' calculations.

FIGURE 5.7
Investment Ratio to Base: Permanent Increase in Foreign Aid, with Borrowing Constraints

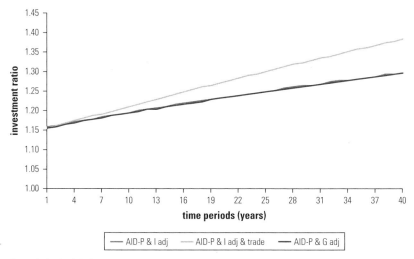

Source: Authors' calculations.

appreciation of the exchange rate. This is the kind of story that is behind much of the standard thinking about the effect of aid. Because the inflows are grants and borrowing is fixed (zero), no debt story is relevant in this simulation.

Sensitivity tests of rising trends in trade shares and trade substitution elasticities result in amplifying somewhat the effect on investment and output while consumption is almost identical or very slightly more (figure 5.6). The appreciation of the exchange rate is more at every point in time. The eventual reduction of the initial appreciation is, therefore, also relatively less over time (figure 5.5—as what would be expected from the static case of changing shares and elasticities).

Much concern has also been made regarding the differences in effect between exogenous flows financing pure government consumption rather than investment. Although not directly productive,[9] the expansion of government consumption as an exogenous component of aggregate demand has a Keynesian effect on prices and income. If the same amount in foreign grants all go to government consumption rather than investment, prices will still be bid up in the same way and the consumer will face the same kind of Ramsey saving decision. Hence, the results with regard to the real exchange rate (see figure 5.5), investment (see figure 5.7), and output are essentially the same as the investment case. The only difference is that with total absorption or aggregate demand also behaving the same way, the consumption curve over the simulation period will shift down to make room for the exact amount of increase in government consumption (see figure 5.6).

Simulation 4: Foreign Official Grants Increase by
2 Percent of Output, Myopic Case
The only way for the case of financing government consumption to differ from the investment case is for the representative consumer to be completely myopic so that no optimization is made about present versus future consumption. The results are confirmed by setting up a recursively dynamic 1-2-3 model. If aid all goes to government consumption, the real exchange appreciation is highest, by as much as 12 percent initially (see figure 5.8), because there is no longer any substitution across time for consumption or supply to moderate the results. As current consumption from the government sector raises domestic prices and causes the exchange rates (equations [5.18] and [5.19] in the annex) to appreciate, the latter

FIGURE 5.8
Real Exchange Rate: Permanent Increase in Foreign Aid, with and without Borrowing Constraints

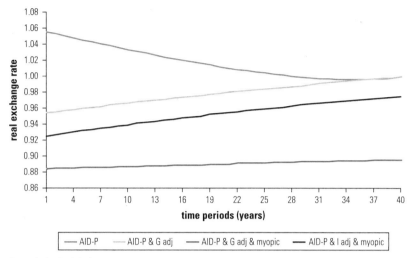

Source: Authors' calculations.

Note: Myopic = agents are myopic.

are no longer linked to the discount rates (equations [5.16] and [5.17]) to affect present and future consumption choices (equation [5.2]) or supply decisions (equations [5.3]–[5.8]). Furthermore, aid does not go to the savings pool to raise investment directly. There is, however, a Keynesian-like expansion from the additional demand, which will raise investment, output, and consumption over time, albeit only marginally. Because the supply response is limited, depreciation remains at 10.5 percent relative to the reference case some 40 years after.

If aid all goes to investment so that supply responds directly over time, the real exchange rate appreciation is less at 7.5 percent initially (see figure 5.8). Relative to the reference path, investment rises by 11.0 percent initially and eventually to 22.5 percent at the end of 40 years (see figure 5.9). Output and consumption both increase eventually by about 10 percent of the reference level (see figure 5.10). However, all the levels regarding investment, consumption, and output are below simulations 1 (permanent aid, no borrowing constraint) and 3 (permanent aid, borrowing constraint). The ideal case is simulation 1 when investment is only

FIGURE 5.9

Investment Ratio to Base: Permanent Increase in Foreign Aid, with and without Borrowing Constraints

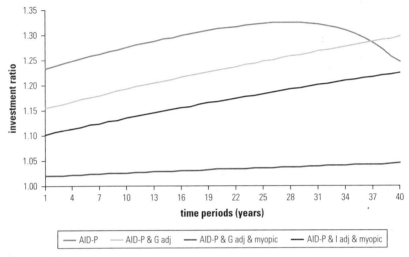

Source: Authors' calculations.

FIGURE 5.10

Consumption Ratio to Base: Permanent Increase in Foreign Aid, with and without Borrowing Constraints

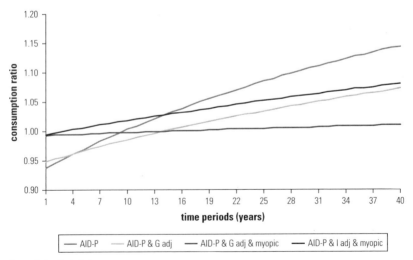

Source: Authors' calculations.

undertaken strictly on a merit basis (as in cost–benefit calculations) and the current account balance is part of the intertemporal optimization. Nonetheless, the comparison of these simple experiments to simulation 3 touches on an important policy implication. If there is a severe borrowing constraint and if donor aid flows are unpredictable so that the representative consumer is unable to smooth consumption over time (for example, myopic or constrained), even if future aid disbursements every year turned out to be constant and at a significant level, the level of consumption and investment (see figure 5.9) and output will still be below the case when these aid flows are fully committed and expected at the outset to allow for expenditure smoothing. In this case, outright debt relief such as the MDRI, which secures a definite resource flow with regard to debt service being forgiven, should be preferable to uncertain aid flows.

If aid is temporary, the results in a myopic case are trivial—all shifts and changes because of aid cease when aid ceases.

Conclusions

If aid is about the future and recipients can plan consumption and investment decisions optimally over time, aid will not only bring about better economic outcomes in output, consumption, and investment but the potential problem of an aid-induced appreciation of the real exchange rate (Dutch disease) does not appear. This result is true not only for a permanent aid shock but also for a temporary aid shock over a period of about 10 years (for a reasonable set of parameters). With greater economic flexibility and an increasing degree of integration to the global economy, the results will be even more dramatic.

This key result does not require extreme assumptions. The economic framework is a standard neoclassical growth model, based on the familiar Salter-Swan characterization of an open economy, with full dynamic savings and investment decisions. It does require that the model is fully dynamic in both savings and investment decisions. The consumption and savings trade-offs follow the usual Ramsey formulation, while supply incorporates the dynamic behavior of firms that is now standard in dynamic macroeconomics. The latter is important in the sense that investment is undertaken only up to the point where the present value of its marginal returns matches the replacement cost of capital; excess aid beyond that point is optimally used to reduce or retire interest-bearing debt.

An important assumption is that aid should be predictable for intertemporal smoothing to take place. If aid volatility forces recipients to be constrained and myopic, Dutch disease problems become an issue. In this case, the levels of consumption, investment, and output are also below the flexible dynamic case. In this constrained and myopic world, greater economic flexibility and an increasing degree of integration into the global economy will reduce the Dutch disease problems as expected and will also improve economic outcomes (but still less than in the flexible dynamic case).

In short, any unfavorable macroeconomic dynamics of scaled-up aid are the result of donor behavior rather than the functioning of recipient economies.

Annex: The 1-2-3Aid Model

Equations

Consumption

$$\frac{C_{t+1}}{C_t} = \left(\frac{PC_{t+1}(1+\rho)}{PC_t(1+r^c_{t+1})}\right)^{-\frac{1}{v}} \tag{5.2}$$

Investment and Tobin's q

$$\frac{I_t}{K_t} = \alpha + \frac{1}{\beta}Q^T_t \tag{5.3}$$

$$Q^T_t = \left[\frac{q_t}{PK_t} - (1 - bb - tc_t)\right] \tag{5.4}$$

$$r_t q_t = R_k(t) + \Delta q - \delta q_{t+1} \tag{5.5}$$

$$J_t = [1 - tc + \theta_t(I/K)]I_t \tag{5.6}$$

$$R_k(t) = rk_t - PK_t(I_t/K_t)^2\theta'_t(I/K) \tag{5.7}$$

$$\theta(x_t) = \left(\frac{\beta}{2}\right)\frac{(x_t - \alpha)^2}{x_t} \tag{5.8}$$

$$K_t = (1 - \delta)K_{t-1} + I_{t-1} \tag{5.9}$$

Terminal Conditions

$$\frac{I_{tf}}{K_{tf}} = \delta^R \tag{5.10}$$

$$PC_{tf}C_{tf} = Y_{tf} \tag{5.11}$$

$$r^c_{tf} \equiv r^p_{tf} \equiv i^*_{tf} \tag{5.12}$$

$$\rho \equiv i^*_{tf} \tag{5.13}$$

Cost of Borrowing and Transformation Rates

$$i^{debt}_t = i^w_t + \omega\left(\frac{DEBT_t er}{Q_t PQ_0}\right) \tag{5.14}$$

$$i^*_t = s_{aid}i^{aid}_t + (1 - s_{aid})i^{debt}_t \tag{5.15}$$

$$r^p_t = i^*_t + \frac{\dot{e}^p_t}{e^p_t} \tag{5.16}$$

$$r_t^c = i_t^* + \frac{\dot{e}_t^c}{e_t^c} \qquad (5.17)$$

$$e_t^p = \frac{PE_t}{PD_t} \qquad (5.18)$$

$$e_t^c = \frac{PM_t}{PD_t} \qquad (5.19)$$

Prices

$$PE_t = \frac{pe_t^* er}{1 + te_t} \qquad (5.20)$$

$$PM_t = pm_t^*(1 + tm_t^c)er \qquad (5.21)$$

$$PMK_t = pmk_t^*(1 + tm_t^k)er \qquad (5.22)$$

$$PMN_t = pmn_t^*(1 + tm_t^n)er \qquad (5.23)$$

$$PK_t = [a_k PMK_t + (1 - a_k)P_t](1 + \phi_t tx_t) \qquad (5.24)$$

$$PC_t = P_t(1 + tx_t) \qquad (5.25)$$

Armington CES Function

$$P_t X_t = PD_t D_t + PM_t M_t \qquad (5.26)$$

$$X_t = X_0 \left[\delta_t^c \left(\frac{M_t}{M_t^{ref}} \right)^{-\rho_t^c} + (1 - \delta_t^c) \left(\frac{D_t}{D_t^{ref}} \right)^{-\rho_t^c} \right]^{-1/\rho_t^c} \qquad (5.27)$$

$$\frac{M_t}{D_t} = \left[\frac{\delta_t^c}{(1 - \delta_t^c)} \frac{PD_t}{PM_t} \right]^{1/(1+\rho_t^c)} \qquad (5.28)$$

$$PM_0 M_t^{ref} = \delta_t^c P_0 X_0 \qquad (5.29)$$

$$PD_0 D_t^{ref} = (1 - \delta_t^c)P_0 X_0 \qquad (5.30)$$

CET Transformation

$$PQ_t Q_t = PD_t D_t + PE_t E_t \qquad (5.31)$$

$$Q_t = Q_0 \left[\delta_t^e \left(\frac{E_t}{E_t^{ref}} \right)^{\rho_t^e} + (1 - \delta_t^e) \left(\frac{D_t}{D_t^{ref}} \right)^{\rho_t^e} \right]^{-1/\rho_t^e} \qquad (5.32)$$

$$\frac{E_t}{D_t} = \left[\frac{(1 - \delta_t^e)}{\delta_t^e} \frac{PE_t}{PD_t} \right]^{1/(\rho_t^e - 1)} \qquad (5.33)$$

$$PE_0 E_t^{ref} = \delta_t^e PQ_0 Q_0 \tag{5.34}$$

$$PD_0 D_t^{ref} = (1 - \delta_t^e) PQ_0 Q_0 \tag{5.35}$$

Value Added

$$PV_t = PQ_t/(1 + ts_t) - a_n PMN_t \tag{5.36}$$

$$PV_t Q_t = w_t L_t + rk_t \overline{K}_t \tag{5.37}$$

$$Q_t = \alpha_v [\delta_v L_t^{-\rho_v} + (1 - \delta_v) \overline{K}_t^{-\rho_v}]^{-1/\rho_v} \tag{5.38}$$

$$\frac{L_t}{\overline{K}_t} = \left[\frac{\delta_v}{(1 - \delta_v)} \frac{rk_t}{w_t} \right]^{1/(1+\rho_v)} \tag{5.39}$$

Household Budget

$$
\begin{aligned}
YH_t = & \; w_t L_t + rk_t K_t \\
& + GTRS_t P_t \\
& + EFLOW S_t er \\
& - (1 - d_g) i_t^* DEBT_t er
\end{aligned}
\tag{5.40}
$$

$$Y_t = (1 - ty) YH_t \tag{5.41}$$

Government Budget

$$
\begin{aligned}
TAX_t = & \; tm_t^c (M_t pm_t^* er) \\
& + tm_t^k (MK_t pmk_t^* er) \\
& + tm_t^n (MN_t pmn_t^* er) \\
& + te_t (E_t pe_t^* er) \\
& + tx_t [P_t (C_t + G_t + J_t)] \\
& + ty_t [YH_t - (PK_t J_t - B_t er - SAVG_t)]
\end{aligned}
\tag{5.42}
$$

$$
\begin{aligned}
SG_t = & \; TAX_t + ts_t/(1 + ts_t) PQ_t Q_t \\
& + FGRS_t er - d_g i_t^* DEBT_t er \\
& - G_t PC_t - GTRS_t P_t
\end{aligned}
\tag{5.43}
$$

Balance of Payments

$$
\begin{aligned}
& pm_t^* M_t + pmk_t^* MK_t + pmn_t^* MN_t + i^* DEBT_t \\
& \equiv pe_t^* E_t + FGRS_t + EFLOWS_t + B_t
\end{aligned}
\tag{5.44}
$$

$$DEBT_t = DEBT_{t-1} + B_t \tag{5.45}$$

$$MN_t = a_n Q_t \tag{5.46}$$

$$MK_t = a_k J_t \tag{5.47}$$

Labor Market

$$L_t \equiv \overline{LS}_t \qquad\qquad (5.48)$$

Goods Market

$$X_t \equiv C_t + G_t + J_t(1 - ak) \qquad\qquad (5.49)$$

Glossary

Parameters

α_v	shift parameter in the CES function for V
a_n	coefficient of intermediate imports
a_n	coefficient of capital imports
d_g	share of public external debt
δ	depreciation rate of capital
δ_t^c	cost share parameter in the CES function for Q
δ_t^e	cost share parameter in the CET function for Q
δ_v	share parameter in the CES function for V
α	parameter in the adjustment cost function
er	nominal exchange rate, price numeraire
g	growth rate
i_t^*	weighted average of interest rates for commercial debt and concessionary loans
i_t^{aid}	interest rate for concessionary loans
i_t^{debt}	world interest rate inclusive of risk premium
i_t^w	world interest rate
ϕ	parameter in the purchase price of investment goods
ρ	rate of consumer time preference
ρ_t^c	exponent parameter in the CES function for Q
ρ_t^e	exponent parameter in the CET function for Q
ρ_v	exponent parameter in the CES function for V
pe_t^*	world export price
pm_t^*	world price of final imports
pmk_t^*	world price of capital imports
pmn_t^*	world price of intermediate imports
s_{aid}	share of concessionary loans in external debt
tc_t	rate of new tax credits to investment
te_t	export tax or subsidies rate
tm_t^c	import duty for final goods

tm_t^k	import duty for capital goods
tm_t^n	import duty for intermediate goods
tx_t	domestic indirect tax rate
ty_t	direct income tax
ω	adjustment parameter for risk premium in debt

Prices

P_t	price of supply
PD_t	price of domestic goods
PE_t	domestic price of exports
PK_t	price of capital
PMC_t	domestic price of final imports
PMK_t	domestic price of capital imports
PMN_t	domestic price of intermediate imports
PQ_t	price of gross output
PV_t	price of value added
e_t^p	real exchange rate for supply
e_t^c	real exchange rate for demand
q_t	shadow price of capital
Q_t^T	tax adjusted Tobin's q
r_t^p	discount rate for supply
r_t^c	discount rate for demand
rk_t	gross rate of return to capital
μ_t	discount factor
w_t	wage rate

Quantities

C_t	aggregate consumption at time t
D_t	domestic goods
D_t^{ref}	reference domestic goods adjusted for changing trade share
E_t	exports
E_t^{ref}	reference exports adjusted for changing export share
G_t	government consumption
I_t	investment
K_t	capital stock
L_t	labor demand
L_0	base-year labor supply
LS_t	labor supply at time t

M_t final imports
M_t^{ref} reference final imports adjusted for changing import share
MK_t capital imports
MN_t intermediate imports
Q_t gross output
V_t value added
RK_t marginal net revenue product of capital
X_t aggregate supply

Values

B_t foreign borrowings or capital inflows
$DEBT_t$ outstanding foreign debt at time t
$EFLOWS_t$ net exogenous flows from abroad (excluding grants and new borrowings)
$FGRS_t$ foreign grants (interest free)
SG_t government savings
$GTRS_t$ government transfers to households
J_t total investment expenditures, including adjustment cost
$\theta(x_t)$ adjustment cost function

Notes

1. A recent survey of the conflicting perspectives is found in Roodman (2007).
2. An adjustment cost to investment is present, however, which raises the cost of investment as investment rises as a ratio to the capital stock. The feature follows the standard q-theory of investment in macroeconomics and also allows for smoother behavior in investment over time.
3. See chapter 3 for a more detailed discussion of some recent approaches and issues.
4. The CFA franc is the currency of the francophone countries in Africa; the CFA franc has a fixed exchange rate with the euro.
5. When changing trade shares, it is assumed that the base utility from the consumption bundle stays at the initial value.
6. Concessionary loans are assumed to have an interest rate of 2.5 percent, which is similar to the effective interest rate for International Development Association–type loans over 40 years at the World Bank. Risk-free commercial loans are assumed to have an interest rate of 5.0 percent. Premium rate γ is calibrated so that i is exactly the average interest paid on the country's external debt in the base year.

7. In reality, there is a range of countries, with the two extreme cases being (1) completely flexible and (2) credit-constrained agents. The two extremes are presented in this section.

8. All simulations are presented as deviations to the levels in the reference run (=1.0), which is defined as a balanced growth or steady-state run.

9. Except for public expenditures on social sectors, which potentially may raise human capital in the long run. Because the trade-offs regarding investments for the development of human and physical capital are not the focus of this chapter, government consumption is considered to be pure consumption expenditures for goods and services.

References

Abel, Andrew B. 1980. "Empirical Investment Equations: An Integrative Framework." In *On the State of Macroeconomics*, ed. K. Brunner and A. H. Meltzer, *Carnegie-Rochester Conference Series on Public Policy* 12: 39–91.

Adam, Christopher. 2006. "Exogenous Inflows and Real Exchange Rates: Theoretical Quirk or Empirical Reality?" In *The Macroeconomic Management of Foreign Aid*, ed. Peter Isard, Leslie Lipschitz, Alex Mourmouras, and Boriana Yontcheva, 171–93. Washington, DC: International Monetary Fund.

Adam, Christopher, and David L. Bevan. 2004. "Aid and the Supply Side: Public Investment, Export Performance, and Dutch Disease in Low-Income Countries." Department of Economics Discussion Paper 201, University of Oxford, Oxford, U.K.

Bardhan, Pranab K. 1967. "Optimum Foreign Borrowing." In *Essays on the Theory of Optimal Economic Growth*, ed. Karl Shell, 117–28. Cambridge, MA: MIT Press.

Benjamin, Nancy C., Shantayanan Devarajan, and Robert J. Weiner. 1989. "Dutch Disease in a Developing Country: Oil Reserves in Cameroon." *Journal of Development Economics* 30 (1): 71–92.

Berg, Andrew, Shekhar Aiyar, Mumtaz Hussain, Shaun Roache, Tokhir Mirzoev, and Amber Mahone. 2007. "The Macroeconomics of Scaling Up Aid: Lessons from Recent Experience." Occasional Paper 253, International Monetary Fund, Washington, DC.

Bhandari, Jagdeep S., Nadeem U. I. Haque, and Stephen J. Turnovsky. 1990. "Growth, External Debt, and Sovereign Risk in a Small Open Economy." *IMF Staff Papers* 37 (2): 388–417.

Bourguignon, François, Carolina Diaz-Bonilla, and Hans Lofgren. Forthcoming. "Aid, Service Delivery, and the MDGs in an Economy-Wide Framework." In *The Impact of Economic Policies on Poverty and Income Distribution: Macro-Micro Evaluation Techniques and Tools*, ed. François Bourguignon, Luiz Pereira da Silva, and Mauritzio Bussolo. New York: Palgrave.

Chenery, Hollis, Jeffrey Lewis, Jaime de Melo, and Sherman Robinson. 1986. "Alternative Routes to Development." In *Industrialization and Growth*, ed. Hollis Chenery, Sherman Robinson, and Moshe Syrquin, 311–47. New York: World Bank and Oxford University Press.

Chenery, Hollis, and Moises Syrquin. 1975. *Patterns of Development: 1950–70*. London: Oxford University Press.

———. 1989. "Three Decades of Industrialization." *World Bank Economic Review* 3 (2): 145–81.

Corden, W. Max, and L. Peter Neary. 1982. "Booming Sector and De-industrialization in a Small Open Economy," *Economic Journal* 92 (368): 825–48.

de Melo, Jaime, and Sherman Robinson. 1992. "Productivity and Externalities: Models of Export-Led Growth." *Journal of International Trade and Economic Development* 1: 41–68.

Devarajan, Shantayanan, 1997. "Real Exchange Rate Misalignment in the CFA Zone." *Journal of African Economies* 6 (10): 35–53.

———. 1999. "Estimates of Real Exchange Rate Misalignment with a Simple General Equilibrium Model." In *Exchange Rate Misalignment: Concepts and Measurement for Developing Countries*, ed. Lawrence E. Hinkle and Peter J. Montiel, 359–80. Washington, DC: World Bank and Oxford University Press.

Devarajan, Shantayanan, and Delfin S. Go. 1998. "The Simplest Dynamic General-Equilibrium Model of an Open Economy." *Journal of Policy Modeling* 20 (6): 677–714.

Devarajan, Shantayanan, Delfin S. Go, Jeffrey D. Lewis, Sherman Robinson, and Pekka Sinko. 1997. "Simple General Equilibrium Modeling." In *Applied Methods for Trade Policy Analysis: A Handbook*, ed. Joseph F. Francois and Kenneth A. Reinert, 156–88. Cambridge, UK: Cambridge University Press.

Devarajan, Shantayanan, Delfin S. Go, and Hongyi Li. 1999. "Quantifying the Fiscal Effects of Trade Reform: A General Equilibrium Model Estimated for 60 Countries." Policy Research Working Paper 2162, World Bank, Washington, DC.

Devarajan, Shantayanan, Delfin S. Go, John Page, Sherman Robinson, and Karen Thierfelder. 2008. "Aid, Growth, and Real Exchange Rate Dynamics." Policy Research Working Paper 4480, World Bank, Washington, DC.

Devarajan, Shantayanan, Delfin S. Go, Sehaput Suthiwart-Narueput, and John Voss. 1997. "Direct and Indirect Fiscal Effects of the Euro-Mediterranean Free Trade Agreements." Paper presented at the Mediterranean Development Forum: Knowledge and Skills for Development in the Information Age, Marrakech, Morocco, May 12–17.

Devarajan, Shantayanan, Jeffrey D. Lewis, and Sherman Robinson. 1990. "Policy Lessons from Trade-Focused, Two-Sector Models." *Journal of Policy Modeling* 12 (4): 635–57.

————. 1993. "External Shocks, Purchasing Power Parity, and the Equilibrium Exchange Rate." *World Bank Economic Review* 7 (1): 45–63.

Devarajan, Shantayanan, Vinaya Swaroop, and Heng-fu Zou. 1996. "The Composition of Public Expenditure and Economic Growth." *Journal of Monetary Economics* 37 (2–3): 313–44.

Easterly, William R. 2001. *The Elusive Quest for Growth: Economists' Adventures and Misadventures in the Tropics.* Cambridge, MA: MIT Press.

————. 2003. "Can Foreign Aid Buy Growth?" *Journal of Economic Perspectives* 17 (3): 23–48.

Eaton, Jonathan, and Mark Gersovitz. 1981. "Debt with Potential Repudiation: Theoretical and Empirical Analysis." *Review of Economic Studies* 48 (2): 289–309.

Filmer, Deon, Jeffrey S. Hammer, and Lant Pritchett. 2000. "Weak Links in the Chain: A Diagnosis of Health Policy in Poor Countries." *World Bank Research Observer* 15 (2): 199–224.

Gelb, Alan H., and associates. 1988. *Oil Windfalls: Blessing or Curse?* New York: Oxford University Press.

Gupta, Sanjeev, Robert Powell, and Yongzheng Yang. 2006. "Macroeconomic Challenges of Scaling Up Aid to Africa: A Checklist for Practitioners." International Monetary Fund, Washington, DC.

Hayashi, Fumio. 1982. "Tobin's Q, Rational Expectations, and Optimal Investment Rule." *Econometrica* 50 (1): 213–24.

Heller, Peter S., Menachem Katz, Xavier Debrum, Theo Thomas, Taline Koreanchelian, and Isabell Adenauer. 2006. "Making Fiscal Space Happen: Managing Fiscal Policy in a World of Scaled-Up Aid." Policy Discussion Paper 06/270. International Monetary Fund, Washington, DC.

IMF (International Monetary Fund). 2007a. "Aid Inflows: The Role of the Fund and Operational Issues for Program Design." IMF, Washington, DC.

————. 2007b. "Fiscal Policy Response to Scaled-Up aid." Fiscal Affairs Department, IMF, Washington, DC.

Jorgenson, Dale W., and Mun S. Ho. 1994. "Trade Policy and U.S. Economic Growth." *Journal of Policy Modeling* 16 (2): 119–46.

Kletzer, Kenneth M. 1994. "Sovereign Immunity and International Lending." In *The Handbook of International Macroeconomics,* ed. Frederick van der Ploeg, 506–34. Cambridge, MA: Basil Blackwell.

Kuznets, Simon. 1959. *Six Lectures on Economic Growth.* New York: Free Press of Gencoe.

————. 1966. *Modern Economic Growth: Rate, Structure, and Spread.* New Haven, CT: Yale University Press.

Mirzoev, Tokhir. 2007. "Modelling Aid Inflows in a Small and Open Economy." In *The Macroeconomics of Scaling Up Aid: Lessons from Recent Experience,* Occasional

Paper 253, ed. Andrew Berg, Shekhar Aiyar, Mumtaz Hussain, Shaun Roache, Tokhir Mirzoev, and Amber Mahone, 87–100. Washington DC: International Monetary Fund.

Obsfeld, Maurice. 1982. "Aggregate Spending and the Terms of Trade: Is There a Laursen-Metzler Effect?" *Quarterly Journal of Economics* 97: 251–70.

Pritchett, Lant. 2001. "Where Has All the Education Gone?" *World Bank Economic Review* 15 (3): 367–91.

Radelet, Steven, Michael Clemens, and Rikhil Bhavnani. 2006. "Aid and Growth: The Current Debate and Some New Evidence." In *The Macroeconomic Management of Foreign Aid: Opportunities and Pitfalls*, ed. P. Isard, L. Lipschitz, A. Mourmouras, and B. Yontcheva, 43–60. Washington, DC: International Monetary Fund.

Roodman, David. 2007. "The Anarchy of Numbers: Aid, Development, and Cross-Country Empirics." *World Bank Economic Review* 21 (2): 255–77.

Sachs, Jeffrey. 2005. *The End of Poverty: How We Can Make It Happen in Our Lifetime.* London: Penguin Books.

Sachs, Jeffrey, and Daniel Cohen. 1982. "LDC Borrowing with Default Risk." Working Paper 925, National Bureau of Economic Research, Cambridge, MA.

Summers, Lawrence H. 1981. "Taxation and Corporate Investment: A Q-Theory Approach." *Brookings Papers on Economic Activity* 1: 67–140.

Turnovsky, Stephen J., and Santanu Chatterjee. 2004."Substitutability of Capital, Investment Costs, and Foreign Aid." In *Economic Growth and Macroeconomic Dynamics: Recent Developments in Economic Theory*, ed. Steve Dowick, Rohan Pitchford, and Stephen J. Turnovsky, 138–70. Cambridge, U.K.: Cambridge University Press.

Tyrangiel, Josh. 2005. "The Constant Charmer." *Time* 166 (26): 46–62.

United Nations Millennium Development Project. 2005. *Investing in Development: A Practical Plan to Achieve the Millennium Policy Development Goals.* New York: United Nations.

van der Ploeg, Frederick. 1996. "Budgetary Policies, Foreign Indebtedness, the Stock Market, and Economic Growth." *Oxford Economic Papers* 48 (3): 382–96.

van Wijnbergen, S. 1984. "The Dutch Disease: A Disease after All?" *Economic Journal* 94 (373): 41–55.

Winters, L. Alan, Neil McCulloch, and Andrew McKay. 2004. "Trade Liberalization and Poverty: The Evidence So Far." *Journal of Economic Literature* 42 (1): 72–115.

World Bank. 2007. "Fiscal Policy for Growth and Development: Further Analysis and Lessons from Country Case Studies." World Bank, Washington, DC.

CHAPTER 6

Foreign Aid, Taxes, and Government Productivity: Alternative Scenarios for Ethiopia's Millennium Development Goal Strategy

Hans Lofgren and Carolina Diaz-Bonilla

The Millennium Development Goals (MDGs) and poverty reduction strategies of the government of Ethiopia focus on achieving the MDGs by 2015 (MOFED 2005a, 2005b). Starting from a very disadvantaged position in the early 1990s, the country has made considerable progress in terms of growth, MDGs, and other social indicators in the context of moderate aid increases. The government now faces the question of what to do to maintain and further accelerate progress. As an input to the evolving design of Ethiopia's development policies, this chapter[1] analyzes alternative scenarios that differ in terms of government spending, financing, and productivity. Most of the scenarios were designed in consultation with the Ethiopian government. The analysis is based on the Maquette for MDG Simulations (MAMS), an economywide simulation model developed by the World Bank to analyze development strategies in different countries, with Ethiopia's MDG strategy as a pilot case study.[2] In Ethiopia as well as in many other countries in sub-Saharan Africa, policies and foreign aid flows targeting MDGs are likely to have strong effects throughout the economy that feed back on the MDG indicators through markets for labor, goods, services, and foreign exchange. Therefore, MDG strategy analysis at the economywide level is often a necessary complement to sectoral analysis.

Our simulation results refer to the period 2006–15. Given considerable uncertainty about the parameters that underpin the long-run responses of the Ethiopian economy to large shocks, our findings should be viewed as indicating rough orders of magnitude. With this in mind, the results clearly show that a considerable expansion in government spending and foreign aid is required to meet the different MDGs. Under our basic MDG scenario[3], government consumption and investment grow at annual rates of approximately 8 and 20 percent, respectively, doubling the share of government demand in gross domestic product (GDP) from 29 percent in 2005 to almost 58 percent in 2015. Foreign aid per capita reaches almost $81 in 2015, which is five times the level in 2005. Although this is a radical increase in aid, this higher level is not out of range when compared with other countries in sub-Saharan Africa. In terms of average official development assistance (ODA) per capita during the period 2003–05, four countries received more than $70 and 10 countries received more then $60 (World Bank 2007c).[4] Moreover, the international community has committed itself to increased aid to sub-Saharan Africa. Most important, at the Gleneagles summit in 2005, the Group of Eight heads of state committed to doubling aid there by 2010, compared with the level in 2004.

Although it is plausible that Ethiopia's foreign aid will increase significantly, the increase most likely will be much smaller.[5] In addition, such a rapid expansion in government services relative to the overall growth of the economy may be very difficult to manage. Given this likelihood, our analysis explores alternative scenarios that differ in terms of financing (including foreign aid levels), government productivity growth, the extent of government expansion, and the relative emphasis on spending on infrastructure versus human development.

In a first simulation, the nonpoverty MDG targets are pursued in full in a setting where the increase in foreign grant aid is cut by half, with per capita aid peaking at $51 in 2015 (corresponding to 27 percent of GDP), while the government budget is balanced via direct tax increases. The main effect is a slowdown in GDP growth (from 5.5 percent to 4.7 percent) and drastic increases in the share of the economy represented by the government, with total taxes as a share of GDP reaching 37.1 percent by 2015 and total government demand at 70 percent. As a result of slower GDP growth, the headcount poverty rate falls by less (reaching about 23 percent, as opposed to 19 percent under the preceding basic MDG scenario). All in all, the results strongly suggest that, in this setting, a balanced development strategy would involve the pursuit of more modest objectives for the MDG indicators.

Government productivity is a key determinant of the cost of providing government services; improvements in productivity reduce foreign aid needs. The next simulation therefore analyzes the full pursuit of the non-poverty MDGs in the context of improvements by 1.5 percent per year in the productivity growth of government labor and intermediate input use and the same gain in government investment efficiency. Compared with the basic MDG scenario, the results include a substantial decline in foreign aid needs, with a peak of almost $62 per capita in 2015, and practically the same GDP growth (only marginally higher, benefiting from the productivity gain but suffering from the decline in aid). In the final year, GDP shares for government demand and taxes are more moderate (at approximately 53 percent and 19 percent, respectively), and the headcount poverty rate is marginally lower. The results suggest that success in the difficult task of improving government productivity (at the same time as the government expands rapidly) is a key factor in making rapid MDG progress feasible.

The final set of simulations looks at Ethiopia's MDG strategy from a different angle, positing that, in the face of insufficient aid, the government will cut down spending growth either on infrastructure or human development. For two scenarios, we limited foreign aid to 85 percent of what was received under the basic MDG scenario (with aid measured in present value [PV] terms). Assuming that the government cuts nonpoverty MDG spending as much as necessary to remain within the more limited budget (given the aid decrease), the results indicate that Ethiopia would realize 90 percent of the nonpoverty MDG gains (relative to 1990) and slightly more poverty reduction than under the basic MDG scenario. However, if the government instead made the required cuts in infrastructure spending, 89 percent of the poverty objective would be achieved whereas the nonpoverty MDG objectives would remain achieved in full. In the final year, the economy under the scenario with human development cuts has a higher GDP and larger stocks of private and public infrastructure capital. However, it has fewer students enrolled and smaller capital stocks in the different areas of MDG-related services. In the remaining simulations, we analyze the consequences of a wider range of foreign aid cuts and a large number of alternative allocations of government spending between infrastructure and human development. All of these simulations suggest that the losses in terms of weaker MDG performance from moderate cuts in the growth of foreign aid and government spending are not very drastic and that it may seem more attractive to scale down spending in a relatively balanced way across infrastructure and human development.

In sum, the findings of this chapter suggest that, for Ethiopia and other countries in sub-Saharan Africa that up to now have made only moderate progress on many of the MDG targets relative to the situation in 1990, very rapid growth in government service provision and spending would be needed to reach the MDG targets by 2015. Even if the required financing could be mobilized, strong efforts would be required to maintain an acceptable level of government productivity. Unless foreign aid is expanded more rapidly than what seems plausible at this point, it may not be feasible to achieve all MDGs by the target date. Governments would face difficult trade-offs under which some MDGs might be achieved, but only at the expense of reduced progress on other MDGs. In such settings, it seems preferable to direct policy analysis toward the design of alternative strategies for different levels of foreign aid. Such strategies should aim at achieving feasible targets emanating from the specific country context. Finally, this chapter strongly suggests that an economywide perspective, like the one taken here, is needed to explore how such strategies influence key aspects of economic performance, including economic growth, the structure of production and incomes, and labor market conditions.

The road map for the rest of this chapter is as follows: First, a brief note on the Ethiopian context of this study is provided. That is followed by a description of the structure and database of the MAMS model, after which the simulations are presented and their results are analyzed.

Ethiopia's Economy and the MDGs

Among the countries of sub-Saharan Africa, Ethiopia has the second-largest population (71 million, second only to Nigeria), and a quarter of the average for GDP per capita (World Bank 2007b, p. 1). Globally, Ethiopia is ranked only 170 out of 177 countries, according to the United Nations Development Programme Human Development Index (UNDP 2006). The country is strongly dependent on agriculture, which accounts for some 75–80 percent of employment and 40–50 percent of value added (World Bank 2007c). Because of volatile rainfall levels, agricultural production is highly variable, with repercussions throughout the economy. Relative to other countries in the region and low-income countries in general, Ethiopia is far below the averages according to most infrastructure indicators, including irrigation, road density, access to water for household consumption, and electricity access and consumption (World Bank 2007a, p. 5).

From this disadvantaged position, Ethiopia has made significant progress in recent years. Since the 1991 regime change, the state has become more development friendly (World Bank 2007a, pp. ix–x, 18). Between 1990 and 2005, many social and economic indicators have improved (see table 6.1). Road infrastructure also has expanded significantly (World Bank 2007c, p. 6). Since 1990, the trend growth rate has been in the range of 4–5 percent, a significant improvement compared with the period that followed the overthrow of the Selassie regime: during the last decade of the Derg regime (which ruled from 1974 to 1991), the annual rate of GDP growth was slightly below 1 percent. In terms of investment climate, the cross-country Doing Business survey indicates that Ethiopia does well relative to its income level (World Bank 2007c, p. 57). Ethiopia is also slightly above the sub-Saharan African average, according to the Country Policy and Institutional Assessment, which the World Bank uses to assess key policies for growth and poverty reduction. However, the events following the 2005 elections constitute a clear setback for governance and the business climate (World Bank, 2007c, pp. 7–8).

In spite of this generally positive evolution, it is clear that Ethiopia is far from reaching the MDGs unless progress is accelerated dramatically (see table 6.1). Such acceleration may be difficult, especially given that progress in the different MDG indicators tends to become gradually more difficult as the indicators improve because the less costly and higher impact options are usually the first to be undertaken. As an example, at low levels of school attendance, a new school building in a dense urban neighborhood would have a large impact on the education MDG. However, once most children are in school, further improvements become more costly as the remaining students tend to become more and more difficult to reach, possibly because of initial conditions that already made it more difficult for them to go to school, such as distance from school, living in less-dense rural areas (thus a lower impact for the same type of school), relatively poorer families in more need of the child's labor, higher rates of illness in the remaining population, and so forth.

Given the broad nature of the MDGs, a significant acceleration of progress toward those goals may require conditions that cover a wide range of areas, including GDP growth, domestic taxation, foreign aid, and government programs. Perhaps most important, GDP growth needs to accelerate. For Ethiopia and most other sub-Saharan African countries, accelerated GDP growth would require more rapid growth in total factor

TABLE 6.1
Selected Social and Economic Indicators

Indicator	1990	2005	2015 target	Annual growth (%) Actual 1990–2005	Annual growth (%) Required 2005–15
MAMS MDG indicators					
MDG 1: headcount poverty rate (%)	38.4	33.8	19.2	−0.8	−5.5
MDG 2: first-cycle primary net completion rate (%)	24.0	29.1	100.0	1.3	13.1
MDG 4: under-5 mortality rate (per 1,000 live births)	204.0	156.2	68.0	−1.8	−8.0
MDG 5: maternal mortality rate (per 100,000 live births)	870.0	580.0	217.5	−2.7	−9.3
MDG 7a: access to safe drinking water (%)	25.0	24.4	62.5	−0.2	9.8
MDG 7b: access to improved sanitation (%)	8.0	12.0	54.0	2.8	16.2
Other indicators					
Primary gross completion rate	26.0	55.0	n.a.	n.a.	n.a.
Primary net enrolment rate	22.0	61.0	n.a.	n.a.	n.a.
Malnutrition prevalence, weight for age (% of children under 5)	47.7	38.4	n.a.	n.a.	n.a.
Prevalence of undernourishment (% of population)	69.0	46.0	n.a.	n.a.	n.a.
Ratio of girls to boys in primary and secondary education (%)	68.0	76.0	n.a.	n.a.	n.a.
Immunization, measles (% of children aged 12–23 months)	38.0	59.0	n.a.	n.a.	n.a.
Mortality rate, infant (per 1,000 live births)	122.0	80.0	n.a.	n.a.	n.a.
Fertility rate, total (births per woman)	6.9	5.3	n.a.	n.a.	n.a.
Life expectancy at birth, total (years)	45.0	43.0	n.a.	n.a.	n.a.
Population, total (millions)	51.2	71.3	n.a.	n.a.	n.a.

Sources: For 1990 values—MDG 1: World Bank 2005; MDG 2: *World Bank Development Indicators*; MDGs 4, 7a, and 7b: World Bank 2004e; MDG 5: 1990–98 national estimates, *World Bank Development Indicators*; authors' simulations with MAMS.

Note: MAMS = Maquette for MAMS Simulations; MDGs = Millennium Development Goals; n.a. = not applicable. The values for 2005 are simulated; the model is solved for 2002–15. The targeted 2015 changes relative to the 1990 values: 50 percent cut (MDG 1), reach 100 percent in 2015 (MDG 2), 66 percent cut (MDG 4), 75 percent cut (MDG 5), 50 percent cut in share without (MDG 7a), and 50 percent cut in share without (MDG 7b).

productivity (TFP) (Ndulu 2007, p. 53). It is unfortunate that in Ethiopia and elsewhere, the "elixir of growth" is not known with any certainty. However, it seems advisable to strive to alleviate identifiable constraints in infrastructure and the investment climate, while reducing inequalities in opportunity (World Bank 2007c, pp. 16–21). More rapid GDP growth would increase the scope for more domestic government resources (taxes and other receipts) and raise private incomes, which cross-country evidence suggests are related to improvements in most MDG indicators (Clemens, Kenney, and Moss 2007, p. 741). For the case of Ethiopia, there also may be some scope for raising domestic taxes relative to GDP (World Bank 2007c, p. 84). In a setting with more rapid GDP growth and slightly higher tax rates, the government would be in a position to scale up social and economic programs in health, education, water, sanitation, and other infrastructure without generating macroeconomic imbalances. If managed well, these programs could play a key role in speeding up progress on the different MDGs and in contributing to further GDP growth. As indicated by earlier analyses, however, even under favorable circumstances, a substantial increase in aid would constitute a necessary condition for the full achievement of the MDGs by 2015 (MOFED 2005b). Although necessary, additional aid and an expanded government role also would pose additional challenges for macroeconomic management and governance. Aid flows tend to be volatile and may lead to undesirable dependency. Rapid aid increases may lead to exchange rate appreciation and reduced incentives to export. In addition, it is particularly difficult to maintain or improve the productivity of the government sector in times of rapid expansion.

The Ethiopian government's recent strategies for the MDGs and poverty reduction focused on full achievement of the goals by 2015 (MOFED 2005a, 2005b). If it becomes evident that the conditions for achieving the MDGs by 2015 are not satisfied, the government will be forced to prioritize, considering trade-offs among different objectives. Indeed, given that the MDG targets are global, it may be advisable for Ethiopia to define national targets that are more suitable to its own conditions, differing from the global MDGs in terms of indicators, timing, or both.

The scenarios that are simulated later in this chapter have been constructed to shed some light on the choices that Ethiopia's government is facing as it tries to speed up progress toward achieving the MDGs.

Model Structure and Database

MAMS integrates a relatively standard (recursive) dynamic general equilibrium model with an additional MDG module that links specific MDG-related interventions to MDG achievements. The core general equilibrium model follows the disaggregation indicated in table 6.2. As shown, the model has a relatively detailed treatment of government activities, which are classified into 10 functions: four types of education (first and second cycle primary, secondary, and tertiary), three types of health services (low-, medium-, and high-tech, divided into government and nongovernment),

TABLE 6.2
Model Disaggregation

Activities/commodities (11)
Nongovernment (4)
Private
Health sector, low-tech
Health sector, medium-tech
Health sector, high-tech
Government (10)
Education first primary cycle
Education second primary cycle
Education secondary
Education tertiary
Health sector, low-tech
Health sector, medium-tech
Health sector, high-tech
Water and sanitation
Public infrastructure
Other government
Factors (17)
Labor with less than completed secondary education
Labor with completed secondary education
Labor with completed tertiary education
Capital (14)—one stock for each model activity
Institutions (4)
Household
NGO
Government
Rest of the world

Source: MAMS version for Ethiopia.

Note: NGO = nongovernmental organization.

water and sanitation, (other) infrastructure, and other government.[6] The rest of the economy (representing agriculture, industry, and private non-health services) is treated as a single production activity. Both government and nongovernment activities use production factors, and intermediate inputs to produce an activity-specific commodity (in the case of the government, different types of services). The factors of production include three types of labor (those with less than completed secondary, those with completed secondary but not completed tertiary, and those with completed tertiary), public capital stocks (used by government activities; one stock per activity), and a private capital stock (used by nongovernment activities).

The government consumes, invests, and pays interest on its domestic and foreign debts. It finances its activities from domestic taxes, domestic borrowing, and foreign aid (borrowing and grants). Government service consumption is either exogenous or determined to meet MDG targets. The latter may apply to first-cycle primary education, health, and water-sanitation, each of which is linked to a specific MDG. Public investments must be sufficient to ensure that public capital stocks grow in proportion to increases in the production of government services; that is, a Leontief relationship with a fixed input coefficient for capital is assumed. Growth in the stock of public infrastructure capital (including roads, energy, and irrigation) contributes to overall growth by adding to the productivity of other production activities. In health, the model accounts for the fact that nongovernmental organizations (NGOs) and the private sector provide part of the services and the investments.

Apart from the government, the institutions of the economy include two domestic nongovernment institutions (a household and an NGO), and the rest of the world.[7] The household receives its incomes from factors and transfers (from the government or the rest of the world). For factors, household incomes reflect its endowments (or stocks). For private capital, its stock at any point in time depends on its base-year stock, depreciation, and new investments. Household incomes are used for consumption, taxes, savings, and transfers. The NGO is similar to the household except that it receives all of its income as a transfer from the rest of the world and its consumption is limited to health services. It also saves and invests in private capital that contributes to private sector production (including production of nongovernment health services). The rest of the world supplies Ethiopia with foreign exchange by buying Ethiopia's exports, lending, providing grant aid (transfers), and investing directly in Ethiopia's economy. Ethiopia uses its foreign exchange to make payments related to imports, interest, and incomes from private capital. The private capital income of the rest of the world in total depends on its initial stock, depreciation, and new foreign direct investment. In international markets, Ethiopia is treated as a price taker: its decisions regarding export and import quantities have no influence on the international price at which the transactions take place.

The model is based on standard assumptions about economic behavior. Households allocate their consumption across different commodities on the basis of utility maximization. Producers make profit-maximizing decisions in competitive markets. The private sector allocates its output between exports and domestic sales on the basis of relative prices. Similarly, domestic demanders respond to relative price changes when they split their demands between imports and domestic output.

As part of its consistency requirements, the model imposes constraints on the markets for factors and domestic commodities (that is, commodities produced and sold domestically). In equilibrium, the quantities supplied and demanded in each market are equal. The same holds for the receipts of the suppliers and the payments of the demanders. Flexible prices (wages) clear these markets. Moreover, the model requires that, for each institution (the household, the NGO, the government, and the rest of the world), total receipts be equal to total payments, including savings. Receipt-payment equality is also required for the savings/investment balance. For the household and the NGO, by design, total spending is always equal to total receipts. A flexible real exchange rate clears the rest-of-the-world balance, assuring equality between inflows and outflows of foreign exchange; by changing relative prices for exports, domestic sales, and imports, it influences export and import quantities. Other rules govern other transactions in foreign currency. The savings/investment balance is cleared by adjustments in private investment; that is, private investment is flexible and depends on the level of available funding defined as the difference between private savings and government borrowing, supplemented by foreign direct investment. All other savings and investment components are either exogenous (as is the case for foreign direct investment) or determined endogenously by various other rules.[8] The mechanism for clearing the government balance varies across the simulations and will be explained in the simulation section later in the chapter.

The model treats GDP growth in a standard manner: it is determined by growth in factor employment and in factor productivity (or efficiency). The latter may be summarized by a measure of TFP. For the labor factors, stock growth is determined by the evolution of the educational system and demographic factors.

For private and government capital, stock growth is endogenous, determined in the ways described above. Factor productivity (in the different production activities) depends on a trend term and terms that respond to changes in economic openness and growth in (government-owned) infrastructure stocks. The strength of these responses depends on elasticity values (with no response if the elasticity is set at zero).[9] The trend term captures what is not explained in the model (among other things, reflecting changes in institutions and the introduction of new technologies). In some of the simulations, a certain rate of GDP growth is targeted; if so, the trend term is endogenously adjusted to make sure that the target is reached. The resulting changes in productivity growth make it possible to assess the feasibility of the target. It also should be noted that, for labor, marginal productivity increases with educational achievement. As a result, when over time the labor force becomes more educated, its productivity will increase independent of productivity changes for individual labor types.

The model is "dynamic-recursive" in structure, meaning that agents are not assumed to make their decisions on the basis of perfect knowledge about relevant aspects of the future; rather, they draw on current and past events. Given that fact, the model may (but does not have to) be solved one year at a time with exogenous or endogenous updating of different stocks (factors, population, and debts). There is one exception to this: in simulations with an exogenous level for the PV of foreign aid and targeting of a uniform degree of achievement of selected MDGs, government decisions in any year depend on the economywide results for the full simulation period and the government is required to have perfect knowledge about all aspects of the economy that influence its decisions and budget. In this setting, it is necessary to solve the model for all time periods simultaneously.

Turning to the MDGs, the model is intended to capture key interactions between the pursuit of these goals and economic evolution. To keep it relatively simple, the model does not cover all MDGs. It focuses on the ones with the greatest cost and the greatest interaction with the rest of the economy: achieving universal primary school completion (MDG 2; measured by the net primary completion rate), reducing under-5 and maternal mortality rates (MDGs 4 and 5), and increasing access to improved water sources and sanitation (parts of MDG 7). Implicitly, health spending packages that achieve MDGs 4 and 5 also would achieve MDG 6, including halting and reducing the incidence of HIV/AIDS. We also address achievements in terms of poverty reduction (MDG 1).

These different MDGs are covered in an additional set of functions that link the level of each MDG indicator to a set of determinants, as summarized in table 6.3. The determinants include the delivery of relevant services (in education, health, and water sanitation) and other indicators, also allowing for the presence of synergies between MDGs, that is, the fact that achievements in terms of one MDG can have an impact on other MDGs. Outside of education, service delivery is expressed relative to the size of the population. In education, the model tracks base-year stocks of students and new entrants through the four cycles. In each year, students will pass their grade successfully, repeat it, or drop out of their cycle. Student performance depends on educational quality (quantity of services per student), household welfare (measured by per capita household consumption), level of public infrastructure, wage incentives (expressed as the ratio between the wages for labor at the next-higher and current levels of education for the student in question; an indicator of payoff from continued education), and health status (proxied by MDG 4). The achievement of MDG 2 requires that (very close to) all students in the relevant age cohort

TABLE 6.3
Determinants of MDG Achievements

MDG	Determinants				
	Level of service delivery[a]	Per capita household consumption	Wage incentives	Public infrastructure	Other MDGs
1		X			
2	X	X	X	X	4
4	X	X		X	7a, 7b
5	X	X		X	7a, 7b
7a	X	X		X	
7b	X	X		X	

Source: MAMS version for Ethiopia developed by the authors.

a. The services covered are first-cycle public education services (MDG 2), different types of health services (both public and private; MDGs 4 and 5), and public water/sanitation services (MDGs 1a and 7b). Education services are expressed to reflect the amount of classroom space, teacher time, and materials inputs per student (an indicator of educational quality).

enter the first primary cycle (four years) and successfully pass each year within this cycle. The functions for education and the other MDGs have been calibrated to ensure that, under base-year conditions, base-year performance is replicated and that, under a set of other conditions identified by sector studies, the target is fully achieved.

The model is built around an Ethiopian database for 2002, much of which is organized in a social accounting matrix, supplemented by more detailed data related to the different MDGs and the labor market (including levels of service delivery required to meet the different MDGs, stocks of students at different educational levels and of labor by educational level, and student behavioral patterns in terms of passing rates and other indicators), as well as elasticities in production, trade, consumption, and in the different MDG functions. The data are based primarily on government and World Bank studies and data sources, including sector studies (MOFED 2005c; Soucat 2005; Tan 2005; World Bank 2003, 2004a, 2004b, 2004c, 2004d, 2005; and World Bank and Ministry of Health Ethiopia 2004). The model is simulated for the period 2002–15. For the initial period, 2002–05, the model is tuned to available data to provide a starting point in 2005 that reflects the state of Ethiopia's economy in that year, according to the preliminary data that were available at the time of the analysis.

The model includes several links between the MDG module and the rest of the economy. An important link is that the provision of the additional government services needed to reach the MDGs requires additional resources—capital and investment, labor, and intermediate inputs—that become unavailable to the rest of the economy. The effects of any program very much depend on how the program is financed: from foreign sources, from domestic taxes (which will reduce consumption), and/or from domestic borrowing (which will crowd out private investment). Even if foreign sources supply the finance, resources available for the rest of the economy are affected as increased demand for labor with a relatively high education level withdraws this labor from employment elsewhere. Increased foreign aid may lead to exchange rate appreciation with economywide repercussions, including consumers' benefiting from lower prices of imports and a loss of competitiveness for producers of tradables (exporters or producers of import substitutes). At the same time, the pursuit of the MDGs generates additional resources as it influences the educational composition of the labor force, raising its average level of education.

The performance of the rest of the economy also will influence the ease with which different Mdgs can be achieved. Higher private incomes provide additional resources that enable private households to draw more benefit from government health and education programs. More rapid growth raises government revenues, strengthening the ability of governments to finance and operate efficient programs.

Simulations and Results

This section presents simulations of alternative MDG strategies and analyzes their effects on the Ethiopian economy. The first simulation (BASE) is a business-as-usual scenario that explores the consequences of continuing present trends through 2015. The second simulation (MDG-BASE) shows the economywide effects of following a strategy that targets all MDGs under a scenario of unlimited foreign aid. This core MDG scenario becomes the new benchmark against which the remaining simulations are compared. The remaining four simulations analyze the effects of increases in government productivity and alternative responses to constraints on foreign aid availability.

The Base Simulation and General Simulation Assumptions

The BASE simulation is a business-as-usual, moderate growth scenario in which specific MDG targets are not pursued. In terms of domestic policy, the different components of government consumption all grow at an exogenous rate of 4 percent per year, slightly above the rate of real GDP and similar to the overall growth trend of the economy in recent years.[10] For the other scenarios, growth rates for selected government services are endogenous, driven by the MDG-related objectives. As will be noted, some of the exogenous growth rates are also more rapid.

Apart from the treatment of government consumption and some scenario-specific alternative assumptions (which will be pointed out), the features of the BASE simulation explained here are identical to those of the other simulations. Over time, direct tax rates and import tariff rates do not change. Starting from 2006, domestic indirect tax rates increase moderately over time, permitting an increase in the total tax burden by 2.4 percent of GDP in 2015, compared with 2005.[11] Foreign borrowing is assumed to stay constant at the 2005 level. Domestic government borrowing from the central bank and domestic households is exogenous. Foreign grants are flexible, increasing sufficiently over time to ensure full coverage of the government financing gap (an assumption that varies across other simulations). In the factor markets, supplies are driven by investment (for private capital) or a combination of demographic factors and the functioning of the educational system (for the different labor types). The consumer price index is the model numéraire—nominal payments and price changes should be interpreted in the context of a fixed consumer price index.

Selected results of the different simulations are summarized in tables 6.4 through 6.7 and figures 6.1 through 6.6.[12] The results all pertain to the period 2005–15. For the BASE scenario, annual real growth is roughly 3.5–4.0 percent for GDP and most other macroeconomic aggregates, that is, a continuation of long-run trends (table 6.4). The growth rate for government investment is the same as for government consumption. Private investment grows at a slightly higher rate than the rest of the economy. For the period as a whole, wage (or rent) growth is positive for labor with tertiary education but slightly negative for private capital, labor with secondary education, and labor with less than secondary education (because the supplies of these factors grow relatively rapidly) (see table 6.4 and figure 6.1). The endogenous annual rate of growth in TFP is marginally below zero.[13] The net incremental capital-output ratio (ICOR) for this scenario, at 3.7, is lower than for other scenarios, reflecting that, for this scenario, growth in the two parts of capital that contribute most directly to GDP growth (private capital and public infrastructure capital) is high relative to other (government) capital.[14] Foreign aid per capita reaches approximately $18.5, slightly more than the $16.2 value of 2005 (table 6.5). Aid channeled through the government budget decreases from almost 11 percent to less than 10 percent of GDP.[15] This scenario registers significant improvements relative to the situation in 2005 for all MDG targets; however, it falls short of achieving any one of them (see table 6.6 and figures 6.2 and 6.3).

Core MDG Scenario

Unlike the base simulation described above, the second simulation, MDG-BASE, is designed to reach the MDGs by 2015, with foreign aid again filling any financing gap. The results provide a first indication of the effects of pursuing an MDG strategy, including its costs and the need for foreign

TABLE 6.4
Real Growth Data, 2006–15
Percent

	2005	BASE	MDG-BASE	MDG-MIX	MDG-GPRD	MDG-INFCUT	MDG-HDCUT
		Real annual growth 2006–15 (%)					
Macroeconomic totals (US$ millions)							
Absorption	10,153	3.5	8.5	6.5	7.8	7.6	7.9
GDP at market prices	8,528	3.5	5.7	4.8	5.9	5.2	5.7
Private consumption	6,734	3.1	5.4	1.8	5.0	4.7	5.5
Government consumption	1,458	4.0	8.4	8.6	8.4	8.7	6.8
Private investment	942	4.4	8.5	3.0	7.6	7.2	8.3
Government investment	1,019	4.0	20.0	20.3	18.2	17.9	18.4
Exports	1,283	3.7	−1.0	1.1	1.0	−0.7	0.6
Imports	2,908	3.4	12.8	9.1	10.7	11.2	11.4
GDP at factor cost (total)	7,704	3.6	5.5	4.7	5.5	5.0	5.5
GDP at factor cost (private sector)	7,101	3.5	5.2	4.3	5.3	4.6	5.4
GDP at factor cost (government)	603	4.0	8.7	8.8	8.6	8.9	7.3
TFP (growth)	n.a.	−0.06	0.25	−0.35	0.30	0.15	0.35
Real exchange rate (indexed)	1.0	0.2	−3.4	−0.9	−1.8	−2.9	−2.5
Government consumption							
First-cycle primary education	95.1	4.0	15.6	15.9	15.7	16.4	9.3
Second-cycle primary education	68.0	4.0	12.9	12.9	12.9	12.9	12.9
Secondary education	55.9	4.0	11.2	11.2	11.2	11.2	11.2
Tertiary education	51.3	4.0	13.1	13.1	13.1	13.1	13.1
Low-tech health	22.0	4.0	14.7	15.5	14.7	16.0	8.3
Medium-tech health	31.0	4.0	11.9	12.6	11.9	13.0	6.8
High-tech health	110.7	4.0	15.5	16.4	15.5	16.9	8.8
Water and sanitation	16.3	4.0	21.4	21.9	21.5	21.9	20.4
Public infrastructure	17.0	4.0	15.4	15.4	15.4	12.3	15.4
Other government	990.8	4.0	4.0	4.0	4.0	4.0	4.0

Source: Authors' simulations using MAMS.

Note: BASE = business-as-usual scenario; ICOR = incremental capital-output ratio; MDG-BASE = core MDG scenario; MDG-GPRD = MDG scenario with government efficiency gain; MDG-HDCUT = MDG scenario with reduced spending on human development (growth focus); MDG-INFCUT = MDG scenario with reduced spending on infrastructure (human development focus); MDG-MIX = MDG scenario with smaller increase in foreign aid and with additional domestic financing; n.a. = not applicable; TFP = total factor productivity. Values for 2005 are simulated; the model is solved for 2002–15. The 1990 values are 38.4 (MDG 1), 24.0 (MDG 2), 204.0 (MDG 4), 870.0 (MDG 5), 25.0 (MDG 7a), and 8.0 (MDG 7b). The targeted changes relative to the 1990 values are 50 percent cut (MDG 1), reach 100 percent in 2015 (MDG2), 66 percent cut (MDG 4), 75 percent cut (MDG 5), 50 percent cut in share without (MDG 7a), and 50 percent cut in share without (MDG 7b).

a. Billions of constant 2002 birr.

resources. This core MDG scenario targets the full achievement of MDGs 2, 4, 5, 7a, and 7b through an expansion of first-cycle primary education, the different health services, and water and sanitation services. The provision of health services is also sufficient to reach the MDG target of halting the increase in HIV/AIDS via preventive services.[16] Spending on higher educational cycles and public infrastructure expands rapidly to generate

	2005	BASE	MDG-BASE	MDG-MIX	MDG-GPRD	MDG-INFCUT	MDG-HDCUT
				Real annual growth 2006–15 (%)			
Government investment							
First-cycle primary education	18.6	4.0	24.1	24.7	24.3	25.6	12.4
Second-cycle primary education	13.6	4.0	24.4	24.4	24.4	24.4	24.4
Secondary education	26.6	4.0	21.1	21.1	21.1	21.1	21.1
Tertiary education	36.7	4.0	24.9	24.9	24.9	24.9	24.9
Low-tech health	16.3	4.0	28.0	29.5	28.0	30.4	14.9
Medium-tech health	23.9	4.0	22.6	23.8	22.6	24.6	11.3
High-tech health	45.3	4.0	29.6	31.1	29.5	32.1	15.9
Water and sanitation	15.4	4.0	40.4	41.1	40.5	41.1	38.6
Public infrastructure	378.4	4.0	24.6	24.6	24.6	18.9	24.6
Other government	444.3	4.0	4.0	4.0	4.0	4.0	4.0
Factor wages (unit rents)							
(thousands of birr/year)				Nominal annual growth 2006–15 (%)			
Labor (secondary education)	0.8	−0.4	3.9	2.4	3.4	3.2	3.4
Labor (secondary education)	2.1	−0.7	1.6	0.2	0.6	1.1	1.1
Labor (tertiary education)	9.6	2.2	3.4	2.2	1.8	3.3	2.7
Private capital	2.7	−0.4	0.4	1.1	0.4	0.1	0.6
Factor quantities (millions of workers)				Real annual growth 2006–15 (%)			
Labor (secondary education)	29.8	3.5	1.9	1.9	1.9	1.9	2.2
Labor (secondary education)	2.3	3.9	5.0	4.9	5.0	4.9	4.8
Labor (tertiary education)	0.2	1.9	4.4	4.2	4.3	4.2	4.4
Private capital[a]	76.7	3.5	4.9	2.9	4.7	4.6	4.8
ICOR	n.a.	3.7	6.8	7.6	6.7	6.5	6.2

balanced growth in the educational system as a whole and to provide the infrastructure services (roads, energy, and irrigation) needed to support more rapid growth. MDG 1 is not targeted but is monitored (using an elasticity of −1 for the headcount poverty rate with respect to real GDP per capita).[17]

In the areas of health and water sanitation, the service growth rate from 2005 to 2015 is constant, at a level that is sufficient to meet the MDG targets. Apart from the first cycle of primary schooling, educational expansion also takes place at a constant rate. For public infrastructure, expansion is frontloaded with growth twice as rapid in the years 2005–09 as during the remaining years. The rationale for this scenario is the need to build up the critical minimum infrastructure needed for productivity-raising network effects. For first-cycle primary education, frontloading is needed to make

TABLE 6.5
Macroeconomic and Government Data in 2005 and, by Simulation, 2015
Percent of GDP

	2005	2015 BASE	MDG-BASE	MDG-MIX	MDG-GPRD	MDG-INFCUT	MDG-HDCUT
Macroeconomic totals							
Absorption	119.1	118.6	141.7	137.4	137.6	138.7	138.5
Private consumption	79.0	76.0	72.1	58.6	72.9	71.2	74.3
Government consumption	17.1	17.9	22.1	24.4	19.0	23.9	19.0
Private investment	11.0	12.1	12.0	8.9	12.1	11.5	12.5
Government investment	12.0	12.6	35.5	45.5	33.6	32.0	32.7
Exports	15.0	15.6	5.7	9.7	8.1	6.4	7.3
Imports	−34.1	−34.2	−47.4	−47.1	−45.7	−45.1	−45.9
Government incomes							
Direct taxes	6.3	6.0	5.8	24.8	5.8	7.9	3.6
Import taxes	6.4	6.2	7.0	6.3	6.8	6.9	6.9
Other indirect taxes	3.3	6.2	5.9	6.0	6.1	5.9	6.0
Central bank borrowing	1.2	1.4	1.1	1.2	1.1	1.1	1.1
Other domestic borrowing	2.0	2.5	1.9	2.2	2.0	2.0	2.0
Foreign borrowing	5.8	4.2	2.4	3.4	2.8	2.7	2.7
Foreign grants	5.1	5.7	34.6	27.4	29.2	30.7	30.7
Net other capital inflows and errors	0.0	0.0	0.0	0.0	0.0	0.0	0.0
Total	30.1	32.2	58.7	71.4	53.8	57.2	53.0
Foreign aid per capita (US$)[a]	16.2	18.5	80.8	51.4	61.9	67.5	67.5
Government recurrent spending							
First-cycle primary education	1.1	1.1	2.7	2.8	2.2	3.0	1.5
Second-cycle primary education	0.8	0.8	1.5	1.6	1.2	1.6	1.5
Secondary education	0.7	0.8	1.2	1.2	0.9	1.2	1.1
Tertiary education	0.6	0.7	1.2	1.3	1.0	1.3	1.2
Low-tech health	0.3	0.3	0.6	0.7	0.5	0.7	0.3
Medium-tech health	0.4	0.4	0.6	0.7	0.5	0.7	0.4
High-tech health	1.3	1.4	3.0	3.7	2.7	3.6	1.7
Water and sanitation	0.2	0.2	0.8	0.9	0.7	0.9	0.7
Public infrastructure	0.2	0.2	0.5	0.5	0.4	0.4	0.5
Other government	11.6	12.2	10.0	10.9	8.8	10.6	10.1
Domestic interest payments	0.2	0.7	0.5	0.6	0.5	0.5	0.5
Foreign interest payments	0.8	1.1	0.6	0.9	0.7	0.7	0.7
Total recurrent government spending	18.2	19.6	23.2	25.9	20.3	25.2	20.2
Government capital spending							
First-cycle primary education	0.2	0.2	0.9	1.2	0.9	1.1	0.4
Second-cycle primary education	0.2	0.2	0.7	0.9	0.6	0.7	0.7
Secondary education	0.3	0.3	1.0	1.3	1.0	1.1	1.1
Tertiary education	0.4	0.5	1.9	2.4	1.8	2.1	2.0
Low-tech health	0.2	0.2	1.1	1.5	1.0	1.4	0.4
Medium-tech health	0.3	0.3	1.0	1.4	1.0	1.3	0.4
High-tech health	0.5	0.6	3.4	4.8	3.2	4.4	1.2
Water and sanitation	0.2	0.2	2.6	3.4	2.5	2.9	2.4
Public infrastructure	4.4	4.7	19.2	24.0	18.2	13.0	20.3
Other government	5.2	5.5	3.7	4.6	3.5	4.0	3.9
Total capital government spending	12.0	12.6	35.5	45.5	33.6	32.0	32.7
Total government spending (recurrent + capital)	30.1	32.2	58.7	71.4	53.8	57.2	53.0

Source: Authors' simulations using MAMS.

Note: Simulations are defined in the note to table 6.4.

a. Foreign aid per capita includes allowance for aid outside the government budget. In per capita terms, aid in the government budget was approximately $11 in 2005.

TABLE 6.6
Impacts on MDG Indicators

MDG indicators	Rate in 2005	BASE	MDG-BASE	MDG-MIX	MDG-GPRD	MDG-INFCUT	MDG-HDCUT	Target
				Rate in 2015				
Headcount poverty rate (%)—MDG 1	33.8	27.8	18.7	22.6	18.6	21.3	18.6	19.2
First-cycle primary net completion rate (%)—MDG 2	29.1	48.1	99.9	99.9	99.9	99.9	93.8	100.0
Under-5 mortality rate (per 1,000 live births)—MDG 4	156.2	110.5	68.0	68.0	68.0	67.9	79.0	68.0
Maternal mortality rate (per 100,000 live births)—MDG 5	580.0	387.2	217.5	217.5	217.5	217.2	260.1	217.5
Access to safe drinking water (%)—MDG 7a	24.4	26.4	62.5	62.5	62.5	62.5	59.5	62.5
Access to improved sanitation (%)—MDG 7b	12.0	14.1	54.0	54.0	54.0	54.0	50.6	54.0

Source: Authors' simulations using MAMS.

Note: Simulations are defined in a note to table 6.4. Values for 2005 are simulated; the model is solved for 2002–15. The 1990 values are 38.4 (MDG 1), 24.0 (MDG 2), 204.0 (MDG 4), 870.0 (MDG 5), 25.0 (MDG 7a), and 8.0 (MDG 7b). The targeted changes relative to the 1990 values are 50 percent cut (MDG 1), reach 100 percent in 2015 (MDG2), 66 percent cut (MDG 4), 75 percent cut (MDG 5), 50 percent cut in share without (MDG 7a), and 50 percent cut in share without (MDG 7b).

FIGURE 6.1
Wages of Labor with Secondary Education, 2005–15

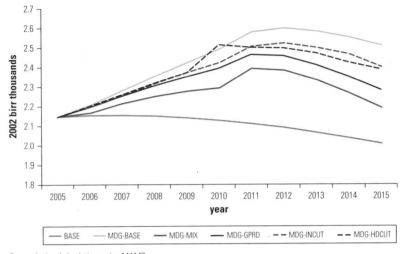

Source: Authors' simulations using MAMS.

Note: Simulations are defined in note to table 6.4.

FIGURE 6.2
MDG 2: Net Primary Completion Rate, 2005–15

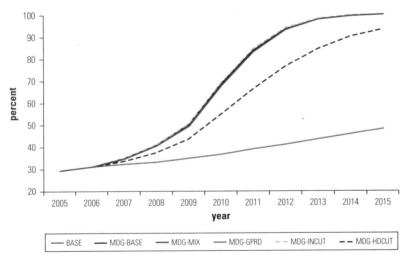

Source: Authors' simulations using MAMS.

Note: Simulations are defined in note to table 6.4.

FIGURE 6.3
MDG 4: Under-5 Mortality Rate, 2005–15

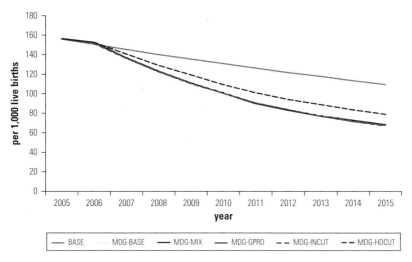

Source: Authors' simulations using MAMS.

Note: Simulations are defined in note to table 6.4.

sure that, by 2012, (close to) every child in the proper cohort enters school and that (close to) every one in this group is able to successfully pass the first grade in 2012 and the remaining three grades in 2013–15. Foreign grants grow apace with government financing needs, whereas domestic financing follows the same rules as under the BASE scenario.

Figures 6.2 and 6.3 show the progress in MDG 2 (net primary completion rate) and MDG 4 (under-5 mortality rate), respectively, in the various scenarios. The results for MDG-BASE in table 6.4 indicate that a rapid expansion of government services is needed to achieve the MDG targets. Government consumption demand (and service production) grows at an aggregate rate of 8.4 percent and at rates ranging between 11 percent and 21 percent a year for the disaggregated government services related to the MDGs. Government investment expands even more rapidly—by 20 percent a year at the aggregate level and by 21–40 percent for MDG-related investments, responding to the need to expand the government capital stock in proportion to service expansion. Growth in total government consumption and investment is kept in check because "other government" (which is not directly related to MDG services) continues to grow at annual rates of 4 percent for each. As a share of GDP, the sum of government consumption and investment increases from 29 percent in 2005 to almost 58 percent in 2015 (see table 6.5).[18]

This government expansion gives rise to a similarly drastic increase in foreign aid requirements, as foreign aid in the government budget increases from 10.9 percent of GDP in 2005 to 37.0 percent in 2015. In per capita terms, total foreign aid reaches almost $81 in 2015, five times the 2005 level (table 6.5, figure 6.4). As Figure 6.4 shows, the expansion in foreign aid per capita increases monotonically, except for a decline in 2011. The latter reflects two factors: First, at this point in time, the period of big investments—in schools and teacher training—to support rapid expansion in primary education comes to an end, reducing government spending needs. Second, the model captures an Ethiopia-specific threshold effect based on expert assessments: private sector productivity is boosted because public infrastructure capital stock exceeds a threshold above which pro-ductivity-enhancing network effects are triggered in the private sector. Compared with the BASE scenario, the PV of foreign aid is 4.5 times larger, reaching almost $31.4 billion[19] (on the basis of a discount rate of 5 percent) (see table 6.7 and figure 6.5).

More rapid growth in factor stocks and TFP (at 0.25 percent, attributa-ble to the increase in public infrastructure) permits real GDP growth to accelerate by close to 2.0 percent, reaching 5.5 percent. The increase in aid inflows imposes a strong increase in the trade deficit, with a drastic appre-ciation of the real exchange rate (by 3.4 percent a year) providing the incentives for import and export growth to accelerate and decelerate, respectively. The combination of an increase in the trade deficit and more rapid GDP growth permits total absorption (the sum of private and gov-ernment consumption and investment demand) to expand at 8.5 percent annually, including private consumption and investment growth at annual rates of 5.4 percent and 8.5 percent, respectively. Growth in GDP per capita leads to a fall in the headcount poverty rate from approximately 33.8 per-cent in 2005 to less than 18.7 percent in 2015.

Across the different scenarios, the private sector grows at rates that are respectable, although clearly more slowly than MDG-related government services. This result reflects the fact that the availability of foreign aid per-mits government expansion to take place without crowding out private investment. For this and the following scenarios, the ICOR is considerably higher than for BASE—between 6.2 and 7.6—reflecting two factors: first,

TABLE 6.7
Total Government Incomes and Spending, 2006–15
2005 US$ millions

	Total 2006–15					
	BASE	MDG-BASE	MDG-MIX	MDG-GPRD	MDG-INFCUT	MDG-HDCUT
Government incomes						
Direct taxes	6,388.6	7,302.8	22,397.4	7,147.6	7,387.1	6,913.6
Import taxes	6,531.0	8,515.8	7,171.3	8,162.7	8,107.2	8,270.1
Other indirect taxes	5,041.8	5,812.9	5,366.7	5,745.8	5,580.4	5,822.0
Central Bank borrowing	1,353.8	1,353.8	1,353.8	1,353.8	1,353.8	1,353.8
Other domestic borrowing	2,517.1	2,517.1	2,517.1	2,517.1	2,517.1	2,517.1
Foreign borrowing	5,024.0	4,112.0	4,729.3	4,316.9	4,212.0	4,317.5
Foreign grants	5,649.3	36,192.1	25,120.2	31,237.6	30,889.9	31,606.8
Net other capital inflows	0	0	0	0	0	0
Total	32,505.6	65,806.6	68,655.8	60,481.6	60,047.6	60,800.8
Present value of foreign aid	6,936.8	31,384.2	20,157.1	26,461.1	26,676.5	26,676.5
Government recurrent spending						
First-cycle primary education	1,164.7	2,564.5	2,427.3	2,189.3	2,670.7	1,717.1
Second-cycle primary education	833.0	1,448.5	1,349.4	1,237.2	1,436.0	1,413.0
Secondary education	737.0	1,138.5	1,083.2	963.5	1,140.6	1,113.5
Tertiary education	654.4	1,101.7	1,069.7	943.1	1,101.1	1,088.1
Low-tech health	274.7	492.3	510.6	444.3	527.1	347.3
Medium-tech health	387.0	592.6	610.4	536.1	626.2	448.8
High-tech health	1,393.9	2,615.4	2,706.5	2,336.9	2,817.1	1,801.7
Water and sanitation	203.7	571.0	554.0	499.5	580.4	528.3
Public infrastructure	212.6	465.9	442.5	410.1	382.3	457.5
Other government	12,369.0	13,021.6	12,578.7	11,718.3	12,953.1	12,870.0
Domestic interest payments	455.3	455.3	455.3	455.3	455.3	455.3
Foreign interest payments	1,027.9	836.3	965.3	881.8	856.1	881.2
Government capital spending						
First-cycle primary education	233.2	1,175.8	1,302.2	1,110.4	1,301.4	544.7
Second-cycle primary education	171.3	660.0	705.3	614.2	666.6	676.8
Secondary education	334.3	1,042.8	1,114.0	971.8	1,053.3	1,068.9
Tertiary education	460.6	1,831.9	1,957.7	1,704.4	1,850.1	1,878.5
Low-tech health	205.1	986.9	1,154.1	915.4	1,152.4	431.1
Medium-tech health	299.4	1,026.8	1,188.3	954.7	1,180.3	488.9
High-tech health	568.3	3,011.6	3,532.6	2,791.4	3,533.1	1,283.0
Water and sanitation	193.7	1,924.2	2,152.4	1,788.7	2,028.2	1,783.1
Public infrastructure	4,749.8	23,763.2	25,380.4	22,250.4	16,603.2	24,328.0
Other government	5,576.9	5,079.9	5,415.6	4,764.8	5,133.0	5,196.4
Total government spending (recurrent + capital)	32,505.6	65,806.6	68,655.8	60,481.6	60,047.6	60,800.8

Source: Authors' simulations using MAMS.

Note: Simulations are defined in the note to table 6.4.

FIGURE 6.4
Foreign Aid Per Capita, 2005–15

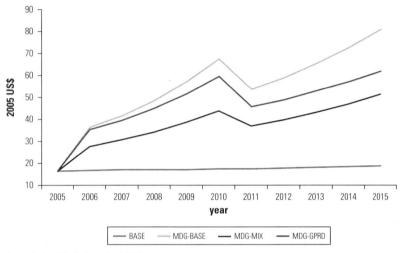

Source: Authors' simulations using MAMS.

Note: Simulations are defined in the note to table 6.4.

FIGURE 6.5
Present Value of Foreign Aid

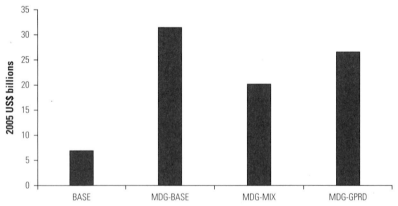

Source: Authors' simulations using MAMS.

Note: Simulations are defined in the note to table 6.4.

in the context of high rates of government service growth, high volumes of government investment are required; second, a large share of these investments is allocated to human development with a relatively low pay-off in growth during the simulation period.

Mixed Financing Scenario

Given that the amount of foreign financing required for MDG-BASE may not be available and/or that such a rapid expansion in government services may not be considered feasible, we constructed a set of simulations that explores alternative scenarios in resource-constrained settings. The first of these alternatives is MDG-MIX, which is identical to MDG-BASE except that the increase in foreign grant aid relative to the base scenario is only half as large. Direct taxes are raised to cover the remaining costs. Therefore, this simulation explores the effects of pursuing the same MDG targets (in health, education, and water sanitation) and maintaining the same real growth in other areas of government spending (including infrastructure), with half the additional foreign grant aid.

The results show that per capita foreign aid reaches $51.4 in 2015 and the PV of total foreign aid between 2006 and 2015 falls from $ 31.4 billion in MDG-BASE to $ 20.2 billion, that is, to a more realistic increase in foreign aid. However, to cover the remaining financing gap, direct taxes have to increase drastically, from a GDP share of 6.3 percent in 2005 to 24.8 percent in 2015.

Such a tax increase has a strong dampening impact on growth in household posttax incomes, consumption, savings, and investments; that impact results in slower growth rates for the private capital stock and private GDP, the latter falling from 5.2 percent under MDG-BASE to 4.3 percent under this scenario. Compared with MDG-BASE, more rapid growth is needed in government spending in education, health, and water sanitation services if the country is to achieve the MDG targets. This is because government services have to make up for the negative impact on MDG performance of slower growth in per capita household consumption. Given more rapid growth in government demand (the sum of government consumption and investment) and slower GDP growth, the share of government demand in GDP reaches 70 percent, an extremely high share.[20] As a result of slower growth in GDP per capita, the MDG target for poverty reduction is not met. One consequence of lower foreign aid is that, compared with the MDG-BASE simulation, the rates of real exchange rate appreciation and import growth are much slower (the latter declines from 12.8 percent to 9.1 percent) while export growth increases (to 1.1 percent).

In sum, compared with MDG-BASE, the results for MDG-MIX show more realistic foreign aid flows and slower GDP growth, while the required expansion in government services and taxes is out of proportion with growth in the rest of the economy.

Government Productivity Scenario

This simulation explores the potential for government productivity in facilitating progress toward the Mdgs. MDG-GPRD is identical to MDG-BASE except that it has more rapid government productivity growth. Under this scenario, the productivity of government labor and government efficiency in intermediate input use and investment are all improved by an additional 1.5 percent annual.[21] Compared with MDG-BASE, the results are noteworthy declines in foreign aid needs (to $26.5 billion; $62 per capita in 2015) and in the GDP share for the government (to 52.6 percent), whereas GDP growth increases marginally (5.55 percent versus 5.53 percent for MDG-BASE), generating a lower poverty rate. In an additional simulation, not reported elsewhere in this chapter, government productivity and efficiency improvement were doubled to 3 percent a year. The results are a further strengthening of these outcomes: the PV of aid declines to $22.4 billion and the government GDP share in 2015 falls to 47.3 percent, without any significant impact on poverty reduction.

In sum, these scenarios highlight that improvements in government productivity can have a major impact on foreign aid needs. At the same time, it should be noted that such productivity gains may be particularly difficult to bring about in the context of rapid government expansion.

A Strategy Focusing on Human Development

The above simulations suggest that, in the face of constraints (on foreign aid, domestic resources, and the scope for productivity improvement), a preferred strategy may involve downward adjustments in the MDG targets the government strives to achieve by 2015. If so, trade-offs among different allocations of government spending will come to the fore. The remaining scenarios anticipate such a situation by analyzing trade-offs between spending on infrastructure and on human development in a setting with reductions in foreign aid relative to MDG-BASE.

The simulation MDG-INFCUT introduces a cut in public infrastructure spending that is sufficient to limit the PV of foreign aid for the full simulation period to 85 percent of the MDG-BASE value. A slight increase in direct tax rates is introduced in 2015 to generate a targeted value of $67.5

for foreign aid per capita, roughly four times the 2005 level. (Per capita aid in 2015 is targeted to ensure comparability with the infrastructure-focused scenario that follows.) The achievement of the targeted (nonpoverty) MDGs is not compromised.

The overall result is a decline in growth rates to levels between BASE and MDG-BASE for all macroeconomic aggregates, except government consumption, because a marginal increase is needed in the different government service sectors to achieve the MDGs. This increase results from declining growth of household consumption and a lower level of infrastructure compared with the MDG-BASE scenario (both are factors that, along with government services, contribute positively to MDG achievements). The fact that the economy fails to achieve the poverty target points to the presence of a short- and medium-run trade-off between expanded human development and poverty reduction. The PV of foreign aid for 2006–15 falls to approximately $26.7 billion (85 percent of the value for MDG-BASE as explained above). The GDP share for government demand reaches almost 56 percent, a slight decrease compared with MDG-BASE. Relative to GDP, total tax revenue in 2015 reaches 20.7 percent, whereas the other scenarios remain between 16.5 and 18.7 (with the exception of MDG-MIX, for which total taxes increase to as high as 37.1 percent in a scenario under which direct taxes cover the remaining financing gap).[22]

A Strategy Focusing on Growth and Infrastructure

The simulation MDG-HDCUT achieves the same cut in the PV of foreign aid as MDG-INFCUT but it does so by reducing expansion in MDG-related government services. This is done in a manner that ensures that a uniform share of the improvement needed to fully achieve the MDGs (other than MDG 1) is attained. To maintain full comparability with MDG-INFCUT, aid levels are fixed at $67.5 per capita in 2015—a moderate cut in direct tax rates is required to balance the 2015 government budget.

The results for this simulation further demonstrate a trade-off between human development versus growth and poverty reduction in a setting where foreign aid is constrained or country absorptive capacity is limited. Compared with MDG-BASE, growth in government consumption and investment shifts down by 1.6 percentage points, whereas growth in total GDP is unchanged and growth in private consumption and private investment change by less than 0.2 percentage points. Private capital grows by slightly less than it does in the MDG-BASE scenario, but growth for the infrastructure capital stock remains the same. The fact that export growth increases noticeably, compared with MDG-INFCUT, is due to slower real exchange rate appreciation and more rapid GDP growth.

Among the Mdgs, the poverty target is achieved. For the nonpoverty Mdgs, this simulation achieves 91.6 percent or more of the gain required relative to the situation in 1990. During the simulation period, it reaches the levels of MDG-BASE and MDG-INFCUT with a lag of only a few years.

The fact that MDG-HDCUT is less costly than MDG-BASE is primarily due to three factors: lower wages of workers with higher education (slower expansion in human development leads to less pressure on this segment of the labor market) (see table 6.4 and figure 6.1), less real appreciation (protecting the purchasing power of aid in foreign currency), and considerable real resource savings from falling slightly short of achieving the nonpoverty MDG targets by the 2015 deadline. Figure 6.6 provides a broader perspective on trade-offs between human development and poverty reduction in the face of foreign aid constraints. It summarizes trade-offs for a larger set of simulations with alternative cuts in foreign aid—the simulations along each curve have identical levels of foreign aid in the final year and, in PV terms, for the period 2006–15.

FIGURE 6.6
Trade-Offs between Human Development and Poverty Reduction

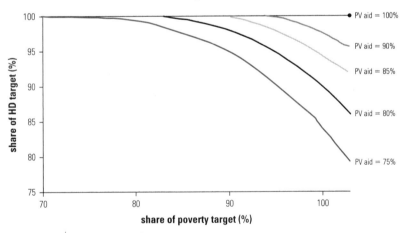

Source: Authors' simulations using MAMS.

Note: HD = human development; PV = present value. Along a given curve, the present value of aid is kept constant. The point at the upper right corner of the graph (PV aid = 100%) corresponds to the MDG-BASE simulation. Simulation is defined in note to table 6.4.

Given more rapid growth than for MDG-INFCUT and a slightly less ambitious agenda than for MDG-BASE, the 2015 GDP share for government demand, at approximately 52 percent, is slightly lower for this simulation than for the other two, both of which landed at close to 56–57 percent of GDP. This observation leads to the related observation that the simulated scenarios involve an expansion in government demand relative to GDP that is extreme by international standards (in spite of relatively optimistic scenarios for GDP growth).

One common feature of the different scenarios presented in this chapter is that the GDP share for total government consumption is only slightly larger than the GDP share for total tax revenues—between 17 percent and 25 percent for the former and between 16 percent and 21 percent for the latter (with the exception of the MDG-MIX scenario). This outcome suggests that, in spite of rapid government expansion, the Ethiopian government need not rely on foreign aid to cover the costs of its recurrent activities.

Annex

TABLE 6A.1
Balance of Payments in 2005 and, by Simulation, 2015
Percent of GDP

		2015					
	2005	BASE	MDG-BASE	MDG-MIX	MDG-GPRD	MDG-INFCUT	MDG-HDCUT
Payments							
Imports	22.3	21.6	22.1	18.9	21.7	22.0	22.0
Factor payments	0.2	2.2	1.7	2.2	1.8	1.7	1.8
Interest payments	0.9	1.1	0.6	0.9	0.7	0.7	0.7
Total	35.2	37.5	49.7	50.2	48.2	47.5	48.3
Receipts							
Exports	15.0	15.6	5.7	9.7	8.1	6.4	7.3
Private transfers	8.5	10.5	6.1	8.4	7.0	6.7	6.7
Foreign direct investment	0.7	1.6	0.9	1.3	1.1	1.0	1.0
Foreign borrowing	5.8	4.2	2.4	3.4	2.8	2.7	2.7
Foreign grants	5.1	5.7	34.6	27.4	29.2	30.7	30.7
Total	35.2	37.5	49.7	50.2	48.2	47.5	48.3

Source: Authors' simulations using MAMS.

Note: Simulations are defined in the note to table 6.4.

TABLE 6A.2
Aggregate Savings/Investment Balance in 2005 and, by Simulation, 2015
Percent of GDP

		2015					
	2005	BASE	MDG-BASE	MDG-MIX	MDG-GPRD	MDG-INFCUT	MDG-HDCUT
Savings							
Private	13.6	14.4	14.1	11.1	14.2	13.7	14.5
Government	2.9	7.5	0.5	18.2	4.3	1.0	1.9
Rest of the world	6.6	2.8	32.9	25.1	27.2	28.9	28.8
Total	23.0	24.7	47.5	54.4	45.7	43.6	45.2
Investment							
Public	12.0	12.6	35.5	45.5	33.6	32.0	32.7
Private	11.0	12.1	12.0	8.9	12.1	11.5	12.5
Total	23.0	24.7	47.5	54.4	45.7	43.6	45.2

Source: Authors' simulations using MAMS.

Note: Simulations are defined in the note to table 6.4.

Notes

1. This chapter draws on Lofgren and Diaz-Bonilla (2006) and Bourguignon, Diaz-Bonilla, and Lofgren (forthcoming), which also present MDG simulation results for Ethiopia. However, this chapter is distinct in terms of focus and analysis.
2. For more information about MAMS, see Bourguignon, Diaz-Bonilla, and Lofgren (forthcoming) and Lofgren and Diaz-Bonilla (2007). After pilot applications to Ethiopia, MAMS has been applied to other countries in the sub-Saharan Africa and Latin America and the Caribbean regions.
3. As will be explained later, this core MDG scenario is designed to reach the MDGs by 2015, with foreign aid filling any financing gap.
4. Forty-four countries were included in this comparison. Four small island countries with very high aid figures (Cape Verde, Mayotte, São Tomé and Principe, and the Seychelles) were excluded from this comparison. In terms of averages for 2003–05, Ethiopia ranked eighth among these 44 sub-Saharan African countries in ODA as a share of gross national income and 30th in per capita terms. Aid figures for Ethiopia tend to vary, depending on source and coverage (government budget versus more inclusive definitions) (World Bank 2007a, pp. 1, 81; World Bank 2007b).
5. According to the assessment of the 2007 World Bank Country Economic Memorandum for Ethiopia, it is plausible that aid to Ethiopia will be twice the 2005 level by 2010 (World Bank 2007a, pp. 1, 81). Further increases are clearly not out of the question after 2010.
6. For MAMS, disaggregations of government and other parts of the economy are application specific, driven by the analytical needs of each application. The category "other government" covers other government programs, some of which may also be essential for growth and/or MDG achievements—for example, measures promoting agricultural growth and targeted efforts directed at poor and hungry people in both rural and urban areas.
7. The household institution includes enterprises, that is, nonconsuming domestic nongovernment institutions that earn capital rents and allocate the rents to the owners of these enterprises after paying taxes and saving.
8. For example, the private savings rate (out of posttax private income) depends on per capita income in a constant elasticity formulation; the product of this rate and total private posttax income defines private savings.
9. Selected values for these and other elasticities are drawn from the literature, with the aim of selecting moderate, "middle-of-the-road" values. For infrastructure investments, it is assumed that a 1.000 birr increase in the capital stock initially leads to a 0.127 birr increase in real GDP (all things being equal), drawing on estimates for sub-Saharan Africa (Dessus and Herrera 1996, p. 27). The full effect will depend on economywide responses and will diminish over time as the capital stock depreciates.
10. For the period 1991–2004 (using the 1990–92 average as a starting point and the 2003–05 average as an end point), annual growth in real GDP at factor cost in constant birr was 3.7 percent (World Bank 2007b).

11. Relevant cross-country comparisons suggest that Ethiopia could raise the share of tax revenues in GDP (World Bank 2007a, p. 84).

12. Annex tables 6A.1 and 6A.2 show additional simulation results.

13. The simulated TFP growth rate (-0.06 percent) is slightly below an estimate for 1990–2003 (0.17 percent). For the longer period 1960–2003, the corresponding estimate is -0.56 percent (Ndulu 2007, p. 53, citing Bosworth and Collins 2003).

14. The net ICOR is defined as the ratio between the change (from 2005 to 2015) in the total physical capital stock (both private and government; valued at the base-year prices of new capital stock) and the change in real GDP at factor cost. This is a net concept because it incorporates the impact of depreciation.

15. In the different simulations, per capita nongovernment aid increases from approximately $5 in 2005 to $7 in 2015, that is, the share of aid that passes through the government budget increases from approximately 70 percent to 90 percent.

16. If donor support is available, these services could be supplemented by HIV/AIDS treatment programs. Given that such programs would be relatively import intensive, their presence would not substantially alter the current analysis.

17. The elasticity of -1 is the central-case elasticity used by Agénor, Bayraktar, and El Aynaoui (2005, pp. 33, 39) and is close to the poverty elasticity of the 1990s in the absence of distributional changes (Christiaensen, Demery, and Paternostro 2003, p. 326). Real GDP per capita was used instead of real household consumption per capita because, at least in the context of these simulations, it provides a better indicator of long-run capacity to maintain a certain level of household consumption per capita. The drawback of using real household consumption per capita is that it is relatively sensitive to temporary changes in foreign aid and differences in aid flows across simulations (due to the immediate influence of these changes on absorption). MAMS applications to other countries have based the poverty analysis on microsimulations linked to household surveys, a preferable approach.

18. Note that the increase in the government share of absorption (also referred to as gross national expenditure or domestic final demand) is more moderate, from 24 to 40 percent. This is due to that absorption grows more rapidly than GDP thanks to an (aid-driven) increase in the trade deficit. As shown in table 6.5, in 2005 and 2015 (for MDG-BASE), absorption is 19 and 42 percent larger than GDP, respectively.

19. A billion is 1,000 millions.

20. In 2003–05, Eritrea had the largest share in the world for the sum of government consumption and investment in any developing country, reaching 70, 71, and 61 percent, respectively. Very few countries exceeded 40 percent (World Bank 2007b).

21. Government investment efficiency is measured by the capital stock input coefficient (commodity input quantities per unit of new government capital that is

created). The efficiency of intermediate input use is measured by the intermediate input coefficient (quantities of intermediate inputs needed per unit of output). In the other simulations, both were unchanged; for MDG-GPRD, they decline by 1.5 percent a year. The improvement in labor productivity is slightly larger than the 1.5 percentage point change in the exogenous productivity term because this term is multiplied by an endogenous productivity term (driven by growth in the capital stock for public infrastructure).

22. Among the 104 countries for which the World Bank Development Data Platform includes information on total tax revenues, 38 had a tax share exceeding 21 percent and 2 had a tax share greater than 37, as an average for 2003–05. The unweighted average for the 104 countries was 17.9 percent.

References

Agénor, P.-R., N. Bayraktar, and K. El Aynaoui. 2005. "Roads Out of Poverty? Assessing the Links between Aid, Public Investment, Growth, and Poverty Reduction." Policy Research Working Paper 3490, World Bank, Washington, DC.

Bosworth, B. P., and Collins, S. M. 2003. "The Empirics of Growth: An Update." *Brookings Papers on Economic Activity* 2.

Bourguignon, F., C. Diaz-Bonilla, and H. Lofgren. Forthcoming. "Aid, Service Delivery and the MDGs in an Economy-wide Framework." In *The Impact of Economic Policies on Poverty and Income Distribution: Macro-Micro Evaluation Techniques and Tools*, ed. F. Bourguignon, L. Pereira da Silva, and M. Bussolo. New York: Palgrave.

Christiaensen, L., L. Demery, and S. Paternostro. 2003. "Macro and Micro Perspectives of Growth and Poverty in Africa." *World Bank Economic Review* 1 (3): 317–47.

Clemens, M. A., C. J. Kenney, and T. J. Moss. 2007. "The Trouble with the MDGs: Confronting Expectations of Aid and Development Success." *World Development* 35 (5): 735–51.

Dessus, S., and R. Herrera. 1996. "Le Role du Capital Public dans la Croissance des Pays en Développement au cours des Années 80." Working Paper 115, Centre de Développement de l'OCDE, Paris.

Lofgren, H., and C. Diaz-Bonilla. 2006. "Economywide Simulations of Ethiopian MDG Strategies." Photocopy. World Bank, Washington, DC.

———. 2007. "MAMS: An Economywide Model for Analysis of MDG Country Strategies—Technical Documentation." Photocopy. World Bank, Washington, DC.

MOFED (Ministry of Finance and Economic Development), Federal Democratic Republic of Ethiopia. 2005a. "Ethiopia: Building on Progress: A Plan for Accelerated and Sustained Development to End Poverty (PASDEP) (2005/06–2009/10)." Addis Ababa.

———. 2005b. "Ethiopia: The Millennium Development Goals (MDGs) Needs Assessment Synthesis Report." Addis Ababa.

———. 2005c. "MDG Needs Assessments for Education, Health, Water, and Sanitation." Addis Ababa.

Ndulu, B. J. 2007. *Challenges of African Growth: Opportunities, Constraints, and Strategic Directions.* Washington, DC: World Bank.

Soucat, A. 2005. "Simulation Results for the Health Sector Based on the Marginal Budgeting for Bottlenecks (MBB) Model Developed by UNICEF, World Bank, and WHO." Personal communication.

Tan, J.-P. 2005. "Simulation Results for the Education Sector Based on the Ethiopia Education Policy Simulation Model (EPSM) Developed by the World Bank in Collaboration with the Ethiopian Ministry of Education." Personal communication.

UNDP (United Nations Development Programme). 2006. *Human Development Report. Beyond Scarcity: Power, Poverty, and the Global Water Crisis.* New York.

World Bank. 2003. "Higher Education Development for Ethiopia: Pursuing the Vision." Africa Region Sector Report 29096, Washington, DC.

———. 2004a. "Education in Ethiopia: Strengthening the Foundation for Sustainable Progress." AFTH3, Human Development Department, Africa Region, Report 28037-ET (draft), Washington, DC.

———. 2004b. "Ethiopia—A Strategy to Balance and Stimulate Growth." Country Economic Memorandum 29383-ET, Washington, DC.

———. 2004c. "Ethiopia: Public Expenditure Review. Volume I: Public Spending in the Social Sectors 2000–2020. The Emerging Challenge." PER Report 29338-ET, AFTP2, Country Department for Ethiopia, Africa Region, Washington, DC.

———. 2004d. "RMSM-X Simulation for Ethiopia." Development Economics Data Group, Washington, DC.

———. 2004e. "World Development Indicators." Online version. Data accessed in August.

———. 2005. "Well-Being and Poverty in Ethiopia—The Role of Agriculture and Agency." Report 29468-ET, AFTP2, Washington, DC.

———. 2007a. "Ethiopia: Accelerating Equitable Growth, Part I: Overview." Country Economic Memorandum, Poverty Reduction and Economic Management Unit, Africa Region, Report 38662-ET, Washington, DC.

———. 2007b. "Ethiopia: Country Brief." Washington, DC.

———. 2007c. *World Development Indicators.* Washington, DC.

World Bank and Ministry of Health, Federal Democratic Republic of Ethiopia. 2004. "Ethiopia: A Country Status Report on Health and Poverty." Draft Report 28963-ET, Washington, DC.

CHAPTER 7

Beyond Aid: New Sources and Innovative Mechanisms for Financing Development in Sub-Saharan Africa

Dilip Ratha, Sanket Mohapatra, and Sonia Plaza

Official aid alone will not be adequate for funding efforts to accelerate economic growth and poverty alleviation and other Millennium Development Goals (MDGs) in Africa. Ultimately, the private sector will need to be the engine of growth and employment generation, and official aid efforts must catalyze innovative financing solutions for the private sector. It is important to stress that financing MDGs would require increasing the investment rate above the domestic saving rate and bridging the financing gap with additional financing from abroad.[1]

This chapter examines the level and composition of resource flows to sub-Saharan Africa: foreign direct investment (FDI), portfolio debt and equity flows, bank lending, official aid flows, capital flight, and personal and institutional remittances. Recognizing that South Africa is expectedly the largest economy and the most dominant destination of private flows, the analysis focuses on the rest of sub-Saharan Africa wherever appropriate.[2] The chapter then examines some new or overlooked sources of financing, some innovative mechanisms such as diaspora bonds and remittances, and some innovative mechanisms such as future-flow securitization and partial guarantees provided by multilateral agencies for raising additional cross-border financing in the private sector. In passing, the chapter also briefly discusses recent initiatives, such as the Global Alliance for Vaccines and Immunization (GAVI) and the International Financing Facility for Immunization (IFFIm), that use innovative methods to frontload future financing commitments from bilateral donors in order to introduce more predictability in aid flows.[3]

Resource flows to sub-Saharan Africa have increased since 2000, a welcome reversal of the declining or flat trend seen during the 1990s. Official development assistance (ODA) to the region excluding South Africa increased from $11.7 billion in 2000 to $30.1 billion in 2005; FDI increased from $5.8 billion to an estimated $13.3 billion in 2006; and net private bond and bank lending flows increased from −$0.7 billion to an estimated $4.3 billion during the same period.[4] Capital outflows from the region have also started reversing in recent years. Workers' remittances to sub-Saharan Africa more than doubled, from $4.6 billion in 2000 to $10.3 billion in 2006, and institutional remittances increased from $2.9 billion in 2000 to $5.3 billion in 2005. New donors and investors (for example, China and India) have increased their presence in the region.

The picture is less rosy, however, when sub-Saharan Africa is compared with the other developing regions. Sub-Saharan Africa continues to depend on official aid for its external financing needs. In 2005, ODA was more than two and a half times the size of private flows received by sub-Saharan Africa excluding South Africa. The recent increase in ODA appears to be driven by debt relief provided through the Heavily Indebted Poor Countries (HIPC) Initiative and Multilateral Debt Relief Initiative (MDRI), and the prospect for scaling up aid is not entirely certain.[5] The relatively small amount of FDI flows to the region went mostly to enclave investments in oil-exporting countries.[6] Portfolio bond and equity flows were almost nonexistent outside South Africa. Private debt flows were small and predominantly relationship-based commercial bank lending,[7] and even these flows were mostly short term in tenor. Less than half the countries in the region have a sovereign rating from the major credit-rating agencies. Of those that are rated, most have below-investment-grade ratings. Capital outflows appear to be smaller than in the previous decade, but the stock of flight capital from the region remains high. Migrant remittances appear to be increasing, but much of the flows are believed to be unrecorded as they bypass formal financial channels. In short, there is little room for complacency; efforts to explore new sources and innovative mechanisms for financing development in the region must continue.

The chapter suggests several new instruments for improving access to capital of sub-Saharan countries. The analysis of country creditworthiness suggests that many countries in the region appear to be more creditworthy than previously believed. Establishing sovereign rating benchmarks and credit enhancement through guarantee instruments provided by multilateral aid agencies would facilitate market access. Creative financial structuring, such as the IFFIm, can help frontload aid commitments, although they may not result in additional financing in the long run. Preliminary estimates suggest that sub-Saharan countries can potentially raise $1 billion to $3 billion by reducing the cost of international migrant remittances, $5 billion to $10 billion by issuing diaspora bonds, and $17 billion by securitizing future remittances and other future receivables.

The chapter is structured as follows. The following section analyzes trends in resource flows to sub-Saharan Africa relative to other developing regions. The next section highlights some new sources and innovative mechanisms for development financing in the region. And the final section concludes with a summary of findings and some recommendations for the way forward.

Trends in Financial Flows to Sub-Saharan Africa

Resource Flows

Resource flows to sub-Saharan Africa have risen in recent years, but the region's external finances are less diversified than in the other developing regions. In one of the largest expansions in private capital flows to developing countries in recent decades, private medium- and long-term capital flows nearly tripled in size, from $196 billion in 2000 to $580 billion in 2006. This period also saw significant diversification in the composition of private flows to developing countries (for FDI, portfolio bond and equity flows, bank lending, and derivative instruments). Official development assistance nearly doubled, from $54 billion to $104 billion, as did migrant remittances, from $85 billion in 2000 to $221 billion in 2006.

Official aid flows to sub-Saharan Africa also rose, from $12.2 billion in 2000 to $30.8 billion (or 38 percent of ODA to developing countries) in 2005. Private resource flows to sub-Saharan Africa, however, have risen at a slower pace, and the region's share of private capital flows to developing regions has continued to remain small and undiversified (table 7.1).

FDI to sub-Saharan countries other than South Africa rose from $5.8 billion in 2000 to an estimated $13.3 billion in 2006, making FDI the second-largest source of external finance. However, a large part of FDI in

TABLE 7.1
Financial Flows to Sub-Saharan Africa and Other Developing Countries, 2005

Type of flow	1990 ($ billions)	1995 ($ billions)	2000 ($ billions)	2005 ($ billions)	2006 estimate ($ billions)	Growth rate, 2000–06 (%)
Sub-Saharan Africa excluding South Africa						
Official flows						
ODA[a]	17.0	17.4	11.7	30.1	29.3	150
Official debt	4.3	3.5	0.7	−0.7	..	..
Private medium- and long-term flows	0.8	3.7	5.1	11.9	14.4	180
FDI[b]	1.3	3.3	5.8	10.3	13.3	128
Portfolio equity	0.0	0.0	0.0	0.1	0.1	..
Bond	0.0	0.1	−0.2	0.0	0.0	..
Bank lending	−0.5	0.3	−0.5	1.5	4.3	..
Private short-term debt	2.3	1.0	−1.4	1.4	1.4	..
Migrants' remittances[c]	1.7	3.1	4.3	8.7	9.6	124
Institutional remittances	1.4	2.3	2.9	5.2	..	..
Capital outflows	3.2	5.3	6.6	6.3	..	..
South Africa						
Official flows						
ODA[a]	0.0	0.4	0.5	0.7	0.7	146
Official debt	0.0	0.0	0.1	0.1	..	..
Private medium- and long-term flows	0.3	4.1	6.1	14.6	18.4	191
FDI[b]	−0.1	1.2	1.0	6.3	2.5	84
Portfolio equity	0.4	2.9	4.2	7.2	12.4	201
Bond[d]	0.0	0.7	1.2	0.4	1.4	40
Bank lending[d]	0.0	−0.8	−0.2	0.7	2.1	..
Private short-term debt[d]	0.0	1.9	0.3	1.8	1.9	..
Migrants' remittances[c]	0.1	0.1	0.3	0.7	0.7	114
Institutional remittances	0.1	0.0	0.0	0.1	..	..
Capital outflows	0.2	4.1	3.3	1.9	..	..
Other developing regions						
Official flows						
ODA[e]	37.3	41.0	41.5	76.0	73.9	78
Official debt	19.8	35.4	−6.6	−69.9	−75.8	..
Private medium- and long-term flows	34.6	159.0	184.4	458.9	544.2	195
Private short-term debt	22.0	54.1	−5.3	63.6	68.7	..
Migrants' remittances[c]	29.2	54.3	79.9	181.9	211.0	164
Institutional remittances	15.7	14.1	26.8	57.4	..	..
Capital outflows	34.6	79.7	168.1	351.0	..	..

Sources: Authors' calculations, based on Global Development Finance Database, September 2007.

Note: FDI = foreign direct investment; ODA = official development assistance; .. = negligible.

a. ODA to sub-Saharan Africa in 2006 is assumed to be the same fraction of ODA to all developing countries as in 2005.

b. FDI flows in 2006 to South Africa and oil exporters from World Bank (2007a). FDI to non-oil exporters assumed to be the same as 2005 at $3.3 billion.

c. Migrants' remittances are the sum of workers' remittances, compensation of employees, and migrants' transfers (World Bank 2005).

d. ODA, bank lending, bond financing, and short-term debt flows to South Africa (and the remaining sub-Saharan countries) in 2006 are assumed to be the same fraction of flows to sub-Saharan Africa as in 2005.

e. Development Assistance Committee donors only.

the region is concentrated in enclave investments in a few resource-rich countries. Portfolio equity flows to sub-Saharan Africa increased from $4.2 billion in 2000 to an estimated $12.5 billion in 2006, but almost all the flows went to South Africa (World Bank 2007a). And debt flows were mostly short-term bank credit secured by trade receivables—medium- and long-term bank lending was concentrated in Angola and South Africa, and international bond issuance was concentrated in South Africa.

Sub-Saharan Africa excluding South Africa received a minuscule 2.5 percent of medium- and long-term flows received by developing countries. Medium- and long-term private capital flows to sub-Saharan Africa excluding South Africa increased from $5.1 billion in 2000 to an estimated $14.4 billion during 2006. Private flows to South Africa alone were significantly larger throughout this period (table 7.1). The low- and middle-income sub-Saharan countries barring South Africa and a few commodity exporters have benefited little from the surge in private debt and portfolio equity flows to developing countries (figure 7.1).

FIGURE 7.1
Resource Flows to Sub-Saharan Africa

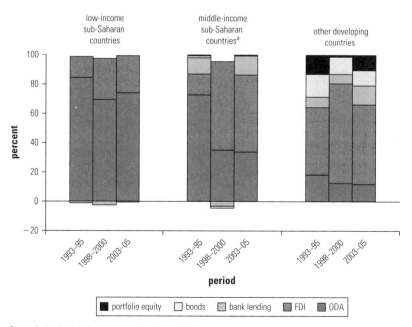

Source: Authors' calculations, based on World Bank 2007a.

a. Excludes South Africa.

Official Aid

Official aid continues to be the dominant source of external finance for sub-Saharan Africa. At $30.8 billion, ODA is the largest source of external financing for sub-Saharan countries, both in dollar amounts and as a share of gross domestic product (GDP). ODA to sub-Saharan countries other than South Africa of $30.1 billion was 4.5 percent of GDP for this group of countries in 2005, compared with 1 percent for all developing countries. While medium- and long-term private capital flows were only a fraction (about 40 percent) of official flows in sub-Saharan countries other than South Africa, they were more than eight times the size of official aid flows in other developing regions (figure 7.1).

Aid flows to sub-Saharan Africa declined until the late 1990s but have increased again in recent years. Official aid to sub-Saharan countries other than South Africa declined between 1995 and 2000, from $17.4 billion to $11.7 billion. ODA has increased again in recent years with a substantial scaling up of aid as a result of the international community's attention on the MDGs. However, debt relief under the HIPC Initiative and the MDRI and exceptional debt relief provided by Paris Club creditors to Nigeria in 2005–06 have contributed a large share of this increase in official flows (World Bank 2007a).[8] Net official debt flows have declined dramatically in recent years (from 1.5 percent of GDP in the early 1990s to 0.3 percent of GDP in 2000–05 for sub-Saharan countries for which data were available in 2005) as debt relief under the HIPC Initiative and MDRI has reduced debt stocks and the stream of future repayments for many sub-Saharan countries.[9]

Although developed countries have pledged to substantially increase aid flows to sub-Saharan Africa over the next decade, recent pledges for scaling up aid have not yet materialized for many donor countries. Excluding the exceptional debt relief to Nigeria, real ODA flows to sub-Saharan Africa fell in 2005 and stagnated in 2006 (IBRD 2007).[10] The promised doubling of aid to Africa by 2010 seems unlikely at the current rates of growth. The lack of predictability of future aid is a cause for concern in addition to the duplication of activities among donors and misalignment of the donor community's priorities with the country's development objectives.

A new group of aid donors—comprising Brazil, China, India, Lebanon, and Saudi Arabia—has emerged on the African scene. In January 2006, the Chinese government issued an official paper on China's Africa policy, and at the November 2006 China-Africa Summit, China promised to double its aid to Africa by 2009.[11] The old relationship between India and Africa is now being refocused to deepen economic collaboration in the areas of trade, technology, and training. Under the Indian Technical and Economic Cooperation Program, India spent more than $1 billion on aid assistance, including training, deputation of experts, and implementation of projects.

With traditional donors still failing to live up to their aid commitments, assistance from new donors could fill some of the funding gap in Sub-Saharan Africa. However, China's and India's approaches of delinking aid from political and economic reforms have raised concerns among traditional donors. These new emerging donors could cause traditional aid institutions to lower their own standards regarding governance and environmental issues, among others, given that China and India have not been involved in the debates on aid effectiveness. In the future, the new aid givers could participate in the global donor system.[12]

FDI Flows

FDI flows to sub-Saharan Africa were comparable to other regions, but appear to be mostly in enclave sectors. FDI to sub-Saharan countries reached an estimated $15.8 billion in 2006, becoming the second-largest source of external financing for the region. Low-income sub-Saharan countries received virtually all medium- and long-term private capital flows in the form of FDI. The region's improved macroeconomic management and growth performance, the commodity price boom, and debt relief have resulted in more investor interest. FDI to sub-Saharan countries excluding South Africa more than doubled from 2000, reaching an estimated $13.3 billion in 2006. Although the amount received by sub-Saharan Africa is tiny compared with the total FDI flows to developing countries, as a share of GDP it is equivalent to 2.2 percent, comparable to the share of FDI in the GDP of other developing regions.

However, FDI flows to sub-Saharan Africa appear to be concentrated in enclave sectors, such as oil and natural resources (McDonald, Treichel, and Weisfeld 2006; World Bank 2007a). FDI flows to oil-exporting and commodities-exporting countries were larger than in other countries in the region from 1990 onward (figure 7.2). Oil exporters received nearly 70 percent of FDI going to sub-Saharan countries other than South Africa in 2005. Net FDI inflows to four major oil-producing countries in sub-Saharan Africa—Angola, Equatorial Guinea, Nigeria, and Sudan—alone

FIGURE 7.2
FDI Flows in Sub-Saharan African Countries, Excluding South Africa

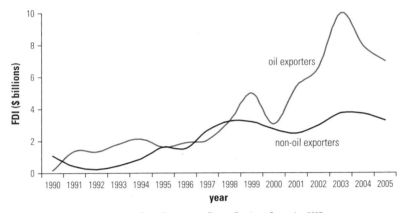

Source: Authors' calculations, based on Global Development Finance Database, September 2007.

were estimated at $10 billion in 2006, half of all FDI to low-income countries in 2006 (World Bank 2007a). Non-resource-intensive countries other than South Africa recorded rising but substantially lower inflows.

Private Debt Flows

Debt flows to sub-Saharan countries are small compared with other developing regions. Countries other than South Africa received an estimated $4.3 billion in 2006 in private medium- and long-term debt flows and $1.3 billion in short-term debt flows (usually in the form of trade credits) from 2004 to 2006, almost half of all short-term debt flows to the region. The high share of short-term debt in private debt flows reflects the high risk of lending on unsecured terms and at longer maturities to sub-Saharan African firms. These short-term flows were relatively volatile and carry the risk of rapid reversal (see box 7.1).

Medium- and long-term flows were mostly bank lending to middle-income sub-Saharan countries. One middle-income oil-exporting country, Angola, appears to account for virtually all medium- and long-term bank lending to sub-Saharan countries other than South Africa in 2003–05.

Bond issuance in sub-Saharan Africa has been almost exclusive to South Africa, which raised more than $2 billion annually from 2003 to 2005. Low- and middle-income sub-Saharan countries other than

BOX 7.1

Reliance on Short-Term Debt in Sub-Saharan Africa

Short-term debt comprises a large share of private debt flows to sub-Saharan Africa.[a] Even as developing countries in other regions reduce their dependence on short-term debt, these flows continue to be a large and volatile component of private debt flows to sub-Saharan Africa (see figure). After a surge in private short-term debt flows to sub-Saharan Africa during the mid-1990s, these flows turned negative from 1998 to 2002 after the Asian financial crisis. They have again increased in recent years as sub-Saharan Africa's growth performance improved. Since 1990, most private debt inflows into sub-Saharan Africa have been short term.

The high share of short-term debt may be partly explained by the severe informational asymmetries and risk perceptions of investing in sub-Saharan Africa. Similar factors also account for the dominance of foreign direct investment (FDI) in private capital flows to Sub-Saharan Africa and the small share of arm's-length financing through bond issuance and portfolio equity. In situations characterized by high risks, investors typically prefer to take direct control of their investment through FDI (Hausman and Fernández-Arias 2001) or resort to relationship-based bank lending that is typically

Short-Term Debt as a Large and Volatile Component of Private Debt Flows to Sub-Saharan Africa

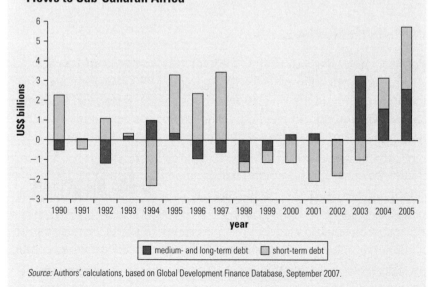

Source: Authors' calculations, based on Global Development Finance Database, September 2007.

BOX 7.1 **(continued)**

short term or can be secured by some tangible collateral, such as trade credits (see box 7.2).

A reliance on short-term debt can be risky for the receiving countries. Short-term debt tends to be pro-cyclical in developing countries, increasing when economic growth is cyclically faster and declining when growth rates falter (Dadush, Dasgupta, and Ratha 2000). Favorable conditions attract large inflows, encouraging potentially unsustainable levels of consumption and investment. Changes in risk perceptions, however, can lead to rapid reversals, imposing larger-than-necessary adjustment costs for the receiving countries.

a. Short-term international debt is defined as cross-border debt falling due within a year. The original maturity concept followed by World Bank (2002) is used here. The Bank for International Settlements, however, uses a "remaining maturity" concept—that is, all cross-border debt falling due within one year is counted as short-term debt, regardless of its original maturity (Dadush, Dasgupta, and Ratha 2000). Although conceptually different, the trends in the two are usually similar.

South Africa received negligible amounts of bond financing from international markets.

Portfolio Equity Flows

Portfolio equity flows were almost absent in sub-Saharan Africa excluding South Africa. Such flows have increased since 1990 to an estimated $12.5 billion in 2006 and are now an important source of external finance for sub-Saharan Africa. However, portfolio flows have gone exclusively to South Africa. When South Africa is excluded, portfolio equity flows are negligible in low- and middle-income sub-Saharan countries. Although South Africa has received more than $4 billion annually since 1995, other sub-Saharan countries received less than $50 million annually during this period. Foreign investors appear to be averse to investing in Africa because of lack of information, severe risk perception, and the small size of the market that makes stocks relatively illiquid assets. One way to encourage greater private investment in these markets could be to tap into the diaspora outside Africa. Some initiatives being prepared by the diaspora is the formation of regional funds to be invested in companies listed on African stock markets.

Personal and Institutional Remittances

Personal and institutional remittances are a growing source of external financing for sub-Saharan Africa.

Recorded personal remittance inflows to sub-Saharan Africa have increased steadily during the last decade, from $3.2 billion in 1995 to $9.3 billion in 2005 and to $10.3 billion in 2006. Most of this flow ($8.5 billion) went to low-income sub-Saharan countries in 2006. Unrecorded flows through informal channels are believed to be even higher (World Bank 2005; Page and Plaza 2006).[13] In six sub-Saharan countries—Botswana, Côte d'Ivoire, Lesotho, Mauritius, Swaziland, and Togo—remittances were higher than ODA flows. In Lesotho, Mauritius, Swaziland, and Togo, remittances were also greater than FDI.

However, remittance flows to sub-Saharan Africa have lagged behind other developing countries. Low-income countries received some $56 billion or 3.6 percent of GDP as remittances in 2006, whereas sub-Saharan countries other than South Africa received 2.2 percent. The relatively low share of recorded remittances to sub-Saharan Africa is mostly attributable to a high share of informal transfers.

Institutional remittances, which include grants by U.S. and European foundations, were another category of resource flows that are large and growing steadily.[14] Institutional remittances to sub-Saharan Africa increased from less than $2 billion in the early 1990s to $5.3 billion by 2005. As with personal remittances, most institutional remittances went to the poorest countries, with low-income sub-Saharan countries receiving $4.9 billion or 1.6 percent of GDP in 2005.

Private foundations, such as the Bill & Melinda Gates Foundation, are increasingly becoming important players in financing development. U.S. and European foundations provide some $4.4 billion in grants annually for international development (Sulla 2007). However, most of the international assistance from U.S. foundations is channeled through global funds, such as GAVI, international institutions, and international nongovernmental organizations, and goes to emerging markets, such as Brazil, China, India, Mexico, the Russian Federation, and South Africa, rather than the poorest countries in sub-Saharan Africa where grants from the

International Development Association (IDA) continue to play a dominant role.[15] This may result partly from a lack of information and difficulties in implementing projects in the poorest countries in sub-Saharan Africa.

Institutional remittances have become increasingly important for financing the most pressing development needs of sub-Saharan Africa, including those essential for reaching the MDGs. However, some of the so-called vertical funds raise challenges because of their focus on specific issues—for example, diseases such as AIDS, tuberculosis, or malaria (see Sulla 2007 for recent trends and issues in grant giving by U.S. and European foundations). Multilateral institutions, such as the IDA, can help channel external assistance in a coordinated manner, provide support for broader sector-specific (education, health) strategies, and align these with sub-Saharan countries' own development priorities.

Capital Outflows

Capital outflows from sub-Saharan Africa have decreased in recent years, but the stock of flight capital abroad remains high.

Capital outflows from sub-Saharan countries averaged $9 billion annually from 1990 to 2005.[16] Capital outflows increased until 2002 but have declined in recent years (figure 7.3). The cumulated stock of outflows from sub-Saharan countries was $173 billion in 2006, nearly 30 percent of

FIGURE 7.3
Capital Outflows from Sub-Saharan Africa

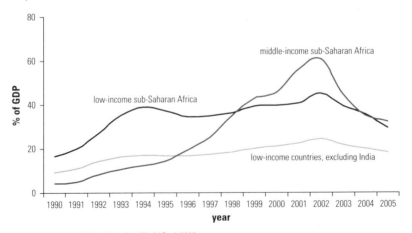

Source: Authors' calculations, based on World Bank 2007a.

GDP—down from a high of 53 percent of GDP in 2002. Capital outflows increased faster from middle-income and resource-rich sub-Saharan countries in the 1990s, reaching 61 percent of GDP in 2002 (figure 7.3).[17]

Several studies have identified a number of factors that encourage capital flight from Africa (see, for example, Ajayi 1997; Boyce and Ndikumana 2001; Collier, Hoeffler, and Pattillo 2001; Hermes, Lensink, and Murinde 2002; Ndikumana and Boyce 2002; Powell, Ratha, and Mohapatra 2002; Salisu 2005; World Bank 2004). Some of the main determinants of capital flight include macroeconomic instability, political instability, external borrowing, risk-adjusted rates of return differentials, and financial development, among others. Consistent with the view of outflows as a portfolio diversification choice (Collier, Hoeffler, and Pattillo 2004), the stock of cumulated capital outflows appears to be negatively related to the country performance rating, including corruption, economic management, and transparency (figure 7.4).

There appears to have been capital flight reversal in the past few years. Improving macroeconomic fundamentals, better growth prospects, and an improving business environment have improved the risk-adjusted returns from investing domestically (see box 7.2).

FIGURE 7.4
Capital Outflows

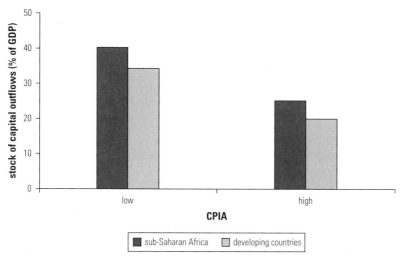

Source: Authors' calculations.

Note: CPIA = Country Policy and Institutional Assessments.

BOX 7.2

New Players in Sub-Saharan Africa: China and India

Emerging creditors such as China—and India on a smaller scale—have increased their financial assistance to sub-Saharan Africa in the form of loans, grants, debt relief, and direct investment. Relevant data are not easily available, but China appears to be the largest of six new creditor nations. By May 2006, China had contributed $5.7 billion for more than 800 aid projects (IMF 2007). In the latest Beijing Summit of the Forum on China-African Cooperation in November 2006, China announced that it would provide $5 billion on preferential credits for 2007–09 ($3 billion in concessional loans and $2 billion for export buyer credits). Counting media reports only, Export–Import Bank of China provided $7 billion in 2004–06. In May 2007, Export–Import Bank of China stated that it planned to provide about $20 billion in infrastructure and trade financing to Africa over the next three years (*Financial Times* 2007b). China's investment in oil and textiles has rapidly spiked upwardly in Angola, Sudan, and Zimbabwe. With the support of the Export–Import Bank of China, Chinese companies have quickly become leaders in the development of roads, railroads, and major public buildings, as well as telecommunications on the continent (Broadman et al. 2007: box 5.12). Chad and China just signed a $257 million economic package to finance several projects in the central African country, including telecommunications, a cement factory, and roads.

Chinese banks are also entering a new phase of involvement in Africa by developing partnerships with and buying equity stakes in African banks.

New Sources and Innovative Mechanisms for Financing Development in Sub-Saharan Africa

This section discusses some new or hitherto-overlooked sources and some innovative structures for development financing in sub-Saharan countries. First, the section discusses two new sources of financing: issuance of diaspora bonds and efforts to increase migrant remittances by reducing money transfer costs. The section then discusses some recent

The Industrial and Commercial Bank of China is acquiring 20 percent of South Africa's Standard Bank for about $5 billion (*Financial Times* 2007a). The two banks will jointly establish a global resources fund to invest in mining, metals, and oil and gas in emerging markets. China Development Bank has formed a partnership with Nigeria's United Bank for Africa to cooperate in financing energy and infrastructure projects in Nigeria and other West African countries (*Oxford Analytica* 2007).

China has offered debt forgiveness to 31 African countries, amounting to $1.27 billion since 2000, and more write-offs are expected. By mid-May 2007, China had signed debt forgiveness agreements with 11 of those countries and expected to conclude agreements with the other 22 by the end of 2007 (Wang 2007).

China's nonconcessional loans to some countries have raised concerns that it may be free riding in countries that received debt relief under the Multilateral Debt Relief Initiative and the Heavily Indebted Poor Countries (HIPC) programs (*Economist* 2007). According to some authors, however, the majority of the projects undertaken by China are in non-HIPC resource-rich countries, such as Angola, Nigeria, and Sudan (Goldstein et al. 2006). In those countries, these loans are part of China's foreign direct investment (FDI) directed to strategic resource seeking.[a] A $5 billion China-Africa Development Fund has been created to support Chinese FDI in Africa.

a. China and India's investments in Africa are examples of a broader South-South investment trend. Aykut and Ratha (2005) show that by the late 1990s, more than a third of FDI received by developing countries originated in other developing countries.

initiatives that involve innovative financial structures—multilateral guarantees that leverage official financing for mobilizing private capital and the IFFIm that frontloads aid commitments—before describing a more generalized financial structuring that allows private entities to issue debt backed by future remittances and other future-flow receivables. Finally, the section argues for establishing sovereign credit ratings for sub-Saharan countries, because ratings are key to attracting private capital.

New Sources of Financing

Diaspora Bonds

A diaspora bond is a debt instrument issued by a country—or, potentially, by a subsovereign entity or by a private corporation—to raise financing from its overseas diaspora. India and Israel have raised $11 billion and $25 billion, respectively, from their diaspora abroad (Ketkar and Ratha 2007). These bonds are issued often in times of crisis and often at a "patriotic" discount. Unlike international investors, the diaspora tend to be less averse to convertibility risk because they are likely to have current and contingent liabilities in their home country. Further, the diaspora usually have a strong desire to contribute to the development of their home country and are therefore more likely to purchase diaspora bonds.

Table 7.2 shows estimates of the diaspora stocks of sub-Saharan countries and their annual savings. The stock of sub-Saharan diaspora is

TABLE 7.2
Potential Market for Diaspora Bonds

Country	Diaspora stock (thousands)	Potential diaspora saving ($ billions)
South Africa	713	2.9
Nigeria	837	2.8
Kenya	427	1.7
Ghana	907	1.7
Ethiopia	446	1.6
Somalia	441	1.6
Senegal	463	1.3
Zimbabwe	761	1.0
Sudan	587	1.0
Angola	523	1.0
Congo, Dem. Rep.	572	0.8
Cape Verde	181	0.7
Uganda	155	0.7
Mauritius	119	0.7
Cameroon	231	0.6
Mozambique	803	0.6
Madagascar	151	0.6
Tanzania	189	0.6
Eritrea	849	0.6
Mali	1,213	0.6
Other sub-Saharan countries	5,285	5.5
Total	15,854	28.5

Source: Authors' calculations.

Note: Diaspora stocks for 2005 include only identified migrants from Ratha and Shaw (2007). Diaspora savings are calculated assuming migrants earned the average per capita income of the host country and saved one-fifth of their income.

estimated to be about 16 million, with 5 million in high-income countries. Assuming that members of the sub-Saharan diaspora earn the average income of their host countries and save a fifth of their income, their annual savings would be more than $28 billion.[18] Presently, the bulk of this saving is invested outside Africa. African governments and private corporations can potentially tap into these resources by issuing diaspora bonds. Diaspora bonds can also provide an instrument for repatriation of Africa's flight capital, estimated at more than $170 billion (as discussed). Diaspora bonds could potentially raise $5 billion to $10 billion annually by tapping into the wealth of the African diaspora abroad and the flight capital held abroad by its residents.[19]

Some of the constraints that sub-Saharan countries may face in issuing diaspora bonds include weak and nontransparent legal systems for contract enforcement; a lack of national banks and other institutions in destination countries, which can facilitate the marketing of the bonds; and a lack of clarity on regulations in the host countries that allow or constrain diaspora members from investing in the bonds (Chander 2001; Ketkar and Ratha 2007). However, because of recent debt relief initiatives and improving macroeconomic management, many sub-Saharan countries are in a better position to access private capital markets than anytime in recent decades.[20]

Reducing Remittance Costs

Reducing remittance costs would increase remittance flows to sub-Saharan Africa. Sub-Saharan Africa is believed to have the highest share of remittances flowing through informal channels among all regions (Page and Plaza 2006).[21] This is partly because of the high cost of sending remittances in sub-Saharan Africa. For example, the average cost, including foreign exchange premium, of sending $200 from London to Lagos, Nigeria, in mid-2006 was 14.4 percent of the amount, and the cost from Cotonou, Benin, to Lagos was more than 17 percent (Ratha and Shaw 2007). Reducing remittance fees would increase the disposable income of remitters, encouraging them to remit large amounts and at greater frequencies. It would also encourage remittance senders to shift from informal to formal channels.

Estimating the additional remittance flows that would result from a decrease in remittance cost is complicated by several factors. For example, remittances sent for an immediate family emergency may not be responsive to costs. However, estimates based on surveys of Tongan migrants indicate the cost elasticity to be in the range of 0.22; that is, a 1 percent decrease in cost would increase remittances by 0.22 percent (Gibson, McKenzie, and Rohorua 2006). For example, halving remittance costs from the current high levels, from 14 percent to 7 percent for the London–Lagos corridor, would thus increase remittances by 11 percent. This change implies additional remittance flows of more than $1 billion every year. Assuming that the reduction in remittance cost also succeeds in bringing in half the unrecorded remittances into formal channels, this reduction would result in an increase in remittances flows to sub-Saharan Africa of $2.5 billion.

Remittance costs faced by poor migrants from sub-Saharan countries can be reduced by improving the access to banking for remittance senders and recipients and by strengthening competition in the remittance industry (Ratha 2007; World Bank 2005). Clarifying regulations related to anti–money laundering and countering the financing of terrorism and avoiding overregulation, such as requiring a full banking license for specialized money transfer operators, would facilitate the entry of new players. It would also encourage the adoption of more efficient technologies, such as the use of Internet and mobile phone technology. Sharing payment platforms and nonexclusive partnerships between remittance service providers and existing postal and retail networks would help expand remittance services without requiring large fixed investments.

Innovative Structuring

Guarantees
World Bank and IDA partial risk guarantees of some $3 billion were successful in catalyzing $12 billion in private financing in 28 operations in developing countries during the past decade (Gelb, Ramachandran, and Turner 2006). These typically cover project financing in large infrastructure projects and other sectors with high social returns. World Bank guarantees include partial risk guarantees and partial credit guarantees that cover private debt for large public projects (typically infrastructure). Although the former typically cover the risk of nonperformance of sovereign contractual obligations, the latter cover a much broader range of credit risks and are designed to lower the cost and extend the maturity of debt (Matsukawa and Habeck 2007).[22] Political risk guarantees issued by

the Multilateral Investment Guarantee Agency (MIGA) have helped alleviate political and others risks in agribusiness, manufacturing, and tourism. The African Export–Import Bank and other agencies provide guarantees for trade credits (see box 7.3). There appears to be potential to increase the use of IDA guarantees beyond large infrastructure projects to small and medium enterprises.

BOX 7.3

Trade Finance as an Attractive Short-Term Financing Option

Trade finance is an attractive way of increasing short-term financing to risky African countries in the presence of asymmetric information. Firms operating in international markets require financing for the purchase of their imports and for the production of their exports. Many African firms, however, have no access to trade finance or instruments to support their operations because of information asymmetries and their perceived greater risk. Larger firms that have access to credit from importers, the banking system (typically from affiliates of European global banking corporations whose core business is often short-term trade finance), or other nonbank financial institutions often provide trade credit to their smaller suppliers, who in many cases have no access to credit.

In recent years, the export credit agencies of China and India have become increasingly prominent in promoting trade finance in sub-Saharan Africa, not only for raw materials, commodities, and natural resources but also for capital goods (machinery, equipment) and manufactured products. In 2006, the Export-Import Bank of India extended a $250 million line of credit to Economic Community of West African States (ECOWAS) Bank for Investment and Development (EBID) to finance India's exports to the 15 member countries of EBID. It has also previously extended trade financing to the Eastern and Southern African Trade and Development Bank (PTA Bank) for $50 million to promote India's exports to 16 eastern and southern African countries. The Export-Import Bank of China is financing a larger set of activities, providing export credit, loans for construction contracts and investment projects (including energy and communication projects), and concessional loans and guarantees.

BOX 7.3 (continued)

The World Bank is supporting an innovative project through its Regional Trade Facilitation Program to address the gaps in the private political and credit risk insurance market for cross-border transactions involving African countries. The project is managed by the African Trade Insurance Agency (ATI), a multilateral agency set up by treaty, and brings together a group of countries in the southern and eastern African regions to develop a credible insurance mechanism. To date, ATI has facilitated $110.7 million in trade and investments in ATI member countries, using only $21.6 million of International Development Association resources—a gearing ratio of almost five to one in sectors that include mining (Zambia), housing (the Democratic Republic of Congo), flowers (Kenya), and telecommunications (Burundi and Uganda). Clients have indicated that without ATI's support, they might not have received the necessary financing.

Although trade finance can facilitate trade and economic linkages with Africa's major trading partners, Africa needs additional longer-term sources of external finance. Trade finance is typically short term and carries many risks associated with short-term debt (see box 7.1). The recent expansion of trade finance may also partly reflect the inability of sub-Saharan countries to obtain unsecured financing at longer maturities. Enhancing the scope and volume of trade finance can facilitate trade and improve regional economic cooperation, but additional external resource flows are required to finance the projects in infrastructure, manufacturing, education, and health that have high social returns and involve significantly longer time horizons.

The first-ever IDA partial risk guarantee in sub-Saharan Africa in 1999 for the Azito power project in Côte d'Ivoire catalyzed private financing of $200 million while keeping IDA support to $30 million, or 15 percent of the project (World Bank 1999). IDA partial risk guarantees are under preparation for the 250-megawatt Bujagali hydropower project in Uganda, a 50-megawatt hydropower project in Sierra Leone, and a project to increase power sector efficiency in Senegal (World Bank 2007c).

There is potential for extending the scope and reach of guarantees to use aid resources to catalyze large volumes of private financing in sub-Saharan Africa beyond the traditional large infrastructure projects and beyond sovereign borrowers. Gelb, Ramachandran, and Turner (2006) suggest that guarantees should be available not only to foreign investors but also to domestic investors, including pension and insurance funds, to raise local-currency financing. Guarantee facilities can be established to support several small projects in the same sector, similar to a "master trust" arrangement. Innovations include service guarantees that can protect investors against service failures in areas such as power, customs, and licensing that discourage private investment in sub-Saharan countries.

IFFIm, AMC, and Other Innovative Structuring by Public-Private Partnerships

Several international initiatives are under way for innovative development financing mechanisms. They include a search for new sources of financing, innovative ways of realizing *future* commitments, and innovative ways of using *existing* resources. IFFIm is an innovative structuring mechanism for realizing future aid commitments to introduce more reliable and predictable aid flows for immunization programs and health system development for GAVI.[23] IFFIm raised $1 billion in 2006 and plans to raise $4 billion more during the next 10 years by "securitizing"—in other words, frontloading—future aid commitments from several donor countries (France, Italy, Norway, South Africa, Spain, Sweden, and the United Kingdom). The donor countries have signed legally binding agreements with the GAVI Fund Affiliate to provide future grants to IFFIm, which issues the bonds in international markets. IFFIm disburses the proceeds as required for GAVI-approved programs to procure needed vaccines and to strengthen the health systems of recipient countries. Future grant flows from donors are used to repay bondholders. The backing of highly creditworthy developed-country donors has enabled IFFIm to issue AAA-rated bonds in international capital markets at competitive spreads.

Such a facility, however, faces several constraints, including the question of "additionality" (whether the countries that bought the bonds will reduce aid), high transaction costs, and whether the coupon yield will be paid for by sovereign bond guarantors or subtracted from the proceeds.

The Advanced Market Commitment (AMC) for vaccines launched in February 2007 is another innovative structuring mechanism that would complement the efforts of IFFIm by providing financial incentives to accelerate the development of vaccines important to developing countries. The donors provide up-front financing for the AMC, which negotiates with the pharmaceutical industry to provide a set level of funding in return for future supply at an agreed price for the manufacturer that first develops the vaccine (GAVI and World Bank 2006). Canada, Italy, Norway, Russia, the United Kingdom, and the Gates Foundation have provided $1.5 billion for the pilot AMC to develop a vaccine for pneumococcal disease, which causes 1.9 million child deaths a year. The AMC is not expected to increase aid flows substantially to poor countries, but it brings together public and private donors in an innovative way to help meet the MDGs (IBRD 2007).[24]

Other public-private partnerships to generate new sources of innovative financing that are under consideration include a currency transaction levy, airline and environmental taxes, and private contributions.[25] Introducing a one basis point levy on currency transactions could yield over $16 billion in revenue annually, according to Hillman, Kapoor, and Spratt (2006). This variation of a Tobin tax, however, is not popular with the financial institutions or with countries that are major financial centers. Such taxes would cause friction in financial transactions and have cascading effects. Airline taxes are already being implemented in some countries (for example, eight countries including France have raised $250 million in 2007), but there are questions as to whether they were new taxes (IBRD 2007).[26]

These public-private partnerships, however, rely on donor government efforts to mobilize financing and are subject to the same concerns about aid allocation, coordination, and effectiveness. These innovative projects are not designed for catalyzing private-to-private flows to developing countries from the international capital markets.

A new initiative by the World Bank Group—the Global Emerging Markets Local Currency (Gemloc) Bond Fund announced in October 2007—proposes to raise $5 billion from international capital markets to invest in local-currency bond markets in developing countries.[27] The Gemloc public-private partnership will mobilize local-currency-denominated resources for governments in selected emerging market countries, thereby eliminating the devaluation risk associated with foreign-currency borrowing. Corporate bonds will be included subsequently, but at least 70 percent of the proceeds of Gemloc would be invested in local-currency bonds issued by sovereign and quasi-sovereign entities.

The creation of an independent and transparent benchmark index and "investability" rankings of countries' local-currency bond markets are expected to facilitate external financing flows to emerging markets. Like portfolio equity flows, however, the Gemloc is likely to favor middle-income countries with market access. Although the Gemloc plans to include Kenya, Nigeria, and West African countries in a subsequent phase, most of the countries selected for the first phase (for example, Brazil, China, India, and South Africa) are countries with sovereign ratings in the BB or BBB category. It is also not entirely clear whether the Gemloc would result in additional funding or whether it might substitute portfolio equity flows.

Future-Flow Securitization
Sub-Saharan countries can potentially raise significant bond financing by using securitization of future flows, such as remittances, tourism receipts, and export receivables. Securitization of future hard-currency receivables is a potential means of improving the access of sub-Saharan countries to international capital markets. In a typical future-flow transaction, the borrower pledges its future foreign-currency receivables—for example, oil, remittances, credit card receivables, airline ticket receivables—as collateral to a special-purpose vehicle (Ketkar and Ratha 2000, 2005). The special-purpose vehicle issues the debt. By a legal arrangement between the borrowing entity and major international customers or correspondent banks, the future receivables are deposited directly in an offshore collection account managed by a trustee. The debt is serviced from this account, and excess collections are forwarded to the borrowing entity in the developing country.[28]

This future-flow securitization mitigates sovereign transfer and convertibility risks and allows the securities to be rated better than the sovereign credit rating. These securities are typically structured to obtain an investment-grade rating. For example, in the case of El Salvador, the remittance-backed securities were rated investment grade, two to four notches above the subinvestment-grade sovereign rating. Investment-grade rating makes these transactions attractive to a wider range of "buy-and-hold" investors (for example, insurance companies) that face limitations on buying subinvestment grade. As a result, the issuer can access international capital markets at a lower interest rate spread and longer maturity. Moreover, by establishing a credit history for the borrower, these deals enhance the ability to obtain and reduce the costs of accessing capital markets in the future.[29]

The potential size of future-flow securitizations for various kinds of flows, including remittances, for sub-Saharan Africa can be estimated on the basis of the methodology of Ketkar and Ratha (2000, 2005) using an overcollateralization ratio of five to one and average flows in 2003–06. These calculations indicate that the potential future-flow securitization is $17 billion annually, with remittance securitization alone in the range of $2 billion (table 7.3). These include only the securitization of remittances recorded in the balance of payments. The actual unrecorded remittances through formal and informal channels are estimated to be a multiple in several countries (Page and Plaza 2006).

Remittances are a large and stable source of external financing that can be creatively leveraged for sub-Saharan Africa's development goals. Remittances can improve capital market access of banks and governments in poor countries by improving ratings and securitization structures (Ratha 2006). Hard-currency remittances, properly accounted, can significantly improve a country's risk rating. It may even encourage many poor countries that are currently not rated to obtain a credit rating from major international rating agencies (see the following for more discussion).

The African Export–Import Bank (Afreximbank) has been active in facilitating future-flow securitization since the late 1990s. In 1996, it coarranged the first ever future-flow securitization by a sub-Saharan

TABLE 7.3
Securitization Potential in Sub-Saharan Africa

	Sub-Saharan Africa		Low income (excluding India)		All developing countries	
	Receivable ($ billions)	Potential securitization ($ billions)	Receivable ($ billions)	Potential securitization ($ billions)	Receivable ($ billions)	Potential securitization ($ billions)
Fuel exports[a]	44.1	8.8	47.7	9.5	417.5	83.5
Agricultural raw materials exports[a]	5.7	1.1	4.4	0.9	46.3	9.3
Ores and metals exports[a]	13.4	2.7	5.0	1.0	106.6	21.3
Travel services[b]	12.4	2.5	4.8	1.0	168.5	33.7
Remittances[b]	8.4	1.7	23.6	4.7	179.4	35.9
Total	84.0	16.8	85.5	17.1	918.3	183.7

Source: Authors' calculations using overcollateralization ratio of 5:1. Data on exports are from the World Bank's World Development Indicators database. Workers' remittances, as defined in Ratha (2003), are calculated from the IMF's Balance-of Payments Statistics Yearbook 2007.

a. Average for 2003–05.

b. Average for 2003–06.

country, a $40 million medium-term loan in favor of a development bank in Ghana backed by its Western Union remittance receivables (Afreximbank 2005; Rutten and Oramah 2006). The bank launched its Financial Future-flow Pre-financing Programme in 2001 to expand the use of migrant remittances and other future flows—credit card and checks, royalties arising from bilateral air services agreements over flight fees, and so forth—as collateral to leverage external financing to fund agricultural and other projects in sub-Saharan Africa. In recent year, the Afreximbank has arranged a $50 million remittance-backed syndicated note issuance facility in favor of a Nigerian entity using Moneygram receivables in 2001, and it coarranged a $40 million remittance-backed syndicated term loan facility in favor of an Ethiopian bank using its Western Union receivables in 2004 (Afreximbank 2005).

There are, however, several institutional constraints to future-flow securitization in sub-Saharan Africa. A low level of domestic financial development; a lack of banking relationships with banks abroad; and high fixed costs of legal, investment banking, and credit-rating services, especially in poor countries with few large entities, make the use of these instruments especially difficult for sub-Saharan countries. Absence of an appropriate legal infrastructure and weak protection of creditor rights (including inadequate or poorly enforced bankruptcy laws) and a volatile macroeconomic environment can also pose difficulties. In the case of remittance securitization, extensive use of informal channels in sub-Saharan Africa can reduce the flows through the formal financial system and thereby the size of potential securitization.

Securitization by poor countries carries significant risks—currency devaluation and, in the case of flexible-rate debt, unexpected increases in interest rates—that are associated with market-based foreign-currency debt (World Bank 2005). Securitization of remittances (and other future flows) by public sector entities reduces the government's flexibility in managing its external payments and can conflict with the negative pledge provision included in multilateral agencies' loan and guarantee agreements, which prohibit the establishment of a priority for other debts over the multilateral debts.

Still, this asset class can provide useful access to international capital markets, especially during liquidity crises. Moreover, for many developing countries, securitization backed by future flows of receivables may be the only way to begin accessing such markets. Given the long lead times involved in such deals, however, issuers need to keep securitization deals in the pipeline and investors engaged during good times so that such deals remain accessible during crises.

Recovery of Stolen Assets

Other innovative ways of using existing resources include recovery of flight capital and stolen assets. The cross-border flow of the global proceeds from criminal activities, corruption, and tax evasion are estimated to be more than $1 trillion annually (UNODC and World Bank 2007).[30] Some $20 billion to $40 billion in assets acquired by corrupt leaders of poor countries, mostly in Africa, are kept overseas. The World Bank and the United Nations Office of Drugs and Crime have launched the Stolen Assets Recovery (StAR) initiative to help countries recover their stolen assets. This initiative will help countries establish institutions that can detect and deter illegal flow of funds, work with the Organisation for Economic Co-operation and Development countries in ratifying the Convention against Corruption, and support and monitor the use of recovered funds for development activities. These recovered assets could provide financing for social programs and infrastructure.[31]

Sovereign Ratings

Establishing and improving sovereign ratings can facilitate market access. Sovereign risk ratings not only affect investment decisions in the international bond and loan markets, but they also affect allocation of FDI and portfolio equity flows (Ratha, De, and Mohapatra 2007). The allocation of performance-based official aid is also increasingly being linked to sovereign ratings. The foreign-currency rating of the sovereign typically acts as a ceiling for the foreign-currency rating of subsovereign entities. Even when the sovereign is not issuing bonds, a sovereign rating provides a benchmark for the capital market activities of the private sector.

Borrowing costs rise exponentially with a lowering of the credit rating (figure 7.5). There is also a threshold effect when borrowing spreads jump up as the rating slides below the investment grade (Ratha, De, and Mohapatra 2007). A borrowing entity with a low credit rating, therefore, can significantly improve borrowing terms (that is, lower interest spread and increase maturity) by paying up front for a better credit rating.

FIGURE 7.5
Launch Spreads and Sovereign Ratings

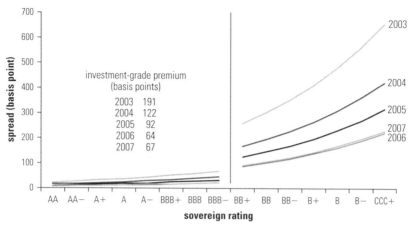

Source: Ratha, De, and Mohapatra 2007, based on Bondware and Standard & Poor's.

Note: Table assumes a $100 million sovereign bond issue with a seven-year tenor. Borrowing costs have fallen steadily since 2003, with a slight reversal more recently, reflecting changes in the global liquidity situation. The investment-grade premium indicates the rise in spreads when rating falls below BBB−. The relationship between sovereign ratings and spreads is based on the following regression: log(launch spread) = 2.58 − 1.20 investment-grade dummy + 0.15 sovereign rating + 0.23 log(issue size) + 0.03 maturity − 0.44 year 2004 dummy − 0.73 year 2005 dummy − 1.10 year 2006 dummy − 1.05 year 2007 dummy; $N = 200$; adjusted $R^2 = 0.70$. All coefficients were significant at 5 percent. A lower numeric value of the sovereign rating indicates a better rating.

Only 20 sub-Saharan countries had been rated by a major international rating agency as of December 2006 (table 7.4).[32] The average rating of sub-Saharan countries remains low compared with other regions, restricting the access of their private sector to international capital. As noted in the previous section, private debt and equity flows to sub-Saharan countries were the lowest among all regions. Some authors have pointed to the existence of an "Africa premium"—equivalent to roughly two rating notches or 200 basis points—even for relatively better-performing countries with above-median growth and low aid dependence (Gelb, Ramachandran, and Turner 2006). At the subsovereign level, few firms in sub-Saharan Africa outside of South Africa are rated by the three international rating agencies.[33] Several firms are highly creditworthy in local-currency terms, but they are constrained by either an absent or low foreign-currency sovereign rating.

Model-based estimates indicate that several unrated sub-Saharan countries would be rated higher than currently believed. Drawing on the

TABLE 7.4
Rated Sub-Saharan Countries

Country	Standard & Poor's		Moody's		Fitch		Predicted shadow rating[a]
	Rating	Date	Rating	Date	Rating	Date	
Botswana	A	April 2001	Aa3	May 2006			AA to AAA
South Africa	BBB+	August 2005	Baa1	January 2005	BBB+	August 2005	BBB to BBB+
Mauritius			Baa1	May 2006			BBB+ to A−
Namibia					BBB−	December 2005	BBB− to BBB
Lesotho					BB−	November 2005	BB to BB+
Nigeria	BB−	Feb 2006			BB−	January 2006	BB to BBB−
Cape Verde					B+	August 2003	BBB−
Ghana	B+	September 2003			B+	September 2007	BB− to BB
Kenya	B+	September 2006					B to B+
Senegal	B+	December 2000					BB to BB+
Seychelles	B	September 2006					BB to BBB−
Cameroon	B	February 2007			B	June 2006	BB− to BB
Benin	B	September 2006			B	September 2004	BB− to BB
Burkina Faso	B	March 2004					B to B+
Madagascar	B	May 2004					B to B+
Mozambique	B	July 2004			B	July 2003	B+ to BB−
Uganda					B	March 2005	BB−
Mali	B	May 2004			B−	April 2004	BB
Malawi					B−	March 2007	CCC+ to B
Gambia, The					CCC	December 2005	B+ to BB−

Source: Ratings from Standard & Poor's, Moody's, and Fitch.

a. These shadow ratings are based on forecasts of explanatory variables for 2007 for the benchmark sovereign rating model of Ratha, De, and Mohapatra (2007).

well-established literature on the empirical determinants of sovereign ratings, Ratha, De, and Mohapatra (2007) find that the predicted or *shadow sovereign ratings* for several sub-Saharan countries that are currently unrated are in a similar range as some established emerging markets (table 7.5).[34]

Sub-Saharan African countries with large remittance inflows can leverage those inflows for raising the sovereign rating (Ratha 2006). Preliminary estimates indicate that including remittances in the debt-to-exports ratio in creditworthiness assessments would result in an improvement in sovereign ratings by up to two notches (World Bank 2005). The securitization of future receivables, including trade payments and future remittances, can further improve the rating of the transaction, typically to investment grade (BBB). For example, the spread saving from improving ratings from B to BBB would be in the range of 320 to 450 basis points (figure 7.5).

TABLE 7.5
Shadow Sovereign Ratings for Unrated Countries in Sub-Saharan Africa

Country	Predicted shadow rating[a]	Rated countries in the same range
Equatorial Guinea	BBB− to BBB	India, Mexico, Romania
Gabon	BBB− to BBB	India, Mexico, Romania
Angola	BB+	El Salvador, Peru
Swaziland	BB− to BB+	Brazil, Peru, Turkey
Zambia	BB− to BB	Brazil, Turkey
Tanzania	BB−	Turkey, Uruguay
Congo, Rep. of	B+ to BB−	Pakistan, Turkey
Niger	B− to B	Argentina, Bolivia, Paraguay
Rwanda	B− to B	Argentina, Bolivia, Paraguay
Togo	CCC+ to B−	Bolivia, Ecuador, Paraguay
Mauritania	CCC to B	Dominican Rep., Ecuador
Côte d'Ivoire	CCC to B	Dominican Rep., Ecuador
Sierra Leone	CCC to B	Ecuador, Pakistan
Ethiopia	CCC to CCC+	Ecuador
Sudan	CCC− to CCC+	Ecuador
Comoros	CCC− to CCC+	Ecuador
Congo, Dem. Rep. of	CCC− to CCC	Ecuador
Guinea	CC to CCC	Ecuador
Chad	C to CCC+	Ecuador
Guinea-Bissau	C to CC	
Zimbabwe	C or lower	

Source: Ratings from Standard & Poor's, Moody's, and Fitch.

a. Shadow ratings use forecasts of explanatory variables for 2007 for the benchmark sovereign rating model of Ratha, De, and Mohapatra (2007).

Sub-Saharan Africa countries that received debt relief and improved their macroeconomic management appear to be better positioned to access international markets. Debt relief under the HIPC Initiative and under the MDRI has reduced the external debt-service obligations for 16 countries in sub-Saharan Africa. Since mid-2005, private foreign investors have started acquiring government debt in local currencies in sub-Saharan Africa (IMF 2006). Investors have been attracted by high yields relative to the perceived risk, better macroeconomic fundamentals, and diversification benefits (IMF 2006, 2007). Countries that have elicited the most investor interest are Botswana, Cameroon, Ghana, Kenya, Malawi, Nigeria, and Zambia. Ghana just became the first post-HIPC debt relief candidate to access international capital markets with a new sovereign bond issue.[35] Also, Gabon, an oil-exporting middle-income African country, is preparing to raise $1 billion in international capital markets; it was rated by Fitch in late October 2007 and by Standard & Poor's in November 2007.[36]

Conclusion

Both official and private flows to sub-Saharan Africa have increased in recent years, a welcome reversal of the declining or flat trend seen during the 1990s. The picture is less rosy, however, when sub-Saharan Africa is compared to the other developing regions and, more importantly, to its enormous resource needs for growth, poverty reduction, and other MDGs. Sub-Saharan Africa outside South Africa continues to depend on official aid. The recent increase in ODA appears to be driven by one-off debt relief provided through the HIPC Initiative and MDRI; the prospect for scaling up aid is not entirely certain.[37] The relatively small FDI flows to the region are concentrated in enclave investments in oil-exporting countries. Portfolio bond and equity flows are nonexistent outside South Africa. Private debt flows are small and dominated by relationship-based commercial bank lending, and even these flows are largely short-term in tenor. More than half of the countries in the region do not have a sovereign rating from the major credit rating agencies, and the few rated countries have subinvestment-grade ratings. Low or absent credit ratings impede not only sovereign but also private sector efforts to raise financing in the capital markets. Capital outflows appear to be smaller than in the previous decade, but the stock of flight capital from the region remains very high. Migrant remittances appear to be increasing, but a large part of the flows bypass formal financial channels.

In short, the development community has little choice but to continue to explore new sources of financing, innovative private-to-private sector solutions, and public-private partnerships to mobilize additional international financing. An analysis of country creditworthiness suggests that many countries in the region may be more creditworthy than previously believed. Establishing sovereign rating benchmarks and credit enhancement through guarantee instruments provided by multilateral aid agencies would facilitate market access. Creative financial structuring such as the IFFIm can help frontload aid commitments, although these commitments may not result in additional financing in the long run. Preliminary estimates suggest that sub-Saharan countries can potentially raise $1 billion to $3 billion by reducing the cost of international migrant remittances, $5 billion to $10 billion by issuing diaspora bonds, and $17 billion by securitizing future remittances and other future receivables.

In raising financing through these means, African countries will face several challenges. Leveraging remittances for sub-Saharan Africa's development will imply efforts to significantly improve both migration and remittances data, including collecting the existing data and making them publicly available. Remittances are private flows, and governments should not try to direct the use of remittances, nor should they think of remittances as a substitute for official aid. Instead, governments should try to reduce costs, increase flows through banking channels, and constructively leverage on these flows to improve capital market access of banks and governments in poor countries by improving ratings and securitization structures.

Efforts to attract private capital to Africa are constrained by shallow domestic financial markets, a lack of securitization laws, a paucity of investment-grade firms and banks in local-currency terms, and an absence of national credit-rating agencies. It is worth mentioning that if Africa were successful in attracting private capital, volatile capital flows could complicate the management of the exchange rate and monetary policy. Foreign-currency denominated debt can lead to currency mismatches. Large inflows can also lead to appreciation of domestic currencies, adversely affecting international competitiveness. Some capital flows can reverse rapidly with potentially destabilizing effects on the financial markets.

The findings in this paper suggest that sub-Saharan countries need to make external finance more broadly based, attract a broader category of investors such as pension funds and institutional investors, and expand the role of public-private partnerships to raise additional external financing.[38] Donors and international financial institutions can play an important role by providing guarantees, political risk insurance, help in establishing ratings, and advice on financial instruments such as securitization of remittances and other future-flow receivables. Accessing private capital markets in a responsible manner will require a sound contractual environment as well as credible monetary, fiscal, and exchange rate policies.

Notes

The authors would like to thank Uri Dadush for extensive discussions and Jorge Araujo, Delfin Go, and Michael Fuchs for useful comments and suggestions. Thanks to Zhimei Xu for research assistance. Comments are welcome, and they may be sent to dratha@worldbank.org.

1. Local borrowing by one investor would lower the availability of capital for another borrower, a point often overlooked in the literature.
2. From 2000 to 2005, almost all portfolio flows went to South Africa. In contrast, the rest of sub-Saharan Africa received the bulk of official development assistance and remittances.
3. Some of the other initiatives under consideration, although in a more preliminary form, include an international airline tax and a levy on international currency transactions. See the discussions of Second and Third Plenary Meetings of the Leading Group on Solidarity Levies to Fund Development at http://www.innovativefinance-oslo.no and http://www.innovativefinance. go.kr. See also Kaul and Le Goulven (2003), Technical Group on Innovative Financing Mechanisms (2004), and United Nations (2006).
4. There is a reporting lag in the transfer items of the balance of payments statistics. Data on ODA and institutional remittances and, in some cases, on debt flows were unavailable for 2006 as of October 2007.
5. Aid effectiveness is hampered by coordination difficulties among donors and by a lack of absorptive capacity among borrowers in the region (see Gelb, Ramachandran, and Turner 2006; IBRD 2006; World Bank 2006).
6. Oil exporters in sub-Saharan Africa comprise nine low- and middle-income countries (Angola, Cameroon, Chad, the Democratic Republic of Congo, the Republic of Congo, Equatorial Guinea, Gabon, Nigeria, and Sudan) with a combined gross domestic product of $255 billion or 37 percent of sub-Saharan Africa's gross domestic product in 2006.
7. Only one middle-income oil-exporting sub-Saharan country, Angola, accounted for virtually all bank lending to sub-Saharan countries other than South Africa from 2003 to 2005.
8. Paris Club creditors provided $19.2 billion exceptional debt relief to Iraq and Nigeria in 2005 and a further $14 billion in 2006 (IBRD 2007; World Bank 2007a). The HIPC Initiative, launched in 1996, has committed $62 billion ($42 billion in end-2005 net present value) in debt relief for 30 highly indebted low-income countries, 25 of which are in sub-Saharan Africa. The MDRI, launched in 2006, deepens this debt relief by providing 100 percent debt cancellation by the International Monetary Fund, International Development Association, and African Development Fund. This debt relief amounts to $38 billion for a smaller group of 22 countries (18 of which are in sub-Saharan Africa) that have reached, or will eventually reach, completion under the HIPC Initiative (IBRD 2006, 2007; World Bank 2007b). These two

initiatives together have reduced debt service to exports from 17 percent in 1998–99 to 4 percent in 2006 (IBRD 2007).

9. The present value of debt stocks would eventually decline by 90 percent for the group of 30 HIPC countries. Lower debt-stock ratios, however, may increase "free rider" risks, that is, new lenders might be willing to finance projects knowing that the borrower would make debt-service payments because of debt relief and concessional loans by official creditors (IBRD 2007).

10. Nigeria has benefited from both debt relief and the commodity price boom. Under an agreement with the Paris Club group of official creditors, Nigeria received $18 billion in debt relief and used its oil revenues to prepay its remaining obligations of $12.4 billion to the Paris Club creditors (and another $1.5 billion to London Club creditors) during 2005–06. This has resulted in a reduction of Nigeria's external debt stock by more than $30 billion (World Bank 2007a).

11. Speech by Chinese President Hu Jintao, Integrated Regional Information Networks, United Nations, November 6, 2006, http://www.worldpress.org/africa/2554.cfm.

12. One first step in this direction has been the memorandum of understanding between the World Bank and the Export–Import Bank of China to improve cooperation in Africa. Initial cooperation would focus on infrastructure lending in the transportation and energy sectors (Jim Adams, interview with Reuters, May 22, 2007, http://africa.reuters.com/top/new/usnBAN222921.html).

13. Page and Plaza (2006) estimate that 73 percent of remittances to sub-Saharan countries were through unofficial channels. Using this estimate, remittances to sub-Saharan Africa through formal and informal channels would be more than $30 billion annually.

14. Institutional remittances consist of current and capital transfers in cash or in kind payable by any resident sector (that is, households, government, corporations, and nonprofit institutions serving households [NPISHs]) to nonresident households and NPISHs and receivable by resident households and NPISHs from any nonresident sector and excluding household-to-household transfers (United Nations Statistics Division 1998). An NPISH is defined as a nonprofit institution that is not predominantly financed and controlled by government and that provides goods or services to households free or at prices that are not economically significant.

15. IDA countries (mostly in sub-Saharan Africa) received an estimated $20 million from U.S. foundations in 2004, which was less than 3 percent of direct cross-border grants of $800 million provided by U.S. foundations in that year (Sulla 2007).

16. See Powell, Ratha, and Mohapatra (2002) and World Bank (2002) for the construction of capital outflows as the difference between sources and uses of funds in the International Monetary Fund Balance of Payments Statistics.

17. Average annual capital outflows from Nigeria have been in the range of $2.5 billion since the late 1980s.

18. Most of these savings would come from the migrants in the Organisation for Economic Co-operation and Development countries, where a third of sub-Saharan diaspora are located because of the larger income differentials. Even if the sub-Saharan diaspora were assumed to earn *half* the average income in the host countries and saved 20 percent, they would still save more than $10 billion annually.

19. South Africa is reported to have launched a project to issue reconciliation and development bonds to both expatriate and domestic investors (Bradlow 2006).

20. Ghana, which benefited from more than $4 billion in debt relief under the HIPC Initiative and MDRI, just concluded a bond issue for $750 million with a 10-year maturity and 387 basis point spread. The resources will finance projects in energy, communications, roads, housing, forestry, and hydropower. Other sub-Saharan countries that are potential candidates for entering the international bond market for the first time include Kenya, Nigeria, and Zambia, all three of which have seen significant increases in the nonresident purchases of domestic public debt in recent years (World Bank 2007a).

21. Page and Plaza estimate that almost three-quarters of the remittances to sub-Saharan Africa were through unofficial channels.

22. Partial risk guarantees have been typically provided for private sector projects in all countries, including IDA-eligible poor countries, and partial credit guarantees have usually gone to public investment projects in countries eligible for International Bank for Reconstruction and Development loans. In addition, policy-based guarantees are extended to help well-performing IBRD-eligible governments access capital markets.

23. GAVI, a public-private partnership for combating disease, was created in 1999 and has received grant commitments of $1.5 billion from the Gates Foundation, with additional contributions coming from Australia, Brazil, Canada, Denmark, France, Germany, Ireland, Luxembourg, the Netherlands, Norway, South Africa, Spain, Sweden, the United Kingdom, the United States, the European Union, and the World Bank. See http://www.gavialliance.org.

24. Birdsall and Subramanian (2007) argue that international financial institutions have traditionally underfunded the provision of global public goods (GPGs) and have not been adequately involved in the development of new GPG products, such as the AMC, preferring instead to provide loans and grants to individual countries.

25. See Skare (2007), Trepelkov (2007), and the discussions of the Second and Third Plenary Meetings of the Leading Group on Solidarity Levies to Fund Development established in March 2006 (http://www.innovativefinance-oslo .no/recommendedreading.cfm and http://www.innovativefinance.go.kr). Among the innovative financing projects, 28 countries of the Leading Group are considering the introduction of an air ticket solidarity levy to funding for improving access to treatments against HIV/AIDS, tuberculosis, and malaria through UNITAID, an international drug purchase facility.

26 The solidarity levy on airline tickets has been implemented by Chile, Côte d'Ivoire, Congo, France, Madagascar, Mauritius, Niger, and the Republic of Korea (see http://www.unitaid.eu).

27. See http://www.gemloc.org for further details.

28. Such transactions also often resort to excess coverage to mitigate the risk of volatility and seasonality in future flows.

29. Obtaining a rating is important for raising not only bond financing or bank loans but also FDI and even official aid (Ratha, De, and Mohapatra 2007). Any improvement in sovereign rating is likely to translate into an improvement in the rating of subsovereign borrowers whose foreign-currency borrowing is typically subject to the sovereign rating ceiling.

30. Every year, African states lose an estimated 25 percent of GDP to corruption, from petty bribe taking by low-level government officials to inflated public procurement contracts, kickbacks, and raids on the public treasury as part of public asset theft by political leaders.

31. For example, Nigeria has successfully recovered half a billion dollars in stolen assets from Swiss sources with the cooperation of the World Bank, civil society, and the Swiss authorities.

32. Ratha, De, and Mohapatra (2007) argue that several factors may make it difficult for poor countries to get rated. The information required for the rating process can be complex and not readily available in many countries. The institutional and legal environment governing property rights and sale of securities may be absent or weak, prompting reluctance on the part of politicians to get publicly "judged" by the rating analysts. The fact that the country has to request a rating, and must pay a fee for that rating, but has no say over the final rating outcome, can also be discouraging.

33. Only five banks in all of sub-Saharan Africa excluding South Africa (four in Nigeria and one in Mauritius) were in Standard & Poor's global debt issuers list. In contrast, South Africa had nearly 30 firms and banks in the list.

34. This literature models sovereign ratings as a function of macroeconomic and institutional variables (see Cantor and Packer 1996; Mora 2006). Interestingly, the benchmark model of Ratha, De, and Mohapatra (2007) performs quite well for sub-Saharan countries. The predicted or shadow ratings for the 11 sub-Saharan countries rated under the recent United Nations Development Programme initiative were within one to two notches of the actual rating assigned by Standard & Poor's, as of the end of 2006. The model successfully predicted the rating of the recent bond issue from Ghana.

35. The 10-year dollar bond issued on September 27, 2007, was sold at par to yield 8.5 percent. The proceeds of the bond would be used to improve Ghana's infrastructure.

36. Both rating agencies assigned Gabon a BB− rating, citing its relatively high income per capita and large external and fiscal surpluses derived from buoyant oil revenues. The proceeds of the bond will be used to buy back outstanding Paris Club debt (AFX News Limited 2007; Reuters 2007). Also, Kenya, a B+

rated country, is reported to be planning a Eurobond issuance in the near future.

37. For the literature on aid effectiveness, see Collier (2006); Easterly (2006); Easterly, Levine, and Roodman (2003); Radelet (2006); Rajan and Subramanian (2005); and Sundberg and Gelb (2006).

38. Because this study has focused on mobilizing new sources of financing, the authors have omitted discussion of structural and investment climate factors that impede private investment in Africa. This literature is summarized in Bhattacharya, Montiel, and Sharma (1997); Bhinda et al. (1999); Gelb, Ramachandran, and Turner (2006); Kasekende and Bhundia (2000); and World Bank (2002).

References

Afreximbank (African Export–Import Bank). 2005. *Annual Report*. Cairo: Afreximbank.

AFX News Limited. 2007. "Gabon Assigned 'BB−' Long-Term Issuer Default Rating with Stable Outlook—Fitch" AFX News Limited, October 30.

Ajayi, S. Ibi. 1997. "An Analysis of External Debt and Capital Flight in the Severely Indebted Low-Income Countries in Sub-Saharan Africa." Working Paper 97/68, International Monetary Fund, Washington, DC.

Aykut, Dilek, and Dilip Ratha. 2005. "South-South FDI Flows: How Big Are They?" *Transnational Corporations* 13 (1): 148–76.

Bhattacharya, Amar, Peter Montiel, and Sunil Sharma. 1997. "How Can Sub-Saharan Africa Attract More Private Capital Inflows?" *Finance and Development* 34 (2): 3–6.

Bhinda, Nils, Stephany Griffith-Jones, Jonathan Leape, and Matthew Martin. 1999. "Scale and Monitoring of Capital Flows." In *Private Capital Flows to Africa*, ed. Jan Joost Teunissen, 19–46. The Hague: Forum on Debt and Development.

Birdsall, Nancy, and Arvind Subramanian. 2007. "From World Bank to World Development Cooperative." Center for Global Development, Washington, DC. http://www.cgdev.org/content/publications/detail/14625.

Boyce, James, and Léonce Ndikumana. 2001. "Is Africa a Net Creditor? New Estimates of Capital Flight from Severely Indebted Sub-Saharan African Countries, 1970–96." *Journal of Development Studies* 38 (2): 27–56.

Bradlow, Daniel D. 2006. "An Experiment in Creative Financing to Promote South African Reconciliation and Development." American University Washington College of Law, Washington, DC.

Broadman, Harry G., Godze Isik, Sonia Plaza, Xiao Ye, and Yutaka Yoshino. 2007. *Africa's Silk Road: China and India's New Economic Frontier*. Washington, DC: World Bank.

Cantor, Richard, and Frank Packer. 1996. "Determinants and Impact of Sovereign Credit Ratings." *Federal Reserve Bank of New York Economic Policy Review* (October): 37–53.

Chander, Anupam. 2001. "Diaspora Bonds." *New York University Law Review* 76 (4): 1005–99.

Collier, Paul. 2006. "Is Aid Oil? An Analysis of Whether Africa Can Absorb More Aid." *World Development* 34 (9): 1482–97.

Collier, Paul, Anke Hoeffler, and Catherine Pattillo. 2001. "Flight Capital as a Portfolio Choice." *World Bank Economic Review* 15 (1): 55–80.

———. 2004. "Africa's Exodus: Capital Flight and the Brain Drain as Portfolio Decisions." *Journal of African Economies* 13 (AERC Supplement 2): ii15–ii54.

Dadush, Uri, Dipak Dasgupta, and Dilip Ratha. 2000. "The Role of Short-Term Debt in Recent Crises." *Finance and Development* 37 (4): 54–57.

Easterly, William. 2006. *The White Man's Burden*. New York: Penguin Press.

Easterly, William, Ross Levine, and David Roodman. 2003. "New Data, New Doubts: Revisiting Aid, Policies, and Growth." Working Paper 26, Center for Global Development, Washington, DC.

Economist. 2007. "Africa and China: The Host with the Most." *Economist*, May 17.

Financial Times. 2007a. "China Pledges US$20 Billion for Africa." *Financial Times*, May 18.

———. 2007b. "$5 Bn S. African Bank Deal Signals China's Ambition." *Financial Times*, October 26.

GAVI (Global Alliance for Vaccines and Immunization) and World Bank. 2006. "Framework Document: Pilot AMC for Pneumococcal Vaccines." Document prepared by the World Bank and GAVI for the second Donor Working Group meeting, London, November 9. http://www.vaccineamc.org/files/Framework%20Pneumo%20AMC%20Pilot.pdf.

Gelb, Alan, Vijaya Ramachandran, and Ginger Turner. 2006. "Stimulating Growth and Investment in Africa: From Macro to Micro Reforms." Paper prepared for African Development Bank–African Economic Resource Consortium Conference, Tunis, November 22–24.

Gibson, John, David McKenzie, and Halahingano Rohorua. 2006. "How Cost-Elastic Are Remittances? Estimates from Tongan Migrants in New Zealand." Working Paper 06/02, Department of Economics, University of Waikato, Hamilton, New Zealand.

Goldstein, Andrea, Nicolas Pinaud, Helmut Reisen, and Xiaobao Chen. 2006. *The Rise of China and India: What's in It for Africa?* Paris: Organisation for Economic Co-operation and Development.

Hausmann, Ricardo, and Eduardo Fernández-Arias. 2001. "Foreign Direct Investment: Good Cholesterol?" In *Foreign Direct Investment versus Other Flows to Latin America*, ed. Jorge Braga de Macedo and Enrique V. Iglesias, 19–60. Paris: Organisation for Economic Co-operation and Development.

Hermes, Niels, Robert Lensink, and Victor Murinde. 2002. "Capital Flight, Policy Uncertainty, and the Instability of the International Financial System." In *Handbook of International Banking*, ed. Andrew W. Mullineux and Victor Murinde. Cheltenham, U.K.: Edward Elgar.

Hillman, David, Sony Kapoor, and Stephen Spratt. 2006. "Taking the Next Step: Implementing a Currency Transaction Development Levy." Paper presented at Second Plenary Meeting of the Leading Group on Solidarity Levies to Fund Development, Oslo, December.

IBRD (International Bank for Reconstruction and Development). 2006. *Global Monitoring Report 2006: Strengthening Mutual Accountability, Aid, Trade, and Governance*. Washington, DC: IBRD/World Bank.

———. 2007. *Global Monitoring Report 2007: Confronting the Challenges of Gender Equality and Fragile States*. Washington, DC: IBRD/World Bank.

IMF (International Monetary Fund). 2006. *Regional Economic Outlook: Sub-Saharan Africa*. Washington, DC: IMF.

———. 2007. *Regional Economic Outlook: Sub-Saharan Africa*. Washington, DC: IMF.

Kasekende, Louis, and Ashok Bhundia. 2000. "Attracting Capital Inflows to Africa: Essential Elements of a Policy Package." In *Finance for Sustainable Development: Testing New Policy Approaches*, ed. Juergen Holst, Donald Lee, and Eric Olson, 159–69. New York: United Nations Department of Economic and Social Affairs, Division for Sustainable Development.

Kaul, Inge, and Katell Le Goulven. 2003. "Financing Global Public Goods: A New Frontier of Public Finance." In *Providing Global Public Goods: Managing Globalization*, ed. Inge Kaul, Pedro Conceição, Katell Le Goulven, and Ronald U. Mendoza, 329–70. New York: Oxford University Press.

Ketkar, Suhas, and Dilip Ratha. 2000. "Development Financing during a Crisis: Future-Flow Securitization." Policy Research Working Paper 2582, World Bank, Washington, DC.

———. 2005. "Recent Advances in Future-Flow Securitization." *Financier* 11/12: 29–42.

———. 2007. "Development Finance via Diaspora Bonds Track Record and Potential." Policy Research Working Paper 4311, World Bank, Washington, DC.

Matsukawa, Tomoko, and Odo Habeck. 2007. "Risk Mitigation Instruments for Infrastructure Financing and Recent Trends and Developments." Trends and Policy Options 4, World Bank and Public-Private Infrastructure Advisory Facility, Washington, DC.

McDonald, Calvin, Volker Treichel, and Hans Weisfeld. 2006. "Enticing Investors." *Finance and Development* 43 (4).

Mora, Nada. 2006. "Sovereign Credit Ratings: Guilty beyond Reasonable Doubt?" *Journal of Banking and Finance* 30 (7): 2041–62.

Ndikumana, Léonce, and James K. Boyce. 2002. "Public Debts and Private Assets: Explaining Capital Flight from Sub-Saharan African Countries." Working Paper 32, Department of Economics, University of Massachusetts, Amherst.

Oxford Analytica. 2007. "Nigeria/China: Deal Will Help Extend Banks' Reach." *Oxford Analytica,* October 31.

Page, John, and Sonia Plaza. 2006. "Migration, Remittances and Development: A Review of the Global Evidence." *Journal of African Economies* 15 (2):245–336.

Powell, Andrew, Dilip Ratha, and Sanket Mohapatra. 2002. "Capital Inflows and Capital Outflows: Measurement, Determinants, Consequences." Working Paper 7, Centro de Investigación en Finanzas, Universidad Torcuato Di Tella, Buenos Aires.

Radelet, Steve. 2006. "A Primer on Aid Allocation." Working Paper 92, Center for Global Development, Washington, DC.

Rajan, Raghuram G., and Arvind Subramanian. 2005. "Aid and Growth: What Does the Cross-Country Evidence Really Show?" Working Paper 05/127, International Monetary Fund, Washington, DC.

Ratha, Dilip. 2003. "Workers' Remittances: An Important and Stable Source of External Development Finance." In *Global Development Finance 2003: Striving for Stability in Development Finance,* 157–75. Washington, DC: World Bank.

———. 2006. "Leveraging Remittances for Capital Market Access." Working paper, Development Prospects Group, World Bank, Washington, DC.

———. 2007. "Leveraging Remittances for Development." Policy brief, Migration Policy Institute, Washington, DC.

Ratha, Dilip, Prabal De, and Sanket Mohapatra. 2007. "Shadow Sovereign Ratings for Unrated Developing Countries." Policy Research Working Paper 4269, World Bank, Washington, DC.

Ratha, Dilip, and William Shaw. 2007. "South-South Migration and Remittances." Working Paper 102, World Bank, Washington, DC.

Reuters. 2007. "International, Domestic Bonds Likely in Gabon—S&P." Reuters, November 9.

Rutten, Lamon, and Okey Oramah. 2006. "Using Commoditized Revenue Flows to Leverage Access to International Finance, with a Special Focus on Migrant Remittances and Payment Flows." Study prepared for the United Nations Conference on Trade and Development Secretariat, Geneva.

Salisu, Mohammed. 2005. "The Role of Capital Flight and Remittances in Current Account Sustainability in Sub-Saharan Africa." *African Development Review* 17 (3): 382–404.

Skare, Mari. 2007. "General Remarks on Major Achievements." Paper presented at the Third Plenary Meeting of the Leading Group on Solidarity Levies, Seoul, September 3.

Sulla, Olga. 2007. "Philanthropic Foundations and Their Role in International Development Assistance." International Finance Briefing Note 3, Development Prospects Group, World Bank, Washington, DC.

Sundberg, Mark, and Alan Gelb. 2006. "Making Aid Work." *Finance and Development* 43 (4): 14–17.

Technical Group on Innovative Financing Mechanisms. 2004. *Action against Hunger and Poverty*. http://www.diplomatie.gouv.fr/en/IMG/pdf/rapportdugroupe-quadripartite.pdf.

Trepelkov, Alexander. 2007. "Reflections on Innovative Financing for Development." Paper presented at the Third Plenary Meeting of the Leading Group on Solidarity Levies, Seoul, September 3.

United Nations. 2006. *Human Development Report 2006: Beyond Scarcity—Power, Poverty and the Global Water Crisis*. New York: United Nations Development Program.

United Nations Statistics Division. 1998. "Recommendations on Statistics of International Migration." United Nations Statistics Division, New York.

UNODC (United Nations Office on Drugs and Crime) and World Bank. 2007. "Stolen Asset Recovery (StAR) Initiative: Challenges, Opportunities, and Action Plan." World Bank, Washington, DC. http://siteresources.worldbank.org/NEWS/Resources/Star-rep-full.pdf.

Wang, Jian-Ye. 2007. "What Drives China's Growing Role in Africa?" Working Paper 07/211, International Monetary Fund, Washington, DC.

World Bank. 1999. "Sub-Saharan Africa Benefits from the first IDA Guarantee for Azito." In *Project Finance and Guarantees Notes*. Washington, DC: World Bank Private Sector and Infrastructure Vice-Presidency.

———. 2002. *Global Development Finance 2002: Financing the Poorest Countries*. Washington, DC: World Bank.

———. 2004. *Global Development Finance 2004: Harnessing Cyclical Gains for Development*. Washington, DC: World Bank.

———. 2005. *Global Economic Prospects 2006: Economic Implications of Remittances and Migration*. Washington, DC: World Bank.

———. 2006. *Global Development Finance 2006: The Development Potential of Surging Capital Flows*. Washington, DC: World Bank.

———. 2007a. *Global Development Finance 2007: The Globalization of Corporate Finance in Developing Countries*. Washington, DC: World Bank.

———2007b. "HIPC At-a-Glance Guide." Economic Policy and Debt Department brief, World Bank, Washington, DC. http://go.worldbank.org/85B908KVE0.

———. 2007c. "World Bank Monthly Operational Summary Guarantee Operations." World Bank, Washington, DC. http://go.worldbank.org/R5XXEKDS70.

PART III

Managing External Shocks

Have External Shocks Become More Important for Output Fluctuations in African Countries?

Claudio Raddatz

African countries are highly dependent on the volatile prices of primary commodities and aid flows. During the period 1985–2000, primary commodities accounted for 73 percent of total exports of African countries, and aid flows averaged 13 percent of gross domestic product (GDP; compared with only 3 percent for the rest of the world). Coincidentally, the economic performance of African countries is also highly volatile. Therefore, it seems intuitive to blame this volatility on the impact of commodity prices, aid, and other external shocks—such as the droughts and famines that have hit these countries with some periodicity.

The evidence, however, suggests that the intuitive appeal of external shocks as an explanation for the unstable performance of African countries is not fully borne out by the data. A recent article by Raddatz (2007) showed that external shocks account for a small fraction of the variance of real per capita GDP in a sample of low-income countries, including most sub-Saharan African countries, during the period 1963–97. This evidence suggests that focusing on mitigating the impact of these shocks, although important, is unlikely to result in large reductions in output volatility.

Since the early 1990s, however, African countries have experienced several important changes that may affect the applicability of conclusions derived from earlier data. On the domestic front, for instance, the volatility of real GDP per capita growth in African countries (measured by its standard deviation) has decreased, and the median growth rate has shown some improvement since the mid-1990s. Standard indicators of democratic accountability, economic management, and control of corruption—such as those produced by the International Country Risk Guide—also have improved during the period 1990–2005. On the international front, commodity prices have experienced an unusual increase since the mid-1990s, especially oil for which the average price during the 1995–2005 period was twice as high as in the 1985–94 period, accompanied by a decline in volatility (as measured by the standard deviation of commodity price indexes). The international business cycle also has shown signals of moderation since the mid-1980s, with exceptionally tranquil times in the United States and Organisation for Economic Co-operation and Development (OECD) countries.

All these ingredients suggest that the relative importance of external shocks as a source of output volatility may have been different post-1990 than in earlier years. For instance, everything being equal, a reduction in policy instability may increase the role of external shocks as sources of fluctuations. On the other hand, a reduced volatility of external shocks may signal a smaller role in the determination of macroeconomic fluctuations. Because the potential gains of mitigating the impact of external shocks depend on shocks' importance as sources of fluctuations, determining whether there have been changes in the role of these shocks and the sources of these changes is an important task from a policy perspective.

This chapter undertakes this task by quantifying and comparing the importance of external and internal shocks as sources of macroeconomic fluctuations in African countries in the 1963–89 and 1990–2003 periods. In particular, I decompose changes in the relevance of each type of shock across periods between changes in the underlying variance of the shock (which I label as changes in *exposure*) and changes in the response of output to a shock of a given size (which I refer to as changes in *vulnerability*). I do so by extending the methodology and time coverage of Raddatz (2007) to estimate a panel vector autoregression (VAR) model in which external shocks can have a different impact in those two subperiods, and using these estimates to perform a series of variance decomposition exercises. I also explore whether oil is a special commodity in either of those periods by treating fluctuations in oil prices separately from variations in other commodity prices. This model therefore includes as external shocks changes in the international business cycle, the international real interest rate, (weighted) oil prices, commodity prices, natural disasters, and aid flows.

The results show an increase in the relative importance of external shocks as sources of output instability in African countries in the last 15 years. This increase is the result of two factors: (1) a decline in the variance of internal shocks, and (2) an increase in the vulnerability of output to external shocks. I also document a decline in the exposure of these countries to external shocks that partly mitigates the effect of those two factors, but is insufficient to compensate for their impact. Looking at individual shocks, we find that the variances of shocks to the international business cycle, oil prices, and commodity prices are lower in the period 1990–2003 than in the period 1960–89, and only the volatility of shocks to real aid flows seems to have increased.

Regarding the role of oil prices, I find that including them separately from measures of commodity price indexes does not increase the relative importance of external shocks for the typical African country in any period. That suggests that the average country does not have a special sensitivity to changes in oil prices, compared with other commodities. However, when looking separately at oil-importing and oil-exporting African countries, I am able to document a special role for oil prices in the latter group. The inclusion of oil prices separately from other commodity prices increases significantly the ability of external shocks to account for output volatility in this group of countries, especially during the period 1990–2003. For these countries, oil has become different than other exporting commodities. I also find that oil exporters experience a larger decline in volatility in the later period—a decline resulting from a greater reduction in the variance of internal shocks.

The rest of the chapter is structured as follows. The next section presents a brief theoretical framework that clarifies the concepts of exposure and vulnerability used throughout the chapter and illustrates why we need a structural empirical approach to determine the differences in exposure and vulnerability across periods. The third section describes my data and takes a first look at the differences in volatility across the various groups of countries considered in the chapter. The fourth section discusses the empirical methodology used to estimate the impact and relative importance of the various external shocks for the different groups of countries. The fifth section reports my results for the decomposition of the change in output volatility in African countries between changes in exposure and vulnerability to external and internal shocks, and for the differential role of oil prices versus other commodities. The chapter concludes with some final remarks.

A Simple Theoretical Framework

Consider the following structural model that describes macroeconomic behavior of a country:

$$\mathbf{x}_t = \mathbf{\Psi}(L)\boldsymbol{\varepsilon}_t \qquad (8.1)$$

where $\mathbf{x} = (x_1,...,x_N)$ is a vector that includes the country's GDP and all other relevant macroeconomic variables, both internal and external to the country; $\mathbf{\Psi}(L)$ is a matrix of distributed lags coefficients; and $\boldsymbol{\varepsilon}$ is a vector that comprises all fundamental, orthogonal shocks that affect this economy, which also may be internal or external to the country. The index t denotes the time period.

This is a very general description of the macro behavior of an economy. The only assumptions required to obtain this kind of expression are that the macroeconomic variables considered are stationary, and that the relations among the variables are linear.[1]

It is straightforward to show that, in this kind of framework, the variance of any variable included in the vector $\mathbf{x}$ is a linear combination of the variances of the fundamental shocks. In particular, the variance of the country's GDP, which we denote by σ_Y^2, can be written as

$$\sigma_Y^2 = \alpha_1\sigma_1^2 + \alpha_K\sigma_K^2 + \beta_1\sigma_{K+1}^2 + \cdots + \beta_{N-K}\sigma_N^2 \qquad (8.2)$$

where σ_i^2 represents the variance of the i-th structural shock ($i = 1,..., N$); the α and β coefficients capture the sensitivity of output variance to each one of those shocks; and I have assumed, without loss of generality, that the K first shocks correspond to "external shocks" (that is, shocks to variables outside of a country's control) and the other $N-K$ correspond to "internal shocks." Thus, the α coefficients measure output's sensitivity to different external shocks, and the β coefficients measure its sensitivity to various internal shocks.

This expression tells us that differences in output volatility across periods (or groups of countries) can result, in principle, from changes in the variances of the fundamental shocks that hit the countries and from changes in the response of output volatility to these various shocks.

A simple example with only one external and internal shock will be useful to define and clarify some concepts that I will use throughout the chapter. In this case, output variance corresponds to

$$\sigma_Y^2 = \alpha\sigma_X^2 + \beta\sigma_I^2 \qquad (8.3)$$

Thus, controlling for the role of internal shocks ($\beta\sigma_I^2$), differences in volatility across periods result from differences in the variance of the external shocks that hit the countries (σ_X^2), which I associate with their degree of *exposure* to these external shocks, and from changes in their *vulnerability* to those shocks (α).

A First Look at the Data

The sample of countries used in the empirical analysis is shown in table 8.1. The sample includes 38 of the 47 sub-Saharan African countries for which there is sufficient coverage of all relevant measures of external shocks and economic performance described below.

The main variables used in the chapter are the following. Real GDP per capita corresponds to the GDP per capita in constant 2000 U.S. dollars, obtained from the *World Development Indicators* (WDI). The reason to use this series instead of the purchasing power parity (PPP)-adjusted ones, despite the reduced international comparability, is that it has more recent coverage than the measures from the Penn World Tables and longer coverage than the PPP series produced by the World Bank. Given the emphasis of this chapter on exploring the differential impact of external shocks during the 1990–2003 period, the trade-off between international comparability and coverage favors the latter.

Commodity price fluctuations are captured by the Deaton-Miller (DM) commodity-based terms-of-trade index (see Deaton and Miller 1996). I updated the data for this index to the year 2004 using weights data from Dehn (2001) and recent commodity price data from the International Financial Statistics database. For each country, I also compute the component of a standard terms-of-trade index associated with oil price fluctuations.[2] This corresponds to the evolution of (log) real oil prices weighted by each country's net share of oil in total commodity exports and imports. Data on oil prices were also obtained from the International Financial Statistics.[3] The reason to use net trade weights is that most sub-Saharan African countries do not export oil, but import it instead. Thus, using only export weights assumes that changes in oil prices have no effect on importing countries. The series for the share of oil exports in total exports and oil imports in total imports were obtained from the World Economic Outlook database.

TABLE 8.1
Summary Statistics for Sample of Sub-Saharan African Countries

Country	Number of available observations (1)	Average real GDP growth (2)	Real GDP growth SD (3)	Average trade-weighted real oil price index (4)	Trade-weighted real oil price index SD (5)	Average DM index (6)	
Angola	20	0.1	9.0	2.81	22.44	−5.7	
Benin	44	0.8	3.2	0.02	0.15	−1.2	
Botswana	45	6.1	4.6	−0.29	2.31	−1.2	
Burkina Faso	45	1.3	3.1	−0.34	2.70	−1.0	
Burundi	45	0.3	6.0	−0.40	3.17	−1.6	
Cameroon	45	0.8	6.0	0.96	7.66	−0.7	
Cape Verde	18	2.6	2.0	−0.19	1.53	−0.7	
Central African Republic	44	−0.9	4.0	−0.26	2.09	−1.4	
Chad	44	−0.3	7.6	−0.04	0.31	−1.1	
Congo, Dem. Rep. of	45	−2.9	6.1	0.20	1.61	−0.2	
Congo, Rep. of	45	1.0	5.8	2.00	16.01	1.9	
Côte d'Ivoire	44	0.3	5.4	−0.11	0.84	−2.2	
Djibouti	18	−3.7	3.8	−0.17	1.39	0.8	
Ethiopia	24	0.4	7.5	−0.45	3.58	−2.4	
Gabon	45	1.9	10.1	1.86	14.85	1.3	
Gambia, The	39	0.7	3.5	−0.29	2.32	−0.3	
Ghana	41	−0.1	4.6	−0.47	3.74	−2.1	
Guinea	19	1.2	1.4	−0.25	1.97	−3.3	
Kenya	45	1.1	4.6	−0.58	4.67	−2.1	
Madagascar	45	−1.1	4.3	−0.14	1.13	0.0	
Malawi	44	1.2	5.4	−0.37	2.95	−1.1	
Mali	37	0.9	5.4	−0.45	3.60	−1.2	
Mauritania	44	1.5	5.6	−0.25	2.00	−2.5	
Mauritius	24	4.3	1.6	−0.29	2.28	0.1	
Namibia	20	0.5	2.5	−0.13	1.07	0.0	
Niger	45	−1.4	6.3	−0.29	2.32	−0.5	
Nigeria	45	0.5	7.3	2.93	23.42	1.8	
Rwanda	41	0.4	8.7	−0.38	3.05	−0.8	
Senegal	45	0.0	4.2	−0.21	1.67	−0.4	
Seychelles	44	2.4	6.2	−0.13	1.02	−1.8	
Sierra Leone	45	−0.1	7.5	−0.53	4.20	−1.5	
Sudan	45	1.0	5.5	1.00	7.96	−1.0	
Swaziland	35	1.9	4.0	−0.40	3.23	1.0	
Tanzania	16	1.3	2.4	−0.45	3.62	−1.6	
Togo	44	1.0	6.5	−0.34	2.75	−1.3	
Uganda	23	2.2	3.1	−0.39	3.15	−2.6	
Zambia	45	−0.8	4.7	−0.32	2.55	−0.6	
Zimbabwe	36	0.2	6.2	−0.39	3.08	−1.2	

Source: Author's calculations using data from *World Development Indicators,* International Financial Statistics, and the Center for Research on the Epidemiology of Disasters.

Note: DM = Deaton-Miller; GNI = gross national income; SD = standard deviation. The various columns report summary statistics for various aspects of macroeconomic performance of the 38 African countries included in the sample during the period 1963–2003. Column (1) shows the number of observations for each country based on the availability of data on all relevant series

DM index SD (7)	Average aid as a percent of GNI (8)	Average growth of real per capita aid (9)	Real per capita aid flow SD (10)	Average number of large geologic disasters (11)	Average number of large climatic disasters (12)	Average number of large humanitarian disasters (13)	Oil exporter (14)
25.4	6.1	5.2	37.6	0.0	35.0	0.0	Yes
15.5	8.2	18.3	80.1	0.0	29.5	0.0	No
13.7	7.4	−1.6	26.8	0.0	26.7	2.2	No
16.3	10.2	20.3	77.1	0.0	22.2	11.1	No
23.8	13.0	5.5	30.0	0.0	6.7	4.4	No
10.0	4.2	12.2	55.1	2.2	2.2	4.4	Yes
12.4	27.4	−3.5	15.3	5.6	0.0	16.7	No
21.7	11.1	11.8	60.4	0.0	6.8	0.0	No
17.6	9.7	16.7	82.4	0.0	36.4	9.1	No
15.1	3.8	5.8	47.6	0.0	4.4	2.2	No
25.5	7.4	12.3	78.6	2.2	8.9	0.0	Yes
11.2	4.2	14.7	94.2	0.0	0.0	0.0	No
16.4	15.1	−9.2	31.9	0.0	50.0	0.0	No
20.0	11.4	7.0	27.2	0.0	66.7	25.0	No
22.3	2.9	14.7	84.8	0.0	2.2	0.0	Yes
19.9	19.0	3.1	42.0	0.0	12.8	5.1	No
9.7	6.1	5.9	34.1	0.0	9.8	2.4	No
19.0	10.6	−0.5	28.9	0.0	5.3	0.0	No
17.0	6.5	1.7	30.1	0.0	22.2	4.4	No
12.6	7.3	6.3	43.2	0.0	62.2	2.2	No
9.1	16.7	6.8	30.5	2.3	25.0	4.5	No
18.6	15.6	3.0	22.8	0.0	16.2	8.1	No
9.7	19.4	19.0	84.6	0.0	36.4	6.8	No
5.0	2.2	−3.4	39.4	0.0	25.0	0.0	No
9.5	3.9	11.6	37.7	0.0	35.0	5.0	No
15.7	10.5	16.8	64.3	0.0	20.0	6.7	No
25.4	0.6	−0.3	41.3	0.0	4.4	0.0	Yes
19.6	16.2	3.8	32.9	0.0	12.2	4.9	No
14.9	10.9	19.6	85.4	0.0	24.4	0.0	No
27.3	10.9	−2.0	41.1	0.0	4.5	0.0	No
13.1	11.7	5.7	41.8	0.0	4.4	0.0	No
14.7	4.1	1.8	54.2	0.0	35.6	4.4	Yes
9.5	5.5	−2.1	43.8	0.0	25.7	2.9	No
19.0	18.3	−0.1	20.0	0.0	56.3	0.0	No
11.9	9.0	11.8	75.2	0.0	11.4	2.3	No
26.0	11.9	6.5	25.4	4.3	30.4	0.0	No
19.7	11.8	9.7	59.5	0.0	20.0	0.0	No
7.7	3.0	11.7	64.7	0.0	22.2	2.8	No

used to estimate the panel vector autoregression model described in the chapter. Columns (2) and (3) show the average and SD of real GDP per capita growth, respectively. Columns (4) and (5) show similar statistics for the trade-weighted real oil price index; and columns (6) and (7) do the same for the DM commodity price index. Columns (8) to (10) show the average level of aid flows (official development assistance) as a fraction of GDP, and the average growth rate and SD of real per capita aid flows. Columns (11) to (13) show the incidence of geologic, climatic, and humanitarian disasters, computed as the average number of disasters of each category per 100 years.

To capture the role of aid flows shocks I use data on real per capita aid flows, which include the flows of official development assistance and official aid in constant 2000 U.S. dollars, obtained from the WDI.

Data on the occurrence of disasters were obtained from the Emergency Disasters Database (EM-DAT; http://www.em-dat.net) maintained by the Centre for Research on the Epidemiology of Disasters. This is a comprehensive database compiled from a variety of sources that includes data on the occurrence and effects of over 12,800 mass disasters in the world since 1900. As a general principle, an event enters into the database if it meets any of the following conditions: there are 10 or more people reported killed; there are 100 or more people reported affected; a state of emergency is declared; or there is a call for international assistance. I classify disasters into three categories to increase the parsimony of the analysis. Geologic disasters include earthquakes, landslides, volcanic eruptions, and tidal waves. An important characteristic of this type of event is its unpredictability and relatively fast onset. The second category is climatic disasters. This category includes floods, droughts, extreme temperatures, and windstorms (for example, hurricanes). Compared with the previous category, some of these disasters can be forecast well in advance (so precautions can be undertaken) and have a relatively long onset. The final category is human disasters, which includes famines and epidemics. These events differ from those of the previous two categories in that these disasters affect mainly human capital instead of physical capital. For each category, I measure the incidence of disasters by counting the number of events in a given year that classify as large disasters according to the following criteria established by the International Monetary Fund (see IMF 2003): the event affects at least half a percent of a country's population, or causes damages of at least half a percent of national GDP, or results in more than one fatality among every 10,000 people.[4]

In addition to commodity price fluctuations, natural disasters, or aid flows, African countries can be affected by fluctuations of international demand or credit market conditions. As mentioned above, exports of African countries tend to be heavily concentrated on primary commodities, whose total demand is largely determined by high-income countries. Furthermore, African countries tend to be heavily indebted and dependent on foreign capital, so they are potentially vulnerable to changes in international credit conditions. Changes in international interest rates may affect significantly the borrowing conditions faced by African countries for two reasons. First, although the actual interest rates that African countries can obtain in private international credit markets certainly will be higher than the observed international market rates (for example, the London Interbank Offered Rate [LIBOR]), the evolution of these rates should be correlated as long as the country premium paid by African countries is not very cyclical. Second, even if African countries obtain most of their financing from international financial institutions, for a given amount of concessionality the rate obtained by these countries should move one to one with the rate at which international financial institutions can finance their portfolios. Therefore, as long as the concessionality is not highly cyclical, the evolution of international interest rates should be associated with the actual cost of borrowing. The variables I use to capture these potential sources of external shocks are the real GDP of high-income countries, and the real international interest rate measured as the six-month LIBOR in U.S. dollars minus the change in the U.S. Producer Price Index. The different columns of table 8.1 show some summary statistics for each of these variables across the sample countries. The table also shows the sample period for which there is data available for each country.

Table 8.2 summarizes the volatility of these variables (measured by their standard deviations) among African countries in each of the subperiods

TABLE 8.2
Output Volatility and External Shocks among African Countries

	1963–89 (SD)	1990–2003 (SD)
Output volatility		
Real per capita GDP growth	0.05	0.04
	(0.02)	(0.03)
External shocks volatility		
Real per capita GDP growth, high-income OECD countries	0.02	0.01
	(—)	(—)
Real DM commodity price index	0.03	0.02
	(0.07)	(0.04)
Trade-weighted real oil price	0.16	0.14
	(0.07)	(0.07)
Real international interest rate	0.03	0.03
	(—)	(—)
Real aid flows	0.35	0.32
	(0.14)	(0.19)

Source: Author's calculations.

Note: — = not available; OECD = Organisation for Economic Co-operation and Development. Each row reports the median and standard deviation of the volatility of the variable described in that row during the periods 1963–89 and 1990–2003, across the sample of 38 sub-Saharan countries. The volatility of each variable in each country corresponds to its SD during a given period.

considered in this chapter. Each entry shows the median and standard deviation (in parentheses) of the volatility of each variable across the sample of countries in each subperiod. It is apparent in the table that the volatility of output and external shocks typically has experienced a small decline in the period 1990–2003, compared with the period 1963–1989. Although the figures reported in parentheses suggest that there are important variations across countries, the typical declines suggested by the median values are a relatively robust pattern of the data. This can be seen in figure 8.1, which plots the standard deviation of each relevant series in the pre- and post-1990 periods, as well as a 45-degree line to facilitate the comparison. It is apparent across panels (except for the panel showing this relation of the shocks to real aid flows) that most of the points fall below

FIGURE 8.1
Volatility of Output and External Shocks in African Countries before and after 1990

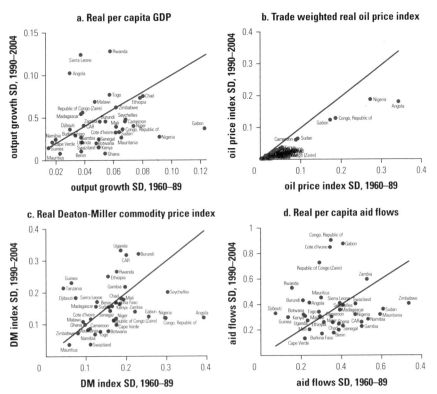

Source: Author's calculations.

the 45-degree line. That implies that the decline in volatility of the different series is a robust pattern of the data across countries.

The figures reported in table 8.2 suggest that the decline in output volatility between the two subperiods may be the consequence of a decline in the volatility of external shocks (that is, a decline in the exposure to these shocks). However, as illustrated in equation (8.3), this conclusion would be true only if the role of internal shocks and the vulnerability to external shocks had not changed between these periods. If, for instance, the vulnerability to external shocks had increased enough to compensate for the lower exposure, then the lower output volatility necessarily would be the result of a smaller effect of internal shocks. To disentangle these different components, we need to go beyond the stylized facts described in table 8.2 and take a structural approach. This is what I do in the following sections.

A Semistructural Approach

The building block of our empirical approach is a panel VAR model that used to estimate the impact of different shocks on a country's GDP growth. For a given country, my semistructural model corresponds to

$$A_0 x_{i,t} = D_{it} + \sum_{j=1}^{q} A_{j,t} x_{i,t-j} + \boldsymbol{\varepsilon}_{it} \tag{8.4}$$

where $x_{i,t} = (z'_{i,t}, y'_{i,t})'$; $z_{i,t} = (GDPH_t, POIL_{i,t}, DMTT_{i,t}, R_t, GEO_{i,t}, CLIM_{i,t}, HUM_{i,t})$ is a vector of exogenous variables that includes the GDP of high-income countries ($GDPH$), the real price of oil weighted by the importance of oil in a country's trade ($POIL$), the real DM commodity-based terms-of-trade index ($DMTT$), the international real interest rate (R), and three dummy variables capturing the occurrence of geologic, climatic, or human disasters (GEO, $CLIM$, and HUM, respectively); $y'_{i,t} = (AID_{i,t}, GDP_{i,t})$ is a vector of "endogenous" variables, in which GDP corresponds to the real GDP per capita (PPP adjusted) and AID is real aid per capita. In the benchmark specification, all the variables (except those capturing the disasters) correspond to the change in the logarithm of the underlying variable, and the matrix $D_{i,t}$ contains country-specific constants.

The main identification assumption in this chapter is that the variables in z do not respond to the y variables at any lags. This assumption is equivalent to imposing the following block diagonal structure in all the A matrices:

$$A_{j,t} = \begin{bmatrix} A^j_{11} & 0 \\ A^{j,t}_{21} & A^{j,t}_{22} \end{bmatrix} \tag{8.5}$$

where the size of the submatrices conforms to the dimensions of z and y. This implies that I assume that neither the terms of trade, the price of oil, the GDP of rich countries, the incidence of natural disasters, nor the international interest rate is affected by the present or past economic performance of any particular low-income country, but that all these variables probably have a contemporaneous and lagged effect on this performance. Aid is included in the vector y because, although foreign aid is not determined by any particular African country, the amount of aid flowing to a country likely responds to its economic performance. Notice that by including aid among the y I am also assuming that the amount of aid flowing to a particular country does not affect its terms of trade, the occurrence of natural disasters, or the conditions of the international economy, but that all these variables do affect the amount of aid a country is receiving.

Although the block-diagonality assumption permits me to identify the effect of the vector of z variables on each y variable, identifying the impact of each individual z variable or the output effect of aid shocks (which are part of the y vector) requires further assumptions. I first assume that the occurrence of natural disasters is fully exogenous—that is, it is unrelated not only to the y variables, but also to the rest of the z variables. For the rest of the z variables, I will follow the standard practice of imposing a lower-triangular structure on the matrix of their contemporaneous relations. In my benchmark case, I assume that the contemporaneous causal order runs from the GDP of rich countries to the oil price, to the terms of trade faced by African countries, and to the international interest rate. This ordering permits the international interest rate to react contemporaneously to the state of the global economy, but imposes that the feedback from the international interest rate to global output operates only with a lag. As pointed out by Ahmed (2003), this assumption is standard in studies of U.S. monetary policy that use quarterly or monthly data, but may be overly strong when using annual data, as in the present case. Placing the price of oil and the terms of trade below the GDP of rich countries assumes that changes in the demand for commodities resulting from changes in the state of the international economy translate into changes in the relative price of these products contemporaneously, but changes in commodity prices affect rich countries' output only with a lag. This assumption is also common in VAR studies of U.S. monetary policy that control for the price puzzle by including indexes of commodity prices (see, for example, Christiano, Eichenbaum, and Evans [1998] and references therein). Given that the price of oil is included in the DM index, the assumption that it precedes the DM index in the ordering is natural. Finally, the ordering of the terms-of-trade index and the international interest rate also follows the typical ordering of commodity price indexes and interest rates in these studies. For the case of aid, I also impose a block-triangular structure in the matrix of contemporaneous relations between the y variables, A_{22}^0, which assumes that output responds contemporaneously to changes in aid, but aid flows to a country respond to changes in its economic conditions only after a year. Given the usual delays in the process of aid allocation (see Odedokun 2003), I believe that this is a sensible assumption.

Several aspects of the model deserve further discussion. In the benchmark specification, I assume that the vector y_{it} is first difference stationary. This contrasts with the benchmark specification used in Raddatz (2007). There are two reasons to prefer the specification in first differences. First, standard tests cannot reject the null of a unit root for most series when performed on a country-by-country basis, and, for some of the series I cannot reject the null either using more powerful panel unit-root tests (Levin, Lin, and Chu 2002). This is particularly the case for the series of oil prices and real GDP per capita. Second, the specification in differences behaves better across periods. In several cases, the impulse responses obtained with the model in levels display unusual behavior in the post-1990 period, in the sense that the impact of some shocks has not decayed after 20 years. This is not surprising considering the short length of the time dimension in the latter period. Thus, we estimate the model as a panel VAR in differences after checking that the Pedroni (1999) panel cointegration test cannot reject the null of no cointegration among the variables.[5] Nevertheless, results obtained for the model in levels (not reported) are qualitatively similar.

The model corresponds to a panel VAR in which it is assumed that the dynamics, represented by the A matrices, are common across cross-sectional units. The advantage of this assumption is that it increases the degrees of freedom of the estimation, which permit me to include more variables and increases the precision of the estimates. The obvious disadvantage is that the model is specified incorrectly if the slope parameters are heterogeneous across cross-sectional units. There are good reasons, however, to believe that this issue is of no first-order importance in this case (see Raddatz [2007] for a discussion).

Regarding the number of lags, I use two annual lags in the benchmark specification, as suggested by standard lag selection tests using the Schwartz information criterion. As a robustness check, I also estimate the parameters of the model with three lags without important changes in the results.

Finally, notice that the t index in the A_{jt} matrices shows that I allow these matrices to vary with time. In particular, as shown in equation (8.4), I permit the coefficients that capture the effect of the exogenous and lagged endogenous variables on the endogenous ones, A_{2i}^{jt}, to be different before and after 1990:

$$A_{2i}^{j,t} = \begin{cases} A_{2i}^1 & t < 1990 \\ A_{2i}^2 & otherwise \end{cases} \quad i = 1, 2 \tag{8.6}$$

Notice that I assume that the dynamics of external shocks (the A_{11}^{jt} matrices) are similar across periods. This is a necessary assumption, given the reduced number of observations that I have to estimate the role of common shocks. The only exception that I make, to capture the spirit of the question being addressed, is that I allow the variances of the variables in the external block, and their contemporaneous relations, to change.

Under the identification assumptions described above, I can estimate the parameters of the model using a two-step procedure in which I first estimate by seemingly unrelated regressions the parameters of each of the following systems of reduced-form equations:

$$z_{i,t}^1 = D_i + \sum_{j=1}^{q} B_j z_{i,t-j}^1 + u_{i,t}^z \tag{8.7}$$

$$y_{i,t} = D_i^y + \sum_{j=0}^{q} B_{j,t}^z z_{i,t-j} + \sum_{j=1}^{q} B_{j,t}^y y_{i,t-j} + u_{i,t}^y \tag{8.8}$$

where $z_{i,t}^1 = (GDPH_t, POIL_{i,t}, DM_{i,t}, R_t)$; and the reduced-form matrices B_{jt} that capture the impact of the exogenous shocks vary with time in accordance with the variation in the A_{2i}^{jt} matrices discussed above. After the estimation, I recover the impulse response functions to each of the structural shocks (the ε in equation [8.4]) using these reduced-form coefficients and the Cholesky decompositions of the corresponding variance-covariance matrices of errors.

Results

I now present the results of the decomposition of the change in output volatility in African countries between changes in exposure and vulnerability to external and internal shocks resulting from the estimation of the panel VAR described in equation (8.4).

Impact of External Shocks

The dynamic responses of output growth to the different external shocks considered in the benchmark specification are depicted in figures 8.2 and 8.3. Figure 8.2, which also displays the 90 percent confidence bands, shows that the dynamic responses have the expected signs when considering the whole 1963–2003 period. A positive shock to commodity prices, world GDP, or aid has a positive impact on growth. A positive shock to the international real interest rate or the incidence of disasters tends to have a negative impact (with the exception of the geologic disasters, which exhibit an expansion). A shock to oil prices has a positive impact. The various panels also show that, except for natural disasters, the response of output growth to the external shocks considered is economically significant. For instance, a one standard deviation shock to both the GDP of rich OECD countries and the oil price index increases the growth rate of output by half a percentage point at their peak. It also is important to remember that the temporary effects on the growth rate reported in the figures imply permanent effects on the level of output. Figure 8.3 compares the dynamic responses to a one standard deviation shock (single-event shock in the case of disasters) to each external variable in the periods 1963–89 and 1990–2003. Thus, differences in the responses across periods are due to both differences in the dynamics and differences in the size of the shocks across periods. The figure shows that, with the exception of the imprecisely estimated effect of natural disasters, the pattern and output impact of signs is similar across periods, except for the shocks to aid flows whose output impact is much larger in the latter period.

Accounting for the Decline in Output Volatility

Using the dynamic responses of output to the different external shocks, and the variances of these shocks estimated above for the different periods,

FIGURE 8.2

Dynamic Responses of Output Growth to Different External Shocks, 1963–2003

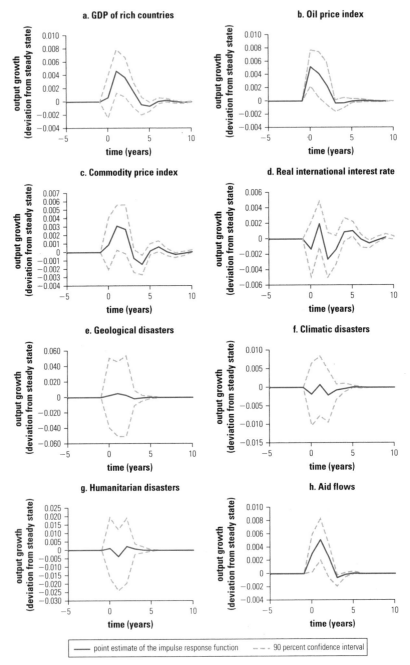

Source: Author's calculations.

Note: The various panels report the impulse response function of output growth to a one standard deviation structural shock to each of the variables indicated in each panel (except in the cases of geologic, climatic, and humanitarian disasters, where the figure reports the impulse response function to the occurrence of one event).

FIGURE 8.3

Dynamic Responses of Output Growth to Different External Shocks, 1963–89 versus 1990–2003

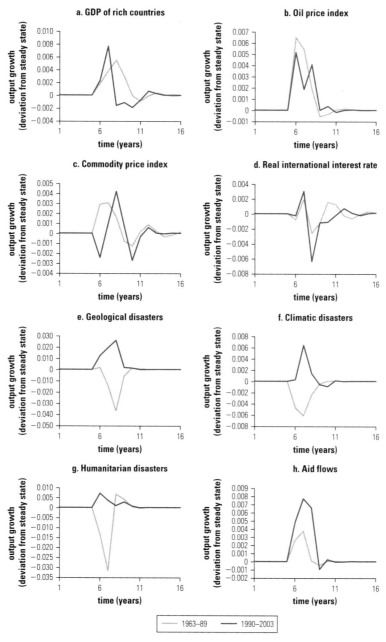

a. GDP of rich countries

b. Oil price index

c. Commodity price index

d. Real international interest rate

e. Geological disasters

f. Climatic disasters

g. Humanitarian disasters

h. Aid flows

1963–89   1990–2003

Source: Author's calculations.

Note: The various panels report the estimated impulse response function of output growth to a one standard deviation structural shock to each of the variables indicated in each panel (in the cases of geologic, climatic, and humanitarian disasters, the figure reports the impulse response function to the occurrence of one event).

I can compute the volatility of output predicted by the model in each period, and decompose its change among changes in exposure and vulnerability to external and nonexternal shocks. I do this by performing a series of counterfactual exercises that allow me to isolate the role of the different components of output volatility as described below.

As discussed in the section describing the theoretical framework, output volatility depends on the variance of external and internal shocks and on the vulnerability of output to these shocks, so that the ratio of output variance across periods of time corresponds to

$$\left(\frac{\sigma_{Y,1}}{\sigma_{Y,0}}\right)^2 = \frac{\alpha_1 \sigma_{X,1}^2 + \beta_1 \sigma_{I,1}^2}{\alpha_0 \sigma_{X,0}^2 + \beta_0 \sigma_{I,0}^2} \tag{8.9}$$

where the indexes 0 and 1 represent the initial and final periods, respectively. My estimates of the dynamic responses of output to external and internal shocks give us information on α and β, and estimates of the size of the external and internal shocks are akin to estimates of σ_X^2 and σ_I^2, respectively. For instance, I can estimate the proportional change in vulnerability to external shocks across periods by determining the dynamic responses of output to a common shock in the first and second periods and computing the ratio of the resulting output variances. By looking at the response to an external shock only, I am looking exclusively at the first term in the numerator and denominator of equation (8.9) (that is, we are implicitly setting σ_I^2 to zero); and by using a common shock, the ratio of the resulting output variances corresponds only to the ratio of vulnerabilities (α_1/α_0). Proceeding similarly, I can estimate relative exposure to external and internal shocks $(\sigma_{X,1}^2/\sigma_{X,0}^2$ and $\sigma_{I,1}^2/\sigma_{I,0}^2)$, and the relative vulnerability to internal shocks (β_1/β_0).

Table 8.3 reports the estimated standard deviations of the various structural shocks for the different subperiods. It shows that the variance of shocks to the GDP of rich countries, oil price index, commodity price index, and own GDP have declined significantly in the latter period; the variance of shocks to the real interest rate exhibits a small increase, and the only important increase is experienced by the volatility of aid flows shocks.[6]

The estimated variances of output, their components, and the relative variances and vulnerabilities to internal and external shocks (as a whole) across periods are presented in table 8.4. Column (1) shows the long-run variance of output predicted by the model in each subperiod. The model is

TABLE 8.3
Volatility of Structural Shocks in African Countries

Period	GDP of rich countries (1)	Oil price index (2)	Commodity price index (3)	Real interest rate (4)	Geologic disasters (5)	Climatic disasters (6)	Humanitarian disasters (7)	Aid flows (8)	GDP (9)
1963–89	0.015	0.081	0.162	0.023	0.056	0.398	0.200	0.311	0.057
1990–2003	0.009	0.052	0.121	0.025	0.056	0.398	0.200	0.371	0.048
Difference	−0.006000**	−0.029000**	−0.041000**	0.002479**	n.a.	n.a.	n.a.	0.060480**	−0.009104**

Source: Author's calculations.

Note: n.a. = not applicable. The entries correspond to the standard deviations of the structural shocks associated with the variables described in the different columns, estimated for the periods 1963–89 and 1990–2003. The exceptions are the entries corresponding to the standard deviations associated with various types of natural disasters, which were computed directly from the data, assuming the occurrence of these disasters follows a Bernoulli process. For these variables, the implicit standard deviations were estimated using data for the whole period, so there is no time variation across columns. The row labeled "Difference" reports the difference between the standard deviations estimated for the 1990–2003 and 1963–89 periods. The significance levels were assessed based on whether the confidence interval of the empirical distribution obtained by parametric bootstrapping contain zero at each specified level.

** Significant at the 5 percent level.

TABLE 8.4
Decomposition of Output Variance in African Countries

Period	Predicted variance (1)	External component (2)	Internal component (3)	External component with pre-1990 shocks (4)	Internal component with pre-1990 shocks (5)	Predicted variance with pre-1990 shocks (6)	External exposure (7)	Internal exposure (8)
1963–89	0.0036	0.0003	0.0034	0.0003	0.0034	0.0036	n.a.	n.a.
1990–2003	0.0027	0.0003	0.0024	0.0005	0.0033	0.0039	n.a.	n.a.
Ratio across periods (1990–2003 divided by 1963–89)	0.7476**	1.3395	0.7023**	2.0169*	0.9922	1.0650*	0.6641*	0.7079*

Source: Author's calculations.

Note: n.a. = not applicable. The various columns of the table present the output variance predicted by the panel VAR model estimated in the chapter, its decomposition among external and internal factors, and estimated changes in vulnerability and exposure to each of these factors. Column (1) reports the long-run variance of output predicted by the model for the 1963–89 and 1990–2003 periods, respectively. Columns (2) and (3) decompose the predicted variance into the components associated with external and internal shocks, respectively. Column (4) reports the output variance that would have been observed in each period if only external shocks hit African countries, and if those shocks had maintained the size they had during the years 1960–89. Column (5) shows an exercise similar to the one reported in column (4), but this time for internal shocks. Column (6) reports the counterfactual output variance that would have been obtained in both periods if all the shocks had maintained the size they had before 1990. Columns (7) and (8) summarize the proportional decline in exposure to external and internal shocks, respectively, by presenting the ratio of the output variances estimated for the last period obtained with the second and first period shocks, respectively (the second rows of column (2)/column (4) and column (3)/column (5), respectively). At the bottom of each column, the row labeled *Ratio across periods* reports the ratio of the value reported in that column for the period 1990–2003 to the one reported for the period 1963–89 (the second row divided by the first row). The values thus correspond to the proportional increase (decrease) in the role of each particular component across periods. The significance levels were assessed based on whether the confidence interval of the empirical distribution obtained by parametric bootstrapping contains the value one at each specified level.

* Significant at the 10 percent level.

** Significant at the 5 percent level.

able to predict the significant decline in output volatility observed in the data, although the predicted proportional decline is somewhat smaller (25 percent in the model compared with 31 percent in the data).[7] This is shown in the row labeled "Ratio across periods," which reports the ratio between the magnitudes reported in each column for the period 1990–2003 to those reported for the period 1963–89. The reason for reporting the ratios (proportional change) instead of the difference is that my counterfactual experiments do not allow me to quantify the level of vulnerabilities and exposures in each period, but only their relative change. Thus, I maintain this convention for all the magnitudes reported in this table and henceforth. In the "Ratio" row, I also report the significance levels (one-sided tests). The significance levels indicate whether the confidence interval of the empirical distribution includes one at that particular level.

Columns (2) and (3) decompose the predicted variance into the components associated with external and internal shocks, respectively ($\alpha \sigma_X^2$ and $\beta \sigma_I^2$). They show that most of the predicted decline in output volatility results from a reduced effect of the internal component. The effect of external shocks exhibits a small, almost negligible, increase, which is not statistically significant (the ratio is not significantly different from one). This small increase may seem paradoxical, given the decline in the variance of these shocks reported in table 8.3. The explanation lies in column (4), which reports the output variance that would have been observed in each period if (1) only external shocks hit African countries, and (2) these shocks had maintained the size they had during the years 1960–89. As explained above, the ratio of these predicted variances measures the proportional increase in the vulnerability of output in African countries to external shocks. The figures suggest that, if such had been the case, the output variance associated with external shocks would have doubled, and this increase is significant at the 10 percent level. This means that, overall, African countries have been more vulnerable to external shocks in recent years. It is this higher vulnerability that compensates for the decline in the variance of external shocks to result in a slightly higher role of external shocks during the last 15 years. Column (5) shows a similar exercise to the one reported in column (4) for the case of internal shocks, and reveals that the vulnerability to these shocks has experienced no change across periods. The information reported in the previous columns is summarized in column (6), which reports the counterfactual output variance that would have been observed in both periods if all the shocks had maintained the size they had before 1990. It can be seen that, in such a case, output volatility would have significantly increased by 7 percent instead of declining by 25 percent. That increase would have been exclusively the result of the higher estimated vulnerability of African countries to external shocks during the latter period. Columns (7) and (8) summarize the proportional decline in exposure to external an internal shocks, respectively. They present the ratio of the output variances obtained for the period 1990–2003 with the second- and first-period shocks, respectively (the second rows of column (2)/column (4), and column (3)/column (5), respectively). As suggested by the figures reported in table 8.3, the exposure of African countries to both types has declined importantly. Although the decline is larger for external shocks, the higher relative importance of internal shocks in both periods, and the increase in the vulnerability to external shocks in the second period, means that the more tranquil internal environment is the main factor responsible for the observed decline in output volatility.

The proportional changes in the vulnerability of African countries to each external shock are reported in table 8.5, which presents the ratio of the vulnerability in the period 1990–2003 to the vulnerability in the period

TABLE 8.5
Relative Vulnerability of African Countries to Various Shocks

Shock	Relative vulnerability (1990–2003 to 1963–89)
GDP of rich countries	3.66**
Oil price index	1.48
Commodity price index	2.51*
Real interest rate	2.55
Geologic disasters	0.73
Climatic disasters	0.66
Humanitarian disasters	0.06
Aid flows	4.30*
GDP	0.99

Source: Author's calculations.

Note: The table reports the estimated ratio of the vulnerability of African countries to each of the structural shocks described in the various rows during 1990–2003 and 1963–89. Thus, a value larger than one indicates an increase in vulnerability. The relative vulnerabilities were obtained by computing the ratio of the response of output variance to a shock of a given size across periods. Significance levels were assessed based on whether the confidence interval of the empirical distribution obtained by parametric bootstrapping contains the value one at each specified level.

*Significant at the 10 percent level.

** Significant at the 5 percent level.

1963–1989. The vulnerability to all external shocks, except natural disasters, has increased in the last 15 years. The largest statistically significant increases correspond to the vulnerability to shocks to aid flows and to the GDP of rich countries, suggesting that African countries have become more sensitive to the international business cycle and aid flows. The relative vulnerability estimated for oil prices also is not statistically different from one, suggesting that the vulnerability to these shocks has not increased for the typical African country.

Taking stock, these results suggest that the decline in output volatility in African countries observed during the last 15 years is largely due to a more stable internal environment. On the external front, there has been a decline in overall exposure, but this decline has been compensated by an increase in the vulnerability of African countries to external shocks, especially to shocks to aid flows and the international environment. Within this sample of countries, these broad patterns are robust to several modifications in my baseline specification, such as changing the number of lags and estimating the model in levels.

Role of Oil Prices

Oil typically is considered a special commodity in policy and academic circles, mainly because its price tends to experience periods of particularly large fluctuations.[8] It is therefore important to determine whether oil is indeed especially relevant to account for the fluctuations of output in African countries versus other commodities. Although in principle the DM index of commodity-based terms of trade includes oil so that fluctuations in oil prices are reflected in fluctuations in the index, the grouping of oil with other commodities in the index assumes that the response of output to shocks to oil prices (properly weighted) is similar to its response to shocks to other commodities. If oil is special, this assumption may be incorrect. A second issue is that the DM index uses only exports weights because it assumes that African countries import few commodities. Although that assumption is correct for many of the commodities included in the index, oil is probably the exception because most countries need to import some amount of oil to accommodate their energy needs. As explained in the third section of this chapter, this is the reason why I used net trade weights instead of export weights to construct our country-specific oil price index.

TABLE 8.6
Relative Importance of External Shocks in Models Excluding and Including Oil Price Index

Period	Model without oil (1)	Model with oil (2)
1963–89	0.06	0.07
1990–2003	0.10	0.13

Source: Author's calculations.

Note: Each entry corresponds to the fraction of the long-run variance of output (the variance of the 20-years-ahead forecast error) that can be explained by shocks to the GDP of rich countries, trade-weighted oil price index (only in column [2]), commodity prices, real international interest rate, natural disasters (geologic, climatic, and human), and aid flows. Columns (1) and (2) present the figures obtained from estimating the panel VAR model described in the chapter, excluding (including) the trade-weighted oil price index.

Table 8.3, which presented the estimated standard deviations of the various structural shocks in my sample of African countries, gave a first indication of the potential role of oil prices for the typical African country. The table showed that, across periods, the trade-weighted oil price index was less volatile than the DM commodity price index among African countries, despite the fact that variance of the latter is smoothed by the averaging of several shocks. The reason for this apparent stability of the oil price index is not that oil prices are less volatile than other commodities, but that the typical net weight of oil in the trade of African countries is small. This suggests it is unlikely that oil will be especially important for African countries as a whole.

Table 8.6 confirms this intuition. For each period, the table compares the fraction of the output variance explained by external shocks in a model including oil prices separate from the standard DM index with the same fraction in a model where oil prices are part of the DM index only. We see that including oil prices separate from other commodities increases only slightly the fraction of output variance explained by external shocks—from 6 percent to 7 percent in the first period, and from 10 percent to 12 percent in the second. None of these changes is statistically different from zero at conventional levels.[9] The similarity between these results confirms that, for the typical African country, fluctuations in oil prices are not significantly more special than fluctuations in the prices of other commodities captured by the DM index.

One could argue, however, that, when looking at the impact of oil prices, the homogeneous treatment of oil-importing and oil-exporting

TABLE 8.7
Output Volatility among Oil-Exporting and Oil-Importing African Countries

Group	1963–89	1990–2003
Oil-importing countries	0.048	0.041
Oil-exporting countries	0.071	0.049
Difference	0.023**	0.008

Source: Author's calculations.

Note: Each entry corresponds to the mean output volatility during the periods 1963–89 and 1990–2003 in the group of African countries indicated in the corresponding row. The volatility of output corresponds to the standard deviation of real GDP per capita growth during a given period. The row labeled "Difference" reports the difference in the mean volatilities across the two groups. Significance levels are based on a *t*-test of equality of means across groups.

** Significant at the 5 percent level.

countries in my panel VAR is inappropriate. Table 8.7 compares the actual standard deviation of output across periods between oil-importing and oil-exporting countries, and it shows that those countries exporting oil are more volatile than those importing it, although the difference is considerably larger and significant only in the pre-1990 period. This finding suggests that separating these two groups may be a good idea.

Based on these arguments, I explore the possibility that oil prices have different effects across these two groups by estimating the baseline model separately in each of them, performing a series of variance decomposition, and computing the incremental effect that considering oil prices separately from the DM index has on the relative importance of external shocks in each group. The results of these exercises are summarized in tables 8.8 and 8.9. Table 8.8 compares the actual standard deviation of the various shocks across periods between oil-importing and oil-exporting countries. The table shows that, although the pattern of standard deviations of the various structural shocks across periods is similar for both groups, there are two main exceptions. First, the decline in the volatility of internal shocks is much larger among oil exporters. Second, the oil price index is always significantly more volatile among oil exporters, it experiences a larger decline across periods, and commodity prices are always more volatile for oil importers. Table 8.9 shows the relative importance of external shocks across periods and groups when oil prices are included (columns [2] and [5]) and excluded from the model (columns [1] and [4]). We see that the pattern for oil importers is similar to the one documented for the whole sample. Including oil prices has little impact on the ability of external

TABLE 8.8
Volatility of Structural Shocks among Oil-Importing and Oil-Exporting African Countries

Group, by period	GDP of rich countries (1)	Oil price index (2)	Commodity price index (3)	Real interest rate (4)	Geologic disasters (5)	Climatic disasters (6)	Humanitarian disasters (7)	Aid flows (8)	GDP (9)
Panel A: oil-importing countries									
1963–89	0.015	0.029	0.154	0.019	0.045	0.427	0.191	0.295	0.048
1990–2003	0.008	0.019	0.125	0.021	0.045	0.427	0.191	0.326	0.042
Difference	−0.006**	−0.010**	−0.029**	0.002**	n.a.	n.a.	n.a.	0.031**	−0.006**
Ratio	0.583**	0.648**	0.814**	1.111**	n.a.	n.a.	n.a.	1.104**	0.876**
Panel B: oil-exporting countries									
1963–89	0.015	0.160	0.091	0.019	0.090	0.332	0.127	0.351	0.077
1990–2003	0.008	0.115	0.069	0.021	0.090	0.332	0.127	0.420	0.044
Difference	−0.006**	−0.045**	−0.022**	0.002**	n.a.	n.a.	n.a.	0.070	−0.033**
Ratio	0.583**	0.717**	0.761**	1.111**	n.a.	n.a.	n.a.	1.198**	0.568**
Differences across groups									
1963–89	n.a.	0.131**	−0.063**	n.a.	n.a.	n.a.	n.a.	0.056	0.029**
1990–2003	n.a.	0.096**	−0.056**	n.a.	n.a.	n.a.	n.a.	0.095	0.001

Source: Author's calculations.

Note: n.a. = not applicable. The entries correspond to the standard deviations of the structural shocks associated with the variables described in the different columns, estimated for the periods 1963–89 and 1990–2003. The exception are the entries reported in columns (5) to (7) corresponding to the standard deviations associated with various types of natural disasters computed directly from the data, assuming the occurrence of these disasters follows a Bernoulli process. For these variables, the implicit standard deviations were estimated using data for the whole period, so there is no time variation across columns. The rows labeled "Difference" report, for each group of countries, the difference between the standard deviations estimated for the 1990–2003 and 1963–89 periods. The significance levels were assessed based on whether the confidence interval of the empirical distribution obtained by parametric bootstrapping contain zero at each specified level. The rows labeled "Ratio" report the ratio of the estimated standard deviations for the 1990–2003 and 1963–89 periods. The significance levels in those rows refer to the hypothesis that the ratio is significantly different from one; they were obtained in a similar manner as those reported for the "Difference" rows. The section labeled "Differences among groups" shows the within-period difference in estimated standard deviations between oil-importing and oil-exporting countries. Because the results for the two groups were estimated separately, the significance levels reported in this section of the table were obtained by checking whether the confidence intervals of estimates for each group overlapped. A 5 percent confidence level then indicates that the 95th percentile of the empirical distribution in one group did not overlap with the 5th percentile of the empirical distribution in the other group.

** Significant at the 5 percent level.

TABLE 8.9
Relative Importance of External Shocks in Models Including and Excluding Oil Price Index for Oil-Importing and Oil-Exporting Countries

Group	1963–89			1990–2003		
	No oil (1)	Oil (2)	Difference (3)	No oil (4)	Oil (5)	Difference (6)
Oil-importing countries	0.15	0.18	0.03	0.14	0.20	0.06
Oil-exporting countries	0.18	0.15	−0.03	0.20	0.57	0.37**

Source: Author's calculations.

Note: Each entry corresponds to the fraction of the long-run variance of output (the variance of the 20-years-ahead forecast error) that can be explained by shocks to the GDP of rich countries, trade-weighted oil price index (only in columns [2] and [5]), commodity prices, real international interest rate, natural disasters (geologic, climatic, and human), and aid flows. Columns (1) and (2) present the figures obtained from estimating the panel VAR model described in the chapter, excluding and including the trade-weighted oil price index, respectively, for the 1963–89 period. Column (3) reports the difference between columns (2) and (1). Columns (4) and (5) report similar figures for the 1990–2003 period. The significance levels were assessed based on whether the confidence interval of the empirical distribution obtained by parametric bootstrapping contains the value one at each specified level.

** Significant at the 5 percent level.

shocks to account for output volatility in either period. However, for oil-exporting countries, including oil prices separately increases significantly the role of external shocks in the last 15 years. Thus, the evidence points out that oil price shocks indeed may be special—compared to other commodities—but only among oil-exporting countries.[10]

Final Remarks

Quantifying the importance of external shocks as sources of output volatility is crucial to assess the potential gains from helping countries smooth these shocks. This chapter has looked at the role of a broad set of external and other (likely internal) shocks in the decline in output volatility observed among African countries in the 1990–2003 period, and has explored whether the changing roles of the different components of output variance have resulted in a larger role for external shocks.

The findings indicate that external shocks indeed have become more important, relative to other causes, during the period 1990–2003. The reason for this increased importance lies in several events. First and most important, the variance of output not explained by external shocks, which I associate with internal factors, has decreased importantly in this sample of 38 countries. This decline alone would mean that, all things being equal, external shocks mechanically would become more important. Second, there is an important increase in the vulnerability of output to external shocks, especially to those associated with aid flows and the international business cycle. Again, this higher vulnerability itself would result in an increased role for external shocks in the latter period. Third, there is a countervailing force to the increase in vulnerability: The exposure of African countries to these shocks has declined. Therefore, although the external environment has become more tranquil, compared with that of the 1963–89 period, the sensitivity of African countries to external shocks has increased enough to compensate for the reduced exposure.

I also document that, for the typical sub-Saharan African country, oil price fluctuations do not play a special role, compared with fluctuations in other commodities, when properly weighted. However, for the small group of countries that are oil exporters, oil does seem to play a special role (especially during the 1990–2003 period) in the sense that a 1 percent fluctuation in (properly weighted) oil prices has a different impact than a 1 percent fluctuation in the (properly weighted) price of other commodities they produce.

These results indicate that the potential proportional gains in terms of reducing output volatility that can be achieved by smoothing the impact of external shocks are larger now than in the earlier part of the post-independence period. However, the importance of these shocks is still small for the typical African country: My point estimates put the magnitude at approximately 13 percent of total output variance (21 percent for the 95th percentile). This is something to keep in mind when setting expectations regarding the potential gains of programs targeted to reduce the impact of these shocks in terms of increased stability. Together with the finding that most of the reduction in output volatility between the two periods analyzed is the result of the nonexternal shocks, this suggests that focusing on internal causes of instability is still where the bigger payoffs probably are.

The methodological approach followed in this chapter is semistructural. This means that I have not fully described the set of potentially relevant macroeconomic variables, nor the links between them. With respect to the first point, I have focused on a relatively broad set of variables that can be reasonably argued to be exogenous or to require relatively noncontroversial identification assumptions. There are, however, other variables—such as the real exchange rate—that were not included as external shocks because they are more likely to be endogenous. To the extent that these variables have an important external component, my model will attribute it to the other causes that I am associating with internal factors. Nevertheless, it seems unlikely that the inclusion of other external shocks may change the qualitative findings of this chapter. With respect to the second point, external and internal causes of instability may be linked in ways that cannot be captured by my model, and that may lead to underestimating the role of external shocks. This could happen, for instance, if there were nonlinearities in the response of output to shocks. Again, my conjecture is that it is unlikely that these second-order effects could result in a qualitative change in results (that is, order of magnitude), but I cannot completely disregard this possibility, and I leave it for future research. Finally, I have to emphasize that the findings on the higher importance of external shocks in the period 1990–2003 do not guarantee that this will remain the case in the future. I have chosen the subperiods in an ad hoc way motivated by the perceived recent changes in performance for African countries after the lost decade of the 1980s and by the need to have a reasonable number of years in each subsample. However, I am agnostic to whether this corresponds to a structural break or a cyclical phenomenon. Given the limited data available, testing this proposition is probably unfeasible.

Notes

I am grateful to Jan Dehn for generously sharing his data; and to Alexandra Tabova for updating the Deaton-Miller terms-of-trade index; and to John Page, Delfin S. Go, and participants at the Chief Economist's seminar of the Africa region for many useful comments.

1. Of course, the linearity may come from a log linearization of a nonlinear model.
2. The index corresponds to $(w_X - w_M) \log (P_{OIL,t}/MUV_t)$, where w_X is the average share of oil exports in total exports during 1970–2003; w_M is the average share of oil imports in total imports during the same period; $P_{OIL,t}$ is the price of oil at time t; and MUV_t is the manufacturing unit value at t, which is used as a deflator for the oil price.
3. I use the average price (series 00176AAZZF from the International Financial Statistics).
4. Although there may be a concern that, given the criteria used to enter an event in the EM-DAT, disasters may be more frequent in poorer countries (see, for example, the evidence in Kahn [2005]), this issue is unlikely to affect my results for two reasons. First, my sample is composed exclusively of low-income countries, and selection bias among low-income countries is less likely

. to be a significant concern. Second, and more important, I will control for the average income level of a country in my specification, and the identification will be provided mainly by the time variation of the data. Selection bias therefore will be a problem only if the probability of registering an event in the database is larger in a year with relatively low income (with respect to each country's average). This is clearly much less likely than having a relation between a country's average income and the probability of registering a disaster. Still, as mentioned above, one of the criteria used in IMF (2003) to classify a disaster as "large" is that it has an impact of half a percentage point of GDP, which certainly can bias the measured impact of disasters. This concern is unlikely to be important because data on the economic impact of disasters are scant, so the classification of a disaster as large typically is based on other criteria. Nevertheless, it is important to keep in mind that this issue would tend to bias upward the estimated impact of a disaster.

5. I focus on the results of the "panel-rho" test. According to Pedroni (1999), that test has better size properties in a sample of the size used in this chapter.

6. Given the low frequency of occurrence of disasters, I do not attempt to estimate their incidence separately for the two subperiods.

7. The decline in the data corresponds to the proportional decline in the average variance across countries. Thus, it is different from the one that can be obtained from table 8.2, which reports the medians. The reason to compare it with the decline in average variances is that the estimation methods (ordinary least squares) are more appropriate to fit the behavior of mean variables than of medians.

8. Although we saw in table 8.3 that the volatility of the oil price terms-of-trade for a typical African country is actually smaller than that of its commodity price index, the reason for this difference is that most African countries are net oil importers and oil represents a relatively small fraction of their trade. This means that the weights associated with oil prices are relatively small in these countries. The high volatility of oil prices is evident again if we compare the coefficient of variations of the oil price terms-of-trade and commodity price indexes (87 versus 17). This difference cannot be explained by aggregation alone. Assuming that all commodity prices are equally volatile, the standard deviation of the DM index would fall with the square root of the number of commodities included. For the typical African country, there are seven commodities in the basket of the DM index, which can only explain a twofold increase in the coefficient of variation between the index and a given independent commodity.

9. The models with and without oil prices are non-nested so my assessment of the significance of the difference is based on determining whether the 90 percent and 95 percent confidence intervals of the empirical distributions estimated for each case through parametric bootstrapping intersect.

10. The tables decomposing the variance of output and the proportional changes in vulnerabilities for each group and period are available on request to the author.

References

Ahmed, S. 2003. "Sources of Macroeconomic Fluctuations in Latin America and Implications for Choice of Exchange Rate Regime." *Journal of Development Economics* 72: 181–202.

Christiano, L. J., M. Eichenbaum, and C. L. Evans. 1998. "Monetary Policy Shocks: What Have We Learned and to What End?" Working Paper 6400, National Bureau of Economic Research, Cambridge, MA.

Deaton, A., and Miller, R. 1996. "International Commodity Prices, Macroeconomic Performance and Politics in Sub-Saharan Africa." *Journal of African Economies* 5 (3): 99–191.

Dehn, J. 2001. "The Effects on Growth of Commodity Price Uncertainty and Shocks." Policy Research Working Paper 2455, World Bank, Washington, DC.

IMF (International Monetary Fund). 2003. "Fund Assistance for Countries Facing Exogenous Shocks." Policy Development and Review Department, Washington, DC.

Kahn, M. 2005. "The Death Toll from Natural Disasters: The Role of Income, Geography, and Institutions." *Review of Economics and Statistics* 87 (2): 271–84.

Levin, A., C.-F. Lin, and C.-S. J. Chu. 2002. "Unit Root Tests in Panel Data: Asymptotic and Finite-Sample Properties." *Journal of Econometrics* 108: 1–24.

Odedokun, M. 2003. "Analysis of Deviations and Delays in Aid Disbursements." *Journal of Economic Development* 28 (1): 137–69.

Pedroni, P. 1999. "Critical Values for Cointegration Tests in Heterogeneous Panel with Multiple Regressors." *Oxford Bulletin of Economics and Statistics* 61: 653–70.

Raddatz, C. 2007. "Are External Shocks Responsible for the Instability of Output in Low-income Countries?" *Journal of Development Economics* 84 (1): 155–87.

CHAPTER 9

Harnessing Oil Windfalls for Growth in the Africa Region

Julia Devlin, Michael Lewin, and Thilakaratna Ranaweera

The recent boom in oil prices poses significant opportunities for accelerating growth and poverty reduction in the Africa region. Sub-Saharan Africa holds 13 percent of the world's proven reserves outside of the Middle East, and it is the fastest-growing reserve base in the world for oil production. These oil reserves are expected to generate a windfall with a net present value (NPV) of nearly $300 billion, discounted at 10 percent—an amount larger than the continent's external debt burden. However, this windfall is temporary: Reserves likely will be depleted among the largest African oil producers by 2035.

Given the significant size and transitory nature of Africa's oil windfall, it is critical for policy makers to harness these resources to sources of growth and poverty reduction. But the challenges are great. An influx of oil revenues tends to be associated with a negative or, at best, an ambiguous effect on per capita income and living standards (Auty 1998; Gelb and Associates 1988; Sachs and Warner 1995). Poor growth performance among resource-rich countries also is linked to rent seeking, corruption (Tornell and Lane 1999), and weak institutional quality (Isham et al. 2003). For the Africa region in particular, existing studies indicate that oil exporters historically have benefited from terms-of-trade gains, but these gains generally have not been used to place countries on a sustainable growth path. During the 1970s and 1980s, poor macroeconomic management of oil revenues resulted in high inflation, large exchange rate appreciation, and the erosion of the competitiveness in non-oil sectors (Collier and Gunning 1996; Gelb and Associates 1988). Commodity windfalls also are associated with the prevalence of conflict (Collier and Hoffler 2002) and rent seeking behavior (Bates 1983; Sklar and Whitaker 1991).

Existing approaches to managing oil windfalls focus on fiscal policy instruments as central to improving economic outcomes and avoiding the problems of the "resource curse" (Davis, Ossowski, and Fedelino 2003; Devlin and Lewin 2005). This chapter builds on this approach by emphasizing the importance of fiscal policy and institutions in managing Africa's oil windfall. The first section outlines factors influencing the size and variability of current oil windfalls and the size of the government "take" from oil. In the second section, we present methods for assessing the impact of Africa's oil windfalls on the macroeconomy. The third section identifies fiscal mechanisms needed to enhance transparency and accountability in the use of oil windfalls and to mitigate rent-seeking behavior.

Estimating the Size of Africa's Oil Windfall

Sub-Saharan Africa is the fastest-growing region in the world in terms of proven reserves, with growth of more than 110 percent in recent years.[1] Since 1980, the Republic of Congo's reserves have increased by 68 percent, Gabon's reserves have increased by 116 percent, and Nigeria's reserves have risen by 1,736 percent. These increases are high compared with reserve growth in North Africa, Central and South America, and Eastern Europe/Former Soviet Union, where reserve growth has averaged 35 percent (table 9.1).

There are three classes of oil-exporting countries in Africa today, including new (for example, Mauritania), mature (such as Nigeria), and declining (for instance, Gabon) producers; each have different profiles of production and revenue flows. Among all three classes of oil producers, estimating the size of Africa's oil windfall is like following a moving target, given varying production horizons and volatile oil prices (tables 9.2 and 9.3).

Variables such as production schedules, capital and operating costs, infrastructure and transport requirements, oil quality, and oil prices are largely external to policy control; whereas factors such as the design of the contractual arrangements, licensing, and the investment climate are within reach of policy makers. The challenge is how to balance these

TABLE 9.1
Africa's Oil Reserves from a Global Perspective

a. World's proven crude reserves

Share of world reserves (2005)/share of world GDP (2003)	Region	Proven reserves (billion bbls), 2005	World share (%)	Share of reserves outside of Middle East (%)	Region's share of World GDP in 2003 (%)
0.13	Asia and Oceania	41.1	3	9	27
1.92	Central and South America	101.2	9	22	4
4.14	Eastern Europe and Former Soviet Union	121.9	10	27	2
31.08	Middle East	733.9	62	n.a.	2
6.48	North Africa	54.5	5	12	1
0.15	North America	60.9	5	13	35
4.34	Sub-Saharan Africa	57.7	5	13	1
0.05	Western Europe	17.4	1	4	27
n.a.	Total world	1,188.5	n.a.	n.a.	n.a.

b. World's proven crude reserve growth

Region	Proven Reserve Growth, 1994–2005 (%)
Asia and Oceania	−19
Central and South America	36
Eastern Europe and Former Soviet Union	34
Middle East	10
North Africa	37
North America	−30
Sub-Saharan Africa	110
Western Europe	−4
Total world	12

Sources: Energy Information Administration; British Petroleum.

Note: bbl = barrel; n.a. = not applicable.

TABLE 9.2
Proven Crude Oil Reserves of Africa's Oil Exporters
Billion barrels

Country	Increase (%)	1980	2005 (estimated)	Ratio of 2005 reserves to 2005 production
Cameroon	0	0.4	0.4	13
Congo, Rep. of	68	0.83	1.5	16
Gabon	116	1.34	2.5	26
Nigeria	1,736	17.9	35.3	36

Sources: Energy Information Administration; Wood Mackenzie.

TABLE 9.3
Typology of African Oil Exporters: Stages of Production

New	Mature	Declining
Angola	Chad	Cameroon
Mauritania	Congo, Rep. of	Equatorial Guinea
Nigeria		Gabon

Source: World Bank staff estimates.

FIGURE 9.1
Oil Production, 2000–35

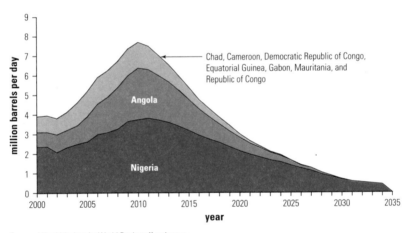

Sources: Wood Mackenzie; World Bank staff estimates.

instruments to enhance the government take from oil revenues, given the volatility and exhaustibility of Africa's oil revenue stream.

Oil reserves do not materialize out of thin air; growth comes from exploration. Increased exploration can be generated by higher prices, allowing for higher exploration costs; by improved technology, making previously uneconomic reserves probable production candidates; and by governments opening new areas for exploration. Reserve growth in sub-Saharan Africa results from all three factors (figure 9.1).

TABLE 9.4
Production Profiles of African Oil Exporters

Country	Estimated total production cycle (years)
Angola	52
Cameroon	42
Chad	25
Congo, Rep. of	55
Equatorial Guinea	33
Gabon	68
Mauritania	22
Nigeria	76

Source: World Bank staff estimates.

Despite the rapid growth in Africa's oil reserves and production, this increase is expected to be temporary. For mature producers such as Nigeria, with approximately 3 percent of world reserves, production is expected to peak at 3.8 million barrels per day in 2010. Gabon, one of sub-Saharan Africa's top five producers, has rapidly declining reserves; production is expected to peak at 304,000 barrels per day in 2009, and end in 2027. In Equatorial Guinea, on the other hand, production has peaked after extraordinarily rapid growth, making it one of sub-Saharan Africa's third largest producers (following Nigeria and Angola) after only 10 years of production. The average years of estimated total production for Angola, Cameroon, Chad, Equatorial Guinea, Gabon, Mauritania, and the Republic of Congo is 42 (table 9.4).

Factors Influencing the Size of Africa's Windfall

The ability to estimate the approximate size and duration of oil revenues is critical for policy makers in oil-exporting African countries. To this end, there are a number of factors that determine the size of Africa's windfall and how this is translated into government revenues—many of them external to government control.

Capital and Operating Costs Vary across Producers
Capital and operating costs depend in part on where the oil is found and on the size of oil fields. For emerging oil producers such as Mauritania,

FIGURE 9.2

Total Operating and Capital Expenditures, Mauritania, 2002–22

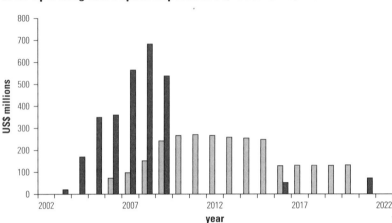

Sources: Wood Mackenzie; World Bank staff estimates.

capital costs per barrel are high—estimated at more than $25 a barrel in some years—because the oil is located primarily in deep water (figure 9.2). As more production comes on line, however, capital costs decline and operating costs rise.

In Cameroon, on the other hand, where production is declining rapidly, there is little investment in new fields, and capital expenses per barrel are low.[2] Producing a barrel of oil becomes increasingly costly as production focuses on marginal fields. Operating costs are the highest toward the end of the production profile—nearly $12 per barrel before production tapers off after 2015.

In Nigeria, the oldest and largest producer, operating costs are estimated at $54 billion. Including capital costs raises this estimate to nearly $62 billion (table 9.5). Annual costs, similar to the discounted total costs, are very large—more than $14 billion in 2007 and 2008 and still more than $7 billion in 2015.

Transportation and Quality Discounts Matter

Transportation and quality discounts also affect the size of oil windfalls and these can vary significantly across oil exporters. In Nigeria, production includes a variety of crude qualities, which deviate from the West Texas

TABLE 9.5
Costs of Production for African Oil Exporters, 2006–16

Country	Total operating costs (US$ millions)	Total capital costs (US$ millions)
Angola	22,283	26,461
Cameroon	985	280
Chad	3,591	121
Congo, Rep. of	3,947	1,782
Equatorial Guinea	4,184	1,216
Gabon	3,226	1,409
Mauritania	2,257	2,196
Nigeria	54,037	61,969

Sources: Wood Mackenzie; World Bank staff estimates.

Intermediate (WTI) price by −9 percent to +1 percent. In Chad, quality discounts are estimated at 20 percent from the WTI price.

Volatile Oil Prices Affect Crude Differentials

Such factors tend to be exacerbated in volatile markets. Typically, when oil prices rise, quality discounts widen. Increased demand for light, sweet crude to suit refining needs leads to wider crude differentials relative to lower grades—that is, heavy, sour crude is more difficult to convert to refined products, and refineries are often built to manage a few specific crude qualities. Higher prices for sweet crude work parallel with lower prices for heavy crude.

Contractual Terms

Alternatively, governments can and do control the contractual framework governing private operators, which also affects the size of the oil windfall. For African oil exporters, the contractual framework is often complex in the way payments are calculated, the number of institutions involved, and the timing of payments.

Policy makers can and do match the contractual terms of exploration and production with producer incentives at varying stages of production. In Nigeria, for example, fees during exploration and development are structured as bonuses paid by the operator to the government. As a result, government earnings typically increase as revenues rise or production increases. Where royalty rates are based on the value of oil rather than on the number of barrels produced, oil prices become important and the calculation of government earnings will be affected similarly.

Exploration and Development Fees

Bonuses are paid by the operator to the government at various milestones in a project, such as signing the contract and starting production. In Nigeria, for example, terms require signature bonuses of $5–20 million; in Mauritania, where the finds are smaller, the typical signature bonus is $10,000 per license. In Chad, the signature bonus is $250,000.

Royalties and Production Sharing

Royalties are calculated on the basis of oil revenues or barrels produced either cumulatively or annually.[3] In Nigeria, for example, royalty rates are 4–20 percent, depending on field location and water depth. In Equatorial Guinea, all new contracts pay royalties of 10–16 percent, depending on production levels.

In a production-sharing contract (PSC), a share of the profit oil[4] also belongs to the government. This may or may not replace royalties in concession contracts. In Equatorial Guinea, for example, profit-sharing arrangements allocate 10 percent to the government at cumulative production levels of less than 50 million barrels and 60 percent for production in excess of 200 million barrels. Often in these arrangements, policy makers choose to have the contractor market the government's oil as well. In Mauritanian PSCs, for example, there is a 25 percent income tax on the contractor's share of profit oil.

For royalties and production sharing, the percentage of revenues allocated to the government typically increases as revenues or production increase. If the royalty rate is based on the value of oil rather than on barrels produced, the oil price becomes important. (figure 9.3)

Corporate Tax

In addition to the petroleum-specific fees and taxes, there are regular corporate income tax payments that accrue to the government. These payments can be linked to the petroleum regime, and, in some cases, oil companies can be exempt from corporate taxes for the first years of production. For example, in the Republic of Congo, the tax rate is approximately 30 percent, in Cameroon 57.7 percent, and in Chad 50 percent.

FIGURE 9.3
Royalty Receipts, Cameroon, 1976–2020

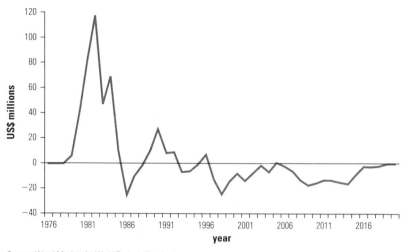

Sources: Wood Mackenzie; World Bank staff estimates.

How Are Government Revenues Affected?

Absolute revenues to African oil-exporting governments are large, but the government take[5] can vary significantly, depending on how contracts are structured. Estimates of total government take range from a low of $4 billion in Mauritania to a high of $151 billion in Nigeria.[6]

In Mauritania, the government's share under the production-sharing contract represents most of the government take, followed by income taxes from contractors. In Nigeria's concessions, on the other hand, the most important elements are taxes followed by royalties and the government's equity share of oil.

Government Take Varies from Year to Year
The total government take is often reported as a percentage of revenues and can vary significantly from year to year. In Chad, for example, production-sharing contracts (PSC) can yield government revenues on the order of 10 percent of total revenues in one year and almost 70 percent in following years when costs have been written off (table 9.6).

In Nigeria, on the other hand, the government take remains stable at around 70 percent; although PSC revenues fluctuate between less than

TABLE 9.6
Government Take from Oil Production and Royalties, 2006–11
US$ millions

Country	Low price	Mid price	High price
Angola	113,208	151,125	219,493
Cameroon	4,646	5,939	7,868
Chad	7,608	9,797	13,945
Congo, Rep. of	11,346	14,601	19,944
Equatorial Guinea	15,158	19,024	24,909
Gabon	13,792	17,505	23,203
Mauritania	3,141	4,369	6,649
Nigeria	204,349	266,120	369,577

Sources: Wood Mackenzie; World Bank staff estimates.

FIGURE 9.4
Government Take and Total Oil and Gas Revenues, 1990–2024

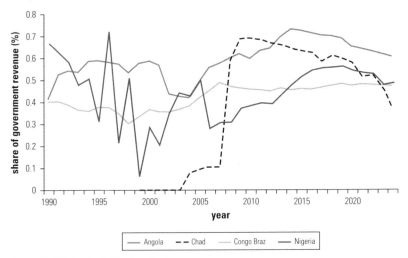

Sources: Wood Mackenzie; World Bank staff estimates.

10 percent and more than 70 percent because of more volatility related to less volume and more cost write-offs (figures 9.4 and 9.5).

Government Take Varies with Oil Price
Government revenues also vary with oil price levels: When prices increase, the government take as a percentage of oil revenues also may increase if policy makers decide to skew windfall profits toward the government

FIGURE 9.5
Nigeria's Split of Oil and Gas Revenues, 1990–2035

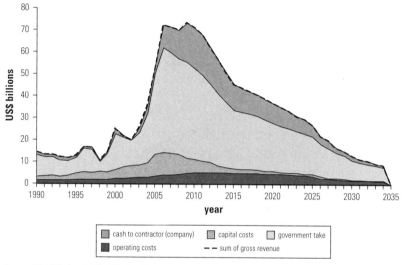

Sources: Wood Mackenzie; World Bank staff estimates.

and/or if cost write-offs do not increase with prices. For most African oil exporters, oil windfalls accrue largely to governments rather than to private operators, and, in all but one case (Equatorial Guinea), the government take is expected to increase with oil prices. This effect is expected to continue and does not reverse as costs are written off for the newest fields.

In Nigeria, for example, most of the revenue flow accrues to the government, with the exception of some years of high relative costs in the early 2000s.

The opposite scenario is found in Chad, where high initial costs led to a write-off against government revenues that makes the government take very low over the first years of production—estimated at 10 percent in 2005 (figure 9.6).

What Is the Value of Africa's Oil Windfall?

Given these factors, Africa's oil reserves are expected to generate a windfall with an NPV of nearly $300 billion, discounted at 10 percent—an amount larger than the continent's external debt burden. In the case of Nigeria, oil revenues would allow for constant annual spending per capita

FIGURE 9.6
Chad's Split of Oil and Gas Revenues, 1999–2029

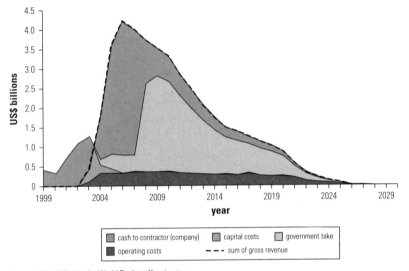

Sources: Wood Mackenzie; World Bank staff estimates.

of $109 for the next 50 years, assuming 2.4 percent per year population growth and 5.0 percent financial asset yield. However, this windfall is temporary: Reserves likely will be depleted among the largest African oil producers by 2035. This estimation is based on a number of price scenarios and discount rates (box 9.1).

In calculating the size of Africa's oil windfall, we estimate and compare high, mid, and low scenarios to a flat price. The flat price is based on the actual oil price until the year 1999 (figures 9.7 and 9.8); then it assumes $20 in 2000 and increases by 2.5 percent per year. In 1999, it appeared reasonable, based on history, to assume oil prices would fluctuate around $20. Shortly after, prices increased to the mid-$30 range; and since the end of 2001, prices have been on an upward trend, reaching $74.62 in May 2006. We then compare the NPV based on a $20 oil price to the NPV of government revenues based on our three price scenarios. This gives us the NPV of the windfall (table 9.7).

Based on these price scenarios, and on the situation where the windfall represents increased revenues compared with a $20 price scenario, the NPV of Africa's windfall is $300 billion and higher than the total outstanding debt of sub-Saharan Africa in 2004 ($235 billion).

BOX 9.1

Oil Price Scenarios

These estimates draw from three WTI price scenarios based on the World Bank's Development Economics Prospects Group base scenario. The middle price scenario assumes that prices average $64 per barrel in 2006 and gradually fall to $35 in 2015. The low price scenario assumes a $52 average in 2006 and a straight line reduction to $25 in 2015. The high price scenario assumes a flat price of $75 until 2008 and, for every year thereafter, $20 above the middle price scenario. After 2015, prices are inflated by 2.5 percent per year to keep up with U.S. dollar inflation. When calculating the oil windfall effect, we compare this to a scenario where the WTI price was $20 in 2000, which is increased by 2.5 percent each year. This price converge crosses the low scenario in 2014.

Source: World Bank staff estimates.

FIGURE 9.7
Oil Price Scenarios (WTI), 2006–15

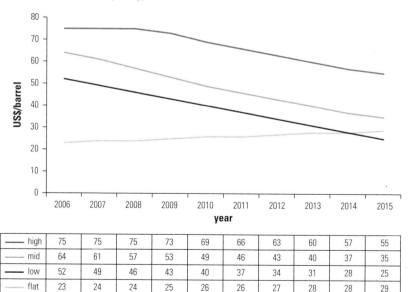

	2006	2007	2008	2009	2010	2011	2012	2013	2014	2015
—— high	75	75	75	73	69	66	63	60	57	55
—— mid	64	61	57	53	49	46	43	40	37	35
—— low	52	49	46	43	40	37	34	31	28	25
—— flat	23	24	24	25	26	26	27	28	28	29

Source: Authors' calculations.

Note: WTI = West Texas Intermediate.

FIGURE 9.8
WTI Spot Prices, 1986–2006

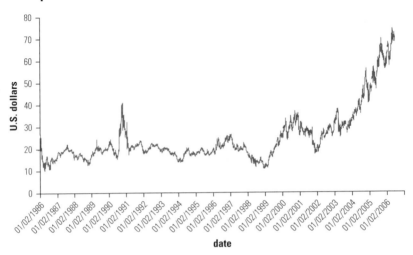

Source: World Bank.

Note: WTI = West Texas Intermediate.

TABLE 9.7
Windfall Estimates, by Country, 2006
US$ millions

Discount rate, price	Angola	Cameroon	Chad	Congo, Dem. Rep. of	Congo, Rep. of
5%					
High	240,053	5,538	13,903	1,498	17,057
Mid	122,374	3,573	6,911	956	9,502
Low	61,235	2,299	3,375	614	5,250
10%					
High	181,413	4,775	10,468	1,284	13,650
Mid	97,021	3,139	5,470	834	7,941
Low	52,110	2,044	2,911	541	4,620

Discount rate, price	Côte d'Ivoire	Equatorial Guinea	Gabon	Mauritania	Nigeria
5%					
High	6,290	18,806	17,559	6,396	427,146
Mid	3,764	11,267	10,626	3,338	204,736
Low	2,271	6,717	6,409	1,778	85,429
10%					
High	5,230	15,471	14,643	4,964	308,257
Mid	3,226	9,609	9,165	2,654	161,665
Low	1,998	5,932	5,707	1,454	80,306

Source: World Bank staff estimates.

Note: Windfall in government oil revenues calculated as of 2006, when compared with a $20 price scenario, US$ millions; net present value as of January 1, 2006.

This is a substantial gain in oil revenues in absolute terms and relative to levels of debt relief at the individual country level. Nigeria, for example, received $18 billion of debt relief in 2005–06, whereas the 10 percent NPV of the projected oil windfall to Nigeria as of 2006 is significantly higher— $162 billion.

However, as the term implies, the oil windfall by itself does not mean a permanent increase in wealth. Consumption expenditure based on current oil revenues will not be sustainable. Hence, policy makers have to balance the needs and welfare of the present with those of the future. This can be done only in the context of a sound macroeconomic/fiscal framework.

Enhancing the Growth Impact of the Oil Windfall

Africa's oil windfall has the potential to bring unambiguous benefits to current and future generations. However, the windfall is large, volatile, and exhaustible. This situation poses particular challenges for Africa's policy makers and requires policies and institutional measures to enhance the windfall's growth impact.

Oil Windfalls and Growth

One of the consequences of an oil windfall, other things being equal, is a real appreciation and fall in competitiveness of the non-oil sectors of the economy. The mechanism is as follows: The windfall brings a rise in income, some of which will be spent on home-produced goods. If the economy is at its natural rate of employment, this will cause some rise in home goods prices relative to import prices, which are determined internationally. Employment is maintained as more home goods are consumed domestically, and non-oil exports fall. Overall, consumption has risen as the increase in imports is financed by the rise in oil revenues.[7]

But how do windfalls affect growth? It is generally accepted that, to a greater or lesser extent, growth depends on capital deepening—that is, investment. Investment is constrained by saving. Foreign saving (that is, capital inflows) can augment domestic saving and help accelerate capital accumulation and growth, but at the cost of servicing the acquired foreign liabilities. Oil revenue increases domestic disposable income and therefore should increase both consumption and saving. So, if saving increases, so does investment and, thus, the rate of growth. This conclusion seems to be at variance with the empirical observation that oil economies (or, more generally, resource-endowed economies) perform worse in terms of long-run growth and poverty reduction.

Although there may be some question about the general validity of these observations, there are clearly many instances where they are true, and so the effect of oil on growth warrants more scrutiny:

- Because government owns the oil and is the recipient of the rent, investment may not increase at all. The total rent may go toward increasing consumption, albeit of government-produced goods and services. Thus, the revenue will have no impact on growth.

- Government investment may be inefficient because of poor governance and supervision and, sometimes, corruption. Additionally, government investment booms following revenue windfalls strain implementation capacity, so the investment is simply wasted. During the boom, aggregate demand will increase; but as the boom subsides, a government now dependent on revenues may borrow to maintain spending, eventually leading to a crisis and growth collapse.

- The poor long-run performance is often attributed to the decline of the traditional exports due to the real appreciation. However, the decline in non-oil exports does not necessarily mean a decline in growth. Indeed, because aggregate demand does not decline during the boom, the fall in non-oil exports is offset (and often more than offset) by the rise in home goods (or in nontraded goods) consumption and production. Because, as noted above, the additional consumption and output often come in the form of government goods and services, the public sector becomes the booming sector. All this reallocation of resources, however, has little to do with long-run growth.

- The decline of the non-oil traded goods or non-oil export sector sometimes is viewed as the culprit for another reason: namely, that it has positive externalities that contribute to accelerating growth and development. However, there is little empirical evidence to support this view.

Strengthening the Growth Impact of Oil Revenues

Given the explanation of the links between oil windfalls and growth outlined above, policy measures for mitigating these risks should focus on the following elements:

- *Governance:* The overextension of government noted above may lead to the deterioration of the quality of investment and to increased waste, corruption, and other unproductive activities (rent seeking). As a government minister put it recently, it is not so much a resource curse as a "governance curse."

- *Volatility:* The foregoing text argued that the real appreciation per se (the Dutch disease) was not an adequate explanation for the deleterious effects of oil. However, the real exchange rate may play a role if it is volatile. Thus, if oil revenue itself is volatile—which is likely because oil prices are volatile—then revenues will be volatile. If the revenues are absorbed in the domestic economy, then the turbulence will spill over to the real exchange rate, leading to a boom/bust cycle. This cycle has the effect of increasing uncertainty in the non-oil export (or traded goods) sector and so may result in an increasing risk premium on investment in that sector. This premium would lead to lower investment and lower growth. The government can sterilize the real exchange rate effect by saving part of the windfall offshore. The question of how much to save is, of course, a very complex one. A fairly rough guideline can be derived from consumer theory. That is, the government should save abroad the "transitory" component of the windfall and spend only the "permanent" part. Doing so will not prevent the real appreciation, but it can help smooth or stabilize it over time. This action is sometimes referred to as de-linking current expenditure from current revenue and thus preventing pro-cyclical fiscal behavior.

- *Exhaustibility:* Oil is an exhaustible resource. Most of the countries surveyed in the first section of this chapter face a fairly short time horizon. Therefore, even in the absence of volatility, the oil revenue is a windfall in the sense of its being transitory. Again as in the case of volatility, expenditure smoothing will contribute to the orderly movement of the real exchange rate. However, if the other deleterious effects of the rents are present, then the non-oil sector will not grow as needed; and, as the oil nears depletion, the economy will require painful adjustment.

Fiscal Policy—The Key to Successful Oil Windfall Management

Fiscal policy therefore becomes a critical element for enhancing the growth impact of oil windfalls. Given that the oil industry in African countries functions as an enclave (in the sense that it employs few domestic factors of production and exports all but a negligible part of output) and that the central government owns oil and gas reserves, practically all the rent derived from oil and gas production accrues to the central government. Hence, the impact of the rents on the domestic economy depends almost exclusively on fiscal policy—on how fiscal policy responds to oil revenues and how this policy in turn influences the overall economy.

Expenditure smoothing is the key to avoiding the transmission of volatility of oil prices to the economy. Smoothing expenditures over time will be an antidote to the Dutch disease—the real appreciation will not be avoided, but its turbulence can be significantly reduced. If budgetary expenditure is planned and implemented according to permanent rather than transitory prices, many of the destructive swings in public expenditure can be avoided. This smoothing will help stabilize the real exchange rate. Also, smoothing expenditures means that some revenue will be saved to provide continued income (either from financial assets abroad or from domestic returns to capital, even in the form of the implicit returns to infrastructure) for the time when oil is exhausted.

Over the medium term, the decline in competitiveness in the non-oil traded goods sector is inevitable and can cause short-run hardship and adjustment. However, it need not be terminal. The effect of the real appreciation can, in time, be more than offset by increases in productivity due to technological progress and investment. Therefore, policies to improve the investment climate in the non-oil economy are central to the antidote for the Dutch disease, although they are not a focus of this chapter. Stable fiscal policy to encourage a stable real exchange rate and a sustainable public investment program is one key element (discussed above). Targeting investment and other government expenditure at productive public goods is another.

Oil Funds and Fiscal Rules

For many oil-exporting countries, the problems of volatility and exhaustibility have provided the rationale for saving all or some of the oil revenues in a revenue management fund. If the fund is meant to combat volatility, it is often referred to as a "stabilization" fund; if it is for intertemporal purposes, it is often referred to as a "savings" fund.

However, it is important to point out that a stabilization fund by itself cannot stabilize the real exchange rate. It can stabilize only revenue. But, as explained above, the problem for the economy is the volatility of the real exchange rate, which is caused by volatile expenditure patterns. The challenge for governments, therefore, is to smooth expenditure. To achieve this smoothing, governments have to accumulate and de-cumulate assets as prices (or volumes) rise and fall, which implies the existence of some sort of fund.

A government that does not base current expenditure on current revenue will be using a fund. A stabilization fund, therefore, is something of a misnomer: The fund is the result of a stable fiscal policy rather than its cause. A government that plans for the day the mineral will be depleted will adopt a similar policy. It will target a sustainable level of expenditure, which implies saving some revenue in the present to finance expenditure in the future. Thus, in both cases, a stable and sustainable fiscal policy aims to de-link expenditure from current volatile revenue and to base it on a stable, sustainable source of revenue—namely, the income from the fund.

Fiscal rules that attempt to accommodate both the savings and stabilization objectives typically are based on projecting permanent or sustainable revenue rather than transitory revenue. One possibility is the "permanent income" fiscal rule, which can help policy makers determine how much of the oil windfall a government should spend. According to that fiscal rule, only the permanent (rather than the transitory) component may be spent. Hence, the government, like a private household, should increase consumption only by the amount of the permanent income.

The permanent income from the oil is defined as the amount of the expected revenue stream that could be spent in perpetuity. In this way the benefits of the oil are spread out over generations, and current expenditures are smoothed over time. This has the desired effect of de-linking current consumption expenditure from current revenue, and therefore addresses the problems of volatility and exhaustibility discussed above. However, there are some problems with the approach:

- Should a government of a poor country really expect to allocate consumption expenditure equally in perpetuity? Even if growth of the non-oil sector does not accelerate but remains positive, then the current generation is likely to be the poorest. It would be very difficult for government to deprive the current generation of significant consumption benefits. For example, assume that oil revenue begins to flow in the current period and that non-oil gross domestic product (GDP) continues to grow at, say, 3 percent a year in real per capita terms. Then, in 24 years, non-oil domestic product will have doubled. Even if the oil is exhausted at that time the cohorts born 24 years from that time will enjoy an income twice that of the current generation, which has not yet begun to enjoy the benefits of the oil. Consequently, even prudent benevolent governments may want to include the natural growth of the economy when deciding how to allocate consumption over time.[8]

• Oil prices and production are notoriously difficult to calculate. Estimates would have to be revised continuously, and government will find it difficult to withstand the pressure to spend as it accumulates assets during a lengthy upturn.[9]

A Macroeconomic Model for Managing Africa's Oil Windfalls

The purpose of this modeling exercise is to demonstrate a simple numerical tool for assessing the quantitative macroeconomic impact of the production of oil.[10] The model used must account for the key macroeconomic elements associated with oil-based economies, discussed above. To summarize, the model should show the impact of the revenue on the real exchange rate, on non-oil production, on growth of the non-oil GDP, and on the development of the balance of payments and aggregate consumption. The exercise is highly stylized and should not be regarded as a forecast or prediction. (See the annex for model description.)

At present, African oil exporters are having some measure of success in de-linking current levels of oil revenues from government spending. In 2006, for example, it was estimated that oil exporting countries, such as Angola, Cameroon, Chad, Republic of Congo, Equatorial Guinea, Gabon, and Nigeria, spent on average approximately half of their oil revenues to finance non-oil deficits (IMF 2007). Will this trend continue? More specifically, what would be the effects on growth of higher rates of government spending?

In applying this model to the cases of emerging and mature producers, it is important to point out that in both Mauritania and Nigeria the structure of the balance of payments is such that current observations make it difficult to assess the real exchange rate effect of the windfall or the likely responsiveness of exports to possible future real depreciations. In the case of Nigeria, this difficulty arises because oil and gas exports already so dominate the export sector that the current boom will have no effect on non-oil exports. And, if the real exchange rate depreciates in the future

FIGURE 9.9
Government Oil Revenues, Mauritania, 2005–25

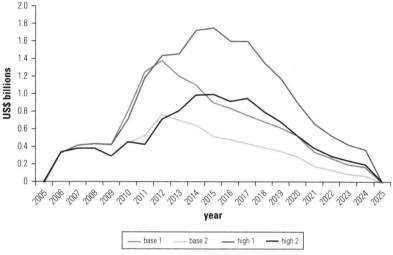

Source: Authors' calculations.

because of investment in the non-oil sector, will non-oil exports materialize? On the basis of experience in many countries—both oil and non-oil exporting—the model assumes that the answer is positive. However, the question warrants further research. An expanded modeling exercise might test the sensitivity of the results with respect to different values for the key elasticities.

The Case of Emerging Producers: Mauritania

Although Mauritania is a new oil producer, its balance of payments is dominated by commodity exports and international aid flows (figure 9.9). Like oil and gas, these flows are not responsive to real exchange rate changes. The real appreciation due to the new windfall is unlikely to have much further effect on noncommodity exports because, to a large extent, these exports already have been squeezed out of the market. Nevertheless, in time, as investment and growth take hold, new noncommodity exports are likely to arise.

Selected results are presented.[11] In the case of Mauritania, there is clear dependence of the real exchange rate on government revenue from oil—simply the government take, equal in domestic currency terms to the net export value of oil[12] (figure 9.10). This dependence results from the specific

FIGURE 9.10
Real Exchange Rate Indexes, Mauritania, 2005–24

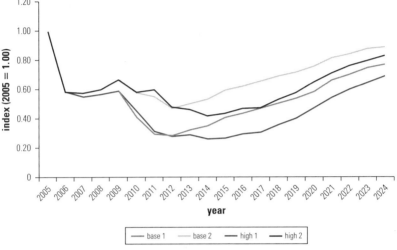

Source: Authors' calculations.

assumption that the government "transfers" the full amount to the private sector, raising disposable income and consumption. Thus, the net revenue is fully absorbed in the domestic economy. If the government were to save all or some of the revenue abroad (for example, in a revenue fund), then the impact on the real exchange rate would be completely or partly sterilized.

The simulations show the potential impact of the oil windfall on non-oil exports, growth, and consumption. According to these results, the real exchange rate will track the absorption of the revenues into the economy, with a smooth path of real appreciation followed by a gradual depreciation.[13] As oil revenues increase, so do non-oil exports, growth, and consumption over the medium term (figures 9.11 and 9.12).

The effect on growth of increasing government consumption from 27 percent of non-oil GDP (the actual estimate for 2007) to 30 percent is to slow growth in all periods until the oil is exhausted. This illustrates the case of shifting some of the benefits to the present (figure 9.13).

At the same time, there are clear vulnerabilities to the macroeconomy. If the simulated time paths do not materialize, the smooth path of the real appreciation followed by a gradual depreciation also will not materialize. Instead, the real exchange rate could be volatile, and the initial decline in

FIGURE 9.11

Non-Oil Exports, Mauritania, 2005–25

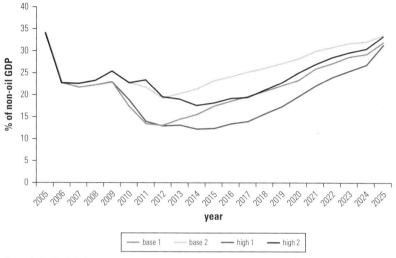

Source: Authors' calculations.

FIGURE 9.12

Non-Oil Growth Rates, Mauritania, 2006–25

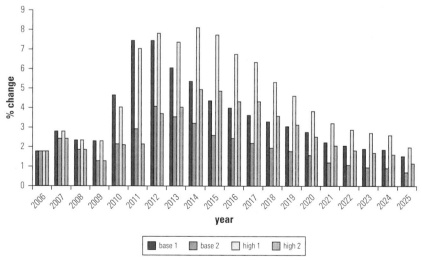

Source: Authors' calculations.

FIGURE 9.13
Non-Oil Growth, Mauritania, 2006–25

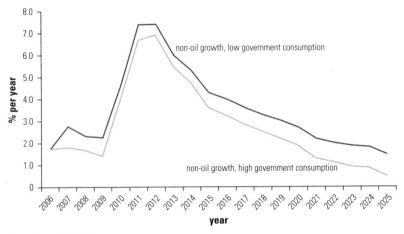

Source: Authors' calculations.

the non-oil sector will not easily be reversed. This outcome suggests that a risk-averse government should avoid at least some of the real appreciation by sterilizing the windfalls.[14]

The Case of Mature Producers: Nigeria

For Nigeria, the model incorporates two cases: In the first case, production of oil and gas was assumed to remain constant at about 3 million barrels per day through 2025 (figure 9.14). In the second case, production declines gradually to about 2 million barrels per day. For both cases, the price (based on the latest World Economic Outlook projections) is assumed to decline gradually over the projection period. Thus, the net rents are assumed to decline gradually, though obviously more steeply, in the second case.

The real exchange rate appreciation is somewhat muted in the initial periods (figure 9.15). Although there is some appreciation, it is less than what would be expected in a new producer. However, the real exchange rate depreciates as the oil revenues decline (figure 9.16). This is due to the combination of the fall in net exports and the relative fall in the price of domestic goods resulting from growth in non-oil domestic goods. (The rate of change in the real exchange rate is shown only for the first case simply to show the slight appreciation initially that is barely discernable from the chart of the real exchange rate indexes.)[15]

FIGURE 9.14
Net Oil/Gas Exports, Nigeria, 2005–25

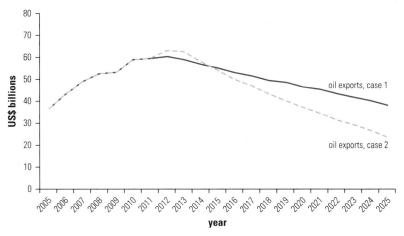

Source: Authors' calculations.

FIGURE 9.15
Real Exchange Rate, Nigeria, 2005–25

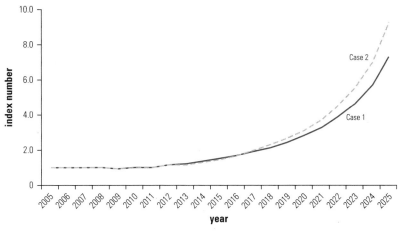

Source: Authors' calculations.

Figure 9.17 shows the correlation between the net revenues to the government and the real exchange rate for both cases.

Finally, in figure 9.18, we show non-oil for the two cases of high and low government consumption.

FIGURE 9.16
Change in Real Exchange Rate, Nigeria, 2005–25

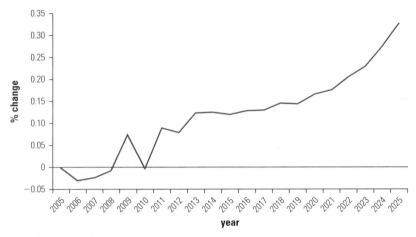

Source: Authors' calculations.

FIGURE 9.17
Real Exchange Rate Index and Net Oil Exports, Nigeria, 2005–25

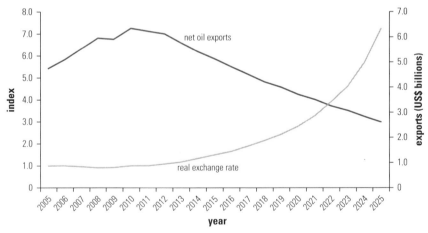

Source: Authors' calculations.

Again, the higher government consumption is, the lower non-oil growth is. Increasing consumption implies lower investment and, therefore, lower growth. This response is a shifting of the benefits from the future to the present. Although in these simulations all increases in saving are domestic, such a situation is unrealistic. In practice, some future benefits are likely to

FIGURE 9.18
Non-Oil Growth, Nigeria, 2005–25

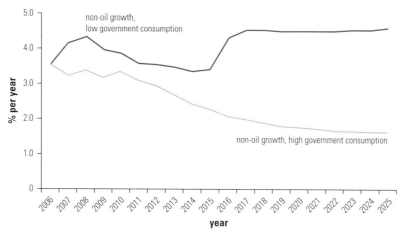

Source: Authors' calculations.

come from income on foreign assets rather than domestic ones (that is, non-oil growth).

Summarizing, to the extent that African oil-exporting governments can break the link between current oil windfalls and current levels of government spending, they will be able to mitigate the damaging effects of volatile real exchange rates on growth. In addition, expenditure smoothing can work to offset the effects of exhaustibility in oil revenues and the associated loss of productivity in the non-oil export sector. The key is fiscal policy and the degree to which governments pass through the effects of oil windfalls into higher levels of saving and investment. This degree can be assessed only in the context of a dynamic macroeconomic framework, which enables policy makers to assess the costs and benefits of varying levels of absorption of the oil windfalls in terms of fiscal deficits and the balance of payments.

Building Transparency and Accountability into the Fiscal Management of Oil Revenues

The ability to smooth fiscal spending in oil-exporting African countries also requires well-functioning fiscal institutions and political incentives conducive to taking into account the welfare of current and future generations.

Doing so is important to align fiscal expenditures with development priorities and to minimize opportunities for rent seeking and corruption. Among the oil exporters surveyed for this chapter, four are in the bottom 5 percent in Transparency International's 2005 Corruption Perceptions Index; Gabon is rated 88/158; and Mauritania was not surveyed. Similarly, among African households, corruption is ranked among the top problems identified as underlying poverty and unemployment (ECA 2005).

Africa's oil windfall poses significant challenges for fiscal institutions. Large oil revenue flows tend to create conditions for rent seeking and corruption in weak institutional frameworks for governance. This finding applies to areas as diverse as (1) the laws governing the uses and controls for oil revenues, (2) government controls over domestic national oil companies (DNOCs), (3) incomplete and low-quality expenditure management processes that fail to effectively target priority areas of expenditure and to deliver the expected outputs and outcomes from the spending, (4) a lack of transparency in government financial reporting, and (5) ineffective auditing of financial management on an ex post basis.

Fiscal Control of Oil Revenues

Control over oil revenues requires a strong public financial management framework based on (1) the fiscal framework within which governments plan and execute their budgets, (2) the budget formulation processes in which spending priorities are established and financed, (3) the budget execution phase where actual spending takes place and where financial controls are executed, (4) the auditing phase that verifies transactions and assesses the robustness of revenue and expenditure processes, and (5) the reporting processes that contribute to transparency and accountability.[16]

One approach to enhancing accountability and transparency in the use of oil windfalls has been to implement specific petroleum-related laws and oil savings/stabilization mechanisms. However, the limitations of such stand-alone mechanisms for improving fiscal management of oil revenues are well documented (Davis, Ossowski, and Fedelino 2003; Devlin and Lewin 2005)—particularly in the case of oil stabilization and savings funds.

In the Africa region, only two countries surveyed have laws in place to govern petroleum management activities: Chad and Gabon. In practice, this legislation has not enhanced the management of oil revenue earnings.

In the case of Chad, legislation governing the use of oil proceeds was highly prescriptive; earmarking of all oil revenue precluded cash management by the treasury and gave rise to arrears, even though there were positive balances in earmarked accounts. The law effectively created a third, parallel budget (IMF 2005, pp. 9–11). It effectively became null and void when parliament adopted amendments to the petroleum revenue management law to increase the government's share of oil revenues (IMF 2006).

Oil revenues enter the budget through a number of taxes that include royalty payments, income taxes, and petroleum profit taxes. These revenues may be paid directly into specific government accounts that are then paid into the consolidated fund and budgeted for expenditures or savings. In some countries, the DNOC receives payments as a participating partner in a joint-venture agreement.

Given that oil revenues constitute such a major percentage of total government revenues, reporting in a full, transparent, and timely manner is essential for the government to prepare accurate revenue forecasts over its planning period, both for direct oil revenues and for related income taxes, value-added taxes, and customs duties arising from oil-related operations. All oil-producing countries should account fully for the activities of their DNOCs.

Of particular concern is the extent to which DNOCs and governments have timely and full access to all relevant information and initiatives. To that issue, the Extractive Industries Transparency Initiative (EITI) has provided a partial answer, Full adherence to EITI's criteria (box 9.2) would make a major contribution to transparency of oil sector operations in implementing countries. To date, however, challenges remain in implementing the EITI. Reporting requirements are large and demand a significant number of entities to operate the process successfully.

The EITI Implementation Advisory Group reported in 2005 that eight countries were in the process of implementing EITI (only Nigeria was among our sample countries), whereas 14 more countries have endorsed the concept and are considering how to proceed with implementation. Our sample countries in the latter category include Angola, Chad, Gabon, Equatorial Guinea, and Mauritania.

Only Nigeria has made significant progress in implementing and submitting an EITI bill to parliament (early 2005). A National Stakeholders Working Group was created; it held consultations with civil society

BOX 9.2

EITI Criteria

1. Regular publication of all material oil and gas payments by companies to governments and all material revenues received by governments from oil, gas, and mining companies to a wide audience, in a publicly accessible, comprehensive, and understandable format.

2. Payments and revenues should be subject to a credible, independent audit by an auditor using international auditing standards.

3. Payments and revenues are reconciled by a credible, independent administrator, applying international auditing standards, who will issue an opinion regarding the reconciliation and the identification of any discrepancies.

4. This approach applies to all companies, including state-owned enterprises (DNOCs)

5. Civil society is actively engaged in the design, monitoring, and evaluation of the process.

6. The government, assisted by international financial institutions, prepares an implementation plan with measurable targets, an implementation timetable, and an assessment of potential capacity constraints.

Source: DFID 2005.

throughout 2005. The first audit examined the operations of the country's oil and gas industry from 1999 to 2004, and reported that 11 companies had underpaid taxes in the amount of hundreds of millions of dollars. In 2002 alone, an estimated $250 million reported by oil companies as payment to the central bank did not appear anywhere in central bank records. The auditor also noted that accounting standards were low in all government agencies audited (Reuters 2006).

In African oil-exporting countries, DNOCs are public enterprises that tend to operate outside of the government's procurement and expenditure control processes. At the same time, however, competencies for oil resource management have developed and remained in the DNOC staff,

TABLE 9.8
Oil Revenue Management Laws and Institutions

Factor	Angola	Chad	Equatorial Guinea	Gabon	Mauritania	Nigeria
Petroleum management law	No	Yes	No. IMF recommended establishment of a clear fiscal policy for oil revenue management.	Yes; also created a FFG.	No	Not yet. FRA was tabled in parliament; not passed.
Revenue accumulation fund	Yes; in the 2005 budget, windfall oil revenues directed to foreign currency reserve account.	No. All oil revenues are budgetary. Direct receipts: 10% to FFG, 72% to PRSP, 13.5% to government, and 4.5% to Doba Basin project.	n.a.	Partial. FFG target is CFAF 500 billion: 10% of oil revenues, 50% of windfall. Has effect of skimming some windfall revenue.	Unknown. Government states it will follow sound oil revenue management principles. IMF calls for strong framework.	Not yet. FRA will require oil windfall revenues to be saved; no current mechanism is in place.
Use of windfall revenues	Offset revenue shortfalls, arrears, and debt reduction	FFG for use after oil reserves are depleted	n.a.	Not specified	IMF recommended an oil stabilization account integrated into the budget.	Offset revenue shortfalls in future budgets

Source: MacDonald 2006.

Note: FFG = Fund for Future Generations; FRA = Fiscal Responsibility Act; n.a. = not applicable; PRSP = Poverty Reduction Strategy Paper.

and, as a result, a number of countries have been assigned responsibilities that really belong to the government. These responsibilities include items such as collection of all receipts due to the government, regulation and enforcement of the oil industry, and management of the concessions granted to individual oil companies. This is the case in Angola, Equatorial Guinea, and Mauritania. Only Nigeria has developed an adequate oversight arrangement for the industry to enhance governance and a degree of transparency (table 9.8, box 9.3).

To deal with this issue and improve accountability with respect to DNOCs, governments must separate the commercial activities of DNOCs from central government functions related to oil revenue management. In

BOX 9.3

Management of Oil Revenues: Important Achievements in Nigeria

1. Separation of commercial responsibilities (Nigerian National Oil Company) from policy and implementation (National Petroleum Investment Management Service) and regulation and monitoring functions (Department of Petroleum Reserves)

2. Legislation of Nigeria EITI (NEITI) to implement the EITI principles (awaiting passage by senate):

    a. NEITI is an autonomous, self-accounting body that ensures due process and transparency in payments made by extractive industry companies to the government; ensures accountability in revenue receipts (by matching to reported payments); eliminates corruption in the determination of revenues due; ensures revenue collection and reporting in the books of the oil companies and the government.

    b. NEITI will develop a framework for transparency in operations and disclosure of revenue due and paid to the government, including operating practices and costs of oil company operations, management

some countries it may be useful to establish an agency to perform the oversight function that is outside civil service salary controls and hierarchical structures (table 9.9). Doing so would enable the entity to compete in the marketplace for high-quality staff skills, while maintaining an accountability link through reporting to a designated minister. Regulatory oversight could be conducted by an internal ministry entity, given that a normal component of government responsibility is regulatory compliance enforcement. The oil industry is simply another application with its own specialized knowledge requirements.

Budgeting Issues

A critical factor for oil-exporting countries is the unity of the government budget and the ability to recognize and track all revenues due to the government.[17] At present, a number of African oil-exporting countries of investments by the federal government, production and sales records details, and monies remitted to the government; it will improve the framework where possible, and publish in transparent fashion reports and information on revenues paid and received.

   c. NEITI will appoint an independent auditor to audit the government revenues paid and due for accuracy and completeness.

3. NEITI reports to the National Stakeholders Working Group (NSWG), which will exercise governance and oversight responsibilities, including approval of plans, the budgets of NEITI, and development of policies and strategies to enhance NEITI's effectiveness as required.

   a. NSWG will have 9–15 members appointed by the president, drawn from the extractive industry, civil society, and labor unions.

   b. Term of office is five years, re-appointment possible.

4. Audit reports are being prepared quarterly as well as annually and are being made public; reports for 2003 and 2004 were published in January 2006.

Source: MacDonald 2006.

maintain extrabudgetary funds, entities, and accounts; in extreme cases, they operate shadow budgets on an informal basis through the DNOC. Most countries have relatively weak accountability links to public enterprises owned and operated by the government, making it possible for the operations of the DNOCs to occur outside the core budget activities of the government.

This problem can be addressed either by full consolidation into the government entity; or by establishing an equivalent reporting regime for budget and actual revenues and expenditures, to be submitted to the government and to parliament at the same time as the regular budget and final accounts are submitted.

Sound budget preparation practices support efficient and effective resource allocations that respond to government priorities. The medium-term expenditure framework (MTEF) is a rolling, three-year framework

TABLE 9.9
DNOC and Government Responsibilities

Factor	Angola	Chad	Equatorial Guinea	Gabon	Mauritania	Nigeria
Domestic national oil company	Sonangol	None	GEPetrol	Société Nationale Pétrolière Gabonaise	Société Mauirtanienne des Hydrocarbures (SMH)	Nigerian National Oïl Company
Separation of DNOC duties from state responsibilities	No. Sonangol performs regulatory and concessionaire functions and QFAs on behalf of government. IMF has recommended that the government functions be repatriated to government.	n.a.	No. GEPetrol performs regulatory and concessionaire functions as agent of the government. IMF recommends clarification of mandate.	—	No. IMF has recommended a framework to formalize SMH responsibilities.	Yes. National Petroleum Investment Management Service and the Department of Petroleum Reserves discharge government's responsibilities.

Source: MacDonald 2006.

Note: — = not available; n.a. = not applicable; QFA = quasi-fiscal activities.

that is updated at least annually and serves as the context for the annual budget. It is comprehensive in scope, provides reasonably accurate estimates of revenue inflows and expenditure outflows, and establishes a firm expenditure ceiling for the next budget cycle and indicative ceilings for the two following years.

In practice, most oil exporters have an MTEF in place for key sectors, with the exceptions of Angola and Gabon. However, in all cases, application of the MTEF to support government priorities is only now being implemented. Nigeria is somewhat the exception with links to government priorities in the 2006 annual budget.

Most African oil exporters maintain fiscal systems characterized by separate and uncoordinated current and investment budgets administered by independent ministries that communicate poorly with each other (table 9.10). This tends to affect the quality of investment when lack of coordination between the two budgets can result in a situation where

TABLE 9.10
Fiscal Processes in African Oil Exporters

Process	Angola	Chad	Equatorial Guinea	Gabon	Mauritania	Nigeria
Budget is unified; all transactions pass through the TSA	No	No	No	No	No	No
MTEF is in place for key sectors	No	Yes	Yes	No	Yes	Yes
MTEF links PRSP priorities	No	—	No	No	No	Yes
Current and investment budgets are integrated	No	No	No	No	No	No
Revenue forecasting and collection are sound and well managed	No	No	—	n.a.	Partial	No
There is functional classification of expenditures	—	Yes	No	No	No	No
Hard budget ceilings and priorities are included in budget call letter	Ceilings only	—	No	No	Indicative ceilings only	Yes
Budget spending is linked to PRSP priorities	No	—	—	No	No	Yes; 75% of outlays in 2006
Budget authorizations are respected in budget spending	No	No	No	No	No	No
Simplified, transparent, and strong expenditure controls exist	No	No	No	No	Yes	No
Computer-based integrated financial management information system is in place	Yes, SIGFE	In upgrade	No	Treasury system	No	Partially; TRRS extended by end 2006
Modern internal audit function is in place in ministries and key agencies	No	No	No	No	No	No
External audit meets INTOSAI requirements	No	No	No	No	No	No; new bill is before parliament
Anticorruption measures are in place	No	—	Yes	No	Yes	Yes
Well-trained financial staff operate the PFM system	No	No	No	No	No	No
There is a culture of accountability for performance	No	No	No	No	No	No
Final budget accounts are accurate and timely, and meet ROSC fiscal transparency requirements	No	No	No	No	No	No

Sources: Various reports by the IMF and the World Bank; MacDonald 2006.

Note: — = not available; INTOSAI = International Organization of Supreme Audit Institutions; MTEF = medium-term expenditure framework; PFM = public financial management; PRSP = Poverty Reduction Strategy Paper; ROSC = Reports on the Observance of Standards and Codes; SIGFE = Integrated State Financial Management System; TRRS = Transaction Recording and Reporting System; TSA = Treasury Single Account.

governments lack sufficient resources to finance a project's ongoing operations. Only Chad has a working functional classification for budgets and expenditures, which is essential for targeting Poverty Reduction Strategy Paper (PRSP) priority areas through the participation of multiple ministries or agencies. In addition, all oil exporters lack adequate revenue forecasting and collection capabilities, a critical shortcoming.

Budgets are designed to reflect government spending priorities within available resources. Use of ceilings and government or ministry priorities is intended to prevent a laundry-list type of approach to budgeting and is particularly critical in the context of oil-exporting African countries. Best-practice countries exercise a budget challenge at each level of aggregation to ensure that requests reflect ministry priorities and respect budget ceilings. This challenge process can help ensure that effective spending priorities will be reflected in the budget (box 9.4).

For individual ministries, budget ceilings force a ranking of priority investments and other resource requests. Effective ceilings provide the basis for a review of budget proposals within the ministry and from the individual ministry to the ministry of finance (MOF). Mandatory budget ceilings should be a standard component of every process in oil-exporting African countries, together with clear statements of the government's priorities in upcoming years. These priorities can be derived from PRSP or

---

BOX 9.4

Best Practices in Budget Preparation

- Determine hard ministry budget ceilings and government priorities.

- Require ministry budgets to respect ceilings in budget proposals.

- Allocate resources consistently to priority areas.

- Determine subceilings and local priorities for ministry budgets.

- Use functional classification to identify priority spending areas.

- Perform internal budget challenge process.

Source: MacDonald 2006.

Millennium Development Goals targets previously agreed by the government, and ministry budget submissions should be strictly reviewed for compliance against these priorities.

Although a number of African oil exporters currently stipulate budget ceilings, only Nigeria attempts to link this ceiling to budget priorities. The effective linking of projects to priorities is an issue currently being addressed in most countries and should continue to be a high priority going forward.

In practice, oil-exporting African countries exhibit problems in compliance with budget ceilings. Whereas some countries maintain a range of expenditures (emergency spending), which can be authorized and subsequently approved by the government on an ex post basis, other countries (such as Angola) have no legal limits on spending, borrowing, or the level of the deficit. Nigeria has maintained a long history of noncompliance with budget limits, without penalties being imposed. Finally, in Gabon, departments have the authority to carry over old-year uncommitted balances into the new budget without subsequent approval by parliament.

Ideally, governments should develop a three- to five-year time series or calendar of budget requests, budgets approved, and budget utilization by individual sectors. Doing so would enable better tracking relative to government priorities such as pro-poor spending patterns in budget plans and in execution, thereby assessing resource planning and utilization efficiency. Given that there are no such data readily available, it would be a good area for further horizontal analysis of oil-exporting countries, along with the development of indicators and targets for benchmarking across countries.

Fiscal transparency Reports on the Observance of Standards and Codes and other analytic studies suggest that all African oil exporters suffer from poor budget reporting practices. Budget reports are uniformly late (some by several periods) and poor data quality prevents reconciliations and audits—a critical area that needs to be addressed to enhance transparency.

Internal Controls

Internal controls guide the spending processes of governments and are particularly critical in the oil-exporting context. Such measures are also vital for reducing the incidence of fraud and corruption. For most African oil exporters, internal spending controls are characterized by heavy ex ante controls at the commitment phase, exercised by multiple parties resulting in overlap and duplication. Only Angola has simplified and streamlined its internal control regime, emphasizing ex post controls as much as ex ante controls. Ex post controls are largely deficient across the board, and that deficiency is problematic, given the potential for increased oil revenue flows through the budget.

Complex expenditure controls and in-year cash rationing by the MOF tend to reduce budget effectiveness in African oil-exporting countries. Only Mauritania has effectively simplified and streamlined its system of commitment controls. Chad, conversely, maintains 14 distinct steps, involving 28 different actions to initiate and complete a purchase and payment transaction (World Bank 2004, pp. 8–9). Processing time varies from one month to nine months, depending on the transaction type and complexity. This delay is a serious deficiency. Because the current budgets are largely salary related, they are less likely to be cash rationed as governments are reluctant to incur payroll arrears for the civil service unless absolutely necessary. This reluctance results in greater cash rationing for the investment budgets with at least two adverse effects: (1) investment projects are generally in programs that deliver services for citizens, and cuts thereby deny citizens the planned outcomes; and (2) unstable government capital expenditure patterns adversely affect private sector productivity through the commercial suppliers to government.

Public procurement is a vital part of the overall system of internal controls and should conform to international standards. International best practice requires the widespread use of international competitive tendering, the use of standardized bidding documents, contracts, and selection procedures. These procedures must be guided by transparency, the absence of conflict of interest, and full disclosure of individual tender results (including the name of the successful bidder and the value of the bid).

In addition, the acquisition of a new financial management information system (FMIS) is an opportunity to scale back and simplify the internal controls and delegate many of the currently centralized approval functions to ministries and districts. A modern and comprehensive FMIS is an essential component of sound oil revenue management and control over budget execution. Lack of such a system is a common shortcoming among African oil exporters. Chad's budget execution system is being upgraded as part of International Monetary Fund conditionality under the three-year Poverty Reduction and Growth Facility arrangement; however, a fully integrated system is still lacking. Angola's system is functioning well, and Gabon has a treasury system in place. All other surveyed countries have serious deficiencies in their FMISs. A critical priority for governments wishing to track, monitor, and control oil revenues and to minimize exposure to corrupt practices and financial loss is the accelerated development of a modern FMIS.[18]

Audits

Although most African oil-exporting countries have internal inspection units that perform ex ante controls over planned spending, often there are several independent entities performing what is essentially the same audit. Another weakness is the bias toward compliance-based audits, focusing on the legality of the transactions, rather than a modern internal audit.

Under the best circumstances, modern internal audit functions include ex post audits to provide management with information as to how well internal controls are performing. At present, however, there is no capacity in any of the African oil exporters to undertake a modern internal audit, and any initiative to implement such a function will represent a major change in the current culture of compliance auditing. This initiative also will require considerable technical training assistance over many years. In the interim, more emphasis should be placed on upgrading the external audit function.

Most external auditor organizations in African oil-exporting countries are relatively young and inexperienced. Few, if any, of these organizations meet the International Organization of Supreme Audit Institutions' (INTOSAI's) requirements for auditor independence in reporting relationships, financing, and other matters (box 9.5).

The Cours des Comptes in Chad, for example, reports not to parliament but to the president of the Supreme Court, who also determines the organization's budget. Its audit program covers the Supreme Court, but does not cover foreign-financed funds in the final budget report; the organization can be affected by specific audit requests from the executive or from parliament, without any budgetary offsets (World Bank 2004).

For many oil exporters, external audit staff skills are not well developed and there is a need for the external audit function to perform in conformance with international standards. The majority of external audit entities do not have the staff levels or supporting equipment necessary to perform their role as external auditors. In this regard, priority activities should be to improve the quantity and the quality of the external audit staff and to

BOX 9.5

INTOSAI Audit Standards for External Auditors

1. Independence

   • The auditors will be outside the entity that they are auditing and protected from undue influence.

   • The auditors have the functional and organizational independence to accomplish their tasks,

   • Establish external auditor independence in the Constitution

   • The auditors have the financial resources necessary to accomplish their task.

2. Relationships to parliament and government

   • Relationships with parliament are established in law.

   • The auditor has a high degree of initiative and autonomy, even when acting as an agent of parliament.

   • The Supreme Audit Institution (SAI) audits all government entities, including extrabudgetary funds, public enterprises, and joint ventures controlled by the state; this includes DNOCs and joint ventures.

   • The SAI reports its findings annually and independently to the parliament; reports are published.

   • Public authorities and other institutions established abroad are audited by the SAI.

   • The auditor gives particular attention to the audit of public works and public contracts.

Source: INTOSAI, Lima Declaration, www.intosai.org.

provide a continuous learning process that will permit them to acquire the necessary knowledge of international audit standards.

In the short term, governments also can make significant improvements to external audit functions a high priority. Doing so will be the fastest and easiest way to acquire an enhanced audit capacity that can respond to the need of an oil-exporting country. Governments should ensure that their external audit organizations meet all of the international standards for external auditors set by INTOSAI; resolve outstanding issues of auditor independence; and ensure the use of modern external audit techniques, staff training, and provision of adequate audit resources.

External auditors then could focus audits on the areas of greatest fiduciary risk within the government reporting entity. Such a focus likely will involve the use of international audit firms skilled in auditing particular aspects of oil revenue management, forensic (fraud) audits, value-for-money studies of PRSP expenditures, and any other specific audit assignment where skill requirements exceed the Supreme Audit Institution's internal capabilities.

Over the medium term, governments should work toward establishing a modern internal audit function initially in the MOF. Such a unit could focus on high-risk areas, such as processes involving the calculation of oil and gas revenues due from international oil companies and the DNOC, the collection of payments, revenue accounting and banking arrangements for all royalties and contractual revenues, as well as the contracting procedures for large-value investment projects. Implementation of internal audits in all ministries is likely to be a long-term project with a time horizon of 5 to 10 years.

Summary of Best Practices and Recommendations
A summary of best practices for oil revenue management effectiveness is presented in table 9.11. In addition, implementation of these recommendations can be tracked in terms of progress achieved by using the relevant public expenditure and financial accountability (PEFA) indicators and a performance-measuring framework for sound public financial management.

For mature producer countries such as Angola and Nigeria, the challenges of improving transparency and accountability in oil windfalls require (1) ensuring a well-developed revenue forecasting and management capacity within the government; (2) implementing the EITI process for all oil producers and the government; (3) fully implementing the MTEF and tracking monthly budget utilization in priority PRSP areas, holding responsible civil servants accountable for progress; (4) ensuring a clear separation of functions between the government and its DNOC; and (5) strengthening external audit to international standards and requiring auditors to focus their audits on areas of greatest fiduciary risk.

TABLE 9.11
Best Practice for African Oil-Exporters and the PEFA Performance Measurement Framework

Best practice	PEFA indicator	How measured
Bring DNOC within a government budget entity, or ensure equivalent disclosure.	Comprehensive budget information in document [PI 6]	Measure against nine information benchmarks
Develop in-house forecasting skills for key economic parameters, especially oil revenues.	Comparison of aggregate expenditures and revenues— actual and budget; planned vs. actual composition of expenditures [PI 1–3]	Measure of variance of actual vs. forecast, as a percentage of forecast
Implement an efficient budget preparation process, using an MTEF with fixed budget ceilings and annual budget priorities; rigidly enforce ministry compliance.	Orderly and participative budget preparation process; multiyear planning and budgeting process [PI 11–12]	Rate against three criteria: fixed budget calendar; comprehensive guidance with political input; timely approval by parliament. Functional analyses; debt sustainability analyses; costed sector strategies and links between investment budgets and multiyear spending estimates
Develop and implement an FMIS, among other things to record and control all oil revenue transfers and PRSP expenditures. Doing so also will enable the restructuring of the financial control and management processes, eliminate overlapping agencies and duplicative functions, increase process efficiency and effectiveness, and reduce staff costs.	Timeliness and regularity of accounts reconciliation, in-year budget reports and annual financial statements [PI 22–24, 25]	Regularity of reconciliations; timeliness, quality, and scope of in-year reports and annual financial statements
Track and report budget utilization, especially on PRSP priority services affecting citizens.	Quality and timeliness of in-year and annual budget reports and financial statements [PI 24, 25]	Regularity of reconciliations; timeliness, quality, and scope of in-year reports and annual financial statements
Decentralize financial controls to ministries and regional offices, thereby simplifying and removing excessive complexity, undue bureaucratic influence, and discretion.	Effectiveness of controls for taxpayer registration, collection of taxes due, payrolls, procurement, and nonsalary expenditures [PI 14, 15, 18–20]	Effectiveness of controls for taxpayer registration, collection of taxes due, payrolls, procurement, and nonsalary expenditures; commitment controls in place; adherence to internal control processes in place or planned; compliance with rules for transaction processing and recording
Impose a system of financial accountability on public officials, including conflict of interest disclosures and civil and criminal penalties for faulty or illegal performance.	n.a.	n.a.

TABLE 9.11
(continued)

Best practice	PEFA indicator	How measured
Apply international standards of procurement practice to all government and DNOC contracting and procurement activities.	Competition, VFM, and controls in procurement [PI 19]	Evidence of use of open, competitive procurement processes, justification for deviations, and existence and effective operation of a complaints process.
Ensure a separation of functions between the DNOC and government so that the DNOC does not perform noncommercial activities that are the responsibility of government.	n.a.	n.a.
Adopt and fully implement the EITI regime for disclosure and reconciliation of oil companies and the government oil revenues and receipts.	Resource extractors tax issues [PI 13–15]	Clarity and comprehensiveness of tax liabilities, good access to data on tax liabilities, administrative procedures, existence of a complaints procedure, controls in the tax registration system, effectiveness of mass registration procedures, audits
Ensure that the government has access to the skills necessary to perform its share of the EITI agreement.	n.a.	n.a
Develop and implement modern internal audits in all ministries and agencies.	Effectiveness of internal audit [PI 21]	Measurement of coverage and frequency of audits, frequency and distribution of audit reports, management acceptance of IA recommendations
Strengthen external audits by establishing full compliance with INTOSAI standards and accelerate staff training in modern audit techniques.	Scope, nature, and follow-up of external audit [PI 21]	Scope and nature of audit conducted, use of international auditing standards
Supplement audit capacity limitations through the generous use of international auditors to audit all key financial process that are corruption prone in an oil-producing country.	n.a.	n.a.

Source: MacDonald 2006.

Note: IA = internal audit; n.a. = not applicable; PI = PEFA indicator; VFM = value for money.

TABLE 9.12
Administrative Conditions Most Susceptible to Rent Seeking and Corruption in African Oil-Exporting Countries

Condition Favoring Rent Seeking and Corruption	Explanation
Excessive concentration of discretionary authority in the hands of individual civil servants	This condition can occur particularly where procurement activities are carried out without an acceptable contracting framework in place.
Complex financial administration with multiple layers of bureaucracy	When many people share responsibility for revenue or other expenditure controls, no one feels responsible. Multiple decision points slow approvals and create an environment for rent-seeking behavior to accelerate a slowly moving approval process.
Weaknesses in organizational and administrative systems	Weak budgeting systems can result in resource allocations that may steer resources away from priority areas and prevent effective spending of allocated funds. Extrabudgetary entities and DNOCs operating outside the budget, overseen by weak, low-capacity government entities, offer the opportunity for detection-free diversion of revenues away from the state.
Excessive organizational concentration or centralization of authority	Separation of functions between those involved in operating an oil-producing company and those relating to the administration or regulation of the country's natural resource base should be mandatory. If necessary, specific new entities should be established to manage the state's oil and gas resources.
Lack of transparency in PFM and inadequate reporting	Public accountability of government generally, and for oil revenues in particular, demands the highest standard of transparency and reporting on the sources and disposition of oil revenues by the government and the DNOC. The latter should be held to the highest standards of transparency and regular reporting to the government and the public on all aspects of its oil and gas production activities.
Inadequate external audit mechanisms	Weak courts of account are unable to properly perform their audits for noncompliance, fraud, and corruption; in the absence of an effective internal audit function, this represents a serious shortcoming. DNOCs that are not subject to annual external audit by a capable, international audit firm using international methods are more able to conceal revenue diversions, side payments, export volume/quality mismeasurements, and other fraudulent activities.

Sources: INTOSAI workshop on Supreme Audit Institutions and corruption, undated; MacDonald 2006.

Five immediate priorities are recommended for emerging oil-producing countries: (1) get a sound fiscal framework in place to stabilize the fiscal environment and insulate it from oil revenue volatility; (2) establish a unified budget, eliminating all extrabudgetary funds, agencies, and accounts; (3) require the DNOC (where it exists), other oil companies, and all government agencies to fully adhere to the EITI process; (4) implement a modern FMIS; and (5) strengthen external audit to international standards and require auditors to focus their audits on areas of greatest fiduciary risk.

Rent Seeking

The extent to which fiscal rules and institutions can enhance transparency and accountability in the use of oil windfalls will depend critically on the degree to which professional administrative bodies can function adequately in a rent-seeking environment. Rent seeking, or the use of scarce resources to compete for access to pure transfers, is a costly form of political competition and tends to be extreme in oil-exporting states.

In identifying appropriate measures to mitigate rent-seeking behavior, it is important to point out that the costs and benefits of such behavior are not static; in fact, they tend to vary with the costs of enforcement and organization, among others. In the case of African oil-exporting countries, the prevalence of weak administrative conditions substantially raises the potential benefits from rent seeking and corruption (table 9.12).

Conclusion

Africa's oil windfall holds significant promise for creating sustainable improvements in living standards. But much will depend on the extent to which policy makers manage the fiscal and political costs and benefits associated with absorption of oil revenues.

Today, Africa's oil reserves are expected to generate a windfall with a net present value of nearly $300 billion, discounted at 10 percent—an amount larger than the continent's external debt burden. However, this windfall is temporary: reserves likely will be depleted among the largest African oil producers by 2035.

Transforming this windfall into the basis for sustainable growth is an urgent but complex process. Africa's oil windfall is large, exhaustible, and volatile. Policy makers, therefore, must be able to estimate and predict oil revenue flows within some bounds of certainty and to identify appropriate levels of saving and investment. Doing so requires accurate and timely information on the government take from oil revenues—an estimate that varies with factors both external and internal to policy control. Using

Wood Mackenzie's Global Economic Model and various price scenarios, we estimate that the total government take from current windfalls ranges from a low of $4 billion in Mauritania to a high of $151 billion in Nigeria between 2006 and 2011.

However, this windfall in and of itself does not translate into a permanent increase in wealth. What is needed is a medium-term fiscal policy framework in which policy makers can make decisions about savings and investment, based on the impact of oil revenues on the real exchange rates, non-oil production, growth of non-oil GDP, the balance of payments, and aggregate consumption. Using a simple macro-model, we show that, for both emerging and mature oil producers, higher rates of government consumption of current oil revenues lead to higher and more volatile real exchange rate appreciation and to lower non-oil growth, relative to a smoother path of consumption spending unrelated to current oil prices. This finding suggests that risk-averse governments can avoid at least some of the real appreciation by sterilizing windfalls while shifting some of the benefits of current oil windfalls partially to future generations.

Implementing such fiscal policy, however, requires a well-functioning system of fiscal control—processes and institutions—as well as political incentives conducive to balancing the welfare of current and future generations. Policy makers can strengthen oil reporting mechanisms, together with budget formulation processes (in which spending priorities are established and financed) and budget execution (where actual spending takes place and where financial controls are executed). Timely and transparent measures for budget auditing and reporting are also critical for enhancing the transparency and accountability in fiscal spending of oil revenues.

However, the extent to which fiscal rules and institutions can enhance transparency and accountability in the use of oil revenues will depend also on the degree to which professional administrative bodies can function adequately in a rent-seeking environment. Rent-seeking or the use of scarce resources to compete for access to pure transfers is a costly form of political competition and tends to be extreme in oil-exporting states.

A number of studies point to the prevalence of rent seeking and clientelism as a major dynamic in African politics. Although many studies rightly point to the importance of constitutional checks and balances, civil society, and the media in improving management of oil windfalls, this chapter has focused primarily on the effectiveness of the budgetary process in addressing governance-related challenges of oil windfalls. The premise is that channeling rent-seeking behavior into well functioning, formal budgetary institutions and processes can provide greater oversight and accountability over competition for resource rents.

Annex: Key Features of the Model

The model used is a dynamic aggregative model. That is, it is based on a single produced good. The basic structure is therefore very simple.[19] The price of this good—the home good—is determined domestically. Purchasing power parity, therefore, does not hold in this model. The domestic good is consumed domestically, invested, or exported. If domestic prices rise relative to foreign prices, exports will decline, and vice versa. The home-good model provides a simple alternative to explicitly modeling the traded/nontraded goods distinction, and it yields similar results with greater economy. The growth process is also modeled. The essentials of the model do not depend on the specific production function used. In this particular case a simple linear function is used (see Lewin 2006).

The real exchange rate is an endogenous variable. The exact solution depends on the import and export elasticities. The real exchange rate then can be used to solve for the implied nominal exchange rate and domestic prices, depending on the exchange rate regime or the nominal exchange rate or inflation targets. For a new discovery, the model shows an initial decline in non-oil exports. However, the model also shows that this is reversed as productivity rises with capital deepening due to the rise in investment.

Money is assumed to be neutral. This is to emphasize that the key impacts of oil or oil windfalls are real in the sense that they affect real variables, such as real consumption, net exports, saving/investment, and growth. However, the model extends the standard World Bank flow of funds framework such as is found in a typical revised minimum standard model–extended (RMSMX). Thus, the output can be used to produce a standard RMSMX output, including the monetary sector, if it is needed. We did not do so in this exercise because the focus here is on the real side.

A key element of this exercise is the assumption that the government saves all the revenue from oil domestically by not increasing expenditure and by holding the fiscal deficit constant. Thus, with expenditure and the fiscal deficit/surplus constant and oil revenue increasing, the windfall finances a reduction in non-oil taxes (or, if these are negligible, an increase in transfers to the private sector). This assumption may seem strange but, in fact, it is an interesting limiting case for the following reason. Other things being equal, the reduction in taxes (or the increase in transfers) to the private sector increases the sector's disposable income; and assuming that the marginal and average propensity to save/consume is constant, then overall savings/consumption ratios of the economy will remain unchanged. It therefore provides a kind of benchmark case for how a windfall could affect an economy if it were saved and consumed in the same proportions as existed in the economy before the windfall.

Notes

1. This section is based on Andreassen (2006). Data analysis is based on Wood Mackenzie's Global Economic Model.
2. The spike in capital costs in 2006 was due to M'Via, the only projected new field to come on line in the near future.
3. In some cases, deductions can be made from the revenues used to calculate royalties. For example costs of handling, storing, and transporting oil to a terminal or refinery in Nigeria can be deducted before royalty is assessed.
4. Profit oil is the amount of production (after deducting the cost of oil production allocated to costs and expenses) that will be divided between the participating parties and the host government under the production-sharing contract.
5. The definition of government *take* includes royalties, corporate income tax, government share of production, state equity cash flow, and any petroleum-specific taxation.
6. Estimates are for the period covering 2006–11. A major source of income for African oil-exporting governments are domestic national oil companies (DNOCs). In some countries, the DNOC receives the government's share of production sharing, or it is in charge of receiving fees and royalties. In other countries, the DNOC operates on a similar basis as other companies, although this is the exception rather than the rule. Estimates of the government take detailed below are likely to be understated because of a lack of adequate information regarding the activities of DNOCs.
7. In the aggregative model, an exogenously caused increase in exports (for example, caused by a rise in foreign income) will raise export prices and therefore the price of home goods. Export supply may be expected to rise in response to the higher prices but at the cost of lower consumption of the home-produced goods. Consumption of the relatively cheaper imports will rise. Thus, the improvement in the terms of trade is clearly welfare enhancing

and, unlike the case of foreign transfers, there is no apparent downside in terms of loss of produced exports.

8. Formally, one could say that government should take into account the permanent or expected income from all assets, oil and capital.

9. Even super-prudent Norway has had great difficulty withstanding the pressure to increase expenditure in the current boom.

10. Thilakaratna Ranaweera contributed to the modeling exercise discussed in this section.

11. For more details in the Mauritania case, see World Bank (2006). Simulations for Mauritania used the latest International Monetary Fund (IMF) data and oil data provided by World Bank staff. The framework was simplified by normalizing all variables with initial (non-oil) GDP equal to 100. Thus, all indicators are proportional to GDP. The initial real exchange rate is set equal to 1. The base case and high case refer to differing oil prospects. For each production profile, a lower price and a higher price were assumed. The model is constrained to balance trade at the end of the projection period.

12. That is, all profit and other remittances and associated imports are netted out. The remaining "rent" is made up from the taxes and royalties paid to the government. Payments to other domestic factors and domestic consumption of oil are considered negligible.

13. In some sense, this is a best-case scenario because the transfer of the rents to the private sector assumes that domestic saving will increase and so growth will increase, and, in time, non-oil exports will rise.

14. Thus, a useful extension of the model would be to model a stochastic time path for oil revenues rather than the smooth ones modeled above. A smooth path could be considered the expected or reference path, and deviations above or below it would elicit accumulation or depletion of foreign assets, respectively.

15. As the real exchange rate depreciates, non-oil net exports will rise. This occurs via a decline in imports, a rise in exports, or some combination thereof.

16. This section is based on MacDonald (2006).

17. There may be several entities relating to the government. These may include the narrowly defined entities financed through the budget (the budget entity): the budget entity plus extrabudgetary funds, entities, and accounts; the previous entity plus public enterprises; and the previous entity plus other levels of government financed directly from the state budget.

18. There are a number of mid-size FMIS software packages on the market that could be implemented relatively quickly; doing so would be preferable to using internally developed software, unless such work is already well under way. Regardless of the system employed, it should be capable of covering all budgetary and extrabudgetary operations of major entities, such as the DNOC and all other resource-based public enterprises.

19. This section is based on Lewin (2006). The technical solution to the model is described in the appendix to that report, which also shows how the model can be tied in to a standard World Bank flow of funds model.

References

Andreassen, O. 2006. "Estimating the Size of Africa's Oil Windfall." Photocopy. Oil, Gas, and Mining Unit, International Bank for Reconstruction and Development, Washington, DC.

Auty, R. 1998. "Resource Abundance and Economic Development: Improving the Performance of Resource-Rich Countries." Research for Action 44. United Nations University/World Institute for Development Economics Research, Helsinki.

Bates, R. 1983. *Essays on the Political Economy of Rural Africa.* African Studies Series. Cambridge, UK: Cambridge University Press.

Collier, P., and J. Gunning. 1996. "Policy Towards Commodity Shocks in Developing Countries." Working Paper 96/84, International Monetary Fund, Washington, DC.

Collier, P., and A. Hoffler. 2002. "Greed and Grievance in African Civil Wars." Photocopy. World Bank, Washington, DC.

Davis, J., R. Ossowski, and A. Fedelino, eds. 2003. *Fiscal Policy Formulation and Implementation in Oil-Producing Countries.* Washington, DC: International Monetary Fund.

Devlin, J., and M. Lewin. 2005. "Managing Oil Booms and Busts in Developing Countries." In *Managing Economic Volatility and Crises: A Practitioner's Guide,* ed. J. Aizenman and B. Pinto, 186–211. Cambridge, UK: Cambridge University Press.

DFID (U.K. Department for International Development). 2005. *Source Book.* http://www.eitransparency.org.

ECA (Economic Commission for Africa). 2005. *African Governance Report.* Addis Ababa.

Gelb, A., and Associates. 1988. *Oil Windfalls: Blessing or Curse?* New York: Oxford University Press.

IMF (International Monetary Fund). 2005. Chad: Request for a Three-Year Arrangement under the PRGF and Additional Interim Assistance under the Enhanced HIPC Initiative. Washington, DC.

———. 2006. Statement by First Deputy Managing Director Anne O. Kruger on Chad. Washington, DC.

———. 2007. *Regional Economic Outlook: Sub-Saharan Africa.* Washington, DC.

Isham, J., L. Pritchett, M. Woolcock and G. Busby, 2003. "The Varieties of the Resource Experience: How Natural Resource Export Structures Affect the Political Economy of Economic Growth." Photocopy. World Bank, Washington, DC.

Lewin, M. 2006. "Notes on Modeling the Macroeconomic Impact of Oil Revenues." Photocopy. World Bank, Washington, DC.

MacDonald, A. 2006. "Fiscal Policy and Revenue Transparency: Public Financial Management Strategy for African Oil and Gas Producers." Photocopy. World Bank, Washington, DC.

Reuters. 2006. "Millions Missing from Nigeria Oil Account Audit." April 12.

Sachs, J., and A. Warner. 1995. "Natural Resource Abundance and Economic Growth." Working Paper W5398, National Bureau of Economic Research, Cambridge, MA.

Sklar, R. L., and C. S. Whitaker. 1991. *African Politics and Problems in Development.* Boulder, CO: Rienner.

Tornell, A., and P. Lane. 1999. "Voracity and Growth." *American Economic Review* 89: 22–46.

World Bank. 2004. "Tchad: Évaluation de la Gestion des Finances Publiques et des Pratiques Comptables du Secteur Prive." Photocopy. Washington, DC.

———. 2006. "Mauritania: Managing Natural Resources: Challenges and Options, Country Economic Memorandum Update." Sector Report 36386. Washington, DC.

CHAPTER 10

Managing Oil Revenue Volatility in Nigeria: The Role of Fiscal Policy

Nina Budina and Sweder van Wijnbergen

Not since the 1979–80 oil price hikes have oil prices been so high above historical averages for so long. Moreover, available forecasts indicate that this latest price boom, which started in 2000, could persist for another five to seven years beyond the time of writing. This boom presents oil-exporting countries with a unique opportunity to remedy what has been labeled the "resource curse." International evidence suggests this is not an easy challenge: resource-rich countries are characterized by slow or stagnating growth, de-industrialization, low savings, lagging human and physical capital accumulation, and stagnating or declining productivity.

Manzano and Rigobon (2001) have suggested a link between debt problems and slow growth in resource-rich countries, but have not identified the specific channels through which this link operates. Indeed, in spite of their resource wealth, a large number of resource-rich countries remain classified by the World Bank as severely indebted countries with high levels of external debt making them vulnerable to exchange rate fluctuations induced by volatile resource prices.[1] Public indebtedness also tends to be high in oil-exporting countries, and a substantial number of them have run into debt problems (for example, Angola, Chad, Ecuador, Iraq, Mexico, the Russian Federation, Sudan, the República Bolivariana de Venezuela, and the Republic of Yemen), mostly when oil prices were in decline but some even in boom periods. Budina, Pang, and van Wijnbergen (2007) have provided econometric evidence showing that the volatility of expenditure was increased by debt overhang problems. This evidence suggests that fiscal policy design should pay special attention to downside risk. Debt overhang problems imply that world capital markets become inaccessible at precisely the moment they are needed most.

This chapter focuses on the role of fiscal policy in managing the volatility of oil wealth and its implications for debt and development. We show that Nigeria's fiscal policy has increased volatility beyond that stemming from oil price variance. The chapter uses the lessons from poor management of oil wealth in Nigeria to derive a framework that can be used to assess fiscal sustainability and vulnerability to debt overhang problems in oil-rich countries. To that end, the case of Nigeria, interesting in its own right, is also of wider interest to other oil-rich countries, given the opportunities and challenges presented by the recent oil boom. We use this framework to assess the oil price fiscal rule (OPFR) recently adopted in Nigeria and show that it is not robust against plausible downside risks.

The next section of this chapter distills lessons for macroeconomic management of the oil windfall, emphasizing the challenge of managing volatility in a poor institutional environment. The third section presents a framework for assessing fiscal sustainability and vulnerability to debt overhang problems in oil-rich countries. The fourth section applies this framework to Nigeria, and the final section offers our conclusions. The chapter annex explains the derivation of public debt decomposition dynamics.

Oil Wealth and the Poor Growth Record: Lessons for the Future

Nigeria discovered oil in 1956 and began to export it in 1958. Since the oil discoveries in the early 1970s, oil has become the dominant factor in Nigeria's economy. Using 1970 as a benchmark, Nigeria gained an extra $390 billion[2] in oil-related fiscal revenue over the period 1971–2005, or 4.5 times 2005 gross domestic product (GDP), expressed in constant 2000 dollars. The sizable oil windfall, of course, presented net wealth and thus additional spending room, but it also has complicated macroeconomic management and led to an extreme dependency on oil—a highly volatile source of income. The share of mining in total GDP increased substantially, representing about a half of GDP in 2005. Oil also accounts for about 90 percent of total exports and approximately four-fifths of total government revenues (see figure 10.1).

FIGURE 10.1
Indicators of Oil Dependence, Nigeria, 1970–2006

a. Oil dependence

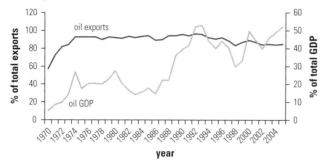

b. Revenue dependence on oil

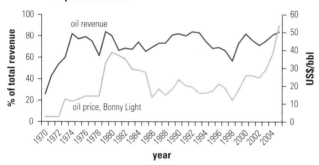

Sources: World Bank 2003; authors' calculations; World Economic Outlook data.

Since the oil discoveries in the early 1970s made Nigeria one of the world's top 10 oil exporters, the Nigerian economy has followed the boom/bust cycles of the world oil market. Yet the many years with oil money have not brought the population an end to poverty nor, at least until recently, have they enabled the economy to break out of what seems like perennial stagnation in the non-oil economy (see figure 10.2).

Is this record the unavoidable consequence of the so-called resource curse, or have misguided policies contributed to slow growth? Traditional among explanations of poor performance in oil-rich countries is the so-called Dutch disease, named after Holland's poor record in managing its natural gas wealth in the 1960s (Corden and Neary 1984; van Wijnbergen 1984a, 1984b). The literature points out that spending out of oil wealth increases demand for nontradables and so draws productive resources into that sector. Because the presumption is that technological progress is faster

FIGURE 10.2
Real Per Capita Income, Nigeria, 1970–2006

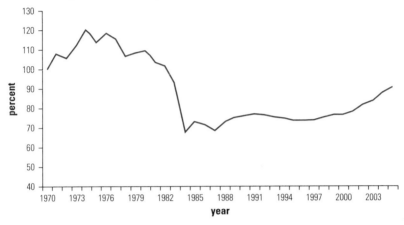

Sources: Authors' calculations; World Bank 2003; World Economic Outlook data.

in traded sectors than in nontraded sectors, the explanation of low growth naturally follows. Moreover, if some of the higher growth is related to effects that are not captured directly by private entrepreneurs, such as sectorwide learning-by-doing effects, there is a case for an explicit government-supported economic diversification strategy (van Wijnbergen 1984b).

However, only when oil revenues are temporary and, critically, capital market failures or misguided spending policies cause an associated tempo- rary spending boom does a strong case for industrial diversification emerge. Countries following a permanent income rule, sharing the oil wealth with future generations and smoothing out expenditure into the far future, do not need to face a near future without oil wealth and with depressed economic activity, and therefore have no need to worry about future declines in exchange rates. In such circumstances, there is no clear- cut case in favor of intensified diversification policies after an increase in oil wealth (van Wijnbergen 1984b).

Nigeria has had periods of excessive spending and periods of under- spending, and it started an explicit expenditure smoothing policy in 2004. As long as that policy is maintained, there will be no real Dutch disease problem now or in the foreseeable future. Moreover, there are other diffi- culties in simply labeling Nigeria as another instance of an oil-rich country (ORC) succumbing to the Dutch disease. In particular, the mechanism through which high spending out of what, in essence, is a tradable resource leads to low growth is a fight for scarce resources drawing labor and capital out of the traded sector. Budina, Pang, and van Wijnbergen (2007) reviewed Nigeria's growth record and indicated that Dutch disease–style resource pull effects out of the traded sector cannot explain a poor non-oil growth record; instead, they point to the extreme volatility of public expenditure.[3]

Poor Growth Record: The Challenge of Managing Oil Revenue Volatility

Several empirical studies also have found that oil-abundant countries' output as well as government revenue and expenditure experience higher volatility due to highly volatile commodity prices combined with undiversified revenue and export bases. Commodity prices and revenues from natural resources tend to be volatile, and they may translate into macroeconomic instability and a highly volatile real exchange rate.[4] Volatility can be seen as a tax on investment. Investment requires irreversible decisions because capital, once installed, cannot be moved to other sectors. Highly volatile relative prices discourage the irreversible commitments to specific sectors that capital investment implies (van Wijnbergen 1985). Aghion, Bacchetta, and Ranciere (2006) have shown empirically that high volatility slows down productivity growth by a substantial margin in countries with a relatively underdeveloped financial sector, like Nigeria. In their sample, a 50 percent increase in volatility slows down productivity growth by 33 percent, on average. And there is substantial evidence that ORCs have more volatile economies than non-ORCs (Hausmann and Rigobon 2002).

Vulnerability problems in ORCs—Nigeria, in particular—may well be exacerbated by apparent volatility clustering in addition to regular oil-price uncertainty (see figure 10.3a). This means there is a significant probability of big outliers and clustering of high-volatility periods. High oil-price volatility results in volatile oil revenue streams and, at the same time, increases the equity characteristics of debt: if a debtor often cannot pay in bad years, debt looks more like equity and debt overhang becomes a real problem (see Budina, Pang, and van Wijnbergen 2007). This situation complicates fiscal management, further increases the vulnerability of the ORCs to debt overhang problems, and therefore underscores the implications of high oil-price volatility for fiscal sustainability.

FIGURE 10.3
The Cost of Volatility

a. Oil prices, 1861–2001

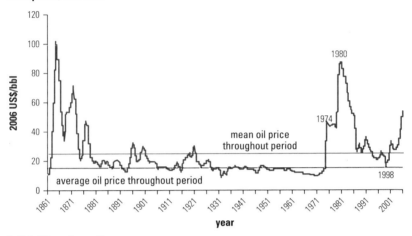

b. Volatility and growth

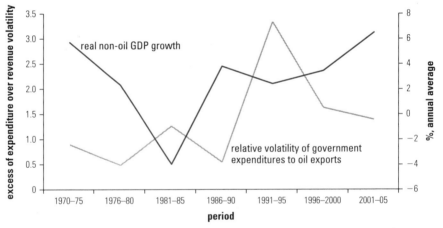

Sources: Authors' calculations; British Petroleum's *Statistical Review of World Energy;* World Bank 2003; World Economic Outlook data.

As illustrated by figure 10.3b, however, fiscal policy has pushed volatility beyond the volatility stemming from variable oil prices; the government itself has become a source of macroeconomic volatility. One plausible explanation for this volatility is the "voracity effect" (see Lane and Tornell 1996). To explain high volatility in ORCs, it has been argued that countries with many interest groups competing for the resource rents are likely to overspend in good years, and underadjust in bad years. Each interest group tries to overexploit windfall gains in an attempt (at least partially) to offload adjustment costs to others while fully capturing the gains from its lobbying efforts. Federal states like Nigeria are thought to be especially vulnerable to what amounts to an equivalent of overgrazing the commons. An expenditure behavior that leads to overspending in good days and underadjustment in bad days may end up with an economy that has even higher volatility than is to be expected on the basis of the volatility in its revenue streams alone.

There is an alternative, or possibly complementary, explanation of high volatility in ORCs—an explanation that starts from the surprising fact that many ORCs have landed themselves in debt problems, their oil wealth notwithstanding. Borrowing may well have been restricted after the sudden reduction in net resource inflows associated with lower oil prices because lenders fear too much of "project returns" will be diverted to the servicing of old debt, thereby undermining the credit quality of any new debt. This is the classic *debt overhang* problem. Manzano and Rigobon (2001) have suggested a link between debt problems and slow growth in resource-rich countries.

And there is another problem in Nigeria and in many ORCs—the problem of too close a link between public expenditure and volatile current oil income. When oil prices unexpectedly drop, it is often difficult and costly to adjust expenditure downward, although, in fact, the need to do so may be larger than the actual decline in income triggering the need for adjustment in the first place. This is because ORCs, and Nigeria very much so, have a peculiar problem concerning capital market access. Obviously, their need to borrow is lowest when oil prices are high, and is high when prices are low. However, their borrowing capacity is inversely related to their borrowing need because the value of their de facto collateral—oil wealth— also peaks when prices are high and drops when they are low. This perverse link among income shortfalls, declining collateral values, and reduced resource inflows is an obvious recipe for debt overhang problems: new lenders will fear too much of their money will be diverted to service old debt, thereby reducing the value of their claims even if projects financed by the new moneys have a sufficiently high rate of return to service new debt in the absence of old claims outstanding. This is the classic debt overhang problem, triggering a larger need for adjustment than just the current fall in income, as debt repayments coming due cannot be refinanced either. In this way, debt overhang problems raise the costs of adjustment substantially and explain why volatility of government expenditure in Nigeria has exceeded the volatility of oil prices.

It is important to note that debt overhang problems can arise in countries with relatively little debt; what matters are short-term cash flow needs. So having a modest debt but with all debt coming due in the near future is more damaging than having a much higher debt with amortization smoothly stretched. And the worse the debt service record, the more likely it is there will be a debt overhang problem. The fact that the existing debt was not serviced actually reinforces the argument: debt overhang exists when debt has strong equity characteristics (that is, when it is serviced only in good times) and accordingly trades at a large discount.

The consistent record of repeated rescheduling and continuing arrears since the early 1980s has effectively shut Nigeria out of international capital markets for most of the past two decades.[5] Evidence of this lack of market access is the prohibitive markups that Nigeria would have had to pay on primary issues that can be derived from secondary market information (figure 10.4). It is only after the most recently concluded debt relief agreement that markups have fallen to manageable, although still high, levels.

The combination of exuberance in good years and debt-overhang-induced, draconian adjustment in bad years makes for disastrous non-oil growth records over longer horizons. Nigeria's pre-2000 fiscal policy actually increased expenditure volatility above levels induced by oil prices themselves, constituting an additional tax on non-oil growth. Moreover, the impact of such policies is much exacerbated if coupled with exchange rate policies that do not accommodate upturns and do not adjust to downturns. Real exchange rate adjustments will take place anyhow, but, when not accommodated through nominal adjustments, they will come about through outbursts of inflation in boom periods and prolonged recessions in down periods. And inflation processes have their own overshooting dynamics, leading to larger collapses and deeper recessions than would have occurred if either more orderly appreciation mechanisms had been found or appreciation pressures had been lessened through expenditure smoothing.

Lessons for the Future

Nigeria's checkered past has important lessons for the future, lessons that should be heeded if the upturn since 2004 is to be more than just a demand-driven upturn foreboding another crash once prices fall again.

FIGURE 10.4
Net Public Debt-to-GDP Ratio and Risk Premium on External Debt

a. Oil price and net public debt

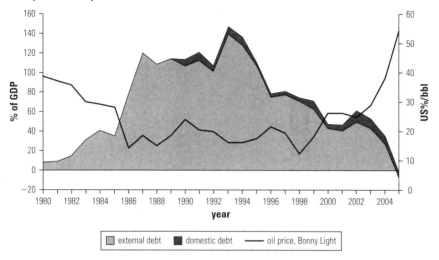

b. EMBI global stripped spreads

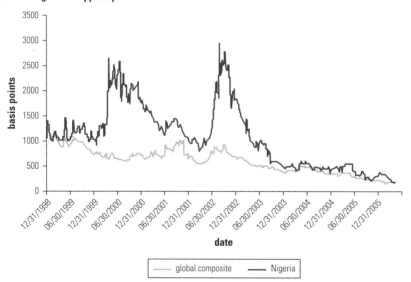

Sources: International Monetary Fund and World Bank staff reports; Data provided by JPMorgan.

As discussed in Budina, Pang, and van Wijnbergen (2007), Nigeria's pre-2000 record of fiscal policy actually increased expenditure volatility rather than reduced it, which led to a series of boom/bust cycles and slowed down non-oil growth.

Moreover, the authors found empirical evidence showing that debt overhang problems also contributed to volatility. They also found evidence of voracity effects that exacerbated expenditure volatility prior to 1984. With the exception of the years leading up to the 1984 crisis, spending in upturns has not been excessive (although perhaps not smoothing volatility enough either), but adjustment in downturns has been harsh as access to capital markets dried up at the very moment it was needed most—when oil prices slumped.

The point is brought out most clearly by the experience of the 1980s and confirmed by the econometric analysis presented. In the beginning of the 1980s, oil prices were substantially higher than they are now in real terms, and predictions of a secular rise in prices abounded, just as some now predict $60+ oil for years to come. Yet a downturn in the West triggered a collapse from which (real) prices have still not recovered. Nigeria followed the optimists' advice then and continued spending, only to find out that capital markets would not accommodate such policies; subsequent adjustment exceeded the decline in oil revenues as short-term debt coming due could not be rolled over. A classic case of debt overhang resulted, and breaking out of it required a new oil boom and substantial debt relief.

Volatility is harmful to economic growth, a problem that is especially relevant in resource-rich countries because of the extremely high volatility of their income streams. Nigeria's experience suggests that managing income volatility to isolate expenditure from it as much as possible is the main challenge in resource-rich economies. Nigeria's experience so far also indicates that managing volatility in a poor institutional environment is especially difficult, thus stressing the need for institutional reform.

Lessons from Nigeria's poor growth record suggest that ORCs, particularly Nigeria, are subject to much bigger vulnerability problems than other countries because of oil price uncertainty and possible volatility clustering (figure 10.3a).

The lesson should be clear. Planning on long-run expenditure commitments low enough to be met from much lower oil revenues than currently projected on the basis of recent price developments is the only way to ensure sustainability and avoid another debt overhang–induced decade of misery. This means non-oil deficits geared toward a sustainable overall balance based on oil prices in a range of $25–35 a barrel. The importance of complementing the OPFR with such a non-oil deficit policy should be clear: putting money aside with one hand but borrowing on the side with the other to sustain incompatible overall deficits makes the OPFR totally ineffective.

Of course, windfall gains in excess of that price range do not need to be carried over exclusively in the form of foreign exchange; physical capital is also a way of sharing wealth with future generations. But no investment projects should be undertaken that cannot be entirely financed from already accumulated and ring-fenced oil fund assets, and whose recurrent costs cannot be met within the long-run sustainability constraints just outlined. Otherwise, the capital market problems that Nigeria will undoubtedly face again during future downturns will make fiscal policy a source of volatility and low growth. Moreover, Nigeria's extraordinarily poor record on public investment productivity suggests substantial improvements are necessary in the institutional infrastructure for project analysis, selection, and implementation before strategies of transforming oil wealth in improvements of public infrastructure should be considered, however necessary such improvements may be.

The second lesson concerns exchange rate management. Unless public expenditure completely smoothes over oil revenue fluctuations, and no private spending boom is triggered, the real exchange rate will have to appreciate when oil prices rise. Not accommodating through nominal exchange rate flexibility implies that high domestic inflation becomes unavoidable. It is unfortunate that, once started, inflation is often difficult to stop, even if pressure for appreciation falls away. The ensuing overvaluation of the real exchange rate then will trigger unemployment and the necessity of overly harsh downward adjustments later on, once a crisis has brought down a then overvalued nominal rate. Thus, a cautious move toward more exchange rate flexibility, coupled with expenditure restraint to reduce pressure toward real appreciation, will be essential if Nigeria wants to avoid the boom/bust cycles of the past.

The extent to which exchange rates will rise with rising oil prices is directly related to the degree to which the government succeeds in smoothing out expenditure levels through the use of an oil fund facility. If such a facility is used, only structural upshifts in oil income require real exchange rate adjustment.

Assessing Fiscal Sustainability in Oil-Rich Countries

Many ORCs, recently including Nigeria, have attempted to use oil funds and/or fiscal rules to de-link public expenditure from volatile oil revenue and to accumulate large foreign exchange reserves/oil fund assets to lower vulnerability to financial crises and debt overhang problems. Experience has shown that high current oil income is in no way a guarantee that these countries will not have to face crisis circumstances at times in future. Thus, managing fiscal risks from oil revenue uncertainty is a key challenge facing policy makers in ORCs. This section proposes an analytical framework for assessing the sustainability of fiscal strategies in ORCs.

Any framework needs to go beyond the routine consistency checks that form the bread and butter of fiscal sustainability analysis (FSA).[6] First of all, doing an FSA in the presence of an oil fund rule requires explicit incorporation of non-oil deficit rules to make the oil fund a meaningful exercise.[7] This requires modifying the government budget constraint and the resulting public debt dynamics equation to isolate the impact of oil on public finances and to reflect the special features of oil discussed above.

The first step in such an approach is to create a baseline scenario of the likely future time path of the oil producer's net financial asset position, using the flow budget constraint equation. This baseline uses the flow budget equation to update future net financial assets as a share of GDP, based on macroeconomic projections of key determinants of public debt dynamics, such as growth, inflation, projected primary surpluses, and interest rates, as well as our projections for the oil fiscal revenues, which involve projections or assumptions of remaining oil reserves, the future rate of oil extraction, future oil prices, and taxation regimes. As mentioned above, customizing the forward looking approach to ORCs requires modifying the government budget constraint and the resulting public debt dynamics equation to isolate the impact of oil on public finances and to reflect the special features of oil.

Once the baseline scenario is created, the next step requires checking the vulnerability of the net debt/net asset dynamics to key debt determinants and, most important, to sudden drops in oil prices. The sensitivity checks to low oil prices are especially important, given the large uncertainty surrounding future oil prices, high oil price volatility, and possible volatility clustering.

Before going into the details, we should consider one important point. To ensure consistency among debt stocks, deficits, and revenue from seigniorage, it is necessary to consolidate the general government accounts with the central bank's profit and loss account (Anand and van Wijnbergen 1988, 1989). Otherwise, seigniorage, an important source of revenue in most developing countries will not show up in the budget dynamics, and debt may be mismeasured by failing to take into account assets held by the central bank.[8] This is especially important if the savings from current oil revenues are deposited at the central bank. Public sector foreign debt is then measured net of the (net) foreign asset holdings of the central bank and net of the assets of the oil fund, if those are deposited outside the central bank. Similarly, deficits and the ensuing liabilities for the state may be seriously mismeasured if the quasi-fiscal deficit of the central bank is excluded. Such mismeasurement is a major shortcoming of the recent International Monetary Fund approach to sustainability (IMF 2002, 2003). Similarly, if the oil fund is set up as an extrabudgetary fund, then one should consolidate the oil fund operation in the general budget. This consolidation may be especially important if the fund is authorized to undertake expenditure outside the consolidated budget.

After that consolidation, increases in net public debt (that is, measured net of the net foreign assets, public debt holdings of the central bank, and oil fund assets) can be decomposed in various contributing factors, which, in turn, can be linked to the macroeconomic projections available. By switching to ratios to GDP, public debt dynamics can be broken down into several components: (1) the primary non-oil fiscal deficit net of seigniorage revenues; (2) growth adjusted real interest rate payments on domestic debt; (3) the real cost of external borrowing, including capital gains and losses on net external debt due to changes in the real exchange rate; and (4) oil fiscal revenue, which is often the most important way of financing a non-oil deficit in countries highly dependent on oil. This can be expressed in the following formula:[9]

$$d = (f - \sigma) + (r - g)b + (r^* + \hat{e} - g)(b^* - nfa^*)e - Roil + OF \qquad (10.1)$$

where d is the net public debt-to-GDP ratio (that is, measured net of the net foreign assets, public debt holdings of the central bank, and oil fund assets); the OPFR is captured by the projections for the non-oil primary deficit as a share of GDP, f; g is the real GDP growth rate; r is the real interest rate on domestic debt; r^* is the real interest rate on external debt; e is the real exchange rate, $\dfrac{EP^*}{P}$ with obvious definitions of variables; and *Roil* refers to projected oil fiscal revenues (at projected World Economic Outlook [WEO]/Development Prospects Group oil prices).

Furthermore, given the oil price uncertainty and the possibility of volatility clustering, many ORCs have introduced fiscal/oil fund rules that aim at stabilizing the oil revenue flow to the budget, using a conservatively chosen budget reference price. In what follows, we are referring to a so-called reference price rule, whereby all revenues due to actual prices in excess of this reference price are diverted to an oil fund. Commensurately, revenue shortfalls due to prices falling short of the reference price can be met from the oil fund.

After adding and subtracting the oil revenue evaluated at the reference price from the right-hand side of equation (10.1), we get

$$d = (f - Roil_{REF} - \sigma) + (r - g)b + (r^* + \hat{e} - g)(b^* - nfa^*)e$$
$$- (r^* + e - g)oa^*e - (Roil - Roil_{REF}) + OF \qquad (10.2)$$

In equation (10.2), $Roil_{REF}$ stands for oil revenue evaluated at a reference price, whereas *Roil* is the oil revenue evaluated at the projected WEO price. We assume that the excess of actual oil revenues over the reference revenues evaluated at the budget reference price and the interest earned on the stock of oil assets are saved in a ring-fenced oil fund. This results in the following two equations, one for the dynamics of the oil fund *oa* and one for public debt:

$$oa^* = (r^* - \hat{e} - g)oa^*e + (Roil - Roil_{REF}) \qquad (10.3)$$
$$d = (f - Roil_{REF} - \sigma) + (r - g)b + (r^* + \hat{e} - g)(b^* - nfa^*)e$$
$$- oa^* + OF \qquad (10.4)$$

As can be seen from equation (10.4), the net public debt-to-GDP ratio can increase as a result of larger non-oil primary deficits, f, net of the revenue from seigniorage; it also can grow as a result of "automatic debt dynamics," which are determined by the difference between the real interest rate and the real growth rate. If a large share of public debt is denominated in foreign currency, the public debt-to-GDP ratio also can change because of capital gains/losses due to real exchange rate fluctuations. It also includes a catchall term, OF (other factors). OF collects residuals due to cross-product terms arising because of the use of discrete time data[10] and the impact of debt-increasing factors that, in a perfect accounting world, would be included in deficit measures but, in the real world, are not included. Examples are contingent liabilities that actually materialize, such as the fiscal consequences of a bank bailout, one-off privatization revenues, and so on. Of course, if countries borrow in more than one foreign currency (for example, dollars and euros or yen), more than one foreign debt stock should be kept track of in an analogous manner.

The modified public debt dynamics equation (10.4) also isolates the impact of oil on public finances. In particular, it reflects the following major changes. First, it renders transparent the fact that a substantial share of fiscal revenues is derived from oil; the primary fiscal deficit (noninterest spending minus revenues) is replaced with the non-oil primary deficit, isolating net oil revenues evaluated at reference price as a financing flow, $Roil_{REF}$. Second, the change in net debt-to-GDP ratio now also accounts for fiscal savings out of oil, accumulated in a ring-fenced oil fund, oa^*–dot.[11] Third, given the higher volatility of the oil fiscal revenue, the uncertainty about the net debt trajectory for ORCs is likely to be much higher; hence, fiscal sustainability assessment should pay much more attention to the issues of uncertainty and risk.

A simplified scheme of the proposed practical framework, which also accommodates a fiscal strategy for de-linking public expenditure from current oil revenue, is presented in figure 10.5. As shown in the figure, besides the traditional automatic debt dynamics, the path of (gross) public debt depends on the projected stream of oil-related fiscal revenues, the level and the trajectory of the non-oil deficit, and the targeted level of foreign exchange reserves (the oil fund).

The fiscal sustainability tool presented in Budina, Pang, and van Wijnbergen (2007), has been extended along the lines of figure 10.5 and incorporates the oil fund rule used in Nigeria, as in many other resource-rich countries.

Note that the implementation of such an OPFR is especially relevant for mature oil producers with a relatively constant oil extraction profile, so it is oil price volatility that matters most. This rule might need to be modified for countries with new oil discoveries (such as Azerbaijan), which might find that they can suddenly and substantially raise the non-oil deficit. Whereas the same considerations—such as absorptive capacity, impact on real exchange rate and non-oil economy, and intergenerational equity—apply, the relative emphasis would be different, with absorptive capacity becoming much more important. For countries where oil is running out (such as Yemen), the emphasis on the non-oil economy and diversification should

FIGURE 10.5
Steps in Conducting Fiscal Sustainability Analysis for ORCs

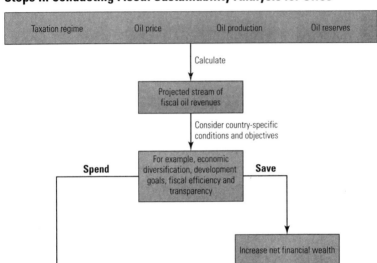

Source: World Bank 2006.

receive more prominence. Finally, it is also important to stress that, to be meaningful at all, such an OPFR should be complemented with targets for the non-oil deficit. Putting money aside with one hand but borrowing on the side with the other obviously would make the OPFR ineffective.

The second extension to regular FSA is the incorporation of uncertainty. So far we have assumed deterministic paths for the variables underlying the debt dynamics, as spelled out in equations (10.1) and (10.3). Given that there is uncertainty attached to projections of variables such as interest and growth rates, exchange rate developments, and so on, how sensitive are the results to a given shock in any of the variables used as input in the exercise? One way to address these uncertainties is to introduce *stress tests* to deal with specific risks. In a stress test, a set of sensitivity tests to the baseline scenario is conducted, assuming that the underlying variables swing away from their means by one or two standard deviations. Stress tests are a useful sensitivity check, but they have their limitations. In particular, they are incomplete because they ignore the endogenous interactions between input variables, and so are not a substitute for a full macroeconomic model–based analysis. But their merit is that they significantly reduce computational complexity and data requirements, and still give meaningful insights about the sensitivity of the model results to exogenous shocks. The most important sensitivity analyses include stress tests with respect to oil prices, real interest rates on domestic and foreign public debt, real output growth, primary balance, and (changes in) the real exchange rate.[12] The purposes of the various alternative scenarios are to facilitate a discussion of key vulnerabilities of the economy and to ensure more realistic fiscal sustainability assessments. In addition, the framework used allows for a fully specified crisis scenario, whereby the fiscal rule is compromised and a country is hit by a severe negative oil price shock.

In the light of Nigeria's recent debt overhang problems (Budina, Pang, and van Wijnbergen 2007), the fiscal rule should aim for long-run expenditure commitments low enough to be met from much lower oil revenues than are currently projected on the basis of recent price developments. Periods with low oil prices are also periods of difficult capital market access for Nigeria. A cautious approach would be to use as reference price a range of $25–35, the long-term average of the (real) price of oil (see figure 10.3a).

Oil Wealth, the OPFR, and Sustainability of Public Debt

Despite its long history of poor economic performance, Nigeria appeared to be experiencing an economic turnaround that began in 2000. Real non-oil GDP grew at an annual average rate of 5.9 percent during 2000–05; together with the significant oil windfall, that growth has more than doubled GDP per capita in current U.S. dollars over the same period. Is this a structural shift toward sustained high growth or just a temporary, demand-induced boom due to an unanticipated jump in oil prices? Has fiscal policy been able to dampen the impact of oil revenue volatility and to lower vulnerability of the economy to debt overhang?

The adoption of an oil price–based fiscal rule in the 2004 and 2005 budgets has been an important step in the implementation of Nigeria's fiscal reform agenda. This rule is designed to link government spending to some notion of a long-run oil price, thereby de-linking government spending from current oil revenues. This action should both lower the volatility of public expenditure and lead to the saving of at least part of the current oil windfall receipts. Indeed, contrary to earlier responses to steep increases

FIGURE 10.6
Benchmarking Marginal Propensity to Spend out of the Oil Windfall,
2000–05

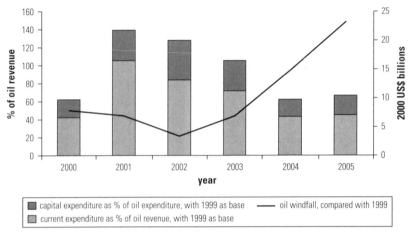

Sources: International Monetary Fund staff reports; World Economic Outlook data; authors' calculations.

in oil revenues, Nigeria has accumulated sizable foreign exchange reserves, external debt has almost disappeared (also because of the recent Paris Club debt deal), and the consolidated government budget registered strong and increasing surpluses.

To check whether there is any change in the spending pattern, we present the share of annual increments in public expenditure (with respect to their 1999 level) as a share of the incremental oil windfall (with respect to the 1999 level of oil revenues) for each year (figure 10.6). Indeed, there seems to be a change in Nigeria's spending pattern before and after 2004, the year when the OPFR was implemented.[13]

In what follows, we will check whether the recently implemented OPFR is robust enough to lower the vulnerability of Nigeria to potential negative shocks to key debt determinants, and we will show that if the fiscal rule is compromised, a negative oil price shock is likely to have severe consequences for the net asset position.

Impact of Adherence to the OPFR on Net Asset Position

This section uses public debt dynamics to create a baseline projection of future trends in the net public debt-to-GDP ratio, utilizing existing macroeconomic projections.[14] The base case scenario for public debt dynamics assumes continued commitment to implementation of the oil price fiscal rule over the projection period. It is not surprising that public debt dynamics are particularly sensitive to assumptions about projected and budget reference oil prices, which determine the net oil revenues and acceptable level of non-oil deficits. As we have seen, the cost of oil price forecasting errors is asymmetric, with the cost of overpredicting being far greater than the cost of underpredicting. To account for this feature, the annual budgets for 2004 and 2005 were built on rather conservative budget reference oil prices. Looking forward, budget reference price is assumed to be roughly constant at slightly above $30 per barrel, despite expectations that oil prices will stay at their current high levels for the projection period (figure 10.7a). Fiscal projections also assume that non-oil tax collection will improve, leading to higher non-oil taxes (an increase of about 3 percentage points of GDP). Public expenditure is assumed to increase by less than the increase in the non-oil tax revenues, so that the entire non-oil deficit is being financed by the oil revenues calculated at the conservative budget reference price. As a result, the non-oil deficit to non-oil GDP ratio is expected to decline from about 41 percent in 2005 to slightly above 36 percent in the medium term, which is consistent with maintaining real wealth over the long run. Finally, using the WEO

FIGURE 10.7
Scenarios for Oil Price and Net Oil Revenue, 1999–2011

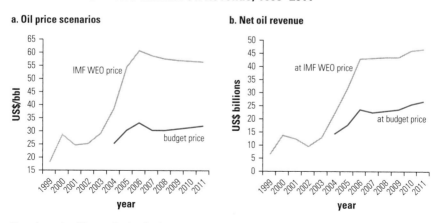

a. Oil price scenarios   b. Net oil revenue

Source: International Monetary Fund staff projections.

Note: IMF = International Monetary Fund; WEO = World Economic Outlook.

projections, oil prices are assumed to hover above $60 a barrel, which implies substantial savings out of oil revenues (figure 10.7b).

In addition, the base case scenario assumes that, under good policies and reforms, the non-oil GDP grows at about 5 percent, underpinned by a strong growth in the non-oil sector (on average, 6 percent over the projection period). External debt-to-GDP ratio is assumed to remain roughly constant—at around 4 percent as a ratio to GDP, with a very low real interest rate on external debt reflecting Nigeria's low-income status. The annual average real interest rate on domestic debt during the projection period is assumed to be somewhat lower (6 percent), accounting for the ample liquidity and increased savings from oil. The base case also assumes a broadly constant real exchange rate, which once again reflects the relatively prudent fiscal stance under the current assumption that high oil prices will prevail. Furthermore, to check the robustness of the baseline scenario to shocks, we also perform a battery of stress tests, as elaborated below. Results from the baseline scenario and the most important stress tests are summarized in figure 10.8.

FIGURE 10.8
Debt Dynamics and Stress Tests, 2005–11

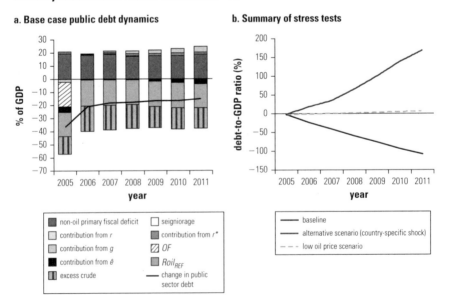

Source: Authors' calculations.

As can be seen in figure 10.8a, if the oil prices remain at their present very high levels (around $60+ a barrel at time of writing)', and if the current OPFR is adhered to, fiscal sustainability is not going to be an issue in Nigeria for many years to come. Following the OPFR would lead to a very fast accumulation of foreign assets: at the end of the projection period, the net asset position will reach 100 percent of GDP! Sizable oil assets accumulation is the chief reason for this favorable debt dynamics. Of course, the strong initial position (as a result of the combination of the Paris Club debt relief and the high oil prices) also helps.

Although the baseline scenario looks rather optimistic, history shows that key determinants of public debt dynamics are highly volatile and subject to external shocks. The fiscal sustainability framework checks the credibility of baseline projections with alternative scenarios (historical scenario, no policy change, alternative country-specific scenario, and low oil price scenario) and bound tests, which are used to assess the behavior of the public debt ratio in the event of temporary shocks on key parameters. Although all the stress tests are presented in table 10.1 for the sake of completeness, the baseline scenario is quite robust to most of the stress tests— including historical, no policy change, and the bound tests. The most important vulnerability of the baseline scenario relates to an unanticipated oil price drop, which is illustrated by the low oil price scenario and by the alternative country-specific scenario (see figure 10.8b and table 10.1). Hence, we concentrate our further discussion on these two scenarios.

As demonstrated by Nigeria's past, the role of fiscal policy in minimizing the impact of oil wealth volatility on the economy by delinking public expenditure from volatile oil revenues is crucial if debt overhang and associated low growth are to be avoided. To check the robustness of the OPFR, we also project the net public debt dynamics on the assumption of a negative permanent oil price shock during the projection period. In particular, we assume that the oil price would permanently drop to a constant $25 a barrel in real terms, which is the oil price observed on average during 1986–99. At the same time, the non-oil deficit trajectory remains unchanged because it is bounded by the reference price of oil, which remains as in its baseline level of around $30 a barrel, or somewhat higher than the

TABLE 10.1
Net Public Debt: Stress Test Results, 2006–11
Percent of GDP

	2006	2007	2008	2009	2010	2011
Baseline scenario	−23.7	−41.8	−59.7	−76.3	−93.2	−108
Alternative scenarios						
A1. Key variables are at their historical averages in 2006–11	−24	−42	−59	−76	−100	−122
A2. No policy change (constant primary balance) in 2006–11	−24	−3.0	−1.7	1.2	−20	−36
A3. Alternative country-specific scenario, modeling a country-specific shock	18	35	65	100	138.3	169.6
A4. Low oil price scenario, 2006–11	−1.0	1.2	2.1	3.5	4.8	7.2
Bound tests						
B1. Real interest rate is at historical average plus two standard deviations in 2005 and 2006	−21.0	−32.2	−52.4	−71.6	−95.1	−113
B2. Real GDP growth is at historical average minus two standard deviations in 2005 and 2006	−22.3	−38.2	−54.1	−69.3	−84.4	−98.3
B3. Primary balance is at historical average minus two standard deviations in 2005 and 2006	−2.5	−12.6	−41.8	−56.9	−71.8	−85.1
B4. Combination of 1–3 using one standard deviation shocks	−15.9	−26.6	−44.1	−60.1	−76.3	−90.7
B5. One time 30 percent real depreciation in 2005	−27.8	−43.3	−57.7	−70.3	−82.8	−93.0
B6. 10 percent of GDP increase in other debt-creating flows in 2005	−14.4	−34.5	−54.6	−73.8	−93.0	−111

Source: Authors' calculations.

projected oil price. Whereas this scenario will result in net outflows from the oil stabilization fund, given the strong initial net asset position and the adherence to the OPFR, Nigeria would be able to survive a sizable negative oil shock of at least five years' duration without requiring dramatic fiscal adjustment and with only modest debt accumulation. This is good news for the fiscal rule and indicates that it is robust enough to withstand a sizable negative oil shock. Of course, if the duration of the shock is much longer (beyond the five-year projection period that we assumed here), this policy rule may need to be reconsidered to avoid over-borrowing.

Robustness Check of the OPFR

To explore the consequences of abandoning the fiscal policy rule, we have constructed an alternative scenario where OPFR is compromised by assuming a much higher budget reference price of oil ($60 a barrel), although, in reality, oil prices would drop permanently to a constant $25 a barrel. In other words, we performed a *robustness check* to see what would be the implications if history repeats itself and Nigeria experiences a shock similar to the one in the mid-1980s. Specifically, this scenario assumes that the government will passively spend its oil revenues, which are estimated on the assumption that current high oil prices ($60 a barrel) will continue to prevail during the projection period, while oil prices actually return to their historical level ($25 per barrel in real terms).

As a result, non-oil deficits will expand drastically, while the oil revenue available for deficit financing will turn out to be much lower than expected. Under such a policy, Nigeria will exhaust its oil fund assets in 2006, after which sizable financing gaps will emerge (shown in figure 10.9 as the difference between projected non-oil primary deficits and oil revenues).

The options available to the government are then to borrow or, more likely when external funds dry up, to print money and see inflation

FIGURE 10.9
Financing Gap in the Alternative Scenario, 2006–11

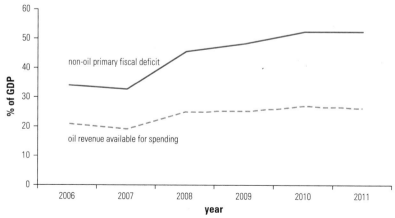

Source: Authors' calculations.

reemerge. Given debt overhang problems for ORCs after price downturns, this situation most likely would lead to confidence crises, credit rationing by external capital markets, sizable depreciation, rapid increases in real interest rates, hyperinflation, and deep recession—the end result of which would be unsustainable levels of public debt only five years after the Paris Club debt agreement. This simulation thus stresses the importance of the fiscal policy rule and the conservative reference price chosen to underpin it. Both are necessary to impart sufficient robustness to Nigeria's macroeconomic policies. Guessing wrong can be very expensive if high oil prices fail to materialize.

Conclusions

This chapter has focused on the role of fiscal policy in managing the volatility of oil wealth and its implications for debt and development. It uses the lessons from poor management of oil wealth in Nigeria to derive a framework that could be used to assess fiscal sustainability and vulnerability to debt overhang problems in ORCs. Whereas Nigeria is an interesting example in its own right, many issues that are familiar from other countries show up here too, making the case of wider interest.

Nigeria's poor record with managing oil revenue volatility has important lessons for the future, lessons that should be heeded if the upturn since 2004 is to be more than just a demand-driven upturn foreboding another crash once prices fall again. The combination of exuberance in good years and debt-overhang-induced, draconian adjustment in bad years makes for disastrous non-oil growth records over longer horizons. Volatility is harmful to economic growth—a problem that is especially relevant in resource-rich countries because of the extremely high volatility of their income streams. Furthermore, the challenge of managing volatility is even greater in a poor institutional environment.

In particular, Nigeria's pre-2000 record of fiscal policy shows two things: (1) Nigeria's own policies increased rather than smoothed volatility, and (2) volatility of expenditure in Nigeria was further increased by debt overhang problems. Debt overhang problems mean that world capital markets become inaccessible at the very moment they are needed most. This suggests that fiscal policy design should pay special attention to down-side risk.

The point is brought out most clearly by the experience of the 1980s. In the beginning of that decade, oil prices where substantially higher than they are now in real terms, and predictions of a secular rise in prices abounded, just as some now predict $60+ oil for years to come. Yet a downturn in the West triggered a collapse from which (real) prices have still not recovered. Nigeria followed the optimists' advice then and continued spending, only to find that capital markets would not accommodate such policies; subsequent adjustment exceeded the decline in oil revenues as short-term debt coming due could not be rolled over. A classic case of debt overhang resulted, and breaking out of it required a new oil boom and substantial debt relief.

Experience has shown that high current oil income does not guarantee that these countries will face no crisis circumstances in future times. Thus, managing oil revenue volatility is a key challenge facing policy makers in oil-rich countries. Many oil-rich countries, recently including Nigeria, have attempted to use oil funds and/or fiscal rules to de-link public expenditure from volatile oil revenue and to accumulate large foreign exchange reserves/oil fund assets to lower vulnerability to financial crises and debt overhang problems.

Adopting an OPFR in the 2004, 2005, and 2006 budgets has been an important step in improving fiscal discipline since 2004, and Nigeria has been able to accumulate sizable foreign exchange reserves, while net public debt virtually disappeared. We have applied a framework for fiscal sustainability to check how robust the newly established OPFR is under different oil price assumptions. First, we used public debt dynamics to create a baseline projection of future trends in the net public debt-to-GDP ratio, using existing macroeconomic projections. Second, given the uncertainty surrounding public debt dynamics, we conducted various sensitivity tests on baseline public debt dynamics, emphasizing the importance of oil price volatility. Finally, we formulated a country-specific alternative scenario whereby fiscal rule is compromised and a country is hit by a severe negative oil price shock, which serves as a robustness check and accounts for oil price uncertainty and volatility.

Assuming that oil prices remain at their present very high levels of around $60+ per barrel, and that Nigeria adheres strictly to its

OPFR (resulting in non-oil deficits geared toward sustainable balance based on oil prices in a range of $25–35), the fiscal rule is sufficiently robust and the country could weather a substantial oil price drop during the projection period without a substantial impact on its net public debt.

However, the fiscal reforms record is still mixed: during the past three years, 2004–06, the non-oil deficit (expressed as a ratio to non-oil GDP) increased rapidly, and the off-budget deficit items of several percentage points indicate that signs of slippage are appearing. To see the impact of a full loss of fiscal control, we assumed that the reference price is increased back to $60 a barrel, or the OPFR is abandoned, while Nigeria is hit by a severe downturn in the international oil prices. Under such a scenario, large financing gaps will emerge throughout the projection period, leading to a rapid exhaustion of the oil savings. The government then has two available options: to borrow or, more likely when external funds dry up, to print money and watch inflation reemerge. Given ORCs' vulnerability to debt overhang problems following price downturns, this scenario probably will lead to a crisis of confidence, the rationing of credit by external capital markets, sizable depreciation, swift increases in real interest rates, hyperinflation, and deep recession. As a result, there will be unsustainable levels of public debt only five years after the debt agreement reached with the Paris Club.

The overall conclusion should be clear. The only way to avoid another debt overhang problem is to plan expenditure levels and commitments low enough to avoid a crisis if and when oil prices come down to earth again and revenues fall. This implies non-oil deficits based on oil prices in a range of $25–35.

Nigeria recently started to adhere to an oil price–based fiscal rule, introduced more exchange rate flexibility, and improved various aspects of the public investment process. But there are clear dangers of slippage: non-oil deficits have been above safe levels, particularly if off-budget commitments and arrears are taken into account. Those signs of slippage need to be reversed. And, finally, Nigeria's poor public investment performance makes it clear that reform of the public investment process, including anti-corruption measures, should remain at the top of the policy agenda. Only if the reform process is brought back on track and maintained in the years to come is there a chance that Nigeria's oil wealth will turn from a curse into a blessing.

Annex: Derivation of Public Debt Decomposition Dynamics

The first section of this annex lists and defines the variables used in the debt decomposition, and the second section derives the debt decomposition equation.

Set of Variables

1. $D_t = B_t + e_t B_t^* - e_t NFA_t^*$: public sector net debt.

2. B_t: domestic debt in local currency units (LCUs).

3. B_t^*: foreign debt in dollar terms.

4. NFA_t^*: net foreign assets in dollar terms.

5. e_t: end-of-period (*eop*) exchange rate, LCU/$.

6. M_t^{bop}: monetary base at the beginning of period in time t (or monetary base *eop* at $t - 1$).

7. i_t^d: domestic interest rate paid over the period $(t - 1, t)$.

8. i_t^f: foreign interest rate paid on foreign debt and reserves on the period $(t - 1, t)$.

9. i_t^1: London interbank offered rate paid on net foreign assets of the central bank on the period $(t - 1, t)$.

10. $P_{t,AV}$: average consumer price index level for period t.

11. $\pi_{t,AV} = (P_{t,AV} - P_{t-1,AV})/P_{t,AV}$: average consumer price inflation in the year t.

12. $\pi_t^* = (P_t^* - P_{t-1}^*)/P_t^*$, where P_t^* is the average U.S. consumer price index.

13. Y_t: real GDP in period t in LCUs.

14. g_t: $(Y_t - Y_{t-1})/Y_t$: real GDP growth rate in the year t.

15. $s_t = (e_t - e_{t-1})/e_{t-1}$.

16. $\hat{e}_t = (1 + s_t)*(1 + \pi_t^*)/(1 + \pi_t) - 1$: rate of change in the bilateral real exchange rate (LCUs per $1) $e_t P_t^*/P_t$, where $+$ denotes real depreciation, and $-$ denotes real appreciation.

17. Small letters, d_t, b_t, b_t^*, and nfa_t^* denote ratios of Dt, Bt, Bt^*, and $NFAt^*$ to GDP.

18. $\sigma_t = (M_{t+1}^{bop} - M_t^{bop})/P_tY_t$: seigniorage revenue.

19. $Roil_{tREF}$, $Roil_t$: net oil revenue evaluated at the budget reference prices, respectively, on projected WEO oil prices.

20. OA^*: oil fund assets.

21. OF_t: other exogenous factors of public debt accumulation that may increase or decrease the outstanding stock of net public debt, such as privatization receipt or recognition of contingent liabilities.

Public Debt Decomposition Equation

In ORCs, a substantial share of fiscal revenues is derived from exhaustible natural resources (oil and gas, referred to simply as "oil"). Hence, we break total tax revenue to Tt (non-oil taxes) and OTt (oil-related taxes). Oil-related taxes are defined as oil revenues evaluated at the reference price assumed in the government budget, net of oil-related expenditure and transfers. Furthermore, net debt is now defined as domestic treasury debt to private sector and external public debt, net of the central bank's net foreign assets and net of the oil assets, assuming that those are separate from net foreign assets.

$$D_t = B_t + e_t \cdot B_t^* - e_t \cdot NFA_t^* - e_t \cdot OA_t^* = (G_t - T_t - OT_t)$$
$$- (M_{t+1}^{bop} - M_t^{bop}) + (1 + i_t^d) \cdot B_{t-1} + (1 + i_t^f) \cdot e_t \cdot B_{t-1}^*$$
$$- (1 + i_t^l) \cdot e_t \cdot NFA_{t-1}^* - (1 + i_t^l) \cdot e_t \cdot OA_{t-1}^* + OF_t \qquad (10.5)$$

Converting all the variables in ratios to GDP and defining lowercase variables as uppercase variables in percent of GDP yields

$$d_t = b_t + b_t^* - nfa_t^* - oa_t^* = (g_t - t_t - Roil_t) - \sigma_t$$
$$+ \frac{(1 + i_t^d) \cdot b_{t-1}}{(1 + g_t) \cdot (1 + \pi_t)} + \frac{(1 + i_t^f) \cdot (1 + s_t) \cdot b_{t-1}^*}{(1 + g_t) \cdot (1 + \pi_t)}$$
$$- \frac{(1 + i_t^l) \cdot (1 + s_t) \cdot [nfa_{t-1}^* + oa_{t-1}^*]}{(1 + g_t) \cdot (1 + \pi_t)} + of_t \qquad (10.6)$$

The next step involves converting all the variables in real terms. To do that, it is also necessary to multiply and divide the last two terms of the right-hand side by $(1 + \pi_t^*)$ and group the real exchange rate components in $(1 + \hat{e}_t)$:

$$
\begin{aligned}
d_t = b_t + b_t^* - nfa_t^* - oa_t^* &= (g_t - t_t - Roil_t) - \sigma_t \\
&+ \frac{(1 + i_t^d) \cdot b_{t-1}}{(1 + g_t) \cdot (1 + \pi_t)} + \frac{(1 + i_t^f) \cdot (1 + \hat{e}_t) \cdot b_{t-1}^*}{(1 + g_t) \cdot (1 + \pi_t^*)} \\
&- \frac{(1 + i_t^l) \cdot (1 + \hat{e}_t) \cdot [nfa_{t-1}^* + oa_{t-1}^*]}{(1 + g_t) \cdot (1 + \pi_t^*)} + of_t
\end{aligned}
\tag{10.7}
$$

Finally, to represent changes in net public debt, it is necessary to subtract d_{t-1} from equation (10.7):

$$
\begin{aligned}
\Delta d_t = (g_t - t_t - Roil_t) - \sigma_t &+ \frac{(i_t^d - \pi_t) \cdot b_{t-1}}{(1 + \pi_t) \cdot (1 + g_t)} - \frac{g_t}{(1 + g_t)} b_{t-1} \\
&+ \frac{(i_t^f \cdot (1 + \hat{e}_t) - \pi_t^*) \cdot b_{t-1}^*}{(1 + \pi_t^*) \cdot (1 + g_t)} + \frac{\hat{e}_t \cdot b_{t-1}^*}{(1 + \pi_t^*) \cdot (1 + g_t)} \\
&- \frac{g_t}{(1 + g_t)} \cdot b_{t-1}^* - \left(\frac{(i_t^l \cdot (1 + \hat{e}_t) - \pi_t^*)}{(1 + \pi_t^*) \cdot (1 + g_t)} + \frac{\hat{e}_t}{(1 + \pi_t^*) \cdot (1 + g_t)} \right. \\
&\left. - \frac{g_t}{(1 + g_t)} \cdot \right)[nfa_{t-1}^* + oa_{t-1}^*] + of_t
\end{aligned}
\tag{10.8}
$$

Given the uncertainty surrounding future oil prices and the possibility of high-volatility periods, this framework introduces the so-called reference price rule, which aims to stabilize the oil revenue flow to the budget, using a conservatively chosen budget reference price. According to this rule, all revenues in excess of this reference price are saved in an oil fund; revenue shortfalls due to prices falling short of the reference price are financed using the accumulated oil fund's assets. To model this rule, $Roil_{REF}$, the oil revenue evaluated at the reference price is added and then subtracted from the right-hand side of equation (10.8) to get equation (10.9):

$$
\begin{aligned}
\Delta d_t = (g_t - t_t - Rroil_t) - \sigma_t &- \frac{g_t}{(1 + g_t)} \cdot d_{t-1} \\
&+ \frac{(i_t^d - \pi_t) \cdot b_{t-1}}{(1 + \pi_t) \cdot (1 + g_t)} + \frac{(i_t^f \cdot (1 + \hat{e}_t) - \pi_t^*) \cdot b_{t-1}^* e_{t-1}}{(1 + \pi_t^*) \cdot (1 + g_t)} \\
&- \frac{(i_t^l \cdot (1 + \hat{e}_t) - \pi_t^*) \cdot [nfa_{t-1}^* + oa_{t-1}^*] e_{t-1}}{(1 + \pi_t^*) \cdot (1 + g_t)} \\
&+ \frac{\hat{e}_t \cdot (b_{t-1}^* - nfa_{t-1}^* - oa_{t-1}^*) e_{t-1}}{(1 + \pi_t^*) \cdot (1 + g_t)} - [Roil_t - Roil_{REFt}] + of_t
\end{aligned}
\tag{10.9}
$$

Next, it is assumed that the excess of actual oil revenue over the reference revenue evaluated at the budget reference price, and the interest earned on the stock of oil assets, are saved in a ring-fenced oil fund:

$$\Delta oa^*_t = \left[\frac{(i^l_t \cdot (1 + \hat{e}_t) - \pi^*_t)}{(1 + \pi^*_t) \cdot (1 + g_t)} + \frac{\hat{e}_t}{(1 + \pi^*_t) \cdot (1 + g_t)} - \frac{g}{1 + g} \right] oa^*_{t-1}$$

$$+ \ [Roil_t - Roil_{REFt}] \tag{10.10}$$

Using (10.10), equation (10.9) can be rewritten as

$$\Delta d_t = (f_t - Rroil_t) - \sigma_t - \frac{g_t}{(1 + g_t)} \cdot d_{t-1} + \frac{(i^d_t - \pi_t) \cdot b_{t-1}}{(1 + \pi_t) \cdot (1 + g_t)}$$

$$+ \frac{(i^f_t \cdot (1 + \hat{e}_t) - \pi^*_t) \cdot b^*_{t-1} e_{t-1}}{(1 + \pi^*_t) \cdot (1 + g_t)} - \frac{(i^l_t \cdot (1 + \hat{e}_t) - \pi^*_t) \cdot nfa^*_{t-1} e_{t-1}}{(1 + \pi^*_t) \cdot (1 + g_t)}$$

$$+ \frac{\hat{e}_t \cdot (b^*_{t-1} - nfa^*_{t-1}) e_{t-1}}{(1 + \pi^*_t) \cdot (1 + g_t)} - \Delta oa^* + of_t \tag{10.11}$$

According to equation (10.11), change in net public debt in percent of GDP is determined by the non-oil primary deficit, oil revenues at budget price, seigniorage revenue, the real interest rate growth differential, capital gains (losses) on net debt from real exchange rate appreciation (depreciation), accumulation of oil assets, and other factors.

Notes

1. Manzano and Rigobon (2001) attributed the resource curse to a "debt overhang" with its origins in the 1970s when oil prices were high and oil-rich countries used commodities as collateral to take on excessive debt. A collapse in oil prices in the 1980s left those countries with no ability to service their debts.

2. A billion is 1,000 millions.

3. The World Bank (2003) also ranked Nigeria as the third most volatile economy in terms of trade volatility (out of 90 developing countries) and the fourth in terms of (real) exchange rate volatility (out of 84 developing countries) during the 1961–2000 period.

4. See also Devlin and Lewin (2005) for a discussion of managing oil booms and busts in developing countries.

5. In 1982 and 1983, Nigeria accumulated trade arrears for the first time. It has been running arrears on its external debt ever since, and the bulk of the

increase of its external debt since the mid-1980s has reflected not so much new lending as converted past commercial debt arrears. Nigeria's arrears on external debt have been rescheduled in successive agreements with the London Club (1984, 1987, 1989, and 1992) and the Paris Club (1986, 1989, 1991, 2000, and 2005). The last Paris Club debt reduction agreement, which was reached in October 2005, has brought significant external debt relief. For more details on this agreement, see IMF (2005).

6. See Burnside (2005) for a good overview of the traditional Word Bank approach.

7. See Davis, Ossowski, and Fedelino (2003) for a discussion of fiscal policy formulation in ORCs, and see Baunsgaard (2003) for a discussion of possible fiscal rules for Nigeria.

8. For debt decomposition derivation in discrete time, see the annex to this chapter.

9. Note that, to simplify the exposition, we present a continuous time formula. As shown in the chapter annex, however, in the fiscal sustainability analysis we use discrete time formulas for deriving public debt dynamics. A similar debt decomposition formula also has been used in World Bank (2005).

10. For an elaboration, see annex A.1 in Bandiera et al. (2007).

11. Ring-fenced oil funds can be successful only if complemented with a rule that limits the non-oil deficit or public debt. Otherwise, the government will accumulate assets in the oil fund while borrowing, so the net asset position may even deteriorate because the cost of borrowing is typically higher than the interest earned on oil fund assets.

12. For a more detailed description of all the stress tests, see Bandiera et al. (2007).

13. The share of the oil windfall that has been spent more than doubled in 2001, relative to 2000, and was quite high in 2002 and 2003; but there seems to be a substantial drop in 2004 and 2005, the years of the OPFR implementation.

14. For more detailed information on this tool, see Budina, Pang, and van Wijnbergen (2007) and Bandiera et al. (2007). All the assumptions underpinning the fiscal sustainability calculations in the base case are derived from the IMF projection framework.

References

Aghion, P., P. Bacchetta, and R. Ranciere. 2006. "Exchange Rate Volatility and Productivity Growth: The Role of Financial Development." Working Paper 12117, National Bureau of Economic Research, Cambridge, MA.

Anand, R., and S. van Wijnbergen. 1988. "Inflation, External Debt and Financial Sector Reform: A Quantitative Approach to Consistent Fiscal Policy with an Application to Turkey." Working Paper 2731, National Bureau of Economic Research, Cambridge, MA.

————. 1989. "Inflation and the Financing of Government Expenditure: An Introductory Analysis with an Application to Turkey." *World Bank Economic Review* 3 (1): 17–38.

Bandiera, L., N. Budina, M. Klijn, and S. van Wijnbergen. 2007. "The 'How to' of Fiscal Sustainability: A Technical Manual for Using the Fiscal Sustainability Tool." Policy Research Working Paper 4170, World Bank, Washington, DC.

Baunsgaard, T. 2003. "Fiscal Policy in Nigeria: Any Role for Rules?" Working Paper 03/155, International Monetary Fund, Washington, DC.

Budina, N., G. Pang, and S. van Wijnbergen. 2007. "Nigeria's Growth Record: Dutch Disease or Debt Overhang?" Working Paper 4256, World Bank, Washington, DC.

Burnside, C. 2005. *Fiscal Sustainability in Theory and Practice: A Handbook.* Washington, DC: World Bank.

Corden, M., and J. P. Neary. 1984. "Booming Sector and Deindustrialization in a Small Open Economy." *Economic Journal* 92: 825–48.

Davis, J. M., R. Ossowski, and A. Fedelino, eds. 2003. *Fiscal Policy Formulation and Implementation in Oil-Producing Countries.* Washington, DC: International Monetary Fund.

Devlin, J., and M. Lewin. 2005. "Managing Oil Booms and Busts in Developing Countries." In *Managing Economic Volatility and Crises: A Practitioner's Guide,* ed. J. Aizenman and B. Pinto, 186–209. Cambridge, UK: Cambridge University Press.

Hausmann, R., and R. Rigobon. 2002. "An Alternative Interpretation of the Resource Curse: Theory and Policy Implications." Working Paper 9424, National Bureau of Economic Research, Cambridge, MA.

IMF (International Monetary Fund). 2002. "Assessing Sustainability." Washington DC. http://www.imf.org/external/np/pdr/sus/2002/eng/052802.htm.

————. 2003. "Sustainability Assessments: Review of Application and Methodological Refinements." Washington DC.

————. 2005. "Nigeria: 2005 Article IV Consultation—Staff Report; Staff Supplement; and Public Information Notice on the Executive Board Discussion." Country Report 05/302, Washington, DC.

Lane, P. R., and A. Tornell. 1996. "Power, Growth and the Voracity Effect." *Journal of Economic Growth* 1 (2): 213–41.

Manzano, O., and R. Rigobon. 2001. "Resource Curse or Debt Overhang?" Working Paper 8390, National Bureau of Economic Research, Cambridge, MA.

van Wijnbergen, S. 1984a. "Inflation, Employment, and the Dutch Disease in Oil-Exporting Countries: A Short-Run Disequilibrium Analysis." *Quarterly Journal of Economics* 99 (2): 233–50.

————. 1984b. "The Dutch Disease: A Disease After All?" *The Economic Journal* 94 (373): 41–55.

————. 1985. "Trade Reform, Aggregate Investment and Capital Flight: On Credibility and the Value of Information." *Economic Letters* 19 (4): 369–72.

World Bank. 2003. "Nigeria: Policy Options for Growth and Stability." Report 26215-NGA, World Bank, Washington, DC.

————. 2005. "Nigeria's Opportunity of a Generation: Meeting the MDGs, Reducing Indebtedness." Anchor Report prepared for Poverty Reduction and Economic Management, Africa Region, World Bank, Washington, DC.

————. 2006. "Debt Sustainability Analysis in Oil-Rich Countries." PRMED Note, Washington, DC.

CHAPTER 11

Evaluation of the Welfare Impact of Higher Energy Prices in Madagascar

Noro Andriamihaja and Giovanni Vecchi

Typical analyses of the economic impact of oil price movements treat them as macroeconomic supply shocks affecting inflation and output. No less important is their distributional impact on different segments of the population, operating through relative prices and real incomes. A rise in petroleum prices is not simply bad news for the economy as a whole, but is particularly bad news for poorer households.

Over the past few years, Madagascar has experienced a substantial increase in oil prices. The relatively low price of international crude oil ($29.8 a barrel) in December 2003 has increased by about 150 percent, to reach $62.0 a barrel by December 2006. To make things worse, the local currency, the ariary (MGA), depreciated considerably during the period 2003–05. A U.S. dollar bought MGA 1,277.0 in January 2003, which became MGA 2,488.5 by mid-2004. Beginning in the second half of 2004, the ariary showed some tendency to appreciate to reach MGA 2,013 at the end of December 2006. Since that time, the exchange rate has stabilized around MGA 2,050 to one U.S. dollar.

Fiscal regimes did not help. Oil products are subject to specific taxes (*Taxes sur les Produits Pétroliers,* [TPP]), and petroleum products are subject to a value-added tax. The oil tax rates were adjusted upward in 2002 and 2006. Diesel was affected the most, with increases of 230 percent in TTP in 2002 and 179 percent in the budget law of 2006.

Given the dynamics of (1) international crude oil prices, (2) the exchange rate, and (3) the fiscal regimes, it comes as no surprise that domestic prices of petroleum products increased significantly between 2003 and the first half of 2006. Prices of gasoline, diesel, and kerosene increased an average of 145 percent between December 2003 and December 2006.

Higher energy prices have adverse consequences for poor people. Real income losses may be substantial because higher oil prices imply not only higher prices for petroleum products directly consumed by households, but also higher prices of other goods that use petroleum as an intermediate good in the production process. In fact, previous studies have shown that the latter, indirect effect is equally or more important than the direct effect (Coady and Newhouse 2005; Kpodar 2006). With the goal of shielding the purchasing power of poor households, governments may consider subsidizing petroleum prices. However, the introduction of price subsidies raises a number of issues that need careful consideration.

First, the introduction of price subsidies is not neutral from the distributive standpoint. The key questions here are (1) Are the poor the real beneficiaries of the price subsidies? (2) What is the exact extent of their benefit? and (3) Is the overall effect progressive or regressive?

Second, there is a concern about the consequences of price subsidies in terms of allocational efficiency. Are subsidies the most effective or efficient way of protecting the real income of the poor? In the presence of binding budget constraints, subsidies are likely to divert resources from other social expenses that may be more effective in reaching the poor. Moreover, by altering the structure of relative prices, subsidies may affect the incentives for households to use their energy efficiently.

Third, there are fiscal considerations. Even if price subsidies are not financed by reductions in other social expenditures, they may eventually cause fiscal distress (increases in budget deficit and debt). Thus it can be argued that they may lead to adjustment policies, for example, increases in taxes, with offsetting effects (Gupta et al. 2000).

To begin addressing the issues defined above in the context of Madagascar, this chapter analyzes how higher petroleum prices impact households, focusing most of the attention on the poor. The simulation exercise is based on an input-output model à la Coady and Newhouse (2005). This approach, besides being relatively easy to implement, efficiently combines micro- and macrodata that are commonly available for most countries.

The chapter is organized as follows. The next section provides background information on the present pricing regime in Madagascar, the petroleum sector market structure, and the pattern of price increases. The third section outlines the method used to assess the welfare effect of higher oil prices and presents the estimates. A summary and final remarks conclude the chapter text, and two annexes follow.

General Background

Madagascar is a net oil importer. It stopped importing crude oil in 2005, after the refinery in Tamatave was closed. It imported, however, 540,106 metric tons of final products in 2006. Besides transport, the lighting and electricity generation sectors are the second-largest users of petroleum. More than half of the electricity produced in Madagascar is derived from fuel. More than 85 percent of the rural population use kerosene for lighting.

The market is dominated by four companies: Total, Shell, Galana, and Jovenna. Prices were set by the Malagasy Petroleum Office, the regulatory agency until June 2004, based on a formula with monthly adjustments. In early 2004, when oil prices started moving upward, the government froze prices for a couple of months. Prices were expected to be fully liberalized by October 2004, but that date was moved forward to July 2005. Since that date, prices at the pump have been set by the operators, with no government oversight whatsoever.

Oil prices have increased dramatically since the beginning of 2004. Figure 11.1 shows that, between January 2003 and December 2006, international prices rose significantly (+1.7 percent per month), if not steadily. From $31.30 a barrel in January 2003, the price of crude oil peaked in July 2006 at $72.45, and closed at $60 in December 2006. Figure 11.2 shows the dynamic of prices for a selection of petroleum products.

To calculate the effect of the exchange rate on the increase of domestic prices of energy products, we define our terms as follows. Let $p^\$_{oil}(i)$ be the international price of a given energy product at the beginning of year i, and $\lambda(i)$ be the exchange rate (ariary/dollar) at the beginning of year i. The change in international price in ariary during year i is given by the following formula:

$$\Delta p^{Ary}_{oil} = \lambda(i+1)p^\$_{oil}(i+1) - \lambda(i)p^\$_{oil}(i) \tag{11.1}$$

FIGURE 11.1
International Versus Domestic Crude Oil Prices, 2003–06

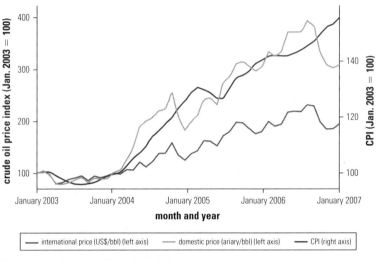

Sources: Malagasy Petroleum Office; authors' calculations.

Note: bbl = barrel; CPI = consumer price index.

FIGURE 11.2
Domestic Prices of Selected Petroleum Products, 2000–06

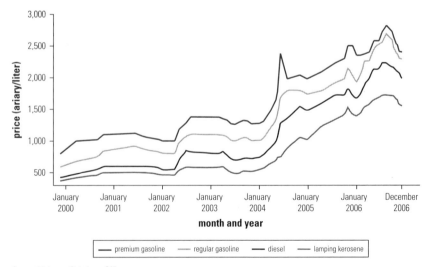

Source: Malagasy Petroleum Office.

TABLE 11.1
Exchange Rate Effect on Domestic Price, 2004–06
Percent

Oil product	2004	2005	2006
Aircraft gasoline	92	1.00	23
Lamping kerosene	61	24	30
Premium gasoline	66	26	26
Regular gasoline	71	24	30
Diesel	66	23	29
Fuel oil	99	12	93
Total	60	22	32

Sources: Malagasy Petroleum Office; authors' calculations.

Note: Domestic prices are assumed to be a linear transformation of international prices.

The (simulated) change of international price in ariary, assuming a constant exchange rate during year i, is

$$\Delta p_{oil}^{Ary}(sim) = \lambda(i)p_{oil}^{\$}(i + 1) - \lambda(i)p_{oil}^{\$}(i) \qquad (11.2)$$

The effect of the exchange rate on the change in domestic prices, therefore, is given by

$$\text{Exchange rate effect} = \frac{\Delta p_{oil}^{Ary} - \Delta p_{oil}^{Ary}(sim)}{\Delta p_{oil}^{Ary}} \qquad (11.3)$$

Table 11.1 shows the proportion of the domestic price change due to the variation of the exchange rate for selected oil products.

The increase in international oil prices caused a net deterioration in the terms of trade by 5.1 percent in 2004 and 6.2 percent in 2005. In addition, the net impact of these international price movements is estimated at 1.57 percent of gross domestic product in 2005 (figure 11.3). This net impact is a measure of the aggregate burden to the economy caused by the increase of the international oil product.

Welfare Impact of Higher Energy Prices

The effects of increasing petroleum prices on household welfare are twofold. First is the *direct* effect: households are affected through increases in the price of petroleum products that they consume directly—for example, kerosene for lighting and cooking, gasoline for private

FIGURE 11.3
Impact of the Increase of International Oil Price on Imports, 2002–06

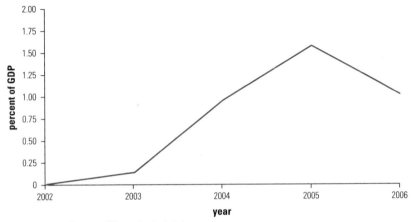

Sources: Malagasy Petroleum Office; authors' calculations.

Note: GDP = gross domestic product.

transport, and so forth. Second is the *indirect* effect: households are affected through increases in the prices of other goods and services as higher energy costs are passed through to the consumer.

One way of assessing the scale of the two effects is by decomposing the total welfare effect (TWE) into its two components—namely, the direct welfare effect (DWE) and the indirect welfare effect (IWE)—and estimating them separately:

$$TWE = DWE + IWE \qquad (11.4)$$

Let w_j^{oil} ($j = 1, \ldots n$) denote the budget share for the j-th petroleum product, and Δp_j^{oil} its price variation (expressed in percent). The DWE of price changes in petroleum products can be calculated by multiplying the price variation by the corresponding household budget share and aggregating across goods:

$$DWE = \sum_{j=1}^{J} \Delta p_j^{oil} w_j^{oil} \qquad (11.5)$$

where J is the number of petroleum products consumed by the households. Equation (11.5) expresses DWE as a percentage of total household expenditure.

The procedure is more involved for the IWE. In the text immediately below, we provide a broad outline of the strategy for estimating IWE; a full account is offered later in the chapter.

Let p^{oil} denote an aggregate (scalar) measure of the price of petroleum products:

$$p^{oil} = \sum_{j=1}^{J} \delta_j p_j^{oil} \text{ with } \sum_{j=1}^{J} \delta_j = 1 \qquad (11.6)$$

where the last term is quantity-share based. The change in this aggregate price is

$$\Delta p^{oil} = \sum_{j=1}^{J} \delta_j \Delta p_j^{oil} \qquad (11.7)$$

Now let us define $\Delta\mathbf{q}$ as a (row) vector of changes in consumer prices:

$$\Delta\mathbf{q} = f(\Delta p^{oil}) \qquad (11.8)$$

Equation (11.8) makes clear that consumer prices for nonpetroleum goods and services depend on prices of petroleum goods because the latter enter the production of the former as intermediate goods.

Once estimates for equation (11.8) are available, calculating IWE is a simple matter:

$$\text{IWE} = \sum_{j=1}^{S} f_j(\Delta p^{oil}) w_j \qquad (11.9)$$

where $f_j(\Delta p^{oil})$ denotes the change in price for the j-th good (or service) consumed by the household. The difficulty, as we will see in a later section, is in calculating $\Delta\mathbf{q}$ because the function $f_j(\cdot)$ in equation (11.9) is a mapping between producer and consumer prices that must account for the production structure of various sectors of the economy—in particular, for the different intensity in the use of petroleum products as inputs by various sectors.

In the following subsections, we discuss equations (11.5) and (11.9) in detail, and obtain estimates for both the direct and indirect effects.

Direct Welfare Effect

Measuring the direct effect of a change in petroleum product prices on households' welfare is a relatively straightforward matter. Schematically, it requires three steps: The first step is identifying the petroleum products

TABLE 11.2
Direct Welfare Effect of Price Changes, by Expenditures Quintile, 2005

Expenditure	Q1 (poorest)	Q2	Q3	Q4	Q5 (richest)	All quintiles
Household budget shares (%)						
Diesel	0.19	0.10	0.08	0.07	0.08	0.10
Electricity	0.06	0.10	0.21	0.45	1.17	0.48
Gasoline	0.02	0.00	0.00	0.02	0.27	0.08
Kerosene	3.18	2.31	1.96	1.64	1.04	1.89
All	3.46	2.51	2.25	2.19	2.56	2.55
DWE (*% of total household expenditure*)	1.19	0.86	0.73	0.64	0.50	0.74
Mean consumption of petroleum products (*ratio to bottom quintile*)	1.00	1.08	1.16	1.34	3.10	1.69

Source: Authors' estimates.

Note: DWE = direct welfare effect. Budget shares are based on the *Enquête Auprès des Ménages* 2005. Quintiles are based on the national distribution of per capita annual expenditures. Estimation of the DWE is based on price increases observed during 2005 (11 percent for gasoline, 13 percent for diesel, and 36 percent for kerosene). The change in the price of electricity is assumed to be one-third of the average change in petroleum prices.

directly consumed by households. According to the *Enquête Auprès des Ménages* 2005, information is available for electricity (*électricité*), gasoline (*essence*), diesel (*gas-oil*), and kerosene (*pétrole*). The second step is identifying the price increases for each petroleum product. Data on prices are available from the Malagasy Petroleum Office. The third step is estimating the direct impact of price increases on households by multiplying the budget share of each petroleum product by its percentage price increase.

The top panel of table 11.2 shows household budget shares for diesel, electricity, gasoline, and kerosene. Overall, petroleum products absorb, on average, 2.6 percent of the household budget. However, the table shows that the consumption of energy products differs significantly across households, according to their expenditure levels. For example, kerosene—the single most important product with, a 1.9 percent budget share—accounts for as much as 3.2 percent of expenditures among the poorest households, but for only 1.0 percent among households in the upper quintile. Consumption of gasoline, by contrast, is negligible for most households, except for the 0.3 percent of expenditures among the richest 20 percent.

Similarly, the budget share for electricity increases dramatically with the household's living standard: from 0.06 to 0.10 percent in the bottom two quintiles of total expenditure to 1.17 percent for the richest 20 percent of households.

FIGURE 11.4
Difference between Urban and Rural Energy Consumption Patterns, by Quintile, 2005

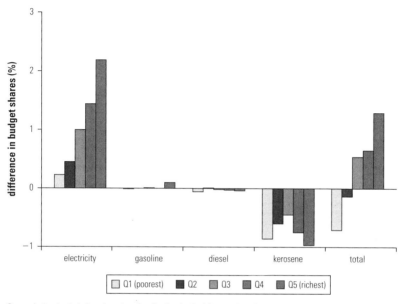

Source: Authors' calculations, based on *Enquête Auprès des Ménages* 2005 data.

Note: The graph charts the average *difference* between urban and rural budget shares for energy products, by national per capita expenditure quintiles. A positive bar implies a higher consumption in urban than in rural areas.

Figure 11.4 investigates the differences in consumption patterns among urban and rural households. Three features stand out. First, the budget share allocated to electricity is always higher for urban households than for rural ones, with a clear pattern across income quintiles. Second, rural households allocate a higher percentage of total consumption to kerosene. Third, the overall pattern in budget shares for energy products differs according to living standards: poor rural households allocate a higher percentage of their total expenditure to energy than do poor urban households, whereas the reverse is true for the richest 40 percent.

Table 11.2 shows estimates of the DWE as defined in equation (11.5). The average direct impact of the increase in the price of energy products on total household expenditure is 0.74 percent. The table shows that the loss of purchasing power is higher for the poor (1.2 percent) than for the rich (0.5 percent). Part of this difference is attributable to differences in

FIGURE 11.5
Components of Direct Effect of Per Capita Expenditure, by Quintile, 2005

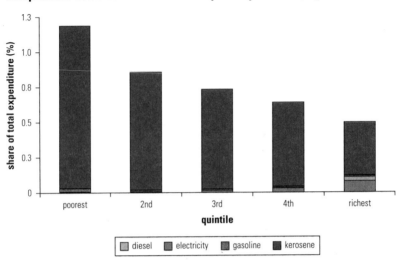

Source: Authors' calculations, based on *Enquête Auprès des Ménages* 2005 data.

the total budget share of all fuels, and the rest is occasioned by the budget share structure.

It is worth mentioning that the estimates in table 11.2 are effectively a Laspeyres index that holds budget shares fixed, overstating the loss in welfare. This issue will be taken up again in the final section of the chapter.

Figure 11.5 clearly shows the regressive nature of the welfare effect of energy price increases. The poor are affected most severely (1.2 percent of their total expenditure), mostly by the increase in the price of kerosene, with other fuels and electricity playing a marginal role only. The negative impact on welfare decreases monotonically with per capita expenditure. Rich households are affected the least (0.5 percent of total expenditure), as a consequence of the increase in prices of both kerosene and electricity.

Indirect Welfare Effect

Measuring the indirect effect of a change in petroleum product prices on households' welfare is *not* a straightforward matter. In this section we use the price-shifting model introduced in Coady and Newhouse (2005). The building blocks of this model are (1) an input-output matrix, and (2) household expenditure patterns, available from the *Enquête Auprès des Ménages* 2005.

Price-Shifting Model

We start by assuming that the technology of the economy is fully described by the input-output (IO) matrix. The IO matrix describes the use of sectoral inputs in the production of sectoral outputs, and, in particular, it provides information on the use of petroleum products as inputs in each sector of the economy. In the case of Madagascar, the IO table contains 30 economic sectors, and was last estimated for the year 1995 (see annex 11B). A stylized representation of the IO matrix is as follows:

$$\mathbf{A} = \begin{bmatrix} a_{11} & a_{21} & \cdots & a_{1S} \\ a_{21} & a_{22} & & \\ \vdots & & \ddots & \\ a_{S1} & & & a_{SS} \end{bmatrix} \tag{11.10}$$

In our application, the matrix $\mathbf{A}$ is a 30×30 square matrix. The generic element of $\mathbf{A}$, a_{ij} $(i,j = 1, 2, \ldots, S)$ represents the cost of the i-th input per one unit of value of the j-th output. Units of output are defined so that they have a user price of unity. Annex 11A shows that the a_{ij} coefficient represents the change in the cost of producing one unit of j due to a unit change in the price of input i.

The next step is modeling each sector of the economy as a producer of an "aggregate" or composite commodity. There are as many composite commodities as the number of economic sectors in the IO matrix. For instance, sector "Agriculture" produces the "agricultural commodity," sector "Animal Production" produces the "animal production commodity," and so on.

Each sector is assumed to face a certain market structure, which determines the mechanism through which changes in *input* prices are passed on to *output* prices. Precisely, we assume that three market structures are enough to describe the sectors of the economy (notation is as follows: $\mathbf{p}$ denotes the $1 \times S$ vector of *producer* prices net of sales taxes and/or tariffs, whereas $\mathbf{q}$ denotes the $1 \times S$ vector of *consumer* prices):

1. **Traded sectors:** These are sectors that compete with internationally traded goods. Foreign goods compete with domestic goods; therefore, higher input costs cannot be passed on to output prices:

$$\mathbf{q}^{ts} = \mathbf{p}^{world} + \mathbf{t}^{ts} \tag{11.11}$$

In equation (11.11), consumer prices ($\mathbf{q}^{ts}$) are determined by world prices ($\mathbf{p}^{world}$), and by trade taxes ($\mathbf{t}^{ts}$, inclusive of tariffs and sales taxes).

2. **Controlled sectors:** These are sectors where output prices are controlled by the government:

$$\mathbf{q}^{cs} = \mathbf{p}^* \qquad (11.12)$$

In equation (11.12), consumer prices ($\mathbf{q}^{cs}$) are determined by pricing controls ($\mathbf{p}^*$). For the sake of simplicity, domestic taxes are set to zero.

3. **Cost-push sectors:** These are sectors where higher input costs are pushed fully on to output prices. This is likely to occur for most government services, construction, public utilities, trade and transportation, and retail and wholesale trade. In general, one would expect this pricing scheme to apply to nontraded commodities. The formula:

$$\mathbf{q}^{cp} = \mathbf{p}^{cp} + \mathbf{t}^{cp} \qquad (11.13)$$

According to equation (11.13), the final price paid by consumers ($\mathbf{q}^{cp}$) is equal to the price set by producers ($\mathbf{p}^{cp}$) plus sales or excise taxes ($\mathbf{t}^{cp}$) imposed by the government.

Having defined the price-setting equations, we now turn to modeling the mechanisms through which factor price *changes* are passed on to output prices. Changes in prices for traded sectors are given by

$$\Delta\mathbf{q}^{ts} = \Delta\mathbf{p}^{world} + \Delta\mathbf{t}^{ts} \qquad (11.14)$$

where both $\Delta\mathbf{p}^{world}$ and $\Delta\mathbf{t}^{ts}$ on the right-hand side are assumed to be exogenous.

For controlled sectors, the formula for the changes in prices is most simple, and is obtained from equation (11.12):

$$\Delta\mathbf{q}^{cs} = \Delta\mathbf{p}^* \qquad (11.15)$$

where the right-hand side variable is exogenously determined by the government pricing controls.

Finally, the change in consumer prices in cost-push sectors is given by

$$\Delta\mathbf{q}^{cp} = \Delta\mathbf{p}^{cp} + \Delta\mathbf{t}^{cp} \qquad (11.16)$$

A problem arises in calculating the term $\Delta\mathbf{p}^{cp}$. Producer prices depend on all factor prices of intermediate goods. Let $\mathbf{w}$ denote the vector containing the prices of production factors *not* included in the IO table (wages, for instance), and let $\mathbf{q}$ be the vector of intermediate goods included in the IO table. Equation (11.16) can then be rewritten as follows:

$$\Delta\mathbf{q}^{cp} = \Delta\mathbf{p}^{cp}(\mathbf{w},\mathbf{q}) + \Delta\mathbf{t}^{cp} \qquad (11.17)$$

Equation (11.17) shows that the difficulty in calculating $\Delta\mathbf{q}^{cp}$ arises because output prices $\mathbf{q}$ are, in fact, input prices for certain industries. That is what the term $\Delta\mathbf{p}^{cp}(\mathbf{q})$ represents. How do changes in $\mathbf{q}$ pass on to final prices? For simplicity, we will ignore changes in $\mathbf{w}$ and will focus on $\mathbf{q}$ so that $\Delta\mathbf{p}^{cp}(\mathbf{w},\mathbf{q})$ is reduced to $\Delta\mathbf{p}^{cp}(\mathbf{q})$.

The solution suggested by Coady and Newhouse (2005) is based on the assumption that each of the composite commodities described above is made up of a certain proportion of cost-push, traded, and controlled commodities. Let α, β, and γ denote these proportions, respectively. To illustrate, let us assume that the producers of the "agricultural commodity" buy α_s percent of inputs from producers in the cost-push sectors, β_s percent of inputs from the traded sector, and γ_s percent from the controlled sector. The suffix s refers to the sector, and ranges from 1 to 30. Obviously, these proportions should sum to unity and never be negative:

$$0 \leq (\alpha_s, \beta_s, \gamma_s) \leq 1 \text{ and } \alpha_s + \beta_s + \gamma_s = 1 \ (s = 1, \ldots 30) \tag{11.18}$$

The change in the price of the j-th commodity (the "agricultural commodity") can be expressed as a linear combination of the three market structures identified above:

$$\Delta p_j^{cp}(\mathbf{q}) = \sum_{i=1}^{S}\alpha_i a_{ij}\Delta q_j^{cp} + \sum_{i=1}^{S}\beta_i a_{ij}\Delta q_j^{ts} + \sum_{i=1}^{S}\gamma_i a_{ij}\Delta q_j^{cs} \ (j = 1, \ldots, S) \tag{11.19}$$

Equation (11.19) can be compacted by using matrix notation:

$$\Delta\mathbf{p}^{cp} = \Delta\mathbf{q}^{cp}\boldsymbol{\alpha}\mathbf{A} + \Delta\mathbf{q}^{ts}\boldsymbol{\beta}\mathbf{A} + \Delta\mathbf{q}^{cs}\boldsymbol{\gamma}\mathbf{A} \tag{11.20}$$

where $\Delta\mathbf{p}^{cp}$ is a $1 \times S$ row vector; $\boldsymbol{\alpha}$, $\boldsymbol{\beta}$, and $\boldsymbol{\gamma}$ are diagonal $S \times S$ matrices; $\Delta\mathbf{q}^{cp}$ is $1 \times S$; $\Delta\mathbf{q}^{ts}$ is $1 \times S$; and $\Delta\mathbf{q}^{cs}$ is $1 \times S$. Equation (11.20) gives the changes in the *producer* prices for the controlled sectors. Now substitute (11.14), (11.15), and (11.16) in equation (11.20):

$$\Delta\mathbf{p}^{cp} = \Delta\mathbf{p}^{cp}\boldsymbol{\alpha}\mathbf{A} + \Delta\mathbf{t}^{cp}\boldsymbol{\alpha}\mathbf{A} + \Delta\mathbf{p}^{world}\boldsymbol{\beta}\mathbf{A} + \Delta\mathbf{t}^{ts}\boldsymbol{\beta}\mathbf{A} + \Delta\mathbf{p}^{*}\boldsymbol{\gamma}\mathbf{A} \tag{11.21}$$

The reduced form of equation (11.21) is given by

$$\Delta\mathbf{p}^{cp} = \Delta\mathbf{t}^{cp}\boldsymbol{\alpha}\mathbf{AV} + \Delta\mathbf{p}^{world}\boldsymbol{\beta}\mathbf{AV} + \Delta\mathbf{t}^{ts}\boldsymbol{\beta}\mathbf{AV} + \Delta\mathbf{p}^{*}\boldsymbol{\gamma}\mathbf{AV} \tag{11.22}$$

where, to simplify the notation, we let $\mathbf{V} = (\mathbf{I} - \boldsymbol{\alpha}\mathbf{A})^{-1}$. Equation (11.22) gives the vector of *producer* price changes in the cost-push sectors. The matrix $\mathbf{V}$ captures both the direct and indirect effects of input price changes on output price changes.

The equation we are interested in is *consumer* price changes:

$$\Delta q = \Delta q^{cp}\alpha + \Delta q^{ts}\beta + \Delta q^{cs}\gamma \tag{11.23}$$

In our application to Madagascar, we further simplify the model by assuming that (1) the only exogenous price changes are changes in the controlled sector (in other words, we assume no changes in producer prices abroad [$\Delta p^{world} = 0$] and no changes in either taxes or tariffs [$\Delta t^{ts} = 0$, $\Delta t^{cp} = 0$]); (2) all petroleum products are within the controlled sector (this poses restrictions on the matrices α, β, and γ); and (3) all other products are cost-push sectors. As a consequence, equation (11.14) is reduced to $\Delta q^{ts} = 0$, and equation (11.16) becomes $\Delta q^{cp} = \Delta p^{cp}$. Under hypotheses (1) through (3), equation (11.23) can be rewritten as

$$\Delta q = \Delta p^{cp}\alpha + \Delta p^*\gamma \tag{11.24}$$

Finally, we substitute equation (11.22) in equation (11.24):

$$\Delta q = \Delta p^*\gamma AV\alpha + \Delta p^*\gamma = \Delta p^*[\gamma AV\alpha + \gamma] \tag{11.25}$$

Equation (11.25) is key for the evaluation of the impact of a change in energy prices on consumer prices for the range of sectors available in the IO table.

Estimates

Table 11.3 shows the impact of higher petroleum prices on the prices in other sectors. Multiplying these induced price increases (column [2]) by the corresponding household budget shares (column [1]) and aggregating across goods and services gives the percentage increase in costs due to the indirect price increases.

According to the estimates in table 11.3, the generalized increase in prices of goods and services caused by a 17 percent increase in petroleum prices implies a drop in household real income of 1 percent (row total of column [3]). This is the estimate of what was referred to previously as the IWE. Table 11.3 also shows that the single most important contribution comes from products in the food industry, which accounts for almost two-thirds of the indirect effect. The aggregate of all food-related sectors accounts for almost 80 percent of the overall indirect effect. The second highest source is the textile sector, which accounts for some 7 percent of the indirect effect.

TABLE 11.3
Indirect Price and Real Income Effects, by Sector, 2005

Sector	Budget shares (%) (1)	Price effect (%) (2)	Impact on expenditure (%) (3)[a]	Percent of total impact (%) (4)
Agriculture	10.17	0.29	0.03	2.94
Farming	0.20	1.13	0.00	0.23
Agro-industry	1.53	2.75	0.04	4.19
Food industry	39.53	1.61	0.64	63.38
Beverage	0.70	1.29	0.01	0.90
Tobacco	2.15	0.95	0.02	2.03
Fats	2.00	3.48	0.07	6.93
Chemical	2.30	2.21	0.05	5.06
Textile	2.97	2.44	0.07	7.22
Metal	0.00	1.69	0.00	0.00
Electrical products	0.00	1.08	0.00	0.00
Paper	0.01	2.81	0.00	0.03
Leather	0.66	1.49	0.01	0.98
Transport (people)	0.94	3.14	0.03	2.94
Transport (other)	0.02	1.26	0.00	0.03
Telecommunication	0.06	0.87	0.00	0.05
Trade	0.30	1.04	0.00	0.31
Services (collective)	3.15	0.87	0.03	2.73
Services (individual)	0.18	0.36	0.00	0.06
Total	66.87	n.a.	1.00	100.00

Source: Authors' estimates.

Note: n.a. = not applicable. Budget shares are derived from *Enquête Auprès des Ménages* 2005, based on commodity groupings that match the more aggregated input-output table sectoral breakdown available for the year 1995. The estimation of the indirect welfare effects are based on price increases observed during 2005 (11 percent for gasoline, 13 percent for diesel, and 36 percent for kerosene). The change in the price of electricity is assumed to be one-third of the average change in petroleum prices.

a. $(3) = (1) \times (2)/100$.

Total Welfare Effect

After separately calculating the direct effect by aggregating real income changes across petroleum products, and the indirect effect by aggregating real income changes across all other commodities, the total effect can be calculated as the sum of the two separate effects.

Table 11.4 presents the key estimates for understanding the distributional impact of higher petroleum prices in Madagascar. A number of findings are worthy of a comment. First, the top panel of the table shows that the TWE is significant in magnitude: an average increase of 17.00 percent

TABLE 11.4
Total Welfare Effect of Energy Price Changes, by Per Capita Expenditure Quintile, 2005
Percent of total household expenditure

Expenditure	Q1 (poorest)	Q2	Q3	Q4	Q5 (richest)	All quintiles
DWE	1.19	0.86	0.73	0.64	0.50	0.74
IWE	0.95	1.01	1.01	1.03	1.02	1.01
TWE	2.14	1.87	1.74	1.67	1.52	1.75
IWE as % of total	44.00	54.00	58.00	62.00	67.00	58.00
Share of the burden						
DWE	13.4	16.0	17.8	20.4	32.4	100
IWE	6.9	11.7	15.5	21.2	44.7	100
TWE	9.2	13.2	16.3	20.8	40.4	100

Source: Authors' estimates.

Note: DWE = direct welfare effect; IWE = indirect welfare effect; TWE = total welfare effect. Budget shares are derived from EPM 2005 based on commodity groupings that match the more aggregated input-output table sectoral breakdown available for the year 1995. Quintiles are based on the national distribution of per capita annual expenditures. The estimation of the total welfare effect is based on price increases observed during 2005 (11 percent for gasoline, 13 percent for diesel, and 36 percent for kerosene). The change in the price of electricity is assumed to be one-third of the average change in petroleum prices.

in energy prices causes a loss equal to 1.75 percent of total household expenditure. The loss is greater for households in the bottom quintile (2.14 percent). It decreases for households in the upper quintile (1.52 percent). The incidence of the increase in oil prices, therefore, is unambiguously regressive.

Second, approximately 60 percent of the total welfare loss is due to the IWE. This implies that the main channel through which households are affected by higher energy prices is the indirect effect on non-oil prices (especially food prices, as noted above). The combination of (1) a relatively high sensitivity of food prices to oil prices (table 11.3, column [2]), and (2) a large budget share devoted to food (table 11.3, column [1]) is largely responsible for the prevalence of the IWE shown in table 11.4.

Third, the share of the indirect effect is lowest for the poorest households, accounting for 44 percent of the TWE, compared with 67 percent for the households in the top quintiles. This result is driven by the pattern observed for the direct effect.

The bottom panel of table 11.4 translates the percentage effects shown in the top panel into shares of aggregate real expenditure loss borne by each quintile. Although energy products may absorb a higher proportion of the total consumption budget of low-income households, high-income households typically consume larger quantities of these products. Hence, it is important to assess the distribution of the total loss, in absolute terms (that is, in local currency units), by quintile. This is precisely what is shown in the bottom panel of table 11.4.

The top two quintiles, representing only 40 percent of the population, account for approximately 60 percent of the total loss, compared with approximately 22 percent for the bottom two quintiles. The pattern observed for the TWE mirrors the pattern for both indirect and direct effects.

The main finding here is that, although price increases hurt the poor more in percentage terms (third row of table 11.4), subsidizing energy prices would involve a substantial leakage in favor of higher-income households (last row of table 11.4). This empirical finding raises the issue of identifying more cost-effective policies to protect the poor households against energy price increases.

Summary and Final Remarks

High on most governments' agendas is the issue of how to deal with the adverse consequences of higher energy prices on living standards of the poorest segments of the population. A hotly debated question is whether governments should introduce price controls or intervene in other ways to mitigate the social costs of oil price increases. In the absence of compelling, unambiguous theoretical arguments, assessing the advisability of price controls must be based on the empirical evidence.

In this chapter, we assessed the distributional impact of the increase in petroleum prices during 2005 by estimating the impact on households' real expenditures. The main findings can be summarized as follows. First, a 17.00 percent rise in the price of energy products leads to a 1.75 percent average decrease in real expenditure. This percentage is higher for low-income households (2.1 percent) than for high-income households (1.5 percent). This finding implies that the benefits of introducing energy price subsidies would be *progressive;* that is, in percentage terms, subsidies would benefit poor households more than rich households. However, subsidizing would involve substantial leakage in favor of high-income households, which account for more than 60 percent of the total burden of price increases. These results raise the issue of identifying more cost-effective policies to protect the poorest households. The relatively large size of the "leakage to the rich" implied by our estimates suggests that improvements in the ability to target social transfers and expenditure should be a priority. The analysis carried out in the chapter suggests that subsidies on kerosene represent one such option worth exploring. Consistent with our results is an overall rethinking of the system of safety nets.

It is well to bear in mind the limitations of the method used here. A first simplification in our analysis is the assumption that all "composite goods" (with the exception of energy products) are produced in cost-push sectors. As noted by Kpodar (2006), this assumption is likely to overemphasize the importance of the indirect price effect, though the bias is hard (if at all possible) to quantify. Second, our analysis does not take into account the fact that consumers are likely to change their consumption behavior in response to the initial price shock. Nor does it account for the fact that producers also are likely to modify their use of factors of production. Dealing with substitution effects would require a different approach, based on the estimation of a computable general equilibrium model, a task that goes beyond the scope of this chapter (see Banks, Blundell, and Lewbel 1996).

That said, it is probably a fair claim that, given the relatively low substitutability of petroleum products among both consumers and producers in the context of Madagascar, the results obtained in the chapter may be deemed reasonable, and possibly realistic, at least for the short term.

Annex 11A: On the Interpretation of the Coefficients of the Input-Output Matrix

This annex shows that the a_{ij} coefficient of the IO table represents the change in the cost of producing one unit of j due to a unit change in the price of input i.

According to equation (11.10) in the text, a_{ij} denotes the cost of input i to produce one unit of output j. Now rescale the unit of measurement of each output so that total value of each output is equal to 1:

$$v_j = \sum_{i=1}^{s} a_{ij} + AV_j = 1 \quad \forall j \tag{11A.1}$$

where v_j is the total value of the j-th output, and AV_j is the added value for output j. Let b_{ij} denote the quantity of input i required to produce one unit of output j, as defined above. By definition, we have

$$a_{ij} = b_{ij} p_i \tag{11A.2}$$

The elasticity of the monetary *cost* of producing j with respect to the price of the input i is

$$\frac{\partial v_j}{\partial p_i} \times \frac{p_i}{v_j} = b_{ij} \times \frac{p_i}{v_j} = b_{ij} p_i = a_{ij} \quad \text{QED} \tag{11A.3}$$

Annex 11B: IO Table for Madagascar, 1995

This annex shows the IO table for 1995, based on a compilation of data from the Ministry of Economy and Finance, the Ministry of Trade, the Ministry of Agriculture, and the Central Bank of Madagascar. External trade data are from the National Institute for Statistics and other surveys sent to enterprises, nongovernmental organizations, the banking sector, and insurance companies.

TABLE 11B.1
IO Table, Madagascar, 1995

	Agriculture	Farming	Hunting	Fishing	Agroindustry	Mining	Energy
Agriculture	0.0137	0.0879	0.0000	0.0141	0.3896	0.0000	0.0000
Farming	0.0194	0.0019	0.0000	0.0000	0.0000	0.0000	0.0000
Hunting	0.0076	0.0328	0.0000	0.0386	0.0018	0.0002	0.0000
Fishing	0.0000	0.0516	0.0000	0.0000	0.0000	0.0000	0.0000
Agroindustry	0.0014	0.0000	0.0000	0.0000	0.0042	0.0016	0.0000
Mining	0.0001	0.0000	0.0000	0.0000	0.0000	0.0000	0.3247
Energy	0.0035	0.0214	0.0497	0.0635	0.1253	0.0756	0.0180
Food	0.0000	0.2091	0.0000	0.0003	0.0000	0.0000	0.0000
Beverage	0.0000	0.0000	0.0000	0.0000	0.0000	0.0000	0.0000
Tobacco	0.0000	0.0000	0.0000	0.0000	0.0000	0.0000	0.0000
Fats	0.0000	0.0257	0.0000	0.0000	0.0000	0.0000	0.0000
Chemical	0.0628	0.0393	0.0093	0.0045	0.1134	0.0594	0.0335
Textile	0.0006	0.0024	0.0023	0.0091	0.0007	0.0003	0.0006
Wood	0.0047	0.0000	0.0000	0.0000	0.0000	0.0297	0.0027
Nonmetal	0.0058	0.0000	0.0000	0.0000	0.0000	0.0000	0.0010
Metal	0.0110	0.0112	0.0346	0.0241	0.0579	0.0221	0.0791
Electrical products	0.0000	0.0005	0.0000	0.0003	0.0034	0.0000	0.0164
Paper	0.0003	0.0025	0.0026	0.0040	0.0077	0.0020	0.0086
Leather	0.0001	0.0007	0.0008	0.0021	0.0197	0.0095	0.0173
Construction	0.0000	0.0000	0.0000	0.0000	0.0000	0.0000	0.0000
Transport (goods)	0.0000	0.0000	0.0000	0.0000	0.0000	0.0000	0.0000
Transport (people)	0.0008	0.0148	0.0056	0.0064	0.0022	0.0068	0.0085
Transport (other)	0.0021	0.0026	0.0073	0.0129	0.0142	0.0404	0.0070
Telecom	0.0001	0.0014	0.0011	0.0041	0.0011	0.0008	0.0008
Trade	0.0000	0.0000	0.0000	0.0000	0.0000	0.0000	0.0000
Banks	0.0006	0.0042	0.0078	0.0095	0.0028	0.0016	0.0011
Service firm	0.0027	0.0274	0.0265	0.0375	0.0878	0.1506	0.0064
Service (collective)	0.0032	0.0121	0.0430	0.0597	0.0472	0.1295	0.0227
Service (individual)	0.0095	0.0340	0.0234	0.0331	0.0480	0.0355	0.0074
Service (public sector)	0.0040	0.0047	0.0115	0.0044	0.0000	0.0075	0.0000

Sources: The Ministry of Economy and Finance, the Ministry of Trade, the Ministry of Agriculture, the Central Bank of Madagascar; external trade data from the National Institute for Statistics and other surveys sent to enterprises, nongovernmental organizations, the banking sector, and insurance companies.

Food	Beverage	Tobacco	Fats	Chemical	Textile	Wood	Nonmetal	Metal
0.3250	0.1476	0.2160	0.0700	0.0049	0.0514	0.0000	0.0000	0.0000
0.2464	0.0000	0.0000	0.0000	0.0000	0.0001	0.0000	0.0000	0.0000
0.0004	0.0003	0.0092	0.0025	0.0035	0.0001	0.1023	0.0042	0.0110
0.0261	0.0000	0.0000	0.0197	0.0000	0.0000	0.0000	0.0000	0.0000
0.0271	0.0166	0.0000	0.0131	0.0013	0.0000	0.0000	0.0000	0.0000
0.0194	0.0000	0.0000	0.0000	0.0000	0.0000	0.0000	0.0000	0.0000
0.0479	0.0433	0.0189	0.0918	0.0251	0.0549	0.0282	0.0704	0.0241
0.1132	0.0000	0.0000	0.0000	0.0002	0.0012	0.0000	0.0000	0.0000
0.0000	0.0008	0.0000	0.0000	0.0002	0.0000	0.0000	0.0000	0.0000
0.0000	0.0000	0.0535	0.0000	0.0000	0.0000	0.0000	0.0000	0.0000
0.0041	0.0000	0.0000	0.3818	0.0253	0.0000	0.0000	0.0000	0.0000
0.0094	0.0419	0.0108	0.1810	0.5608	0.0072	0.0295	0.0076	0.0620
0.0001	0.0006	0.0008	0.0035	0.0016	0.5602	0.0008	0.0000	0.0000
0.0003	0.0012	0.0016	0.0000	0.0000	0.0006	0.1657	0.0000	0.0107
0.0000	0.0000	0.0000	0.0022	0.0000	0.0004	0.0014	0.0311	0.0015
0.0041	0.0612	0.0445	0.0060	0.0247	0.0144	0.0583	0.0579	0.5472
0.0001	0.0012	0.0000	0.0000	0.0000	0.0000	0.0018	0.0267	0.0118
0.0088	0.0069	0.0896	0.0084	0.0153	0.0061	0.0017	0.0397	0.0033
0.0006	0.0497	0.0101	0.0089	0.1025	0.0090	0.0041	0.0269	0.0107
0.0000	0.0000	0.0000	0.0000	0.0000	0.0000	0.0000	0.0000	0.0000
0.0000	0.0000	0.0000	0.0000	0.0000	0.0000	0.0000	0.0000	0.0000
0.0107	0.0164	0.0051	0.0050	0.0404	0.0102	0.0003	0.0411	0.0199
0.0005	0.0315	0.0253	0.0070	0.0308	0.0050	0.0123	0.0204	0.0488
0.0007	0.0052	0.0052	0.0033	0.0073	0.0047	0.0009	0.0112	0.0023
0.0000	0.0000	0.0000	0.0000	0.0000	0.0000	0.0000	0.0000	0.0000
0.0007	0.0099	0.0103	0.0095	0.0043	0.0072	0.0016	0.0069	0.0013
0.0050	0.0666	0.0722	0.0096	0.0101	0.0104	0.0937	0.0553	0.0195
0.0092	0.0525	0.0480	0.0176	0.0347	0.0152	0.0705	0.0651	0.0244
0.0003	0.0287	0.0171	0.0449	0.0192	0.0049	0.0276	0.0248	0.0111
0.0000	0.0000	0.0080	0.0000	0.0000	0.0000	0.0000	0.0000	0.0002

(Continues on the following spread.)

TABLE 11B.1
(continued)

	Electrical products	Paper	Leather	Construction	Transport (goods)	Transport (people)	
Agriculture	0.0000	0.0000	0.0000	0.0000	0.0000	0.0000	
Farming	0.0000	0.0000	0.0009	0.0000	0.0000	0.0000	
Hunting	0.0000	0.0068	0.0002	0.0040	0.0000	0.0000	
Fishing	0.0000	0.0000	0.0403	0.0000	0.0000	0.0000	
Agroindustry	0.0000	0.0001	0.0140	0.0000	0.0000	0.0000	
Mining	0.0000	0.0000	0.0234	0.0214	0.0000	0.0000	
Energy	0.0056	0.0468	0.0421	0.0203	0.1780	0.1483	
Food	0.0000	0.0000	0.0331	0.0000	0.0000	0.0000	
Beverage	0.0000	0.0000	0.0000	0.0000	0.0000	0.0000	
Tobacco	0.0000	0.0000	0.0000	0.0000	0.0000	0.0000	
Fats	0.0000	0.0000	0.0001	0.0000	0.0000	0.0000	
Chemical	0.0003	0.2271	0.0935	0.0735	0.0204	0.0241	
Textile	0.0000	0.0003	0.0001	0.0002	0.0000	0.0001	
Wood	0.0021	0.0000	0.0173	0.0877	0.0050	0.0039	
Nonmetal	0.0258	0.0006	0.0036	0.1776	0.0000	0.0000	
Metal	0.0128	0.0111	0.0181	0.3708	0.1068	0.2425	
Electrical products	0.7410	0.0242	0.0291	0.0222	0.0030	0.0029	
Paper	0.0135	0.4596	0.0167	0.0065	0.0004	0.0004	
Leather	0.0146	0.0283	0.0951	0.0259	0.0001	0.0002	
Construction	0.0000	0.0000	0.0000	0.0009	0.0000	0.0000	
Transport (goods)	0.0000	0.0000	0.0000	0.0000	0.0000	0.0000	
Transport (people)	0.0070	0.0056	0.0137	0.0126	0.0074	0.0123	
Transport (other)	0.0099	0.0380	0.0004	0.0131	0.0234	0.0172	
Telecom	0.0081	0.0044	0.0067	0.0050	0.0067	0.0069	
Trade	0.0000	0.0000	0.0000	0.0000	0.0000	0.0000	
Banks	0.0021	0.0060	0.0041	0.0045	0.0587	0.0985	
Service firm	0.0098	0.0460	0.0239	0.0155	0.0249	0.0980	
Service (collective)	0.0079	0.0492	0.0492	0.0100	0.0244	0.0321	
Service (Individual)	0.0058	0.0028	0.0298	0.0198	0.0315	0.0402	
Service (public sector)	0.0000	0.0000	0.0000	0.0022	0.0024	0.0017	

Transport (other)	Telecom	Trade	Banks	Service firm	Service (collective)	Service (individual)	Service (public sector)
0.0000	0.0000	0.0000	0.0000	0.0000	0.0906	0.0000	0.0006
0.0000	0.0000	0.0000	0.0000	0.0000	0.0196	0.0000	0.0003
0.0000	0.0000	0.0000	0.0000	0.0000	0.0112	0.0004	0.0000
0.0000	0.0000	0.0000	0.0000	0.0000	0.0586	0.0000	0.0002
0.0000	0.0000	0.0000	0.0000	0.0000	0.0187	0.0000	0.0006
0.0000	0.0000	0.0000	0.0000	0.0000	0.0066	0.0000	0.0000
0.0398	0.0297	0.0533	0.0089	0.0123	0.0120	0.0198	0.0324
0.0000	0.0000	0.0000	0.0000	0.0000	0.1787	0.0000	0.0018
0.0000	0.0000	0.0000	0.0000	0.0000	0.0305	0.0005	0.0000
0.0000	0.0000	0.0000	0.0000	0.0000	0.0000	0.0000	0.0000
0.0000	0.0000	0.0000	0.0000	0.0000	0.0122	0.0000	0.0000
0.0062	0.0014	0.0018	0.0000	0.0003	0.0043	0.0009	0.0090
0.0000	0.0000	0.0000	0.0000	0.0000	0.0041	0.0005	0.0002
0.0000	0.0000	0.0021	0.0000	0.0000	0.0014	0.0006	0.0025
0.0000	0.0034	0.0000	0.0000	0.0000	0.0000	0.0005	0.0003
0.0470	0.0073	0.0009	0.0022	0.0287	0.0105	0.0028	0.0182
0.0059	0.0000	0.0004	0.0000	0.0005	0.0005	0.0004	0.0004
0.0764	0.0642	0.0065	0.0285	0.0056	0.0011	0.0002	0.0392
0.0069	0.0397	0.0006	0.0062	0.0005	0.0006	0.0003	0.0176
0.0013	0.0047	0.0000	0.0000	0.0000	0.0002	0.0003	0.0032
0.0000	0.0000	0.0000	0.0000	0.0000	0.0000	0.0000	0.0000
0.0114	0.0042	0.0102	0.0149	0.0209	0.0044	0.0010	0.0257
0.0029	0.0000	0.0172	0.0000	0.0040	0.0062	0.0000	0.0009
0.1124	0.0000	0.0123	0.0140	0.0096	0.0014	0.0007	0.0082
0.0000	0.0000	0.0000	0.0000	0.0000	0.0000	0.0000	0.0000
0.0406	0.0004	0.0094	0.0112	0.0075	0.0011	0.0015	0.0552
0.1059	0.0236	0.0612	0.0255	0.0113	0.0629	0.0034	0.0559
0.0735	0.0855	0.0247	0.0064	0.0212	0.0096	0.0077	0.1094
0.0423	0.0134	0.0251	0.0275	0.0249	0.0010	0.0008	0.0352
0.0011	0.0000	0.0000	0.0000	0.0000	0.0022	0.0000	0.0000

Note

This chapter is the product of a joint effort by the Government of Madagascar and the World Bank to investigate the poverty and social impacts of key policy reforms and economic events. The authors would like to thank the Poverty and Social Impact Analysis Group at the International Monetary Fund, and Benu Bidani and Stefano Paternostro of the World Bank for advice and comments. We are also grateful to Brian A'Hearn and Nicola Amendola for many helpful discussions. Thanks also to Laza Razafiarison for help at various stages of the project.

References

Banks, J., R. Blundell, and A. Lewbel. 1996. "Tax Reform and Welfare Measurement: Do We Need Demand System Estimates?" *Economic Journal* 106 (438): 1227–41.

Coady, D., and D. Newhouse. 2005. "Evaluating the Distribution of the Real Income Effects of Increases in Petroleum Product Prices in Ghana." Photocopy. International Monetary Fund, Washington, DC.

Gupta, S., M. Verhoeven, R. Gillingham, C. Schiller, A. Mansoor, and J. P. Cordoba. 2000. *Equity and Efficiency in the Reform of Price Subsidies. A Guide for Policymakers.* Washington, DC: International Monetary Fund.

Kpodar, K. 2006. "Distributional Effects of Oil Price Changes on Household Expenditures: Evidence from Mali." Working Paper WP/06/91, International Monetary Fund, Washington, DC.

CHAPTER 12

Economywide and Distributional Impact of an Oil Price Shock on the South African Economy

B. Essama-Nssah, Delfin S. Go, Marna Kearney, Vijdan Korman, Sherman Robinson, and Karen Thierfelder

As crude oil prices reach new highs, there is a renewed concern about how external shocks will affect growth and poverty in developing countries and how this effect should be modeled and anticipated. The links between the two aspects—macroeconomics and poverty/income distribution—surely have become a major focus of economic research and modeling in recent years.[1] However, the main challenge has been the reconciliation of potentially very detailed and large information sets from microeconometric modeling of individual or household behaviors about income and employment opportunities with the more aggregative behavior in a macroeconomic model.

A promising approach for researchers is to employ computable general equilibrium (CGE) modeling as a meso framework because CGE models generate from macroeconomic changes a set of consistent relative prices, wages, and profits at the sectoral level that provides the vital sources and changes of household incomes and expenditures for further analysis of poverty impact and income distribution (see figure 12.1). There have been several ways of utilizing CGE models and household analysis to establish the links between macroeconomic changes and poverty analysis, depending on the level of simplification and the level of information retained for both macroeconomic and microeconomic components. At one end of the spectrum, where data constraints and technical capacity of policy analysts are issues, the "123PRSP Model" in Devarajan and Go (2003) simplifies

FIGURE 12.1
Disaggregated Framework Linking Macroeconomic Events to Poverty Reduction Issues

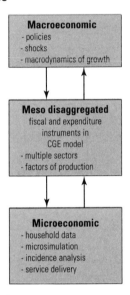

Source: Authors' illustration.

Note: CGE = computable general equilibrium.

the CGE framework into an aggregative distinction of tradable and non-tradable goods. Effects of external shocks are first derived in terms of movements of the real exchange rate between tradable and nontradable goods, and those movements are then mapped to the expenditure and income sources of various household groups (for example, income deciles). Growth impact is derived from either short-term vector autoregressive analysis or long-term growth regression of various determinants. More information is provided in CGE models with higher levels of disaggregation, such as the South Africa model in Go et al. (2005), which combines a rich structure of the economy and a good number of household groupings—49 industries, 3 labor categories, and 13 household groups.

Another type of simplification is found in Essama-Nssah (2005), which distills the income distribution from household surveys into a parameterized Lorenz model of income distribution and which then can easily be linked to macroeconomic models to examine policy and external shocks.

The approach provides the flexibility of choosing the macroeconomic framework from among simple macroeconomic consistency models (like the World Bank's RMSM-X or the International Monetary Fund's financial programming model) to more sophisticated econometric or CGE models.

However, none of the models mentioned so far makes full use of household information, which is a significant feature in microsimulation models. As an example at the other end of the spectrum, Bourguignon, Robilliard, and Robinson (2002) merged a disaggregative macroeconomic framework in a CGE model with a microsimulation model that makes full use of the complete household data, with explicit treatment and full individual heterogeneity of labor skills, preferences, and characteristics at the individual and household levels.

Although the various approaches of combining CGE models and household data are distinguished by the level of sophistication and information retained in either the macroeconomic or microeconomic component, there is one drawback. The integration of the macroeconomic and microeconomic components is often a one-way, top-down approach because of the inherent complexities of a full integration.[2] To be sure, there are attempts at full integration. Cogneau and Robilliard (2000) implemented a version for Madagascar. However, the general equilibrium macroeconomic framework has very few sectors. Heckman and Lochner (1998) did an overlapping-generations general equilibrium model of labor earnings with heterogeneous agents; but to present both integration and dynamics, the macroeconomic part is aggregative. A classic econometric method for the integration of a CGE model with detailed household analysis is provided by the work of Jorgenson, Lau, and Stoker (1980), whereby exact aggregation of the representative consumer from heterogeneous households is econometrically estimated from survey data; and whereby, under certain demand restrictions, demand functions of heterogeneous groups are recoverable from the representative consumer. Given an overall representative household, however, stable or fixed household distribution underlying the econometric results is implicitly assumed. A promising and practical link between the macroeconomic and the microeconomic has been provided by Savard (2003, 2006), who uses a recursive iteration between the two approaches without the need to simplify each of them. A similar approach has been adopted in this chapter and will be described below.

The purpose of this chapter is to assess the potential impact of a large oil price shock on the economy, poverty, and income inequality in South

Africa, using a combination of a disaggregative CGE model and microsimulation analysis of household surveys. The framework employed is a valuable tool to sort out the wide-ranging impact of an external shock on the economy as well as on the various sectors, industries, and heterogeneous households. We implement a recursive two-way feedback mechanism similar to Savard (2003, 2006) and devise an efficient reconciliation between the CGE and microsimulation models to derive a consistent or integrated analysis of the shocks from the two approaches while retaining the particular advantages provided by each approach—that is, the detailed structure of an economy in the CGE model and the full heterogeneity of households and labor in the microsimulation. At the end, we draw some possible lessons about where the multilayered analysis may be most useful and where simpler approaches would be sufficient, including a one-way, top-down approach; a more clear-cut decomposition of the vertical and horizontal impact on inequality, such as Roy's method in Ravallion and Lokshin (2004); and a simpler summary of the household characteristics by income deciles or a parameterized Lorenz curve.

The outline of the rest of the chapter is as follows. The second section describes the simulation framework used to analyze the issues raised in this introduction. Basically, the framework links a CGE model for South Africa to two types of microsimulation models of household welfare and occupational choice. The third section analyzes the distributional implications of a large oil price shock to the economy. A summary and conclusions are presented in the fourth section.

Simulation Framework

For an oil-importing country, a significant increase in the price of this commodity not only will have consequences on various macroeconomic aggregates but also will have structural and distributional implications because of changes in relative prices of goods and factor costs due to the pass-through of oil costs throughout the economy. Thus, we need a framework that accounts not only for the *interdependence* among stabilization, structural, and distributional issues, but also for the *heterogeneity* of the stakeholders that underpins distributional concerns. This section describes the macro-microsimulation framework used to track the macroeconomic, structural, and distributional implications of a sizable oil price shock for the economy of South Africa. A disaggregated CGE model is used for the macroeconomic and structural implications whereas the microsimulation component accounts for agent heterogeneity and the impact on distribution.

CGE Model of the South African Economy

The CGE model has 43 production activities.[3] For reporting purposes, the output results by activity are aggregated into three categories: agriculture, industry, and services (see table 12.1 for the composition of the aggregate categories). As seen in figure 12.2, agriculture accounts for 4 percent of value added, industry accounts for 27 percent, and services accounts for 69 percent.

Labor categories are combinations of labor types (formal, self-employed, and informal), and skill levels (high-skilled, semi-skilled, and low-skilled).[4] Each activity can use these labor categories and capital in production. For reporting purposes, all skill levels of self-employed are aggregated into a single input, self-employed labor; the same is true for informal labor.[5]

TABLE 12.1
CGE Model Sectors

I. Agriculture	II. Industry (cont'd)	III. Services
Agriculture	Basic chemicals	Electricity, gas, and steam
II. Industry	Other chemicals and man-made fibers	Water supply
Coal mining	Rubber products	Construction and civil engineering
Gold and uranium ore mining	Plastic products	Catering and accommodation
Other mining	Glass and glass products	Wholesale and retail trade
Food	Nonmetallic minerals	Transportation and storage
Beverages and tobacco	Basic iron and steel	Communication
Textiles	Basic nonferrous metals	Financial services
Wearing apparel	Metal products excluding machinery	Business services
Leather and leather products	Electrical machinery	Health, community, social, and
Footwear	TV, radio, and communication equip	personal services
Wood and wood products	Professional and scientific equipment	Other producers
Paper and paper products	Motor vehicles parts and accessories	Government services
Printing and publishing	Other transport equipment	
and recorded media	Furniture	
Coke and refined		
petroleum products		

Source: South Africa SAM 2003 Database.

Note: CGE = computable general equilibrium.

FIGURE 12.2
Aggregate Activity Share of Value Added

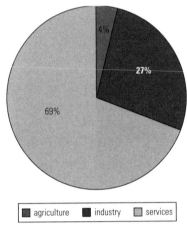

4%

27%

69%

◼ agriculture   ◼ industry   ▨ services

Source: South Africa SAM 2003 Database.

In the production technology, it is assumed that substitution possibilities among inputs differ and the following structure is used: (1) it is difficult to substitute low-skilled labor for high-skilled labor in any of the three labor categories; (2) it is easy to substitute across labor categories for the same skill (that is, a high-skilled formal worker is a good substitute for a high-skilled informal worker or a high-skilled self-employed worker); and (3) as the skill level of labor increases, it is more difficult to substitute capital for labor.[6]

Structural unemployment is specified for low-skilled and semi-skilled formal workers, with sticky real wages. There is full employment in the other labor markets. The peculiarities of the labor markets in South Africa are treated in a fashion similar to that in Go et al. (2005) and Lewis (2001). In a separate analysis of the possible impact of a wage subsidy scheme contemplated by the South African authorities, we examine the labor market structure and markets in much more detail (Essama-Nssah et al. forthcoming).

It is assumed that all resources in coal, gold, and other mining are activity specific, consistent with the notion that the supply of these mineral products is relatively inelastic. For the other activities, we assume that capital is activity specific.

TABLE 12.2
Value-Added Shares

Factor	Agriculture	Industry	Services
Capital	0.76	0.54	0.45
High-skilled formal labor	0.03	0.12	0.25
Semi-skilled formal labor	0.02	0.12	0.18
Low-skilled formal labor	0.11	0.15	0.04
Self-employed labor	0.04	0.03	0.04
Informal labor	0.04	0.04	0.04

Source: South Africa SAM 2003 Database.

Value added is allocated to primary factors according to the shares shown in table 12.2.

In the base data, the category "other mining" includes crude oil as well as diverse mineral inputs, such as diamonds and iron ore. To focus on the impact of an oil price shock, we create an additional category, "crude or unrefined oil," which is the amount of other mining inputs used in the production of refined petroleum and basic chemicals. It is assumed that all crude oil is imported and that there is no tariff on crude oil.[7]

As noted above, crude oil imports account for 100 percent of crude oil consumption. Refined petroleum imports account for 17 percent of oil consumption, and basic chemical imports account for 29 percent of basic chemical consumption in South Africa. In addition to crude oil, the region is heavily dependent on imports of commodities such as communication equipment (70 percent of consumption), other transportation equipment (65 percent of consumption), and machinery and equipment (56 percent of consumption).

Crude oil, petroleum, and basic chemicals are primarily purchased as intermediate inputs.[8] Direct household purchases of petroleum are quite low, with expenditure ranging from 4 percent to 6 percent, depending on household; for basic chemicals, the household expenditure shares are 1 percent or less.

Given the structure of the economy, the effects of an oil price shock (which is modeled as an increase in the world price of imported crude oil, refined petroleum, and basic chemicals) on households will be felt primarily through the effects on prices of final goods that use refined petroleum and basic chemicals as intermediate inputs (see table 12.3). Note that

TABLE 12.3
Direct and Indirect Input Requirements of Refined Petroleum per Rand Spent on Final Demand

Final product/service	Rand	Final product/service	Rand
Coke and refined petroleum products	1.16	Nonmetallic minerals	0.07
Basic chemicals	0.18	Footwear	0.07
Transportation and storage	0.18	Health, community, social, and personal services	0.06
Rubber products	0.14	Furniture	0.06
Basic nonferrous metals	0.14	Wood and wood products	0.06
Other chemicals and man-made fibers	0.11	TV, radio, and communication equipment	0.06
Plastic products	0.11	Other industries	0.06
Agriculture, forestry, and fisheries	0.11	Beverages and tobacco	0.06
Electrical machinery	0.10	Other transport equipment	0.05
Construction and civil engineering	0.09	Wearing apparel	0.05
Basic iron and steel	0.09	Glass and glass products	0.05
Food	0.09	Catering and accommodation	0.05
Textiles	0.08	Printing, publishing, and recorded media	0.05
Machinery and equipment	0.08	Business services	0.04
Motor vehicles parts and accessories	0.08	Wholesale and retail trade	0.04
Leather and leather products	0.07	Water supply	0.04
Professional and scientific equipment	0.07	Electricity, gas, and steam	0.04
Other mining	0.07	Other producers	0.04
Metal products, excluding machinery	0.07	Government services	0.03
Coal mining	0.07	Gold and uranium ore mining	0.03
Paper and paper products	0.07	Financial services	0.02
Communication	0.07		

Source: South Africa SAM 2003 Database.

production of electricity and gas does not depend heavily on refined petroleum. Instead, coal is a more important intermediate input.

Modeling Household Response to Macroeconomic Events

Fundamentally, we can think of the observed poverty and inequality in a given society as an outcome of individual behavior subject to endowments and the institutions that govern social interaction. Indeed, Bourguignon and Ferreira (2005) noted three groups of determinants of the size distribution of economic welfare: (1) the distribution of factor *endowments* and socioeconomic characteristics among the population, (2) the *returns* to these assets, and (3) the *behavior* of socioeconomic agents with respect to resource allocation subject to institutional constraints. Thus, we would expect the distributional impact of macroeconomic events to have three types of effects on the distribution of economic welfare: (1) *endowment effects* due to changes in the amount of resources available to individuals, (2) *price effects* reflecting changes in the reward of these resources, and (3) *occupational effects* linked to changes in resource allocation.

For the purpose of our study, we consider two alternative approaches to simulating these effects at the household level. The first approach, as applied by Ravallion and Lokshin (2004) to the case of a trade reform in Morocco, relies on the *envelope theorem* to downplay the endowment and occupational effects and focus on the welfare implications of price effects. The second approach, explained in Bourguignon and Ferreira (2005), tries to account for the endowment and occupational effects through a *model of earnings generation*.

Our empirical implementation of the second approach relies on a data set that combines information from the 2000 Labor Force Survey (LFS) with data from the 2000 Income and Expenditure Survey (IES).[9] Given that both surveys are based mostly on the same sample of households, the combined data set provides comprehensive information on household expenditures, labor and nonlabor income, labor supply, employment, and several socioeconomic characteristics of individuals and households. The IES sample contains 26,687 households and 104,153 individuals. The LFS sample consists of 105,792 individuals. When the two data sets are combined and observations with missing sampling weights are dropped, the remaining number of individuals in our combined database drops to 103,732 from 26,214 households.

Envelope Model of Household Welfare

Just as in the context of the general equilibrium model, we rely on the optimization principle to model economic welfare at the household level. Following Ravallion and Lokshin (2004), we assume that each household's preferences can be represented by a utility function of the quantities of commodities demanded and labor supplied to both external and own production activities. In addition, the household earns a profit from a productive activity. The optimal behavior of household h can be represented by an envelope function known as the *indirect utility function*. This is the maximum attainable welfare, given the level of resources and prevailing prices. Formally, we write

$$v_h(p_h^s, p_h^d, w_h) = \max_{q_h^d, L_h}[u_h(q_h^d, L_h) | p_h^d q_h^d = w_h L_h + \pi_h(p_h^s)]$$ (12.1)

In the above expression, q_h^d stands for a vector of commodities demanded by the household, L_h is the vector of labor supplies by activity, and w_h is the corresponding vector of wages. In addition, p_h^d and p_h^s stand for vectors of consumption and production prices, respectively; while $\pi_h(p_h^s)$ is the maximum profit achievable from own production, given prevailing prices.

The indirect utility is a function of prices. According to the envelope theorem, as manifested by Roy's identity, the change in the maximum utility induced by a change in one of its arguments is equal to the partial derivative of the indirect utility with respect to the argument. The money metric of this change is obtained by normalizing the partial derivative on the basis of the marginal utility of income. The following expression of the overall welfare change induced by price changes provides a framework for assessing the impact of shock or policy reform on a household:

$$g_h = \sum_{j=1}^{m}\left[p_{hj}^s q_{hj}^s \frac{dp_{hj}^s}{p_{hj}^s} - p_{hj}^d q_{hj}^d \frac{dp_{hj}^d}{p_{hj}^d}\right] + \sum_{i=1}^{n}\left[w_i L_{hi} \frac{dw_i}{w_i}\right] \qquad (12.2)$$

Equation (12.2) says that a first-order approximation of the welfare impact in a neighborhood of the optimal behavior of the household is equal to a weighted sum of proportionate changes in prices. The weights are the initial patterns of demand or supply as revealed by expenditure and sales patterns. These patterns help us account for heterogeneity to the extent that they are based on sociodemographic characteristics of households and because households may face different prices for the same commodity.

Depending on the application, the benefit of being able to derive an elegant closed-form approximation from the envelope approach must be weighed against the limitation stemming from the fact that it assumes away endowments and occupational effects. In what follows, we therefore also consider a model of earnings generation that would allow for such effects.

Household Earnings-Generation Model

To account for endowment and occupational effects, we need a framework that links both earnings and occupational choice to sociodemographic characteristics of the household. That is, we need a model of the income generation process at the individual or household level. We base the specification of our model on the general framework described in Bourguignon and Ferreira (2005). The model has three components: (1) a multinomial logit model of the allocation of individuals across occupational states, (2) a model of the determinants of earnings, and (3) an aggregation rule for computing household income from the contribution of its employed members.

OCCUPATIONAL COMPONENT

The occupational component contains 16 categories: (1) inactive and unemployed; (2) formal sector workers, low skilled in agriculture; (3) formal sector workers, semi-skilled in agriculture; (4) formal sector workers, high skilled in agriculture; (5) formal sector workers, low skilled in industry; (6) formal sector workers, semi-skilled in industry; (7) formal sector workers, high skilled in industry; (8) formal sector workers, low skilled in services; (9) formal sector workers, semi-skilled in services; (10) formal sector workers, high skilled in services; (11) informal sector workers, agriculture; (12) informal sector workers, industry; (13) informal sector workers, services; (14) self-employed workers, agriculture; (15) self-employed workers, industry; and (16) self-employed workers, services.

Table 12.4 shows the distribution of employment by sector and occupation. These results show that about six people out of ten are employed in the services (or tertiary) sector. About the same ratio represents those engaged in formal sector work. About 24 percent of working individuals are self-employed. Although, the data are available for disaggregating informal and self-employment sectors by skill types, analysis was performed by economic sectors for informal and self-employed categories.

With respect to the distribution of skills, the results show that about 15 percent of employed people are highly skilled. Furthermore, the highest

TABLE 12.4
Distribution of Employment by Sector and Occupation

Workers	Agriculture	Industry	Services	Total
Formal sector workers				
Low-skilled	6.0	2.9	5.7	14.6
Semi-skilled	6.2	8.7	16.5	31.3
High-skilled	0.7	1.3	9.6	11.6
Informal sector workers	2.7	2.5	13.9	19.2
Self-employed	9.1	2.8	11.5	23.4
Total	24.6	18.2	57.2	100.0

Source: Authors' calculations.

TABLE 12.5
Distribution of Employment by Sector and Skill Level
Percent

Sector	Low-skilled workers	Semi-skilled workers	High-skilled workers	All workers
Agriculture	8.9	14.9	0.6	24.4
Industry	3.5	13.0	1.7	18.2
Services	19.9	25.0	12.4	57.4
All	32.4	52.9	14.7	100.0

Source: Authors' calculations.

percentage of people at any skill level is found in the tertiary sector (table 12.5).

Now, let P_{ij} stand for the probability of observing individual i engaged in activity j. Then, selecting one category as a reference (here, inactive and unemployed), we can express this probability as

$$P_{ij} = \frac{\exp(z_i \gamma_j)}{\left[1 + \sum_{j=2}^{16} (\exp(z_i \gamma_j)) \right]} \tag{12.3}$$

where z_i is a vector of observable characteristics of individual i. In our case, z includes the following variables: a constant, gender, years of education, education squared, experience, experience squared, a dummy for residence in the urban area, the number of children who are aged 9 or less, a dummy for marital status, a dummy indicating whether a member of the household owns a family business, years of schooling for the head of household, and a dummy indicating whether the individual is head of household.

When the multinomial logit model is motivated in terms of utility-maximizing behavior, the utility[10] associated with activity j is given by $z_i \gamma_j + \varepsilon_{ij}$, where the second term represents the unobserved determinants of the utility of activity j. The utility of the reference activity is arbitrarily set to zero. It is usually assumed that the random component of the activity-utility follows the law of extreme values and is independently distributed across individuals and activities.

In principle, the participation component (12.3) of the earnings generation model should be estimated jointly with the earnings equations defined in the next subsection of this chapter. For the occupational model to be considered as a structural model of labor supply, its specification must include the wage rate, the productivity of self-employment, and nonlabor income. To avoid the difficulties associated with joint estimation, we follow Bourguignon and Ferreira (2005) in their reduced-form interpretation of the framework. Thus, the components can be estimated separately with the possibility of testing for selection bias at the level of earnings equations. This interpretation precludes any causal inference, and the resulting parameter estimates are simply statistical descriptions of conditional distributions based on the chosen functional forms. The reduced-form estimates for the occupational model are presented in table 12.6.

Overall results show that gender has significant impact on the probability of being employed in different sectors. However, gender is not a statistically significant explanatory variable for being employed for the formal low-skilled and formal high-skilled individuals in the services sector. Among formal workers, people in the industry and services sectors are more likely to be living in the urban areas than are people in the agriculture sector, as expected. It is also true for the informal and self-employed sectors. Similarly, the number of children (aged 9 years or less) has a significant impact on the choice to participate in the labor force. People with children aged 0 through 9 years are less likely to participate as formal workers. They are more likely to be self-employed. Similarly, individuals living in households owning a family business are more likely to be self-employed than to be paid workers. Being head of the household also plays a significant role for participating in the labor force. Furthermore, married people are more likely to be active in the labor force than are unmarried couples.

EARNINGS

The earnings block of the microsimulation model consists of three equations explaining formal wages, informal wages, and self-employment income in terms of observable and nonobservable individual characteristics. The specification of these equations follows the Mincerian model. The wage equation is written as

$$\log w_i = x_i \beta_w + u_{iw} \tag{12.4}$$

The set of observable characteristics used as explanatory variables includes a constant, gender, years of education, education squared, experience, experience squared, a dummy indicating whether the individual is head of household, a dummy for residence in the urban area, a dummy for union membership, and a dummy for marital status. We estimate this equation separately for the primary, secondary, and tertiary sectors using ordinary least squares (OLS).[11] The results are presented in table 12.7.

TABLE 12.6
Occupational Choice Models for Individuals

Variable	Formal employees									Informal employees			Self-employed		
	Agriculture			Industry			Services								
	Low-skilled	Semi-skilled	High-skilled	Low-skilled	Semi-skilled	High-skilled	Low-skilled	Semi-skilled	High-skilled	Agriculture	Industry	Services	Agriculture	Industry	Services
Gender	0.82	2.442	1.563	0.909	1.192	1.043	-0.057	0.583	-0.102	0.993	1.762	-0.78	0.123	0.25	-0.321
	[14.06]**	[24.12]**	[7.22]**	[11.31]**	[22.85]**	[7.31]**	[1.01]	[15.74]**	[1.75]	[11.88]**	[17.31]**	[19.00]**	[2.70]**	[2.88]**	[6.24]**
Eduyear	-0.01	-0.086	-0.222	0.062	0.07	-0.055	0.071	0.002	0.221	-0.072	0.035	-0.038	-0.073	-0.144	-0.143
	[0.43]	[3.40]**	[3.16]**	[1.85]	[3.22]**	[0.77]	[2.99]**	[0.14]	[3.68]**	[2.25]*	[1.02]	[2.60]**	[4.18]**	[4.81]**	[7.78]**
Eduyear2	-0.009	0.003	0.029	-0.003	0.002	0.023	-0.002	0.011	0.021	-0.003	-0.004	0.001	0.009	0.015	0.015
	[4.44]**	[2.11]*	[8.67]**	[1.29]	[1.31]	[7.45]**	[0.95]	[10.82]**	[8.74]**	[1.04]	[1.57]	[0.78]	[6.92]**	[8.02]**	[12.76]**
Expyear	0.124	0.221	0.215	0.18	0.214	0.219	0.19	0.167	0.254	0.132	0.212	0.184	0.032	0.205	0.168
	[14.39]**	[20.72]**	[7.62]**	[15.19]**	[27.79]**	[10.63]**	[22.19]**	[30.57]**	[26.83]**	[10.93]**	[16.12]**	[32.38]**	[5.37]**	[15.69]**	[24.11]**
Expyear2	-0.003	-0.004	-0.004	-0.003	-0.004	-0.004	-0.003	-0.003	-0.005	-0.003	-0.004	-0.003	0	-0.003	-0.003
	[18.58]**	[23.53]**	[7.30]**	[15.48]**	[27.53]**	[9.77]**	[21.48]**	[29.52]**	[23.27]**	[12.93]**	[16.53]**	[32.70]**	[0.53]	[14.91]**	[22.26]**
Urban	-2.181	-1.119	-0.366	0.781	0.891	1.549	0.691	0.816	0.449	-1.91	-0.237	0.408	-2.468	-0.108	0.128
	[26.83]**	[18.97]**	[2.21]*	[9.13]**	[16.14]**	[7.57]**	[11.37]**	[18.94]**	[6.95]**	[17.41]**	[2.91]**	[10.41]**	[33.99]**	[1.29]	[2.51]*
Nchild09	-0.292	-0.485	-0.332	-0.08	-0.084	-0.129	-0.07	-0.107	-0.049	-0.172	-0.063	-0.204	0.107	-0.159	-0.071
	[12.96]**	[16.55]**	[4.04]**	[2.69]**	[4.45]**	[2.35]*	[3.31]**	[7.10]**	[2.11]*	[5.91]**	[2.04]*	[13.49]**	[8.39]**	[5.00]**	[4.06]**
Married	0.903	1.282	1.297	0.526	0.711	1.248	0.283	0.663	0.656	0.657	0.222	0.236	0.274	0.488	0.503
	[14.45]**	[18.18]**	[6.55]**	[6.37]**	[13.80]**	[9.03]**	[4.91]**	[16.85]**	[11.29]**	[7.53]**	[2.45]*	[5.98]**	[5.41]**	[5.48]**	[9.46]**
Fambusiness	-1.081	-0.624	-0.567	-0.333	-0.197	-0.223	-0.242	0.004	-0.427	-0.661	-0.135	-0.08	0.685	4.088	4.845
	[7.42]**	[5.05]**	[1.98]*	[2.47]*	[2.55]*	[1.26]	[2.51]*	[0.07]	[5.01]**	[3.80]**	[0.98]	[1.28]	[12.03]**	[38.58]**	[66.28]**
Eduyearhd	-0.026	0.04	0.058	-0.025	-0.01	0.05	-0.03	0.035	0.045	-0.036	-0.006	-0.013	0.003	-0.005	0.005
	[2.64]**	[2.62]**	[1.75]	[2.02]*	[1.22]	[2.10]*	[3.31]**	[6.22]**	[5.12]**	[2.53]*	[0.43]	[2.11]*	[0.43]	[0.35]	[0.70]
Headd	1.44	2.11	1.27	1.073	1.279	1.316	1.349	1.237	1.292	1.26	1.294	1.342	0.708	1.946	1.976
	[21.86]**	[23.83]**	[5.89]**	[12.12]**	[22.83]**	[8.76]**	[21.47]**	[29.83]**	[20.11]**	[13.47]**	[13.05]**	[32.23]**	[12.89]**	[19.72]**	[33.48]**
Constant	-3.485	-7.37	-10.084	-6.969	-7.324	-11.818	-6.223	-6.268	-11.408	-4.552	-7.326	-4.059	-3.474	-8.943	-7.735
	[26.98]**	[41.28]**	[20.77]**	[35.02]**	[54.59]**	[24.27]**	[43.17]**	[59.43]**	[29.90]**	[24.12]**	[33.54]**	[44.72]**	[34.49]**	[38.92]**	[57.81]**
Sample size	65113	65113	65113	65113	65113	65113	65113	65113	65113	65113	65113	65113	65113	65113	65113

Source: Authors' calculations.

Note: For descriptions of the variables, see table 12A.1 in the annex to this chapter. Absolute value of z-statistic appears in brackets.

* Significant at 5%.

** Significant at 1%.

TABLE 12.7
OLS Estimates of the Formal Wage Equation

Variable	Agriculture sector			Industry sector			Services sector		
	Low-skilled	Semi-skilled	High-skilled	Low-skilled	Semi-skilled	High-skilled	Low-skilled	Semi-skilled	High-skilled
Gender	0.227	0.154	0.512	0.298	0.29	0.233	0.245	0.142	0.092
	[6.34]**	[2.08]*	[1.99]*	[5.83]**	[8.69]**	[1.97]*	[5.89]**	[5.76]**	[2.70]**
Eduyear	0.007	−0.03	0.107	−0.01	−0.077	−0.002	−0.015	0.014	−0.047
	[0.57]	[2.15]*	[1.20]	[0.46]	[5.83]**	[0.04]	[0.95]	[1.27]	[2.26]*
Eduyear2	0.004	0.01	0.001	0.006	0.011	0.007	0.005	0.006	0.007
	[3.59]**	[8.96]**	[0.24]	[3.81]**	[12.97]**	[3.14]**	[4.23]**	[9.01]**	[8.10]**
Expyear	0.033	0.065	0.009	0.032	0.038	0.051	0.038	0.031	0.034
	[6.06]**	[8.72]**	[0.31]	[4.06]**	[7.45]**	[3.15]**	[5.50]**	[8.13]**	[6.11]**
Expyear2	0	−0.001	0	0	0	−0.001	0	0	−0.001
	[5.30]**	[7.74]**	[0.00]	[2.33]*	[4.76]**	[2.13]*	[4.06]**	[5.04]**	[4.55]**
Headd	0.056	0.112	0.216	0.051	0.058	0.189	0.149	0.117	0.218
	[1.49]	[1.83]	[0.88]	[0.97]	[1.77]	[1.60]	[3.44]**	[4.60]**	[6.31]**
Urban	0.408	0.362	0.658	0.31	0.295	0.395	0.273	0.303	0.309
	[8.35]**	[9.82]**	[4.53]**	[5.92]**	[8.80]**	[2.43]*	[6.47]**	[10.86]**	[8.17]**
Union	0.569	0.556	−0.033	0.408	0.272	−0.108	0.624	0.404	0.056
	[11.83]**	[15.51]**	[0.22]	[8.59]**	[9.85]**	[1.18]	[15.32]**	[17.82]**	[1.89]
Married	0.033	0.094	−0.077	0.089	0.193	0.018	0.038	0.253	0.173
	[1.00]	[2.16]*	[0.35]	[1.78]	[6.32]**	[0.18]	[0.93]	[10.70]**	[5.27]**
Constant	7.792	7.674	8.368	8.039	8.229	8.41	7.943	8.031	9.174
	[97.87]**	[62.41]**	[13.84]**	[60.69]**	[98.18]**	[22.51]**	[71.85]**	[115.94]**	[62.64]**
Sample size	1,665	1,713	123	804	2,412	368	1,588	4,544	2,649
R^2	0.26	0.42	0.41	0.29	0.31	0.37	0.28	0.32	0.24

Source: Authors' calculations.

Note: OLS = ordinary least squares. For descriptions of the variables, see table 12A.1 in the annex to this chapter. Absolute value of *t*-statistic appear in brackets.

* Significant at 5%.

** Significant at 1%.

These results indicate that variables such as education and experience have expected signs and are consistent with the standard human capital approach and economic theory. Estimate coefficients for education (eduyear2) are statistically significant at 1 percent, except in the primary high-skill group. The relationship between the education variable and wage is mostly nonlinear. In the agriculture low-skill segment, an additional three years of schooling increase formal wage income by 5.7 percent for formal wage earners.

In the industry sector, three years of additional schooling will bring 2.4 percent more wage income for the low-skilled formal workers. The returns to education are the highest in the tertiary sector medium-skill segment, with a 9.6 percent increase in wage income for an additional three years of schooling.

Empirical literature suggests that union membership is an important determinant of wages, labor market behavior, and the unemployment rate in South Africa. Our results show that union membership has a strong positive impact on the income of members, except for high-skilled individuals across economic sectors. The associated coefficient is very significant statistically (at the 1 percent level). In agriculture, membership in a labor union brings about 60 percent more income than does nonmembership for low-skill workers in the tertiary sector and 37 percent more income for medium-skill formal workers, other things being equal in the same sectors with similar characteristics. The pattern is similar in the other sectors. For example, wage increases of about 40 percent for low-skilled workers in manufacturing, 28 percent for semi-skilled workers in manufacturing, and 62 percent for low-skilled workers in the tertiary sector.

Another interesting result relates to the effect of urbanization on wages. People living in the urban areas are earning, on average, 30 percent higher wages. This finding may be due partly to a relatively higher cost of living in urban areas as well as to the structure of the labor markets—for example, higher skills in urban and nonagricultural sectors. We draw on empirical literature in selecting a model specification for the wage function. Another important determinant of wages is gender differences. Everything else being equal, male employees are paid, on average, 9 percent to 51 percent higher wages.

Next, we specify the informal wage equation (iw), which is analogous to the formal wage equation:

$$\log iw_i = x_i \beta_{iw} + u_{iiw} \tag{12.5}$$

TABLE 12.8
OLS Estimates of the Informal Wage Equation

Variable	Agriculture	Industry	Services
Gender	0.095	0.347	0.254
	[1.34]	[3.88]**	[8.43]**
Eduyear	−0.01	0.041	−0.045
	[0.49]	[1.44]	[4.73]**
Eduyear2	0.007	0.002	0.011
	[4.00]**	[1.08]	[14.53]**
Expyear	0.029	0.023	0.043
	[3.01]**	[1.86]	[9.33]**
Expyear2	0	0	−0.001
	[3.12]**	[1.39]	[7.68]**
Headd	0.153	0.11	0.121
	[2.05]*	[1.47]	[4.36]**
Urban	0.311	0.397	0.177
	[3.68]**	[5.84]**	[6.55]**
Married	0.124	0.184	0.055
	[1.99]*	[2.59]**	[1.99]*
Constant	7.665	7.594	7.331
	[52.30]**	[37.71]**	[98.81]**
Sample size	758	693	3,860
R^2	0.21	0.22	0.28

Source: Authors' calculations.

Note: OLS = ordinary least squares. For descriptions of the variables, see table 12A.1 in the annex to this chapter. Absolute value of t-statistic appears in brackets.

* Significant at 5%.

** Significant at 1%.

The explanatory variables in this equation include a constant, gender, years of education, education squared, experience, experience squared, a dummy indicating whether the individual is head of household, a dummy for residence in the urban area, and a dummy for married. Table 12.8 contains the results of the OLS estimation of this equation.

As noted earlier, the specification of the equation explaining self-employment earnings (π) is entirely analogous to that of the wage equation. We express that equation as follows:

$$\log \pi_i = x_i \beta_\pi + u_{i\pi} \tag{12.6}$$

The explanatory variables in this equation include a constant, gender, years of education, education squared, experience, experience squared, a dummy indicating whether the individual is head of household, a dummy for residence in the urban area, a dummy for high skill level, and a dummy

TABLE 12.9
OLS Estimates of Self-Employed Earning Equation

Variable	Agriculture	Industry	Services
Gender	0.146	0.605	0.45
	[3.52]**	[7.40]**	[10.81]**
Eduyear	−0.059	0.027	−0.024
	[4.12]**	[1.02]	[1.79]
Eduyear2	0.011	0.004	0.007
	[10.44]**	[2.60]**	[8.66]**
Expyear	0.042	0.049	0.078
	[8.62]**	[4.06]**	[13.74]**
Expyear2	0	−0.001	−0.001
	[3.83]**	[3.35]**	[12.52]**
Headd	0.352	0.065	0.182
	[7.00]**	[0.74]	[4.20]**
Urban	0.131	0.158	0.27
	[1.91]	[1.96]*	[6.78]**
SkillH	0.361	0.811	0.556
	[1.85]	[5.92]**	[10.42]**
Formallab	1.451	0.798	0.703
	[17.45]**	[7.05]**	[13.58]**
Constant	6.926	7.215	6.982
	[83.49]**	[34.98]**	[72.40]**
Sample size	2,544	776	3,217
R^2	0.44	0.42	0.42

Source: Authors' calculations.

Note: For descriptions of the variables, see table 12A.1 in the annex to this chapter.

* Significant at 5%.

** Significant at 1%.

for working in the formal sector. Table 12.9 contains the results of the OLS estimation of equation (12.6).

We observe many patterns for self-employment that are similar to the case of wage employment. For instance, in the primary sector, heads of household earn 35 percent more from self-employment than those who are not heads of household. This is much higher than the 20 percent premium they earn as wage employees in the same sector. Similarly, self-employment pays more (15 to 30 percent) in the urban area than in the rural area. However, this premium is lower than the one estimated for formal wage employment. Finally, we observe that self-employment pays much more for highly skilled individuals than for the other skill categories. The findings are similar for people engaged in the formal sector of the economy.

AGGREGATION

Given individuals' earnings, household income is aggregated according to the following formula:

$$y_h = \sum_{i\in h} w_i L_{iw} + \sum_{i\in h} iw_i L_{iiw} + \sum_{i\in h} \pi_i L_{i\pi} + y_{0h} \qquad (12.7)$$

As equation (12.7) shows, total household income is a sum of three components. The first two components add all earnings (wage and self-employment) across individuals and activities, whereas the last element is an exogenous unearned income, such as transfers and capital income (see table 12.10). Real income is obtained by deflating total income by a household-specific consumer price index CPI_h. This is a weighted sum of the prices of various commodities purchased by the household. The weights are given by the budget shares, which vary across households.

Household's annual total income is defined as total annual income including wage income, self-employed income, and all other income.[12] Average values vary significantly among income deciles. On average, 9 percent of the household income is coming from other sources of income—nonwage income for laborers and non-self-employed income for self-employed people. When compared among income deciles, the ratio of other income to the total income varies between 12 percent in the lowest decile and 9 percent in the richest decile of the income distribution.

TABLE 12.10
Household Income Distribution between Labor and Nonlabor Income

Population decile	Nonlabor income/total annual income (ratio)	Total annual household nonlabor income (rand/year)	Total annual household income (rand/year)	Annual nonlabor income per capita (rand/year)	Annual total income per capita (rand/year)
1	0.12	720.35	6,025.79	107.24	723.94
2	0.13	949.01	7,164.21	133.37	990.21
3	0.13	1,258.22	9,519.38	182.21	1,420.86
4	0.12	1,467.23	12,381.75	233.49	1,801.05
5	0.11	1,637.85	15,365.86	299.38	2,443.36
6	0.10	2,256.26	22,175.89	429.49	3,795.05
7	0.08	2,497.54	31,152.63	543.68	6,044.95
8	0.09	3,414.77	39,702.75	817.71	9,067.07
9	0.08	5,650.85	67,829.13	1,498.38	16,997.32
10	0.09	15,061.66	159,162.60	5,589.73	53,806.32
Total	0.09	3,491.71	37,050.35	983.65	9,710.38

Source: Authors' calculations from Income and Expenditure Survey (2000) and Labor Force Survey (2000).

Linking the Microsimulation Components to the CGE Model

Assessing the *endowment, price,* and *occupational* effects of an oil price shock in a way that fully accounts for heterogeneity at both individual and household levels requires appropriate channels of communication between the CGE model and the microsimulation components. This communication works in the following way. The CGE model translates the impact of the shocks and policies through changes in relative prices of commodities and factors and through levels of employment. The microsimulation module takes these changes as exogenous and translates them into change in household behavior, which underpins changes in earnings, occupational status, and welfare.

To obtain meaningful results from the simulation framework, one must ensure that outcomes from the microsimulation model are consistent with the aggregate results from the CGE model both before and after the shock. This implies that the links between the two modules must respect a set of consistency constraints, which requires that the observed occupational choices predicted by the microsimulation module match the employment shares in the CGE model. Similarly, simulated earnings at the microeconomic level must match macroeconomic predictions.[13] A key consideration here stems from the fact that occupational choice depends on the random utility function, which is a *latent variable.* For example, a shock might cause unemployed or inactive individuals to become employed in one of the segments of the labor market. Implementation of the consistency constraints, therefore, requires information on both the observable and nonobservable components of the occupational choice and earning models. The observable components of these models are calculated on the basis of estimated parameters and data on observable characteristics. For those showing zero earnings, counterfactual earnings are computed on the basis of their observable characteristics, estimates of the relevant coefficients, and residuals drawn from a normal distribution with the same standard deviation as the distribution of residuals for those individuals with nonzero earnings.

In practice, differences underlying the microeconomic and macroeconomic data (sampling weights, coverage, imputed values, and so forth) make it very difficult to enforce fully the consistency constraints described above. Therefore, we adopt several steps to achieve the consistency. First, because of the importance of the labor market structure in South Africa, we ensure that the occupational choices in the microsimulation have the same classification as the labor categories in the CGE model and capture the appropriate taxonomy, structural, and unemployment issues in South Africa. Second, the base years for the social accounting matrix (SAM) (2003) and the survey data (2000) in our study of South Africa are different. To retain the more recent numbers in the macroeconomic accounts as well as the familiar poverty and inequality measurements of the microeconomic data, we employ percent changes to communicate changes in employment, wages, and prices from the CGE to the microsimulation.[14]

As noted by Bourguignon, Robilliard, and Robinson (2002), reconciliation in the postshock microsimulation means adjusting the intercepts (or constant terms) of the wage and occupational functions to ensure that changes predicted by the income generation model are consistent with those predicted by the CGE model.

Impact of a Large Oil Price Shock

The nominal price of crude oil increased by about 125 percent during the period from 2003 to 2006. In May 2007, for example, the global oil price averaged over $65 a barrel. In real terms, however, the recent price increase is only a cyclical recovery and has yet to reach the peaks of 1979–80. Moreover, non-oil commodity prices, such as those for metal and minerals (for example, gold and other metals), also have risen significantly and have contributed very positively to the balance of payment positions of countries like South Africa. As a result, the ratio of oil and non-oil commodity prices so far has not risen as sharply as it did for oil-importing countries, when compared with the previous shock of 1999–2000. The trend of rising prices, however, is worrisome. In what follows, we analyze the marginal impact of a large increase in the price of oil similar to the price hike in 2003–06 (holding other things constant unless otherwise specified).

To analyze the effects of an oil price shock on prices and the structure of production in South Africa, we consider two experiments:

1. A 125 percent increase in the world price of imported crude and refined oil

2. A 125 percent increase in the world price of imported crude and refined oil, a 30 percent increase in the world price of imported basic chemicals, and a 6 percent increase in the world price of all other imported goods.

TABLE 12.11
Macroeconomic Results for South Africa

Real variables	Oil price shock (% change)	Oil and general price shock (% change)
Real exchange rate	16.2	22.4
Total absorption	−5.6	−7.8
Exports	7.7	9.1
Imports	−6.2	−10.3
Household consumption	−6.5	−8.8
Total investment	−7.0	−10.8
GDP (at market prices)	−1.8	−2.5
Total employment	−2.1	−2.7
Consumer price index	1.9	2.7

Source: Authors' calculations.

Note: GDP = gross domestic product.

The second experiment takes into account the spillover effects of an oil price increase on other commodities.

Macroeconomic Results

The macroeconomic results are shown in table 12.11. When world prices of imported goods increase, the currency depreciates; the real exchange rate, measured as local currency units per world currency unit, increases from 16.2 percent to 22.4 percent, depending on the magnitude of the price shock (that is, an oil price increase alone or an oil price increase plus a general price increase). In effect, the currency depreciates to shift resources into exports, increasing export earnings to pay for the more expensive but essential crude oil imports.[15] Total absorption and real gross domestic product (GDP) at market prices decline as imported oil becomes more expensive. The world price shocks reduce employment, which also contributes to the decline in real GDP.

Despite a dramatic increase in the world price of crude oil imports, the quantity of crude oil imported—a commodity with no domestic substitute—declines slightly by approximately 1 percent in either price shock scenario. Imports of refined petroleum decline by approximately 20 percent. Imports of all other goods fall as a result of the currency depreciation.

Output responds to the direct effects of an increase in input costs as crude and refined petroleum prices increase. See figures 12.3–12.6 for output results by activity and price shock.

FIGURE 12.3
Output Adjustment in the Services Activities: Oil Price Shock

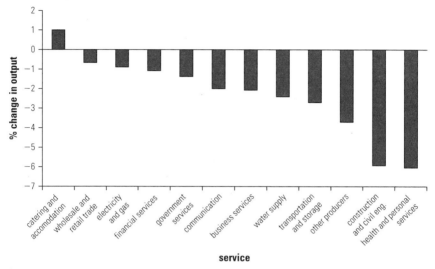

Source: Authors' calculations.

FIGURE 12.4
Output Adjustment in the Services Activities: Oil and General Price Shock

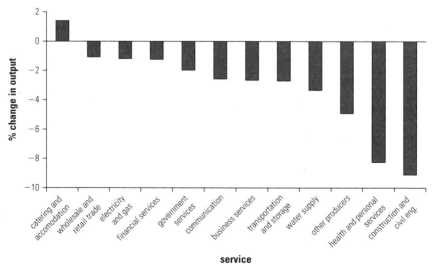

Source: Authors' calculations.

FIGURE 12.5
Output Adjustment in the Industry Activities: Oil Price Shock

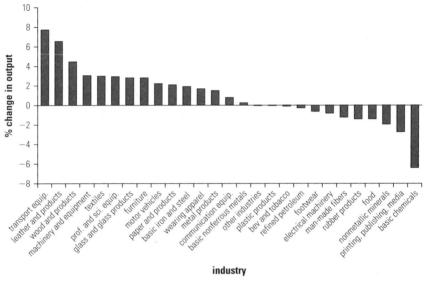

Source: Authors' calculations.

FIGURE 12.6
Output Adjustment in the Industry Activities: Oil and General Price Shock

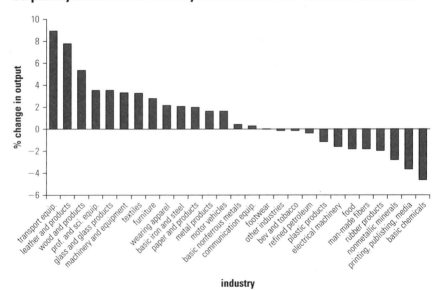

Source: Authors' calculations.

For price shock, refined petroleum and basic chemicals—the sole users of crude oil—contract when the price of imported oil increases because the input cost increases. Other sectors with strong indirect intermediate input use of petroleum (such as printing and publishing, rubber products, transportation and storage, and food) also contract. (See table 12.3 for a ranking of intermediate input demand for refined petroleum, accounting for direct and indirect effects.) Output also responds to economywide changes induced by the world price shocks. As a result of the depreciation, output of services activities—which are primarily nontraded (with the exception of catering and accommodations)—decline.

Consistent with the output changes, employment in services activities declines and labor moves to agriculture and industry activities. Overall employment declines as the demand for semi-skilled and low-skilled labor declines following the import price shocks (the direction of the results is the same for either price shock; the magnitude of the shock is higher when there is an increase in oil and other commodity prices). The percent changes in employment are presented in table 12.12. (Note that there is movement of resources within the industry and services activities, but here we report only the aggregate changes.)

Real wages decline for all labor categories with the exception of semi-skilled and low-skilled formal workers who receive a constant real wage, and the quantity employed adjusts downward in the price shocks considered here (table 12.13).

As wages decline, household demand for goods and services also declines. The commodity price changes result from shifts in both the demand and the supply curves for each activity. The net effect of an increase in oil prices (as well as for oil and a general price shock) is a dramatic increase in the price of fuel (see table 12.14). Prices also increase for food and transportation.

Welfare and Distributional Implications of the Oil Price Shock

Having identified the macroeconomic effects of an oil price increase, we now address the poverty and distributional implications. We measure poverty with members of the Foster, Greer, and Thorbecke (1984) family of decomposable indexes. Our analysis of inequality is based on the Gini coefficient and general entropy indexes. We discuss, respectively, the baseline distribution of welfare and the distributional implications of a severe oil price shock.[16]

TABLE 12.12
Employment Changes

Workers, by sector	Oil price shock (% change)	Oil and general price shock (% change)
Agriculture		
Formal high-skilled workers	3.5	4.9
Formal semi-skilled workers	−1.5	−1.4
Formal low-skilled workers	1.0	1.9
Self-employed	3.6	5.2
Informal workers	8.0	11.8
Industry		
Formal high-skilled workers	2.1	2.5
Formal semi-skilled workers	−1.7	−2.6
Formal low-skilled workers	0.5	0.1
Self-employed	2.6	2.8
Informal workers	4.2	5.2
Services		
Formal high-skilled workers	−0.5	−0.7
Formal semi-skilled workers	−8.6	−11.4
Formal low-skilled workers	−8.4	−11.6
Self-employed	−3.4	−4.8
Informal workers	−2.3	−3.3
Economywide employment		
Total	−2.1	−2.7
Formal semi-skilled workers	−5.3	−7.0
Formal low-skilled workers	−2.8	−3.7

Source: Authors' calculations.

TABLE 12.13
Wage Changes

Workers, by wage type	Oil price shock (% change)	Oil and general price shock (% change)
Real		
Formal high-skilled workers	−11.3	−15.2
Formal semi-skilled workers	0	0
Formal low-skilled workers	0	0
Self-employed	−10.5	−13.8
Informal workers	−9.6	−12.8
Nominal		
Formal high-skilled workers	−9.6	−13.0
Formal semi-skilled workers	1.9	2.7
Formal low-skilled workers	1.9	2.7
Self-employed	−8.8	−11.6
Informal workers	−7.9	−10.5

Source: Authors' calculations.

TABLE 12.14
Price Changes

Expenditure category	Oil price shock (% change)	Oil and general price shock (% change)
Food	0.6	1.6
Beverages	–1.7	–1.6
Alcoholic beverages	–1.7	–1.6
Cigarette and tobacco	–1.7	–1.6
Personal care	–7.2	–9.2
Housing operations	–3.8	–5.1
Fuel	65.9	68.1
Housing, energy, and water	–3.1	–3.7
Clothing and footwear	–0.9	0.3
Furniture	–0.2	1.4
Health	–7.2	–9.2
Transportation	4.5	7.3
Communication	–1.7	–1.5
Education	–7.2	–9.2
Reading	0.2	2.0
Entertainment	–7.2	–9.2
Miscellaneous	–3.8	–5.1

Source: Authors' calculations.

Baseline Distribution of Economic Welfare

The available survey data provide information on both household income and consumption expenditures. Figure 12.7 and table 12.15 describe the distribution of these two variables by decile. We combine information on household size and the sample household weights to estimate poverty and inequality at the population level. At the national level, average per capita consumption was a little more than R 10,000 and per capita income was about R 9,700 in 2000.

Moreover, the average values of income and expenditures vary significantly by decile and locality. Comparing average consumption levels across rural and urban South Africa shows disparities between rural and urban sectors (table 12.15). Similar disparities exist in per capita expenditure levels among deciles and between urban and rural locations.

Figure 12.8 and table 12.16 provide a poverty profile for South Africa in 2000, based on a poverty line set at $1 per day, which amounts in South Africa to R 2,533 per capita per year. Figure 12.8 contains a set of TIP[17] curves, one based on the distribution of per capita expenditure and the other one based on that of per capita income. TIP curves offer an alternative way to test for unanimous poverty comparisons across time and across

FIGURE 12.7
Distribution of Income and Expenditure, by Decile

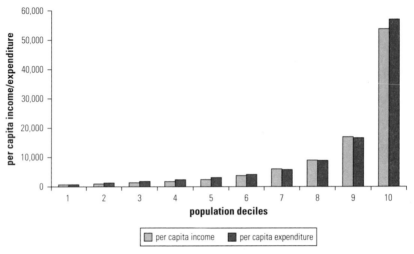

Source: Authors' calculations.

TABLE 12.15
Per Capita Household Expenditures and Income, by Decile
Rand

	Expenditure		Income		Urban/Rural Ratio	
Income decile	Urban	Rural	Urban	Rural	Expenditure	Income
Poorest	759.0	741.6	724.4	723.8	1.02	1.00
2	1,346.4	1,321.2	992.7	989.1	1.02	1.00
3	1,842.2	1,827.9	1,604.2	1,312.2	1.01	1.22
4	2,399.6	2,389.6	1,980.5	1,643.0	1.00	1.21
5	3,129.6	3,102.7	2,757.1	2,093.1	1.01	1.32
6	4,174.7	4,115.0	3,853.8	3,685.0	1.01	1.05
7	5,794.8	5,733.5	6,385.0	5,151.1	1.01	1.24
8	8,984.7	8,917.5	9,232.4	8,436.0	1.01	1.09
9	16,744.7	15,807.2	16,528.3	21,353.3	1.06	0.77
Richest	56,017.3	72,562.9	53,167.3	63,415.5	0.77	0.84

Source: Authors' calculations.

regions and countries, based on a wide class of poverty indexes. The TIP curve provides a graphical summary of incidence, intensity, and inequality dimensions of aggregate poverty, based on the distribution of poverty gaps (Jenkins and Lambert 1997). On the basis of this poverty profile, we note that about 37 percent or 49 percent of the population was poor in 2000, as welfare is measured by expenditure or income.

FIGURE 12.8
A Picture of Poverty in South Africa, 2000

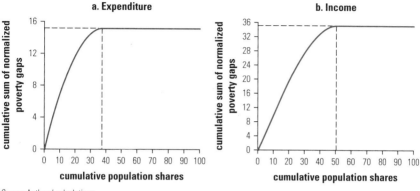

Source: Authors' calculations.

TABLE 12.16
Poverty Profiles, 2000

a. Expenditure-based profile

Measure	Estimate	Scale-elasticity	Gini elasticity	Trade-off
Head count	0.37	−0.95	2.88	3.03
Poverty gap	0.15	−1.45	8.42	5.81
Squared poverty gap	0.08	−1.70	13.20	7.78

b. Income-based profile

Measure	Estimate	Scale elasticity	Gini elasticity	Trade-off
Head count	0.49	−0.44	1.22	2.76
Poverty gap	0.34	−0.43	4.96	11.45
Squared poverty gap	0.28	−0.40	8.64	21.48

Source: Authors' calculations.

Inequality is also quite high in South Africa. Using the distribution of expenditure by decile, we find that the richest 20 percent of the population, on average, spends 35 times more than the poorest 20 percent of the population in 2000 prices. The Gini coefficient associated with the distribution of expenditure is about 67 percent and that for the distribution of income is about 72 percent. These baseline case results are in line with other studies of South Africa (for example, Jenkins and Thomas 2000). The high level of inequality is certainly a constraint to the responsiveness of poverty to economic growth. Table 12.16 presents information on two types of poverty elasticities computed according to the Kakwani (1993) method.

The scale elasticity measures the responsiveness of poverty to changes in the mean value of the welfare indicator (expenditure or income). The Gini elasticity indicates the extent to which poverty responds to changes in inequality as measured by the Gini coefficient. The trade-off indicator is known as the proportional rate of substitution (marginal proportional rate of substitution) between mean welfare and inequality. This rate is the rate at which income needs to grow to compensate for an increase of 1 percent in the Gini coefficient to keep poverty constant. Thus, the information presented in table 12.16 reveals that income would have to grow at least 3 percent to keep poverty incidence constant at the 2000 level.

Distributional Impact of the Severe Oil Price Shock

We now focus our attention on the case of the severe oil price shock. The distributional implications of this shock are obtained by comparing the baseline distribution of income or expenditures to the one that accounts for gains and losses arising from changes in wages, self-employment income, occupational choices, and consumer prices. To enforce the consistency constraint discussed earlier, we adjust the constants (or intercepts) of the set of equations estimated from the household and labor surveys so that the modified equations respect changes from the CGE model. Recall that the microsimulation model has three economic sectors and three skill types for formal wage workers, 16 occupational choices (including a base category of inactive and unemployed), and three types of incomes (formal wages, informal wages, and self-employment income). Overall, the model has a total of 30 equations with 30 constants (15 constants for income equations and 15 constants for occupational choice equations (the constant for the base category in the multilogit model is set to zero).

The microsimulation calculates the formal wages, informal wages, self-employment incomes, and occupational choices at the microeconomic units (that is, for each individual) that are consistent with the post-shock relative prices, wages, and employment levels by broad categories generated from the CGE model. After aggregating all incomes within the households, per capita income and expenditures are deflated by a new household-specific consumer price index. As the price index reflects household-specific consumption baskets, changes in prices of consumer goods and services will have differential impact on individual households, based on their allocation of budget to these components of the consumer basket.

TABLE 12.17
Household Expenditure Shares, by Income Quintile

Quintile	Food	Beverage	Alcoholic beverage	Cigarette and tobacco	Personal care	Housing operation
Poorest	0.45	0.01	0.01	0.01	0.05	0.03
2	0.42	0.01	0.01	0.01	0.05	0.03
3	0.38	0.01	0.02	0.01	0.05	0.03
4	0.31	0.01	0.02	0.02	0.05	0.03
Richest	0.17	0.01	0.01	0.01	0.03	0.04
Average	0.35	0.01	0.01	0.01	0.05	0.03

Quintile	Fuel	Housing, energy, and water	Clothing and footwear	Furniture	Health	Transportation
Poorest	0.05	0.23	0.05	0.01	0.01	0.03
2	0.04	0.21	0.06	0.02	0.01	0.03
3	0.03	0.20	0.06	0.03	0.01	0.05
4	0.02	0.20	0.06	0.03	0.02	0.07
Richest	0.01	0.21	0.04	0.03	0.04	0.10
Average	0.03	0.21	0.05	0.02	0.02	0.06

Quintile	Communication	Education	Reading	Entertainment	Miscellaneous
Poorest	0.01	0.03	0.0001	0.002	0.04
2	0.01	0.02	0.0002	0.002	0.06
3	0.01	0.02	0.0003	0.003	0.08
4	0.02	0.03	0.0007	0.004	0.12
Richest	0.03	0.03	0.0012	0.008	0.23
Average	0.02	0.03	0.0010	0.004	0.10

Source: Authors' calculations.

The survey shows that households' budget allocation on different types of consumer goods and services varies significantly (table 12.17). For example, the poorer households spent a larger share of their incomes on food and utilities like water, energy, and rent for housing. On the other hand, the richer households spent relatively more on health, transportation, and communication, and other goods and services. The oil price shock has directly increased prices for energy and transport, but also has affected prices of other goods and services through second-round effects. Although the overall price level has gone up slightly, we observed significant variation in prices within the consumer basket. For example, prices for food, fuel, and transportation have gone up, but prices for many other goods and services have declined slightly. Consequently, households had been affected differently, depending on their spending patterns. Because

TABLE 12.18
Wage Impact of Oil Shock on Formal Workers, by Decile
Rand, 2000 prices

Income decile	Formal wage, postshock	Formal wage, preshock	Ratio of postshock to preshock wage
Poorest	3,824.85	4,101.92	0.93
2	7,724.03	8,157.37	0.95
3	11,895.97	12,409.63	0.96
4	16,163.26	16,540.06	0.98
5	21,572.56	21,915.76	0.98
6	27,394.34	27,768.17	0.99
7	33,806.99	34,605.13	0.98
8	44,793.30	46,425.38	0.96
9	65,200.57	68,435.89	0.95
Richest	180,520.80	194,553.30	0.93
Overall average	32,967.42	34,511.12	0.96

Source: Authors' calculations.

poorer households spend relatively more on food, they are expected to be adversely affected by the oil price shock. This issue of changes in households' welfare is discussed next.

IMPACT ON THE FORMAL LABOR SECTOR

The adverse impact of the oil price shock was most obvious in the formal labor sector. Following the shock, formal workers' wages, on average, declined by 4 percent of their preshock earnings (table 12.18). Although, the wage loss varies by income decile, the differences are significant only for the poorest and the richest deciles of formal workers.

In addition to a decline in wages, formal sector labor also experienced increased unemployment in the tertiary sector. Most of those who became unemployed were low- and medium-skill workers of the tertiary sector. These unemployed workers lost their earnings completely following the shock (table 12.19). Almost 70 percent of these newly unemployed formal wage earners belong to the bottom three deciles (based on preshock per capita incomes).

WELFARE IMPACT ON LOW-SKILL HOUSEHOLDS

As noted above, the poorest deciles were disproportionately adversely affected by the shock because they tend to have low skills. Figure 12.9

TABLE 12.19
Unemployment Impact of Oil Shock on Formal Workers, by Decile

Income decile	Percentage of people	Average annual wage, preshock	Average annual wage, postshock	Loss (%)
Poorest	31.07	3,742.64	0	−100
2	19.11	8,253.35	0	−100
3	18.39	12,127.46	0	−100
4	9.11	16,562.43	0	−100
5	10.18	21,893.82	0	−100
6	4.46	27,403.68	0	−100
7	3.39	33,850.42	0	−100
8	2.50	45,794.71	0	−100
9	1.25	70,534.29	0	−100
Richest	0.54	97,081.67	0	−100
Overall average	n.a.	18,306.53	0	−100

Source: Authors' calculations.

Note: n.a. = not applicable.

FIGURE 12.9
Gains and Losses from Oil Price Shock for Low-Skill Households

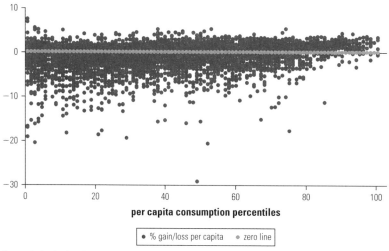

Source: Authors' calculations.

shows that households with low skill levels tend to lose more than they gain from the shock. Losses are more pronounced than the gains; also, losses are more clustered around the lower end of the distribution (poorer households with low skill levels).

FIGURE 12.10
Gains and Losses from Oil Price Shock for High-Skill Households

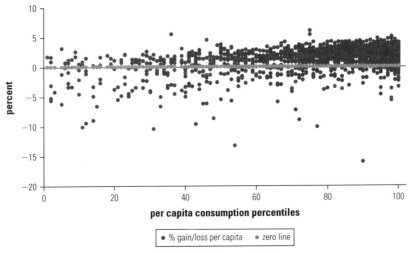

Source: Authors' calculations.

WELFARE IMPACT OF THE OIL PRICE SHOCK ON HIGH-SKILL HOUSEHOLDS
In contrast to low-skill households, those with a high skill level are, on average, gaining from the shock. As figure 12.10 shows, there are relatively few households that are experiencing losses from the shock and they are scattered across the income deciles. However, most high-skill households have gained more income after the shock and these gainers are concentrated on the higher end of the income distribution. In our view, high-skill workers are less likely to be laid off when unemployment increases as a result of an oil price shock, or they can move relatively easily to different jobs. Moreover, these households, which are already mostly in higher income quintiles, are also less affected by the price changes following the oil price shocks. To start with, they are richer and spend relatively less on food and other goods affected most by the changes in oil prices.

OVERALL WELFARE IMPACT OF THE OIL PRICE SHOCK
Figure 12.11 presents an overall picture of gainers and losers from the oil price shock. It is clear that the poorer segment of the population is more adversely affected by this shock. For instance, households below the seventh decile of income per capita are losing and becoming poorer, whereas the richest 35 percent of households are gaining even higher incomes as a result of the shock. On average, shock results in a decline of about 1.5 percent of initial per capita income for the poorer segments of the population.

FIGURE 12.11
Distribution of Gains and Losses to Households, by Decile

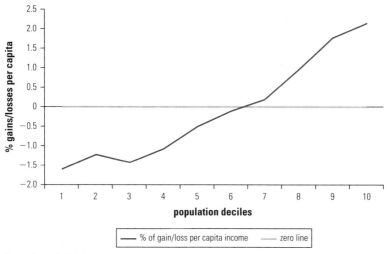

Source: Authors' calculations.

Following the shock, not only did the extent of poverty increase slightly but also the distribution of household welfare became less equal.

Table 12.20 presents our results on poverty and inequality indicators, along with some disaggregations of the baseline profile. Thus, when regional disparities are considered, over 70 percent of people living in rural South Africa were poor, whereas only 33 percent of urban population had income below the poverty line (the equivalent of $1 a day). The simulation results for oil price shock have an adverse impact on poverty. The proportion of individuals living under poverty (based on a $1 a day poverty line and the income measure of welfare) increases slightly less, from 49.0 percent to 49.5 percent (it increases 37 percent to 38 percent if we consider expenditure per capita as a welfare measure). Poverty rates also increased at the regional level. The poverty gap index increased from 15 percent to 16 percent (result not reported), which indicates that there is a 1 percent increase in the difference between actual income and income required to sustain a minimum standard of living.

As far as inequality is concerned, we use both general entropy indexes and the Gini coefficient for the whole population and decomposition at the regional levels. The simulation results also show some increase in inequality. The overall Gini coefficient increases by about 1 percent, the same increase as the Gini coefficient for the urban and rural sectors. Thus, following the oil price shock, income distribution worsened slightly. The

TABLE 12.20
Impact of Oil Shock on Poverty and Income Distribution

Indicator	Base case			Simulation 1: oil price shock		
	National	Urban	Rural	National	Urban	Rural
Poverty indicator, using expenditure						
Head count ratio	0.37	0.21	0.60	0.38	0.22	0.61
Poverty gap	0.15	0.08	0.26	0.16	0.08	0.27
Poverty severity	0.08	0.04	0.15	0.08	0.04	0.15
Poverty indicator, using income						
Head count ratio	0.49	0.33	0.72	0.49	0.33	0.72
Poverty gap	0.33	0.22	0.51	0.33	0.22	0.51
Poverty severity	0.28	0.17	0.43	0.28	0.18	0.43
Inequality Indicator, using expenditure						
General entropy(0)	0.87	0.77	0.60	0.89	0.78	0.61
General entropy(1)	0.98	0.80	1.04	1.00	0.81	1.06
Gini coefficient	0.67	0.63	0.58	0.68	0.64	0.59
Inequality Indicator, using income						
General entropy(0)	1.22	1.02	1.14	1.23	1.03	1.15
General entropy(1)	1.20	1.00	1.46	1.21	1.02	1.48
Gini coefficient	0.71	0.67	0.71	0.72	0.68	0.72

Source: Authors' calculations.

distributional impact, as measured by changes in the Gini coefficient, deteriorated both for rural and urban areas. These results suggest that the impact on heterogeneous households tends to average out when the households are collected by income groups. The separation of impact by household would be meaningful for the macroeconomic-microeconomic linking if the household classification were based on characteristics other than income, and if the data were rich enough in such characteristics for the construction of the SAM underlying the CGE model. However, aggregative poverty and income inequality measures do not vary much. The oil price shock tends to increase the disparity between rich and poor—that is, the mean welfare or consumption of various household groups. This finding means that the impact on different household types will tend to be the same if they have more or less the same mean welfare or income prior to the shock—that is a significant finding.

Finally, we decompose the overall change in inequality into its vertical and horizontal components. We follow Ravallion and Lokshin (2004) in using the mean log deviation (MLD) measure of inequality. This measure is a member of the generalized entropy class with the focal parameter set to zero. Members of this class are defined by the following expression:

$$GE(\theta) = \frac{1}{\theta^2 - \theta}\left[\frac{1}{n}\sum_{i=1}^{n}\left(\frac{x_i}{\mu}\right)^{\theta} - 1\right] \tag{12.8}$$

When the focal parameter θ is equal to 1, we get Theil's measure; and when the parameter is equal to 0, we get the MLD defined as follows:

$$GE(0) = \frac{1}{n}\sum_{i=1}^{n}\log\left(\frac{\mu}{x_i}\right) \tag{12.9}$$

To see clearly what the decomposition entails, let y_i and x_i stand, respectively, for the post- and prereform welfare per person in household i, and let g_i stand for the gain (or loss) to household i as a result of the shock. Thus, $y_i = x_i + g_i$. The vertical component relates to inequality among people at different preshock welfare levels, whereas the horizontal component measures inequality between people at the same preshock welfare level. The decomposition involved here requires an estimate of the average impact for the distribution of gains at given preshock welfare (x). In other terms, we need an estimate of the conditional mean impact defined by $g_i^c = E(g_i|x = x_i)$. It would be difficult to observe significant dispersion in impact at given preform welfare within a data set from a household survey. This conditional expectation can be estimated using a nonparametric regression of the gains on x (for example, locally estimated scatter plot smooth). On the basis of the MLD, it can be shown that the overall change in inequality can be written as

$$\Delta I = \frac{1}{n}\sum_{i=1}^{n}\ln\left(\frac{1 + \bar{g}/\bar{x}}{1 + g_i^c/x_i}\right) + \frac{1}{n}\sum_{i=1}^{n}\ln\left(\frac{1 + g_i^c/x_i}{1 + g_i/x_i}\right) \tag{12.10}$$

The first term on the right-hand side of equation (12.10) measures the contribution to the change in total inequality of the way conditional mean impacts vary with preform welfare levels, and is called the vertical component. The horizontal component, the second term, measures the contribution of the deviations in impacts from their conditional means.

Table 12.21 shows the decomposition of the impact on inequality. In the case of a shock produced by increased oil prices, aggregate results show that the horizontal component is inequality reducing whereas the vertical impact is inequality enhancing. A closer look at the components of this

TABLE 12.21
Decomposition of the Impact on Inequality

Decomposition	Vertical component	Horizontal component	Total
Gains from consumption[a]	137.0	−37.0	100.0
Gains from changes in formal wages[a]	120.4	−20.4	100.0
Gains from changes in informal wages[a]	104.1	−4.1	100.0
Gains from changes in self-employed income[a]	77.0	23.0	100.0
Aggregate gains[a]	135.0	−35.0	100.0
Aggregate gains[b]	119.0	−19.0	100.0

Source: Authors' calculations.

a. Using per capita consumption as an explanatory variable in the locally weighted scatter plot smooth regression.

b. Using per capita income as an explanatory variable in the locally weighted scatter plot smooth regression.

aggregate result reveals (except in the case of self-employment income), that the horizontal impact is inequality decreasing, whereas the vertical effect is inequality enhancing. Because self-employed individuals are a relatively smaller share of the total employed population (about 23 percent) and their contribution to household income is not high enough (about 16 percent), it is unlikely that the impact of changes in the self-employment income will change the sign of the horizontal impact.

Summary and Conclusions

This chapter has developed a macroeconomic-microeconomic framework for examining the macroeconomic and distributional consequences of an oil price shock for the South African economy. In so doing, it gave simultaneous quantitative expressions to the impact of an external shock on macroeconomic aggregates such as GDP, real exchange rate, total absorption, exports, imports, various subsectors of interest to policy makers, as well as the household distributional response to the shocks with the full heterogeneity of household and labor characteristics normally found only in household and labor surveys. This framework was accomplished by implementing and merging (1) a highly disaggregative CGE model that captures important economywide consequences of relative price and income effects, as well as labor market adjustment arising from a significant external shock or policy change; and (2) a microsimulation component linking both earnings and occupational choice to sociodemographic characteristics of the household, as in Bourguignon and Ferreira (2005).

We emphasize that the application to the oil price shock should be taken as illustrative because offsetting factors are not considered. Although the magnitude of the shock would be similar to that of 2003–06, there were several other factors at play in South Africa—like the strong macroeconomic policy in place, the overall favorable terms of trade, the relative strength of the South African rand, and strong investment programs in the public sector.[18] In fact, economic growth in South Africa has been very high during that period. The scenarios should be taken as the marginal impact of a similar severe price hike without the benefit of offsetting factors—that is, a conservative case. It also assumes that the labor market structure and rigidities, particularly about the real wages of the low- to medium-skill workers, will continue to be operating along the shocks. Under those circumstances, the two scenarios indicate that total absorption would fall between 5 and 8 percent. Real GDP would decline 1.8 to 2.5 percent. The real exchange rate depreciation that would be necessary ranges from 16 to more than 20 percent. The impact on industries can vary widely, with most of the negative impact falling on fuel-intensive sectors, such as construction, rubber, and plastic products, various chemicals, electrical machinery, and health services.

With respect to the distributional impact of these shocks, we find that aggregative poverty and income inequality measures do not vary a lot numerically. However, a look beyond these aggregate results enables us to identify various groups of winners and losers. The adverse impact of the oil price shock was mostly felt by the poorer segment of the formal labor market in the form of declining wages and increased unemployment. Unemployment hit mostly low- and medium-skill workers in the tertiary sector, and about 70 percent of those workers belonged to the bottom three deciles of the formal labor force.

Our findings show that losses are more pronounced in the low-skill group than are the gains. On the other hand, high-skill households, on average, gained from the oil price shock. Most high-skill households gained more income after the shock. Moreover, the gainers are concentrated on the higher end of the income distribution, but the relatively small number of losers is scattered across the income deciles. In addition, the shock has a limited impact on high-skill households for another reason: the spending basket of these relatively rich households is less skewed toward food and other goods affected most by the changes in oil prices.

Evidence also suggests that high-skill workers are less likely to be laid off when unemployment increases as a result of the oil price shock, or they can move relatively easily and quickly to different jobs. In fact, the opportunity cost of not working is typically higher for the highly skilled individuals. Therefore, in response to a job loss, high-skill workers quickly will seek another employment. Workers with more years of schooling and experience may also be better able to adapt to new jobs and have better access to information on vacancies and opportunities than are low-skill individuals. Thus, an adverse shock is like a poverty trap for low-skill workers unless there are polices and institutional arrangements to mitigate the adverse impact of the shock on this group of households.

The overall welfare impact shows that the poorer, and generally low-skill, segment of the population is more adversely affected by this shock. Thus, the oil price shock tends to increase the disparity between rich and poor. This conclusion is also supported by the observed changes in the mean welfare or consumption of various socioeconomic groups considered in this study. Furthermore, a decomposition of changes in inequality reveals that the horizontal component tends to decrease inequality. This comparison of aggregate and disaggregate results suggests that the impact on different household types will tend to be the same if they have more or less the same mean welfare or income prior to the shock—a significant finding.

Finally, the relative stability of the aggregate measures of poverty and inequality also poses an issue for the recursive linking between the CGE model and the microsimulation module. If the distributional effects collected and pulled together from the microsimulation are aggregative in nature (such as the income groupings currently specified in the CGE model), the broadly defined structures of households and labor supplies for the bottom-up feedback are likely to be relatively stable. This is consistent with empirical findings that, without long-term economic growth, productivity change, and factor accumulation (as can be found in a more dynamic CGE setting), poverty and inequality measures will likely not vary significantly. Hence, in the static setting found in current implementation of the CGE model, no recursive feedback into the macroeconomic model was found to be necessary. In the end, what constitutes an appropriate or meaningful classification of the households for a two-way feedback likely would depend on the policy issue and external shock under investigation. The trade-offs between greater sophistication and simplification also will depend on data constraints as well as the needs and capacity of policy makers.

Annex

TABLE 12A.1
Description of Variables

Variable name	Description
Demographic variables, *individual-level data*	
Gender	Dummy variable:1 male, 0 female
Age	Years of age
Nchild09	Number of children aged 0–9 in household
Nchild01	Number of children aged 0–1 in household
Headd	Dummy variable: 1 household head, 0 otherwise
Married	Dummy variable: 1 married couple, 0 otherwise
Urban	Dummy variable: 1 urban, 0 rural
Prov	Regional province variable
Hhsize	Household size
Education and experience, *individual-level data*	
Eduyear	Number of years spent in school. Highest education completed.
Eduyear2	Number of years spent in school-squared
Expyear	Experience measured as ($=$age-eduyear-5)
Expyear2	Experience-squared measured as ($=$age-eduyear-5$)^2$
Eduyearhd	Years of schooling of head of the household
SkillH	Professional, semiprofessionals, technical occupations, managerial, executive administrative occupations, and certain transport occupations, such as pilot navigator
SkillM	Clerical occupations, sales occupations, transport, delivery and communications occupations, service occupations, farmer, farm manager, artisan, apprentice and related occupations, production foreman, production supervisor
SkillL	Elementary occupations and domestic workers
Income from employment and occupational *categories, individual level data*	
Fwage	Yearly wage income in rand, formal workers
Fwagelog	Log of yearly wage income, formal workers
Iwage	Yearly wage income in rand, informal workers
Iwagelog	Log of yearly wage income, informal workers
Selfincr	Yearly total self-employed income in rand
Seinclog	Log of yearly self-employed income
Fambusiness	Dummy variable: 1 someone in the household owns family business, 0 otherwise

(*Continued on the following page*)

TABLE 12A.1

(continued)

Variable name	Description
Occhoice1	Dummy variables: 0 unemployed and inactive; 1 self-employed, agriculture; 2 informal wage employee; 3 formal wage employee
Occhoice2	Dummy variables: 1 Inactive and unemployed; 2 formal sector workers, low-skilled in agriculture; 3 formal sector workers, semi-skilled in agriculture; 4 formal sector workers, high-skilled in agriculture; 5 formal sector workers, low-skilled in industry; 6 formal sector workers, semi-skilled in industry; 7 formal sector workers, high-skilled in industry; 8 formal sector workers, low-skilled in services; 9 formal sector workers, semi-skilled in services; 10 formal sector workers, high-skilled in services; 11 informal sector workers, agriculture; 12 informal sector workers, industry; 13 informal sector workers, services; 14 self-employed, agriculture; 15 self-employed, industry; and 16 self-employed, services
Economic sectors	
Primary sector	Includes agriculture, forestry, and fishing, mining and quarrying
Secondary sector	Includes manufacturing, electricity, other utilities, and construction
Tertiary sector	Includes trade, transport, financial, and business services; and social, personal, and community services
Formallab	Dummy variable for formal labor: based on question asked in labor force survey
Informallab	Dummy variable for Informal labor: based on question asked in labor force survey
Household aggregate expenditures and income variables, household-level data from income and expenditure survey 2000	
Household expenditures and consumer price index for 17 household expenditure categories	Food; nonalcoholic beverages, alcoholic beverages; cigarettes, cigars, and tobacco; clothing and footwear
	Housing, fuel and power, furniture and equipment, household operations, health, transport
	Communication, recreation and entertainment, education, miscellaneous personal care,
	Other miscellaneous goods and services
Household aggregate income	Includes formal wage income, informal wage income, and self-employed income from labor force survey, and other income from income and expenditure survey .

Sources: Labor Force Survey (2000) and Income and Expenditure Survey (2000).

Notes

This paper is issued simultaneously as a working paper at the World Bank and the Institute of Development Studies (IDS), Sussex University. The framework used in the paper is based on a World Bank technical assistance to develop a computatble general equilibrium-microsimulation model for South Africa's National Treasury in a collaborative effort with IDS and the U.S. Naval Academy. The work is jointly managed by Delfin Go at the World Bank and Marna Kearney at the South Africa National Treasury. The purpose of the exercise is to illustrate the potential use of the framework for analysis of policy and external shocks. The views expressed are those of the authors and do not necessarily reflect those of their respective institutions or affiliated organizations. The authors would like to thank Maurizio Bussolo, David Coady, Alan Gelb, Jeffrey Lewis, Hans Lofgren, John Page, and James Thurlow for helpful comments on an earlier version of this paper.

1. See, for example, Bourguignon and Pereira da Silva (2003) or Essama-Nssah (2006) for a compilation and evaluation of various approaches, techniques, and tools.
2. There are also other issues, such as introducing dynamics and growth, incorporating individual firm behavior, and so forth. See, for example, the conclusion chapter in Bourguignon and Pereira da Silva (2003).
3. Full details of the South Africa CGE model can be found in Kearney (2004); for a version of the model used to analyze value-added taxes, see Go et al. (2005). In this description, we comment on features of the model important for an analysis of the oil price shock.
4. More specifically, the employment data in the CGE have been calibrated to match the employment share data from the household survey in which there are five labor types (high-skilled formal, semi-skilled formal, low-skilled formal, self-employed, and informal) and three activities (agriculture, industry, and services).
5. To match the 15 occupational choices in the household data, we report results for five labor categories and aggregate economic activities (agriculture, industry, and services).
6. All activities, except coal, gold, other mining, and refined petroleum, use a translog production function; coal, gold, other mining, and refined petroleum use a constant elasticity of substitution production function with the assumption that it is difficult to substitute among inputs so the elasticity of substitution is low (less than 0.5 in each activity).
7. McDonald and van Schoor (2005) also adjusted the "other mining" category to properly account for crude oil. They supplemented the social accounting matrix with data on imported crude oil. In this chapter, we assert that all inputs of other mining into refined petroleum are actually imports of crude oil.
8. By construction, crude oil is used only as an intermediate to the refined petroleum sector and it is not produced domestically.

9. These surveys are published by Statistics South Africa, and are available at http://www.statssa.gov.za.

10. This is the latent variable that governs occupational choice to the extent that people are believed to move to the activity with the highest level of utility. However, Bourguignon and Ferreira (2005) noted that such an interpretation would not be valid in cases where occupational choices are constrained by the demand side of the market.

11. We also tried the Heckman method on both the wage and self-employment equations to account for possible selection bias due to the fact that estimation is based on subsamples of individuals with observed earnings in the given activity. There was no significant difference in the results. We therefore stick with OLS.

12. "All other income" is income derived from the sale of vehicles, fixed property, other property, rents collected, payments received from boarders and other members of the household, lump sums resulting from employment before retirement, gratuities and other lump-sum payments received from pension, provident and other insurance or from private persons, life insurance and inheritances received, claims, grants, total withdrawals from savings, remittances, and other sources of income.

13. Bourguignon, Robilliard, and Robinson (2002) explained that benchmark consistency could be achieved by ensuring that the calibration of the CGE is compatible with the consistency constraints.

14. Savard (2006) discussed a way to achieve consistency in a case where the SAM of the CGE model and the survey data of the microsimulation have the same base year.

15. The elasticity of substitution between imports and the domestic variety in consumption for refined petroleum is 0.73; for basic chemicals, it is 0.677. Crude oil is not produced domestically. A value less than 1 indicates that the imported variety is not a good substitute for the domestic variety. See Devarajan, Lewis, and Robinson (1993) for a more detailed discussion of the real exchange rate in CGE models.

16. We also estimate poverty indicators at sectoral levels (urban, rural) and by provinces, but the latter are not reported.

17. TIP stands for "three 'I's of poverty"—that is, incidence, intensity, and inequality. The length of the nonhorizontal section reveals poverty incidence, intensity is represented by the height of the curve, and the concavity of the nonhorizontal section translates the degree of inequality among the poor.

18. The increase in the dollar price of crude oil was counterbalanced significantly by the strong South African rand during much of the recent trend in crude oil prices. The nominal rand per dollar, for example, appreciated by about 20.0 percent from end-2002 to end-2006 and by as much as 42.5 percent from end-2001 to end-2006.

References

Bourguignon, F., and F. H. G. Ferreira. 2005. "Decomposing Changes in the Distribution of Household Incomes: Methodological Aspects." In *The Microeconomics of Income Distribution Dynamics in East Asia and Latin America*, ed. F. Bourguignon, F. H. G. Ferreira, and N. Lustig, 17–47. New York: Oxford University Press.

Bourguignon, F., and L. A. Pereira da Silva. 2003. *The Impact of Economic Policies on Poverty and Income Distribution: Evaluation Techniques and Tools.* New York: Oxford University Press.

Bourguignon, F., A.-S. Robilliard, and S. Robinson. 2002. "Representative versus Real Households in the Macroeconomic Modeling of Inequality." Photocopy. International Food Policy Research Institute, Washington, DC.

Cogneau, D., and A.-S. Robilliard. 2000. "Income Distribution, Poverty and Growth in Madagascar: Micro Simulations in a General Equilibrium Framework." Trade and Macroeconomics Discussion Paper 61, International Food Policy Research Institute, Washington, DC.

Devarajan, S., and D. S. Go. 2003. "The 123PRSP Model." In *The Impact of Economic Policies on Poverty and Income Distribution: Evaluation Techniques and Tools,* ed. F. Bourguignon and L. A. Pereirra da Silva, 277–99. New York: Oxford University Press.

Devarajan, S., J. D. Lewis, and S. Robinson. 1993. "External Shocks, Purchasing Power Parity, and the Equilibrium Real Exchange Rate." *World Bank Economic Review* 7 (1): 45–63.

Essama-Nssah, B. 2005. "Simulating the Poverty Impact of Macroeconomic Shocks and Policies." Policy Research Working Paper 3788, World Bank, Washington, DC.

———. 2006. "Macroeconomic Shocks and Policies." In *Analyzing the Distributional Impact of Reforms,* ed. A. Coudouel and S. Paternostro, 355–435. Washington, DC: World Bank.

Essama-Nssah, B., D. S. Go, M. Kearney, V. Korman, S. Robinson, and K. Thierfelder. Forthcoming. "The Macroeconomic and Poverty Implications of a Wage Subsidy in South Africa." Photocopy. World Bank, Washington, DC.

Foster, J., J. Greer, and E. Thorbecke. 1984. "A Class of Decomposable Poverty Measures." *Econometrica* 52 (3): 761–66.

Go, D. S., M. Kearney, S. Robinson, and K. Thierfelder. 2005. "An Analysis of South Africa's Value Added Tax." Policy Research Working Paper 3671, World Bank, Washington, DC.

Heckman, J., and L. Lochner. 1998. "Explaining Rising Wage Inequality: Explorations with a Dynamic General Equilibrium Model of Labor Earnings with Heterogeneous Agents." *Review of Economic Dynamics,* 1: 1–58.

Jenkins, C., and L. Thomas. 2000. "The Changing Nature of Inequality in South Africa." Working Paper 203, United Nations University/World Institute for development Economics Research, Helsinki.

Jenkins, S. P., and P. J. Lambert. 1997. "Three 'I's of Poverty Curves, with an Analysis of UK Poverty Trends." *Oxford Economic Papers* 49 (3): 317–27.

Jorgenson, D. W., L. J. Lau, and T. M. Stoker. 1980. "Welfare Comparison under Exact Aggregation." *American Economic Review* 70 (2): 268–72.

Kakwani, N. 1993. "Poverty and Economic Growth with Application to Côte d'Ivoire." *Review of Income and Wealth* 39 (2): 121–39.

Kearney, M. 2004. "Restructuring Value-Added Tax in South Africa: A Computable General Equilibrium Analysis." PhD diss., University of Pretoria, South Africa.

Lewis, J. D. 2001. "Reform and Opportunity: The Changing Role and Patterns of Trade in South Africa and SADC." Africa Region Working Paper 14, World Bank, Washington, DC.

McDonald, S., and M. van Schoor. 2005. "A Computable General Equilibrium (CGE) Analysis of the Impact of an Oil Price Increase in South Africa." Working Paper 2005:1, PROVIDE Project, Elsenburg.

Ravallion, M., and M. Lokshin. 2004. "Gainers and Losers from Trade Reform in Morocco." Policy Research Working Paper 3368, World Bank, Washington, DC.

Savard, L. 2003. "Poverty and Income Distribution in a CGE-Household Micro-Simulation Model: Top-Down/Bottom-Up Approach." Working Paper 03–43, CIRPEE, Université Laval, Quebec, Canada.

————. 2006. "Analyse de la pauvreté et distribution des revenus dans le cadre de la modélisation en équilibre général calculable." PhD diss., Ecole des Hautes Etudes en Sciences Sociales, Paris.

Contributors

Noro Aina Andriamihaja has been an Economist for the World Bank Country Office in Madagascar since 2005. Prior to that, she spent five years as an Economist at the Resident Representative's Office of the International Monetary Fund in Madagascar. She holds a master's degree in economics (macroeconomic option) from the Université d'Antananarivo, Madagascar. Her work is related to macroeconomics and poverty reduction.

Jorge Saba Arbache is Senior Economist in the World Bank's Office of the Chief Economist, Africa Region. Before joining the Bank, he was Professor of Economics at the University of Brasilia (1991–2005). He also served as an Economist at the International Labor Organization in Brasilia (1989–1991). Mr. Arbache holds a Ph.D. in economics from the University of Kent, England. He has published on development economics, including issues on growth, labor economics, international trade, and industrial economics.

Nina Budina completed her Ph.D. in economics at the University of Amsterdam, Netherlands. She is a Senior Economist at the Economic Policy and Debt Department of the World Bank's Poverty Reduction and Economic Management (PREM) Network, where she is currently working on the issues of fiscal sustainability and on the specific issues of macro/fiscal management in oil-rich countries. Prior to this assignment, she worked as an Economist on Azerbaijan and Kazakhstan in the Europe and Central Asia unit of PREM. Her research record also includes articles on the transition economies of Eastern Europe.

Punam Chuhan-Pole is a Lead Economist in the Development Economics Vice Presidency. She is a member of the core team that produced the 2007 *Global Monitoring Report*. Her current work includes analyzing trends and developments in official development assistance, addressing issues in the scaling up of aid to poor countries, and exploring the links between donor allocations and recipient policies. She also has worked on monitoring and assessing vulnerability to external shocks, analyzing the determinants of private capital flows, and evaluating the debt defaults of the 1980s and 1990s. She holds a Ph.D. in economics from Georgetown University.

Shantayanan Devarajan is the Chief Economist of the World Bank's South Asia Region. Since joining the World Bank in 1991, he has been a Principal Economist and Research Manager for Public Economics in the Development Research Group, as well as the Chief Economist of the Human Development Network. He was the Director of the *World Development Report 2004: Making Services Work for Poor People*. Before joining the World Bank, he was on the faculty of Harvard University's John F. Kennedy School of Government. Shantayanan Devarajan's research covers public economics, trade policy, natural resources and the environment, and general-equilibrium modeling of developing countries. He also maintains a Web blog that is open to public opinion: http://endpovertyinsouthasia.worldbank.org/.

Julia Devlin is an Economist and Senior Strategy and Operations Officer at the World Bank. She is currently working on development effectiveness and partnerships with regional donors in the Middle East and North Africa region. She is also Senior Research Fellow at the University of Virginia. Julia has worked and published on oil revenues and economic development—notably in the areas of fiscal policy, trade, and financial management—in her capacity as an Economist and Senior Private Sector Development Specialist at the World Bank for nearly nine years. Prior to joining the Bank, Julia was on the faculty of the Georgetown School of Foreign Service and she has continued to teach courses on economic development in the Middle East and North Africa at Harvard University, the University of Virginia, and others.

Carolina Diaz-Bonilla is an Economist for the Development Prospects Group of the World Bank. She works on economywide country strategy analysis including poverty reduction and the Millennium Development Goals. Previously, she was at the International Food Policy Research Institute. She has worked on trade policy, poverty, income distribution, and labor market issues in Africa, Asia, and Latin America. She holds a Ph.D. in economics from the Johns Hopkins University.

B. Essama-Nssah is a Senior Economist with the Poverty Reduction Group at the World Bank. He works on the development and application of simulation models for the study of the impact of economic shocks and policies on poverty and income distribution. He is the author of a book on analytical and normative underpinnings of poverty, inequality, and social well-being. He was a Senior Research Associate with the Cornell University Food and Nutrition Policy Program from 1990 to 1992. From 1984 to 1989, he was Vice Dean of the Faculty of Law and Economics, and head of the Economics Department at the University of Yaoundé (Cameroon). He holds a Ph.D. in economics from the University of Michigan (Ann Arbor).

Brendan Fitzpatrick was a Junior Professional Associate in the Development Economics Vice Presidency. His major research areas were aid effectiveness and environmental economics. He holds a master's degree in public administration in international development from Harvard's John F. Kennedy School of Government. He also holds bachelor's degrees in bioengineering and economics from the University of Illinois at Urbana-Champaign. Brendan recently left the World Bank to work for Keybridge Research LLC in Washington, DC.

Delfin S. Go is Lead Economist in the Chief Economist Office of the World Bank's Africa Region. Previously, he served as the Bank's Country Economist for South Africa and Zambia. He first joined the Bank as Research Economist, Public Economics, Development Research Group. Delfin Go's work focuses on macroeconomics, investment and growth, public finance, aid effectiveness, trade liberalization, public expenditure analysis, debt and adjustment problems, and general-equilibrium modeling of developing countries. He received his Ph.D. in political economy and government from Harvard University.

Marna Kearney is a consultant in economywide modeling in South Africa. She has previously been employed by the National Treasury as Director, Economy-wide Policy Modelling. She holds a DCom (Economics) degree from the University of Pretoria. Her work so far has focused on determining the impact of economic events and policies on the economy of South Africa in the promotion of economic growth, employment, and reducing poverty.

Vijdan Korman is an Economist at the World Bank. Her recent work focuses on the poverty impact assessment of policies and shocks using a micro-simulation framework. At the Chief Economist Office of the Africa Region, she also helps coordinate the Country Policy and Institutional Assessment for the region. Previously, at a consulting firm in Cambridge, she conducted appraisals of infrastructure projects, contributed to a book and a manual on appraisal issues in the public sector, and delivered lectures in training workshops at Harvard University and many multilateral development banks. She holds a Ph.D. in economics from Boston's Northeastern University.

Michael Lewin teaches economics at Middlebury College in Vermont. He was a Senior Economist at the World Bank when this piece was written. He holds a Ph.D. from Johns Hopkins University. He has worked in both operations and in the research complex and was the task manager for macroeconomic modeling at the Bank. His current work focuses on macroeconomic modeling and macroeconomic and fiscal issues in mineral dependent developing economies.

Hans Lofgren is a Senior Economist in the Development Prospects Group of the World Bank. His work is focused on the strengthening of tools for economywide analysis of development policies, including policies aimed at achieving the Millennium Development Goals, and the application of these tools in World Bank analytical work. He joined the World Bank in June 2004. Prior to this he was a Senior Research Fellow at the International Food Policy Research Institute. Mr. Lofgren holds a Ph.D. in economics from the University of Texas at Austin.

Sanket Mohapatra is an Economist in the Development Prospects Group of the World Bank. He has previously worked in the Debt Department of the World Bank and in the Africa Department of the International Monetary Fund. He holds a Ph.D. in economics from Columbia University and an M.A from the Delhi School of Economics. His research encompasses capital flows to developing countries, financial liberalization and corporate financial structures in emerging markets, and various issues regarding sovereign ratings, remittances, and migration.

John Page is the Chief Economist for the Africa Region at the World Bank. He has been a World Bank Economist and Manager since 1980, and has undertaken a wide range of research, policy, and operational assignments including Director, Poverty Reduction; Director, Economic Policy; Chief Economist of the Middle East and North Africa Region; and Director of its Social and Economic Development Group. He obtained his doctorate from Oxford University, where he was a Rhodes Scholar. He has published three books and more than 70 scholarly papers on growth, poverty reduction, trade, migration and remittances, and industry and technology in developing countries.

Sonia Plaza is a Senior Economist in the Development Economics Prospect Group of the World Bank. Ms. Plaza worked on science and technology projects in Latin America. In the Africa Region, she coauthored a major analytical survey of migration and development. Ms Plaza also worked at the Chase Manhattan Bank and at the Peruvian Ministry of Trade as a manager responsible for trade and debt swap agreements. She has a dual degree from Yale University and the University of Pennsylvania in International Economics and Development.

Claudio Raddatz is an Economist in the Development Economics Research Group of the World Bank. He holds a degree in engineering from University of Chile and a Ph.D. in economics from the Massachusetts Institute of Technology. His work focuses on the macroeconomic aspects of economic development, especially on the institutional determinants of macroeconomic volatility and growth.

Thilakaratna Ranaweera is a consultant and Senior Economist in the Development Data Group, Development Economics and Chief Economist Office of the World Bank. Both in and outside the World Bank, he has done extensive empirical work on macroeconomic models and medium-term frameworks for oil-rich countries. He holds a Ph.D. in economics from the University of Birmingham, England.

Dilip Ratha is a Senior Economist in the Development Prospects Group of the World Bank. Previously, he worked as a consultant in the Financial Policy and Country Risk Department of the World Bank, as a Regional Economist for Asian emerging markets at Credit Agricole Indosuez, and as an Assistant Professor at Indian Institute of Management, Ahmedabad. He has a Ph.D. in economics from Indian Statistical Institute, New Delhi. His work focuses on remittances and migration, country risk analysis, future-flow securitization, and development finance.

Sherman Robinson has a joint appointment as a Professor of Economics at the University of Sussex and a Research Fellow at the Institute of Development Studies (IDS). He received a Ph.D. in economics from Harvard University. He has served as a Division Director at the International Food Policy Research Institute, a Professor at the University of California, and a Division Director at the World Bank. He has had visiting senior staff appointments at the Economic Research Service, U.S. Department of Agriculture; the U.S. Congressional Budget Office; and the President's Council of Economic Advisers (in the Clinton Administration).

Karen Thierfelder is a Professor of Economics at the United States Naval Academy. She received her Ph.D. in economics from the University of Wisconsin (Madison). She has worked as a Visiting Research Fellow at the International Food Policy Research Institute and as a consultant to the World Bank. In her research, she uses general equilibrium models to analyze trade reforms, tax policies, and labor market issues.

Sweder van Wijnbergen is a Professor of Economics at the University of Amsterdam, Netherlands. Prof. van Wijnbergen received his Ph.D. from the Massachusetts Institute of Technology in 1980 under the guidance of Stanley Fischer. He is one of the main contributors to the literature on fiscal sustainability and the fiscal origins of exchange rate crises. He also has considerable experience in advising oil-exporting countries and he is by now an academic authority in the field—papers and books produced by him are part of the standard references on this topic. He has served as a Secretary General at the Ministry of Economic Affairs in the Netherlands and as advisor to a number of market access and oil-rich countries, and as Lead Economist on Mexico and Eastern Europe, which has given him the practical experience necessary to blend high theory with pragmatic realism.

Giovanni Vecchi is Professor of Economics at the University of Rome "Tor Vergata," where he specializes in the theory, measurement, and history of welfare, as well as in economic history. He is a regular visiting professor at the Universidad Carlos III de Madrid, Spain, and a consultant to the World Bank on issues related to poverty and inequality measurement. He has published widely and his scholarly articles have appeared in a number of international, peer-reviewed journals.

Xiao Ye is an Economist in the African Chief Economist Office of the World Bank. She holds a Ph.D. in agricultural economics from University of California at Davis. She has worked in the areas of economic growth, public resource management, access to public services, and debt sustainability, among others.

Index

Boxes, figures, notes, and tables are indicated by *b, f, n,* and *t,* respectively.

Uganda (*Continued*)
  in MDRI, 82*n*29
  predictability of aid to, 214
  as PRS-II country, 230*n*9
United Bank for Africa, Nigeria,
    315*b*
United Kingdom, 202, 203*f*, 216,
    321, 322
United Nations
  Joint United Nations Programme
    on HIV/AIDS, 225
  Office of Drugs and Crime, 326
United States, 202, 203*f*, 217
U.S. Overseas Private Investment
    Corporation, 71

vaccines and immunizations,
    financing, 301, 303,
    321–22
van Wijnbergen, Sweder, 7, 49, 73,
    156, 427
Vecchi, Giovanni, 8, 45, 461
Venezuela, República Bolivariana
    de, 427
verticalization of aid funds,
    226, 227*f*
Vietnam, 61, 230*n*9
voice and accountability.
    See governance indicators
volatility in aid
  analysis of, 209–10, 210*t*, 211*f*
  growth volatility, as correlate
    of, 124
  macroeconomic management of,
    155–56, 156*f*, 162–63, 185
volatility of growth in Africa
  correlates of, 121–24, 123*t*

economic performance and,
    119–21, 121*f*
historical volatility of growth
    cycles, 25. *See also* cycles of
    growth in Africa
internal vs. external shocks
    causing, 343–45. *See also*
    internal vs. external shocks
    as sources of macroeconomic
    fluctuation in Africa
long-term patterns of, 119–24,
    121*f*, 123*t*, 125
oil revenues in Nigeria, 431–37,
    432*f*
oil windfall management
    and, 391

WDI *(World Development Indicators)*,
    88, 347
West African Economic and
    Monetary Union (WAEMU),
    18*t*, 20, 51*b*, 81*n*18, 151
widespread nature of, 14–16,
    16*f*, 17*t*
Wijnbergen, Sweder van, 7, 49, 73,
    156, 427
women's access to production
    factors, 77, 78*f*
World Bank
  Africa Action Plan, 219
  CPIA. *See* Country Policy and
    Institutional Assessment
  effectiveness of aid, improving,
    227–29
  Export-Import Bank of China,
    memorandum of
    understanding with, 224